```
HM        Fernandez, Ronald
251          I, the me, and you
.F38
```

DATE DUE

DEC 15 1984
DEC 10 1990
APR 11

The I, the Me, and You

The I,
the Me,
and You

An Introduction to Social Psychology

RONALD FERNANDEZ
Central Connecticut State College

Praeger Publishers
New York

Published in the United States of America in 1977
by Praeger Publishers, Inc.
200 Park Avenue, New York, N. Y. 10017

© 1977 by Praeger Publishers, Inc.
All rights reserved

Library of Congress Cataloging in Publication Data

Fernandez, Ronald.
  The I, the me, and you.

  Includes index.
  1. Social psychology. I. Title.
  HM251.F38   301.1   76-41957
  ISBN 0-275-22080-X

Printed in the United States of America

TO SALLY AND MILTON,
with much love and a huge thank you

PREFACE

This text was written for five reasons. The first was a desire to put "social" back into social psychology. Overwhelmingly, texts in the field are written by psychologists, and this disciplinary bias inevitably overlooks concepts and insights that are important to sociologists and all social psychologists. In this volume, while including a wide variety of topics, I have consistently stressed concepts of particular interest to sociologically minded social psychologists.

The second reason was the wish to show students the relevance and importance of social psychology in their everyday lives. Throughout the book, short passages from imaginative literature are used before the discussion, for example, of socialization or reference groups; the purpose of these excerpts is to show students that the concepts are not the esoteric products of people who know nothing about life. On the contrary, the passages are meant to provide a basis for proving that the concepts do in fact relate to life as people actually live it.

The third reason was a desire to write a book that was free from what one editor has called "academic anemia." Only readers can say if the prose is successful, but I have tried to write a lively text without sacrificing substance or coverage.

The fourth reason is the work of George Herbert Mead and the school of thought now labeled "Symbolic Interactionism." Consistently, Mead's insights and emphases have been overlooked by many social psychologists. This volume is rooted in his work and, I believe, far better for being so.

Finally, *The I, the Me, and You* was written because the social sciences have a unique potential: they can enable people to begin a radical yet peaceful reevaluation of self and world, and help them to use social psychological concepts as tools for understanding better why men and women think and act as they do. I hope, then, that this text allows any who have the desire, to use social psychological concepts as a basis for understanding the future through a consciously reevaluated yesterday and today.

Substantial parts of the research for this volume were done while I taught at Bingley College in Bingley, Yorkshire, England. To Thomas

Brennan, head of Bingley's Social Science Division, I owe a large debt of gratitude. He was unfailingly kind and always able to provide an atmosphere conducive to scholarly research. I shall always remember Tom's constant efforts to make a stranger feel welcome. To Peter McKay, a very able and conscientious assistant who made my work much easier, I also say thank you.

Professors Ralph Turner of the University of California, Los Angeles, and Joseph Zygmunt of the University of Connecticut did prepublication reviews of the manuscript that were comprehensive, critical, and quite helpful. Obviously, neither of these scholars bears any responsibility for what is now between these covers.

Professor Bill Harrell was an invaluable guide and critic in helping to formulate the overview of obedience to authority that is the second half of Chapter Nine.

This is the second book I have done with Praeger's sociology editor, James Bergin. Without a doubt Jim is one of the ablest editors in college publishing and a pleasure to work with.

Nancy Ferguson Fernandez knows the important part she played in the book's writing.

R.F.

CONTENTS

Introduction: What Is Social Psychology?   1
The Origins of Social Psychology 3
Social Psychology—So What? 8

PART ONE: SOCIALIZATION AND HUMAN DEVELOPMENT   13

Chapter One   Beyond Stimulus and Response   15
Other Animals and Us 16
Brains and Gains 20
Language 23
The Influence of Genes 29
Personality and the Self 34
The Self 37

Chapter Two   Childhood Socialization   50
Trust versus Mistrust 51
Is a Mother Mandatory? 54
Competence Motivation 56
Infant Cognitive Development 60
Negativism, Egocentrism, and Role-Taking 63
Parent-Child Relations 70
Identification 74
Private Speech and the Generalized Other 77
Stabilization of Concepts 83
Sex Roles 87
Conscience 93
School 97
Peer Groups 98
Overview 100

Chapter Three   Three A's: Adolescence, Adulthood, and Aging   109
Egocentricism in Adolescence 110
Occupational Identities 112

x/Contents

Generation Gap: Canyon or Crack?   115
Sex in Adolescence   117
Peer Relations in Adolescence   120
Early Adulthood   124
Middle Age   133
Work and Self-Image   141
Widowhood in Old Age   145
Family Relations of Aged People   146
Identity in Old Age   148
Death   148

Chapter Four   Problems in Living   155

The Myth of Mental Illness   157
Schizophrenia as a Human Process   163

PART TWO: PERSONALITY IN CULTURE   181

Chapter Five   How Is Society Possible?   183

How Is Society Possible?   185

Chapter Six   Roles   198

Roles: A Definition   200
Roles: Freedom versus Determinism   203
Role-Making   205
Role Involvement   208
Role Conflict   211

Chapter Seven   Frames and the Presentation of Self in Everyday Life   227

Frame Analysis   229
Presentations of Self   236
Presentation Problems   239
Watergate and Structural Problems in Fabrications   243

Chapter Eight   Reference Groups   253

Reference Groups and the Generalized Other   255
Types of Reference Groups   256
Some Determinants of Normative Reference Groups   259
Some Determinants of Comparative Reference Groups   262
Prejudice and Comparative Reference Groups   266
Reference Others   271

PART THREE: SOCIAL PSYCHOLOGICAL PROCESSES — 279

Chapter Nine   Attitudes, Beliefs, Opinions, and Change — 281

What Is an Attitude?   283
Dissonance, Commitment, and Self-Justification   284
Inadequate Justification   292
Public Opinion   295

Chapter Ten   Obedience to Authority — 307

The Milgram Experiments   308
An Overview of Obedience to Authority   317
Ultimate Reasons for Obedience to Authority   327

Chapter Eleven   Leadership — 334

Leadership Traits   336
Charisma and Social Situation   338
Leadership, Power, and Authority   341
Emergence of Leadership   344
Leadership: Style and Effectiveness   347

Chapter Twelve   Aggression and Social Conflict — 355

Aggression: A Social Psychological Analysis   357
Manhood and Aggression   364
What Is War?   368
Propositions about War   370

Chapter Thirteen   Collective Behavior — 383

What Is Collective Behavior?   385
Crowds   386
Riots   393
Social Movements   399
Origins of Social Movements   400
Types and Concerns of Social Movements   402
Social Movements: Growth, Decay, Change   406
Motives of Movement Members   409

Glossary — 417

Index — 423

The I, the Me, and You

INTRODUCTION
What Is Social Psychology?

The next day Rastignac dressed himself very elegantly, and about three o'clock in the afternoon went to call on Mme. de Restaud. On his way through the streets he began to think about what he should say to her. He equipped himself with wit, rehearsed repartees in the course of an imaginary conversation, and prepared certain neat speeches conjuring up a series of small events which should prepare the way for the declaration on which he had based his future. . . .

At last he reached the Rue du Hilder, and asked for the Countesse de Restaud. He bore the contemptuous glances of the servants, who had seen him cross on foot and . . . he understood the meaning of their glances at once, for he had felt his inferiority as soon as he entered the court, where a smart cab was waiting. . . .

"This way to the drawing-room sir," said the servant, with the exaggerated respect which seemed to be one more jest at his expense.

"Oh! is that you, M. de Rastignac? I am very glad to see you, the Countess said, but there was something in her manner that a shrewd observer would have taken as a hint to depart.

Eugène assumed an amiable expression.

"Madame," he began, "I hastened to call upon you—"

He stopped short. The door opened and the owner of the tilbury suddenly appeared. . . .

"M. de Restaud," said the Countess, introducing her husband. . . .

Eugène bowed profoundly.

"This gentleman," she continued presenting Eugène to her husband, "is

> M. de Rastignac; he is related to Mme. la Vicomtesse de Beauseant through the Marcillars. . . ."
> Related to Mme. la Vicomtesse de Beauseant through the Marcillars! *These words, on which the Countess threw ever so slight an emphasis, by reason of the pride that the mistress of a house takes in showing that she only receives people of distinction as visitors in her house, produced a magical effect. The Count's stiff manner relaxed at once as he returned the student's bow.*
> "Delighted to have an opportunity of making your acquaintance," he said.
>
> Honoré de Balzac, Le Père Goriot (1901)

Eugène's meeting lends itself to at least three interpretations. Focusing on group factors, sociologists might stress social class. Since the countess and her husband are aristocrats, they set the standard for everyone else and this is obvious from the servant's reaction. Arriving on foot, Eugène is common, an average man who fools no one. But remember the count's reaction; although he too is initially cool, Eugène's ancestry produces an immediate smile of recognition: "Eugène is one of *us*."

Psychologists will stress the individual. What kind of man is Eugène? Does he have a poor self-image? If so, is his poor self-image the reason for his meeting with the countess? For *his* psychological well-being, in order to counter his lack of self-esteem, does Eugène need to see himself as a member of a powerful social group?

The third interpretation belongs to social psychology. Interested in both the individual and the group, in both psychology and sociology, social psychologists try to understand and explain how the actual, imagined, or implied presence of others influences a person's thoughts and actions (Allport, 1968). First, take Eugène's walk. On his way to the countess, not yet in her actual presence, he imagines what he will say to her. And although the dialogue is Eugène's creation, its content is influenced by the imaginary countess.

Second, consider the servant's reaction. Only Eugène and the butler are actually present, but when the servant scorns Eugène's means of transportation, his judgment is based on the implied presence of aristocrats. They set standards, and since no aristocrat would ever arrive on foot, Eugène is common and must be treated as such.

Third, remember Eugène. Although no indication is given in the quoted passage, he reacts to the servant with anger. Actual and implied scorn from others produces a fervent desire to succeed at all costs. Eugène will "make it" or die trying.

Why? Is Eugène's reaction simply a response to the servant? Or does his desire have deep roots? Did his parents teach, and did Eugène accept, that the only worthwhile life is an aristocrat's life? Was he taught in school that poverty was a "sin"? Does the culture closely link social mobility and a sense of self-worth?

Although no answers are possible without detailed knowledge of Eugène's life and society, possessing that kind of knowledge is the social psychologist's ultimate goal. For social psychology is a junction between two sciences: sometimes it overlaps psychology and sociology, but it always uses the aims and insights of each to achieve knowledge that neither pursues single-mindedly. Like a bridge, social psychology fosters free passage from one science to the other, but it always stands between the two, using the data of each to build something different, to build a science that tries to understand and explain how the actual, imagined, or implied presence of others influences the thoughts, feelings, and behavior of people (Allport, 1968).

THE ORIGINS OF SOCIAL PSYCHOLOGY

All modern social science has the same point of origin: the seventeenth-century revolution in our knowledge of the universe. Of course, physical scientists such as Copernicus, Galileo, Kepler, and Newton never set out to deliberately create psychology or sociology. In the 1600s that would have been "impossible." But hindsight shows that when scientists undermined religious explanations of the universe, they also undermined religious explanations of why people think, feel, and act as they do. Before the scientific revolution, God was the axis upon which explanations of human behavior securely revolved. After the revolution, after Galileo showed the sun to be the center of the universe, God was pushed to the side, and the resulting vacuum was filled with explanations firmly rooted not in the hereafter but in the here and now. Soon, some even argued that human thought and action were the result of only social and biological influences (see, for example, Koyre, 1958; Geymonat, 1965; Russell, 1961).

Conceivably, rejecting traditional explanations meant only despair and humility. After all, before Galileo and Newton, the Earth was the center of a finite universe, created by God, for people. But in the Newtonian world, "the Earth was a minor planet of a not specially distinguished star," and it seemed unlikely that this "immense apparatus"—the universe—was designed only "for the good of certain small creatures" on a pinpoint called Earth. So, in response to such a discovery, people could have focused on their own nothingness. They could have felt like aliens in a world created for . . . only God knew who.

Some did adopt this view; overwhelmed by the new discoveries, they were unhappy with the idea of universal insignificance. But others were ignited, overjoyed, by science's potential. The universe's demonstrated lack of purpose produced a sense of pride in human accomplishments.

Paradoxically, people undermined the ultimate explanations of their existence and came to this conclusion: "Nature and Nature's laws lay hid in night. / God said 'Let Newton be,' and all was light" (Russell, 1961).

Today, as then, all is not light, but it is the spirit of the phrase that is significant. Science produced optimism, for some people felt that science, rooted in reason, could actually uncover the laws that made the universe work. And not only that. Science even led men and women to believe that they could understand the causes and course of human social life. Although God's significance, and that of original sin, was inevitably reduced by efforts to explain human life in scientific terms, sociology, psychology, and social psychology are the direct descendants of those scientists who, fired up by the possibilities of the Enlightenment, tried to apply "scientific" standards in explaining why people think and act as they do (see, for example, Gay, 1966; Cassirer, 1966; Salomon, 1961).

Since Enlightenment thinkers were rooted, above all, in philosophy, "sociology" reaped great benefits from the powerful desire to seek truth through reason. For philosophers often focused attention on politics, and now, rejecting religious explanations, they had no choice: interpretations of political thought and action had to be based in this world, in the societies made and remade by human beings.

One famous example of Enlightenment thought is French philosopher Jean Jacques Rousseau's *Discourse on Inequality*, first published in 1754. Rousseau (1712–78) began by stressing the distant past. Granted, in 1754 a "state of nature" no longer existed, and even though it "perhaps never existed," it was still necessary to have "just ideas" about the past "in order to judge well our present state." Tragically, any fair assessment of the present was inevitably harsh. People constantly killed, fought, and starved; it was anything but the peaceful state of nature. However, only their own social institutions, especially private property, made people act badly and only—as set forth in Rousseau's *Social Contract* (1762)—new institutions could create a world resembling the blissful state of nature (Rousseau, 1961; Nisbet, 1956; Russell, 1961).

Rousseau's version of the remote past is an hypothesis. Today we know it is wrong, but consider the positive insights embedded in Rousseau's thought. First is the origin of society. Like Montesquieu before him, Rousseau assigned the responsibility for its creation to people. God is in the background, and men and women are the primary makers of all social institutions. Second is the possibility of social change. Rousseau says yes. People make society and, within limits, they can remake it. Third is the "inevitability" of social inequalities. Aristotle said slavery was "natural"; along with many others, Rousseau said no. Inequalities are created by society, and under a proper "social contract" inequalities can be, if not eliminated, at least mitigated.

Rousseau was only one of many brilliant Enlightenment thinkers. As early as 1720, Montesquieu (1689-1755) broached the idea of cultural relativity (in *The Persian Letters*), and in *The Spirit of the Laws* (1748), he also put God aside when he wrote that human thought and action were best explained by a variety of social influences, for example, climate, custom, law, and religion. However, specific thinkers are less important to us than the Enlightenment's results. For example, could the elimination of social inequalities be a central political goal until men and women decided that society was a human product? And could sociology or social psychology arise until human beings "knew" that, instead of God, the actual, imagined, or implied influence of others was the key factor in explaining anyone's thought and action? Hindsight indicates no. For the growth of specific sciences devoted to explaining the influence of others on the individual, it was first necessary for "scientists" to believe that social factors were a central influence in the development of self and society.

While Enlightenment philosophers often focused on politics or society, they never neglected psychology or, more accurately, "mental philosophy." Spurred on by the drive to understand all, these thinkers sought "a psychological foundation for philosophical discussions" (Thomson, 1968). But since the aim of "psychology" was to help philosophers build a theory of knowledge and ethics, a distinct science of mind developed slowly. First, because mental philosophers said that men knew their mental life by introspection, there was no need for "elaborate techniques" of analysis; they could observe psychology's subject matter in their own states of consciousness (Thomson, 1968). Second, and more important, since psychology and sociology were subordinate to philosophy, neither discipline could begin to develop as a specific science until theoretical models were furnished that did two things: mapped out the science's subject manner and provided the conceptual overview needed for systematic analysis.

Why were models needed? According to Thomas Kuhn, they provide the order required for focused research (1971). Before the appearance of models, say, Freud's theory of psychoanalysis, reality resembles an unsolvable puzzle; nothing fits together coherently. Models change this. In fact, by creating order out of chaos, they furnish explanations of reality that are the basis of everyday science. Remember, while many models— the grand model of Auguste Comte in sociology, for instance—supposedly explain everything, they normally provide no more than the skeleton of a solution. What happens is that scientists adopt one model or another and then devote their energies to proving or disproving the model. And, yes, models are constraining; they limit the world of experience by providing scientists with "tunnel visions" of reality (Reese and Overton, 1970). Yet, despite their faults, they are the basis of scientific research, for systematic analysis of reality is very difficult unless models somehow order the mass of otherwise chaotic facts (Kuhn, 1971).

In psychology, German philosopher Johann Herbart (1776–1841) was the "first" writer (*Text Book of Psychology*, 1816) to stress the need for a distinct science of mind. Herbart envisioned a psychology rooted in experience, metaphysics, and mathematics. He felt that the components of mental states could be measured and their relationships statistically treated; he also saw the possibility of mathematically analyzing the way ideas combine, conflict, and modify one another (Thomson, 1968). Regarding the content of mind, Herbart said ideas were active, and instead of being associated together in a "passive and mechanical way," those ideas actively struggled with one another for a place in consciousness. In fact, given the number of ideas, conflict was inevitable. But "inhibited ideas were not destroyed." They remained active "below the threshold of consciousness," and while ideas only rose if they fit in with conscious notions, Herbart said that unconscious ideas were "just as important" as any other material in explaining the "composition of consciousness." For whether through cooperation with an ally, or through a weakening of conflicting ideas, unconscious notions could overcome formerly strong resistance (Flugel, 1964; Thomson, 1968).

Herbart's influence on subsequent thinkers was great. For example, Freud later developed the notion that unconscious ideas actively strive to be heard, and one basis for experimental research is the idea that mathematics can be used to study mental events. However, in his own work Herbart rejected experimental psychology, failing to see how scientists could experiment on the mind (Flugel, 1964). To the extent that researchers adopted Herbart's model, psychology tended to be rationalistic, introspective, mentalistic—in short, as metaphysical as many philosophies were (Allport, 1968).

Auguste Comte (1798–1857) was bothered by psychology's emphasis. Since his law of three stages declared that history moved from a theoretical to a metaphysical to *the* positive stage of science, psychology was one stage behind. So, when Comte constructed his hierarchy of the sciences and sought a name for the "highest" science of all, the science "that would preside over the reorganization of society," he rejected psychology and invented instead one called "sociology" (Allport, 1968; Aron, 1966). Now Comte's thought was always guided by his philosophy; history definitely moved toward the positive stage of science and industry. But, in analyzing the causes and course of historical progress, Comte underlined the influence of social forces. And while he often attached too much importance to society—in his work men and women were sometimes *only* social products—he asked the question that became the basis for the first sharp focus on what is now called social psychology.

The question was: "How can the individual be at once cause and consequence of society?" How can people create religious or political institutions and yet still be influenced—perhaps even determined—by them?

Comte had no single answer to the question, but since he felt that people were more than biological beings, more than "cultural culminations," he sought to create a new science. Dependent on biology and sociology, "*la morale*," as the new science was called, focused on the "individual unity" of human beings, which meant that while it sought to understand the uniqueness of each person, it never turned away from generalizations common to everyone. In effect, *la morale* was "a science of human nature in general, but one that adopted itself to the phenomenon of individuality" (Allport, 1968).

Gordon Allport rightly notes that Comte was the "founder" of social psychology. However, in Comte's own time, no one was vitally interested in yet another social science. Besides grappling with the meaning of psychology and sociology, scientists were also trying to assimilate a host of startling discoveries. This was "Darwin's Century" (see Eiseley, 1966), and evolutionary doctrines had a profound effect; for example, in England Herbert Spencer's model of society was tied to the idea of survival of the fittest, and Charles Darwin's cousin, Francis Galton, firmly rooted his analysis of genius in hereditary factors. In Germany, Wilhelm Wundt laid a solid foundation for experimental psychology, and remember too the feverish attempts to explain behavior in terms of "racial" groupings (see, for example, Barzun, 1962).

In sum, it was a busy and productive century. Theoretical models, in both psychology and sociology, were abundantly available, and it was not until 1908 that two texts appeared about a science called social psychology.

Although the first text, *Social Psychology*, was written by a sociologist— E. A. Ross—the book reflected its origins: some libraries still catalog the volume as philosophy. More important, since Ross followed the nineteenth-century pattern of relying heavily on one explanation of thought and action—he stressed suggestion or imitation—his model of social psychology looked backward as well as forward. For however slowly, researchers were coming to the conclusion that no one principle could ever explain the complex relationship that existed between individuals and their society (Allport, 1968).

William McDougall's *Introduction to Social Psychology* reflected this process of slow change. Echoing the late nineteenth-century stress on biological determinism, McDougall rooted his work in a totally instinctual explanation: instincts "are the essential springs or motive powers of all thought and action." But, McDougall qualified his enthusiasm for one explanation by noting that "these primary innate tendencies have different relative strengths," and, besides, instincts "are favored or checked in very different degrees by the very different social circumstances of men in different stages of culture." So, while McDougall relied heavily on one explanation, his work looked forward. For in stressing the importance of other mechanisms (for example, imitation) and motives (for instance, cultural), he pointed to one of today's dominant conclusions: no model that rests on unitary explanations will ever explain the influence of others on an individual's thought and action.

This conclusion is involuntary. Among others, Freudians and behaviorists tried to fill the gap left by a rejection of instinct models. But human beings are stubborn, and their refusal to think and act according to one mechanism or motive has made the twentieth century a graveyard for unitary explanations. Of course, it would be nice—although much less fascinating—if simple answers sufficed, but time, the complexity of life, and a search for truth forced researchers to see that no one model, mechanism, or motive explained the questions posed by people.

Today virtually all social psychologists use models based on more than one mechanism or motive, but no one model is accepted by all—and many scholars feel that a grand model is a long way off. So, while a text's purpose is to summarize a science's accepted principles and insights, remember that, while social psychologists know a great deal, the discipline is still young. Symbolic interactionism, cognitive development theory, psychoanalysis, balance theory, behaviorism all have something to offer, and at least for now all these models combine to produce the principles and insights widely accepted by social psychologists.

SOCIAL PSYCHOLOGY—SO WHAT?

Like all words, *freedom* means different things to different people. Some quickly add an adjective and talk of *political freedom;* people have the right to assemble where they please or worship as they wish. Others think the word is an illusion. People are never free; any individual's thoughts and actions are determined by others, and freedom is only "a matter of the contingencies of reinforcement." Like pigeons, people lack the ability to make free choices (Skinner, 1971; 1953).

Perhaps. But even a denial of freedom points to a thread that runs through all discussions of the word: freedom needs a barrier. No one is free in a vacuum. One is free of something, free from something, or free to do something; but the word loses its thrust—its sense of liberation— unless there is a barrier to be scaled, with freedom on the other side.

So? What has this to do with social psychology? A great deal. First, since freedom is possible (see Chapter One), it is necessary to distinguish between two types. *External* freedom refers to freedom of speech, of worship, of assembly and is a political right granted to some or all of a state's citizens. In contrast, *internal* freedom means insight into one's self and the world, plus the ability to act on those insights. It means the capacity to reflect on why we think and act as we do *and* the ability to change if we are unhappy with what we see. Probably, internal freedom is always a relative achievement; does anyone ever know everything about the causes and course of his personal development? Still, even small amounts of internal freedom are often a prized possession. For if we see how the past (for example, our parents, our sex role, our social class) shapes our present, we can consciously decide whether or not we wish to enter the future on the basis of "new" beliefs, values, and practices.

Let us take an example. Say you are a twenty-year-old woman in contemporary American society. You want to get married, you hesitantly believe a woman's place is in the home, you think men are smarter than women (even though you know some very foolish men), and when it comes to setting sexual limits, the job is yours: "I mean because guys can't help it. I mean they are born that way . . ." (Grinder, 1973). However, you unintentionally come across Masters and Johnson's findings on sex and that leads you to read feminist literature, say, Kate Millet's *Sexual Politics*. Slowly, you begin to see things in a new light. You gradually start asking how many of your beliefs, values, and practices are only a result of readily accepting—in childhood and adolescence—what others told you about the "proper" roles of women and men. Undoubtedly, rethinking your sexual identity brings pain and anxiety—rejecting the past means you now lack a set of beliefs and practices—but it also equals the freedom to reject an arbitrarily inherited plan for *your* life.

Social psychology often does this by providing the information or, equally important, the conceptual tools that allow us to ask and answer a very radical question: Why do I think and act as I do? The question is radical because we are very often unaware, or unwilling to admit, the actual, imagined, or implied influence of others. "Me? I'm an individual. I think for myself. I don't conform to anybody's dictates." Perhaps, but at best it is quite unlikely. We are all constantly influenced by others (see Chapter Five, for example), and the only way to consciously say yes or no to that influence is to first become aware of it. No one rejects the unknown.

So, my belief is that, like sociology (see Fernandez, 1975), social psychology is a "revolutionary" discipline. And by "revolutionary" I mean that social psychology provides an important basis for radical yet peaceful change of self and society. On an individual level, it furnishes the concepts and information needed to begin the process of gaining internal freedom. And, to repeat, internal freedom can be revolutionary because one is often unaware of the influence of others. Like the aged woman who unquestioningly said her place was in the home, we can sometimes live—and die—without conscious knowledge of the determining influence of others.

Although social psychology often focuses—rightly—on the development of the unique individual, the discipline also offers potentially radical insights about society. For example, to the extent that social psychology understands and explains obedience to authority (see Chapter Ten), it furnishes the insights needed if people are to begin to build societies that forever avoid the social conditions that led to Auschwitz and Dachau. Or, to the extent that social psychology understands and explains personal and group aggression, it provides the insights needed if people are to begin to abolish war. Since the world has seen over sixty wars since 1945, help in reducing social conflict would be a revolution welcomed by "all."

Social psychology—so what? The answer is insight. The answer is a discipline that has the potential to provide its students with conscious knowledge of the actual, implied, and imagined influence of others on the development of self and society.

Bibliographical References

Allport, Gordon W. "The Historical Background of Modern Social Psychology." In *Handbook of Social Psychology*, edited by Gardner Lindzey and Elliot Aronson. Vol. 1. Reading, Mass.: Addison-Wesley, 1968.

Aron, Raymond. *Main Currents in Sociological Thought.* 2 vols. New York: Basic Books, 1966, 1967.

Barzun, Jacques. *Race: A Study of Myth.* New York: Harper & Row, 1962.

Blumer, Herbert. *Symbolic Interactionism: Perspective and Method.* Englewood Cliffs, N.J.: Prentice-Hall, 1969.

Cassirer, Ernst. *The Enlightenment.* New York: Random House, 1966.

Eiseley, Loren. *Darwin's Century.* Garden City, N.Y.: Doubleday, 1966.

Fernandez, Ronald. *The Promise of Sociology.* New York: Praeger, 1975.

Flugel, J. C. *A Hundred Years of Psychology.* London: Methuen, 1964.

Gay, Peter. *The Enlightenment: The Rise of Modern Paganism.* Vol. One. New York: Random House, 1966.

Geymonat, Ludovico. *Galileo Galilei.* New York: McGraw-Hill, 1965.

Grinder, Robert. *Adolescence.* New York: Wiley, 1973.

Koyre, Alexandre. *From the Closed World to the Infinite Universe.* New York: Harper & Row, 1958.

Kuhn, Thomas. *The Structure of Scientific Revolutions.* 2d ed. Chicago: University of Chicago Press, 1970.

McDougall, William. *An Introduction to Social Psychology.* 14th ed. London: Methuen, 1915.

Montesquieu, Charles de Secondat. *The Persian Letters.* New York: Meridian, 1961.

Nisbet, Robert. *Community and Power.* New York: Oxford University Press, 1956.

Reese, Hayne W., and Overton, Willis F. "Models and Theories of Devel-

opment." In *Life-Span Developmental Psychology*, edited by L. R. Goulet and Paul Baltes. New York: Academic Press, 1970.
Ross, E. A. *Social Psychology*. New York: Macmillan, 1908.
Rousseau, Jean Jacques. *Discourse on Inequality* and *The Social Contract*. New York: Washington Square Press, 1961.
Russell, Bertrand. *History of Western Philosophy*. New York: Simon and Schuster, 1961.
Salomon, Albert. *In Praise of Enlightenment*. New York: Meridian, 1961.
Skinner, B. F. *Beyond Freedom and Dignity*. New York: Knopf, 1971.
Skinner, B. F. *Science and Human Behavior*. New York: Macmillan, 1953.
Thomson, Robert. *The Pelican History of Psychology*. London: Penguin Books, 1968.

PART ONE

SOCIALIZATION AND HUMAN DEVELOPMENT

CHAPTER ONE

Beyond Stimulus and Response

Then there was a vicious snarling in the mouth of the shelter and the plunge and thump of living things. Someone tripped over Ralph and Piggy's corner became a complication of snarls and crashes and flying limbs. Ralph hit out; then he and what seemed like a dozen others were rolling over and over, hitting, biting, scratching. He was torn and jolted, found fingers in his mouth and bit them. A fist withdrew and came back like a piston, so that the whole shelter exploded into light. Ralph twisted sideways on top of a writhing body and felt hot breath on his cheek. He began to pound the mouth below him, using his clenched fist as a hammer . . . a knee jerked up between his legs and he fell sideways, busying himself with his pain, and the fight rolled over him. Then . . . dark figures drew themselves out of the wreckage and flitted away, till the screams of the littluns and Piggy's gasps were once more audible.

Ralph called out in a quavering voice.

"All you littluns go to sleep. We've had a fight with the others. Now go to sleep. . . ."

Samneric came close and peered at Ralph.

"Are you two all right?"

"I think so—"

"—I got busted. . . ."

"That was Jack and his hunters," said Ralph bitterly. "Why can't he leave us alone?"

. . . Far off along the bowstave of beach, three figures trotted toward the Castle Rock. . . . Occasionally they sang softly; occasionally they

turned cartwheels down by the moving streak of phosphorescence. The Chief led them, trotting steadily, exulting in his achievement. He was a chief now in truth; and he made stabbing motions with his spear. . . .
William Golding, Lord of the Flies (1959)

Ralph's question is important: "Why can't he leave us alone?" Golding's answer has to do with human nature. People are innately aggressive. Often civilization puts a check on violent conflict, but, stripped of societal restraints, people affirm their true natures. Like the boys on the island, people "in the Raw" fight one another, exult in their killing, and make stabbing motions with their spears, guns, and bombs.

Blaming violence on human nature, on innate and unalterable instincts, places a great burden on biology. For if men and women are unavoidably driven by their biological inheritance, they suddenly lose their uniqueness. Granted, people create ideas, pyramids, and spaceships, but, at bottom, they are just like dogs, cats, and horses. For all animals, biology is destiny and if people are willing to face this fact, they will work within the behavioral limits set by their evolutionary inheritance.

Perhaps. But is it a fact? Is it true that in terms of possibilities, people's lives are biologically closed? To begin to answer these questions, we must consider animals besides ourselves. For if we are unique, that judgment can only be based on a comparison with Earth's other animal inhabitants.

OTHER ANIMALS AND US

The aim in this section is to show that the world of infrahuman animals is biologically padlocked in terms of its possibilities. Naturally, some animals are more capable than others, but despite differences in abilities between, say, a horse and a chimpanzee, the overall conclusion is the same: biology closely limits the world-making possibilities of all infrahuman animals.

Take as a first example "the almost universal tendency of animals" to become attached to certain specific localities. Salmon yearly trek from the ocean to spawn in the streams where they first hatched and birds fly enormous distances to return year after year to the same nesting place. Often, animals not only return to a particular location, but also many always remain in the same areas or home ranges (Scott, 1969). The beautiful blue and red wall creeper lives only in Europe, and at that its local distribution is exclusively confined to the middle and southern parts of the Continent. In the case of the waxen chatterer, the bird lives in Norway, Sweden, Germany, Japan, China, and America, but, for all its wanderings, it always stays between the fortieth and seventieth degrees latitude (Gould and Kolb, 1970).

If biology often places set limits on where animals live, as well as when and where they move, biology also determines the "continuous cohesion" seen in many animal groups. During the first twenty-four hours of life, chicks become attached to virtually anything, another chicken, an animal of another species, and even an inanimate object. Although the process continues for about twelve weeks in dogs, they too form critical attachments in the first weeks of life, and rhesus monkeys reared away from their mothers become attached to inanimate objects, preferring comfortable models, even when another, not so comfortable model, furnishes rewards (Scott, 1969; Rutter, 1974).

Primary socialization is the name given to this process of gaining social attachments, and studies show that the process is "largely internal." In fact, in contrast to behavior controlled by external reinforcements, many animals have no choice about these attachments—bonds are formed because they must be. Often neither external stimulation nor reinforcement changes attachments made during the critical period, for the process is biologically primary, not socially derived (Scott, 1969).

Another way of focusing on infrahuman animal abilities is to ask how much and what animals can learn. In one study of Japanese rhesus monkeys, a new behavior pattern spread to the entire species. Normally fed in the wild, the troop was fed grain on a sandy beach. Eventually one monkey learned that by placing mixed grain and sand under water, the grain floated to the top. Quickly, other members of the troops picked up the new method, although younger monkeys learned faster than their elders (Scott, 1969).

Other examples of malleable behavior patterns are easily available (for example, the blue tit now knows how to open the top of milk containers), but these patterns "are largely connected with food-gathering." Beyond these, other animal behavior is relatively stable. For example, raccoons, comparatively wise animals, were tested for delayed reactions. Placed in a wire mesh cage, facing three identical exit doors, each with its own electric grid and light bulb, the raccoon must learn that to choose a lighted exit equals food, a darkened exit a shock. So the raccoon learns to associate food with light, while the position of light is randomly changed over the series of trails. Now, once the raccoon consistently goes to the light, a new experiment asks the raccoon to remember where the light *was*. Still in the cage, the raccoon sees the lighted exit for a moment, then the light is turned off, and the light is also off when the cage is opened. Does the raccoon recall the light's position? For a period of up to twenty-five seconds, yes. The raccoon goes directly to the lighted exit and obtains food, proving that it can represent an absent stimulus in its brain. But after twenty-five seconds, the raccoon's memory fails; unable to represent the stimulus, the raccoon achieves no more than chance accuracy on the test (Munn, 1971; Scott, 1969).

Although rats did poorly on the same test, monkeys and chimpanzees do exceptionally well on tests of delayed reaction. In one experiment, monkeys sat in their cages while two cups that looked and smelled alike were placed to the cage's right and left. Experimenters caught the monkey's attention, placed food under one cup, and then placed a screen between animal and cups. From trial to trial the baited cup was moved around, and since the cups looked and smelled exactly alike, if the animal uncovered the food, the cause was not an external stimulus. Like the raccoon, only the capacity to represent an absent stimulus in the mind explains the monkey's ability to locate the food after delays of up to twenty-four hours. In a slightly altered test, chimpanzees remembered for as long as forty-eight hours (Munn, 1971).

Forty-eight hours is a long time. But a person of average intelligence could easily recall the food's location—via a stored image—for forty-eight days, forty-eight months, or even forty-eight years. Put differently, no other animal remotely approaches a person's ability to store and recall via images and symbols (for example, words) the reality experienced. And this is significant because it is hard to overestimate the importance of an ability to symbolically represent reality via images, words, and gestures. For example, if we use the word *mind* to refer to "inner control based on information acquired by the individual" (Munn, 1971), the amount of storable information, and thus the possibility of inner control, is tremendously increased if we can represent hundreds of things (say, the varieties of dogs) by one symbol (the word *dog*). Remember, too, that with the ability to symbolically store information for many years, an animal need not relearn, time after time, which lighted exit leads to food or which cup contains a reward. With the ability to approach reality via symbols, plus the capacity to remember those symbols, knowledge is permanent. Indeed, the animal can even try to learn something new.

Experiments such as those with the raccoon or chimpanzee show that the capacity to store symbols is poor in even the most advanced infrahuman animals. Another factor that severely limits their world-making possibilities is the infrahuman animal's inability to use complex symbols in communication. Take the bees and the birds. Bees "talk" by grading their messages, "by moving the signal along a physical dimension in correlation with a shift in content." For example, a worker bee returning from a hunting expedition performs a dance on the beehive wall. If the food is within ninety meters of the hive, the bee does a "round dance"; if the food is over ninety meters, the bee does a "wiggle dance," tracing a figure eight and indicating distance by the dance's speed. Other bees understand the wiggle dance quite well because, after seeing it performed, they fly directly to the food (McNeil, 1972).

This is remarkable. But remember the limits of bee "talk." When they receive the message, "they have no option as to behavior. . . . Communication depends on the lock-step adjustment of bees to other bees. . . . The entire system is so rigid that nothing is required beyond a method of referring to biologically important states. . . ." (McNeil, 1972). So, within their biologically set limits, bees "talk" perfectly, but lacking the ability to *combine* complex symbols, bees could never develop sentences, the most obvious manifestation of people's ability to communicate with indefinite creativity or open-endedness (Lyons, 1970; Chomsky, 1973).

Birds can combine elements in communicating with one another; they can make new combinations that stand for new messages. For instance, in order to distinguish between high and low intensity of alarm, passerine birds do not grade their messages—they do not move the signal along a physical dimension. Instead, "each call is a distinct acoustic category, unrelated to the other." And among mistle thrushes, this ability reaches a high degree; for thrushes combine about twenty basic themes in their communications. Again, this is remarkable. But songbirds only combine sounds: unlike people, they do not combine messages, and they never use our complex symbols of communication: words (McNeil, 1972).

As a final example, let's turn to monkeys. Like bees, they grade their messages, but instead of talking about external happenings, monkeys use their rich repertoire of calls to focus on internal events. When threatening an animal of inferior rank, monkeys roar—a long, loud noise. But when threatening a superior, they screech, making abrupt pitch changes. And in the wild, where dense vegetation makes visual contact difficult, monkeys use calls to indicate their location. Naturally, these calls make them conspicuous targets for predators, so, to cut down on the risks, they use short calls which fade in and out. In addition, the calls use few frequencies, making it very difficult to precisely pin down an animal's location (Rowell, 1972; McNeil, 1972).

In the wild, monkeys rely on grading. Acoustically, they fail to combine elements, and, most important, in sharp contrast to people, monkeys lack a predicative system of communication. Where the open-endedness, the creativity of language is its ability to predicate, to root communication in the assumption that a set of arbitrary symbols—words—refers to external events, internal states, or both, monkeys are biologically locked into a grading system that focuses on internal states (McNeil, 1972; Farb, 1974).

However, because monkeys are similar to people in so many ways, a number of researchers have tried to teach them to use language. Most attempts have failed, but after ten years of instruction, Beatrice and Allen Gardener have taught their chimpanzee Washoe to use hundreds of words. Although this is an achievement, for all her talk Washoe combines words spontaneously (children's combinations of words make grammatical relations explicit) and, most important, shows little ability to organize her words into sentences. As McNeil notes, monkeys are probably at the "threshold" of a genuine linguistic system, but ten years of labor with

Washoe has shown that biological limits keep them at the threshold. They are forever unable to use the communication system willed in evolution only to human beings (McNeil, 1972).

BRAINS AND GAINS

Let's begin with a conclusion. People are unique, different in kind from every other animal on Earth. This is so for a number of inextricably linked reasons. First, people lack the biological chains that closely limit the world-making possibilities of infrahuman animals. Instincts, defined as innate, unalterable, fixed action patterns, are absent in people; in fact, one human problem is to transcend biological *underdevelopment* by building a cultural world that ensures survival (Berger, 1969; Fernandez, 1975). Second, humans are born with a brain that allows them to store symbolically enormous amounts of information, and, because of its unique structure, that brain also allows people to use language, a tremendously creative form of communication. Third, with language, people can "arbitrarily impose signification"; by creating and bestowing value on ideas, places, things, humans can make a world for themselves. That is a unique ability; it is also a tremendous responsibility. Fourth, and perhaps most important, because they can acquire, store, and use complex symbols for inner control, people can actually talk to themselves, about themselves and their world. Remembering via symbols what happened yesterday, or ten years ago yesterday, people can use their memories to look backward or forward; they can even consciously change themselves if a look at past or present convinces them that change is needed (see, for example, Eiseley, 1957 and 1961; Mumford, 1967; Munn, 1971; Birney and Teevan, 1961; Montagu, 1968).

No other animal uses symbols as people do. We alone have this ability. We are also the only animal able to consciously change ourselves and our world (White, 1949).

Although life began to evolve in the sea about 2 billion years ago, the oldest fish fossil goes back only 400 million years, youngsters such as the dinosaur are about 280 million years old, and human evolution dates from the appearance of the insect-eating shrew about 60 to 75 million years ago. Precursors of the modern anthropoid ape go back 28 million years, the first advanced hominid lived in Africa about 2 million years ago, creatures such as ourselves roamed Southern Africa about 400,000 years ago, and *Homo sapiens*—man and woman—put in an appearance about 30,000 years ago (Munn, 1971).

Undoubtedly, other animals noticed our arrival, but the full evolutionary significance of our appearance, the basis of our uniqueness, is clear only if we can do something other animals cannot do—use our brain to analyze our brain.

Size is not the crucial variable. People do have large brains, but an elephant's brain is three times larger than any human's, and a whale's brain is nearly five times larger. However, in comparing the ratio of brain size to body weight, people have about 1 pound of brain to every 50 pounds of bulk; gorillas weigh in with a ratio of 1 to 250, elephants 1 to 500, and whales 1 to 10,000. Finally, in comparing the brain's weight to that of the spinal cord, human uniqueness begins to show itself. For example, an ape's brain is 15 times as heavy as its spinal cord; the human brain is 55 times as heavy as the spinal cord (Munn, 1971).

Since the nervous system develops as "one single neural tube," people use the unity of the brain's processes to control complex thought and action. Humans exercise control better than any other creatures primarily because evolution gave people so much gray matter. Recall that nervous tissues are gray or white, that white tissue transmits impulses, and that gray matter, which results from tightly packed nerve cell bodies, is the locus of decision making, *the* place where people interpret messages received from others. Now in most parts of the nervous system, gray matter wears a coat of white tissue, but the mass of brain known as the cerebrum is covered in gray and, as the accompanying illustration shows, during evolution the cerebrum grew and grew until, in humans, it enveloped the rest of the brain (Gurney, 1973).

A gray cerebral covering, the cortex, made its first appearance among the reptiles, but most of their external gray matter, the paleo or old cortex, dealt with smell. Only a minute portion was equivalent to our gray matter, the neocortex, and, most important, as our neocortex grew, the old cortex was either shoved aside or internalized in the brain. Not surprisingly, people paid for this pushiness; in contrast to other animals, our sense of smell is poor (Gurney, 1973; Eiseley, 1957). But if we lost the ability to sniff with precision, we gained something else—the gift of mind, the power of inner, conscious control of thought and action.

Consider some gains of a large cortex. First, humans are able to control old functions in new ways. Estimates are that the cortex contains 14 billion tightly packed cells—but remember that cell density in the cortex decreased during evolution. The result was greater inner control because, if the space between cells is greater, mutual electrical influence decreases, and "the reflex response can be set aside in favor of the learned" (Gurney, 1973; Childe, 1951). Second, the cerebral hemispheres of the human brain perform associative functions; they allow us to interrelate information received, to recall plus to relate past and present, and to reason. In the brains of infrahuman vertebrates, the associative areas are relatively small. In people "the association areas are larger than the areas given over to sensory and motor functions," with the frontal lobes of the cerebral hemi-

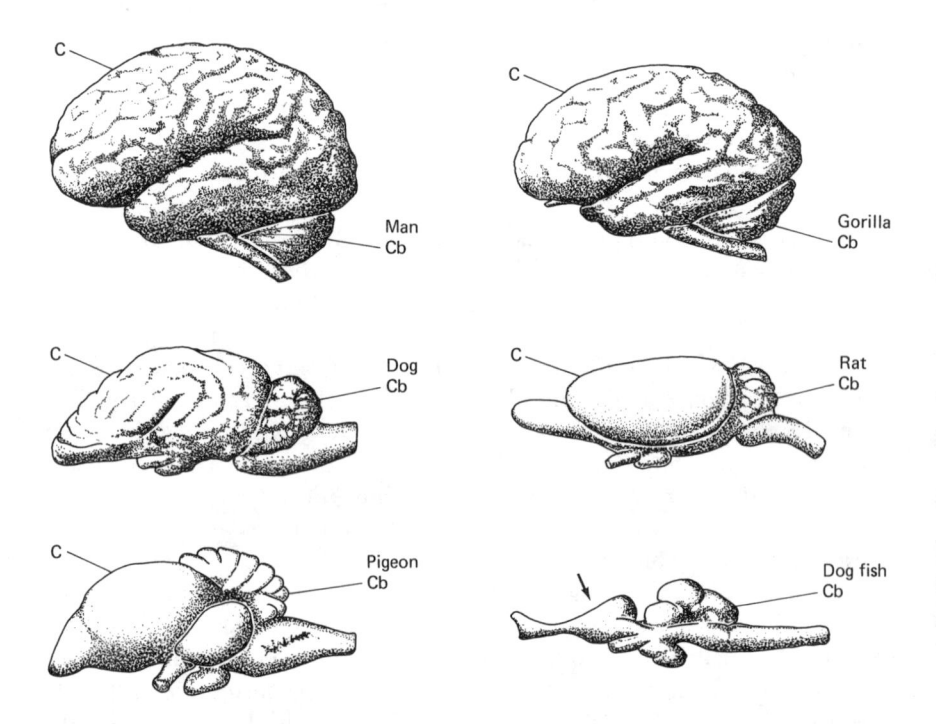

The brain from fish to man. Brains are drawn the same length to show adequate detail in smaller ones. Relative sizes are shown by approximate weights, in grams: man, 1500; gorilla, 400; dog, 130; rat, 2; pigeon, 2.2; and dogfish, 3. The cerebrum (C) not only grows heavier, it also enlarges in proportion to body weight. The dogfish has no cerebrum (arrow shows comparable structure). The gorilla, much heavier than man, has only about one-fourth the human brain weight. Note invaginations shown in the dog's brain; these are more pronounced in the gorilla and human brains. The smell brain, prominent at the left of the three lower brains, recedes in higher brains. Cb is cerebellum. Note its prominence in the pigeon, which exhibits behavior notable for its complex coordinations. In the pigeon the optic thalmus is seen below the cerebellum.

spheres especially large. This is significant because the frontal lobes deal with "voluntary motor action and association" (Munn, 1971).

Third, and last, since changes in brain parts give a good indication of the importance of those parts, speech must be particularly significant for men and women. No muscular system of the body, not our legs, arms, or eyes, has more tissue devoted to receiving and controlling impulses than the tongue and vocal organs (Gurney, 1973). Perhaps some of us are loud mouths, but that is in keeping with the structure of our most remarkable organ—the human brain.

Lewis Mumford rightly notes that "brain and mind are non-comparable aspects of a single organic process" (Mumford, 1967). The brain is necessary to store and use large amounts of symbolic information, but what the brain holds and uses is the result of people's world-building activities. Women and men daily bestow meaning and value, store their work in their minds, and use this acquired knowledge as a basis for inner control of themselves and their world. Inextricably, then, brain and mind are linked, married with no possibility of divorce.

But, despite the links between mind and brain, one must always credit our human legacies. "Civilization" began about ten thousand years ago and since that time mind has passed on its work in books, buildings, wars, paintings, and cities. Often we embrace our particular cultural legacy; sometimes we flee it. However, whether we accept or reject, rethink or rebuild the mind's legacies, all people use the same process and tool. People think, they talk to themselves about themselves and their world, using as their tool a set of arbitrary symbols, a human language.

So if the brain is the biological basis of our uniqueness, and mind the symbol we use to refer to inner control based on acquired information, then language is the indefinitely creative tool that allows us to use our brain to create mind's legacies. By far, language is the most important means of human communication.

LANGUAGE

"We'll all come over to your next party, Mr. Gatsby," she suggested. "What do you say?"

"Certainly, I'd be delighted to have you."

"Be ver' nice," said Mr. Sloane, without gratitude. "Well—think ought to be starting home."

"Please don't hurry," Gatsby urged them. . . . "Why don't you stay for supper? I wouldn't be surprised if some other people dropped in from New York."

"You come to supper with *me*," said the lady enthusiastically. "Both of you."

This included me. Mr. Sloane got to his feet.

"Come along," he said—but to her only.

"I mean it," she insisted. "I'd love to have you. Lots of room."

Gatsby looked at me questioningly. He wanted to go, and he didn't see that Mr. Sloane had determined he shouldn't. . . .

"I haven't got a horse," said Gatsby. . . . "I'll have to follow you in my car. Excuse me for just a minute."

. . . "My God, I believe the man's coming," said Tom. "Doesn't he know she doesn't want him?"

"She says she does want him."

"She has a big dinner party and he won't know a soul there."

. . . Suddenly Mr. Sloane and the lady walked down the steps and mounted their horses.

"Come on," said Mr. Sloane to Tom, "we're late. We've got to go." And then to me: "Tell him we couldn't wait, will you?"

F. Scott Fitzgerald, *The Great Gatsby* (1925)

Gatsby's mistake was to take a clear and exact statement—"You come to supper with me"—at face value. He should have known the lady was only being "polite"; he should have known she did not mean what she said. But Gatsby misinterpreted her remark, put a strain on all concerned, and wound up being offended—all because he took an exact phrase at face value.

Gatsby's problem is also our problem. For any human language is a system of symbols and signs that must be interpreted by the people who use it[1] (Aranguren, 1967). Symbols are arbitrary representations of an experience (love) or an event (Watergate); dictionaries exist to provide the specific meaning of every word in a language, but if people bestow many meanings on a word dictionaries can only list the products of such word building. It then becomes the individual's task to decide what words mean. For instance, *Webster's Seventh Collegiate Dictionary* lists seven different meanings for *love*. In talking with another person, one must decide how the word is being used. Conceivably a score in tennis (*love* is "zero" in tennis) could be interpreted as a sign of affection. Following Gatsby, one could easily misinterpret the "precise" words of another.

J. L. Aranguren uses the word *decipher* to stress the unavoidable gambles of communication (Goffman, 1955; Aranguren, 1967). People say this, but mean that. We must decipher, through facial expressions, voice inflections, knowledge of the person, situational variables, what is actually meant. If the communication is face-to-face, the gamble is less risky. Misunderstandings can be avoided by subtle probings or explicit questions.

---

[1] Any word is both symbol and sign. It is *first* a symbol because people use words to represent things, experiences, events. Meaning is humanly bestowed and represented in symbols. But, after a symbol is established, it functions as a sign, as a physical form, whose purpose it is "to indicate some other thing, object, quality, or event" (White, 1949).

But, when one turns to the printed page to read what an author has written, the risks increase greatly. If the author is unclear, if he uses a word without defining it, both reader and writer are in trouble. The reader's problem is unresolvable uncertainty about meaning: "How can I pass an exam when this guy is in a fog?" The writer's problem is twofold: the reader might slap down the book in disgust or the reader might think the writer meant the opposite of what he intended to say.

So, remember this: dictionaries contain a record of a language, the accumulated word-makings of countless human beings. In appearance dictionaries seem to "stop the action"—to say that this is *the* meaning of that word. Don't be fooled by appearance. Words are alive; they are the ongoing creation of human beings. Often we do "settle" on one accepted meaning for a word; if we did not, human communication would be chaotic. But two factors jointly cause communication via language to be an interpretative process. One, words very often have many meanings. Two, words are never used in a vacuum. People use words, in certain situations, in certain moods, and on the basis of certain ethnic and class influences. All these factors determine the meaning of words in action; indeed, all these factors guarantee that communication via language is always an interpretative, a deciphering process.

Today, no one is certain why children acquire a language so quickly. Born wordless, children often speak well by the age of three or four, and by five or six they "produce and understand" an indefinitely large number of phrases they have never met before. This amazing ability to master language has led some to turn to biology for answers. Noam Chomsky suggests that all languages contain "invariant properties," "deep-seated and rather abstract principles of a very general nature that determine the form and interpretation of sentences in all human languages." Chomsky says these language universals are genetically determined, and while environment is still very important for explaining language acquisition and development, all people get off to a flying start because of their "innate language facility." In fact, "if an artificial language were constructed which violated some of these general (universal) principles, then it would not be learned at all, or at least not learned with the ease and efficiency with which a normal child will learn human language" (Chomsky, 1973; Lyons, 1972; Farb, 1974).

Time and study will prove or disprove Chomsky's hypothesis, but even if it is true, Chomsky refers to universals of an "abstract and very general nature." His focus is syntax, his universals are "regularities governing the combinations of words" (for example, where nouns, verbs, and verb-phrases are placed). No mention is made of specific languages; no mention is made of semantics, of that aspect of linguistics that describes the meaning of words and sentences. In short, while biology may determine how all people put words together, meaning is still humanly bestowed. Any particular language is the result of human endeavor, and any particular language shapes our thoughts while simultaneously giving us the ability to create new ones.

Language is often seen as a "mold shaping the mind," as a major element in the formation of thought," as a programmer of people's perceptions about self and world (Brown, 1965; Sapir, 1960; Hall, 1969; Ervin-Tripp, 1964). Let's take two examples. First the Hanunoo, a group that has names for ninety-two varieties of rice. Now such precise word-making obviously reflects the importance of rice to the Hanunoo; but the words enable them to see things the outsider is blind to. The English language talks of brown and white rice. That is it. Granted, with effort one could get beyond two types of rice, but a Hanunoo learns ninety-two types as a matter of course, and those ninety-two types are an acute programmer of Hanunoo perceptions about the world of rice (Brown, 1965). Incidentally, the Hanunoo are typical: Eskimos have several words for snow, the Lapp languages of northern Scandinavia have many words for reindeer, and the Bedouin Arabs possess "a large camel vocabulary" (Trudgill, 1974).

Our second example is drawn from the Australian aboriginal language Njamal. Here one word, *mama*, is "used for all males of the same generation as the father." Njamal makes no distinction between father and uncle; these relationships are relatively unimportant in Njamal society. So, because of the language, because of the mold shaping the mind, all Njamal lack uncles. *Mamas* they have, but no Njamal can say, "I love my uncle" or "My father is just like my uncle." The word is absent in the Njamal language, and it is *mama* that furnishes the mold for Njamal thinking about all males of the same generation as the father (Trudgill, 1974).

One main reason why language shapes our thought is that it exists before we do. We inherit the word-makings of others—our near and distant ancestors—who used words to symbolically represent certain events, experiences, relationships, ideas. This enabled them to impose a measure of order on reality; it gave them the ability "to convey information, warn of dangers, transmit values, and guide action" (Brown, 1965). That is a significant achievement, but the rub is that *their* word-building shapes *our* thought. In fact, if the semantic arrangement of a language corresponds to the typically relevant experiences dominant in a society (Schutz and Luckmann, 1974), then what was typical for them is also typical for us. Wordless at birth, we must at least begin with the word-makings of others.

Another more basic reason why language shapes our thought is that words are by far the prime means people use in thinking. Thinking is internalized conversation (Mead, 1934); it is talking to ourselves about ourselves and our world. So, if like the Vietnamese, we lived for thousands of years without the pronoun *I*, plus lacked the opportunity or incentive to rethink our inherited language (Fitzgerald, 1972), we would talk to ourselves about ourselves within the limits set by the inherited mold. We would not say, "I did this" or "I think that." Referring to ourselves, we *would* say, "Your brother went there" or "Your nephew likes school." Without the desire or opportunity for change, there is little choice in our terms of reference. For we think by means of words, via the symbolic representations of others.[2]

Perhaps all this is very confusing. Language shapes thought; language is indefinitely creative. The paradox is real, but it is not new. The paradox is life's. Consider this. Theoretically any person's world is wide open in terms of possibilities. Owning the ability to symbolically represent reality, to think with words, people can build any version of self and society. However, since all people are wordless at birth, they must rely initially on the word-makings of others. And those inherited words are undoubtedly an important factor in shaping thoughts and programing perceptions. But, if language is a mold, the mold is both pliable and breakable. For words do not stand alone. People make words, and variables such as temperament, personality, social class (see, for example, Bernstein, 1972), ethnic group, skin color, religion, occupation, and experience all play a part in deciding the meaning of a word for any specific individual or group. The result is a dialectical relationship between ourselves and our inherited language; it molds us and we mold it.

Our ability to make language, to bestow meaning, assures creativity on at least three fronts. First, based on the meanings provided by others, any person can use old words to mean new things. Take the word *Amazon*. To many of us, *Amazon* refers to a group of female warriors who continually fight with the gods of Greek mythology. But to Eldridge Cleaver, an Amazon is a subfeminine woman. Monopolizing all the "good" traits for themselves, upper-class women—ultrafeminine females—have enhanced their own image by projecting all "the domestic components of their nature" onto lower-class women. The result is the subfeminine woman, in social imagery, an Amazon (see Cleaver, 1968).

A second side of creativity via language is the human ability to use words as symbolic representations of new experiences. For example, the following symbols were nonexistent in 1859 America: unemployment, lockout, genocide, corporate state, totalitarianism, master race, cold war, iron curtain, bomb shelter (Schattschneider, 1969). Each word or phrase represents something new. Civilians were not systematically bombed be-

---

[2] While the absence of a word does not mean an inability to perceive, words sharpen our perceptions immeasurably. For example, try assessing the significance of some event or experience without using words.

fore World War II, and corporations assumed great power only toward the end of the nineteenth century. But, when people produced these changes, when they decided to bomb anyone, they were able to use words to represent their decisions and actions. Unfortunately, many of the new words and phrases refer to the horrors of war, but that is not the fault of language. Language is a creative tool in the hands of people that can be used to represent beauty or horror, peace or war. Human beings make the choices; language represents in symbols the products of their world-making efforts.

The third side of creativity via language is probably the most important. Reference is to the ability to use language as a means of gaining conscious control over self and society. Consider the consequences of literacy. Before people could write, culture was passed on orally, one result being a continual failure to perceive personal and societal contradictions. Since they were passed on orally, conceptualizations of the past could not help being governed by the concerns of the present, merely because there was no body of chronologically ordered statements to which reference could be made (Goody and Watt, 1972). But once people could write, awareness of contradictions was much harder to avoid. People could rise above the present and use the written word to "objectively" compare yesterday and today. For many, what they saw was a shock; they noticed "so many inconsistencies in the beliefs and categories of understanding handed down to them that they were impelled to a much more conscious, comparative, and critical attitude to the accepted world picture. . . ." (Goody and Watt, 1972).

Historically, this critical attitude led to at least two lines of thought. The Skeptics of ancient Greece applauded "dogmatic doubt"; eying the past, they became disgusted with it and approached the future on a foundation of distrust and disbelief (Russell, 1961). But in *The Republic*, Plato dared to imagine something startlingly new: Utopia. For Plato, an awareness of contradictions led to the conclusion that the future could be different. In fact, elated by the possibilities of tomorrow, Utopians faced the future with a perfect plan.

Perfect plans are always at a premium, and today most people seriously doubt the possibility of such plans. But Skeptics and Utopians symbolize the polar reactions to the conscious discovery of inconsistencies and contradictions in the approach to self and society. More important, they illustrate the human ability to move into the future on the basis of a conscious look—via language—at the past and the present. Naturally we need not look back to move forward, but the power is there to be used; employing words, all people have the potential to consciously build the futures on the basis of a corrected past. Paradoxically, language shapes our thought while providing the means (words) of its own destruction.

THE INFLUENCE OF GENES

So far the emphasis of this chapter has been on the uniqueness of people, the open-ended possibilities of human life. Now we reverse course and turn to genetic constraint. For if people are not biologically determined, they do inherit certain predispositions that "color" the abilities and traits acquired through learning (White, 1972; Allport, 1937).

Let's begin with constitution, for the size and shape of our bodies are closely determined by genetic factors. Studies of identical twins reared apart show that when they reach adulthood, differences of more than one inch (about 1.5 percent) are unusual. For identical twins reared together, the differences are the same and much less than those height differences between fraternal twins reared together (Carter, 1970).

Since height is the result of more than one gene pair, interesting differences occur between fathers and sons. Sons of tall men tend to be tall, but not as tall as their fathers; and sons of short men tend to be short, but not as short as their fathers. For example, 72-inch fathers had one-sixteenth of their sons at 72 inches, another sixteenth at 64 inches, but the large majority ranged between 66 and 70 inches (Carter, 1970).

Although proper nutrition can influence height, its overall effect appears to be small. Studies in London over the last seventy-five years show a possible increase of one inch in the height of the average English man or woman. However, nutrition can influence the *rate* of growth. Eleven-year-olds in London are now four inches taller than their predecessors in 1900. Apparently, a better environment steps up the pace of growth, so that full height is now reached earlier than ever before (Carter, 1970).

Height is genetically determined, but its effect on personality is the result of a social response to a biological fact. Take two examples. If a culture, say America, puts a great value on social success in adolescence, the very tall or very short person is at a distinct disadvantage. Unable to find dancing partners, much less dates, they may begin to feel odd or even inferior. Either way, they respond to the society's definition of their constitutional worth. Or, take a 64-inch son of a 72-inch father. Suppose dad is a real "he-man," a father who expects his son to follow in his virile footsteps. Well, the 64-inch son is in trouble. Constitutionally, he is going to have difficulties in meeting his father's expectations. One possible result may be the son's feeling that he has let his father down, that he is not worth all the time his father spends in trying to help him to be a "real man."

Besides height and body build (see Carter, 1970), people are genetically susceptible to a large number of diseases. This is especially true of men, the weaker sex. Recall that a woman's sex chromosomes are XX, a man's XY. The problem is the puny Y chromosome. It is one-fifth the size of an X chromosome, and, of great importance, the Y chromosome carries few genes. So, when a disease (for example, hemophilia) is inherited as a single, sex-linked recessive gene, men have a problem. Unlike women, they lack another X chromosome which, if it is normal, easily suppresses the recessive gene. Men depend on their Y chromosome, and it is unable to prevent the appearance of various sex-linked diseases. For example, besides hemophilia, men are much more susceptible to dense hairy growth on the ears, the absence of teeth enamel, skin cysts, double eyelashes, red-green color blindness, day blindness, night blindness, progressive deafness, barklike skin, and the loss of hair (Montagu, 1974; Hutt, 1972; Potts, 1970).

All these susceptibilities are obviously biological facts but, once again, their effect on personality is often the result of social forces. Take the loss of hair. Society says that a man needs a full head of hair to be attractive to women. Like Samson, the loss of hair supposedly saps a man's sexual strength. To counteract baldness, and the sense of "inferiority" which it brings, some men use toupees, others begin to comb whatever hair is left forward or sideward. Either way, the response to the biological fact of hair loss is a result of society's scorn for those without a head of wavy hair.[3]

If biological factors directly determine a person's height or susceptibility to baldness, the role of biology decreases when we turn our attention to the causes of intelligence. However, before we take that turn, let's first discuss the meaning of the word *intelligence,* as well as the meaning and interpretation of I.Q. tests.

Intelligence is generally defined "as the ability to benefit from experience." It is a person's capacity to perceive facts and propositions, to reason about the relations between those facts and propositions, as well as to use the acquired knowledge for adaptive purposes (Kagan, 1971; Mussen, 1973). Now, if this is the definition of intelligence, the next question becomes: What does the normal means of measuring intelligence, the I.Q. test, tell us about intelligence?

I.Q. tests measure one aspect of intelligence; they focus on verbal skills and abilities. In addition, most tests measure knowledge and skills already possessed by the child. Few tests contain questions requiring children to learn new responses or ideas, and as such they cannot be treated as "pure

---

[3] Women also have biological difficulties. Menstruation is often quite painful, and severe problems do have psychological consequences (see Montagu, 1974). The focus here has been on men because our society has given so little recognition to the biological weaknesses of males. Sheer physical strength does not equal biological superiority.

measures of native ability or intellectual potential" (Mussen, 1973; Kagan, 1971). On the contrary, it could be argued that the I.Q. test's focus on verbal skills and abilities does not measure the most important aspect of intelligence (Jencks et al., 1973). For example, a person could have weak verbal abilities but continually show a capacity to use knowledge, say about farming, for adaptive purposes. Because I.Q. tests do not measure this ability, is the person to be considered stupid? And more importantly, which is the most crucial aspect of intelligence: verbal ability or the capacity to use knowledge for adaptive purposes?

I.Q. tests have faults, but they still reveal something about the biological basis of intelligence. For example, in one study of identical twins reared together, the correlation of I.Q. tests for 95 pairs of twins was .92; for 53 pairs of identical twins reared apart, the correlation was .87 (Bayley, 1970). Both of these figures are *impressively* high, and other investigators obtain similar results. Mussen cites a study which shows that identical twins reared *apart* had test correlations of .76, while fraternal twins reared *together* could muster test correlations of only .55 (Mussen, 1973). Finally, studying 50 pairs of identical twins reared together, Newman et al. found I.Q. differences of no more than 9 points on 84 percent of the pairs; fully 48 percent had differences of no more than 4 points. In tests of pairs of brothers and pairs of sisters reared together, only 60 percent had I.Q. differences of 9 points or less (Carter, 1970).

These results provide solid and impressive evidence that heredity plays a part in determining human intelligence. The question is: How much? No one knows for sure. Consider the following three examples. First, tested at 21 months, a shy boy from an unhappy home scored 106; at 4, in an improved home situation, he had an I.Q. of 140; at 6, with the reappearance of home problems, it dropped to 123; at 12, it jumped to 163, and at 18, when he was very depressed about himself and his family, his I.Q. had fallen to 122 (Bayley, 1970). Second, a group of black preschool children from poverty families in the South went to preschool classes for the summer. The average I.Q. gain for those with tutoring five days a week was 15 points; for those with tutoring three days a week, the average gain was 7 points; and children in the control groups generally made no I.Q. gains. Third and last, remember that very different environments can also seriously affect the I.Q.'s of identical twins reared apart. In one instance, the first twin was adopted into a home that stressed education and achievement; her sister lived in an isolated mountain setting and dropped out of school at a very early age. The difference in I.Q. between the girls was 24 points, with the deprived twin fully 7 years behind her sister in educational achievement (Mussen, 1973).

These results offer considerable evidence that environment plays a part in determining intelligence. Children who are not motivated to learn, children who, like migrant youngsters, feel that teachers dislike them (see Coles, 1971), and children who are anxious about school or home life, have great difficulty in making their latent abilities manifest. Often, children's environments inhibit intelligence to such a great extent that the I.Q. brand of "below average" or "stupid" bears no resemblance to abilities that are actually present.

In sum, heredity sets flexible limits on intelligence, and the "best estimate" is that "genes explain about 45 percent of the variance in American's test scores, that environment explains about 35 percent, and that the tendency of environmentally advantaged families to have genetically advantaged children explains the remaining 20 percent" (see Jencks et al., 1973; also Mussen, 1973; Bayley, 1970).

Temperament is the last topic in this section. Defined as a person's characteristic inclinations or modes of emotional response, temperament deals with individual susceptibility to emotional stimulation, customary strength and speed of response, quality of prevailing mood, as well as peculiar fluctuations and intensity of mood (Buss et al., 1973). In everyday language, temperament refers to the level and quality of a person's emotions, activity, sociability, and impulsiveness. Because of temperament, people tend to be active or passive, outgoing or reserved, deliberate or impulsive, even-tempered or moody.

A solid body of evidence shows that genetic factors influence a person's temperament. For example, one study makes a distinction between "easy" and "difficult" infants (Thomas et al., 1968). From birth, easy children enjoy a regular rhythm; they nap, remain awake, eat, and eliminate as if on schedule. Generally they are quite sociable; it makes little difference who feeds the child, and even visits to new and strange places go smoothly. Moodiness is rare; these children generally cry only when they are hungry or sleepy. The case is somewhat different with difficult children. As infants they seem to need much less rest than the average baby. Sleep is irregular; they may wake up two or three times during the night. There is no schedule—unpredictability is the rule! Moodiness is common; exposed to new places, difficult children often become fearful and negative. Placed in a bathtub, the child responds with kicks and screams, and, when finally accustomed to the tub, difficult children may scream and kick when parents try to take them out of it (Thomas et al., 1968; see also Bell, 1968).

One rule is to hope for an easy child, but is hope realistic? How much does inheritance determine temperament? In an attempt to answer this question, Buss et al. studied more than 100 pairs of identical and fraternal twins. They found considerable support for a genetic influence on temperament, but finally concluded that "the data argue strongly not only that the four temperaments (that is, emotionality, activity, sociability, impulsivity) are in some degree inherited, but also that they are in some degree altered by socialization." Although this is obviously not a clear-cut, clean conclusion, it does have one thing in its favor: it is rooted in the empirical evidence that social psychologists possess.

Consider evidence from two longitudinal studies. In Topeka, children were studied at birth and then some years later by another group of researchers. This made it possible to arrange an experiment in which the "blind" predictions of the first researchers, made within the first thirty-two weeks of the children's lives, were compared with the appraisals of the later workers. On activity level, the original predictions were 67 percent correct. Although not a remarkable figure, it is a lot better than chance guesses (White, 1972).

In another study, covering the period from birth to early maturity, the authors noted "that the tendency toward passivity during preadolescence was already apparent during the first two years of life." Moreover, passivity was significantly associated with a "consistent cluster" of school-age behaviors. Passive children tended to avoid dangerous activities, to conform to parents' wishes, and to refrain from physical and verbal aggression. However, Kagan and Moss also found that the prediction of adult passivity-activity worked only for girls. Boys were unpredictable, and the authors rightly noted that social factors acted to confound their predictions. Society teaches girls to be passive, so girls found little resistance to their temperamental inclination. But boys have to be tough, aggressive, active. Passivity was not tolerated in the boys; on the contrary, social pressures demanded that they cast temperament to the winds and act like the men they would become (Kagan and Moss, 1962; White, 1972).

Yes and no: once again that is our conclusion. For the evidence shows that while temperament is inherited, genes furnish predispositions rather than finished products. Paraphrasing Robert W. White, inherited temperament tips the learning scale in one direction or another, increasing the chances that some behaviors will be learned well, others not so well. But inherited temperament does not ensure one result rather than another. Instead, because it provides "a gentle persistent slanting of experience," inherited temperament's main influence is "to color traits acquired through learning" (White, 1972).

One last point. As evidence from longitudinal studies increases, social psychologists will learn more about temperament's role. However, it is hard to see how new evidence will undermine the overall conclusion. After all, with words, people can talk to themselves about their temperaments, and if they try hard, people can change. This would not be possible if genetic influences alone determined our modes of emotional response.

PERSONALITY AND THE SELF

Although biology influences human development, it by no means determines our beliefs, values, and practices. On the contrary, people develop over time, in society, and through a wide variety of actual, imagined, or implied social influences. At birth people are essentially potential. We become what we are (Allport, 1955), and other people always have a great deal to do with the course and causes of my, your, anyone's becoming.

Let's begin with the concept of personality. Psychologists say that personality is equivalent to individuality; it is what makes people distinctively themselves; it is a man or a woman's "unique adjustment" to his/her environment (Murphy, 1968; Allport, 1937; White, 1972). "Sam is mean, aggressive, and abrupt." "Alice is kind, considerate, and affectionate." "Paul is a pain—he has no sense of humor; he's moody, argumentative, and domineering."

Definitions of personality that stress individuality dominate social psychology. This is acceptable because it is true; even identical twins reared together make unique adjustments to their environment. However, when equating personality with individuality, we must also stress that it is often the typical that makes us distinctive. Personality is shaped by biological predispositions, situational variables, a history of unique experiences with others, and culture (Mussen, 1973). The last is common to everyone; like language, it is an arbitrary inheritance from the worldbuilders who went before. So, if you know someone whose individuality rests on being materialistic, acquisitive, and competitive, those characteristics are distinctively Tom's, Dick's, or Harry's; but those characteristic are also common to many people socialized in and by American culture. Each of us is simultaneously unique and typical; it is even possible that many of the characteristics that make us distinctive are shared with thousands of other "unique" personalities.

Take another example. Paul Mussen notes that personality is partly shaped by the individual's history of unique experiences with others. Now it is correct to say that any person's experiences with others are unique; your parents treated your brother as they treated you—but not in *exactly* the same way. However, while recognizing this uniqueness, social psychologists still try to typify it. Parents are loving or hostile, overprotective or neglectful, indulgent or indifferent. The basic assumption underlying these generalizations about parental attitudes is that they influence people in similar ways. Exposed to hostile, authoritarian parents, a person might easily develop into an aggressive, self-righteous, antagonistic personality (see, for example, Adorno et al., 1950). No one can say for certain that this will occur, only that it is more or less probable. But, once again we uncover typical forces that are the basis of individuality; once again we are forced to accept that many characteristics that make us distinctive are shared with others.

In sum, while personality *is* equivalent to individuality, one's distinctiveness is always rooted in a solid foundation of beliefs, values, parental attitudes, and child-rearing practices that are common to an ethnic group, social class, or religion. Inevitably, these typical forces shape distinctive personalities in similar ways.

In discussing personality, social psychologists sometimes seem contradictory. Personality is dynamic; it is the ongoing process of making distinctive adjustments to an environment. However, personality is also "demonstrated consistency" in behavior; granted, Freud overemphasized the links between infancy and adulthood, but people do show continuity in personality development and so consistency of behavior. Over time, individuality does manifest durability and even a "basic oneness" (Allport, 1937).

How can social psychologists stress both dynamism and consistency, both activity and stability? The answer is they must. Life leaves no choice. On the one hand, dynamism is a fact; if only because of situational variables (for example, being in school as opposed to home as opposed to a party), people constantly adjust personality to environment. On the other hand, people do show continuity and consistency in personality development. Stability is relative, and personality theory must make room for variability and change (Mischel, 1969).

Normally three types of continuity are cited. First is complete continuity: the basic psychological process (say, a feeling of inferiority) and the manifest form of behavior (say, an attempt to excel in sports) remain stable. Based on certain beliefs and attitudes, a person always does the same thing. Second is genotypic continuity: the psychological process (say, anxiety about parental rejection) remains stable, but the form of behavior changes. Where the six-year-old refused to go to school, the twelve-year-old now substitutes excessive obedience to parents. Third and finally is phenotypic continuity: the behavior remains stable, but the underlying psychological process changes. For example, a boy could join the army to escape his parents, discover he liked military life, and then decide to make the army his career. Over time the behavior remains stable, but the motives for behavior change (see Kagan, 1969).

When social psychologists stress personality continuity and consistency, genotypic continuity is often the model used. In childhood, people adopt a set of beliefs about self and world (for example, "I'm intelligent, well-liked, anxious about sex") and use this set of dispositions as a basis for behavior. Consistency arises because, whether children or adolescents, middle-aged or elderly, people rely on the same set of underlying psychological processes to guide their behavior.

Recently the notions of consistency and continuity have been criticized. Walter Mischel suggests that consistency is often an illusion. Citing the case of a man who steals on one occasion, lies on another, donates generously to charity on a third, cheats on a fourth, and still thinks of himself as a basically honest and moral person, Mischel feels that the human mind often "functions like an extraordinarily effective reducing valve, creating and maintaining the perception of continuity even in the face of perpetual observed changes in actual behavior" (Mischel, 1969).

This criticism has merit. For example, while most social psychologists stress the interaction between people and environment, some fail to follow this stress to its logical conclusion: interaction is a formative process in its own right (Blumer, 1969). A person might enter interaction owning certain underlying beliefs (for example, "I'm honest") but discover in the course of interaction that he can steal something with no possibility of getting caught. This discovery, in interaction, might move the person to steal, and, despite his dishonesty, the man might continue to believe that he is basically honest.

Interaction is only one of the variables that affect personality continuity and consistency. A second is that personality traits[4] often contradict one another. People might be submissive to symbols of political authority, domineering to everyone else. Or a person might be generous with his time, tight with his money. In "the ever changing environment," and along with situational variables, one trait appears here, another there (Allport, 1937). The social psychologist's task is to locate whatever continuity and consistency exist, knowing all the while that like a continually moving ramp, the *process* that is life often makes continuity and consistency difficult to achieve.

Our conclusion is twofold: "perfect consistency will never be found and must not be expected." Trait consistency is always a matter of degree (Allport, 1937). A person is generally nervous or typically compulsive, but the determining power of interaction, the contradictions between traits, *and the power of conscious personality change* all guarantee that even the most thorough search for perfect consistency will never achieve it.

Conceivably, a view of personality that makes "conceptual room" for variability and major change could be cause for gloom. Few people enjoy discarding theoretical models (for example, Freud's) that seem to hold the truth. But, if we seek to discuss reality, we have no choice. Trait in-

---

[4] A trait is defined as a distinguishing quality. A person is patient or impatient, generous or tight, active or passive.

consistency is a fact, and people often make personality changes that add discontinuity to their development. So, "to be more than nominally dynamic, our personality theories" must make "as much room for human discrimination as for generalization, as much place for personality change as stability, and as much concern for people's self-regulation as for their victimization by either enduring intraphysic forces or by momentary environmental constraints" (Mischel, 1969).

At best, this is a difficult task. But it is possible, and much of the formative work has already been done by those theorists who focused research interest on the development of the self.

THE SELF

"The mercy that I speak of," replied Don Quixote, "is that which God is showing me at this moment—in spite of my sins, as I have said. My mind now is clear, unencumbered by those misty shadows of ignorance that were cast over it by my better and continual reading of those hateful books of chivalry. I see through all contained in them, and my only regret is that my dillusionment has come so late . . . I find myself, niece, at the point of death and I would die in such a way as not to leave the impression of a life so bad that I shall be remembered as a madman; for even though I have been one I do not wish to confirm it on my deathbed. And so, my dear, call in my good friends . . . for I want to confess my sins and make my last will and testament."

The niece, however, was relieved of this errand, for they came in just then.

"I have good news for you, kind sirs," said Don Quixote the moment he saw them. "I am no longer Don Quixote de la Mancha but Alonso Quijano . . . I am the enemy of Amades of Gaul and all his innumerable progeny; for those profane realize how foolish I was and the danger I courted in reading them; but I am in my right sense now and I abominate them."

. . . At this point he turned to Sancho. "Forgive me, my friend," he said, "for having caused you to appear as mad as I by leading you to fall into the same error, that of believing that there are still Knights-errant in the world."

"Ah, master," cried Sancho through his tears, "don't die, your Grace, but take my advice and go on living for many years to come; for the greatest madness that a man can be guilty of in this life is to die without good reason, without anyone's killing him, slain only by the hands of melancholy. . . ."

"Not so fast, gentlemen," said Don Quixote. "In last year's nests there are no birds this year. I was mad and now I am sane. I was Don Quixote de la Mancha, and now I am, as I have said, Alonso Quijano the Good.

May my repentance and the truth I now speak restore to me the place I once held in your esteem. And now, let the notary proceed." [Miguel de Cervantes, *Don Quixote* (translated by Samuel Putnam, 1951)]

The self refers to a person's representation of himself (or herself) as an object in the world of experience; over time and based on the beliefs, attitudes, and actions of others, I look at myself and come to positive, negative, or ambiguous conclusions about *my* self. Some conclusions breed indifference—who cares if I have no mechanical ability?—but others are a vital guide to understanding people and human interaction. For Don Quixote his image of self as a knight-errant was all-important; it was *the* foundation for his perception of reality, for his perception of others, and for his self-esteem. Tragically, experience and constant humiliation by others "forced" him to reach a terrible conclusion: "They are right about me. I am not who I think I am. I am not Don Quixote, I am only Alonso Quijano. And when I believed I was Don Quixote, I was mad."

This conclusion about self, about Don Quixote as an object in the world of experience, is devastating. Sancho Panza asks his master to live with his new image of self, but Alonso Quijano refuses. And his refusal underlines the significance of self-image by suggesting what can happen if an important image of self and world collapses: apparently, a meeting with reality can produce, not only melancholy, but willing death.

Defined as a person's representation of himself as an object in the world of experience, the self is abstract, it is insufficiently tied to reality. So, to more accurately assess the significance of the self, let us try to be more specific. Globally, the self is the "organization of qualities" (Kinch, 1967) that the person thinks he possesses; it is the (more or less) organized set of beliefs and attitudes the person has about himself. Always, a global or overall view of self is positive, negative, or ambiguous, but no matter what the evaluation, virtually everyone comes to a conclusion ("Man, I'm a pretty nice guy") that sums up the many images that are, altogether, the self-concept.

What are these many images? First are identities. I'm a man, I'm a woman, I'm a Protestant, I'm an American, I'm a slave. What links these images of self is their social origin. Identities establish what and where we are in social terms (Stone, 1962), and they generally do this on the basis of institutionalized beliefs and practices—what sociologists call "culture." For example: I'm a Protestant and Protestants are better than Catholics and Jews. So, I'm on top of the religious scale and that means I'm better than they are. Or, traditionally, black was ugly, white beautiful. So, since I'm black, I must be ugly, lazy, shiftless, third class (see, for example, Griffin, 1961; Malcolm X, 1965).

Any person owns a number of identities. Some are more important than others (for example, man or woman as opposed to student), but all are a basis for self-evaluation, attitude formation, and behavior to self and others. As one steelworker said: "I want my kid to look at me and say, 'Dad, you're a nice guy but you're a fuckin' dummy.' Hell yes, I want my kid to tell me he's not gonna be like me" (Terkel, 1974).

Besides a host of identities, all people also own "unique" images of self. These are normally acquired from parents, but no matter how one gets them, these "unique" images of self were first gained in childhood. Say, for example, that you are white, Protestant, and middle class. Say, too, that your father has personal resentments that he takes out on you. Often your father yells and uses his hands, with the result that he makes you feel unwanted, inferior, a pain in everyone's rear end. Now, because these images of self—I'm a loser; I'm troublesome—are the result of your *singular* experiences with the people who socialized you, they are "unique," they are the conclusions you drew about yourself from the beliefs, attitudes, and actions of others toward you.

Identities and "unique" images of self are linked in the most varied ways. For instance, a boy might feel inferior, and in order to gain esteem, he might try to become a "real man." By developing muscles and the presumed admiration of others, the person tries to make up for his poor "unique" image of self. Or, say you are lower class, black, and your parents gave you a poor "unique" image of self. Here, these important aspects of self mesh, with the probable result being a very poor global image of self.

Without detailed knowledge of a person's history, it is impossible to understand the way identities and "unique" self-image were and are combined. Normally, we can say that certain identities produce positive or negative images of self (for example, woman, black, lower class, illiterate), but to comprehend any specific person we must try to learn how these identities were linked to biological predispositions, situational variables, historical conditions, and, of course, "unique" self-image.

Finally, a distinction must be made between self-images and self-percepts (Smith, 1968). Here, self-images refer to relatively enduring representations of self. Man, woman, black, white, smart, dumb, inferior, superior: frequently these images are acquired in childhood and often they are carried with us for many, sometimes all, of our years. In contrast, self-percepts refer to transitory representations of self. Say I'm eating in a restaurant, I manage to spill food over everyone and conclude, "I'm a clumsy ox." Or, say I'm a young faculty member, I go to the registrar for information, and am treated as if I were a student. Conceivably, I may not care. It is a simple mistake that anyone could make. But, suppose I make a big fuss, produce my Ph.D.—I'm Doctor Smith—and make the registrar feel very uncomfortable. Conceivably, the self-percept has acted back upon important and enduring self-images (that is, I'm a Ph.D.; I'm a faculty member); conceivably, I make a big fuss because the transitory self-percept threatens self-images that are crucial to me: "I'm a faculty member, and it's important to me that no one forget it."

Sometimes self-percepts call up enduring self-images. Sometimes they do not. Always the essential importance of the self for personality rests on enduring images that are important to the person.

Look at it this way: the global self and the images that are its building blocks are the most basic and essential part of anyone's individuality because, like strands of rope, so many of our decisions, judgments, beliefs, values, and personality traits are organized around the core that is our important self-images. Let's consider two examples, the first relating to global self-image. Paranoids are characteristically ashamed, "sometimes to the point of delusional preoccupation," about body odor, weak muscles, the size of their genitals, the softness of their hands. Often this shame attaches itself to some external feeling, but "one can be sure that it is actually quite pervasive and continuous and reflects a general lack of self-respect" (Shapiro, 1965). In short, feeling little or no sense of self-worth, feeling instead worthless, paranoids are continually ashamed of themselves. And while the object of shame (for example, body odor or the size of the genitals) varies, the constant core is the lack of self-esteem.

For an example of self as identity, let's return to our steelworker. Embracing society's definition of his occupation, he feels little esteem: "It's the not-recognition by other people. To say a woman is just a housewife is degrading, right? Okay. *Just* a housewife. It's also degrading to say *just* a laborer." In sum, the identity *steelworker* is so degrading to this man that key attitudes toward himself and his son are based upon it: "I want my kid to tell me he's not gonna be like me" (Terkel, 1974).

At the core of personality, self-images are consistently the crucial variable in explaining any person's thought and action, as well as the influence of others on any person. However, even very important self-images are *always* one variable among others, and to avoid any misunderstandings about the significance of self-images, let's examine two examples where they are *not* crucial for explaining thought and action.

Consider first Vietnam draftees. Undoubtedly many had positive, many negative self-images, but the evidence shows that most men served for one reason: exile or jail was not a viable alternative (see, for example, Moskos, 1969; Polner, 1971; Parks, 1968). Here self-image cannot explain action; the crucial variable is power, the government's ability to threaten and enforce severe sanctions for those who disobey. As a second example, consider mousetraps. Say someone wants to sell you a better mousetrap. In terms of importance, your self-image moves to the side; mousetraps are not "your thing." So, since you are in the market for the product, and since you lack the personal problems that might move you to misinterpret the salesperson's arguments (for example, "Everybody's out to get me; this guy's just trying to take my money"), you will objectively analyze the product's worth. On the periphery where mousetraps and salespeople are concerned, your self-image is not crucial for guiding your thought and action.

In sum, self-images are the core of personality; they are overall the most important variable for explaining a person's thoughts and behavior because they are *trans-situational* variables, images that are important at home, at work, at school, at play, anywhere a person interacts (Smith, 1968). But we want to avoid the problems that impeded early social psychology (see the Introduction). Life, human beings, seems to deny unitary explanations of anything. For all their importance, self-images act in concert with other variables, and sometimes these other variables (for example, power) and not self-images are the most important in understanding and explaining human behavior.

Imagine a week-old infant, the baby is healthy, has an inherited predisposition toward activity, stays awake for nine hours a day, and lacks any self-images.

Now imagine our infant (a girl) at six years of age. She knows she is a girl and even understands many of the consequences that occur as a result of gender identity. She knows men have the social power, she realizes "daddy is the boss," and in contrast to decisions made at three or four, she now feels boys are superior to girls. How did she learn these things? How did she come to believe that as an object in the world of experience, she, a girl, is inferior (see Kohlberg, 1966; Emmerich, 1961)?

Our answer is that she learned to feel inferior. The self is absent at birth. It develops only in the process of social experience; it develops only in the process of taking the role of the other, of using the attitudes and evaluations of others as a basis for attitudes and evaluations about ourselves (Mead, 1934).

Recall that the self refers to one's representation of him/herself as an object in the world of experience. *Object* is the key word. For the self is reflexive; it has the ability to be subject and object to itself *at the same time* (Mead, 1934). Consider the following example of self-percept. Assume that I've just given what I think is a terrible lecture and I'm driving home. No one else is in the car, I'm intensely analyzing the lecture, and I'm not talking out loud. Instead, I'm thinking, I'm having a private conversation with myself about myself. On one side of my head, I'm the subject of my own speculations, Fernandez giving the terrible lecture. But, on the other side of my head—I'm in the car remember—I'm Fernandez thinking about Fernandez. I'm now the object of my own thoughts and my conclusion is, after looking at myself in the classroom, "My God, I am a terrible lecturer." Or, if I'm trying to protect a self-image, I could conclude: "Ah, it's not me. It's those students. I gave a great lecture, but they're so apathetic they slept through it. I am a good lecturer. It's just that students are terrible."

The ability to split our heads into two, to be subject and object to ourselves at the same time, is pregnant with human possibilities. For example, this ability of the self is a great help in explaining variability and major change in personality. If people have the ability to consciously perceive themselves as objects, they can split their heads into two, deliberately examine their own personalities, and decide to change. Indeed, with a good memory, people can actually perceive the causes and course of their personality development. Comfortably seated in an armchair (or reclining on a psychiatrist's couch), they can reflect on their childhood, see why they own the self-images they do, and, once again, decide to change.

This ability only develops over time. We lack any concept of the self at birth and that makes us so dependent on others that we are unable to become an object to ourselves *until we are first the subject of some other person's beliefs, attitudes, and actions.* Remember: initially we do not experience ourselves directly. Instead, since we must take the role of the other (for example, Mommy always says I'm a bad boy) to have self-images and percepts, our initial experience of self is indirect, it is mediated by what others say about us and do to us.

No one, even the child of the most "progressive" parents, has any choice in this matter. For before our liberated child is out of the womb, he or she is already the subject of other people's thoughts, and, once born, our child becomes an object to itself only on the basis of what others say (Ms. as opposed to Miss) or fail to say, and on the basis of what others do (for example, about toilet training) or fail to do.

One important consequence of our dependence on others is social determinism. For example, even if we say no to others (for example, girls are inferior; no, they're not), our no is a response to their yes, and that means that we are still unwittingly being determined by what others have said (see Mannheim, 1969). However, we will return to the question of determinism later, and must first ask: Who are these other people who have such a profound effect on the development of our personalities?

George Herbert Mead placed "other people" into two categories: generalized and significant others.[5] Significant others refers to anyone who has had (or still has) an important influence on a person's thoughts about self and world. Parents are the most obvious significant others, but anyone, living or dead, can be significant to us. For the great Greek poet-novelist Nikos Kazantzakis, friendship with "Zorba the Greek" taught him "to love life and have no fear of death"; after Zorba, Kazantzakis's work always had "dramatic *élan* and form . . . no matter how much I strug-

---

[5] Experimental evidence supporting Mead's theories is, for example, Manis, 1955; Reeder, 1960; Rosenberg, 1965, 1973.

gled to give a balanced form to what I wrote, it quickly assumed (like Zorba) a vehement dramatic rhythm" (Kazantzakis, 1971). And for an example of a long-dead significant other, consider this remark from a member of the Jesus movement: "I said, God, I give it up; I turn my whole life over to you. You're it. You're the only one, and if that means being a missionary in Tibet . . . or whatever you want with my life, you just take over from here. It's yours" (Mauss and Petersen, 1973).

Where significant others refers to one or more specific people, Mead said the generalized other was "the organized community or social group" that gives individuals their "unity" of self. Imagine yourself a black slave in early nineteenth-century Georgia. The white community is your most important generalized other, and it does furnish unity of self: blacks are inferior, whites superior; blacks follow, whites lead. Now, imagine you are black in late twentieth-century Georgia. Many whites still feel about blacks as their ancestors did, but others believe that blacks and whites are equal. More important, the black community has at least three images of self available for its members: black is beautiful, black is ugly, I'm not certain what black is or means (see, for example, Frazier, 1962; Jackson, 1970).

Mead assumed that the generalized other transmitted unity of self (Mead, 1934). He was incorrect. Like today, the organized community can live "between past and future," unsure of everything from correct gender identities to proper sexual practices to the existence of God and the ultimate meaning of human life. The generalized other need not be unified; it can transmit confusion and that means that individuals unsure of themselves (for example, about the meaning of man or woman) are normal. After all, we get our self-images from others. And if the generalized and significant others who are the agents of our socialization are confused, we should be too. Our initial thinking about self and world is an inheritance from them.

To extend our understanding of the self's development, Mead used two original concepts: the "me" and the "I." The "me" consists of the attitudes of others that one assumes. Remember: Mead knew we must take the role of the other to be an object to ourselves; so, he conceptualized that role-taking process in his notion of the "me." The "I" is the person's response to the attitudes of others. Yes, no, or maybe are the three possible responses, but if we assume a yes, the dialectic *can* proceed as follows: "My mother says I'm handsome and intelligent. My father agrees and my grandparents think my parents underestimate my abilities and good looks. Now that's *me* all those *other* people are talking about, and they all agree about my good looks and intelligence. Well, why be difficult? *I* think they're right about me. *I* am a brilliant, handsome person. Couldn't be any doubt about it because other people always say the same things about *me*."

The example is an exaggeration. Few people find that all others think alike about them; and even fewer find that everyone thinks they are handsome and intelligent! But the example emphasizes Mead's main point: through the "me" we assume the attitudes of others, and through the "I" we respond to the attitudes of others. We can agree, disagree, hesitate, or become confused by others, but if we are to have a self-concept, if we are to become objects to ourselves, we must make some response to what others say about us—about "me."

Although a person responds to the attitudes of others, any response *follows* a process of interpretation. Refer again to our discussion of language when it was argued that, because words have many meanings, people have to interpret what others say. A dictionary definition of words is often insufficient. Another, more basic, reason why people interpret before responding is rooted in the nature of human perception: perception is always an interpolated act (Sullivan, 1968). Based on temperament, our unique history of experiences with others, our social class, the particular social situation, we insert ourselves, our individuality, between the stimulus and the response. Always this process of altering, refurbishing, or corrupting the messages of others gives people the ability to turn any message into its opposite. Once, when diapering our then year-old son, he would not be still. Frustrated, I got angry and yelled: "Stop it." His response, after a process of interpretation, was one huge belly laugh! Clearly, the voice of authority had spoken.

The interpolated nature of perception is important for at least three reasons. First, it helps personality theory to "make room for human discrimination." For one important reason that we cannot expect perfect continuity or consistency in personality is that people always interpolate the messages of others. It is true if a person says so; black is green if I say it is, and so long as I remain adamant, all the facts in the world cannot alter my perception. So, no theory can lock up the freedom to interpolate as we wish. What theory can do is recognize that the nature of human perception is one important variable that facilitates human discrimination and assures the impossibility of perfect consistency.

A second reason to stress the interpolated nature of perception goes back to the "I" and the "me." Mead stressed that the relationship between the "I" and the "me" was dialectical, one acted back upon the other. Based on temperament, social class, situation, significant and generalized others have no assurance that children will respond in the appropriate manner. On the contrary, studies of neurotics indicate that one of their responses is a loud no to the attitudes of others: "You tell me I'm worthless and unwanted. I say no. You're the problem. I'm actually one of the kindest, nicest people on earth" (see, for example, Horney, 1950).

A third and final reason to stress the nature of human perception is that it helps us explain personality continuity and change. Mead said freedom resided in the "I." Splitting myself into subject-object, I can see what they (my parents, my teachers) did and said to me, decide if those experiences are the reasons for my images of self, and, if my answer is yes, I can decide if I want to continue to think as they told me to. However, to use my freedom, I must be able to interpret reality with some measure of objectivity. If I defend myself or my parents with a host of lies and rationalizations, I am unlikely to change. On the contrary, in order to feel secure, I will see what I wish or need to see. Reality be damned. Change is too painful!

Self-images are the core of personality: they are overall the most important basis for an individual's thought and action. But to understand any self's development, to begin to comprehend a person's continuities, consistencies, and changes, it is necessary to know how and why he interprets reality as he does. Given certain biological predispositions, unique experiences with others, cultural and situational variables, did Tom or Jane, John or Mary get locked into a certain view of self and world? Is their life one continual *no* to the attitudes and beliefs of others? Is their consistency built on a firm foundation of insecurity? "You tell me I'm worthless. I say no. And nothing is going to change my mind!" Or, did Tom or Jane's childhood lead to a sense of self-esteem, plus a belief to think for themselves, to be open to new and novel experiences, to applaud self-actualization and societal change?

Only detailed life histories can furnish precise answers to these questions. But in the absence of specific details, the next two chapters—on childhood, adolescence, adulthood, and old age—generalize about factors that lead human development down various paths. Always we will use and amplify the basic concepts developed in this chapter. And that is good. For the value of a theory is its ability to deal with real life, with infancy, with middle childhood, with adolescence, with adulthood, with old age.

Bibliographical References

Adorno, T. W.; Frenkel-Brunswik, Else; Levinson, Daniel J.; and Sanford, R. Nevitt. *The Authoritarian Personality*. New York: Norton, 1969.

Allport, Gordon. *Becoming: Basic Considerations for a Psychology of Personality*. New Haven: Yale University Press, 1955.

Allport, Gordon. *Personality*. New York: Henry Holt, 1937.

Aranguren, J. L. *Human Communication*. New York: McGraw-Hill, 1967.

Bayley, Nancy. "Development of Mental Abilities." In *Carmichael's Manual of Child Psychology*, edited by Paul Mussen. New York: Wiley, 1970.

Bell, Richard Q. "A Reinterpretation of the Direction of Effects in Studies of Socialization." *Psychological Review* 75, no. 2 (March 1968): 81–95.

Berger, Peter. *The Sacred Canopy*. Garden City, N.Y.: Doubleday, 1969.

Bernstein, B. "Social Class, Language, and Socialization." In *Language and Social Context*, edited by Pier Gigliolo. London: Penguin, 1972.

Birney, Robert, and Teevan, Richard, eds. *Instinct*. New York: Van Nostrand Reinhold, 1961.

Brown, Roger. *Social Psychology*. New York: Free Press, 1965.

Buss, Arnold; Plomin, Robert; and Willerman, Lee. "The Inheritance of Temperaments." *Journal of Personality* 4-1 (November 4, 1973): 513–24.

Carter, C. O. *Human Heredity*. Rev. ed. London: Penguin, 1970.

Childe, V. Gordon. *Man Makes Himself*. New York: Mentor, 1951.

Childe, V. Gordon. *What Happened in History?* Baltimore: Penguin, 1964.

Chomsky, Noam. *Problems of Knowledge and Freedom*. London: Fontana, 1973.

Cleaver, Eldridge. *Soul on Ice*. New York: McGraw-Hill, 1968.

Coles, Robert. *Uprooted Children*. New York: Harper & Row, 1971.

Eiseley, Loren. *Darwin's Century*. Garden City, N.Y.: Doubleday-Anchor, 1961.

Eiseley, Loren. *The Immense Journey*. New York: Vintage, 1957.

Emmerich, Walter. "Family Role Concepts of Children Ages Six to Ten." *Child Development* 32 (1961): 609–24.

Ervin-Tripp, Susan. "An Analysis of the Interaction of Language, Topic, and Listener." *American Anthropologist* 66 (1964): 86–107.

Farb, Peter. *Word Play*. New York: Knopf, 1974.

Fernandez, Ronald. *The Promise of Sociology*. New York: Praeger, 1975.

Fitzgerald, Frances. *Fire in the Lake*. Boston: Little, Brown, 1972.

Frazier, E. Franklin. *Black Bourgeoisie*. New York: Macmillan, 1962.

Goffman, Erving. "On Face Work." *Psychiatry* 18 (1955): 213–31.

Goody, J., and Watt, I. "The Consequences of Literacy." In *Language and Social Context*, edited by Pier Gigliolo. London: Penguin, 1972.

Gould, John, and Kolb, Annette. *Colorful Birdlife*. Berne: Hallway, 1970.

Griffin, John. *Black Like Me*. New York: Signet, 1961.

Gurney, Roger. *Language, Brain, and Interactive Processes*. London: Edward Arnold, 1973.

Hall, Edward T. *The Hidden Dimension*. Garden City, N.Y.: Doubleday-Anchor, 1969.

Horney, Karen. *Neurosis and Human Growth*. New York: Norton, 1950.

Hutt, Corinne. *Males and Females*. London: Penguin, 1972.

Jackson, George. *Soledad Brother: The Prison Letters of George Jackson*. New York: Bantam, 1970.

Jencks, Christopher, et al. *Inequality: A Reassessment of the Effect of Family and Schooling in America.* New York: Harper & Row, 1973.

Kagan, Jerome. *Personality Development.* New York: Harcourt Brace Jovanovich, 1971.

Kagan, Jerome. "The Three Faces of Continuity in Human Development." In *Handbook of Socialization Theory and Research,* edited by David Goslin. Chicago: Rand McNally, 1969.

Kagan, Jerome, and Moss, H. A. *Birth to Maturity.* New York: Wiley, 1962.

Kazantzakis, Nikos. *Report to Greco.* New York: Bantam, 1971.

Kimmel, Douglas. *Adulthood and Aging.* New York: Wiley, 1974.

Kinch, John W., "A Formalized Theory of the Self Concept." In *Symbolic Interaction,* edited by Jerome G. Manis and Bernard N. Meltzer. Boston: Allyn & Bacon, 1967.

Kohlberg, Lawrence. "A Cognitive-Developmental Analysis of Children's Sex-Role Concepts and Attitudes." In *The Development of Sex Differences,* edited by Eleanor Maccoby. Stanford: Stanford University Press, 1966.

Krauss, Robert M. Language As a Symbolic Process in Communication. *American Scientist* 56 (1968): 265–78.

Labov, W. "The Logic of Nonstandard English." In *Language and Social Context,* edited by Pier Gigliolo. London: Penquin, 1972.

Lyons, John. *Chomsky.* London: Fontana, 1970.

McNeill, David. *The Acquisition of Language.* New York: Harper & Row, 1972.

Malcolm X. *Autobiography of Malcolm X.* New York: Grove Press, 1965.

Manis, Melvin. "Social Interaction and the Self-Concept." *Journal of Abnormal and Social Psychology* 51 (1955): 362–70.

Mannheim, Karl. "The Sociological Problem of Generations." In *Studies in Social Movements,* edited by Barry McLaughlin. New York: Free Press, 1969.

Mauss, Armand, and Petersen, Donald W. "The Cross and the Commune: An Interpretation of the Jesus People." In *Social Movements,* Chicago: Rand McNally, 1973.

Mead, George Herbert. *Mind, Self, and Society.* Chicago: University of Chicago Press, 1934.

Mischel, Walter. "Continuity and Change in Personality." *American Psychologist* 24, no. 11 (1969): 1012–18.

Montagu, Ashley, ed. *Man and Aggression.* New York: Oxford University Press, 1968.

Montagu, Ashley. *The Natural Superiority of Women.* New York: Macmillan, 1974.

Moskos, Charles. *The American Enlisted Man.* Hartford: Russell Sage, 1969.

Mumford, Lewis. *Technics and Human Development: The Myth of the Machine.* New York: Harcourt Brace Jovanovich, 1967.

Munn, Norman. *The Evolution of the Human Mind.* Boston: Houghton Mifflin, 1971.

Murphy, Gardner. "Psychological Views of Personality and Contributions to Its Study. In *The Study of Personality,* edited by Edward Norbeck, Douglas Price-Williams, and William McCord. New York: Holt, Rinehart & Winston, 1968.

Mussen, Paul. *The Psychological Development of the Child.* 2d ed. Englewood Cliffs, N.J.: Prentice-Hall, 1973.

Parks, Michael. *GI Diary.* New York: Harper & Row, 1968.

Polner, Murray. *No Victory Parades.* New York: Holt, Rinehart & Winston, 1971.

Potts, D. M. "Which Is the Weaker Sex?" *Journal of Biosocial Science,* supplement 2 (1970): 147–57.

Reeder, L. G.; Donohue, G. A.; and Biblarz, A. "Conceptions of Self and Others." *American Journal of Sociology* 66 (September 1960): 153–59.

Robinson, W. P. *Language and Social Behavior.* London: Penguin, 1972.

Rosenberg, Morris. *Society and the Adolescent Self-Image.* Princeton, N.J.: Princeton University Press, 1965.

Rosenberg, Morris. "Which Significant Others?" *American Behavioral Scientist* 16, no. 6 (July–August 1973): 829–60.

Rowell, Thelma. *The Social Behavior of Monkeys.* London: Penguin, 1972.

Russell, Bertrand. *History of Western Philosophy.* New York: Simon & Schuster, 1961.

Rutter, Michael. *Maternal Deprivation Reassessed.* London: Penguin, 1974.

Sapir, Edward. *Culture, Language, and Personality.* Berkeley: University of California Press, 1960.

Schattschneider, E. E. *Two Hundred Million Americans in Search of a Government.* New York: Holt, Rinehart & Winston, 1969.

Schutz, Alfred, and Luckmann, Thomas. *The Structures of the Life-World.* London: Heinemann, 1974.

Scott, J. P. "The Social Psychology of Infrahuman Animals." In *Handbook of Social Psychology,* edited by Gardner Lindzey and Elliot Aronson, vol. 4. Reading, Pa.: Addison-Wesley, 1969.

Shapiro, David. *Neurotic Styles.* New York: Basic Books, 1965.

Smith, M. Brewster. "The Self and Cognitive Consistency." In *Theories of Cognitive Consistency,* edited by R. P. Abelson, E. Aronson, W. J. McGuire, T. N. Newcomb, M. J. Rosenberg, and P. Tannenbaum. Chicago: Rand McNally, 1968.

Stone, Gregory. "Appearance and the Self." In *Human Behavior and So-*

cial Processes, edited by Arnold M. Rose. Boston: Houghton, Mifflin, 1962.
Sullivan, Harry Stack. *Interpersonal Theory of Psychiatry.* New York: Norton, 1968.
Terkel, Studs. *Working.* New York: Pantheon, 1974.
Thomas, Alexander; Chess, Stella; and Birch, Herbert. *Temperament and Behavior Disorders in Children.* New York: New York University Press, 1968.
Trudgill, Peter. *Sociolinguistics.* London: Penquin, 1974.
White, Leslie A. *The Science of Culture.* New York: Farrar Straus Giroux, 1949.
White, Robert W. *The Enterprise of Living.* New York: Holt, Rinehart & Winston, 1972.

CHAPTER TWO

Childhood Socialization

> ... I doubt whether anyone can ever have raged against his surname as I have all my life; this is stupid, of course, but so it has been. Every time I entered a school or met persons whom I had to treat with respect as my elders, every wretched little teacher, tutor, priest—anyone you like—on asking my name and hearing it was DOLOGORUKY, for some reason invariably thought fitting to add, "Prince Dologoruky?" And every single time I was forced to explain to these futile people, "No, simply Dologoruky."
>
> That simply began to drive me mad at last.... My comrades and school fellows were the most insulting of all....
>
> "What's your name?"
>
> "Dologoruky."
>
> "Prince Dologoruky?"
>
> "No, simply Dologoruky."
>
> "Ah, simply! Feel."
>
> And he was right; nothing could be more foolish than to be called Dologoruky without being a prince. I have to bear the burden of that foolishness through no fault of my own. Later on, when I began to get very cross about it, I always answered the question "Are you a prince?" by saying, "No, I'm the son of a servant, formerly a serf."
>
> At last, when I was roused to the outmost pitch of fury, I resolutely answered:
>
> "No, simply Dologoruky, the illegitimate son of my former owner."[1]
>
> Fyodor Dostoyevsky, *A Raw Youth* (1875)

---

[1] Prince indicated legitimacy; its absence meant illegitimacy.

With a woman's pain and to everyone's joy, children emerge from the womb. Sometimes they cry at once; sometimes they need prodding. Always, by crying too much or rarely, by sleeping endlessly or never, they have an effect on other people. Biological helplessness never equals an inability to affect others. From birth, the relationship between an infant and others is dialectical, one is always acting back on the other (Schaffer, 1966; Bell, 1968).

However, all infants do have a problem: they must fit into a set of social relations created, maintained, and defined for them by others (Mayamoto, 1970). Often this preexisting set of social relations wills them a terrible self-image; like DOLOGORUKY, simply Dologoruky, their lives can be determined by an arbitrarily inherited social identity. Before birth, others *place* the infant as a social object, and during socialization, others teach the child to accept inherited identities. If they are "successful," when the child says illegitimate, he announces to himself and others a very poor image of self (Stone, 1962).

Our social identities (for example, lower class, man-woman) establish *what* and *where* we are in social terms; they are meanings of the self (Stone, 1962). But social relations give us more than identities. Mothers and fathers are happy and loving, or they are bored with one another, their careers, and their unwanted children. Or, like some schizophrenic families, the father is extraordinarily narcissistic, the mother bends to his wishes, "and the parents' delimitation of the environment and their perception of events to suit their needs result in a strange family atmosphere into which the children must fit themselves and suit this dominant need or feel unwanted. . . . The world as the child should come to perceive or feel it is denied" (Lidz et al., 1958).

In sum, any infant must fit into a set of preexisting social patterns that arbitrarily furnish the foundation for the image of self. More specifically, based on the social relationships that exist between significant others, as well as the numerous social identities that are intertwined with those relationships,[2] children act on others with far less power than others act on them.

TRUST VERSUS MISTRUST

No social psychologist doubts the profound importance of infancy (0 to 18 months) for human development. Perhaps it was Freud who "began" by arguing that infant identifications had lasting and general effects

---

[2] For example, the father who is bitter because he was born poor or the mother who feels inferior, and teaches her daughter to feel inferior, because society says that women are inferior. (On the latter, see Hoffman, 1972; Horner, 1972; Gump, 1972.)

(*The Ego and the Id,* 1923), but today Freudians and non-Freudians alike stress the great significance of infancy for the development of humans with few problems in living.

Given this stress, it is surprising that so much of the evidence for infancy's importance is negative rather than positive. Reference is to the body of studies about institutionalized infants. We have learned much about what to do by first seeing what not to do. Consider this example from an early study. Believing that crying was an infant's way of indicating need or distress, doctors worried that hospitalized infants cried too much. Two hours crying a day was far more than necessary to show need or distress. So, doctors changed the hospital's routine. Instead of no blankets, and a possible feeling of insecurity, children were loosely wrapped in blankets. Instead of 6 P.M. feeding trays, they now arrived at 5 P.M., allowing infants to get their 6 P.M. feeding on time, rather than one hour later. Finally, and most important, extra nurses were added to the nursery staff, and since all nurses were now sensitized to the baby's cry, they tried to satisfy infants as soon as possible. The results were quite encouraging. After the changes, babies cried less than one hour a day, and where 35 percent of the previous crying was due to unknown causes, now only 23 percent occurred without obvious cause. Doctors were pleased that their changes stopped much of the crying due to "less compelling causes," even if it did not calm babies from crying for a need like hunger (Aldrich et al., 1946).

This example makes two points. First, environment is a crucial variable in explaining infant happiness or unhappiness. Simple changes in schedule and staff cut crying time in half. Second, infants cry, show signs of distress or need, for many reasons. Some are internal; hungry or thirsty babies will often cry until others satisfy them. But some crying is due to external causes. A door slams, a doctor or nurse speaks too loudly, an attendant drops a tray: all of these are external to infants and all are capable of inducing anxiety in them. Consider the position of infants. They do not know it was *just* a door slamming or a tray dropping; cognitively, they are years away from such understanding (see, for instance, Piaget, 1974). So, since they lack the ability to deal with the experience in rational terms, emotion dominates their perception. Affect, how they feel about things, is the "perceptual ground" for their apprehension of these anxiety-inducing events, and infants often cry until others reduce their unmanageable anxiety by hugs, cuddling, soft words, anything that allows them to feel that all is well (Sullivan, 1953; Solley, 1966).

Aware of infants' dependence on others for a sense of physical and psychological well-being, Erik Erikson argues that above all babies need to develop basic trust in others. Cognitively, they cannot know this, the word *trust* is only a sound in the air, but they do need to sense that others will consistently and continually satisfy their physical needs, as well as calm them when unmanageable anxieties produce feelings of insecurity (Erikson, 1964; also Lidz, 1968). Consider the position of infants. They have no sense of self; that develops over time, and most children wait eighteen months before they say something like *me, mine, self, I* (see Lewis, 1963). So, trust in others is crucial because it is the basis for trust in the developing self. Able to depend on others, have faith in their love, the infant enters early childhood without a weight of unmanageable, unexplainable anxiety. At the core of the infant's "personality," based on day-to-day experience, is an established sense of security about the world and the people who inhabit it. That is a solid foundation for a positive image of self. In its absence, in the presence of distrust, the way is paved for tendencies toward restlessness, dependency, a thirst for affection, and hyperactivity (see, for example, Bell and Ainsworth, 1972).

What is the proof for these assertions? Again, it comes from studies of institutionalized infants. Getting less, often far less, handling and cuddling than children living at home, infants in hospitals and orphanages later show a need to affiliate with others. However, where this need could have its roots in a past which said that others were "dependable sources of pleasure and gratification," among institutionalized infants the need for others has its roots in an absence of trust. Inadequate staff, impersonal care, long bouts of fright, these make institutionalized infants anxious about people and their effect on people. So, lacking a sense of trust in others, and a developing sense of trust in self, the children later hunger for the proof that will give them a solid sense of self-esteem. And since they need others for that proof, they seek to affiliate with others (see Youngelson, 1973; Rutter, 1974; Montagu, 1967).

Other characteristics of institutionalized infants include "an unusual degree of apathy or emptiness of emotional response," as well as retarded language development and poor cognitive skills. Seemingly, one follows from the other. Lacking the stimulation often provided by parents at home, institutionalized children respond to a bland, dull environment by imitating it. And why not? Other people give them little reason to be excited about life, and they are often alone, so why be excited about nothing?[3] And how can they develop language skills, the basis for a good score on I.Q., tests, if few people talk to them for any length of time (Goldfarb, 1945, 1955; Leach, 1975)? The answer, of course, is that it is very hard to learn skills without teachers. Remember, too, that poor language development and poor cognitive skills later have an effect on self-image. Entering school, the child is slated to do poorly, and that will unfortunately confirm the already established poor image of self. Obviously, development for an institutionalized child often takes the form of a vicious circle.

---

[3] In an orphanage in Iran, infants received so little attention that, at the age of two and one-half, only 8 percent of the children could walk (Dennis, 1960).

Another, and last, point about institutionalized infants is the restlessness, inability to concentrate, and unmanageability that often characterizes them. McCarthy notes that where infants learn to trust others, they also learn to control themselves, to plan, to have foresight, and even to delay immediate gratification (McCarthy, 1966). For example, if parents consistently satisfy an infant's needs, he learns to wait. Hearing the bottle being made, or seeing Mommy unfastening her bra, the infant learns over time that food is coming, and that knowledge eventually leads to patience. Or, if a child awakes crying, a trusted voice often produces an immediate smile. The child feels secure. Or, if cuddled during a thunderstorm or hugged while a brother imitates a police siren, the infant seemingly develops a rudimentary sense of foresight: "I can depend on hugs and kisses the next time I'm scared."

Where the lucky child learns about patience and love, the institutionalized child often learns little. Why not be restless if one feels no sense of trust in others or the environment? And how does one learn to concentrate if the basis of one's developing sense of self is unmanageable, unexplainable anxiety?

Three qualifications are needed. First, institutional care provides an *example* of emotional and cognitive deprivation in infancy. The same thing can and does often happen in the family; and some institutions avoid many of the problems associated with living in hospitals or orphanages. Second, reversal of infancy deprivations is possible. Although the chances seem better where cognitive abilities are concerned, pessimism about reversing the psychological effects of infancy deprivation comes essentially from clinical accounts. Hopefully, systematic studies will show cause for optimism (Rutter, 1974; Leach, 1975). Finally, some infants weather the desert that is deprivation better than others. Temperamentally active infants provide stimulation for themselves and so avoid at least some of the ill effects associated with poor environments in infancy (Schaffer, 1966).

The overall conclusion is short: Infant experiences of warmth, security, pleasure, stimulation, and satisfaction furnish the basis for trust in others, as well as the basis for trust in the developing self. We know this to be true because, in the absence of these experiences, people develop many psychological and cognitive problems (for instance, White, 1972; Kagan, 1971).

IS A MOTHER MANDATORY?

In 1953 British psychiatrist John Bowlby published a report entitled *Maternal Care and Mental Health*. Based on evidence from institutional studies, Bowlby stressed that infants and young children needed "a warm, intimate, and continuous relationship with a mother . . . in which both find satisfaction and enjoyment." He also noted that a mother-substitute was acceptable if she steadily cared for the child, but many chose to disregard Bowlby's qualification. Instead, some said *only* Mother was good enough. She had to remain at home—work was out of the question—and she had to avoid day nurseries and crèches since they had "permanently" bad effects on child development (Bowlby, 1965; Rutter, 1974).

Is Mother actually mandatory? Is she the only one able to provide a sense of basic trust? The evidence says no. First, infants do not know who gave birth to them. Even sexually well-informed children take years to figure this out (Kohlberg, 1966), so, unless we assume a sort of magic in the blood tie between mother and infant, there is no reason to assume that only the biological mother can provide love and security. That is normally the case. And it is also true that babies choose to establish a special relationship with whoever furnishes love and security (Leach, 1975). But, if that special person is normally the mother, sociological, not biological, factors are at work. For example, since only 11 percent of mothers breastfeed beyond one month, no biological tie keeps a mother at her baby's side. And if men learn to control their emotions, they can speak softly, provide love, and change diapers. If they do not, it is the result of living in societies which teach that men are policemen, women are meter maids; men are presidents, women are first ladies; men invent things, women use what men invent.

This conclusion is not the clarion call of a "liberated" man. It is the truth. Consider these examples. Michael Rutter and his colleagues sought to assess the long-term effects of separation of parents and children. They found that separations, especially from both parents, were associated with "anti-social" behavior, but they also found "that this is due, not to the fact of separation, but to the family discord which accompanies separation." Children can be away from a mother or father without ill effects if the relationship between parent and child is good (Rutter, 1971; see also Caldwell et al., 1970).

In a recent summary of the findings since publication of Bowlby's book, Mary Ainsworth (1965) distinguishes between different patterns of childrearing. She finds deprivation where a major mother figure is absent and infants were cared for by a number of people, none furnishing the sense of continuity and security needed for the development of trust. But Ainsworth finds no evidence that only the natural mother will do. She does believe that infants "tend to attach themselves primarily to one specific person," and that person must be female, but a psychologically secure and cognitively advanced child does develop when there is "a partial dispersal of responsibility for the care of a child among a few figures who have a high degree of continuity and who together give sufficient care" (Ainsworth, 1965).

Finally, there is evidence from children placed in strange environments. They naturally become anxious and seek security. Is a mother the only one able to provide it? No, others will do if they are familiar to the child. For example, although children from a residential nursery showed signs of distress when brought to a strange place, their distress was often reduced by the presence of a familiar nursery helper. And when children are admitted to a hospital, their anxiety is often greatly reduced by the presence of a loved brother or sister. So, while children are normally less distressed with the mother than with anyone else, "there is no evidence that it is being a mother that is important" (Rutter, 1974). On the contrary, if the bonds are stronger with someone besides this mother, then that person should have the greatest ability to reduce the child's stress.

Let us try to avoid any misunderstandings. Evidence shows that the natural mother is not the only person able to provide a sense of basic trust. But, evidence also shows that it is often vital for a child to experience a loving sense of continuity and consistency from others. In its absence, the child "must" be confused. "Will they do that again? Can I depend on being cuddled when that happens? Why does she laugh and he scream when I do that?" Trust can only develop when infants have faith in the consistency and continuity of their environment. Working together, mothers and fathers, or mothers and fathers and kibbutzim staff, can provide a sense of trust, but as the circle of significant others expands, so do the chances for discontinuity, inconsistency, and distrust. The circle seems to have limits.

One last point. If child-rearing is shared by a limited number of like-minded people, the chances for the infant's psychological well-being are probably increased. For example, to the extent that infants are familiar with both parents, separations are no problem. Daddy takes over where Mommy left off. And, if child-rearing is shared among like-minded people, its burdens should lead to fewer frustrations taken out on the child. If fathers spell mothers, and vice versa, perhaps both will reach the screaming stage—"This baby is gonna drive me up a wall"—less often.

COMPETENCE MOTIVATION

Since Freud, many social scientists think of infancy as the oral phase of psychosexual development. The argument goes something like this. Since an infant's life centers on taking in food through sucking, the "first critical relationships" with others are formed when infants are fed. For Erik Erikson infants "live through and love with their mouth"; mothers "live through and love with their breasts." This mutuality is vital for an infant's physical well-being but, equally important, it is crucial for the development of personality. The act of sucking is full of erotic pleasures and if infants are denied their necessary oral gratification, problems are sure to arise. For example, oral gratification leads to a sense of optimism; an infant who sucks happily is likely to be sociable, generous, positive toward life. But a lack of oral gratification leads to pessimism; deprived infants are likely to be dependent, anxious, in need of constant reassurance (Freud, 1962; Erikson, 1964; Lidz, 1968).

This theory lacks only one thing: proof that it is true. First, to the extent that theorists place emphasis on breast-feeding,[4] most of us should be unconsciously in search of missed oral gratifications. Few women breast-feed at all, and the crucial weaning stage, which when handled badly may give "a depressive undertone to the whole remainder of life" (Erikson, 1964), is not a part of most people's development. So, on the one hand, we have a crucial stage of development missed by most people; and, on the other, we reach the conclusion that the absence of breast experience prevents nearly 90 percent of the population from being sociable, optimistic, and generous.

Second, in reviewing more than thirty years of research, Bettye Caldwell noted that "no clear adjustment patterns had been demonstrated to appear as a consequence of any aspect of infant feeding experience" (1964). However, she did cite one study which showed "that prolonged sucking was associated with a preference for a confection which could be sucked (lollipop) rather than chewed (chocolate) in a candy choice situation." And it was also found that prolonged sucking was associated with a tendency toward constipation. Unfortunately, in psychoanalytic theory this trait supposedly has its origins in the anal, not the oral, stage of development (Caldwell, 1964).

Third, and most important, it is incorrect to argue that an infant's life *centers* on taking in food through sucking. This is perhaps true for the first month or six weeks of life, but infants quickly do much more than suck and sleep. From birth most infants are awake for eight or more hours a day, and even if we assign four of those eight hours to sucking, that still leaves, in the very first weeks, four hours of nonsucking. What happens in those four hours? Infants are changed, bathed, and cuddled; that takes a lot of time and it forms a basis for trust in others. The infant's arms are pulled; clothes are placed over its head; parents hold the child close while pacing the floor. All these involve tactile stimulation, and they take about two to four hours of time a day. Finally, remember that as early as one month, infants imitate adults; they happily repeat simple actions, say the sticking out of a tongue (Piaget, 1962a). And if complex patterns or in-

---

[4] For example, Harry Stack Sullivan's remark that "the good mother begins as a discrimination of the good and satisfactory nipple" (1953).

teresting shapes are placed close enough—up to the age of two months, infants see clearly for a distance of only eight inches—they respond, particularly if movement is added to the complex shape (Leach, 1975).

Seeking to restore some balance to our view of infancy, Robert W. White suggested that besides oral gratification, infants seek a sense of competence; they are motivated to interact effectively with their environment. They want, because they can and because others ask them to do it, to discover the effects they can have on the environment, as well as the effects the environment can have on them. In the early months "effantance motivation" is limited by the infant's abilities, but as the months go by oral gratification increasingly takes a back seat to the infant's desire to interact effectively with others and the world (White, 1959, 1960, 1972).

Consider three examples, two of motor, the third of cognitive capacities. Infants want to crawl and walk. As early as five months, they will try to stand when sitting on someone's lap, and precocious infants often spend hours of their sixth and seventh months in trying to stand and walk. When they fail, they often cry, seemingly from frustration. But when they stand on the side of the couch, or reach the mountain that is one side of their crib, the sense of satisfaction, the pride in achievement, is obvious. Their eyes light up; they have interacted effectively with their environment.

As a second example, take White's comment on "the battle of the spoon." Generally this occurs at one year, but our daughter (not that uncommon) began periodic battles at six months. Essentially what happens is that infants want to feed themselves. Rather than accept oral gratification from others, they risk getting less food to their mouths—and more on the floor!—so long as they do it themselves.

For a third example, consider the learning of hand-eye coordination. Most infants cannot coordinate until they are two months old but, once achieved, infants show a desire for competence. In one experiment, some infants had mobiles and other toys hanging above their cots; the control group had nothing over their cots. The result was that the babies with toys reached out and grasped for objects efficiently nearly five weeks ahead of the control group. Apparently, if stimulation is provided, even very young infants want to have an effect on the world (Leach, 1975; also Goodman, 1970).

Our examples point to two conclusions. First, infants' attempts to gain competence have an effect on personality and self-image. Especially when infants begin to crawl and walk, they are often a source of worry. For safety's sake they can be put into a playpen, but even prisoners are allowed time off for good behavior, and when they try to stand against a dangerous table, begin to eat a valuable book, or quietly fondle an electric outlet, it is the significant other's definition of the situation that is decisive. Parents can yell and scream, or even hit the child. But "if you start them on tantrums—I know a good example of it, of a child who's been made to leave things alone while his mother got on with the work—he must always keep out of the way, the work must be done, it's the first thing; with the result that he's been pushed around while the housework's been done, and now he's full of tantrums; because nobody *loved* him out of a situation, he was *bullied* out of the situation. Yet they thought they were being kind to him, but I don't. You shouldn't *make* them do things that way" (Newson and Newson, 1965).

Why? Because the child does not know what you are talking about. Electric outlets or books are meaningless sounds. However, since affect is the basis for infants' perceptions (Solley, 1966; McCarthy, 1966),[5] they do grasp anger, hostility, and rage. And the result is that in reacting to others, infants must deal with unmanageable anxiety. Some respond with tantrums and defiance; others, like ostriches, stay below ground, passive witnesses to their development. But no matter what the child's eventual response, an imaginative reconstruction of their interpretation of the situation is: "What are they yelling for? When I crawled before she hugged and kissed me. Now I touch this thing—a book?—and they're screaming? Why are they mad at me? What did I do wrong?"

Naturally, infants do not talk like this. If they did, they could *begin* to deal with their feelings. But they cannot talk, nor can they understand the parent's anger. In fact, repeated on an everyday basis, infants exposed to anger and rage have no choice but to root their personalities in distrust of others and of themselves.

Our second conclusion goes back to competence and oral gratification—which is *the* center of infant development? The answer is neither. Both are very important aspects of infant development and each dominates particular periods of infancy. Most important, we want to avoid a mistake noted by Robert W. White. In watching a child try to walk, "it is equally possible to discuss a theme of mastery, power, or control, perhaps even a bit of primitive self-assertion. . . ." But giving priority to any of these goals, "arbitrarily" stops "the cycle of transaction between child and environment." We say: "This is the real point." White asks, "Is it?" and his answer is no. For competence motivation "the real point is the transaction as a whole." The real point is the infant's trys to interact effectively with the environment in a wide variety of areas and tasks, plus the sense of "self-esteem" that infants gain if their attempts are successful (White, 1959).

White cautioned against arbitrarily giving priority to one side of competence motivation. The same caution is needed in arbitrarily making one

---

[5] McCarthy cites the case of an infant who was quite hard of hearing. Pleasant sounds were missed; she only heard the harsh "no's" and the scoldings. The result was a refusal to talk until she was fitted with a hearing aid (McCarthy, 1966).

series of infant experiences *the* crucial determinant of personality. Oral gratification *is* vital but from birth infants do much more than suck, and while theory must underline the experiences that dominate specific periods of infancy, perhaps the soundest view is to stress interactions as a whole. For example, in their study, *Patterns of Infant Care*, the Newsons recorded the following comment: "Well, I smack her for temper; and then if she puts things in her mouth, I smack her; or if she slops with her food. If I see her doing *anything* I don't want her to do, then I smack her; I don't think it hurts her, not just a smack. She knows when I'm going to smack her anyway, I just raised my hand, and she clears at the run (Newson and Newson, 1965).

By "clearing at the run," this one-year-old showed she knew what to expect. But, because she is smacked for anything, it is doubtful if even perfect oral gratification will produce trust in others and trust in self. Infants live day to day; their personalities and the beginnings of their self-images develop day to day. So, while some experiences are more important than others, *it is interaction as a whole that produces trust or distrust.*

INFANT COGNITIVE DEVELOPMENT

Cognitive development. The words are forbidding; they seem to call attention to a mysterious process, complex in its workings, difficult to understand, impossible to master. Like the prospect of an algebra course, study of cognitive development often puts people off before they take their seats.

Refuse to be put off. Study of cognitive development is essential for any understanding of the development of personality and self. This is so because, like temperament or religion or social class, cognitive abilities help mediate a person's interpretation of a particular comment, event, or action (Ziegler, 1968). In effect, the structure of children's thoughts, their developed and age-related abilities to grasp this (the danger of electric plugs) or comprehend that (the cultural meaning of morality), is a crucial variable in understanding their response to the words and actions of others. It is even possible that an infant's refusal to listen to parents is often due, not to stubbornness or willfulness, but simply to the child's cognitive inability to know what others mean by their words and actions.

Any study of cognitive development begins with the work of the brilliant Swiss psychologist, Jean Piaget (1962a and b, 1974). Separating cognitive development into four successive stages, Piaget says the first is the sensory-motor period (0 to 18 months), the second the period of representation (18 months to 6 or 7), the third the period of concrete operations (7 to 12), the fourth the period of formal operations (13 +). To enter a higher stage, any child must pass through a lower one; the stages are "precisely characterized by their set order of succession." In fact, while cultural and personal differences make it impossible to set one age as the beginning of concrete operations or the end of the sensory-motor period,[6] nothing alters "the constant order of succession." Present and future build on the past; to advance to a higher stage, a person must already own the abilities required of an earlier stage(s) (Piaget, 1974).[7]

What happens during the sensory-motor period? Well, if we agree that a person "knows" something in three ways, through doing it, through a picture or image of it, and through a symbolic means such as language (Bruner, 1966), initially infants can know only by doing. Study shows that an ability to represent images in the mind first appears at about fifteen months, and any proficiency in language takes years. So, infants must begin with action; they must first learn by doing, "for a long practice of pure action is needed to construct the substructure of later speech." In that first year or so, infants do not *think* about things; via the stimulation furnished by others and themselves, infants *live* with things, and that living is the bridge which allows them to cross over into the world of thought (Piaget, 1962a; 1974; Bruner, 1966).

Let's take some examples. Piaget notes that between one and four months children acquire a number of "primary circular reactions." The idea is that in this period infants generally focus on themselves; not yet oriented to the outside world of couches, chairs, and toys, they learn by keying on themselves. Piaget's son begins "systematic grasping"; he scratches and tries to grasp, scratches and grasps again. Six days later (0;2 months 11 days), the child spends nearly fifteen minutes scratching and grasping. The action is circular because the child repeats and repeats the same movements; it is primary because action is not yet oriented to the world outside the "self" (Piaget, 1954; Flavell, 1973).

But, between four and eight months, children begin to repeat actions that lead to effects in the outside world. Intention, the deliberate pursuit of a goal by means of action, is not yet present but infants are well on the way toward gaining this ability. For they are now learning to pull, strike, kick, swing, and rub things. As above, actions are repeated for their own sake, for example, the child kicks and kicks a toy rabbit hung over his crib, but now he deals with externals. At times it even seems as if the infant intends to do this or that; seeing that a plastic glass drops from his high chair to the floor, the infant continues to throw down things—as long

---

[6] For example, American children tend to reach each of the stages about a year earlier than Swiss children, the subjects for most of Piaget's experimental work.

[7] Piaget links the stages of development to specific ages. Generally, I have followed his lead because the evidence supports his predictions. But development can be speeded up or slowed down. Moreover, most studies in cognitive development take place in western societies. Other cultures could have different timetables for the growth of cognitive abilities.

as others provide the ammunition! However, this is not yet true intention. Here the interesting event becomes a goal only *after* the means are put into effect. Intention is still post hoc; it came only after the goal was discovered; intention was absent in the original act (Flavell, 1973; Piaget, 1954).

Intention normally appears somewhere between eight and twelve months; its developmental importance rests on the infant's acquired ability to *coordinate* two or more independent actions, one serving as a means, the other as a goal. Finally, the infant deals with more than one action at a time; he is on his way toward "fusing" actions in a manner "that is more genuinely a representation of the world" (Bruner, 1966). One example is an infant's removal of an obstacle that prevents her from reaching, say, a desired toy. At eleven months Piaget's daughter took his hand, placed it against a doll she was unable to move, and put pressure on Piaget's finger to do what was needed. Clearly, this infant was well on the way toward a genuine *internal* representation of reality (Piaget, 1954).

With the ability to coordinate actions firmly in hand, infants between twelve and eighteen months engage in an active process of trial-and-error; not only do they coordinate two or more actions, they now "manage to solve problems which demand new and unfamiliar means." This is still done without *internal* representations, but these "experiments in order to see" are the solid foundation needed for the symbolic capacity. For example, Piaget placed his watch on a cushion, and his son pulled the cushion forward in order to reach the watch. Then Piaget placed two cushions in front of the child, with the watch on the extreme end of the second cushion. The child pulled the first one forward, but no watch! Then, with his eye fixated on the watch, the child grabbed the second cushion and its treasure. It is *as if* the child said, "Well, when I pulled the first one, no watch. But if I pull this other cushion, I'll get the watch" (Piaget, 1954; Flavell, 1973).

Evidence for a symbolic capacity appears somewhere around fifteen months. Consider these two examples. Piaget's daughter watched him quickly cross and uncross his arms, hitting his shoulders with his hands. His daughter imitated him, and later, with no action on Piaget's part, she imitated him again. This "deferred imitation" showed she was no longer entirely dependent on actual action; now she could internally represent a model in the form of an image and imitate the image without any need to witness actual action (Piaget, 1962a). In another case Piaget's twenty-month-old daughter wanted to open a door while holding two blades of grass. Putting the grass on the floor, she began to grasp the door knob, but then realized that the opening door would "chase away" her grass. So, without the aid of action, she internally explored ways and means. Finally, she picked up the grass, moved it out of the door's reach, and proceeded to go on her way, unmolested grass and all (Piaget, 1954).

Piaget's daughter showed the ability to represent actions rather than perform them. This is the "end" of sensory-motor development. The child is already using words and, over time, the ability to represent via images is dominated by the ability to use those most sophisticated of symbols—words. However, before ending this discussion of cognitive development, two points need to be made.

First, like the self, and along with the self, cognitive structures develop through a process of interaction with others (Kohlberg, 1969). Genetically, some people are more intelligent than others, but without the stimulation that makes actions turn into images into words, children are often impeded in their cognitive development. The tragic example is the average institutionalized child.

Second, our knowledge of cognitive development provides essential insights into the development of self and personality. Taking the role of the other, responding to what they say about "me," any child reacts on three separate yet interrelated levels. First is an *evaluative* orientation; based on what they tell me, I'm good or bad, pleasant or a pest. Second is the *affective* orientation; based on what they tell me, I feel good about myself, or I'm overloaded with feelings of insecurity. Third is the *cognitive* orientation; based on what they tell me, I can define and understand the events and situations that characterize my life, or I'm unable to know or comprehend the meaning of others' actions toward me (Miyamoto, 1970).

Piaget's work shows that the child is poorly equipped to deal with others on a cognitive level. For the child, barely able to represent images at eighteen months, conceptual understanding is still years away. This means that in their early years children's evaluations and feelings about themselves are based quite heavily on their emotional understanding of the words and actions of others. Freud overemphasized the determinism supposedly inherent in human development, but the potential for genotypic continuity is present in all women and men. Unable to satisfactorily deal with others on a cognitive level, all children must hope that their significant and generalized others show empathy. For if empathy is absent, the stage is set for problems. This is clear when we turn to what is commonly called the "period of negativism," the "terrible two's."

NEGATIVISM, EGOCENTRISM, AND ROLE-TAKING

No! Many parents continually hear this word like a loud and persistent drum when their children approach or reach two years of age. Toddlers get balky or contrary, seemingly overnight. They boss others around and even when no one is bothering them, they may act as if *they* are being ordered about too much. Often, the child says one thing and two minutes later contradicts himself. Sometimes offers of help are vehemently refused: "Me, me," or "I, myself," as the parent's hand is pushed away. And if the child is asked, "Do you want to go shopping with Daddy?" responds "Yes," and is taken along, cries may erupt in the car, or, better, in the supermarket. Seemingly, two-year-olds do not know what they want or when they want it (Spock, 1968; Leach, 1975; Ausubel, 1950).

Although this is a difficult period for parents, especially for mothers who are with the child all day, the real burden of being two years old falls on the weak shoulders of the child. For this is a period when parents begin to make many demands on girls and boys. Toilet training is probably the most conspicuous example (for example, Wolff, 1969), but a child's no during the "terrible two's" is a response to the attitudes and actions of others: "Don't play with the electric plugs. Never." "No. Don't ever touch that vase. Mommy and Daddy love it." "Keep out of the garbage." "My God! No! Don't eat the scouring powder!" "Peter. Watch the ironing board. It'll fall on you and hurt you. Peter, please stay away from the ironing board. Peter!! Keep away from that ironing board. Now! Or else!"

Parental demands spring from at least two sources. First, by the age of two children have developed some competency in walking, grasping, opening, closing, and climbing. They can easily "get into" a number of valuable things or dangerous activities. If parents are to protect the children and themselves, they often have little choice: *No* is the order of the day! Second, aware of the child's developing cognitive and motor skills, parents often seek a modicum of "civilization." Children are asked to eat with a spoon or fork, brought to a "potty chair" for a bowel movement, and no longer laughed at when they scream at the top of their lungs.

If we follow Harry Stack Sullivan and separate the attitudes of others into "good-me," "bad-me," and "not-me" (1953), the child's difficult situation becomes clear. *Assuming* parents the child learned to trust, those first twenty-four months[8] were overwhelmingly filled with "good-me" experiences; other people tended to the child's needs and other people made the child happy about being alive. It is *as if* the child was able to conclude: "Everyone tells me I'm nice. It must be so. I'm nice." Now, suddenly, others continually tell the child no. If he does that, he's a bad boy (bad-me) and if she doesn't stop that, she's a bad girl (bad-me). Most important, parents sometimes scream, fume, and hit children. In their role-taking, in their assuming the attitudes of others, toddlers often take these experiences (for example, a boy being hit and screamed at for touching his genitals. Newson and Newson, 1965) to be "not-me's." These are things children *never* do—under any circumstances. They must be ter-

---

[8] Twenty-four months is obviously an arbitrary figure. Some parents begin to make demands much earlier, and the child has heard the word *no* from his or her earliest steps. The figure is meant to symbolize that period when others—all at once—make a number of new demands on the child.

rible, evil, disgusting, dreadful, because Mommy and Daddy have never acted that way before; the child concludes: "I must have done something horrible!"

In response to this host of "bad" and "not-me" experiences, children react by being balky, contradictory, and negative. This perfectly legitimate reaction is due to their interpretation of the situation. They don't like breaking comfortable habits (say about the toilet); they don't understand what their parents are doing. So, they react like most adults placed in an untenable and anxiety-provoking environment: they get nervous, frustrated, angry, and eager to establish control over their uncontrollable situation. Unfortunately, if others are unable to emphathize with the child, the unequal battle between toddlers and their significant others spells defeat for the young boy or girl. For this is a period in childhood when it is very, very easy to produce serious problems in living, not to mention a poor self-image.

Consider first the concept of egocentrism. This is not the "unbounded self-love," the narcissism that Freud said all children possessed (1962). At two, at three, at five, children fail to make a clear distinction between self and others; unlike most adults, toddlers are just learning to think about themselves as subjects (I) and objects (me). So, if children love themselves, it is not because they know self in any precise cognitive sense. On the contrary, if children love themselves, it is because they are egocentric; it is because they ignore "all that is outside their dreams and desires"; it is because they fail to distinguish with any precision between subjective and objective; it is because they "confuse their own point of view with that of others" and because they confuse the "activity of things and persons with their own activity" (Piaget, 1973, 1962a and b).

Begin with the activity of things. A child is asked if the sun came at the same time as people or after. She answers: "It started as soon as there were little children." "Why?" "So that children should have fresh air." Another says the sun is alive because "it keeps coming back." He is asked "Does it know when the weather is fine? "Yes, because it can see it." "Does the sun have eyes?" The child answers: "Of course! When it gets up it looks to see if it is bad weather and if it is, it goes off somewhere else where it's fine" (Piaget, 1929). In each example the children confuse their own activity with that of things. Children get up, so the sun must also. Children need fresh air to grow big and strong, so that's why the sun exists: to give children fresh air. Conceivably, these interpretations mean narcissism, but before making up our minds, let's first ask another question: Why should a child know that the sun does not get up in the morning and that the origin of the sun is obscure? Children must learn these facts; they must learn to distinguish between animate and inanimate, between a thing that revolves on its axis and an animal that rises from a bed.

That learning takes time and until children acquire knowledge about things, they seem narcissistic. In reality they are only unable to distinguish between the activity of things and their own activity.

Children's confusion about things assures misunderstanding between themselves and others; parents can explain, explain, explain, but do the children understand? Often they do not, and their confusion is even clearer when we turn from things to a toddler's role-taking abilities.

Now in role-taking, people have two general options. They can identify with the other's role, using it as a model or standard ("They tell me that's bad; I agree"), or they can "retain a clear separation of identity" between the self-attitudes and the attitudes of others ("They tell me that's bad; now, what do I think?") (Turner, 1956). Initially children must identify with the other's role; again, to be an object to ourselves, we must first be the subject of other people's thoughts. However, do children, especially toddlers, make a clear separation between self and other? Can they "search out the role attributes of others, compare them with one's own, and make effective use of the comparison in any of a variety of adaptations" (Flavell, et al., 1968)?

No, they cannot. And the evidence comes from a number of sources. Consider first a two-year study of nursery school children between the ages of eighteen months and four years. The aim was to uncover the toddlers' sense of self in relation to others (Ames, 1952). At eighteen months children grab objects from the teacher "without regarding her," and generally they show an "utter disregard" for other children. If another child is in the way, they "impersonally" push past him. At twenty-four months the children occasionally exchange greetings like "Hi" and "Hello," but for as long as fifteen minutes "no inter-child behavior is observed," and often children "climb right onto another child, brush right by him, or bump right into him, without seeming to notice the child is there."[9] By three, things begin to change. Aggressive threats are diminishing, the idea of sharing makes an appearance ("O.K., you have it. Then it's my turn"), and some children "not only cooperate but *adjust.*" For example, three children are playing on trains and all in each other's way. Doug says to Jim: "Go around this way." Jim does not move, so Doug says, "I'll go this way" and gets out of the way (Ames, 1952).

Doug's kindness rests on his developing ability to take the role of the other, as well as make effective use of his knowledge "in any of a variety of adaptations." Three-year-olds are still only on the "verge of cooperative play," but in sharp contrast to the extreme egocentrism of the two-year-

---

[9] Working with English nursery school children, twenty years before the Ames study, Susan Issacs said egocentrism involved "a recognition of the *presence* of other children, but not their personalities or independent purposes" (1933).

old, the three-year-old has developed a rudimentary ability to retain a "clear" separation between self and others.

Keep in mind that this ability is only basic. It is not until the child is much older that he or she takes on a role with any degree of objectivity. Consider the following examples. A three-year-old is riding in a car and asks his father "What was that?" when "that" is already out of sight. Or a three-year-old asks his father to tell him a story when the father's mouth is full of toothpaste. Or a mother on the telephone does not realize that her four-year-old's calls meant she was on the toilet and needed help. "Didn't you know?" said the child in an outraged tone. Or, finally, in an experiment, five- and twelve-year-olds learned a game and then had the job of teaching it to a blindfolded adult. Generally, the older children did much better than the younger ones, and none of the twelve-year-olds showed a role-taking failure common to the five-year-olds: the young children sat in front of the blindfolded person and blandly told him that to play the game "You pick up *this*" (points to cube), "put it in here" (points to cup), and . . ." (Flavell, et al., 1968; Flavell, 1966).

Now, let's return to the period of negativism. David Ausubel wrote that when approaching the age of two, the child feels "omnipotent." Parents rarely said no and their deference to the child's wishes produced, "as a naturalistic product of actual interpersonal experience," a sense of power, a feeling of control over one's wishes and desires (Ausubel, 1957). Perhaps? But another interpretation is that to the extent that parents met the child's every need, there was no reason for the child to begin to develop role-taking abilities. After all, one important way children learn to take the role of the other is through conflict; one child wants this, the other wants that, and never will the roles of the other meet. Well, if children rarely need to take the role of the other, they are not going to begin the development of this ability. On the contrary, when they *are* forced to take the other's role, via a constant barrage of bad and "not-me" experiences, they are likely to respond with anger, frustration, and contradiction. Their predicament is "What's going on?" And their problem is that, with poor cognitive abilities, their chances of finding out are slim.

Recall the young child's failure to clearly distinguish between the activity of things and his own activity. This weakness is only one side of a child's problem in communicating with self and others. For progress with words is uneven. Two-, three-, and four-year-olds are beginning to think but, for all their progress in syntax, in how words are put together "properly," young children lag far behind in semantics, in the meaning and reference of words. Apparently, young children first learn words as signs rather than symbols (Bruner, 1966; Vygotsky, 1962). Asking Albert if he could have been called Henry, he says no. Well, could the moon have been called the sun and the sun, the moon? "No." "Why not?" "Because they are not the same thing" (Piaget, 1929). To a young child the word and the object it denotes are tightly linked; boys and girls *learn* that meaning is relative, arbitrarily bestowed by people via symbols; and, like the seven dictionary definitions for the word *love*, they must also learn the senses a word has, as well as "the contexts into which it fits" (for example, love between people; love in tennis). This takes time. It takes about seven years (Bruner, 1966). And while they are learning the meaning of words, children's—especially young children's—cognitive grasp of the situation is often inaccurate or wrong. Without understanding from others, they will have no answer to their crucial question: "Why are they doing this to me?" (For example, hitting me for urinating in my pants.)

Children have problems with the meaning of words; they also show marked weaknesses in role-taking. Together these two intertwined characteristics of the young child help to explain his negativism, rage, frustration, anger, and tantrums. What is the child to do? Can she request a precise definition of the situation? Can she perceive that Mommy and Daddy have learned that "if eighteen months loomed up, you know, and I was nowhere near tackling the problem (toilet training), I would think, Oh dear, I must spend *all day over this*, I mean I think I would, I should spend the whole day . . ." (Newson and Newson, 1965, emphasis in original).

Since children cannot ask or answer these questions, they try to gain control with the means at their disposal: crying, screaming, kicking, yelling. Remember, though, that children's reactions are more than a response to cognitive weaknesses. The stress is made here to empathize with toddlers, to try to understand the cognitive basis of their "I's," of their reaction to the attitudes of others. However, in those first two years children have developed habits; based on the actions of others, they "expect" certain things to happen and not happen. Perhaps parents have always comforted the child when he awoke at night; now that he is two, he may not understand, indeed, he may fiercely resent, being told that "big boys" sleep alone. Or, perhaps parents have generally said yes to the child's wishes; well, the child may get quite angry when told at the supermarket that she cannot have that toy: "Daddy doesn't have enough money."

Besides habits, there is a child's striving for competence (White, 1959). Especially if a child has been applauded with each step or newfound sign of genius, she will continue to seek to discover, explore, uncover. Attempts to stop this are bound to be resented. Cognitively the child cannot perceive why it is all right to play with this but not that. She wants to do both and will—or scream trying.

Probably, some balkiness is unavoidable. Children must learn the cultural and parental rules of the game; conflict is inevitable when, for instance, children are asked to give up habits for reasons they fail to understand. However, the crucial points for the development of self and personality are the amount of conflict, as well as the way conflict is handled. During the second year (and the third too), children continually face a host of bad and not-me experiences that may form the basis for a weak or poor self-concept. Children are often assaulted by others with charges of ineptness, naughtiness, willfulness, and even evil. They are bound to be sensitive. This normally reaches its peak during the second year, but Lewis notes that three-year-olds rarely criticize themselves and Ames adds that *"we may surmise from his (the four-year-old's) excessive boasting and bragging about himself, his abilities, his relatives, and his possessions that his sense of self may need strengthening*—that he may not feel as secure as he appears at first glance" (Lewis, 1963; Ames, 1952, emphasis in original).

Ames is right. Just the *number* of bad and not-me experiences is a good foundation for a poor self-image. However, whether this solidifies, and becomes a continuous and consistent basis for judgment about the self, depends primarily on the attitudes and actions of others. Children are behind the cognitive eight ball; they are unable to grasp others meanings or roles. So, if others respond to the child's confusion with screams, yells, and force, the child's first reaction is anxiety, with the second a poor or even terrible self-image. First, the child is worried: "What did I do?" "Why are they yelling at me?" "Why are they yelling at me again?" Second comes the child's response to the attitudes of others. Based on temperament, class, religion, this reaction takes many forms. Some children say yes to others and become passive; others say no and become aggressive. But, underlying both of these responses is a yes—the child's weak sense of self-esteem, his agreement with others that he *is* inept, willful, difficult to deal with.

This conclusion does not occur overnight. Although one brutal experience can of course leave permanent scars, normally a self-image is built up or torn down day by day, experience after experience. Often the results of everyday life are obvious: the child is comfortable and confident with others, or the child bites his nails to the quick. But, whether the results are obvious or hidden, the dialectic is the same: if others refuse to empathize with toddlers and add to the *number* of bad and not-me experiences, to the feelings of unmanageable anxiety, children have little choice but to root the concrete development of their self-concepts—the word *I* is first used with frequency at about twenty-seven months (Ausubel, 1957; Lewis, 1963)—in the obvious dislike shown to them by others.

Theoretically, the most vulnerable period is the year from two to three. Forced to give up habits and suppress strivings for competence at a time when cognitive abilities are minimal, the intensity of the child's reaction indicates the threats which others pose. This is a period when it is very easy to produce lasting problems in living. However, recall the comments of Ames and Lewis on three- and four-year-olds. Although the intensity of their response to others, their negativism, has lessened considerably, they still often walk on eggs. Day in and day out, they confront bad and not-me experiences ("don't ever go into the street"; "don't touch the stove"; "it's not good to pull your infant sister by the arms"; "please don't yell, your brother is sleeping"). So, since others provide criticism as daily fare, it is not surprising that three- and four-year-olds rarely criticize themselves. The last thing they need to do is echo others by asserting their own ineptness or inferiority.

For children and parents alike, getting from year two to year five is often difficult. But it can be done without lasting harm to anyone, and it is even possible to enjoy children and their development (see, for example, Ginott, 1965; Faber and Mazlish, 1975). The crucial variables are the attitudes and actions of others, particularly significant others. For the evidence here is substantial. We are in fact well on the way toward knowing which attitudes and actions help or hinder the development of a positive self-concept, as well as a relatively problem-free personality.

PARENT-CHILD RELATIONS

Parental attitudes are generally discussed in terms of two dimensions. The first is *warmth* versus *hostility*. Warm others are accepting, affectionate, understanding, often use explanations in disciplining, rarely or never use physical punishment; hostile others exhibit the opposite characteristics.

The second is *control* versus *autonomy*. Generally this refers to the way in which parents set and enforce rules plus foster or inhibit a child's sense of individuality and autonomy. However, time and research show that this dimension has two distinguishable patterns, for parents sometimes exert firm control but applaud a sense of individuality while other parents practice lax control but hold a tight rein on the child's chance to think for himself. So, parents are *permissive* or *restrictive;* they make rules and regulations, set limits to the child's activities, and enforce these rules and limits; or they do not. Finally, parents practice *psychological control* versus *psychological autonomy:* they are willing and happy to let the child be an individual apart from the parents, or they are overprotective, intrusive, and eager to foster a sense of dependence on the child's part (Schaefer, 1959; Mussen et al., 1974; Becker, 1964).

What do we know about the effects of these various parental attitudes? On the warmth versus hostility dimension, a child's sense of self-esteem is intimately related to acceptance and approval by others. Coopersmith found that children with high self-esteem had mothers who showed their love and approval in many ways. Mothers were sensitive to the child's needs, concerned about his friends and activities, supportive when he failed or experienced distress. Children perceived this warmth and interpreted it as a sign of significance: "She spends so much time caring about and for *me, I* must be worth the effort" (Coopersmith, 1967; Sears, 1970).

On the negative side, hostility often produces aggressive children. But whether aggressive reactions to the attitudes of others are taken out on the self (a shy, withdrawn personality) or others (a bully) depends on many variables; hostility only assures the need for some explanation of others feelings of dislike, hatred, or resentment. Hostility demands that children fit into a set of social relations that loudly proclaim they are unwanted. This is always difficult. For children are forced to root personality development in a world flooded with bad and not-me experiences. Although that is conducive to many things, self-esteem is *not* one of them (for instance, Becker, 1964; White, 1972).

Warmth, approval, affection: all are critical antecedents of self-esteem and such personality traits as competence, responsibility, self-reliance, and independence (Mussen, 1973). However, since warmth always operates in conjunction with parental attitudes toward control and autonomy, to begin to understand the total effect of parental attitudes, it is necessary to locate those variables that operate alongside warmth, approval, and affection.

First is firm control by the parents. Now this does not mean rigid rules, inflexibly enforced by fiat or "the rod." It does mean self-esteem is closely related to rules that are firm, clear, and demanding. As usual, consider the child's position. He or she must fit into a set of social relations made by others; parents set the rules and part of a child's sense of self-esteem comes from doing well by them. So, if parents set no rules, either through indifference or a belief in the value of freedom, the children are given no definitions of life's many situations. There is no way to tell "good-me" from "bad-me," no way for the "I" to clearly react to others, because others have provided no basis for decisions about self and world. In the extreme, the child lives in a definitional vacuum (see Coopersmith, 1967; also Neill, 1960, 1966).

If firm rules provide guidelines, they are also a sign of parental concern. Here we meet a mesh between warmth and control. For as long as parents are reasonable in setting and enforcing guidelines (for example, parents explain why the rules exist; they do not resort to force or threaten loss of love; they reward rather than punish), children seem to "interpret these limits and demands as expressions of concern." Significantly, Coopersmith found no relationship between self-esteem and frequency of demands. However, the means of control were related to self-esteem. Parents who used reward, praise, and support tended to have children with high self-esteem; parents who used force and punishment tended to have children with poor self-images (Coopersmith, 1967; also Ginott, 1965).

These results are consistent with theory. For even if they were cognitively unable to understand their parents, children who were *loved* into obeying rules had no cause to develop basic anxieties. Learning the bad and not-me's of their parents and society, these children undoubtedly felt, like most four-year-olds, unsure and anxious, but they were always able to return to warm parents, significant others who were unwilling to bully them into submission. In the case of children with punitive parents, even warmth is often unable to overcome the effects of harsh, forceful discipline. In studying mothers who were warm but very restrictive during the first three years, Kagan and Moss found the children conforming, aggressive, submissive, and unlikely to show mastery behavior (Kagan and Moss, 1962; also Mussen and Kagan, 1958). From our standpoint, the reaction of the children is "reasonable." Unable to understand why their parents are yelling or hitting, they react by seeking the warmth they sometimes receive. It is as if the child says: "She's often nice to me. I don't know why she's yelling or screaming and I'm really scared and frightened. There's probably something wrong with me—Mommy's usually so nice—so maybe if I do exactly what she wants, she'll be nice again." If this is the child's response to others, the child has developed certain personality traits, all rooted in the poor self-image derived from Daddy and Mommy.

High self-esteem is closely linked to warmth and firm rules; it is also tied to "respect and latitude for individual action" within the limits set by others (Coopersmith, 1967). After all, if parents try to exert psychological control over the child, he or she is unlikely to feel a sense of self-reliance or independence. If others fail to respect a child's judgments, how is the boy or girl to learn respect for them? And if others allow the child no latitude, no freedom to make mistakes and achieve success, the child has no experience in thinking for himself. Always others set the rigid and inflexible rules and maintain a set of social relations that foreclose opportunities for developing self-confidence. The child never gets the chance to discover that she can make wise choices, produce things on her own, face the world of others, and come out on top. Unfortunately, without such experiences, children are unlikely to develop a crucial aspect of self-esteem: confidence in one's abilities and aptitudes, whatever they may be (Coopersmith, 1967; Mussen et al., 1974; White, 1972).

While parental attitudes never result in personal or social life changing into utopia—at least some misunderstanding and impatience between adults and children seem to be everyone's legacy—attitudes of warmth, firm rules, and respect plus freedom do produce a sense of self-esteem. And that is vital. For what happens when self-esteem develops is that parents keep anxieties to a minimum, and, through love and empathy, help children do a very difficult thing—"happily" to fit into a set of arbitrarily inherited social relations.

Remember, though, that even the best intentions need not lead to self-esteem. First, besides parental attitudes, culture is also an important determinant of personality and self-image. For example, try as hard as they might, parents of a black child in the Deep South would have a very difficult time producing a sense of self-esteem. And until recently, anywhere in America a black woman often had difficulty in gaining self-esteem. For if the culture defines beauty as a white, blue-eyed, straight-haired blonde, a black woman was ugly; and even the finest parents rarely defeat a culture (Greir and Cobbs, 1968). So, for all their importance, parental attitudes operate in conjunction with cultural variables, and sometimes culture proves more significant than warmth, firm rules, and respect plus freedom.

Second, unless the attitudes of others are tied to the "proper" messages, parental actions may undermine the hopefully beneficial effects of parental attitudes. For example, a loving parent might try to produce self-esteem by telling his child: "You're an angel" or "You're such a wonderful little boy." Seemingly the child should respond in this way: "He's telling me I'm an angel. I agree. I'm an angel." However, recall two points made in Chapter One: our freedom resides in the I, and perception is always an interpolated act. Confronted with such a wonderful image of self, the child may experience anxiety. "He may feel he is far from being wonderful and that he is unable to live up to this label" (Ginott, 1965). In fact, the child may try to eliminate conflict ("He's telling me I'm an angel, but I know I often do bad things") by accepting a negative image of self, and he may also begin to reevaluate the worth of others: "If he thinks I'm so great, he can't be very smart" (Ginott, 1965; Faber and Mazlish, 1975).

Always, perception is an interpolated act; always, I am relatively free in responding to what you say about me. So, along with warmth, firm rules, and respect plus freedom, others must tell the child things he is likely to interpret in a positive way and they must use techniques of control that are not an assault on self-esteem. For example, Ginott argues that praise for a child should be specific and descriptive. If a child washes the car, instead of saying, "You're an angel," say, "Thank you for washing the car, it looks new again." In this way, the child has no problems with an ideal image and he is also likely to arrive at a positive yet realistic response to the attitudes of others: "I did a good job. My work is appreciated." Or, take rule setting. Instead of challenging the child's sense of self by saying, "You know you can't go to the movies on school nights" or "You are too young to stay up that late. Go to bed," say, "No movies on school nights" and "It's bedtime." Obviously, there is no guarantee that the child will listen, but at the least an impersonal setting of limits tries to avoid challenging the child's sense of independence or assaulting his sense of esteem. Ideally, an impersonal setting of rules produces a modicum of order in the home, tries to avoid implicating the child's images of self, and, assuming obedience on the child's part, fosters a sense of esteem because the child acts in a manner others define as good and proper (Ginott, 1965; Faber and Mazlish, 1975).

Stated differently, whether it is washing a car or not going to the movies, these situations often produce self-percepts, transitory representations of self (see Chapter One). Eventually, these self-percepts produce enduring images of self. And Ginott's point is that, along with the "correct" attitudes, others must use messages and techniques of control that allow children to experience the long series of positive self-percepts which over time produce the positive, unique image of self.

Our discussion in this section focused on the core of personality, the self-concept. However, any particular cluster of parental attitudes produces tendencies toward certain traits (for example, hostility, rigid control, and lack of respect are often associated with aggressiveness, paranoid tendencies, and closed-mindedness). The problem is to locate the parental attitudes, understand their effects, and keep in mind that, like the self-concept, trait development is influenced by biological predispositions, culture, and situational variables. For example, two Americans could have "competitiveness" as a personality trait. For one, the trait's roots are culture and a positive self-image; for the other, the trait's roots are culture and a negative self-image.

IDENTIFICATION

I was sorry I hated the mate so, because it was not in (young) human nature not to admire him. He was huge, muscular, his face was bearded and whiskered all over; he had a red woman and a blue woman tattooed on his right arm—one on each side of a blue anchor with a red rope to it; and in the matter of profanity, he was sublime. When he was getting out cargo at a landing, I was always where I could see and hear. He felt all the majesty of his great position, and made the world feel it too. When he gave even the simplest order, he discharged it like a blast of lightning, and sent a long reverberating peal of profanity thundering after it. I could not help contrasting the way in which the average landsman would give an order with the mate's way of doing it. If the landsman should wish the gangplank moved a foot farther forward, he would probably say: "James, or William, one of you push that plank forward, please"; but put the mate in his place, and he would roar out: "Here, now, start that gangplank forward! Lively now! What're you about! Snatch it! Snatch it! There! There! Aft again! Aft again! Don't you hear me? Dash it to dash! Are you going to *sleep* over it! Vast heaving. Vast heaving, I tell you! Going to heave it clear astern? Where're you going with that barrel! For-ard with it 'fore I make you swallow it, yore dash-dash-dash-dashed split between a tired mud turtle and a crippled hearse horse!"

I wished I could talk like that . . . I sat speechless, enjoying, shuddering, wondering, worshipping. [Mark Twain, *Life on the Mississippi* (1883)]

Robert W. White says identification is a form of imitation. The latter is a general process of "wanting to do something that someone else has done." Twain could have cursed like the mate or grown a beard when he was able. But, if Twain identified with the mate, mere imitation is unsatisfactory. Identification means wanting to be like another person, it means "wanting *to create in one self* the model's social competence, effectiveness, and attractiveness to other people" (White, 1972, emphasis added; Mussen, 1973). So, if Twain identifies with the mate, a beard or steady stream of dash-dash-dashes symbolizes his desire to use the beliefs, attitudes, and actions of the mate as a model for himself.

Identification is important for at least two reasons. The first is personality development. We think and act according to the rules laid down by our model; we evaluate and judge ourselves by his or her standards. If all goes well, this is satisfactory. But identification is a gamble. Conceivably, the model has many faults; this could have serious effects if we root our self-image in the model's, and then discover, like Mark Twain, "that he was a low, vulgar, ignorant, sentimental, half-witted humbug. . . ." Or, what if social forces prevent us from becoming like the model? Many Americans identify with the ideal of the self-made man, only to discover that conditions in the modern factory make them otherwise. Tragically this identification with the impossible produces a poor self-image; the person feels that he, not the society, has failed (Chinoy, 1965; Wyllie, 1966).

Identification directs personality development down the model's path; it is also important as a means of socialization and bondage. Assume that a child identifies with his father. Through this identification, he learns what men do and do not do, what men wear and do not wear, what men seek and do not seek. This is a form of socialization; the child learns and applauds the recipes for living that society says all men use. However, via this identification, the child roots one important aspect of his self-image—his gender identity—in inherited definitions of man and woman. Perhaps these are unjust, unequal, even slavelike? No matter. The boy has based his self-image on them and change demands a difficult and painful admission: "What my father told me was all wrong. I can't continue to think and act like a man. It's unfair to half the people on earth!" Conceivably, such an insight produces change. But if the model is still revered, and the person roots his self-image in the model's beliefs, change is unlikely. Few people embrace threats to established beliefs, identities, or self-image. It's easier to lie. Remember, too, that to give up a belief or identity leaves a person in a social vacuum; the individual is without one definition of self.

That is uncomfortable. In fact, since very few people enjoy confusion, one common reaction to threatening insights is to applaud the old, rather than to build the new (Festinger, 1957).

Identifications are common in the period from three to six years of age. Cognitively, children are beginning to make sense of their world; slowly, they are starting to perceive who has social power, as well as which competencies are valued (Kohlberg, 1969). When this growing ability is linked to the child's developing sense of self, identifications are to be expected. Unsure of their identities, even confused about who they are, children seek clarity; and taking the roles of others, four-, five-, and six-year-olds are able to see with some precision those roles valued by their significant and generalized others: "They tell me that's good, powerful, wonderful, essential." Then, when children see those desirable roles, they can make a choice for themselves. Using the other's role as a mirror, they can identify with the reflected image and say, "I want to be like that." Choice of models is relative, but the process of identification always means using the role of the other as a basis for creating in oneself the model's desirable qualities (Turner, 1956; Cooley, 1922).

Although no one is yet certain why specific identifications take place, it is generally agreed that many factors are at work. One is *warmth*. Boys, for example, seem to identify with loving fathers. High masculinity, self-acceptance by the fathers, encouragement of the son: all were much less important than the son's feeling that the father loved him (Mussen and Rutherford, 1963; Payne and Mussen, 1956). A second factor is *power*. In Belfast many Catholic children identify with IRA soldiers because these men have the power to hurt a hated enemy, and many Irish boys identify with their fathers because women have no power in Ireland. There the male is taught "to daily give thanks to God that he was not born a woman" (Fraser, 1974). A third cause of identification is *cultural:* any group places certain figures on a pedestal, and children learn from others the privileges and esteem that go with a particular role. In Twain's day it was the riverboat sailor; today it is the astronaut, and in many lower-class areas it is the criminal or sports figure. Fourth is the *frequency of interaction*. When seeing someone every day, children are forced to learn the content of the other's behavior; so, when they want or need a model, those well-known to them have an advantage (Maccoby, 1959). Finally is the *perceived similarity of the other*. Kagan cites a study in which boys watched a female experimenter dispense rewards, while a male experimenter sat quietly. In the end, the boys imitated the ignored male rather than the rewarding female. Seemingly, children are more likely to imitate and identify with others who have characteristics (sex, clothes, religion) similar to their own (Kagan, 1971).

All of these factors cause identifications to occur and the importance of any one variable is hard to estimate. Significant others provide obvious models for children but boys and girls often copy selectively, and how can we know which of the television figures will be copied? or which of the school friends? or which of the parents' friends? For now, we do not know. Our only guarantee is that the child's identifications represent a "fit" between "inner needs and outer models" (White, 1972).

Although identification is often of great help in understanding personality development, its significance is limited. The term refers to a motivated desire to be like someone else; that is it. And when the concept is "stretched" to include situations where children learn from others or do what others want, the value of identification is "washed out." For we all perceive "many important aspects of the personal world through experiences in which there is no element of wanting and trying to be like another person" (White, 1972). For example, entrance into school is often a humiliating experience for lower-class children, and traditional religions teach their child members that they are sinners, people unalterably stained by evil. Neither of these experiences includes an identification; yet both give children important knowledge about self and world.

PRIVATE SPEECH AND THE GENERALIZED OTHER

One fascinating topic in child development is "private speech"; three-, four-, and five-year-olds meet in a public place and loudly talk to themselves. For example, in nursery schools many children are often gathered around a table, seated or standing side by side, the room is humming with conversation, with none of the children talking to each other. Oblivious to the social implications of their talk (that is, if an adult were to try it, he might be called crazy), the children are happily and busily talking to themselves.

Since Piaget first called attention to children's public yet private speech (see Piaget, 1962b), its meaning has been debated. There is agreement that private speech begins about three, increases in use till about five, and disappears by age seven. Children are then able to silently say in their minds what they previously needed to say out loud. But why do the children speak privately in public? And what of the forms of private speech? Sometimes children simply repeat words; at other times they talk to things; and on still other occasions children have a dialogue with themselves. Assuming the role of robber and police officer, the child pretends to steal something and then catches herself!

Piaget said that private speech was egocentric; children sat with others and talked to themselves because they were unable to differentiate their point of view from that of others. In response to Piaget's argument, Vygotsky said private speech had a specific function: cognitive self-guidance. When the child says, "The wheels go here, the wheels go here," there is a "communicative intent" behind the public statement. The child is using speech to guide action, thus differentiating herself from others. Her "mistake" is in not distinguishing between self-guiding speech and social speech. Unable to internalize her words, the child's cognitive weaknesses make it seem as though her speech is egocentric (Piaget, 1962b; Vygotsky, 1962; Luria and Yudovich, 1971; Kohlberg et al., 1968).

Like so many disputes in social psychology, both writers are correct, but neither accounts for all the observed forms of behavior. First, some private speech is egocentric. When four or five nursery school children engage in a collective monologue, none taking account of the other, their inability to differentiate themselves from others is clear. Second, some private speech does serve as a form of self-guidance; in task situations children do use words to direct themselves. However, the problem is that neither of these views provides a basis for understanding the other. If all private speech guides, how does one account for collective monologues? And if all private speech is egocentric, what about "The wheels go here, the wheels go here"?

George Herbert Mead's work provides a basis for bringing the observed facts under one theoretical umbrella (Kohlberg et al., 1968). Recall the argument that no one is an object to himself until he is first the subject of other people's thoughts and actions. For Mead there is the assumption that speech and thought always have "implicit, if not explicit," dialogues, forms, and functions. "If I wear this, what will they say?" "If I do this, will she do that?" "I'm a nice boy," with the implicit assumption that this knowledge was gained from others: "They told me so." Or "I can't play with dolls; boys aren't supposed to," with the implicit assumption that this rule is part of the generalized other's recipes for living.

Now, if we adopt Mead's point of view, collective monologues, dialogues, and self-guidance are all way stations along a road that leads—by about the age of seven—to thought, to internalized conversation. Children are not born with the ability to silently talk to themselves about themselves and their world. This ability and the knowledge it presupposes (for instance, about good-me's, bad-me's, and not-me's; about how things work) are all acquired in the process of social development. Children "practice" before they are able to think silently, and their practice tells us much about the process of becoming a person.

Consider the collective monologue. Seated beside other children, a four-year-old boy is loudly talking to himself: "I'm awful strong. I can even box." "See! I ride with my hands off. Ain't I smart?" (Ames, 1952). Such talk is egocentric but it has a purpose: in telling others about his activity, the boy is also establishing its meaning for himself. Indeed, such talk indicates that "the awareness of the meaning of his action to himself arises in the process of communicating it to the other" (Kohlberg et al.,

1968). Why should the child know what he is doing? At this stage of life, he still sees himself primarily from another's perspective. So the collective monologue is like a series of questions. Unsure of the meaning of his activity, or his place in it, the child describes his action to others and thus implicitly calls out in himself the response of the others. The child wants others to confirm that he is doing this or that; so he makes a statement ("I'm awful strong") or asks a question ("Ain't I smart?") and implicitly answers it himself. In sum, even though the child talks to himself, the monologue is confirmation from others of the meaning of his activity and his self.

Monologues are the basic form of private speech. Some sophistication comes when children begin to have dialogues with themselves. Consider the following two examples. While lying in bed, the solitary child says: "Do you know what this model plane is, Brain? It's a Cessna. Now you can have it, but you can't take it home or break it or I'll get mad. Now can I go to your house and play? O.K." Sitting in a room also occupied by mother and father, this four-year-old says: "I'll pretend I'm in this building and it's on fire. Fire! Fire! Fire!" (Child makes noise of siren, then proceeds to become a fire chief, furiously giving orders to a number of firefighters.) "You take out hoses and put them on the fire hydrant." "You turn up the hook and ladder" (Kohlberg et al., 1968; personal experience).

In these public yet private dialogues children show the ability to simultaneously assume two or more roles. They know what to do when a fire occurs and they know what firefighters do when they arrive at the fire. On the one hand, this ability represents knowledge; the child had to learn what happens at fires, as well as what different people do to combat them. On the other hand, the dialogue shows abilities absent in the monologue. Private speech is still an attempt at self-defining (breaking a plane is bad-me) or self-communicating (this is what happens at a fire), but in the monologue the child relied on others to confirm the meaning of action. Now both self and others are explicitly represented in the child's speech. In fact, in fighting the fire, the child shows the ability to step outside of his own mind and imaginatively assume the roles of other people. Here the child no longer depends on confirmation from others. His dialogue indicates that he knows what happens when a plane is broken or a fire erupts. Again, his speech is a form of "practice," of cementing this acquired knowledge, but the dialogue contains a script that is far more complex than any collective monologue.

Theoretically, the final stage in private speech occurs when the child makes self-guiding statements. One example was given before: "The wheels go here, the wheels go here." Another is: "This red one! I have to press this!" And finally: "I must clean this up" (Luria and Yudovich, 1971). In each statement "speech precedes and controls activity rather than following it" (Kohlberg et al., 1968). Here children do away with confirmation from the other, as well as the dialogue. Both are now—at about the age of six—taken for granted. For the children's speech shows they no longer need to engage in dialogue; they are so certain of the reasons for action ("I have to press this!") or they have analyzed the situation so well ("Daddy will be angry if I don't clean up"), that they can dispense with questions and begin with answers. Using the "extraordinary supplement" called words, children show they have internalized the knowledge acquired from others by using speech to "synthesize reality" as well as guide and regulate their behavior (Luria and Yudovich, 1971; also Lewis, 1963).

Eventually children even dispense with self-guiding statements. By about seven, thinking is internalized conversation; children now rarely make private speeches in public. Like adults, they rely primarily on silent inner speech, or thought.

Consider the profound implications of this development. Mead said that the self developed in two general stages. First, it included "an organization of the particular attitudes" of others toward the self ("I'm a good boy," "I'm a nice girl") and toward one another in specific acts (say, eating or sleeping). Then, second, "the self is constituted not only by an organization of these particular individual attitudes (for example, of father or mother), but also an organization of the social attitudes of the generalized other or the social group as a whole to which he belongs" (Mead, 1934). Well, when speech proceeds from the collective monologue to thought, children show they have taken this second step. Based on the actions and attitudes of others, the girl or boy learns good-me's, bad-me's, and not-me's. When, by seven, children need only supply answers, they show that their use of private speech for the purposes of self-defining or self-communicating has been successful. They know the rules of the game, the society's recipes for living, so well that by seven they already take them for granted.

Mead tried to show this by contrasting play with the organized game. In play where the boy is both policeman and robber, the child takes a number of roles but responds to "immediate stimuli"; the role-taking is not organized into a whole. But in an organized game such as baseball, the child "must be ready to take the attitude of everyone else involved," plus know "that these different roles have a definite relationship to each other." In baseball (or football or volley ball) the roles are organized as a whole, and at times the child has to have three or four present in his own mind. Otherwise he will not know who throws the ball, who catches it, or who catches a fly ball in right field (Mead, 1934).

Mead's point is that through the generalized other any society provides a set of *organized rules* that all its members must learn if they are to interact successfully. For example, boys learn what they do, they learn what girls do, and they also learn the rules and regulations that guide reactions between the two sexes. This knowledge is acquired from various sources (parents, friends, books, television), but where the four- or five-year-old *played* the roles of husband-wife, the seven-year-old dispenses with private speech and substitutes taken-for-granted knowledge acquired from others over time.

In summary, private speech is important for at least two reasons. First, its rise and fall show how children learn to silently talk to themselves. Second, and equally important, when children begin to think, they show they now take the *content* of private speech for granted. We focused on forms, monologues, dialogues, self-guiding speech, but it is the taken-for-granted content that is at the root of the thinking child's conceptions of self and world. Consider, for example, the prospects of change. This is difficult when children need no longer even supply questions; answers are assumed and it will be difficult to undo the work of six or seven years. Successfully socialized, the thinking child knows the organized rules of the game. These provide the basis for thinking about self and world. Children know this because others have told them it is so. And how much doubt can there be if children meet few people who disagree about the rules of the game, the society's recipes for living?

A final point concerns the relationship between the particular attitudes of others and the generalized other. Do the two mesh? Or, does what significant others tell us about self and world conflict with images and rules derived from the larger society?

No precise answer is possible. Harmony is likely but by no means assured. First, any distinction between the attitudes of parents and the attitudes of society is somewhat arbitrary. Parents, significant others, provide us with specific images of self, but our parents are also representatives of the larger society. For example, their good-me's and bad-me's are shared by other parents, and in the process of developing a self-concept in reaction to these attitudes, the child is also learning the "organized community's" rules of the game. So, while the decline of private speech is one indication that the child takes society's rules for granted, this process of learning began at birth, and it is one cause of the harmony that often exists between what parents and society say about self and world. For instance, if parents say good-me is being polite, courteous, and speaking well, this should be reaffirmed in school. Teachers often applaud these qualities and one result for the child is a positive self-image, as well as confirmation that the rules work outside the family.[10]

---

[10] Mead makes this point when he writes that the structure of the self is conventional, shared with other people; for example, consider the similarities between men and women, blacks and whites, Americans and Japanese (Mead, 1934).

Second, remember that as our social identities establish what and where we are in society's terms (Stone, 1962), they also limit or extend life's possibilities. For example, parents could give a migrant child a relatively positive image of self, but that image has to *fit into* identities derived from the generalized other. Society says migrants are lower class, dirty, unreliable, and lazy. These images are also internalized during the decline of private speech, and for migrant children they often prove more important than the specific attitudes toward self derived from parents. Robert Coles notes that migrant children score low on I.Q. tests but high on knowledge of society's image of self. The children feel they are "worthless, blamed, frowned upon, spoken ill of" (Coles, 1971). And the children are right. For them, social identities are likely to undo even the strongest efforts by their significant others.

Third, primarily because of institutionalized inequalities, the probability is that specific images derived from others will fit into identities derived from the generalized other. With less money, fewer opportunities, less education, and more need to work long hours, lower-class parents are more likely to engage in child-rearing practices that foster a poor self-image. This is not inevitable, and middle- and upper-class parents often produce children with negative self-images and disutrbed personalities. However, at birth society gives those with money and the "proper" skin color advantages denied to members of the lower classes or minority groups. One result of this is a vicious circle: parents have a poor self-image and they pass this on to their children through child-rearing practices as well as acceptance of society's definition of self and world (Williams and Steth, 1974; Pavenstedt, 1965).

Fourth, and last, probability is not certainty. Harmony between the messages of significant others and the messages of society is never assured. Children are typical and unique; their reactions to others are shaped by a number of variables, and there is no reason why those variables cannot produce children who say no to their significant or generalized others. Remember, too, that parents can disagree with the generalized other; they can foster a positive self-image in their daughter, while informing her that what society says about women is all wrong. Here parents intentionally foster conflict between self and society.

Finally, what is the pace of social change? Groups such as the Amish (in Pennsylvania) are an extreme example, but in a fast-moving society it is possible for significant others to prepare their children for a world that does not exist. If, like the Amish, homogeneity is maintained, the decline of private speech need not symbolize confused thought. But if significant others prepare children for a world they can never find, the content of their thought is likely to include not a host of assured recipes for living, but a jumble of contradictory and muddled ingredients. The result for the child is confusion about self and world.

STABILIZATION OF CONCEPTS

Middle childhood (the years from six to twelve) is often characterized as a period of "relative tranquillity" (Stone and Church, 1968), a time when children "consolidate and adjust to past gains in preparation for the increased pace of change and transformation that is wrought by adolescence" (Weiner and Elkind, 1972). One sign that this view is accurate is the decline of private speech; the ability to think shows that children now take many of society's rules for granted. Naturally, children can reject or disobey the rules, but they are still unwittingly determined by them. For the "good girl" who thinks of herself as an angel and the "bad girl" who thinks of herself as horrible have both given the same answer to others' definitions of their behavior: that answer is yes.

Another important sign of consolidation during middle childhood is the stabilization of concepts. Defining *concept* as an idea of something or some person formed by mentally combining all its characteristics (for example, a boy, a black, a dog, a hammer), concepts are important because they serve as filters for the perception of people, things, experiences. When a white child learns the meaning of black in American society, the concept is often a guide to perception. For the white child who owns and understands the concept, the black child is no longer a unique human being; now he or she is lazy, stupid, inferior. This is true because the learned concept says it is, because the learned concept acts as a filter for the perception of people.

Concepts are learned. And the evidence indicates that they begin to stabilize about the seventh year, with stability often increasing as the child approaches adolescence. As a first example, take children's conceptions of their religious denomination. David Elkind asked a six-year-old Jewish boy, "What is a Jew?" The answer was "a person." And when asked, "How is a Jewish person different from a Catholic?" the child responded "cause some people have black hair and some people have blonde." Talking to a boy nearly eight, Elkind said, "What is a Jew?" The answer was "a person who goes to temple and Hebrew school." Finally, discussing his religion with a ten-year-old, the child said a Jew was "a person who believes in one God and doesn't believe in the New Testament" (Elkind, 1961).

Since Elkind found very similar responses among Catholic and Protestant children (Elkind, 1962a, 1963), he concluded that the answers represent a developmental trend from "vague, undifferentiated conceptions to abstract, clearly demarcated conceptions!" Where eight-year-olds differentiated their religion concretely and absolutely by the *behavior* of their members, ten-year-olds based their distinctions on abstract differences in the content of religious *beliefs*. Echoing the Jewish child, a six-year-old

Catholic said a Catholic was a person, but ten- and eleven-year-olds responded on the basis of abstract beliefs. A Catholic was someone who believes in the Pope, "someone who believes in the truths of the Roman Catholic Church" (Elkind, 1962a).

Elkind focused on religious concepts. Other studies have tried to understand the development of racial identities. By four or five, children are aware of racial differences; they know the relevant words, concepts, and phrases used to describe themselves and others. But until eight or nine, the child's understanding of these words is generally "more apparent than real." Children slowly learn to understand the meaning of racial concepts, and for black children, increased cognitive abilities often lead to a poor evaluation of self. For many black boys and girls, forced to acknowledge and accept their inherited racial identities, an abstract understanding of the social meaning of black and white leads to "ambivalence, self-doubt, and lowered self-esteem" (Proshonsky and Newton, 1968; Stevenson and Stewart, 1958).

Besides religious and racial conceptions, gender identities and brother-sister concepts also become increasingly abstract and differentiated as children approach adolescence (see Kohlberg, 1966; Elkind, 1962b). The general conclusion is clear: middle childhood is typically a period in which a wide variety of conceptions about self and world stabilize, as they become more abstract and differentiated.

This has at least three consequences for the developing child. One, as conceptual understanding increases, children sharpen their image of self and use this acquired knowledge to more accurately locate themselves in society. For black children the result is a poorer self-image, but for whites self-esteem is typically increased. Too, white children with poor self-images may use this new knowledge to increase their own sense of self-esteem; always, the self-image derived from significant others and the self-image derived from generalized others are intimately related.

Two, increased conceptual understanding symbolizes a consolidation of the knowledge gained from significant and generalized others. Between six and twelve, children acquire new abilities and knowledge, but the *content* of their thought is still deeply rooted in the attitudes of their significant and generalized others. One reason that middle childhood is a period of "relative tranquillity" is because children are "only" gaining a better understanding of things they have heard all their lives. Although this is necessary if children are to act successfully in society, it is a six-year period in which children learn to root their images of self and world even more firmly in the attitudes of others. Seemingly, human development proceeds along a path that makes personal and social change quite difficult. Although children are often told to think for themselves, each day of their development makes it harder to base their thinking in anything other than the arbitrarily inherited attitudes of others.

Three, increasingly abstract concepts tell us something about the child's ability to think. Words are symbols and as children develop their ability to use words (that is, concepts such as black and white, Protestant and Catholic), they show they are well on their way toward taking advantage of the symbolic capacities willed to them in evolution. Where the eight-year-old tied his definition of Jewishness to action (going to Hebrew school), the ten-year-old begins to relinquish his ties to concrete reality and to substitute increasingly abstract representations of it. This is a marvelous ability, for the growing child is developing the capacity to symbolically represent *anything*.

In adolescence children push this capacity to its limits: they dare to think hypothetically, they dare to imagine different recipes for living, different organized rules of the game. However, in middle childhood the capacity to think in terms of hypotheses is only developing. For example, an eight-, nine-, or ten-year-old has no trouble in ordering a series of dolls or sticks according to height. But, if asked to solve a problem such as, "Edith is taller than Susan; Edith is shorter than Billy; who is the tallest of the three?" these same children generally fail to furnish correct answers. Able to manipulate objects and concepts, they are still unable to reason on propositional, verbal statements. Wedded to concrete reality, they are still unable to completely divorce the word from concrete events and assume another's role "without believing the propositions on which they reason" (Piaget, 1974; Mussen, 1973).

Not surprisingly, Piaget calls the years from seven to twelve the period of concrete operations. Expressing relationships in terms of pure language is a very complicated process; children need time to acquire this ability, and for Piaget the period of concrete operations lays the cognitive groundwork for the reasoning abilities that fully blossom only in adolescence (Piaget, 1974, 1954; Richmond, 1970).

One aspect of the period of concrete operations was discussed above: concepts are consolidated into increasingly abstract and differentiated forms. Another cognitive development of middle childhood is class inclusion. Refer again to our discussion of Protestants. When six-year-olds were asked if they could be American and Protestant at the same time, children said no. When asked if all girls and boys were Protestant, children said yes. These answers show the six-year-olds' inability to handle class inclusions and exclusions. Compatible classes (Protestants and Americans) were incompatible; and incompatible classes (all children and all Protestants) were compatible. Clearly the children had problems with their cognitive understanding of self and world (Elkind, 1963).

By eleven or twelve, children's abilities to deal with classes has advanced greatly. When asked if all boys and girls in the world are Protestant, the eleven-year-old says, "No, because there are different faiths in the United States." When asked if one can be an American and a Protestant at the same time, the child says, "Yes, because there are different faiths in the United States." These answers show an accurate assessment of class inclusions and exclusions; they also indicate the eleven-year-old's ability to multiply classes. For when the child says that people can be Americans and Protestants at the same time, the studies indicate the child knows "that the class of Americans and the class of Protestants multiplied yields all those Protestants who are also American, and vice versa" (Weiner and Elkind, 1972: Elkind, 1963). This knowledge is essential for consciousness of kind. How can a child or adult say with any understanding, "I am a Protestant-American" or "I am an Afro-American" until they are able to multiply classes?

A final example of an ability gained during middle childhood is reversibility, the capacity to coordinate relations, plus group them into systems. Consider an experiment performed by Piaget. A seven-year-old is given a set of wooden beads; eighteen are brown, two are white. The question is: "Are there more wooden beads or more brown beads?" The seven-year-old answers, "More brown ones because there are two white ones." An eight-year-old answers correctly when he states that "there are more wooden ones because the two white ones are made of wood as well"; but consider what the eight-year-old had to do to answer this problem correctly. He had to group the class of brown and white beads to form the inclusive class, wooden beads. Then he had to reverse this question mentally, separating white beads from wooden ones, to reform the class, brown beads. Simultaneously, the child had to maintain in his mind the class of wooden beads so that the class of brown beads could be included in it. When the eight-year-old, probably very tired, answers correctly he shows that he is able to reverse himself and compare part (brown beads) with whole (wooden beads).

Now, let's turn from beads to brothers. Children are typically nine years old before they have an abstract and differentiated conception of brother. At seven, a brother was the "littlest boy" or "someone who lives with you"; at nine, a brother belongs to a family or was born from the same mother (Elkind, 1962b). But what about "having-a-brother"? Asked at six, "How many brothers do you have?" the child said, "One, David." Asked how many brothers David had, the child said, "He don't have no brothers." But, "Are you David's brother?" "Yes." "So, how many brothers does David have?" "None" (Elkind, 1962b). Although this six-year-old was sure that he had a brother, and that he was a brother, the child denied that his brother had a brother. This mistake stems from the child's inability to "coordinate two relations at the same time." To both be a brother and have a brother, the child "had to think simultaneously of having a brother (from his brother's viewpoint) and of being a brother (from his own viewpoint)" (Elkind, 1962b). To perform this task, the child had to be able to reverse himself; he had to be able to *be* a brother and then, at the same time, turn around and *have* a brother. Studies show that children in Western societies do not have this ability until they reach the age of nine (Piaget, 1974; Weiner and Elkind, 1972).

All of these cognitive abilities assume great importance for any discussion of what has been called internal freedom. Clearly it is quite hard to understand the causes and course of our development unless we understand, for instance, class inclusion, the multiplication of classes, and the relation between classes. How can *I* see and understand what happened to *me* until and unless I am able to see, for example, how my conceit and self-esteem are tied to my being a white, Anglo-Saxon, Protestant? Or, if my parents hated me and favored my sister, how can I deal with this unless I first know that I can simultaneously be a brother and *have* a sister?

Besides freedom, an understanding of cognitive development between six and twelve reaffirms the importance of parental attitudes of warmth, empathy, firm rules, and respect plus freedom. Like infants and toddlers, juveniles too are in the process of making cognitive sense of others' attitudes, beliefs, and practices. Eight- and nine-year-olds are immeasurably more advanced than infants, but their perception of others and their evaluation of self are still loaded with affective content. They do not understand the world; they are trying to make sense of it. But, if others fail to respond to their efforts with warmth and empathy, the child's limited abilities force him to evaluate self and world on the basis of feelings and emotions derived from others. Naturally, the dependence on emotion varies with age and the particular child, but it seems fair to conclude that weak cognitive abilities cause children to rely heavily on feelings for their evaluation of self and world.

SEX ROLES

People are born male or female. They become men and women, and often the learning process begins at birth. In America and Great Britain, boys wear blue, girls wear pink. Boys cry and within a few weeks they are often allowed to continue; boys need to be strong. Girls cry and they are generally picked up and cuddled; girls need to be cared for. Boys are shy; girls are coy. Boys are expected to be "fussy"; they need a rough-and-tumble childhood. Girls are expected to be "ladylike"; rough play has no important place in the life of a person who wears frilly dresses in the "soft" colors of white or yellow (Leach, 1975; Moss, 1967; De Beauvoir, 1953; Lewis, 1975).

Naturally, infancy only furnishes one basis for learning appropriate sex roles. Study shows it takes six or seven years for sex-role identities to solidify (for example, Kohlberg, 1966), and right into adolescence children are still learning sex-appropriate values, beliefs, and practices. However, no matter when the formal learning process ends, and even in cultures that lack a distinct period of adolescence, one thing is clear: always generalized and significant others demand that children, born male or female, become men and women (Barry et al., 1957; Goodman, 1970).

Is environment the only cause for learning appropriate sex roles? Are others alone responsible for making physiological differences one basis of children's life fates? Or, is anatomy also a determinant of sex-role identities? Does physiology play an important part in our becoming men and women?

Twenty years ago some doctors proposed a definite answer to the question of biological determinism: No. The basis for this very clear answer was work with hermaphrodites.[11] Studying children whose dominant sexual characteristics were female, or children whose dominant characteristics were male, doctors found the children readily accepting the identities given them by others—even when their external genitalia contradicted what others said. In short, if a child had the sexual characteristics of a boy, but others said the child was a girl, he became a she. And he did so without developing any form of psychoses (Money et al., 1957).

Since hermaphrodites were so malleable, Money and his colleagues hypothesized that at birth people were psychosexually neutral; men and women embraced sexual identities only on the basis of their response to the attitudes and actions of generalized and significant others. Today, this hypothesis has had to be rejected. Beginning with frogs and working their way up to people, doctors were able to show that, one, some part of the brain is characteristically different in males and females; two, the difference is closely associated with the way "sex hormones affect the developing brain pathways of the human fetus"; and three, because of the differential effects of sex hormones—the male androgens, the female estrogens and progesterone—males and females are biologically predisposed to engage in different types of behavior (Money and Tucker, 1975; Hutt, 1972).

Consider this example. Money and his colleagues found ten females who were normal except for prenatal androgens which were given to their mothers during pregnancy and then stopped at birth. Generally the androgens had little effect on appearance, and surgery easily corrected whatever masculine characteristics the androgens produced. But what about behavior? What was the effect of the androgens on thought and action? In terms of sexual identity, the androgens had no effect. The females became girls; "they don't pretend to be boys and they don't wish to change sex." However, the difference in behavior between the ten girls

---

[11] An hermaphrodite is a person who has both male and female physiological characteristics.

and a control group that received no androgens was summed up in one word: tomboys. Generally, the prenatally "androgenized" girls liked "strenuous physical activity, cavorting about on their bicycles, climbing trees, hiking, and exploring." They joined in rough games such as football, they enjoyed competition, and while wanting and expecting marriage and a family, their ambitions centered on their careers, both before and after marriage (Money and Tucker, 1975).

Now, before anyone jumps to extreme conclusions, let's try to assess the meaning of these findings. First, remember that *both* sexes normally have all three sex hormones in circulation. Men are dominated by androgens, women by estrogens, "but the wiring for all the affected behavior is present in both sexes." Second, while it is reasonable to assume that hormones make it easier for the sexes to practice certain types of behavior (say, athletics), the evidence negates the reasonable assumption. Once a woman decides to be athletic, or a man nonviolent, hormones do not seem to make the behavior any harder to achieve for one sex than the other. Third, and perhaps most important, consider another patient of Money's. A seven-month-old boy went to the hospital for circumcision. Tragically, while using an electric cauterizing needle, the physician burned off the boy's penis. Overwhelmed, the parents took the child home, but eight months later decided the boy should be a girl. Now, remember, this was a boy with normal amounts of androgen in his system. Surgery was performed to avoid any obvious genital signs of maleness, and the boy was treated like a girl. Happily, the parents were diligent and empathic; they simply acted as if the child were a girl. And in reaction to the attitudes and actions of her significant others, the child agreed. She is more active than other girls her age but, in sharp contrast to her twin brother, a doll and doll carriage headed her Christmas list at five; she is neat, dainty, experiments happily with styles for her long hair, and she often tries to help in the kitchen. In sum, born male, there was little problem in convincing the child to become a girl (Money and Tucker, 1975).

So, while it is wrong to argue that people are born psychosexually neutral, it is also wrong to attach too much importance to the effect of hormones. Essentially, what prenatal hormones do is "lower the threshold so that it takes less of a push to switch you on to some behavior and raise the threshold so that it takes more of a push to switch you on to other kinds" (Money and Tucker, 1975; Hutt, 1972). But members of each sex can easily cross any threshold if they want to, or are pushed to; and no hormonal predisposition determines that women stay home while men work. That is a cultural decision, an inherited result of the men and women who created our culture. After all, if biology determines social roles, then women should run the economy and men do the housework. Certainly, a woman with two children and a house to care for engages in much more strenuous physical activity than a man who drives to work, sits tied to his desk all day long, and then drives home. Perhaps feminists are actually doing men a biological favor?

If the argument seems exaggerated, the point has been made. Males and females are biologically predisposed to engage in certain forms of behavior, but people—the only makers of culture—determine the significance of predispositions and they also decide whether children are asked to cross thresholds or, at all costs, stay behind them. For besides the four reproductive functions—to menstruate, gestate, lactate, and impregnate—*none* of the differences between the sexes is "immutably ordained" by biology. In terms of sex roles and their social-psychological consequences, people are biologically underdeveloped and that means the social world of men and women is open in terms of its possibilities. People are born male or female; they become men and women (Money and Tucker, 1975; Montagu, 1974; Dangzier, 1971).

The process of becoming takes time; like virtually all knowledge about self, others, and world, children acquire their sexual identities over a period of years, and the evidence strongly indicates it takes about seven years for children to grasp with clarity the social significance of being labeled a boy or a girl. For example, where many two-and-a-half-year-olds answer incorrectly when asked their sexual identity, by three, a large majority know the right answer, and by four almost all children accept the identity willed to them by significant and generalized others. Or, where three- and four-year-olds often make mistakes about power and prestige, the stabilization of concepts and the ability to nest classes within classes (for example, men and women within the larger class people) seem to lead many seven-year-olds to accurate assessments of social reality: by about seven both sexes know that men have much more power and prestige than women. And by about seven girls make fewer judgments than boys that their own sex is better (Kohlberg, 1966; Emmerich, 1959, 1961; Gesell and Ilg, 1943; Garai, 1966; Hartley, 1964; White, 1972).

Essentially socialization into sexual identities focuses on three things: physical attributes, overt behaviors, and covert behaviors, such as feelings, beliefs, attitudes, motives (Kagan, 1971). Girls learn to be careful about their appearance; others want and expect them to be pretty. Boys learn to be rugged; others want and expect them to be strong. So, where the girl shuns muscles, the boy seeks them. Or, where the girl is encouraged to experiment with a variety of hair styles, even most long-haired boys learn that such experiments lead others to make a very negative judgment about self: "You're a sissy." Or, where the young girl learns to use make-up as a way of enhancing her appearance, the boy learns to do without. Seemingly, a woman's body needs work, a man's does not. She has to soften her hands and body with creams; he should not. She has to use lipsticks in a variety of becoming shades; he should not. She has to strip herself of hair; he can bask in and display it.

Still, the body is a cover. And for all the instruction boys and girls receive about packaging it, the key focus of others' teaching efforts are the beliefs, attitudes, feelings, and behavior "proper" for each sex. Simone De Beauvoir views the essential differences (in Western societies) in terms of activity versus passivity, daring versus watching, doing versus pleasing. Boys inherit a social identity that asks them to assert themselves; inventing, risking, venturing, boys are told they create their existence by doing; in America myth has it that men are self-made. But girls, very young women? Here De Beauvoir sees a basic and tragic contradiction. For while any girl is able to invent, dare, and assert, she learns that "to please she must try to please." She learns that her self-esteem is rooted in the judgments of men and they demand she appear weak and docile, they demand she act like a satellite whose main function is to revolve around and bask in the light created by "man's work." Eventually most girls accept the attitudes of others and so complete a vicious circle: "For the less she exercises her freedom to understand, to grasp and discover the world about her, the less resources will she find within herself, the less will she dare to affirm herself as subject" (De Beauvoir, 1953). And the more will she accept as the foundation for the crucial social identity a passive approach to self, others, and world.[12]

Boys and girls learn about themselves in a variety of ways and circumstances. Often teachers are explicit: girls cry, boys do not; boys fight, girls do not; boys bring home the bacon, girls cook it and say thank you. However, sometimes instruction is subtle; it can easily take place outside the home and even in the absence of a significant other of the same sex. In discussing the socialization of ghetto males, Hannerz notes that boys without fathers are still "real men." Whether it is watching people on street corners, quietly listening to women talk about men, or gaining the knowledge from slightly older peers, the boys soon manage to learn, internalize, and act on the basis of masculine assumptions about self and world (Hannerz, 1976). In effect, the generalized other quickly fills the void left by the death or departure of the significant other.

Naturally, others sometimes fail; today some people are confused about, or in disagreement with, the sex roles inherited from others. However, as the ghetto example suggests, sex roles are important; they spill over into so many areas of life, into so many everyday situations that society normally gets its point across: within relatively broad limits, most of us ac-

---

[12] As Marabel Morgan writes in *The Total Woman*, "it is only when a woman surrenders her life to her husband, reveres and worships him, and is willing to serve him, that she becomes really beautiful to him. She becomes a priceless jewel, the glory of femininity, his queen" (Morgan, 1975).

cept the sex role attitudes of others. For example, I will be the man you want me to be and if I am not, if I fail at sports or run from a fight, I will be sure to embrace a negative image of self: loser or coward.

Although others teach us to become men and women, studies show that the attitudes and actions of others operate in conjunction with cognitive development (Kohlberg, 1966; Dangzier, 1971). Through childhood we normally gain an increasingly sophisticated grasp over the knowledge we acquire and that firm hold on, for example, language and concepts often acts to harden the sex-role knowledge acquired from others.

Consider language. Today we argue about changes in terms: fireman to firefighter, chairman to chairperson, salesman to salesperson. Many think these suggested changes are ridiculous, the ravings of feminists. However, evidence indicates there is good cause for feminist concern. First, if language is a mold shaping the mind (see Chapter One), then women's minds are shaped by words that symbolize man's power, prestige, and superiority. And second, if children engage in private speech from about three to about seven, when they finally begin to think, to silently talk to themselves, this new cognitive ability symbolizes a synthesis of reality that "allows" children to guide themselves by means of words that take for granted the world and sex roles inherited from significant and generalized others. In sum, when by about seven children think like boys and girls, they are thinking about themselves and their futures on the basis of words that say yes to the society's decisions about sex roles.

As a second example, consider the stabilization of concepts and the developed ability to nest classes in classes. Like the identities *Protestant* and *Catholic*,[13] children should gain an increasingly abstract and differentiated conception of the classes *men* and *women* as they get older. Moreover, as they gain the ability to nest classes in classes (*men* and *women* in the larger class *people*), children should be able to more clearly distinguish the relative amounts of power and prestige attached to each sex. And overall the result could easily be a decrease in self-esteem for girls and an increase in self-esteem for boys. For example, while it found no decrease for girls, a recent study did find that boys' self-esteem increased as they approached adolescence (Fein et al., 1975). And Kohlberg cites studies which found that as girls get older, their preferential evaluations for their own sex decrease. Consistently, many more girls would rather be boys than vice versa (see Kohlberg, 1966; Garai, 1966).

To summarize: while biology does provide males and females with innate predispositions toward certain forms of behavior, any normal child can easily cross biological thresholds with no psychological damage. But

---

[13] See the previous section on "Stabilization of Concepts."

whether or not children are allowed to cross thresholds is a decision made by others. Sex roles are the result of people's world-building. People decide the significance of predispositions (e.g., who says stronger is better, superior?) and people make males and females into men and women. Always the process of becoming operates in conjunction with cognitive development, but always the content of our sex-role thinking is rooted in the attitudes and actions of the significant and generalized others who socialize us.

CONSCIENCE

"Hush, Sonia! I am not laughing. I know myself that it was the devil leading me. Hush, Sonia, hush!" he repeated with gloomy insistence. "I know it all, I have thought it all over and over and whispered it all over to myself, lying there in the dark. . . . And how sick, how sick I was then of going over it all! I have kept wanting to forget it and make a new beginning, Sonia, and leave off thinking. . . . Understand me! Perhaps I should never have committed a murder again. I wanted to find out . . . whether I can step over barriers or not, whether I dare stoop to pick up or not, whether I am a trembling creature or whether I have the *right*. . . ."

"To kill? Have the right to kill?" Sonia clasped her hands.

"Ah Sonia!" he cried irritably and seemed about to make some retort. . . . "Don't interrupt me, Sonia. I want to prove only one thing, that the devil led me on then and he has shown me since that I had not the right to take that path. . . ."

"And you murdered her!"

". . . I murdered myself, not her! I crushed myself once for all, forever. . . . But it was the devil that killed that old woman, not I. Enough, enough, Sonia, enough! Let me be!" he cried in a sudden spasm of agony, "let me be!"

"What suffering!" A wail of anguish broke from Sonia. [Fyodor Dostoyevsky, *Crime and Punishment* (1886)]

Raskolnikov's pain underlines the difference between shame and guilt. Shame is a person's unpleasant reaction to an actual or imagined negative judgment of self by others. Shame needs others to make its appearance; if only in fantasy, others are essential to getting "red in the face," ashamed of ourselves and our behavior (Ausubel, 1955).

Raskolnikov is not ashamed; he is guilty. And while his feelings of self-reproach, self-disgust, self-contempt, and remorse are tied to moral standards learned from others, guilt is relatively independent of others. It does not rely on expecting or feeling disapproval from others. Instead, guilt occurs when the *self* disapproves of a contemplated or already completed act. Guilt is essentially internal; it is a negative self-evaluation, a "reprimand," that occurs when people accept that their behavior is at variance with moral values they feel obligated to accept (Kagan, 1971; Ausubel, 1955).

If people feel guilty, we assume they have a conscience. Somehow they came to accept a set of moral values and beliefs that guide their behavior. Somehow they learned an obligation to conform to these beliefs, to their conscience; and, when they fail to conform, guilt makes an appearance. People reprimand themselves for violating accepted standards of right and wrong.

Like the self and personality, a conscience develops over time and in the process of social experience. In the following paragraphs we will examine some of the factors associated with developing a conscience and feeling guilt. But, before we try to explain why a conscience appears, we must first examine the stages of moral development. For internal reprimands—guilt feelings—normally make their first conspicuous appearance in middle childhood. Before then, moral standards are generally determined by external rewards and punishments. Apparently a close relationship exists between the general course of cognitive development and the development of moral judgment. The appearance of guilt is related to the cognitive ability to think of morality in terms of generalized standards (Kohlberg, 1969; Piaget, 1965; Dangzier, 1971).

Jean Piaget was perhaps the first to link cognitive abilities to the development of morality. In *The Moral Judgment of the Child* (1965), Piaget made at least four points which subsequent research has consistently confirmed (for example, Graham, 1972). First, where young children (aged three, four, and five) judge an act as bad in terms of physical consequences, older children root their judgments in intention: "Did she mean it?" "Was it only an accident?" Second, young children are unaware of relativity in moral judgment; they also generally fail to admit others' views of right and wrong. Lying is bad. Period. Third, young children regard acts as bad because *they* will be punished; older children discuss bad acts in terms of rule-breaking or harm to others. Fourth, young children generally fail to use empathy in their judgments; still egocentric, young children are unable to take the other's role and use it as a reason to consider others' attitudes or welfare (Piaget, 1932; Dangzier, 1971).

Taken together, these facts led to a conclusion: the growth of moral judgment proceeds along a regular sequence of developmental stages. Indeed, in the chart below Lawrence Kohlberg breaks down moral development into three levels and six stages:

LEVEL I   Pre-moral Level
  1)—Punishment and obedience orientation (obey rules to avoid punishment)

2)—Naïve instrumental hedonism (conform to obtain rewards, have favors returned)

LEVEL II   Morality of Conventional Rule—Conformity
3)—"Good boy" morality (conform to avoid disapproval and dislike by others)
4)—Authority-maintaining morality (conform to avoid censure by legitimate authority and the resulting guilt)

LEVEL III   Morality of Self—Accepted Moral Principles
5)—Morality of contract and democratically accepted law (conformity to contract, general avoidance of violation of the will or rights of others, and majority will and welfare)
6)—Morality of individual principles of conscience (conform to avoid self-condemnation) (Kohlberg, 1963, 1969)

Kohlberg presents cross-cultural data which show that these levels and steps do make up developmental stages. Children reach levels at similar ages and they employ their particular orientation across situations. Naturally, the stages tell us nothing about content; their aim is to show *how* children think and to underline that moral development is closely linked to cognitive abilities. For example, Kohlberg argues that the transition from preconventional to conventional morality occurs during the last years of elementary school; and that it is only in adolescence that youngsters root moral judgments in self-accepted principles (Kohlberg and Gilligan, 1971).

The appearance of conscience and guilt is related to cognitive development. But a person can know right from wrong, do wrong, and feel no guilt. To have the ability to think in terms of moral standards is no guarantee that the ability will be used. In short, while conscience is related to cognitive maturity, commitment to moral values depends on a number of factors.

One is disciplinary measures that rely on induction. Instead of asserting their power (say, by spanking) or withdrawing their love (for example, the parents say, "I couldn't love a person who does that"), parents focus children's attention on the consequences of their actions for the parent, for the other, for a third party. Children are specifically requested to take the other's role, and where the assertion of power or the withdrawal of love stresses the results of wrongdoing *for the child,* induction emphasizes the consequences *for others.* Taking the other's role, children are directed to the other's pain, as well as informed that they caused the pain. In Meadian terms, children are asked to conclude: "They're telling me, *I* did that. They're also telling me that I should feel bad because inflicting pain is wrong. Would I like it if someone did that to *me*?" (Hoffman and Saltzstein, 1963; Aronfreed, 1963; Graham, 1972; Kohlberg, 1969).

Induction must be accompanied by parental warmth. On the one hand, if parents use love, no roadblocks to understanding appear. Where power arouses feelings of anger, dismay, or confusion (for example, "What did I do? Why are they hitting me?"), and love withdrawal easily produces intense feelings of anxiety over the loss of love, warmth keeps tension to a minimum. On the other hand, warmth is a motive for listening to the parents' requests and explanations. Especially if children identify with the parent, they should pay attention when parents ask them to take the other's role. The result is children able to "focus attention on the harm done others as the salient aspect of their transgressions"; over time children learn to accept certain standards, as well as feel self-contempt or remorse when they violate those standards (Hoffman and Saltzstein, 1963; Williams and Steth, 1974; Mussen et al., 1974).

Experiments have consistently confirmed that warmth and the use of induction are causal factors in the development of conscience (see, for example, Graham, 1972). Another factor associated with conscience is identification. If children use parents as models, they should seek to adopt the parental standards as their own; too, if they violate those standards, the result is a weaker self-image: "I'm supposed to act like they do, but I did that. That is awful and so am I" (Mussen et al., 1974; Kagan, 1971). Finally, intelligence and culture are also associated with the development of conscience. Brighter children tend to make more sophisticated moral judgments and, along with love and induction, this ability should make it easier to develop conscience. The evidence for culture is sketchy, but Boehm found Catholic schoolchildren (of all classes) ahead of public schoolchildren in learning the distinction between motivation and the results of an action. Perhaps children exposed to a religion that stresses personal responsibility for behavior—"We are all sinners; if you do that, you're a sinner"—are able to internalize feelings of self-contempt more easily than children never exposed to such a stress (Boehm, 1962a, b). Again, this evidence is only suggestive; but it is logical to assume that, like induction, a religious stress on personal responsibility informs children that, since they caused the pain, they should feel bad about it.

Remember: even the best conscience is no guarantee of moral behavior. Studies show that a number of situational factors affect the chances of values actually being used in everyday life. For example, people behave differently when the risk of detection is high or low; they can be induced to cheat in school when frustrated by the teacher; and with a poor self-image, even people with strong consciences may fail to translate moral principles into unpopular actions (Wright, 1971; Dangzier, 1971). So, we cannot equate conscience with moral behavior; conscience is obviously an important cause of "right" action, but conscience operates in concert with other variables. All together, these factors determine whether moral principles become moral action.

SCHOOL

Today school is important. Cognitive skills are an essential basis for making judgments about self and world; like union cards, diplomas are needed for "good" jobs; and, if only because of the time children spend in school, teachers have the chance to influence the development of a person's life.

Some children come to school with a lunch pail. All arrive with a self-concept that affects school performance. In one study, measures of self-concept taken at kindergarten predicted reading achievement two and one-half years later. Children with positive images of self were better readers, and the authors concluded that "as early as kindergarten, self-concept phenomena are antecedent to and predictive of reading accomplishments at the least" (Wattenberg and Clifford, 1964). In another study, although children with positive self-images had higher school achievement, Caplin found that generalized feelings about the self were less important than a positive attitude toward school-related traits. Apparently, it helps a great deal if schoolchildren feel positive about their abilities in say, math or English (Caplin, 1969).

Children get their self-concepts from significant and generalized others. And while a wealthy child can easily enter school with a poor self-image, studies show that the higher the social class, "the more favorable the self-concept of school ability." Indeed, not only do children in the middle and upper classes have more positive images of their school ability, they also generally have more positive attitudes toward school. This could mean a "love of knowledge," or it could mean knowledge that "lots of school equals lots of money." Either way, children from the higher classes enter school with advantages denied to those from the lower classes (Mussen et al., 1974; Jencks et al., 1971).

These facts are important because a school or a teacher's influence is intimately related to a willingness to take preschool factors into account. In *Inequality*, Christopher Jencks and his colleagues show "that the character of a school's output depends largely on a single input, namely the characteristics of the entering children. Everything else—the school budget, its policies, the characteristics of the teachers—is either secondary or completely irrelevant" (Jencks et al., 1971). Now Jencks and his colleagues focus on educational attainment and achievement, but when they stress the importance of outside influences for success in school, they underline the difficulty any school or teacher has in influencing most children's images of self and world. Children come to school with a self-image, and throughout the school years that image is still being shaped by significant and generalized others who are more important than most schools and teachers. So, if teachers fail to recognize the barriers that prevent them from helping children to change, they are likely to do only one thing: confirm the images already possessed by the child.

Consider a study of children who entered school with learning difficulties. Generally they had poor self-images, coupled with problems in language and speech. Their grammar was "far from the expected norm," and with little experience in taking verbal instructions, they were unlikely to respond "properly" to verbal directions within the school or examination setting. However, teachers taught these children by conventional methods. Mistakes in grammar were corrected in front of other students and when children were unable to make themselves understood, they retreated into a shell and said nothing. Over a period of time, school became an echo for these children; coming out of a family atmosphere of discouragement, they met the same thing at school. Daily their images of self and world were reconfirmed by teachers acting in the role of generalized others (Vosk, 1966; see also Kozol, 1967).

Teachers are often said to be substitutes for mothers and fathers (see, for example, Mussen et al., 1974). Perhaps this is so. Perhaps teachers do often serve as significant others. But first and foremost, teachers are generalized others, representatives of the organized community that gives people their "unity" of self. Put differently, while education gives teachers cognitive skills and abilities, it often fails to prevent them from harboring the same biases and assumptions held by many uneducated people. Given the power of parents and other outside influences, the effects of school and teachers on children are generally limited. But if teachers believe that bad English spells stupid, if they accept the conventional wisdom, their overall effect is to confirm the bad or good images children acquire outside the classroom.

PEER GROUPS

Many people grow up without peer groups. In medieval society the idea of childhood was lacking; as soon as young people could live without constant care, they belonged to adult society. Philippe Aries notes that "there is not a single collective picture of the times in which children are not to be found." Either they are urinating in a corner, playing their part in a festival, working as apprentices, or serving as a knight's page; somehow, someway, "children" belonged to adult society (Aries, 1962).

Today childhood exists in full bloom; it is an extended period of social development in which children frequently spend long hours away from adults and with peers. Often it is assumed that peer groups inevitably exert pressures that force children into conflicts with their parents; parents say one thing, peers another, and never shall the two meet.

Perhaps. But the influence of peer groups is socially relative. In Russia "an explicit effort is made to utilize the peer group as an agent for socializing the child and bringing about an identification with the values of the adult society" (Bronfenbrenner, 1967). In contrast, Americans and British adults allow their children a good deal of independence; systematic attempts to influence peer groups are rare, with the result that in America and Great Britain peer groups seem to serve as independent sources of children's beliefs and values.

Appearances are deceiving. Just as they enter school, children enter peer groups with a host of beliefs and values; and while American adults may generally allow children to play alone, the influence of significant and generalized others is substantial. Consider, for example, the sex-segregated groups that still dominate peer relations from middle childhood to adolescence. These clearly reflect inherited gender identities. Boys do this, girls do that, and the two stay apart because they have so little in common. Nonconformists exist, but acceptance by peers is linked to proper sex-role performance (Campbell, 1964; Williams and Steth, 1974), and generalized others are often blunt about demanding allegiance to adult beliefs and values. For example, a popular board game (like "Monopoly") among girls aged eight to fourteen is the "Bride Game." On the box is a picture of a bride dressed in a long white veil and carrying a bouquet. Inside is a game whose instructions declare that the winner is "the first girl to get her complete matching wedding party along with the necessary accessories for the wedding ceremony." Apprentice brides get "wedding cake cards, bridal bouquet cards, ring cards, something old, something new cards," and, using dice, girls move quickly—if they are lucky—from the bridal salon to the pastry shop to the jewelry store to the aisle (Seligson, 1973).

Although subtlety is not one of the "Bride Games'" selling points, this game is one conspicuous sign that even "independent" peer groups often mirror the beliefs and values sanctioned by adults. Children play alone, but unless relations between parents and child are bad, or parents provide no direction, or parents are unable to help because they must work, peer groups in middle childhood generally direct children down those paths marked by a large sign: culturally approved.

If peer groups generally fail to furnish a basis for significant conflicts between parent and child, they do provide a forum for gaining, or not gaining, social status. Peer groups are the first place in which children's self-concepts undergo expansion and differentiation in terms other than as a child of their parents. "In sports, in school, in clubs, peer groups furnish the only cultural institution in which children are central, in which their activities and concerns reign supreme" (Ausubel, 1957).

Status with peers depends on many factors. Studies show that popular children have "strong, aggressive" characteristics; they are outgoing, self-confident, good sports, good looking, cooperative with group rules and routines, kind to others. Children with low status tend to have the opposite characteristics; they are loud, uncooperative, boastful, perhaps the "wrong" color or body build, unable to approach others with ease (Mussen et al., 1974; Williams and Steth, 1974).

Generally, the characteristics associated with social status show a "great resemblance" to those that result from warm, rewarding, early interactions in the family (Mussen et al., 1974). However, class, skin color, and inherited constitution also play a part in gaining social status, and even the warmest family cannot win popularity for a child if others make inherited characteristics a basis of popularity. Finally, success in peer relations could help children with poor self-images; a child who gains success in school or sports could lay the basis for thinking about self and world from a different, positive perspective.

Overall, peer groups take a back seat to the family as a determinant of self-image and social values. Along with school, they are the child's only basis for an independent status, but the evidence shows that success in peer groups is intimately related to the images of self and world first learned at home (Ausubel, 1957).

OVERVIEW

Harry Stack Sullivan once wrote that "the self-system is an organization of educative experience called into being by the necessity to avoid or minimize incidents of anxiety (1953). Hopefully this chapter has shown that Sullivan was both right and wrong. Whether the child is learning to walk, being hugged and kissed, or achieving success at school, self-concepts develop from the positive as well as the negative, from the good as well as the bad. However, Sullivan was perfectly correct on two counts. First, the self-system is an organization of educative experience. Others "teach" us what we are and, by responding to their lessons, we organize our images of self and world. Unfortunately, even a no to the attitudes of others means that we are still unwittingly determined by them.

Second, whether in infancy, the "terrible two's," or middle childhood, anxiety can be a powerful force in shaping our image of self. Particularly if we lack any cognitive basis for understanding the actions and attitudes of others, anxiety can easily channel our perceptions down a road that leads to a lack of self-esteem. In response to the negative attitudes of others, I can, for example, withdraw or react, become passive or boastful. Either way, when I respond to others, I try to come to terms with their attitudes toward me. Tragically, the general rule is the greater the anxiety, the greater the need for security, the greater the need to defend self against the negative attitudes of others.

Since all children must learn others' rules of the game, there seems no way to avoid anxiety in any child's life. But if self-esteem is the goal of educative experience, others cannot allow anxiety a prominent place in child development. On the contrary, the evidence is clear: if self-esteem is the goal, the dominant attitudes of others must be warmth, empathy, respect for children, and a willingness to grant them independence.

Bibliographical References

Ainsworth, Mary. "Further Research into the Adverse Effects of Maternal Deprivation." In *Child Care and the Growth of Love*, edited by John Bowlby. London: Penguin, 1965.

Aldrich, C. Anderson; Norval, Mildred A.; Knop, Catherine; and Venegas, Francisco. "The Crying of Newly Born Babies." *Journal of Pediatrics* 28 (1946): 665-70.

Ames, Louise Bates. "The Sense of Self of Nursery School Children as Manifested by Their Verbal Behavior." *The Journal of Genetic Psychology* 81 (1952): 193-232.

Aries, Philippe. *Centuries of Childhood*. London: Penguin, 1962.

Aronfreed, Justin. "The Nature, Variety, and Social Patterning of Moral Responses to Transgression. *Journal of Abnormal and Social Psychology* 63, no. 2 (1963): 223-40.

Ausubel, David. "Negativism as a Phase of Ego Development." *American Journal of Orthopsychiatry* 20 (1950): 796-805.

Ausubel, David. "Relationship Between Shame and Guilt in the Socializing Process." *Psychological Bulletin* 62, no. 5 (1955): 378-90.

Ausubel, David. *Theory and Problems of Child Development*. New York: Grune and Stratton, 1957.

Barry, Herbert; Bacon, Margaret K.; and Child, Irvin. "A Cross-Cultural Survey of Some Sex Differences in Socialization." *Journal of Abnormal and Social Psychology* 55 (1957): 327-32.

Beadle, Muriel. *A Child's Mind*. Garden City, N.Y.: Doubleday-Anchor, 1971.

Becker, Wesley. "Consequences of Different Kinds of Parental Discipline. In *Review of Child Development Research*, edited by Martin L. Hoffman and Lois W. Hoffman. New York: Russell Sage, 1964.

Bell, Richard Q. "A Reinterpretation of the Direction of Effects in Studies of Socialization." *Psychological Review* 75, no. 2 (March 1968): 81-95.

Bell, Silva, and Ainsworth, Mary D. Salter. "Infant Crying and Maternal Responsiveness." *Child Development* 43 (1972): 1185-89.

Bernstein, Anne C., and Cowan, Philip. "Children's Concepts of How People Get Babies." *Child Development* 46 (1975): 77-91.

Boehm, Lenore. "The Development of Conscience: A Comparison of American Children of Different Mental and Socioeconomic Levels." *Child Development* 33 (1962a): 575–90.

Boehm, Lenore. "The Development of Conscience: A Comparison of Students in Catholic Parochial Schools and in Public Schools." *Child Development* 33 (1962b): 591–602.

Bowlby, John. *Child Care and the Growth of Love*. 2d ed. London: Penguin, 1965, first published in 1953.

Bronfenbrenner, Urie. "Response to Pressure from Peers Versus Adults Among Soviet and American School Children." *International Journal of Psychology* 2, no. 3 (1967): 199–207.

Bruner, Jerome S. "On Cognitive Growth." In *Studies in Cognitive Growth*, edited by Jerome Bruner, Oliver Rose, and Patricia Greenfield. New York: Wiley, 1966.

Caldwell, Bettye. "The Effects of Infant Care." In *Review of Child Development Research*, edited by Martin L. Hoffman and Lois W. Hoffman. New York: Russell Sage, 1964.

Caldwell, Bettye; Wright, Charlene; Honig, Alice; and Tannenbaum, Jordan. "Infant Day Care and Attachment." *American Journal of Orthopsychiatry* 40 (April 1970): 397–412.

Campbell, John D. "Peer Relations in Childhood." In *Review of Child Development Research*, edited by Martin L. Hoffman and Lois W. Hoffman. New York: Russell Sage, 1964.

Caplin, Morris D. "The Relationship Between Self-Concept and Academic Achievement." *The Journal of Experimental Education* 37, no. 3 (1969): 13–16.

Chinoy, Eli. *Automobile Workers and the American Dream*. Boston: Beacon Press, 1965.

Coles, Robert. *Uprooted Children*. New York: Harper & Row, 1971.

Cooley, Charles Horton. *Human Nature and the Social Order*. New York: Scribner's, 1922.

Coopersmith, S. *The Antecedents of Self-Esteem*. San Francisco: Freeman, 1967.

Dangzier, Kurt. *Socialization*. London: Penguin, 1971.

David, Deborah S., and Brannon, Robert, eds. *The Forty-Nine Percent Majority*. Reading, Mass.: Addison-Wesley, 1976.

De Beauvoir, Simone. *The Second Sex*. New York: Knopf, 1953.

Dennis, Wayne. "Causes of Retardation Among Institutional Children: Iran." *Journal of Genetic Psychology* 96 (1960): 47–59.

Elkind, David. "The Child's Conception of His Religious Denomination: I. The Jewish Child." *The Journal of Genetic Psychology* 99 (1961): 209–25.

Elkind, David. "The Child's Conception of His Religious Denomination:

II. The Catholic Child." *The Journal of Genetic Psychology* 101 (1962a): 185–93.

Elkind, David. "The Child's Conception of His Religious Denomination: III. The Protestant Child." *The Journal of Genetic Psychology* 103 (1963): 291–304.

Elkind, David. "Children's Conception of Brother and Sister: Piaget Replication Study V." *The Journal of Genetic Psychology* 100 (1962b): 129–36.

Emmerich, Walter. "Family Role Concepts of Children, Ages Six to Ten." *Child Development* 32 (1961): 609–24.

Emmerich, Walter. "Young Children's Discriminations of Parent and Child Roles." *Child Development* 30 (1959): 403–19.

Erikson, Erik. *Childhood and Society*. Rev. ed. New York: Norton, 1964.

Faber, Adele, and Mazlish, Elaine. *Liberated Parents, Liberated Children*. New York: Avon, 1975.

Feffer, Melvin, and Gourevitch, Vivian. "Cognitive Aspects of Role-Taking in Children." *Journal of Personality* 28 (1960): 383–96.

Fein, Deborah; O'Neill, Sylvia; Frank, Constance; and Velit, Kathryn McColl. "Sex Differences in Preadolescent Self-Esteem." *The Journal of Psychology* 90 (1975): 179–83.

Festinger, Leon. *A Theory of Cognitive Dissonance*. Stanford: Stanford University Press, 1957.

Flavell, John. *The Development Psychology of Jean Piaget*. New York: Van Nostrand Reinhold, 1973.

Flavell, John. "The Development of Two Related Forms of Social Cognition: Role-Taking and Verbal Communication." In *Perceptual Development in Children*, edited by Aline Kidd and Jeanne Rivoire. London: University of London Press, 1966.

Flavell, John; Botkin, P. T.; Fry, C. L.; Wright, J. W.; and Jarvis, P. E. *Development of Role-Taking and Communication Skills in Children*. New York: Wiley, 1968.

Fraser, Morris. *Children in Conflict*. London: Penguin, 1974.

Freeberg, Norman, and Payne, Donald. "Parental Influence on Cognitive Development in Early Childhood." *Child Development* 38 (1967): 65–87.

Freud, Sigmund. *The Ego and the Id*. New York: Norton, 1960, first published in 1923.

Freud, Sigmund. *Three Essays on the Theory of Sexuality*. New York: Norton, 1962.

Garai, Josef Ernest. "Formation of the Concept of Self and Development of Sex Identification." In *Perceptual Development in Children*, edited by Aline Kidd and Jeanne Rivoire. London: University of London Press, 1966.

Gesell, Arnold, and Ilg, Frances L. *Infant and Child in the Culture of Today.* New York: Harper & Brothers, 1943.

Ginott, Haim. *Between Parent and Child.* New York: Avon, 1965.

Goldfarb, William. "Effects of Psychological Deprivation in Infancy and Subsequent Stimulation." *American Journal of Psychiatry* 102, no. 1 (1945): 18–33.

Goldfarb, William. "Emotional and Intellectual Consequences of Psychologic Deprivation in Infancy." In *Psychopathology of Childhood,* edited by Paul Hoch and Joseph Zubin. New York: Grune and Stratton, 1955.

Goodman, Mary Ellen. *The Culture of Childhood.* New York: Teachers College Press, 1970.

Graham, Douglas. *Moral Learning and Development.* London: B. T. Batsford, 1972.

Grier, William, and Cobbs, Price. *Black Rage.* New York: Bantam, 1968.

Gump, Janice Porter. "Sex-Role Attitudes and Psychological Well-Being." *Journal of Social Issues* 28, no. 2 (1972): 79–91.

Hannerz, Ulf. "What Ghetto Males Are Like: Another Look." In *The Forty-Nine Percent Majority: The Male Sex Role,* edited by Deborah S. David and Robert Brannon. Reading, Mass.: Addison-Wesley, 1976.

Hartley, Ruth E. "A Developmental View of Female Sex-Role Identification." *Merrill-Palmer Quarterly* 10 (1964): 3–16.

Hartley, Ruth E. "Sex-Role Pressures and the Socialization of the Male Child." *Psychological Reports* 5 (1959): 457–68.

Hoffman, Lois W. "Early Childhood Experiences and Women's Achievement Motives." *Journal of Social Issues* 28, no. 2 (1972): 129–55.

Hoffman, Martin, and Saltzstein, Herbert. "Parent Discipline and the Child's Moral Development." *Journal of Personality and Social Psychology* 63, no. 2 (1963): 223–40.

Horner, Matina. "Toward an Understanding of Achievement-Related Conflicts in Women." *Journal of Social Issues* 28, no. 2 (1972): 157–75.

Hutt, Corinne. *Males and Females.* London: Penguin, 1972.

Issacs, Susan. *Social Development in Young Children.* London: Routledge and Kegan Paul, 1933.

Jencks, Christopher et al. *Inequality.* New York: Harper & Row, 1972.

Kagan, Jerome, and Moss, H. A. *Birth to Maturity: A Study in Psychological Development.* New York: Wiley, 1962.

Kagan, Jerome. *Personality Development.* New York: Harcourt Brace Jovanovich, 1971.

Kidd, Aline, and Rivoire, Jeanne, eds. *Perceptual Development in Children.* London: University of London Press, 1966.

Kohlberg, Lawrence. "A Cognitive Developmental Analysis of Children's Sex-Role Concepts and Attitudes." In *The Development of Sex Differences,* edited by E. E. Maccoby. Stanford: Stanford University Press, 1966.

Kohlberg, Lawrence. "The Development of Children's Orientations Toward a Moral Order." *Vita Humana* 6 (1963): 11–33.

Kohlberg, Lawrence, and Gilligan, Carol. "The Adolescent as Philosopher: The Discovery of Self in a Post-conventional World." *Daedalus* (1971): 1051–86.

Kohlberg, Lawrence. "Stage Sequence: The Cognitive-Developmental Approach to Socialization." In *Handbook of Socialization Theory and Research*, edited by David Goslin. Chicago: Rand McNally, 1969.

Kohlberg, Lawrence; Yaeger, Judy; and Hjertholm, Else. "Private Speech: Four Studies and a Review of Theories." *Child Development* 39 (1968): 691–736.

Kozol, Jonathan. *Death at an Early Age*. Boston: Houghton Mifflin, 1967.

Lazowick, Lionel M. "On the Nature of Identification. *Journal of Abnormal and Social Psychology* 51 (1955): 175–83.

Leach, Penelope. *Babyhood*. London: Penguin, 1975.

Lewis, M. M. *Language, Thought, and Personality in Infancy and Childhood*. London: Harrop, 1963.

Lewis, Michael. "Early Sex Differences in the Human." *Archives of Sexual Behavior* 4, no. 4 (1975): 329–35.

Lidz, Theodore. *The Person: His Development Throughout the Life Cycle*. New York: Basic Books, 1968.

Lidz, Theodore; Cornelison, Alice; Terry, Dorothy; and Fleck, Stephen. "Intrafamilial Environment of the Schizophrenic Patient." *Archives of Neurological Psychology* 79 (1958): 305–16.

Luria, A. R., and Yudovich, F. LA. *Speech and the Development of Mental Processes in the Child*. London: Penguin, 1971.

McCarthy, Dorothea. "Affective Aspects of Language Learning." In *Perceptual Development in Children*, edited by Aline Kidd and Jeanne Rivoire. London: University of London Press, 1966.

Maccoby, Eleanor E. "Role-Taking in Childhood and Its Consequences for Social Learning." *Child Development* 30 (1959): 239–52.

Maccoby, Eleanor E. "The Taking of Adult Roles in Middle Childhood." *Journal of Abnormal and Social Psychology* 63, no. 3 (1968): 493–503.

Mead, George Herbert. *Mind, Self, and Society*. Chicago: University of Chicago Press, 1934.

Milgram, Norman, and Goodglass, Harold. "Role Style Versus Cognitive Maturation in Word Associations of Adults and Children." *Journal of Personality* 29 (1961): 81–93.

Miyamoto, S. Frank. "Self, Motivation, and Symbolic Interactionist Theory." In *Human Nature and Collective Behavior*, edited by Tamotsu Shibutani. Englewood Cliffs, N.J.: Prentice-Hall, 1970.

Money, J.; Hampson, J. G.; and Hampson, J. L. "Imprinting and the Establishment of Gender Role." *Archives of Neurological Psychiatry* 77 (1957): 333–36.

Money, John, and Tucker, Patricia. *Sexual Signatures*. Boston: Little, Brown, 1975.
Montagu, Ashley. *The Natural Superiority of Women* 2d ed. New York: Mentor, 1974.
Montagu, Ashley. *On Being Human*. New York: Hawthorn, 1967.
Morgan, Marabel. *The Total Woman*. New York: Pocket Books, 1975.
Moss, H. A. "Sex, Age, and State as Determinants of Mother-Infant Interaction." *Merrill-Palmer Quarterly* 13 (1967): 19–36.
Mussen, Paul. *The Psychological Development of the Child*. 2d ed. Englewood Cliffs, N.J.: Prentice-Hall, 1973.
Mussen, Paul; Conger, John; and Kagan, Jerome. *Child Development*. New York: Harper & Row, 1974.
Mussen, Paul, and Kagan, Jerome. "Group Conformity and Perceptions of Parents." *Child Development* 29 (March 1958): 57–60.
Mussen, Paul, and Rutherford, Eldred. "Parent-Child Relations and Parental Personality in Relation to Young Children's Sex-Role Preferences." *Child Development* 34 (1963): 589–607.
Neill, A. S. *Freedom—Not License!* New York: Hart, 1966.
Neill, A. S. *Summerhill: A Radical Approach to Child Rearing*. New York: Hart, 1960.
Newson, John, and Newson, Elizabeth. *Patterns of Infant Care in an Urban Community*. London: Penguin, 1965.
Pavenstedt, Eleanor. "A Comparison of the Child-Rearing Environment of Upper-Lower and Very Low Lower-Class Families." *American Journal of Orthopsychiatry* 35 (1965): 89–98.
Payne, D. F., and Mussen, Paul. "Parent-Child Relations and Father Identification Among Adolescent Boys." *Journal of Abnormal and Social Psychology* 52 (1956): 358–62.
Pervers, Barbara Hollands, and Secord, Paul F. "Developmental Changes in Attribution of Descriptive Concepts to Persons." *Journal of Personality and Social Psychology* 27, no. 1 (1973): 120–28.
Piaget, Jean. *The Child and Reality*. New York: Viking, 1974.
Piaget, Jean. *The Child's Conception of the World*. London: Paladin, 1973, first published in 1929.
Piaget, Jean. *The Language and Thought of the Child*. London: Routledge and Kegan Paul, 1962b, first published in 1925.
Piaget, Jean. *The Construction of Reality in the Child*. London: Routledge and Kegan Paul, 1954.
Piaget, Jean. *The Moral Judgment of the Child*. New York: Free Press, 1965.
Piaget, Jean. *Play, Dreams and Imitation in Childhood*. London: Routledge and Kegan Paul, 1962a, first published in 1951.
Proshansky, Harold, and Newton, Peggy. "The Nature and Meaning of Negro Self-Identity." In *Social Class, Race and Psychological Develop-*

ment, edited by M. Deutsch, I. Katz, and A. R. Jensen. New York: Holt, Rinehart & Winston, 1968.

Richmond, P. G. *An Introduction to Piaget.* London: Routledge and Kegan Paul, 1970.

Rutter, Michael. *Maternal Deprivation Reassessed.* London: Penguin, 1974.

Rutter, Michael. "Parent-Child Separation: Psychological Effects on the Children." *Journal on Child Psychology and Psychiatry* 12 (1971): 233–60.

Schaefer, E. S. "A Circumflex Model for Maternal Behavior." *Journal of Abnormal and Social Psychology* 59 (1959): 226–35.

Schaffer, H. R. "Activity Level as a Constitutional Determinant of Infantile Reaction to Stimulation." *Child Development* 37 (1966): 595–602.

Sears, Robert R. "Relation of Early Socialization Experiences to Self-Concept and Gender Role in Middle Childhood." *Child Development* 41 (1970): 267–89.

Seligson, Marcia. *The Eternal Bliss Machine.* New York: Morrow, 1973.

Sigel, Irving. "The Attainment of Concepts." In *Review of Child Development Research,* edited by Martin L. Hoffman and Lois W. Hoffman. New York: Russell Sage, 1964.

Solley, Charles M. "Affective Processes in Perceptual Development." In *Perceptual Development in Children,* edited by Aline Kidd and Jeanne Rivoire. London: University of London Press, 1966.

Spock, Benjamin. *Baby and Child Care.* New York: Pocket Books, 1968.

Stevenson, Harold W., and Stewart, Edward C. "A Developmental Study of Racial Awareness in Young Children." *Child Development* 29, no. 3 (1958): 399–409.

Stone, Gregory. "Appearance and the Self." In *Human Behavior and Social Processes,* edited by Arnold Rose. Boston: Houghton Mifflin, 1962.

Stone, L. Joseph, and Church, Joseph. *Childhood and Adolescence.* 2d ed. New York: Random House, 1968.

Sullivan, Harry Stack. *Interpersonal Theory of Psychiatry.* New York: Norton, 1953.

Turner, Ralph H. "Role-Taking, Role Standpoint, and Reference Group Behavior." *American Journal of Sociology* 61 (1956): 316–28.

Vosk, Jeannette S. "Study of Negro Children with Learning Difficulties at the Outset of Their School Careers." *American Journal of Orthopsychiatry* 36 (1966): 32–40.

Vygotsky, Lev Semenovich. *Thought and Language.* Cambridge, Mass.: MIT Press, 1962.

Wattenberg, William W., and Clifford, Clare. "Relation of Self-Concepts to Beginning Achievement in Reading." *Child Development* 35 (1964): 461–67.

Weiner, Irving B., and Elkind, David. *Child Development: A Core Approach.* New York: Wiley, 1972.

White, Robert W. "Competence and the Psychosexual Stages of Development." In *Nebraska Symposium on Motivation,* edited by M. R. Jones. Omaha: University of Nebraska Press, 1960.

White, Robert W. *The Enterprise of Living.* New York: Holt, Rinehart & Winston, 1972.

White, Robert W. "Motivation Reconsidered: The Concept of Competence." *Psychological Review* 66, no. 5 (1959): 297–333.

Williams, Joyce Wolfgang, and Steth, Marjorie. *Middle Childhood: Behavior and Development.* New York: Macmillan, 1974.

Wolff, Sula. *Children Under Stress.* London: Penguin, 1969.

Wright, Derek. *The Psychology of Moral Behavior.* London: Penguin, 1971.

Wyllie, Irvin. *Self-Made Man in America.* New York: Free Press, 1966.

Youngelson, Martin L. "The Need to Affiliate and Self-Esteem in Institutionalized Children." *Journal of Personality and Social Psychology* 26, no. 2 (1973): 280–86.

Ziegler, Edward. "Socialization." In *Handbook of Social Psychology,* edited by Gardner Lindzey and Elliot Aronson. Vol. 3. Reading, Mass.: Addison-Wesley, 1968.

CHAPTER THREE

Three A's: Adolescence, Adulthood, Aging

I beg of you—you see, it is all up with me, I can bear it no longer! Today I was sitting with her—sitting, and she was playing on her piano, various melodies, and all that expression! All!—All! What would you?—Her little sister was on my knee dressing her doll. Tears came into my eyes. I bent down, and her wedding ring struck my gaze—My tears flowed—And all at once she dropped into that old, divinity sweet melody, all of a sudden, and through my soul passed a feeling of consolation, and a recollection of things past . . . I walked up and down the room, my heart suffocating under all that flooded into it—"For God's sake," I said, going up to her in an impetuous outburst, "for God's sake, stop!" She stopped and stared at me. "Werther," she said with a smile that pierced my soul, "Werther, you are very sick, . . . Go now! I beg you, calm yourself." I tore myself away from her, and—God! You see my misery, and you will end it.

How that figure pursues me! Walking and dreaming, it fills my whole soul! Here, when I close my eyes, here in my brow, where the power of inner vision unites, are her black eyes. Here! I cannot put it into words for you. If I close my eyes, there they are; like an ocean, like an abyss they lie still before me, in me, filling all the thoughts within my brow.

What is man, the eulogized demigod? Does he not lack force at the very point where he needs it most? And when he soars upward in joy, or sinks down in suffering, is he not checked in both, is he not returned again to the dull, cold sphere of awareness, just when he was longing to lose himself in the fullness of the infinite?

Johann Wolfgang von Goethe, *The Sorrows of Young Werther* (1771)

Sturm und Drang. Storm and Stress. Somehow the words sound more powerful in German, but either way Goethe's novel (first published in 1771) is the historical starting point for one dominant view of adolescence. Young people don't just feel things; they are suffocated, flooded, pierced, overwhelmed, mesmerized by inner visions of black eyes. It's ecstasy or despair, bliss or oblivion. It's true love or, like young Werther, suicide with drama:

"They are loaded—The clock strikes twelve! So be it, then!—Lotte! Lotte! Farewell! Farewell!"

Young people are too diverse for any one perspective to capture *the* reality of adolescence. Forced to work, some young people lack the time for Werther's problems; and study shows that while many male adolescents experience serious problems about an occupational identity, most women do not (Douvan and Adelson, 1966). However, if most young people lack an adolescence filled with such constant storms, virtually all experience some anxiety about self and society. For adolescence is characterized by intellectual, physical, and social changes that ask young men and women to consider their past, ponder their future, and live with new responsibilities in the present. Adolescents respond to this request. Always, variables such as class and sex affect their response, but in rethinking self and society, adolescents are fated to experience varying degrees of storm and stress about sex, work, parents, society.

EGOCENTRISM IN ADOLESCENCE

One reason for tension is the adolescent's developing ability to think in terms of possibilities. Based on their growing capacity to deal with reality in increasingly abstract terms,[1] adolescents are no longer tied to the environment, to concrete reality; instead, somewhere between twelve and fifteen, young people are able to accept contrary-to-fact hypotheses. Dealing with reality indirectly, they are able to sit in a room and use speech to discuss life in terms of its possibilities. For example, confronted with the statement, "Let's suppose coal is white," a child normally responds with "But coal is black." Tied to reality, the child is unable to intellectually escape it. But adolescents can discuss coal in any color; as they begin to understand the arbitrariness, the relativity of their own views, adolescents are developing the ability to use words to imagine anything (Piaget, 1972; Elkind, 1967; Richmond, 1970).

---

[1] Recall the discussion in Chapter Two of concepts such as Protestant, Catholic, and brother.

Contrast the child with the adolescent. By ten or eleven, children often possess a number of competencies, along with the ability to verbally deal with reality on a relatively abstract basis. However, since they are unable to think in terms of possibilities, all children are chained to the inherited world of their significant and generalized others. For example, how can children consider different male-female relations until they first learn the relativity of all social relations? And how can they free themselves from harsh, vindictive parents until they are able to think hypothetically, until they are able to say, "They told me that, but, *all other things being equal,* I could have had another set of parents who might have said different things about me. So, perhaps I'm not to blame? Perhaps I could be different? Perhaps I only think like I do because I was unlucky enough to have those parents?"

These are radical questions. And in sharp contrast to children, adolescents can ask them because they are learning that their views and the views of others are socially and historically relative. Life need not be as it is. It, I, could be different!

Remember that the capacity to think hypothetically is a change in intellectual structure; the content of an adolescent's thought is still dependent on twelve or thirteen years of living with certain significant and generalized others. What happens in adolescence is that a tremendously important intellectual ability begins to blossom at a time when physical (puberty) and social (entrance into junior or senior high school; the need to think about a future job) pressures also direct adolescents to rethink their attitudes toward self and world. The result is adolescent egocentrism —a group of people often preoccupied with themselves and their behavior. For example, using *your* ability to think in terms of possibilities, suppose a fourteen-year-old boy is very anxious about relations with girls; this is in part a result of deep-seated insecurities; in part it is a result of ignorance about sex. Now already focusing on self, this young man can use his ability to think hypothetically as a means of becoming preoccupied with himself. Taking the role of the other, he has the ability to *imagine* anything; anxious about himself, he can translate those anxieties into many terrible possibilities. He can even imagine that others are as preoccupied with his sexual problems as he is (Elkind, 1967; Conger, 1973).

To repeat: this change in cognitive structure occurs at a time in the life cycle when social pressures direct adolescents to think about self and society. So, if "the central phenomenon of adolescence" is the discovery of the self as something unique, uncertain, and curious about the future (Kohlberg and Gilligan, 1971), this is the result of a complex linkage between intellectual and social changes. Sometimes intellect is in the saddle; witness our young friend's ability to imagine anything. More often, intellectual changes furnish a *potential* that a wide variety of social influences do or do not applaud. For example, able to think in terms of possibilities, adolescents have the ability to imagine new political institutions. But whether and how this ability is used depend on social factors. Studies show that leaders of student protests in the sixties generally came from families with liberal political values (Kenniston, 1967; Flacks, 1967), and student focus on political change was significantly reduced when the Vietnam War "ended." Apparently, "the war and the draft forged an intensely personal link between students and far-off war." This link inspired political radicalism while the war continued; when it died down, so did one significant cause of student activism (Yankelovich, 1974).

In sum, adolescents' ability to think hypothetically is one cause of their preoccupation with self, their personal storms and stresses, as well as their attempts to experiment with various images of self and society. But this intellectual ability never operates in a social vacuum. Class, sex, religion, parents, immediate social problems: they all influence the amount of preoccupation with self, the intensity of storm and stress, as well as the degree to which adolescents try to revolutionize self and society.

OCCUPATIONAL IDENTITIES

Recall that identities are meanings of the self; they refer to what and where we are in social terms (Stone, 1962). Well, one supposedly important aspect of development during adolescence is confusion about occupational identity. Erik Erikson argues that "in most instances, it is the inability to settle on an occupational identity which disturbs individual young people" (1964, 1968). Unable to decide what they want to be, and where they want to go, young people experience tension and confusion when they try to solve one of adolescence's critical developmental tasks: finding a vocation.

Occupational identity is a focus of attention for many young people. And middle-class boys "orient to the future primarily in terms of an occupational identity." Studies show that males have a high degree of sensitivity to the job sphere; they approach the area in an active spirit, committing large amounts of energy and thought to their plans. Moreover, where middle childhood saw them focus on fantasy jobs (for example, cowboy, explorer), by adolescence they are rapidly learning about their interests, capacities, and values. In one study of high school students, boys had not only made a tentative occupational choice, 90 percent already had a "fairly realistic idea of the training required" for their particular job selection. Only one in ten saw an educational future out of line with his job aspiration (Douvan and Adelson, 1966; Conger, 1973).

Since traditional sex roles teach that men "bring home the bacon" as a result of their occupational achievements, it comes as no surprise that boys worry about their future vocation. Generalized and significant others say that a man's self-esteem is closely linked to his work; to turn away from a focus on occupational identity is to risk a future where a most important basis of self-esteem provides none.

Problems set in for many reasons. One is the number of possible jobs. *The Dictionary of Occupational Titles* lists over 47,000 different occupations. Although adolescents (and vocational counselors) are perhaps familiar with some of these jobs, they must plead ignorance about most of them. The problem is to make a choice based on ignorance. Remember, too, that in advanced industrial societies new technologies quickly change the skills needed for particular jobs. Adolescents must be careful to avoid learning obsolete skills (Conger, 1973).

A second cause of problems concerns the basis of early occupational choices. Generally high school students select a vocation because of a particular interest or convenient model, say a father or uncle. Over time boys learn that their early choices may have little to do with their own capacities and values. For example, a boy could decide to be an engineer and then discover that he has no aptitude for math. Or a boy could decide to be a teacher and then find that this choice conflicts with his desire to earn a lot of money. Either way, maturity often comes with the knowledge of conflict between interests, capacities, and values. The adolescent's problem is to resolve the conflict.

A third cause of conflict concerns "the new morality." Evidence here is scarce, but Yankelovich argues that young people are trying to do something very difficult: achieve a synthesis between new and old values. Focusing on self-fulfillment and personal satisfaction as key factors in job selection, young people also want to enjoy the kinds of financial rewards that equal a high standard of living. Whether this is possible remains to be seen. However, it is quite possible that in trying to strike "their bargain with society," many adolescents will experience difficulty in finding an appealing occupation (Yankelovich, 1974).

Theory says that confusion about a future vocation is the chief cause of identity problems in adolescence. This is true for many, perhaps most, boys. To date, it has not been true for the other half of the human race, with the mistake probably resulting from male dominance over theory. Generally the tendency has been to neglect women; men's experiences decide *the* characteristics of adolescence. If women also have those characteristics, so much the better; if not, their adolescent experience about occupations rarely gets to be a part of theory.

A conspicuous exception is Douvan and Adelson's *The Adolescent Experience.* They found middle-class girls concerned with occupational and educational planning, but they also found that girls' plans were "not dominated by a long-range or binding commitment to a special talent or skill." On the contrary, showing they had learned the lessons of socialization quite well, girls failed to look at the occupational sphere "as a source of life meaning or life work." For them, an occupational identity was secondary; primary was marriage and motherhood. So, in contrast to boys, girls' plans lacked a focus on the skills associated with a particular job. In addition, their plans showed a lack of coherence, and they also managed to harbor seemingly irreconcilable goals. For example, over 30 percent of the girls who planned to go to college had selected jobs for which college was unnecessary—four years of study were superfluous if a person's goal was to be a bookkeeper or telephone operator (Douvan and Adelson, 1966).

This seeming contradiction is explainable. For these girls showed little concern about work, and for them college was not a means of occupational advancement. College was a place to meet the "right" man, or it was an achievement expected by parents. But the "central fact" for these girls was that "although they focused on work and schooling, very few were strongly invested in work or school per se." Future life began when they married, and the what and where of their social identity was determined by their husband and his occupational achievements (Douvan and Adelson, 1966).

Change is occurring. The women's movement is forcing both sexes to rethink women's place in society (for example, Goldman, 1974; Komarovsky, 1972). But change is slow and, to date, most women are not experiencing an identity crisis about job prospects. Socialized to accept the beliefs and values of a sexist society, most adolescent girls still focus attention on goals laid down by the generalized other: marriage and a family (for example, Grinder, 1973; Yankelovich, 1974). Again, the future holds promise of change, but it is hazardous to theorize about patterns that have not yet developed.

One last point concerns the way different classes of adolescent boys focus on occupational identity. For the poor, a choice is made early, and it is normally made without the same kind of attention, concern, and opportunity felt by middle-class boys. For example, in 1968 fully 75 percent of English adolescents left school by age fifteen[2] (Smith, 1970). In theory, a youth employment service helped those who left to find suitable work; in fact, the majority found jobs through friends or relatives. Here boys took little time to consider the mesh between their interests, their capacities, and their values. Generally boys took jobs because they wanted the independence that came with a paycheck. Over time most "settled in" to a job, and while those in dead-end positions often struggled to find decent work, social class generally put a check on the problems associated with finding an occupational identity. First was the perceived lack of opportunity; these boys knew their poor education equaled poor job opportunities. Second was the relatively low concern with self-fulfillment and self-

---

[2] The age for leaving school is now sixteen.

satisfaction; many boys expected little from work and having their expectations confirmed created no problems (Willmott, 1966).

So, lower-class boys generally end their search for an occupational identity sooner than their middle- and upper-class contemporaries. Whether it was finding a good job, or giving in to reality, most boys in the study cited ended their search by age nineteen or twenty. Nearly 50 percent of the boys remained in jobs found at age fifteen. And, with few opportunities, plus lower expectations, these adolescents generally experience less storm and stress in finding the right occupational identity. As one twenty-year-old said, "I'm a fish porter and that's what I expect to go on being. It's not really a promotion job at all. I suppose I could go on to be a salesman, but I'd rather have no worries. As it is, when I get home from work I'm finished. I prefer it like that" (Willmott, 1966).

GENERATION GAP: CANYON OR CRACK?

Perhaps it was the "sudden" appearance of adolescents? In 1900 this group was relatively small in numbers; by 1970, it was a gigantic group, with nearly 16 million Americans between the ages of fourteen and seventeen, and another 14 million between eighteen and twenty-one (Bakan, 1971; Gordon, 1971). Or, perhaps it was the similar style of dress and taste in music? Or, perhaps it was the presence of so many young people in the same places: junior and senior high schools? Or, perhaps it was youth's prominence in dissent? From Allen Ginsberg in the fifties to Bob Dylan in the sixties, young people have assumed conspicuous roles as dissenters.

For whatever reasons, analysts have been writing for at least twenty years of a "youth culture." Supposedly adolescents manifest a "compulsive independence of and antagonism to adult expectations and authority." Always young people conform to the expectations of their peers and, at times, the gap between parents and children is so wide that "adolescents represent subcultures" (see, for example, Elkin, and Westley, 1955).

This view of adolescence is incorrect. It makes sense when we recall the adolescent's ability to think hypothetically, as well as the societal stress on questioning self and society, but, despite the emphasis on a canyonlike gap between parents and children, "there is overwhelming evidence of congruity" between, for example, parents and children's educational plans aspirations, and performance; between parents' social class and the social class of the adolescents' dates and friends; between the political and racial views of adolescents and their parents (Campbell, 1969; Grinder, 1973; Conger, 1973; Kenniston, 1967; Coleman, 1971; Douvan and Adelson, 1966).

At least five factors account for this general congruity. The first is childhood. People only gain the ability to think hypothetically at about age thirteen; before then, youngsters root their thinking in the beliefs and attitudes furnished by significant and generalized others. The result is that "early impressions tend to coalesce into a *natural view* of the world." Because they were children, adolescents take certain things for granted; for example, boys do this, girls do that; democracy is the best form of government, communism our worst enemy. So, when they begin to think in terms of possibilities, even a generally unified culture stacks the deck in favor of the past. To change, an adolescent must say, "They told me this was true and I believed them. Now I'm not so sure. Perhaps what they told me, about sex, politics, religion, is a lot of nonsense. Perhaps I'm right and they're wrong?" Adolescents do think in these terms, but since "all later experiences tend to receive their meaning" from beliefs and attitudes internalized in childhood, change requires that adolescents say no to *their* own beliefs and practices. This is difficult, especially when change means scrapping beliefs about important aspects of self and world, say, sex roles or social class (see Mannheim, 1969; Ortega y Gasset, 1962).

Second is the set of beliefs and attitudes that others ask adolescents to question. In America "the major ideological dragons to be tamed" center around family, religion, sexuality, drugs, and school (Kagan, 1971). And when adolescents ask these questions, and experience storm and stress, they are often imitating rather than disagreeing with their parents. For example, 40 percent of the American people never attend church at all, and where 49 percent of the population attended church during an average week in 1955, only 40 percent did so in 1972 (Eitzen, 1974). Not surprisingly, a study of social identities among Anglo- and Latin-American adolescents found that "both male and female Anglos have significantly higher proportions of negative religious identities than do the Latins" (Gecas et al., 1973). So, in many cases adolescent questioning reflects adult questioning; the gap disappears if both generations are uncertain about the same aspects of self and world.

Third, in those instances where adolescents do radically question the larger society, studies show that parents and children share similar beliefs and values. In the sixties, student activists came "largely from upper-status families" with high incomes and high levels of education; more important, activists seemed to be "living out expressed but unimplemented values of their liberal, socially conscious parents . . ." (Conger, 1973). In short, radical dissent is much less a gap between parents and children than it is a gap between different *groups* of parents and children.

Fourth, many adolescents' questions concern their immediate identities, and these problems need not cause or reflect any generation gap. For example, Rosenberg found a "general pattern of self-image disturbance in early adolescence; compared to younger children, twelve- and thirteen-year-olds were distinctly more self-conscious, more unstable, and more negative about their self-images." However, the prime factor causing disturbance was entrance into junior high school. Moving from a "protected elementary school" into the more impersonal junior high setting, students were expected to behave more independently, more responsibly, as well as make their first career choice: whether to take an academic, commercial, or vocational course (Rosenberg, 1973). These pressures resulted in disturbances in self-image, but even the most intense questioning need not cause or reflect a generation gap. For these adolescents were anxious about a universal problem: fitting into a new social situation, with new demands, and being accepted by a group of peers who already had social esteem and prestige.

Finally, radical questioning of parents' beliefs and practices is greatly aided by social crises or particular social problems. In the sixties the civil rights movement and the peace movement "forced" many adolescents to rethink inherited beliefs and attitudes. Even then, relatively few adolescents created a large gap between their parents and themselves, but the point is that in the absence of crises or problems, the chances of a substantial gap decrease. Consider, for example, the period of the 1950s.

To deny a canyonlike gap between generations is not to deny social change. On the contrary, one argument has it that *both* parents and children are changing, at least about religion and sex; and another has it that student activists reflect the values of their change-seeking, independently minded parents. However, the general absence of a large gap is important because it underlines why the potential to think in terms of possibilities is not used to generate radical social change. In effect, most significant and generalized others do not applaud major change, and for a variety of reasons (for example, the taken-for-granted assumptions of adolescents, the absence of social crises, the focus on immediate problems) they are generally able to obtain agreement from adolescents. The result is that, in terms of radical social change, the ability to think hypothetically lies dormant; within broad limits, most adolescents accept the social world they inherited.

If adolescents generally agree with their parents' beliefs and practices, they do think about self and society. In terms of the future, tension about occupational identity was (and is) of great concern to boys. In terms of the present, adolescents worry a great deal about sex and about acceptance into adolescent social groups.

SEX IN ADOLESCENCE

In America sexual behavior often lends itself to mythmaking. From Puritan times to the present, sex has aroused anxiety in the minds of children, adolescents, and adults. It is sinful, evil, not to be discussed in public; it is practiced to perpetuate the human race, or, as Benjamin Franklin thought, sexual intercourse is needed for good health (Franklin, 1960).

When change occurs in such a sensitive area, it is often blown out of proportion. For example, a new morality, a sexual revolution is supposedly occurring among America's young people: free love, promiscuity, women taking the sexual initiative. It is all a bit strange. The only certainty is that adolescents practice what adults never preached.

Although adolescent attitudes, values, and practices about sex *are* changing, any generalizations to all, or even a majority, of adolescents are risky. Yankelovich found that 53 percent of noncollege and 47 percent of college youth did *not* welcome more sexual freedom. And in a study of politically conservative youth, only 18 percent wanted more sexual freedom, and fully 70 percent viewed premarital sex as a moral issue. In contrast, no "revolutionary" youth thought sex a moral issue, and only 33 percent of moderate youth did so (Yankelovich, 1974; Conger, 1973). In short, since "the differences between some subgroups of youths appear wider than those between youth in general and adults in general" (Conger, 1973), it is very difficult to say just what storms and stresses about sex *all* adolescents undergo. Seemingly, the only choice is to root our discussion of today in yesterday.

Traditionally, the double standard has dominated male-female sexual relations. Both sexes learned that "guys can't help it. I mean they are born that way" (Grinder, 1973). And this "need" was one justification for boys seeking what "good girls" were not allowed to provide. Another was the male's sense of self-esteem. In childhood, boys somehow learned (on the street, from their fathers) that real men often had sexual intercourse; the result was that one important means of growing up, of becoming a man, was to engage in intercourse with any available partner. Boys with real or imagined experiences gained esteem in the eyes of others and thus themselves; those without experience anxiously looked up to the beacons of masculinity, for if they missed what real men must have, self-esteem was bound to suffer. They were less than real men.

If sex was one important and necessary source of male esteem, girls received the opposite message. Their task was to sympathetically understand the male's position, and to assume responsibility if things got out of hand. Again, boys could not help themselves. But girls were traditionally forced to walk a sexual tightrope. "Good girls" did not allow boys to go too far; although they were sometimes permitted to engage in heavy petting, they were supposed to know what was enough, what was too much. If they failed, boys gave girls a poor image of self; they were "easy marks," "good lays," "subjects of male boasting and fantasy." They were not the type of girl boys got serious about, the type a boy took home to mother.

Remember that this peculiar standard—a boy showed mother the prize father said to destroy—was often built on a foundation of ignorance. Traditionally many adolescents received partial or little knowledge about sex, and this meant that an area of behavior important for adolescent self-esteem was shrouded in mystery. So, added to anxieties about proving oneself a real man or a good girl was anxiety about sex itself. Both boys and girls often knew little about an aspect of life society, not to mention puberty, made conspicuously important for all adolescents.

This traditional model is the basis for the emerging new morality. Like their predecessors, contemporary adolescents know what *was* right and wrong; the reality today is that adolescents are at varying points along a road between past and future. Some still experience the old problems and anxieties; others try to make adjustments in the traditional model; and still others believe they have produced a sexual revolution.

What is the evidence? On sexual intercourse, indications are that both sexes are engaging in more intercourse, at an earlier stage in the life cycle. For example, where fewer than 20 percent of their mothers had engaged in sexual intercourse by age nineteen, fully 46 percent of all unmarried adolescent girls had had intercourse by nineteen. Among college students alone, the changes were even more dramatic. Where 49 percent of their fathers had had intercourse by twenty-one, the figure for today's male student was 82 percent. And where 27 percent of their mothers had had intercourse before twenty-one, 56 percent of today's college women had done so (Conger, 1973).

Increased premarital sex does not mean promiscuity. More sexual intercourse has decreased the prostitute's business,[3] but among college males, 70 percent of those having intercourse are doing so with one partner. For females, the figure is 77 percent, plus emotional involvement with the boy. Overall only 30 percent of the men, and 7 percent of the women had had intercourse in one-night affairs (Conger, 1973).

One way of describing the social psychological effects of increased sexual intercourse is in terms of a "transitional double standard." Coitus is still sanctioned for men under any conditions, and this freedom has now been extended to women, without loss of self-esteem, so long as the women are in love. In one study "female sexual expression was primarily and profoundly related to being in love and going steady," while in another, adolescents said it was no longer necessary for girls to be virgins at the altar; virginity was important only till the girl fell in love, which normally meant going steady or becoming engaged (Grinder, 1973).

Although this transitional ethic should remove some of the pressure from adolescents, especially adolescent girls, old pressures may be re-

---

[3] Where 20 to 22 percent of their fathers had visited a prostitute, only 4 percent of today's college males had done so.

placed by new ones. The difficulty of living in a period of transition is that the generalized other furnishes no one answer. Years ago people knew this was right, that wrong. Today adolescents hear about the old and live with the new. Statistics indicate that more people are having sexual intercourse, but they tell us little about the anxieties that probably accompany earlier intercourse. Between past and future, adolescents receive a number of views on sexual right and sexual wrong. Ultimately it is their problem to make sense of inherited confusion. So, while many contemporary adolescents are less anxious about sex, as well as freer to engage in it, they may pay a price for their freedom. Where their parents' anxiety centered on breaking established codes, today's adolescents may have anxiety about the relative absence of established codes. In transition, today's adolescents have to make decisions without the support of institutionalized answers; this gives them both freedom and anxiety. For what is right is now often a relative matter.

No one knows with any certainty what the future holds. Increases in sexual intercourse have occurred mainly in the middle and upper-middle classes. Lower-class adolescents always had a much higher incidence of sexual intercourse, and the "new morality" has allowed the classes to behave in similar ways (Conger, 1973). However, despite their behavior, lower-class adolescents traditionally voiced support for the established ethic. Now that support seems to be waning, with both middle- and lower-class adolescents moving toward the adoption of much more freedom in sexual attitudes and beliefs. For example, 83 percent of college, and 67 percent of noncollege females believe that women should be free to take the initiative in sex. College and noncollege youth have the same general feeling about premarital sex (66 percent believe it is not morally wrong), and where 58 percent of college youth thought relations between consenting homosexuals was morally correct, the figure for noncollege youth was 53 percent. Finally, 64 percent of college youth and 52 percent of noncollege youth saw nothing morally wrong with having an abortion (Yankelovich, 1974).

These figures are only suggestive but, along with the evidence given above, they give rise to a conclusion: change promises to make all adolescents less anxious about sex itself and more anxious about defining what is "proper" in the sexual situations that characterize everyday life.

PEER RELATIONS IN ADOLESCENCE

Adolescents spend a great deal of time together. Often they have no choice. Adults make little provision for their presence among "grown-ups" (for example, can adolescents go to work with their parents?), and with school attendance required by law, most young people must be together for at least five or six hours a day. Added to this mandatory togetherness is the school's importance in extracurricular activities; from football, baseball, and basketball to clubs of all sorts, to dances and proms, schools act to affirm adult decisions: adolescents should "pal around" with one another.

Besides institutionalized segregation, adolescents often have their own reasons for staying together. First, adolescent peer groups furnish a forum for young people to think and act on their own; parents stay away! Second, if only because adults often forget the pains of adolescence, young people need each other for understanding; socialization makes girls more open than boys, but both sexes often want to talk to someone with similar questions, problems, and potential. Finally, adolescent peer groups are the source for a young person's *immediate* social identity. Probable confusion about future occupation coexists with the need to succeed in the here and now. Thrown together for long hours, and forbidden to be adults, adolescents find in peer groups the source of their immediate sense of social esteem and prestige.

Given the importance of peer groups to adolescents, it is no surprise to find a series of studies that document widespread conformity to group norms (for example, Douvan and Adelson, 1966; Coleman, 1971). Adolescents follow group dictates, and few fail to use group standards as one basis for judgments about self and others. But, are parental and peer group values contradictory, incompatible, at war with one another? Do parents pull adolescents in one direction while the requirements of group conformity push adolescents in another?

The answer is yes and no. First, adults set up the world of adolescent peer groups. They cannot exercise total control, but adults can establish a society in which their children meet friends from similar social, economic, and religious groups. And it is clear that a white, lower-class, blue-collar adolescent has more in common with his parents than with his suburban, upper-middle-class, white-collar contemporaries (Conger, 1973). Second, adults often push their children into peer groups. Interested in their children's social standing, parents want to see them succeed, as well as be popular (Coleman, 1971). Third, studies show "that responses of adolescents to parent-peer cross-pressures are a function of the content of the alternative and that peer-conformity in adolescence, rather than being diffuse, tends to vary systematically across situations" (Brittain, 1963).

Adolescents move along two tracks, and their choices—parents or peers?—tend to reflect their dual orientation. Confronted with questions of immediate social identity, of clothes, hair styles, music, entertainment, language, adolescents normally say yes to their peers. A no singles them out from the group, and while theory applauds those who stand against the herd, reality makes it quite hard to be "the weirdo" among the normals. Especially when views of self and world are uncertain, nonconformity has little appeal. But when choices relate to questions of basic values or long-term prospects (say, whether to report an adult who damages public property or how to be selected for a school honor), adolescents tend to rely on their parents. Rooted in the beliefs and values of others, and aware that parents possess knowledge that peers do not, adolescents tend to choose parents over peers when the question revolves around basic attitudes, beliefs, and practices (Brittain, 1963; Conger, 1973).

If peer groups are normally not hotbeds of major problems between parents and children, the situation can change under certain conditions. If parents and children do not get along, if parents say one thing and do another, if parents are unrealistic, if they fail to empathize with the adolescent, if the young person has a poor self-image and needs the peer group for esteem: any of these conditions can increase the power of the peer group, reduce the influence of parents, and alter our overall conclusion that the power of adolescent peer groups is rooted in questions of immediate social identity.

Adolescent peer groups tend to follow a pattern. Beginning with the unisexual groups of very early adolescence, there is a movement toward groups with both sexes present. Initially, contact takes place in the presence of same sex support; still wary of each other, girls and boys require a period of transition before the boldest begin the dating that produces heterosexual cliques. Normally these "small intimate groups" are themselves associated with other cliques, to form an extended heterosexual group, "the crowd." Crowds are the focal point for adolescent interaction, but over time even they disintegrate, giving way to cliques of couples who are going steady or engaged. Finally, adolescence ends and, as welcome or unwelcome freight, people carry into adulthood the sense of self established in about eight years of day-to-day interaction with peers (Dunphy, 1969).

Here we focus on the crowd. Centered in the school, it furnishes the collective values used by adolescents to judge themselves and others. Equally important, members of crowds tend to stay in them. Dunphy writes that boundaries "are most rigidly defined" and crowd members normally mix only with other crowd members. When asked to choose friends to join them in various situations, over 60 percent chose members of their own cliques and only 6 percent of the choices included people outside the crowd (Dunphy, 1969). Obviously, some adolescents never join a crowd, not to mention "the" crowd, but nonmembership is often an identity problem. Based on the beliefs and values of the generalized other, crowds are the distinctive groups built by adolescents, and young people outside them lose the collective support of the most important source of immediate adolescent social identity. Condemned to attend school, nonmembers find it very hard to escape dominant definitions of self. Called "clods," "duds," or "lame" by others, nonmembers may well conclude "They're right about me. I am a loser."

Research indicates that dominant crowds in high schools place major value on athletic success for boys and club activities for girls. Generally good grades take a back seat to success on the sports field, with popular girls assuming a subordinate role as pretty applauders of boys' abilities[4] (Coleman, 1971; Poveda, 1972). Coleman expressed concern about the stress on athletics as a source of social esteem, but he rightly called attention to a conspicuous fact of school life: athletes are perhaps the only symbol that all school groups may collectively support. Good grades are fine, but "school spirit" is built on symbols everyone can share. Athletes are those symbols, and since school leaders and parents often only furnish support for young people's choices, athletes are assured their place as "top guns" on the totem pole of adolescent social esteem.

In his study of ten high schools, Coleman found an apparent contradiction: high-status adolescents had a greater interest than others in going to college and a lesser interest in scholarly achievement. Coleman eventually resolved the paradox by noting that high-status youths often came from middle- and upper-middle-class families. Before they entered high school, these adolescents expected to go on to college. What they did not expect was a college environment different from that found in high school. In college, too, athletics would be more important than grades; in college, too, the greatest social esteem would attach to those who were symbols that "everyone" could applaud (Grinder, 1973).

If the leading crowds place greatest emphasis on sports as the road to adolescent (and often adult) social esteem, those with other characteristics, boys who only have brains, or girls with brains, fall short of the standards set by their peers. One option for the less successful is to judge self on the basis of peer group values. Another, very difficult, option is to disregard dominant sources of social esteem. And a third is to join another type of crowd: "the hoods."

In one study "hoods" represented 24 percent of the senior class. They gave little serious attention to school or athletics and tended to accord social esteem to boys who were "hard," good fighters. Generally "hoods" looked down on those who participated in established school activities. For them social esteem came from taking risks, perhaps with drugs or minor forms of vandalism, and "hoods" were not oriented toward college. As one might expect, hoods tended to be from the lower classes. So, like the values of the "leading crowd," hood values were as much a result of inheritance from others, as a consequence of unique adolescent world-building (see Poveda, 1972).

---

[4] Since boys' athletics receives the lion's share of funding for sports, the girls' subordinate position is institutionalized. Undoubtedly this will soon begin to change.

Crowds are the major source of immediate social esteem in adolescence. But in closing our discussion of peer relations, we turn from the general to the particular, from a focus on many friends to a focus on one special friend. Now not every adolescent has this relationship and since boys learn to keep things in, to be "strong," they often miss one of the most satisfying means adolescents have for coming to terms with self and society.

Probably the special friend is a member of the adolescent's clique or crowd. Somehow many young people meet another person of the same sex, and the two do each other a great favor: they act as mirrors for the other's crystallizing sense of self. Often the two friends are inseparable, but Douvan and Adelson correctly note that a good part of the intimacy is instrumental; by means of common experiences and seemingly endless conversation, the two examine themselves, their plans, their ambitions, their parents, and even their most intimate secrets. In the end, by explaining themselves to each other, they "complete" an examination of self; by asking the friend to tell that "I'm right in thinking as I do," the adolescent comes to a very reassuring conclusion: "I am who I think I am" (Osterrieth, 1969; Douvan and Adelson, 1966).

With luck, warm and understanding parents, and a good friend, adolescents may "complete" an examination and definition of self. This is a solid basis for beginning the next fifty years of life. But it is still only a basis. For even if people refuse to change the self-images garnered from parents, society will never leave them alone. Life is always a process of acquiring and discarding social identities. Continually others tell us what and where we are in social terms; and continually we must respond to what others say about us—even as adults.

EARLY ADULTHOOD

Her relations with Julien had completely changed; he was an entirely different man since their return from their honeymoon, like an actor who has finished his part and resumed his ordinary life. He scarcely noticed her; he hardly spoke. Every trace of love had disappeared and it was only rarely that he came to her room at night. He had assumed control of the family finances and the running of the house. . . . Now that he was playing the part of the gentleman farmer, he had lost all the polish and elegance which he had had during the engagement. He now always wore, though it was badly stained, an old velvet shooting jacket which he had come across in a wardrobe of his young days; . . . he had given up shaving, so that a long badly trimmed beard made him incredibly ugly. He no longer attended to his hands and after every meal he drank four or five glasses of brandy. Jeanne tried mild protests but he replied crossly: "You had better leave me alone, hadn't you?" so that she risked no further comment.

She accepted the change in her husband to an extent that surprised herself. He had become a stranger, whose heart and thoughts were a closed book to her. . . . Why did this estrangement not cause her more pain? Was life like this? Had they made a mistake? Did the future hold anything for her? [Guy de Maupassant, *A Woman's Life* (1888)]

Yes, it did. In nineteenth-century France, divorce was relatively out of the question. Only twenty when she married, Jeanne is committed to her spouse. She sees no way out and stoically endures even the most unhappy relationship. For in childhood she learned that marriage was an unbreakable bond; now she looks to an adult life filled with unavoidable pain and suffering.

Commitments are constraints; like a long chain, commitments tie people to particular beliefs or patterns of behavior. Sometimes, as with Jeanne, commitments are acquired in childhood. Generalized and significant others teach us cultural recipes for living and we say yes: "I will think and act as you tell me to." Sometimes, commitments are the result of "impersonal bureaucratic arrangements," say, a person who hates her job but does not quit because of accumulated pension benefits. Finally, commitments arise because of "individual adjustment to social positions"—that is, people who remain married because they are comfortable with one another or people who work at a job because they refuse to learn a new one (Becker, 1960).

Commitments are an important basis for understanding consistency in adult behavior. For, if like Jeanne, people accept commitments as lifelong bonds, social identities (for example, husband-wife, mother-father, doctor-laborer) set definite limits to the amount and type of personality change. Locked into certain forms of behavior, people continually think of self and world in similar terms. They cannot or will not say "Perhaps I am not who I think I am?" Or "Perhaps I could be different tomorrow than I am today?"

Based on human labor, and through the generalized other, society establishes the overall conditions for both change and stability in adult life (Becker, 1968). If its recipes for living are cementlike, its economic institutions bound to tradition, people accept in early adulthood "permanent" commitments. They are today what they will be tomorrow. But, if society applauds change, if its formulas for living are flexible, its economic institutions rooted in innovation and the acquisition of new skills, then society establishes an atmosphere conducive to change. Perhaps people marry, knowing they can easily dissolve their commitment. Or, perhaps people begin a job, knowing that retraining is inevitable. Change could even make them obsolete.

Today society creates an atmosphere conducive to identity change in adult life (for example, Neugarten et al., 1968a). As in the past, early adulthood is still characterized by commitments to another person, to a family, and to a job, but today our outlook on self and world is more open in terms of its possibilities. For example, even if she accepts her assigned role as "housewife," a woman knows that when her children leave home she could easily live for thirty years longer. At twenty-five she might be prepared for change; something new will have to fill up the last thirty years of life. Or, take a man who at twenty-five becomes a policeman. Pensions begin after twenty years of service and our policeman expects to retire. He will put in twenty years, but after that life and he will change.

Remember, too, that change in social identities often means change in the self-image acquired from others. A woman affected by women's liberation could easily rethink more than her marriage. She could go back to childhood and try to establish the links between her assigned gender identity and the self-image acquired from her parents. Always the relationship between social and personal identity is dialectical. One acts back on the other and sometimes society actually requests change on both levels. For example, books entitled "Creative Divorce" ask readers to use their change in social identity as a basis for change in unique self-image.

Now, modern society's acceptance (if not applause) of looser commitments in adulthood is a historical fact. Some societies demanded lifelong commitments to marriage and family. Most modern societies do not, and that fact acts to qualify the "grand theories" of adulthood discussed below.

Theoretically, the dominant view of adulthood is in terms of expansion and contraction. During our early years, we learn new roles, as well as gain new identities. Reaching out to the world, young adults (that is, those between twenty-one and forty) try to enlarge their opportunities and increase their knowledge, pleasures, and activities. While achieving new social identities, young adults are kept busy building their careers and raising their families. Then, in middle age, people slowly stop expanding activities and interests. Basking in the sunlight called success or bemoaning the darkness known as failure, middle-aged adults (those between forty-one and sixty) manage to establish a relative balance between their involvement in the world and their view of self. They may not be satisfied or happy, but the period of focusing on the outside world is over. Finally, in old age (sixty and over) people reduce the number of their social identities (for example, retirement), make less use of their physical abilities, and generally turn away from the world to a level of contracted activity that often produces a sense of worthlessness. Sometimes this sense of worthlessness makes the aged happy to meet life's partner: death (see Buhler, 1932, 1959; Bischof, 1969; Kuhlen, 1964; Kimmel, 1974).

If we remember that this "decline and fall" of the person is only a metaphor, there is nothing wrong with using it. It sensitizes us to the experience of many, probably most, people in contemporary society. But, this pattern is neither inevitable nor unalterable (for example, a minority of aged people work until they die), and change in it can come from the person, the society, or both. For example, a fifty-year-old man who felt that work on an automobile assembly line was alienating could easily find support for his view in the larger society. And, together with that support, this middle-aged man could decide to establish a new social identity when theory says he should not (see, for example, Terkel, 1974).

Theory says that young adults spend their time in learning new identities. Data from many sources support this conclusion and data also show that modern society's acceptance of change produces some young adults who often accept and reject new social identities at a rapid pace.

Consider two examples, marriage and work roles. Men marry for the first time at twenty-three, women at twenty-one, and despite incessant talk of new life styles, 1971 saw 650,000 more marriages than 1961. This increase kept pace with population growth and it also kept pace with the tendency for marriages to become more, rather than less, organized. For example, in 1971 80 percent of all first-time weddings were formal; in 1967 the figure was 73 percent. In 1971, 96 percent of marrying couples held a reception; in 1967, 85 percent. And where 1963 saw 67 percent of the couples begin married life with a basic set of china, the figure for 1973 was 84 percent (Seligson, 1973).

These figures show the success of both childhood socialization and the advertising industry. But if people still marry as often as ever, the number of divorces and separations in young adulthood indicates that many people find it necessary to change achieved social identities. About 8 percent of white women and 5 percent of white men are divorced or separated in young adulthood. And among black women and black men, the respective figures are 30 percent and 15 percent.[5] Overall the chances of divorce are greatest between the second and fourth years of marriage. For couples marrying before the age of twenty, 17 out of 1000 divorce during this period. For couples marrying between twenty and twenty-

---

[5] For one good explanation of the very high rates among black people, see Eliot Liebow's *Tally's Corner*.

four, the figure is 15 out of 1000. For those between twenty-five and twenty-nine, 7 of 1000 divorce. And for couples thirty and over (first marriages), the figure is 11 divorces for every 1000 marriages (Kimmel, 1974).

Incidentally, estimates are that 75 percent of divorced people remarry within five years. Generally, second marriages are happier than first ones, but many who divorce again, remarry again. For all the talk of its imminent collapse, marriage is still the accepted pattern for adults. Only 4 percent of the population never marries (Kimmel, 1974).

Turning from marriage to work, we find frequent changes throughout young adulthood. Typically job mobility means change within an occupation, but men and women who gain degrees later in life are one group who use diplomas to change occupations. Overall the figures show that job stability increases with age: where 60 percent of those under twenty-five change jobs or occupations, the figure for those between twenty-five and thirty-four is 30 percent, and for those between thirty-five and forty-four, 20 percent (Hurlock, 1968).

Mobility occurs for many reasons. Sometimes sexism is at work. Women are 42 percent of the labor force, but 55 percent of those working women are married. What happens is that married women often shift job plans and interests to fit their home responsibilities or their husbands transfers to other communities (Neugarten, 1968a; Hurlock, 1968). Besides sexism, people change jobs or occupation because of economic conditions (say, layoffs), lack of education, a desire for more money and better opportunities, or a work world that teaches people to remain "basically uncommitted to any organization." In *Future Shock* Alvin Toffler argues that many executives now expect temporary positions with their corporate employers. Taking economic security for granted, these men "move from slot to slot in a complex pattern that is largely self-motivated." And Toffler feels that as corporations become less rigid and more adaptable, the turnover of people and jobs will markedly increase (1970).

This brief discussion of marriage and work furnishes support for theory: young adults do look out to the world; they do learn new roles, acquire new identities, and a minority do maintain relatively loose commitments to the identities they achieve. But what is the social psychological effect of these identities? What is the actual, imagined, or implied influence of others (for example, husband, children, in-laws, work mates) on the thoughts and actions of young adults? And what is the relationship between new social identities and "old" self-images? Do the new identities inevitably foster major changes in the self-images acquired in childhood and adolescence?

Apparently not. Theory on young adulthood is weak, but Robert White argues that one growth trend between the ages of twenty and forty is a stabilization of the global self-image.[6] By, say thirty, people have had a wide variety of personal experiences. The result is that this accumulated mass of encounters consistently channels perceptions about self down the same road. Experience equals a sharper, clearer image of self, as well as acting to free the self "from transient influences." Lectured on impatience in childhood, a girl might respond with anger. But, at thirty, the woman knows the judgment to be true. Years of experience prove this and there is little use in denying reality: thirty years of impatience (White, 1966).

Naturally, people need not face reality. Someone with feelings of inferiority can respond in childhood with a loud no: "You tell me I'm a loser. I say you're wrong. I'm really a winner." And assuming a continuing need to defend the self (that is, genotypic continuity), accumulated experience can show the adult that the child was right: "Everyone seems to feel I'm a loser. Jealousy and envy are terrible traits! People tell me one thing, but I know their remarks are a cover to avoid facing my genuinely excellent qualities."

So, a stabilizing image of self need not be accurate. White argues that young adults do become objects to themselves, surveying aspirations in relation to abilities, presenting goals in relation to possible goals and their opinion of self in relation to the opinions others have of them. All this is true. But a crucial variable determining any young adult's response to insights is the need to defend self from reality. Facing impatience or an absence of mechanical ability or a hatred of housework is unlikely to crucially affect the self-image of most young adults. But it could. And that means that for most young adults the stabilizing self-image is a complex of truth and lies. Theoretically, truth wins out to the extent that people have no deep-seated need to defend self. However, to the extent that needs are serious, the result of accumulated experience could be a stabilized image that bears little resemblance to the reality that is actually there. Undoubtedly, the result for most young adults is varying degrees of truth and lies, with truth the overall winner.

If the direction of growth is toward stability, the *process* is greatly aided by the newly acquired social identities. Especially if the person is committed to the new roles, experience "accumulates more and more selectively." And this has two effects. First, "stability comes increasingly out of behavior within roles" (White, 1966). Women who see themselves only as wives and mothers achieve a stable identity because there is no choice; whether voluntary or involuntary, the absence of alternative roles generally leads to only one place: a stable set of identities. Second, if the new identities equal stability, they reduce the chances for major changes in

---

[6] White uses the phrase "stabilization of ego identity," which he defines as the "self or person one feels oneself to be." For the purpose of consistency of terms, this text uses the phrase "stable self-image."

the self-image acquired in childhood. Selective experiences narrow the opportunities for fresh insights about self. And while, for example, husbands and wives often help each other to gain a different view of childhood, stable identities reduce the desire to radically rethink the past. Particularly if people are happy in their new roles, but even if they are only resigned to them, what is the motive for rethinking childhood and adolescence? Happiness and resignation both generally produce the same result—people with no strong need to rethink the past.

Remember, too, that to seek major changes in the self-image acquired in childhood is to embrace anxiety. It is ironic but true—in order to change, people need to make threatening assertions: "I am not who I think I am!" or "I am not what my parents told me I am!" or "What my parents told me about me was motivated by *their* problems!" Normally comments such as these threaten established self-images. To change is to substitute one view of self for no view of self. This is a difficult and painful process. People do it; it is the goal of clinical psychologists. But it is a very trying path *under any circumstances.* And when young adulthood produces relatively stable identities, plus selective experiences, the chances of young adults rethinking childhood are substantially reduced.

If young adulthood normally produces no major rethinking of childhood, people do change, they do manage to think about self and world. For example, Robert White argues that another growth trend in young adulthood is toward "the freeing of personal relationships." People now relate to one another as unique human beings. Suddenly sons and daughters no longer need to assert their individuality or "break ties of dependency" (White, 1966; Kimmel, 1974). These are now a reality, allowing young adults to view their parents as distinct people. Often this produces empathy for the parents, acceptance of their personalities, and so a freeing of this very personal relationship. But, sometimes maturity allows young adults to gain insights that result in unhappiness. Free to see parents or friends as unique personalities, young people may decide they do not like what they see. A father revered in childhood and adolescence may turn out, on second glance, to be a rigid, egotistic personality. This insight frees the personal relationship in an unhappy way, sometimes producing change in the young adult. He or she may say: "Boy, I hope I never get to be like that. You (husband, lover, friend) make sure and tell me if I do. God forbid!"

Another factor that causes young adults to think about self and world is the result of new identities. Sometimes this enhances self-esteem. A person who earns a degree(s) and then gets a good job, with a fine office, may conclude: "I'm somebody. I've got my degree and others must think a lot of me; otherwise why give me such a good job, such a nice office, such a high salary? I'm a pretty important person."

If some identities result in increased self-esteem, there is evidence that others cause young adults serious problems. One is becoming a mother or father. A woman might be thrilled about the birth of her child, but one study showed "that mothers with professional training and with extensive work experience *all* suffered extensive or severe crisis with the birth of their first child" (Kimmel, 1974). Reflect on the woman's role. She has an education, plus an occupational identity that affords her some sense of self-esteem. Now, society says that she, the woman, must stay at home with the baby. And, more important, our new mother accepts society's judgment of self. She is only a housewife, and from now on her sense of self-esteem is derived from her husband. At once her identity outside the house is taken from her and she is given in return an identity that says she is only a housewife. No wonder these women experience a crisis. No wonder they rebel against an identity that strips them of one important source of self-esteem, greatly narrows the range of their everyday experience, and furnishes, in return for these sacrifices, a decreased sense of self-esteem.

If motherhood is initially bad for the woman, many men can worsen the situation. Jealousy springs up when husbands accuse their wives of neglect. Before the birth of the baby, the man was the center of the woman's attention; now the baby inevitably occupies that position, and many men complain about the change: "What about me?" Besides jealousy, children often bring other problems. Many women consider breast-feeding, only to find their husbands opposed. Breasts are sexual objects, not bottles of milk; in extreme cases women who breast-feed find they have suddenly become ugly. Men do not think they are feminine until they once more become "attractive." Or, couples who are both happy about the child find they make love with much less frequency. Exhausted by the time they reach bed, sleep, not sex, is the only thing on the couple's mind.

Douglas Kimmel sums up the situation by noting that many parents had little preparation for their new identities. In one study, most new arrivals were "planned" babies, but the couples romanticized child-rearing. Assuming no major change in their marital relationships, men and women were angry, frustrated, upset when they discovered the extent to which baby set the pace of life. Before, the couple could go anywhere, anytime. Now they must stay home and even when they later trust the child to a babysitter, they do not leave: calls to and from the babysitter are a frequent fact of parental life. So, "the role shift at parenthood is a crucial turning point that involves considerable potential for emotional crisis" (Kimmel, 1974). With understanding, couples manage to weather the storm, but the change lasts for about twenty years. Husbands and wives must share each other with children, a "fact of life" that creates identity problems of the most diverse and serious kind. For example, a thirty-five-year-old man or woman might want to change jobs, but refuse to do so because children impose responsibilities. Before, who cared about risks? Now, security is a must, and that consideration might equal bitterness: "My life could be, would have been, different if it weren't for the kids."

A final example of an identity change in young adulthood is divorce. Often this change is drawn out, with "separated" the identity bridge between married and divorced. But, whether the separation period is long or short, one important fact about divorce is the relative absence of recipes for living. Where marriage was an "institutionalized status passage," with a host of prescribed social norms, society still has few rules for the divorced person to follow. So, divorcees must define self and world with little social support. Generally, this is difficult. Turmoil often precedes the breakup of a marriage, and just when a person is trying to sort out his ambiguous feelings (of relief and sadness, of love and hate), he must come to terms with a relatively undefined identity, plus the loss of old ones (for example, married, father, or daughter-in-law). Increasingly, divorce is no longer regarded as failure, but in-laws or children often blame one partner—"They're telling me it was my fault. I broke up this marriage"—and even in the absence of blame, divorcees must still adjust to being alone. Studies show that loneliness is often a "major reaction" to divorce, with time providing the friends needed for adjustments to the new identity. The rate of remarriage for divorcees is higher than for single persons at all ages, but dating often means identity problems: "Am I still attractive?" "What do I say to her, to him?" "What will the children think about me if I leave for the weekend?" Eventually, divorced people answer these questions, but they do so in a society that furnishes few guides or support. Perhaps this is a major reason for the high rate of remarriage? Embracing an old, established identity provides a sense of self that is absent in the limbo now known as divorce (Bischof, 1969; Kimmel, 1974).

Incidentally, divorce does seem to produce greater insights into self. This does not necessarily mean a reexamination of the unique image acquired in childhood, but loneliness does furnish time for thought. Often people gain insight into their own problems and faults, with the result being a new ability to face the self that is actually there. Generally, the "new" person uses this knowledge to embrace old identities. For if one reason for remarriage is the undefined nature of divorce, another is the divorced person's "deeper motivation" to succeed the second time around. Echoing the generalized other by accepting married as the best identity for an adult, the divorced person uses his or her hard won insights to assure success in remarriage (Bischof, 1969).

Marriage, Work, Parenthood, Divorced: all of these identities underline the dialectical relationship that exists between young adults and their significant and generalized others. Between twenty and forty, people do turn outward to the world by establishing a number of important, if not permanent, commitments. Generally these commitments produce few major changes in the self-images carried along from childhood, but always they include attitudes of others that demand a response from the young adult. Sometimes, as with many women and motherhood, the response is frustration, a lowered sense of self-esteem, and resignation, but always the response young adults make to their achieved or imposed identities is the basis for the evaluative process so characteristic of middle age.

MIDDLE AGE

Middle age (from forty to sixty) has at least four sides: it is a dreaded period ("Will you look at those wrinkles!"), it is a time of transition (the change of life), it is a period of readjustment (the children are leaving), and, especially for men, middle age is a time for self-evaluation, a stage of life for happily or unhappily viewing "how the sequence and pattern of events" in young adulthood have led to a "web of circumstances" that is very difficult to change (Hurlock, 1968; Bromley, 1967, 1974).

Let's begin with dread. Physically the obvious signs of middle age include the graying or loss of hair, poorer vision or hearing, loss of skin elasticity (wrinkles, shadows, lines), loss of teeth, and an inability to keep off excess weight. Accompanying the obvious changes are a number of common health problems: tendency to fatigue easily, buzzing or ringing in the ears, general aches and pains, the increased probability of a heart attack. Normally these changes occur over time; people need not perceive them all at once. But at some variable point in middle age, men and women must come to terms with the obvious: they are getting old (see Bromley, 1967; Hurlock, 1968).

Awareness of middle age comes in many forms. One man saw a "cute chick" and then thought: "My God, she's about the age of my son, it was a real shock; it made me realize that I was middle-aged." Another man still felt young mentally, "but suddenly one day my son beat me at tennis. . . ." For one woman middle age arrived at a supermarket checkout counter as she was standing with her twenty-five-year-old friend, and the checker asked the friend if "Mother" needed help with her packages. Finally, for one man "it was a friend's sudden heart attack that made the difference. I realized that I could no longer count on my body as I used to . . ." (Neugarten, 1968b).

"They're telling me, I'm middle-aged." This response to the attitudes of others often means a poor self-image, along with an attempt to avoid the obvious. For example, realizing the decrease in physical strength, people could now root self-esteem in acquired wisdom. One of Neugarten's respondents said "true maturity doesn't come until around 45. . . . And while some of the young men (in this business) are excellently educated, we middle-aged men are no longer learning from a book. We've learned from past experience" (Neugarten, 1968b; Peck, 1968). But the problem with this evaluation of self is childhood; men and women learned to base part of their self-esteem on physical abilities and attributes. When time inevitably saps those capacities, it also comes with a potentially damning insight: "I'm now less than a man" or "I'm no longer attractive to men."

Consider the supposed relationship between sex and baldness. Tradition has it that hair, on face, body, arms, anywhere, is a sign of virility. Well, when some men begin to lose hair, they believe it means the loss of sexual powers. In reality baldness has nothing to do with sexual capacity, but Hurlock notes that "anxiety about virility is one of the chief causes of its decline." Preoccupied with worry, men have trouble with sex and that unfortunately confirms their fears and their poor images of self: "they are no longer 'real' men" (Hurlock, 1968).

Another example is provided by those men who begin to dress, talk, and act like young adults. Refusing to face any decline in physical powers, they respond with a no: "You tell me I'm getting old. I'll show you who's getting old. Just watch me move." At times this technique works but the middle-aged man puts himself in a dangerous situation. Traveling around with youngsters makes him conspicuous; using them as a mirror leaves the looking glass no choice: it has to respond with a middle-aged reflection! Also, when he competes with twenty-five-year-olds, chances are that the middle-aged man will lose. Perhaps he does have skill, but a supple body and sharp reactions stack the cards in favor of youth. Unfortunately, if the middle-aged man refuses to accept the stone wall that is age, the result is often depression and bitterness: "I am not who I think I am" or "I am not who they tell me I should be" (Peck, 1968; Hurlock, 1968; Bromley, 1974).

Women also dread middle age but, instead of focusing on physical abilities, many worry about physical attributes. Probably this concern is relative to a woman's acceptance of traditional gender identities. With a work life of her own, esteem lost through aging can be "picked up" at work. But if house and husband are the woman's whole life, wrinkles, lines, and shadows can be frightening. Her husband is her only important mirror. She tries to stay young and pretty for him and finds a number of cosmetics firms eager to supply "the fountain of youth." Like Ponce de Leon and middle-aged men, she never finds it, but if she continues to root self-esteem in waning physical attributes, one likely result is despair for what was, along with ridicule from those who demand that she act her age.

If middle age is thought of with dread, it is also a time of transition, a period of preparation for old age and death. As Robert MacIver notes, "time does not pass; the passage is ours through time" (1963). And one side of middle age is people's perception of time; suddenly many begin to think in terms of "time-left-to-live rather than time-since-birth." In one study comparing young and middle-aged adults, older people had reduced their level of activity but increased the value they gave to time (Wallach and Green, 1968). Now it was "finite," death was real and coming. To some this insight acted as a "brake"; they slowed down their pace to prolong their lives. But, to others, the perceived end of time was a "prod"; along with a certain anxiety, they experienced a certain zest in seeing how much pleasure could still be obtained, how many good years one could still arrange, how many new activities could be undertaken . . . (Neugarten, 1968b).

Although all middle-aged people must somehow prepare for death and old age, only women have the added experience of menopause.[7] This period of transition, this release from the responsibilities of fertility, typically occurs at age forty-five, but the start, intensity, and duration of menopause varies widely among women. In fact, while a wide range of symptoms (for example, dizzy spells, depression, anxiety, hot flashes) are commonly thought to be associated with menopause, "the frequency and severity of menopausal symptoms in the general population are unknown" (Kimmel, 1974). First, analyses in medical textbooks are based on women who see physicians; if they did not have problems, these women would not consult doctors. Second, some women have no problems at all. And third, because menopause has long been a sensitive topic, women fail to discuss their experiences. Clearly, it is hard to generalize about a subject people refuse to discuss.

If precise knowledge about the medical aspects of menopause is lacking, studies do give good indications of its social-psychological effects. Neugarten et al. found that women over forty-five are more likely than younger women to feel that menopause creates no major changes in life nor any inevitable crises. More important, studies show that middle-aged women vary greatly in their attitude toward menopause. On the negative side, 58 percent of the women surveyed (between forty-five and fifty-five) said menopause was unpleasant, 51 percent thought women worry about losing their minds during menopause, and 40 percent agreed that "nearly every woman is depressed about the change of life" (Neugarten et al., 1968c). However, fully 74 percent said that menopause failed to change women in any important way, and over 70 percent argued that trouble often had its roots in the generalized other. Apparently many women believe the societal assumptions about menopause and so enter middle age anticipating the worst. Over 75 percent of the women said that "women

---

[7] The male "change of life normally occurs during the sixties or seventies." More important, it is normally quite gradual (Hurlock, 1968).

who have trouble in the menopause are those who are expecting it" (Neugarten et al., 1968c).

As discussion and analysis of menopause become more widespread, women (and men) should experience less anxiety about it. Probably an increasing number of women will adopt a position taken by one of Neugarten's respondents: "I remember one time, in the kitchen, I had a terrific hot flush. . . . I went to look at myself in the mirror. I didn't even look red so I thought, 'All right . . . the next time I'll just sit there and who will notice?' And if someone notices, I won't even care . . ." (Neugarten et al., 1968c).

If time increases our knowledge of menopause, it should also begin to underline its positive aspects. Once the menopausal period was over, many women were happy about the end of menstruation, and while a few did experience sadness about the impossibility of motherhood, the majority expressed relief that fears of pregnancy were for others. "Now they were free from the responsibilities, the stresses, the hazards, and trials associated with childbirth" (Hurlock, 1968). Perhaps life was no oyster, but at least many of a woman's discomforts, pains, and fears would be a thing of the past.

Readjustment is a third concern of middle-aged people. For one thing, children leave the home and parents must then make a dual adjustment: to daily life without the children and to each other without the children. Conventional wisdom says this readjustment often equals divorce, depression (especially for women), and conflict, but studies prove conventional wisdom wrong. In fact, most parents relish the freedoms that come with their children's departure. All at once they are free of economic responsibilities, free to come and go as they please, and free from housework, chauffeuring, and a host of adolescent quests (Deutscher, 1962; Rollins and Feldman, 1970).

A large number of women seem particularly happy about the absence of children. Especially when they have an education and possess some money, women embrace the sense of increased freedom and "the satisfying change in self-concept." Before their children left home, they were committed to being a mother, with the result that their interests came second. In addition, their self-concept was rooted in the notion that "I'm only a housewife." Now women are relatively on their own. As one woman put it, "I'm old enough to admit to myself the things I could do well and to start doing them. I didn't think like this before. . . . It's a great new feeling . . ." (Neugarten, 1968b).

Women use their freedom in a number of ways. One is to find a job. For some women this is a return to an old occupation; for others a job in middle age is their first work experience. Whichever it is, in 1968, 51 percent of the women between forty-five and fifty-four were in the labor force, and the estimate for 1980 is at least 60 percent (Hurlock, 1968). Given the institutionalized inequalities between the sexes, women are often forced to accept menial jobs, but in many cases even menial positions afford a better self-concept than housewife and mother. However, it is true that women tend to retire earlier than men, and Hurlock is probably correct when she suggests that a major reason for this occurrence is the woman's experience with institutionalized inequality (Hurlock, 1968).

A second response of women (and men) to the absence of children at home is to join or increase participation in various community groups. The type of group (for example, the Chamber of Commerce as opposed to the Elks as opposed to a bridge club) varies with sex, education, money, and interest, but for both sexes membership in community groups increases significantly during middle age, and one study showed that about 25 percent of married middle-aged women (between forty-five and sixty) held two or more offices or committee memberships within community groups. Naturally the amount of social esteem derived from this participation varies but especially for the women these groups furnish them at least some opportunity to be on their own. Here, they, and no one else, are making things go well (Pressey and Kuhlen, 1957).

Since men normally work while the children are growing up, the absence of children need not require the major readjustments made by many women. However, studies show that some men react by working longer hours, and both men and women use their "postparental" life for new forms of recreation. Freedom is normally a blessing, and middle-aged people use it for everything from travel to gardening, from watching television to reading, from visiting to hobbies of all sorts. Typically these recreational activities produce little change in basic beliefs about self and world, but especially when the middle-aged person has the financial resources, the ability to do as he or she wishes is conducive to a positive attitude toward life.

Another major readjustment during middle age is the death of a spouse. Fully 50 percent of the women in Neugarten's study said the prospect of widowhood was their main fear. And no wonder. Nearly 15 percent of white women and over 25 percent of black women (between forty-five and sixty-four) lose their husbands in middle age. The figures for black men and white men (between forty-five and sixty-four) are, respectively, 7 percent and 3 percent (Kimmel, 1974; Chevan and Korson, 1972).

Widowhood is hardest on the woman. First, because of the great difference in the numbers of widowed men and women, the chances of remarriage are slim. Only 18 percent of widows find another spouse. Second, while both sexes grieve for the loved one, men have a better chance of meeting other people. Without an escort, and suffering from years of staying at home, widows are often reluctant to get out and meet people socially. Third are the financial problems that often affect women the hardest; suddenly, and probably with little training, they must find work. This obviously requires a major adjustment and especially when the family's standard of living drops significantly, the adjustment to widowhood is that much harder. Finally comes loneliness. Widowed at fifty, three out of four women can expect to live twenty years longer! Unfortunately those twenty years are unlikely to be filled with "happy" times. If the widow carries grief too far, people soon begin to avoid her. And while many couples continue to invite widows to parties, those invitations are often built around the idea of the "extra." Widows "fill out" couple-oriented evenings, and when two women are invited as a couple, or a widow assumes the man's spot at bridge, taking the role of the other leads to a sad conclusion: "They're telling me I'm out of place, an alien among the normals, alone when I should be accompanied." Over time the widowed entertain less and less in their own homes, and especially for the women, adoption of society's definition of self—"I'm an extra"—leads to the establishment of a small group of "unattached like-aged women." This group need not share similar interests; what ties them together are middle age, widowhood, and the need to mitigate the harsh effects of loneliness (Bischof, 1969; also Hurlock, 1968; Kimmel, 1974).

Another point must be made. Widowhood and its consequences are one reason that theories of aging focus on the expansion and contraction of life interests and activities. To the extent that widowed people entertain less, as well as see only family and a few friends, their world does contract, they do turn inward. However, remember that this is a broad generalization. A minority of the widowed remarry and many who remain widows do go out to work. Seemingly, the identity "widow" dominates their thinking about self and world, as well as others' attitudes toward them, but work is still one aspect of the widowed experience that expands rather than contracts the person's contacts and activities.

A final side of middle age is the significance people attach to evaluations of young adulthood. To some extent everyone has unique standards for judging "progress" in life, but we all use typical criteria as well, and middle age is one period when the unique and typical combine to ask pointed questions: "What have I done with my life? Have I achieved the goals I set at twenty-five? If I haven't, is there anything I can do about it?"

Consider first what Douglas Kimmel calls the "career clock" (Kimmel, 1974; Dennis, 1968). People start at twelve noon but as time goes by darkness sets in and at each hour on the clock, specific achievements are supposed to be made. If physicists generally make their important discoveries between the ages of thirty and thirty-five, a forty-eight-year-old physicist is late. In all likelihood, he or she must conclude: "I'll never amount to much." Or, if via the generalized other, age norms say that "most men hold their top jobs between forty-five and fifty" (Neugarten, 1968a), a fifty-two-year-old, still ambitious, middle-level executive is in trouble. Perhaps he will find scapegoats, perhaps not, but in some way he must come to terms with the attitudes of others: he has failed.

Naturally, people need not come to sad conclusions about self and world. For example, studies show that for many adults life satisfaction is closely related to socioeconomic status, family income, and participation in community activities (see Edwards and Klemmack, 1973; Dykman et al., 1952). Well, if people reach middle age, look back, and see a long line of successes, they are likely to react with pleasure, along with a heightened sense of self-esteem. As the middle-aged president of a large broadcasting company said: "I've always felt throughout my lifetime that if you have any ability at all, go for first place. . . . I had to create my own paths. Sure. I've been second vice-president, first vice-president, and executive vice-president. But I had only one goal in life and that was to be president. . . . I don't feel any pressure. . . . I'm not under tension. I go to bed at night and I sleep well. The company is doing well. My people are functioning as a team. The success story is not Ward Quaal. It's a great team of people" (Terkel, 1974).

Perhaps. But whether it is Ward Quaal or the team, this middle-aged man has few problems with his present or future image of self. Goals and reality are one; he is what he wanted to be. However, for those who receive a negative evaluation, the prospects for self-esteem are intimately related to the way job or family commitments determine the future. If an unhappy person sees no viable alternative to his or her present way of life, the process of self-evaluation could easily produce depression and bitterness. After all, each of us is unique and when a look back reveals unfulfilled expectations, a host of unrealized dreams, the extreme conclusion is that "I wasted my one and only life!"

Few people embrace this view of self; it is too painful. Instead, faced with a negative evaluation of self, people normally manufacture a number of plausible explanations: "My family stopped me"; "I never wanted that job anyway"; "Successful people are always unhappy." The extent and number of defenses vary with the importance of the conclusions to the particular middle-aged person, but there seems no way to avoid the evaluative process. For one reason or another, middle-aged people look back and come to conclusions that happily or unhappily point them toward old age and death.

OLD AGE

Enter Goneril.
LEAR.   Who comes here?

O heavens,
If you do love old men, if your sweet sway,
Allow obedience, if you yourselves are old,
Make it your cause! Send down, and take my part!
(*To Goneril.*) Art not asham'd to look upon this beard?
O Regan, wilt thou take her by the hand?
GONERIL.   Why not by the hand, sir? How have I offended?
All's not offense that indiscretion finds
And dotage terms so.
LEAR.   O sides, you are too tough!
Will you yet hold? How came my man i' the stocks?
DUKE OF CORNWALL.   I set him there sir, but his own disorders
Deserv'd much less advancement.
LEAR.   You? Did you?
REGAN.   I pray you, father, being weak, seem so.
If, till the expiration of your month,
You will return and sojourn with my sister,
Dismissing half your train, come then to me.
I am now from home, and out of that provision
Which shall be needful for your entertainment.
LEAR.   Return to her, and fifty men dismiss'd?
No, rather I abjure all roofs, and choose
To wage against the enmity o' the air,
To be a comrade with the wolf and owl—
Necessity's sharp pinch! Return with her?
Why, the hot-blooded France, that dowerless took
Our youngest born, I could as well be brought
To knee his throne, and, squire-like, pension beg
To keep base life afoot. Return with her?
Persuade me rather to be slave and sumpter
To this detested groom.
[Shakespeare, *King Lear,* II, 4, 192–220]

King Lear is hurt. But most of all, he is threatened. "They're telling me I'm nothing. They're telling me, a king, the man who gave them everything, that I must retire to a life without purpose or self-esteem. Why, they're even taking away the trappings of my esteem. Half my train is to be dismissed. I will not accept it. I refuse your definition of my self."

Shakespeare published *King Lear* in 1608. In 1838 Honoré de Balzac published a modern version of Lear in his novel, *Le Père Goriot*. And, as in Lear, Balzac's novel depicted reality. In fact, French children treated their parents so badly that laws were established to protect the aged. Fathers who gave property to their children received in return a life annuity; this legal right was the parent's guarantee against starvation. Unfortunately, the law often furnished, along with food, a motive for murder. Prior to the law, children were content to deprive their parents of self-esteem. But the law said children must provide money. This was a tangible obligation and one result was the death of aged parents. Statistics are unavailable—murderers generally fail to record their actions—but Simone De Beauvoir thinks that murders of parents were frequent. French public opinion was uneasily aware of the killings, and whether this concern reflected guilt or worry that the murderers were increasingly careless, the killing of aged parents was a reality in nineteenth-century France (De Beauvoir, 1973).

Greedy children are one reason that aged people are deprived of their self-esteem and even their lives. But sometimes greedy children are not necessary; sometimes societies institutionalize the demand for aged people to make "role exits" (Blau, 1973). Sometimes societies select an age and say, "After this, no more work. After this, you can go on living and you will even receive enough money to survive, but work must stop. 'Retired' is now your identity until you die."

What is the effect of retirement on aged people? Does it invariably lead to a loss of self-esteem, a sense of worthlessness? And does the demand for retirement symbolize the overall attitude of others toward aged people? Do the aged hear, at work and in their clubs, from their offspring and from the mass media, that they are now, like children, in need of guidance from adults? And, finally, if scorn and toleration do characterize the attitudes of others, do aged people say yes? Do they accept a harsh image of self?

WORK AND SELF-IMAGE

Only a minority of men and women continue working after age sixty-five. In America 32 percent of the men over sixty-five are working; in Great Britain the figure is 28 percent, and in Denmark, where the statutory retirement age is sixty-seven, the figure is 38 percent. For women the figures are 13 percent in America, 8 percent in Great Britain, and 8 percent in Denmark (Shanas et al., 1968).

Remember that these figures are for people sixty-five and over. If the statistics are broken down, they reveal decreasing participation over the life span. For example, for men between sixty-five and sixty-nine, the proportion in the labor force is, in Denmark, 64 percent, in Great Britain, 44 percent, and in America, 46.5 percent. And, if we compare white-collar and blue-collar workers, statistics show that a white collar means a greater chance of working after age sixty-five. For example, in America 43 percent of aged white-collar workers continue to be employed, while the figure for blue-collar workers is 20 percent. In Denmark and Great

Britain, 42 percent and 27 percent of white-collar men continue working; the figures for blue-collar men are 33 percent and 25 percent (Shanas et al., 1968).

Since these statistics reveal a complex reality, they allow us to draw one immediate conclusion: generalizations about the effects of retirement on all aged people are impossible. First, a minority of aged people never retire at all. And second, variables such as class and education affect the chance of retirement, as well as the reaction to it. For instance, common sense suggests, and studies show, that money is one weapon that mitigates the possibly harsh effects of retirement (for example, Crawford, 1972).

Now that we are prepared for many reactions to retirement, what is it that makes this role exit so potentially damaging to self-esteem? First is an obvious fact: work gives meaning to a person's life. Especially for men, work is often the most important source of self-esteem. So, to deprive men of their work is to possibly deprive them of meaning. Second, retirement rests on a judgment made by the generalized other: society is better off without aged workers. Thus, not only do retired people lose meaning, they are also potentially left without any defense of self. Where widowhood is due to natural causes, retirement is often avoidable—if the society says yes (Blau, 1973). Third is a crucial point made by Zena Smith Blau: retired is a "roleless status." It designates a *former* position without conferring any new rights or obligations upon the person or others. Perhaps this is because large numbers of aged people are such a recent phenomenon,[8] but, whatever the reason, society lacks precise guidelines for the last twelve to fifteen years of life. People lose their jobs and then enter a role that lacks the "clear-cut set of social expectations that might support a person in this new and unfamiliar position." No wonder inactivity and boredom are a common complaint among retired people. No wonder aged people say: "Do you know what my biggest problem is? Finding something to keep me busy two or three hours every day. Not a damned thing to do. What am I supposed to do?" (Blau, 1973). Tragically, society has no answer to this question. If it did, if it furnished reasons for a positive sense of self, many aged people could more easily accept the loss of their occupational identities. Fourth, and last, when people retire, they lose one important source of friends. Especially if workmates are an aged person's only companions, retirement could equal loneliness and that could easily magnify the effects of having nothing to do. As one seventy-one-year-old man said: "It took me a long time to get used to not working." And I miss "the fellows the most of anything—the association. The first year or two I was lost . . ." (Shanas et al., 1968).

Potentially, retirement is devastating on three interrelated fronts: to a

---

[8] In 1850, 2.5 percent of America's population was over sixty-five. In 1900, the figure was 4.1 percent. Today the figure is 9 percent and rising (De Beauvoir, 1973).

person's self-esteem, mood, and friendships (Blau, 1973). However, many factors reduce the possibly harsh effects of retirement and, in trying to assess the actual reactions to the loss of work, these must be considered.

Do a person's friends retire at the same time? Study shows that activity is related to high morale among the aged (Maddox, 1963; Rosow, 1971). But if people retire out of step with their friends, their chances of interacting with others are reduced. So, one factor mediating between the person and the potentially damning effects of retirement is the prevalence of this role exit among others of similar age, sex, and socioeconomic position (Blau, 1973). When a person's best friends are also partners at work, this loss is avoided if they are also retiring.

Does the retired person also face the loss of a wife or husband? Must the person accept two major role exits at the same time? If so, the chances[9] of retirement having a negative impact are greater—and this is especially so for men. Since childhood taught them to keep their feelings locked up, men often discuss intimate problems only with their wives. So, if the wife is absent, the man must bear her loss, adapt to an everyday life that overloads him with free time, as well as discuss his problems only with himself. None of this is easy. And the loss of an intimate friend could be crucial, for study shows that a confidant can sustain morale even "against such decrements as the loss of role or the reduction of social interaction" (Lowenthal and Haven, 1968).

What preparations has the person made for retirement? Crawford found many men who welcomed retirement. They already had a variety of leisure-time roles ready for occupancy, and retirement was their opportunity to move in to a future they had anticipated and planned. But Crawford also found many men who "dreaded" retirement. Depending "almost exclusively" on work for friends and interests, they saw their lives "collapsing." Work was their all and "they felt either unable or unwilling" to plan for a future with a restructured existence (Crawford, 1972).

What is the effect of social class on the morale of the retired? In the cross-cultural study of America, Denmark, and Great Britain, the amount of retirement income played "a major role in affecting men's attitudes toward retirement" (Shanas et al., 1968). And it is not difficult to see why. With money, retirement brings no change in the person's standard of living; in conjunction with free time, money gives retired people the chance to travel or join country clubs or live in New York in the summertime and Florida in the winter. That may not be the retired person's ideal way of life, but it is far better than the life afforded by the average income of many aged people. For example, nearly 22 percent of all families

---

[9] About 10 percent of the men between sixty-five and seventy-four are widowers. The figure for women is 70 percent (Kimmel, 1974).

with heads sixty-five years of age or older have an annual income of less than $2,500; and over 43 percent have incomes of less than $4,000 (Fernandez, 1975). That kind of money may equal survival; it will never mean a high standard of living.

What about education? Does more schooling generally lead to a happier retirement? The answer is yes. First, education usually means a higher income, and second, education is one factor that often broadens people's interests, plus making them aware of the role options society offers. Aged people with education tend to read more, as well as have more skills, more organizational affiliations, more participation in politics, more hobbies and nonwork interests. In short, aged people with an education have a better chance than the non- or little educated to fill the time that retirement thrusts upon them (Blau, 1973).

Finally, what is the effect of good or bad health? Here the evidence seems to indicate that either has the capacity to produce a desire for the world of work. Summarizing the results of their cross-cultural study, Shanas et al. said that "the more incapacitated the man, the more likely he is to be nostalgic for the world of work." Apparently sickness asks the person to recall health. Now he is useless; then he was vital, important. Now he does nothing; then, when he worked, he was something. However, health also acts to recall the world of work. In Denmark, America, and Great Britain, it was the healthy who most wanted work. Apparently, good health makes men wonder why they do not or cannot work. "They're telling me I can't have a job. But why not? I'm as healthy as I ever was" (Shanas et al., 1968).

Although the preceding shows that retirement is a role exit with potentially devastating effects, our discussion also shows that some aged people never retire (perhaps because they fear its effects[10]), while those who do react to their exit in different ways. Generally retirement has the worst effects on those who lack money, education, family, friends, and intimates to whom they can reminisce and complain. Here the most acute attacks on self-image and morale *are* damning: "I have no family. . . . I have no money, and all my close friends are dead. No one cares what happens to me. My fling is over, and I would just as soon die as not. My life is perfectly meaningless—I expect nothing of it except more of the same and the prospect doesn't please me. There's nothing in this kind of life that is worthwhile" (Blau, 1973).

---

[10] Sixty-nine-year-old Mr. Sterling was "always at work." He hoped he would never have to stop and said that if he did he would miss most "the feeling of being useful." And a seventy-seven-year-old Danish man had turned over the business to his son, but he still went to the factory every day. If he did not, he would find his life "terrible" (Shanas et al., 1968).

Although this reaction is extreme, it is not uncommon.[11] And more important, even if money, education, a spouse, and a family furnish high morale for the aged, many of their self-concepts are rooted in the identity "retired." We will return to this problem. But as Blau so correctly stresses, this new identity is based on a *former* identity. It is not *as if* society said retirees were imitations of themselves; society actually says this. It asks aged people to face the future on the coattails of a former role. It provides no identity that is a positive basis for esteem. On the contrary, the generalized other's message is clear: "They're telling me I was something. Now I'm supposed to find a sense of satisfaction in what I was and not in what I am. I'm supposed to move forward by looking backward. I'm supposed to find esteem in what I did rather than in what I'm doing. I'll try; I have little choice, but it won't be easy."

WIDOWHOOD IN OLD AGE

The number of widowed people increases dramatically among the aged. Where 3 percent of the men in a recent study between fifty-five and sixty-four were widowers, the figure jumps to 10 percent for men between sixty-five and seventy-four, and to over 20 percent for men past seventy-five. For women the rise is even greater. Twenty percent of the women between fifty-five and sixty-four are widows, between sixty-five and seventy-four the figure is 40 percent and for those over seventy-five the statistic is nearly 70 percent (Kimmel, 1974).

Like "retired," "widowed" is an identity that points the person backward. But, where the young or middle-aged adult sees the prospect of changing identities, people over sixty-five face a series of age norms that constrain them to root the present in the past. Perhaps 2 percent of the widowers and hardly any of the widows remarry (Kimmel, 1974). Although factors such as desire, health, and opportunity help produce these figures, the generalized other also bears responsibility. For example, harboring false beliefs about the sexual capacities of aged people (see Masters and Johnson, 1966), others cast a dark eye on sexual relations— "They're telling me I'm a dirty old man"—and family members often frown on aged parents who speak of remarriage. The result is few remarriages; the result is aged people defining who and what they are in terms of who and what they were.

Since many of their contemporaries are also widowed, this role exit

---

[11] In Denmark 50 percent of retired men said they enjoyed nothing in retirement. In America the figure was 35 percent; in Great Britain, 40 percent. And Kimmel cites a large study which found that over 25 percent of the retired reported feelings of uselessness (Shanas et al., 1968; Kimmel, 1974).

does not make the widowed conspicuous. Many others are in the same predicament, and they furnish a potential pool of friends. However, despite the availability of friends, class acts as a barrier in developing friendships. Normally, middle- and upper-class women engage in extensive interaction with others throughout their lives. Whether in clubs or associations, middle- and upper-class women accumulate a number of friends and when, after a husband's death, age-sex peers are needed, they are also available. But the social life of the lower-class woman is often restricted to neighbors and relatives. When a husband dies, there is no reservoir to be tapped, with the result that lower-class widows often lose a, if not the, source of high morale among aged people: friends, especially of the same sex (Blau, 1973; also Rosow, 1971; Lowenthal and Haven, 1968).

As noted above, if aged men lose both a wife and a job, the chances of maintaining high morale greatly decrease. However, men have always left the house, and this lifelong experience does give them one distinct advantage over women in using the pool of available peers. Probably men refrain from "opening up" to friends, but if consistently followed, even superficial interaction with age peers is a tonic to morale.

One last point. Over 40 percent of aged widows and widowers live alone. Generally, this is by choice; aged people want to be on their own. But study shows that the widowed with money and education are three times as likely to live alone as those without money and education (Chevan and Korson, 1972). So, those who most need a sense of integrity are least able to attain it.[12] Moreover, living with family is likely to reduce even more the chances for lower-class widows to use the available pool of age-sex peers. Dependent on their children, these women are unlikely to get out as much as they might want to.

FAMILY RELATIONS OF AGED PEOPLE

In the study made of Denmark, America, and Great Britain, the living arrangements of aged people included: about 25 percent of the aged lived alone; about one-third in Great Britain and slightly less than half in Denmark and America lived as married couples, in their own houses, without other people; and 27 percent in Denmark, 45 percent in Great Britain, and 35 percent in America lived in households that included an adult child, especially an unmarried or previously married child (Shanas et al., 1968).

---

[12] The question of integrity may be unimportant to those aged people who view the extended family as the ideal.

Whether they live alone or with a spouse, aged people generally stay close to at least one of their children. In all three countries studied, over 75 percent of the aged lived within thirty minutes of a child, and in all three countries nearly or over 30 percent of the aged lived within ten minutes of a child. Equally important, proximity translates into contact. About 70 percent in Denmark, 67 percent in Great Britain, and 70 percent in America had seen a child within the previous week, and except in Britain (47 percent), over 50 percent of the aged had seen a child that day or the day before. In breaking the figures down for social class, we find that although blue-collar and agricultural workers see their children more often than white-collar workers, the difference is relatively small. Where 71 percent of the blue-collar workers (in all three countries) had seen a child within the previous week, the figure for white-collar workers was 69 percent in Denmark, 57 percent in Britain, and 65 percent in America (Shanas et al., 1968).

Aged people live near their children and they see one another. What does it mean for the morale of aged people? Apparently, it is beneficial, but not crucial. First, quantity says nothing about quality; seeing a child daily often means no more than a five-minute encounter that does little to bolster morale. Second, a number of studies (for example, Blau, 1973; Kerchoff, 1966) indicate that peer friendships are the most important factor determining morale in old age. Blau rightly notes that "because friendship rests on mutual choice and mutual need and involves a voluntary exchange of sociability between *equals,* it sustains a person's sense of usefulness and self-esteem more effectively than filial relationships" (Blau, 1973). For example, while study shows that one intimate confidant can sustain high morale among the aged, study also shows that "siblings or other relatives as confidants are comparatively rare." Men rely on their wives, while women generally rely on other aged women (Lowenthal and Haven, 1968).

If children take a back seat to peers as a source of morale in old age, children are nonetheless important. When health fails, they often care for the aged,[13] and both parents and children exchange favors. In Britain and America, over 60 percent of the aged received help from children and over 60 percent of the children received help from the aged. Probably it is more important for their morale and esteem that the aged help their children, rather than vice versa. Help from children underlines dependency; help to children furnishes a sense of need and usefulness, especially important to aged people who are retired.

---

[13] Of the 20 million aged people in America, "only" 7 percent live in any kind of institution (Curtin, 1973).

IDENTITY IN OLD AGE

Do young people hate older people? Do they shy away for fear of realizing they too are fated to be old? Answers are not readily apparent, but this much is clear. Our society views aging as a "negative process" (see Chown and Heron, 1965; De Beauvoir, 1973), and many older people are aware of the attitudes of others. One study found older people feeling "set apart, considered different, rejected." Overall, the authors felt that the attitudes of others made aged people a "quasi-minority" and, unfortunately, this study found aged people acting like a minority. Saying yes to the attitudes of others, the aged person "emphasizes certain characteristics and values (and suppresses others) in order to achieve acceptance and ward off rejection by the dominant majority of younger persons" (Kogan and Shelton, 1962). As one aged woman who was learning to adapt said: "But they made me feel guilty about loving that child, as if an old fool like her couldn't have any need to love and be loved. They said we had to do things just so, and that took all the love out. . . . Maybe they were right. . . . They made me feel that I'd done something wrong" (Curtin, 1973).

Often, the "something wrong" is simply being old. Always, those people who accept the identity—"I'm old"—will have a difficult time in maintaining self-esteem. Society does have a negative view of aged people and it caps this view by adding the identities "retired" and "widowed." In short, the person receives a negative image of self because of age, and then, to add to his or her burden, society asks aged people to maintain self-esteem, not for what they are, but for what they were. This is very difficult to do. With friends, family, money, and education, aged people can maintain morale, but based on the attitudes of others isn't the reaction of "Aunt Jenny" an accurate response: "Where is the compensation? What's the *good* of being old? I love being alive, I want to live fully. But I just don't see any logic to old age. Being young, being middle-aged, they had rewards, compensations. You made sacrifices, chose to do without freedom to have children . . . but always before, always, there was a balance of joy and happiness. Where is it now? I don't know what to look forward to, or how much time I will have, . . . of what use is there in going on" (Curtin, 1973).

DEATH

Since death is the end of life, aged people often think about the coming of their end. Robert Butler calls it "the life review." Aware that death is near, people consciously focus on the past, especially on "unresolved conflicts." Success spells reintegration, the look back gives the aged person's life a new sense of meaning and significance. But, often, the look back leads to anxiety, guilt, despair, and depression. Saddened by the past, and with death the only future, life reviews lead to the seemingly common phenomenon of "mirror-gazing." In the case of one hospitalized eighty-year-old woman, others found her "berating her mirror image for her past deeds and shaking her fist at herself." Apparently, as the life review forced her to become an object to herself, this woman became "preoccupied by past deeds and omissions." In the end, although she purposely avoided mirrors, gloom and bitterness were her only response to everyday life (Butler, 1968, 1970; also Hinton, 1972; Jeffers and Verwoerdt, 1970).

Butler suggests that all people approach death with a life review. Perhaps this is so.[14] But life review or not, any aging person facing death today lives in a society that attaches increasingly less significance to dying. Geoffrey Gorer discusses the "pornography of death." Aging is supposedly a negative process and death the obscenity that is aging's end. Like sex yesterday, death is today's taboo topic. In fact, Gorer argues that while we smother death in prudery, violent death plays an ever-increasing part in the fantasies offered to us—in detective stories, thrillers, Westerns, war stories, spy stories, science fiction, and even horror comics (Gorer, 1967). Apparently, our refusal to openly face natural death causes us to approach it via pornography of all sorts.

Gorer has a point. But added to our silence about death is a sociological fact: aged people are increasingly less important to the functioning of modern society (Blauner, 1968). Already retired and dying in a society where religious imagery (the Greeks had Charon ferry souls across the river Styx leading to Hades) is generally weak, what collective significance do the dying have for the living? The answer is less and less. And the result is a society with problems on two fronts. First, we lack a notion of an appropriate death. Where the nineteenth-century (sexist) ideal was that of the patriarch dying in his own home, in full possession of his faculties, and surrounded by family, heirs, and the material symbols of success, we today lack a model for death, a proper way to gain esteem from the inevitable (Blauner, 1968).

Second, as the collective significance of death decreases, "the increasing lack of conventionalized stages in the mourning process results in an ambiguity as to when the bereaved person has grieved enough and thus can legitimately and guiltlessly feel free for new attachments and interests" (Blauner, 1968). Before, society's rituals gave survivors recipes for living. People mourned within a culturally defined situation, for example, the Jewish custom of *shivah* where relatives and friends visit the bereaved for

---

[14] A marvelous example in literature is Leo Tolstoy's, *The Death of Ivan Ilyich.*

an entire week. Today, as old recipes collapse, they are replaced with nothing and the result is ambiguity for survivors. Society furnishes no basis for telling me when I have mourned enough, if I am terrible when I socialize after two months, if I am scandalous in wearing red after only three months (see Gorer, 1967).

What is to be done? Hopefully we will make natural death a topic of everyday life and begin to reattach collective significance to it. If we do not, aged people must continue to endure a life review and death with little actual influence from others; instead of gaining "esteem" in a collective process, the aged die alone in hospital beds. And the living? They learn few norms for grief and mourning and, by refusing to attach collective importance to death, make life that much harder.

Bibliographical References

Bakan, David. "Adolescence in America: From Idea to Social Fact." *Daedalus* (Fall 1971): 979-95.

Becker, Howard. "Notes on the Concept of Commitment." *American Journal of Sociology* 66 (1960): 32-40.

Becker, Howard. "Personal Change in Adult Life." In *Middle Age and Aging*, edited by Bernice L. Neugarten. Chicago: University of Chicago Press, 1968.

Bischof, Ledford J. *Adult Psychology*. New York: Harper & Row, 1969.

Blau, Zena Smith. *Old Age in a Changing Society*. New York: New Viewpoints, 1973.

Blauner, Robert. "Death and Social Structure." In *Middle Age and Aging*, edited by Bernice L. Neugarten. Chicago: University of Chicago Press, 1968.

Brim, Orville, and Wheeler, Stanton. *Socialization After Childhood*. New York: Wiley, 1966.

Brittain, Clay. "Adolescent Choices and Parent-Peer Cross-Pressures." *American Sociological Review* 28 (1963): 385-91.

Bromley, D. B. "Middle Age: An Introduction." In *Middle Age*, edited by Roger Owen, pp. 7-21. London: BBC Publications, 1967.

Bromley, D. B. *The Psychology of Human Aging*. 2d ed. London: Penguin, 1974.

Buhler, Charlotte. "The Curve of Life as Studied in Biographies." *Journal of Applied Psychology* 19 (1932): 405-9.

Buhler, Charlotte. "Theoretical Observations About Life's Basic Tendencies." *American Journal of Psychotherapy* 13 (1959): 561-81.

Butler, Robert N. "The Life Review: An Interpretation of Reminiscence in the Aged." In *Middle Age and Aging*, edited by Bernice L. Neugarten. Chicago: University of Chicago Press, 1968.

Butler, Robert N. "Looking Forward to What?" *American Behavioral Scientist* 14 (September 1970): 121–28.
Campbell, Ernest Q. "Adolescent Socialization." In *Handbook of Socialization Theory and Research*, edited by David Goslin. Chicago: Rand McNally, 1969.
Chevan, Albert, and Korson, J. Henry. "The Widowed Who Live Alone." *Social Forces* 51 (1972): 45–53.
Chown, Sheila, and Heron, Alastair. "Psychological Aspects of Aging in Man." *Annual Review of Psychology* 16 (1965): 417–50.
Coleman, James S. *The Adolescent Society*. New York: Free Press, 1971.
Conger, John. *Adolescence and Youth: Psychological Development in a Changing World*. New York: Harper & Row, 1973.
Conger, John. "A World They Never Knew: The Family and Social Change." *Daedalus* (Fall 1971): 1105–38.
Crawford, Marron. "Retirement and Role-Playing." *Sociology* 6, no. 2 (1972): 217–35.
Curtin, Sharon. *Nobody Ever Died of Old Age*. Boston: Little, Brown, 1973.
De Beauvoir, Simone. *The Coming of Age*. New York: Warner, 1973.
Dennis, Wayne. "Creative Productivity Between the Ages of 20 and 80 Years." In *Middle Age and Aging*, edited by Bernice L. Neugarten. Chicago: University of Chicago Press, 1968.
Deutscher, Irwin. "Socialization for Postparental Life." In *Human Behavior and Social Processes*, edited by Arnold M. Rose. Boston: Houghton Mifflin, 1962.
Douvan, Elizabeth, and Adelson, Joseph. *The Adolescent Experience*. New York: Wiley, 1966.
Dunphy, Dexter. "The Social Structure of Adolescent Peer Groups." In *Studies in Adolescence*, edited by Robert Grinder. 2d ed. London: Macmillan, 1969.
Dykman, A. A.; Heimann, E. K.; and Keer, W. A. "Lifetime Worry Patterns of Three Diverse Adult Groups." *The Journal of Social Psychology* 35 (1952): 91–100.
Edwards, John N., and Klemmack, David L. "Correlates of Life Satisfaction." *Journal of Gerontology* 28 (1973): 497–502.
Eitzen, D. Stanley. *Social Structure and Social Problems in America*. Boston: Allyn & Bacon, 1974.
Elkin, Frederick, and Westley, William A. "The Myth of Adolescent Culture," *American Sociological Review* 10 (1955): 680–84.
Elkind, David. "Egocentrism in Adolescence." *Child Development* 38 (1967): 1025–34.
Erikson, Erik. *Childhood and Society*. Rev. ed. New York: Norton, 1964.
Erikson, Erik. *Identity: Youth and Crisis*. New York: Norton, 1968.
Fernandez, Ronald. *The Promise of Sociology*. New York: Praeger, 1975.

Flacks, Richard. "The Liberated Generation: An Exploration of the Roots of Student Protest." *Journal of Social Issues* 23, no. 3 (1967): 52–75.
Frankel-Brunswik, Else. "Adjustments and Reorientation in the Course of the Life Span." In *Middle Age and Aging,* edited by Bernice L. Neugarten. Chicago: University of Chicago Press, 1968.
Franklin, Benjamin. *The Autobiography of Benjamin Franklin.* New York: Washington Square Press, 1960.
Gecas, Viktor; Thomas, Darwin L.; and Weiger, Andrew J. "Social Identities in Anglo and Latin Adolescents." *Social Forces* 51 (June 1973): 477–84.
Goldman, Nancy. "The Changing Role of Women in the Armed Forces." *American Journal of Sociology* 78, no. 4 (1974): 892–911.
Gordon, Chad. "Social Characteristics of Early Adolescence." *Daedalus* (Fall 1971): 931–57.
Gorer, Geoffrey. *Death, Grief, and Mourning.* New York: Doubleday, 1967.
Grinder, Robert. *Adolescence.* New York: Wiley, 1973.
Hinton, John. *Dying.* London: Penguin, 1972.
Hurlock, Elizabeth. *Developmental Psychology.* 3d ed. New York: McGraw-Hill, 1968.
Jaques, Elliot. "The Mid-Life Crisis." In *Middle Age,* edited by Roger Owen. London: BBC Publications, 1967.
Jeffers, Frances C., and Verwoerdt, Adrian. "How the Old Face Death." In *Behavior and Adaptation in Late Life,* edited by Ewald W. Busse and Eric Pfeiffer. Boston: Little, Brown, 1970.
Kagan, Jerome. "A Conception of Early Adolescence." *Daedalus* (Fall 1971): 997–1012.
Kenniston, Kenneth. "The Sources of Student Dissent." *Journal of Social Issues* 23, no. 3 (1967): 108–37.
Kerchoff, Alan C. "Family Patterns and Morale in Retirement." In *Social Aspects of Aging,* edited by Ida Harper Simpson and John C. McKinney. Durham, N.C.: Duke University Press, 1966.
Kimmel, Douglas. *Adulthood and Aging.* New York: Wiley, 1974.
Kogan, Nathan, and Shelton, Florence. "Belief About Old People." *The Journal of Genetic Psychology* 100 (1962): 93–111.
Kohlberg, Lawrence, and Gilligan, Carol. "The Adolescent as a Philosopher: The Discovery of the Self in a Postconventional World. *Daedalus* (Fall 1971): 1051–86.
Komarovsky, Mirra. "Cultural Contradictions and Sex Roles." *American Journal of Sociology* 76 (1972): 873–84.
Kuhlen, Raymond. "Developmental Changes in Motivation During the Adult Years." In *Relations of Development and Aging,* edited by James Birren. Springfield, Ill.: Charles Thomas, 1964.
Lowenthal, Marjorie Fiske, and Haven, Clayton. "Interaction and Adap-

tation: Intimacy as a Critical Variable." *American Sociological Review* 23 (1968): 20–30.

MacIver, R. M. *The Challenge of the Passing Years.* New York: Pocket Books, 1963.

Maddox, George. "Activity and Morale: A Longitudinal Study of Selected Elderly Subjects." *Social Forces* 42 (1963): 195–204.

Mannheim, Karl. "The Sociological Problem of Generations." In *Studies in Social Movements,* edited by Barry McLaughlin. New York: Free Press, 1969.

Masters, William, and Johnson, Virginia. *Human Sexual Response.* Boston: Little, Brown, 1966.

Neugarten, Bernice L. "The Awareness of Middle Age." In *Middle Age and Aging,* edited by Bernice L. Neugarten. Chicago: University of Chicago Press, 1968b.

Neugarten, Bernice L. "The Old and Young in Modern Societies." *American Behavioral Scientist* 14 (September 1970): 13–24.

Neugarten, Bernice L.; Moore, Joan W.; and Lowe, John C. "Age Norms, Age Constraints, and Adult Socialization. In *Middle Age and Aging,* edited by Bernice L. Neugarten. Chicago: University of Chicago Press, 1968a.

Neugarten, Bernice L.; Wood, Vivian; Kraines, Ruth J.; and Loomis, Barbara. "Women's Attitudes Toward the Menopause." In *Middle Age and Aging,* edited by Bernice L. Neugarten. Chicago: University of Chicago Press, 1968c.

Ortega y Gasset, José. *Man and Crisis.* New York: Norton, 1962.

Osterreith, Paul A. "Adolescence: Some Psychological Aspects." In *Adolescence: Psychological Aspects,* edited by Gerald Caplan and Serge Lebovici. New York: Barie Books, 1969.

Owen, Roger. *Middle Age.* London: BBC Publications, 1967.

Peck, Robert. "Psychological Developments in the Second Half of Life." In *Middle Age and Aging,* edited by Bernice L. Neugarten. Chicago: University of Chicago Press, 1968.

Piaget, Jean. "Intellectual Evolution from Adolescence to Adulthood." *Human Development* 15 (1972): 1–12.

Poveda, Tony G. "A Perspective on Adolescent Social Relations." *Psychiatry* 35 (February 1972): 32–47.

Pressey, Sidney L., and Kuhlen, Raymond G. *Psychological Development Through the Life Span.* New York: Harper & Row, 1957.

Richmond, P. G. *An Introduction to Piaget.* London: Routledge and Kegan Paul, 1970.

Rollins, Boyd C., and Feldman, Harold. "Marital Satisfaction Over the Family Life Cycle." *Journal of Marriage and the Family* 32 (1970): 20–28.

Rosenberg, Morris. "Disturbance in Self-Image at Adolescence." *American Sociological Review* 38 (1973): 553–68.

Rosow, Irving. "Old People: Their Friends and Neighbors." *American Behavioral Scientist* 14 (1971): 59–69.

Seligson, Marcia. *The Eternal Bliss Machine*. New York: Morrow, 1973.

Shanas, Ethel; Townsend, Peter; Wedderbuin, Dorothy; Fris, Henning; Milhoy, Paul; and Stehouwer, Jan. *Old People in Three Industrial Societies*. London: Routledge and Kegan Paul, 1968.

Smith, Cyril. *Adolescence*. London: Longman's, 1970.

Stone, Gregory. "Appearance and the Self." In *Human Behavior and Social Processes*, edited by Arnold M. Rose. Boston: Houghton Mifflin, 1962.

Strib, Gordon R. "Old Age and the Family." *American Behavioral Scientist* 14 (September 1970): 25–39.

Terkel, Studs. *Working: People Talk About What They Do All Day and How They Feel About What They Do*. New York: Pantheon, 1974.

Toffler, Alvin. *Future Shock*. New York: Random House, 1970.

Wallach, Michael, and Green, Leonard. "On Age and the Subjective Speed of Time." In *Middle Age and Aging*, edited by Bernice L. Neugarten. Chicago: University of Chicago Press, 1968.

Willmott, Peter. *Adolescent Boys of East London*. London: Penguin, 1966.

White, Robert. *Lives in Progress: A Study of the Natural Growth of Personality*. 2d ed. New York: Holt, Rinehart, & Winston, 1966.

Yankelovich, Daniel. *The New Morality: A Profile of American Youth in the Seventies*. New York: McGraw-Hill, 1974.

CHAPTER FOUR

Problems in Living

So far our focus has been on "normal" people. Now we turn to a consideration of men and women with problems in living, people who are labeled by others (and often by themselves) as sick, crazy, mentally ill. Hopefully a focus on people with problems does two things: it questions the concept of mental illness and it shows that the roots of normality and abnormality are generally the same. Like everyone else, I must respond to what others say about me and if the others I inherit are contradictory, ambiguous, and mean, perhaps I have few chances to react in anything other than a neurotic or schizophrenic manner. Naturally no response is inevitable, but the main thrust of this chapter is the contention that, like "normality," the development of problems in living is an interactive, a very human, process.

> "Man, what they got going on in there?" McMurphy asks Harding.
> "In there? Why, that's right, isn't it? You haven't had the pleasure. Pity. An experience no human should be without." Harding locks his fingers behind his neck and leans back to look at the door. "That's the Shock Stop I was telling you about some time back, my friend, the Est, Electro-Shock Therapy. Those fortunate souls in there are being given a free trip to the moon. You pay for the service with brain cells instead of money, and everyone has simply billions of brain cells on deposit. You won't miss a few."
>
> He frowns at the one lone man left on the bench. "Not a very large clientele today, it seems, nothing like the crowds of yesteryear. But then,

c'est la vie, fads come and go. And I'm afraid we are witnessing the sunset of Est. Our dear head nurse is one of the few with the heart to stand up for a grand old Paul Kernerian tradition in the treatment of the rejects of sanity: Brain Burning."

". . . What they do is "—McMurphy listens a moment—"take some bird in there and shoot electricity through his skull?"

"That's a concise way of putting it."

"What the hell for?"

"Why, the patient's good, of course. Everything done here is for the patient's good. You may sometimes get the impression, having lived only on our ward, that the hospital is a vast efficient mechanism that would function quite well if the patient were not imposed on it, but that's not true. . . . A number of supposed irrecoverables were brought back into contact with shock, just as a number were helped with lobotomy and leucotomy. Shock treatment has some advantages; it's cheap, quick, entirely painless. It simply induces a seizure."

"What a life, Sefelt moans." Give some of us pills to stop a bit, give the rest shock to start one."

Ken Kesey, *One Flew Over the Cuckoo's Nest* (1962)

Today about three hundred thousand people live in asylums. And although that figure alone means more people are found in asylums than in prisons, in reality the patient population is much larger than three hundred thousand. Over the last twenty years, many states have transferred asylum patients to residential facilities in their own communities. Standards vary, but in many cases the community centers are simply asylums in a new location. Nationwide, perhaps seventy-five to one hundred thousand people live in community homes for the mentally ill (Brandt, 1975; Chesler, 1973).

Overall these statistics argue that mental illness is a serious social problem. So, as such, perhaps we should begin to seek out the mentally ill before they cause trouble? As Senator Abraham Ribicoff has said, "We need an all-out effort to make sure that potentially dangerous youngsters are identified early, effectively brought into treatment, and continuously treated as long as necessary to assure decent lives for themselves and safety for society" (Szasz, 1970b).

Senator Ribicoff's suggestion is based on at least two assumptions: mental illness exists and those who contract the disease need help from others—even if they do not want it. Fully 90 percent of hospitalized patients are involuntary inmates (Szasz, 1970a), and this tremendous power to "help" patients exists only because they are mentally ill. Granted, psychiatrists number no more than 5 percent of a hospital's staff; granted, most are part-time employees; and granted, over 65 percent of the full-time staff are nonprofessionals (Chesler, 1973). No matter. Hospital inmates are ill—would they be there if they were not sick?—and society has to help in whatever ways possible.

But what if mental illness is a myth? What if our society has given psychiatrists and psychologists great power on the basis of an illusion? What if Thomas Szasz is right "that what people now call mental illnesses are, for the most part, *communications* expressing unacceptable ideas, often framed in an unusual idiom" (Szasz, 1970b).

THE MYTH OF MENTAL ILLNESS

Let's begin with history. Asylums have their roots in the seventeenth century when political, religious, and social authorities decided to confine various groups of people. Motivation was multiple, but we find little mention of illness. Instead, political and economic rationales were used. Society contained a host of unemployed and idle and poor and immoral and mad people. To provide work for the able-bodied, to maintain social order, to rid society of beggars, to deal with immorality and antisocial behavior, people were confined, thus protecting society from the sin of disorder. In France, 1647 saw a "Hospital General" at Toulouse, one at Béziers in 1654, at Caen in 1655, and, in 1656 a royal decree founded the "Hospital General" of Paris. Suddenly, society established an institution "which combined the characteristics of a penal institution, an asylum, a workshop, and a hospital (Rosen, 1967; Foucault, 1967).

Change occurs for many reasons, but the main one is the increasing dominance of science. Scientists are value-free, objective to the core. Morality, economic problems, poverty: these are no basis for medical classifications. And as scientists gained knowledge and power in the eighteenth and nineteenth centuries, so did "objective" views of madness. Where the practice of witchcraft was heresy in the seventeenth century, it is mental illness in the twentieth. Where gods played a part in seventeenth-century madness, they are excluded in the twentieth. Indeed, even though study failed to confirm Freud's hope that all mental problems had physiological roots, psychiatrists generally see no difficulty. Whether physical or mental, certain forms of behavior are objectively classified as illnesses. Why? Because doctors say so. And who can disagree with objective facts? Doctors base their judgments on science and if they tell us asylums are only for the ill, that is a fact. Doctors say so (Foucault, 1967; Szasz, 1970a; Freud, 1960).

Doctors are wrong. Since virtually all forms of thought and action labeled mental illness are not caused—at a minimum—primarily by physical problems (see, for example, Coleman, 1972), doctors root their diagnoses of supposedly symptomatic behavior in an analogy. Granted, mental problems often have no physical causes, but mental problems resemble illnesses in some ways and that resemblance is the basic justification that doctors (and other people) use in labeling certain types of thought and action as sick, diseased, unhealthy, and ill.

The analogy between physical and mental problems breaks down for many reasons. First, if mental problems were a "disease entity, like an infection or malignancy," we could *catch* schizophrenia or *get* hysteria. Also, a person might *have* paranoia or *transmit*, as if it were germlike, delusions of grandeur. Finally, if mental problems were really illnesses, people could get rid of them. Perhaps we still lack the proper serums, but it is hard to imagine people taking shots that make them immune from psychosis (Szasz, 1970b).

Second, when doctors discuss illness and disease, they continually refer to signs (such as fever) or symptoms (for example, pain) that alert them to the physical problem. Being human, doctors can diagnose symptoms improperly, but signs and symptoms of physical problems are objective and universal; for a competent physician, fever is fever anywhere in the world. However, subjectivity enters when we turn to "symptoms of mental illness." Here doctors "refer to a patient's communications about himself, others, and the world about him." Perhaps the man says he is Christ (see Rokeach, 1964) or Napoleon or Hitler. Manifestations of mental problems are many, but where fevers or tumors or spotted lungs are "tied to an anatomical and genetic context," declarations of identity or constant fears of persecution are "inextricably tied to the social, and particularly the ethical, context" in which they occur. So, consider the contradiction: signs and symptoms of mental illness are measured in terms of deviations from culturally relative *psychosocial* and *ethical* norms, but "the remedy is sought in terms of *medical* measures" that are supposedly objective and universal (Szasz, 1970b, 1961; also Scheff, 1966, 1974, 1975).

This makes no sense. Values and beliefs are "up front" in any diagnosis of mental problems, the main reason being the nature of our relationship to social and ethical norms. Where our ties to medical norms (for example, dress warmly in cold weather, eat properly) are basically physical, our ties to social norms are basically political[1] (Goffman, 1971). Having learned in childhood that men and women wear clothes to work, I can decide in adulthood that this is a silly or perhaps a bourgeois norm. "I will go to work nude!" This decision to be abnormal is political; it is rooted in my refusal to accord *legitimacy* to an inherited social norm. Conceivably, my decision to wear nothing is a result of problems caused by

---

[1] The word *political* is used in the widest sense possible. It does not refer to Democrats, Republicans, or Socialists. It does refer to the sense of legitimacy people do or do not accord particular social norms.

significant others; or, it could be a dramatic gesture of revolutionary consciousness. Whatever the motivation, a diagnosis of this behavior as a sign or symptom of mental illness is neither objective nor universal. On the contrary, such a diagnosis inevitably reflects the doctor's political relationship to the norm in question. Obviously, wearing nothing in a society that demands clothing is abnormal. But to label this behavior as sick is to use a medical classification for a political decision; it is to argue that, presto, the subjective and culturally relative equal the objective and universal (Goffman, 1971; Szasz, 1970a).

If the basis of our relationship to medical and social norms is fundamentally different, why has this very weak analogy gained such prominence? One reason is Sigmund Freud. Certainly the most influential of early researchers on mental difficulties, Freud labeled various problems in living (for example, hysteria) as mental illness, and his classifications furnished the basis for most early thinking about mental problems (Szasz, 1961). Second is the importance of science in the industrial societies of the twentieth century. Freud never worked in a vacuum. He worked in a society (and so de we) dominated by the "mindscape of scientific rationality" (Roszak, 1973). It was only "natural" to adopt a scientific stance when interpreting odd forms of behavior (for example, witchcraft or homosexuality), and it was only "natural" for others to accept supposedly scientific classifications of mental problems. For, in contrast to ancient Greece or Rome, modern industrial societies *are* disenchanted; we *do* consistently refuse to accept explanations rooted in faith or irrationality. At times, our allegiance to science produces peculiar diagnoses of behavior—"If you talk to God, you are praying; if God talks to you, you have schizophrenia" (Szasz, 1973)—but the point is that a medical classification of mental problems was likely to achieve widespread acceptance in societies dominated by science.

A third factor accounting for the acceptance of the weak physical-mental analogy is the kind of behavior normally labeled mentally ill. Scheff calls it "residual rule-breaking" (Scheff, 1966, 1975), with the idea that thought or action generally labeled sick refers to norms where the culture provides no firm definition of the situation. For example, if a person declares, "I am God," the "formal means of social control do not apply" (Goffman, 1971). People cannot be jailed for such a claim, nor can they lose their right to vote. But what do we call this behavior? It is not immoral or illegal or probably even rude. It is only a proclamation of divinity. Say, too, that "the offender makes little effort to conceal this offense or ritually neutralize it" (Goffman, 1971). One can see the person asserting his divinity in a public place; he makes no effort to hide his abnormal claim, nor is he embarrassed or ashamed when approached by others. On the contrary, instead of trying to neutralize his behavior with an explanation ("I'm rehearsing for a play") or an apology ("Sorry, I don't feel well today; I'm having family problems"), "God" makes an effort to bring us into the fold.

Again, what do we call this claim? Today we label it mental illness, but Goffman brilliantly argues we do so primarily because this type of residual rule-breaking[2] threatens to create "organizational havoc." Generally, mental symptoms refer to behavior where the formal means of social control do not apply, where the person makes no attempt to conceal or neutralize the behavior, *and* where, for various reasons, the offender and offended cannot "resolve the issue by physically withdrawing from the organization (for example, a corporation, a family, a church, a school) and relationship (husband-wife, employer-employee) in which the offense occurs, and the organization cannot be reconstituted to legitimate the new self-assumptions of the offender—or, at least, the participants strongly feel that these adaptations are not possible" (Goffman, 1971).

So, what do we label a loved father who thinks he is Napoleon? Goffman's answer is that although we lack a label—the "grammar" of conduct is nonexistent—we create social order by filling the void with scientific terms that are, if nothing else, consistent with dominant cultural assumptions. Remember the person is openly making statements about self and world "which the relevant bit of social organization can neither allow him nor do much about" (Goffman, 1971). Naturally, there is the option of permitting the person to freely think and act like Napoleon. But to take this option is to deny the relevant bit of social organization (that is, Napoleon is dead and he cannot be Napoleon) or to redefine cultural norms in a way that permits people with problems to remain with "the normals." For example, if I say "I am God," but I do not interfere with your public freedoms, legal norms could say it is all right for me to live in society rather than an asylum.

Such tolerance is unlikely. First is the question of public order. Most societies refuse to allow manifestly "abnormal" people to freely roam the streets. Second, and much more important, people with problems in living attack "the syntax of conduct." Normally people meet with "workable" definitions of self and others: You are a student, I am a teacher, and even though we may disagree about aspects of the two roles, normally our defi-

---

[2] For other examples, consider the person who frantically fears that priests and nuns are "out to get him." Or the person who, after twenty-five years of business success, turns hippie and moves lock, stock, and guitar to a commune. Or the person who suddenly decides he is rich, spends thousands of dollars on his family, and, since he is actually broke, sends the family into the poorhouse. In each instance, the behavior is bizarre or abnormal but, if we do not employ medical terms, what labels do we use? Does "irresponsible" suffice for our big spender? Is "peculiar" enough to account for a frantic fear of nuns?

nitions of self and others are workable enough to permit comfortable interaction. But people with problems refuse to make "working agreements" (McCall and Simmons, 1966). Daddy is not Napoleon! And this *expression* of self dramatically fails to confirm what his role implies (Goffman, 1971; also Laing, 1960). So, because paranoids or catatonics refuse to cooperate, they undermine the very syntax of conduct by "deranging" the usual agreement between posture and place (for example, "You may be Adam, but nobody walks around stores in the nude"), between expression and position (that is, "You are my father—my husband, my son, my employee—you are not Napoleon!"). This makes the rest of us very uncomfortable, and in order to somehow sustain the grammar of activity, we resort to the medical analogy and label the uncooperative as mentally ill.

If schizophrenics are not mentally ill, what are they? Is it true that people with problems in living are anything the society labels them (see, for example, Scheff, 1966, 1975)? On one level, the answer is yes. In Russia people with mental symptoms were often labeled "malingerers" (Szasz, 1961), and while American psychiatrists traditionally labeled homosexuality as an illness, they have now reversed course and decided homosexuality is no longer a sickness. Or, consider the sexist bias of medical terms. Studies show that clinicians have different concepts of health for men and women, with these differences paralleling the sex-role stereotypes dominant in our society. So, if a woman acts like a woman, she is sick because she does not act like a man; but, if she acts like a man, doctors often say she is sick because she does not act like a woman (Broverman et al., 1970; Chesler, 1973)!

On the level of the actual term used (for instance, *malingerer* as opposed to *mentally ill*), the labels given to people with problems in living *are* socially and historically relative. However, to the extent that people's behavior meets Goffman's criteria,[3] the labeling theory of mental illness is insufficient. Any society in any period of history contains people who have assumptions about self and world "which the relevant bit of social organization can neither allow him nor do much about." Labeling of this behavior is culturally relative, but the persistence of people whose peculiar assumptions threaten the syntax of conduct is a cultural universal. For example, the Hippocratic book on *The Sacred Disease* cites people imitating goats, people foaming at the mouth, and people who wake in a delirium, "jumping from the bed and rushing out of doors" (Rosen, 1967). In ancient Greece, explanations were religious (and so the label "sacred

---

[3] That is, the formal means of social control do not apply, the person makes no attempt to hide or neutralize his behavior, and the offender and offended cannot resolve the issue by withdrawal.

disease") but, like today, anyone who imitates a goat threatens to disrupt the working agreements that normally sustain everyday life. So, like the Greeks, we use the labels dominant in our society to try to sustain the grammar of activity.

What is to be done? Well, since mental illness is a myth, we need another label to refer to people with peculiar assumptions about self and world. This new label will not be any less culturally relative than the "sacred diseases" of the ancient Greeks, but it will at least rescue people from the medical classifications that often deprive them of their civil rights. Again, 90 percent of the people in asylums are involuntary inmates, and various authors argue that few of these people pose any danger to those who live outside asylum walls (see, for example, Goffman, 1961; Rosenhan, 1975; Brandt, 1975).

One promising suggestion for a new label is "problems in living" (Szasz, 1961). Here, the label underlines the pain and anxiety that fill the lives of people with mental symptoms, but, avoiding the use of the words illness or sickness or disease, "problems in living" stresses that mental symptoms are basically a legal problem. How far does the society go in forcing people into hospitals? What are the legal rights of people said to have problems in living? Why can't people who proclaim their divinity, but never interfere with the public freedoms of others, be permitted to do as they please?

Answers to these questions are anything but matters of objective fact. For example, a political libertarian, Thomas Szasz, is against all forms of involuntary hospitalization. Theoretically, this is an admirable position in a democratic society, but what about people with problems in living who daily try to kill themselves? Or what about a mother and father who have driven their child into a catatonic state? Can society leave the child alone? Should people be permitted to kill themselves if they want to? I have my answers (no, yes), Doctor Szasz has his, and you have yours. Unfortunately, the three of us have not gotten together to create a label that rescues people from the tyranny of mythical medical classifications and, simultaneously, provides satisfactory answers to the ticklish questions raised by refusing to label mental symptoms as mental illness.

Over thirty years ago, Harry Stack Sullivan discussed the "one-genus postulate." The notion derived from a failure: Working all his professional life with schizophrenics, Sullivan found "nothing to substantiate" the argument that physical factors were the primary cause of schizophrenia (Sullivan, 1961). So he came to the conclusion that explanations of schizophrenia required "for their complete exposition nothing different in essential quality from the elements of commonplace human life." People *got* schizophrenia and they *got* normal. Everyone developed his view of, and response to, self and world in the process of social experience, and while it was "preposterous" to argue "that the individual in the depths of schizophrenic processes was to be understood by a reference to an average individual. . . . ," Sullivan stressed that everyone developed through a process of interaction with others. The problem was to discover how and why schizophrenics developed such painful, such agonizing problems in living.

Since thirty years of research have lent considerable support to Sullivan's postulate, we will examine the evidence below. Hopefully it shows how the concepts and principles discussed in earlier chapters shed light on people with problems in living. Hopefully it shows how the thoughts and actions of schizophrenics are generally a very legitimate response to the bizarre world created by others. For research conducted in many parts of the world makes one thing clear: "There has never been a schizophrenic who came from a stable family" (Lidz, in Boyers and Orrill, 1972).

SCHIZOPHRENIA AS A HUMAN PROCESS

What is schizophrenia? From one perspective it is the general term used to group people whose behavior is characterized by gross distortions of reality, disorganized and fragmented perceptions, thoughts, and emotions, and in many cases total withdrawal from reality (Coleman, 1972). From another perspective schizophrenia is "the name we have for the other person in a disjunctive relationship of a particular kind." One person is sane by common consent and in interaction with another, the other does things (for example, never speaks; has delusions of influence, persecution, sin; hears voices heard by no one else) that cause the sane person to use the term *schizophrenic* (Laing, 1960; Haley, 1959a, b).

Although the chart below shows many forms of schizophrenia, our discussion will focus on two features common to all the various types. First, whether paranoid or hebephrenic, simple or acute, schizophrenics manifest disturbed relations with others. Consistently, they explode the usual agreement between posture and place, between expression and position; consistently, schizophrenics are unable to interact effectively with others. Second, all schizophrenics show varying degrees of personality disorganization. Thought is unintegrated, and delusions or hallucinations or catatonia prevent adaptive behavior (White, 1964).

Since schizophrenia often occurs in the family backgrounds of schizophrenic patients, researchers have continually sought to explain it only in terms of heredity. To date no one has succeeded. Various studies find strong support for a possible genetic predisposition to schizophrenia, but accepting this as a cause still leaves the exact contribution of genes a matter of debate. Remember, too, there are basic problems with the genetic argument. Coleman notes that while a vitamin deficiency disease such as beriberi also runs in families, no one argues it is genetically transmitted. And what about the low reproductive rate of schizophrenics? Only 70 percent have children of their own, but the rate of schizophrenia is a societal constant. So perhaps the pool of pathological genes is always subject to mutations? Or perhaps some forms of schizophrenia are caused entirely by social factors (Coleman, 1972; White, 1964; Lidz et al., 1963)?

While the exact role of genetic factors is still unknown, the evidence about the influence of others is so dramatic that the author (for one) finds it hard to believe genes do more than predispose people to schizophrenia. For example, one legitimate question raised by those who criticize interaction approaches to schizophrenia is, "Why don't the other children also become schizophrenic? If the mother and father are so terrible, why aren't all the children affected?"

The answer is, they are. In studies conducted at Yale, Theodore Lidz and his colleagues studied the twenty-four brothers and sisters of sixteen schizophrenic patients. They found: three clinically schizophrenic, seven borderline schizophrenics, eight emotionally disturbed, three adequately adjusted, and 3 well adjusted. However, the greatest interest of these findings comes when we go beyond statistics. Children who adjusted used two defensive maneuvers: they literally fled the family, and three of the best adjusted "suffered from marked constriction of their personalities, with notable limitations in their range of emotional maturity, their perceptiveness, and the use of their intellectual resources." Among brothers and sisters of the same sex as the patient, the Lidz group found much more personality disturbance than siblings of the opposite sex. And, finally, study showed schizophrenic children were treated differently from the others. In some cases the child was a scapegoat for the parents; in others the child tried to satisfy two parents who hated one another by being a different person for each parent. But, no matter what the pattern, study showed "that the patient's involvement commonly relieved the other children of many burdens" (Lidz et al., 1963; also Wynne et al., 1968; Bateson, 1956; Laing and Esterson, 1970).

Genes furnish one possible biological explanation for schizophrenia. Another is a biochemical imbalance. In studies done at the Tulane Medical School, two volunteers were injected with taraxein, a substance found in the blood of schizophrenic patients. Over time one patient developed a catatonic-type reaction, the other a paranoid-type (Coleman, 1972). Naturally, such findings generated great interest but other researchers failed to confirm the effect of taraxein, and to date "there is no conclusive evidence that the basic etiological pattern in schizophrenia can be explained in terms of biochemical irregularities" (Coleman, 1972).

Still other biological explanations of schizophrenia exist, for example, in terms of neurophysiology. It is enough for us, however, that to date biology accounts for no more than a predisposition to schizophrenia. Conceivably, new studies will alter this conclusion, but perhaps it is well to remember a suggestion first made in 1956: "Year after year papers appear which purport to distinguish between the state of schizophrenia and that of normalcy. The sum total of the differences reported would make the schizophrenic patient a sorry specimen indeed: his liver, brain, kidney, and circulatory functions are impaired; he is deficient in practically every vitamin; his hormones are out of balance, and his enzymes are askew. Fortunately many of these claims of metabolic abnormality are forgotten in time . . . but it seems that each new generation . . . has to be indoctrinated—or disillusioned—without benefit of the experiences of its predecessors" (Horwitt, in Coleman, 1972).

Entering the family world of schizophrenics is overwhelming (no other word will do). Researchers use terms like "transmission of irrationality" (Lidz et al., 1958), the "double-bind" (Bateson et al., 1956), "pseudo-mutuality" (Wynne et al., 1968), "marital schism and marital skew" (Lidz et al., 1957a), fathers whose striking characteristic is the "constant derogation of the son" (Lidz et al., 1957b), mothers who are characterized by a capacity for denial, distortion, and a virtually total inability to accept or recognize the child's individuality (McGhie, 1961a, b). Overall, the child's family world is flooded with anxiety, lies, bickering, double messages, hatred, and contradiction. Somehow, the child is supposed to gain a sense of self-esteem and a firm hold on reality from the frightening and bizarre world created by his significant others.

This is impossible. For children cannot become objects to themselves until they are first the subject of other people's thoughts and actions. Tragically, the child who develops into a schizophrenic inherits others who make him or her a subject of constant derogation or a subject of perpetual contradiction or a subject whose self-image is rooted in the quicksand of the parent's serious problems in living. In the end a schizophrenic's significant others succeed in only one thing: driving the child away from the reality that is actually there (Searles, 1959).

Researchers who focus on the role of significant others in producing schizophrenia approach the problem from a variety of perspectives. One is communication, the way in which significant others talk to, and act toward, the child who becomes schizophrenic. Here we meet the notion of the "double-bind." People simultaneously receive, often from the same person, two contradictory messages. For example, first is "a primary negative injunction"; the child is told "Don't do this" or "If you do this, I'll punish you." Then, while the child is being punished, he is told "Do not see me as the punishing agent" or, better, "Do not think of what you must not do." Sometimes, the first comment is verbal, the second transmitted by

Summary of Types of Schizophrenia

ACUTE TYPE—Characterized by a sudden onset of undifferentiated schizophrenic symptoms, often involving perplexity, confusion, emotional turmoil, delusions of reference, excitement, dreamlike dissociation, depression, and fear. The individual seems to undergo a massive breakdown of filtering processes, with the result that experience becomes fragmented and disorganized, taking on the qualities of a nightmare.

PARANOID TYPE—A symptom picture dominated by absurd, illogical, and changeable delusions, frequently accompanied by vivid hallucinations, with a resulting impairment of critical judgment and erratic, unpredictable, and occasionally dangerous behavior. In chronic cases, there is usually less disorganization of behavior than in other types of schizophrenia, and less extreme withdrawal from social interaction.

CATATONIC TYPE—Often characterized by alternating periods of extreme withdrawal and extreme excitement, although in some cases one or the other reaction predominates. In the withdrawal reaction there is a sudden loss of all animation and a tendency to remain motionless for hours or even days, in a stereotyped position. The clinical picture may undergo an abrupt change, with excitement coming on suddenly, wherein the individual may talk or shout incoherently, pace rapidly, and engage in uninhibited, impulsive, and frenzied behavior.

HEBEPHRENIC TYPE—Usually occurs at an earlier age than most other types of schizophrenia, and represents a more severe disintegration of the personality. Emotional distortion and blunting typically are manifested in inappropriate laughter and silliness, peculiar mannerisms, and bizarre, often obscene, behavior.

SIMPLE TYPE—An insidious depletion of thought, affect, and behavior, beginning early in life and gradually progressing until the individual impresses others as being curiously inaccessible, isolated, colorless, and uninteresting. Because psychological disorganization is typically less severe than in other types of schizophrenia and some superficial contact with reality is usually maintained, hospitalization is less frequent.

SCHIZO-AFFECTIVE TYPE—Characterized by a mixture of general schizophrenic symptoms, in conjunction with more pronounced obvious depression or elation—not typical of the usual surface pattern of "flattened affect."

LATENT TYPE—Characterized by various symptoms of schizophrenia but lacking a history of a full-blown schizophrenic episode.

CHRONIC UNDIFFERENTIATED TYPE—Although manifesting definite schizophrenic symptoms in thought, affect, and behavior, not readily classifiable under one of the other types.

RESIDUAL TYPE—Mild indications of schizophrenia shown by individuals in remission following a schizophrenic episode.

CHILDHOOD TYPE—Preoccupation with fantasy, and markedly atypical and withdrawn behavior prior to puberty.

posture, gesture, or tone of voice. Children are often acutely sensitive to these nonverbal communications and perhaps they are even more disturbing to the child than verbal contradictions. For instance, the mother asks the child to hug and kiss her but when the child does so, the mother freezes up, her anxiety or dislike quite apparent. Or the mother says, "Go to bed, you're very tired and I want you to get your sleep," in a manner and with a tone of voice that indicates, not concern for the child's welfare, but the opposite: "Get out of my sight because I'm sick of you" (Bateson et al., 1956; Bateson, 1960).

Double-bind is the child's position. Locked into an "intense" relationship where it is crucial for the child to accurately assess what is being said, but getting two contradictory messages from the other, and because the other forbids it or because of emotional blocks or intellectual inability, the child is unable to understand which message to respond to and so responds in a way that sane people call insane. Perhaps the child denies that anything was said. Or perhaps the child (over time) decides to be somebody else. Or perhaps the child responds by shifting to a metaphor. All these are characteristic forms of communication for schizophrenics and all symbolize the child's position. "Terribly on the spot," forced to respond—the other will not disappear—and unable to discuss the messages of significant others without considerable help from different others, the child reaches for responses and definitions of the situation that offer a measure of security in a world that permits none (Bateson et al., 1956; Haley, 1959a, b; Goldfarb et al., 1972).[4]

Probably, all parents sometimes put their children in a double-bind situation. What happens in the families of schizophrenics, however, is that "when family members interact, they confine themselves *almost entirely to disqualifying* their own statements" (Haley, 1959b, emphasis added; Laing and Esterson, 1970). This means that the basis for the child's learning to communicate with others, the foundation for his abilities in role-taking, is incongruence, incoherence, absurdity, and contradiction. In an instance reported by Haley, a hospitalized patient had sent his mother a Mother's Day card with the inscription, "For someone who has been like a mother to me." When the patient's mother visited him, she was obviously angry about the card but disqualified the obvious with laughter and statements such as: "I'll take all—Simon, believe me, I'll take all the hurt in the world if it will help you—you see what I mean?" The patient responded to his mother by imitating her double message. He apologized for sending the card but disqualified his apology by making it in a manner and tone of voice that indicated it was no apology at all. In-

---

[4] Relevant here is a suggestive study which found that, "when confronted with a conflicting message, children resolve the incongruity by assuming the worst" (see Bugenthal et al., 1970).

cidentally, while the son and mother were busy disqualifying what they said, the father responded by stating "that the son didn't mean what he said, and the card didn't say what he didn't mean anyhow" (Haley, 1959b).

If we remember that it is very characteristic of schizophrenic families to maintain a homogeneous environment for the children—in one instance a sixteen-year-old girl had never gone out on the street unaccompanied (Laing and Esterson, 1970)—the probable effect of communication via double-binds is clear. Based on role-taking experiences with significant others, the child responds, the child builds up a pattern for interaction, in which most communication with others is via incongruence and incoherence. And why not? That is the child's experience, it provides a measure of security, a "definition" of a situation others refuse to unambiguously define, and in its own way the child's response is a reasonable reaction to irrationality. After all, if others make no sense, why should the child? If they respond "almost entirely" by incongruence, how is the child supposed to gain a basis for communicating in a sane manner?

The answer is he or she cannot. The child must respond, and significant others furnish the basis for his acquired abilities in communicating with others. So, by continually putting the child in a double-bind situation, others often succeed in creating serious problems for the child. Like "Mrs. Church," they may repeatedly say they forget things, precisely recount twenty-year-old incidents, and then end with, "I think of those things, Claire—I mean I forget it and let it pass" (Laing and Esterson, 1970; also Tietze, 1949).

Inevitably, children fail to make sense of constant incongruence, and should parents load their *form* of communication with a *content* of hostility, the developmental result may be a paranoid personality. The child might think that "behind every statement there is a concealed meaning which is detrimental to his welfare." He might anxiously search for "hidden meanings, determined to demonstrate that he could not be deceived—as he had been all his life." He might think others are "out to get him" and, based on this reaction to the attitudes and actions of others, he might develop personality traits such as an obsessive suspiciousness and defiance (Bateson et al., 1956; Laing, 1965; Laing and Esterson, 1970; Schatzman, 1975).

Might is a big word. It is stressed to show that double-bind refers only to the form of communication found in the families of schizophrenics. Conceivably, that form is enough to produce a reaction such as catatonia, but in reality form always appears with content, for example, other people who are hostile, a dominant mother and a passive father, a mother and father who hate each other and use the child to "settle" their own conflicts. So, to better understand the child's reaction to the attitudes and actions of others, we need to ferret out some of the specific things significant others say and do to children who become schizophrenic. Today we still lack the knowledge of how form and content interact to produce specific types of schizophrenia. And perhaps this exact knowledge will always be missing; temperamental and situational variables affect the response of the person to the attitudes of others. However, the theoretical point is that form and content always work together; jointly, they produce the problems in living labeled schizophrenia (Fleck, 1960).

Let's begin with a specific example, the Grau family. From the outset this family was a forum for bitter conflict. Dominated by a man who "always believed his way of doing things to be right," everyday life was punctuated by violent arguments because Mrs. Grau had somehow failed to satisfy her husband's demands. And, as if personality problems were not enough, Mr. Grau was a Protestant who was opposed to Catholicism. Unfortunately, Mrs. Grau was a Catholic (Lidz et al., 1957a).

Soon after they married, Mrs. Grau said they would avoid child-rearing problems by avoiding the presence of children. However, Mrs. Grau became pregnant after three years and even though Mr. Grau assumed responsibility for birth control, the pregnancy so angered him that he struck his pregnant wife in the abdomen. The unwanted child grew up in a home where her most important significant others continually gave her the most contradictory knowledge about self and world. Mr. Grau always made it clear to Nancy (the child) that he hated and scorned his wife, using Catholicism as the prime basis for his contempt. Toward his daughter, Mr. Grau was a model of contradiction. He tried to win the child away from the mother, but he managed to combine permissiveness with harshness, criticism, and cynicism. For example, although he forbade dating before she was sixteen, he was lax about supervision, and then linked his indifference to anger and disappointment if the girl mentioned dates with a Catholic (Lidz et al., 1957a; Lidz et al., 1958c).

Mrs. Grau was very rigid with Nancy, "following to the letter strict schedules taught in her (child-rearing) book and she was apprehensive of any initiative the girl showed." Nancy responded with docility and conformity; when small, she never stood up to her mother or her friends. However, while passiveness was an answer to her mother's actions, Nancy had more trouble with her mother's attitude toward her father. For Mrs. Grau responded to her husband in kind; she continually criticized him to Nancy and began a long and bitter fight when she secretly had Nancy baptized. Mr. Grau later learned of the baptism, and it only increased his distrust of Mrs. Grau.

Now, let's try to put ourselves in Nancy's position. Others filled her life with anxiety, with fears, dangers, and situations that made her very uncomfortable with self and about world (on anxiety, see May, 1950; Rycroft, 1968). In an attempt to evade the constant tremor that is anxiety,

Nancy tried to avoid or minimize its incidence. Just before hospitalization, she engaged in fantasies that had her mother leaving home, her father remaining. However, because she inherited contradictions on so many crucial issues, Nancy never achieved security, nor did she respond to the problems of others with a sane view of self and world. First, satisfying one parent meant rejection by the other (Lidz et al., 1963). Nancy had no choice about a very poor "unique" image of self. Remember, too, that this poverty was combined with child-rearing practices that produced a passive child. Apparently, Nancy's mother frightened her into submission and that fear was another basis for a poor image of self. Second, since the father dominated the family, his outlook won out. He "trained Nancy to hate her mother," with the result that Nancy must hate herself if she resembled her mother. "He told me she's horrible. I agree. But, I'm like her in some ways. So, maybe I'm horrible too." Third, since Nancy chose to escape the daily double-binds by taking her father's side, his continually incongruent messages furnished no solace at all. Often he was simultaneously kind and cruel. Always, even though he favored Nancy, Mr. Grau also managed to communicate disappointment in her. Sometimes he did this by telling Nancy she acted like her mother (Lidz et al., 1957b; Lidz et al., 1958c).

Eventually Nancy became schizophrenic. Only by escaping into a world of fantasy could she avoid the unresolvable conflicts and profound insecurities inherited from others. Living in a world filled with hatred, conflict, and double-binds, Nancy passively faced it by fleeing it. She faced it by imagining it would go away.[5]

Nancy's response to others is understandable only in the context of her "unique" family history. Double-binds are constant and the anxiety they create is one cause of Nancy's problems in living. But she is incomprehensible without knowledge of the attitudes and actions of her significant others. Double-binds occur about specific things and Nancy must respond to specific things. In this case she must respond to two significant others constantly pulling her in opposite directions.

The case of Nancy and her parents is typical. Lidz and his colleagues call it marital schism, a situation in which two people with serious problems in living aggravate themselves "to the point of desperation" by marrying each other. Such marriages are filled with bitter conflict, recurrent threats of separation, and "a particularly malignant feature of these marriages is the chronic undercutting of the worth of one partner to the

---

[5] This is a simplified history of a complex family. For example, Nancy had a sister and there were still other problems associated with that relationship. I have only tried to underline Nancy's essential conflicts and her primary response to the attitudes and actions of others.

children by the other." Sometimes the undercutting is done to gain from the children the affection missing from the spouse; sometimes it is done to hurt and spite the other. Either way the battle between significant others creates "insurmountable" problems for the children (Lidz et al., 1957b; Fleck, 1960).

Schismatic families may be dominated by men or women and they create an environment in which catatonia is one sensible reaction to the attitudes of others. In another male-dominated family, the daughter sided with the mother but, like Nancy Grau, this girl found no security in her choice. In fact, when her problems became overwhelming, "the hospitalization and treatment all offered more opportunities for mutual nagging, for undermining the other's plans and hopes, and for holding each other responsible for this disaster" (Fleck, 1960). Like a turtle under attack, the daughter responded to her significant others by hiding; she simply remained mute at all times.

One last point about schismatic families. Fleck notes that breakdowns often occur when the child faces young adulthood. At twenty-one, the child is supposed to know who he or she is, to have a sense of self on a foundation of independence. So, when age and society ask the child to assume a role outside the home, he or she is forced to resolve an unresolvable situation. Since others always provided contradictory beliefs, no answer exists to the question, "Who am I?" And, since others furnished no basis for self-esteem or independence, the child is unable to deal with his or her problems. Nancy reacted with a withdrawal into delusions; the other woman embraced muteness. Both reacted to problems in living by creating more serious problems in living (Fleck, 1960; Laing, 1965; Birley and Brown, 1970).

In contrast to schismatic families, another pattern uncovered by Lidz and his colleagues was "marital skew." Here, one partner who was "extremely dependent or masochistic" married a spouse who seemed to be "a strong and protecting parental figure." In everyday life the dependent spouse went along with the other and "a striking feature in all cases was the psychopathology of the partner who appeared to be dominant," creating an environment that the "healthier" spouse accepted and taught to the children as normal. Always the dominant figure lived in a world of sham and unreality. Unfortunately no one told the children. In fact, sometimes the entire family shared beliefs and attitudes that had little relationship to the world labeled "sane" (Lidz et al., 1957a).

An example is the father-dominated Dolfuss family. Coupled with realistic abilities was Mr. Dolfuss's "paranoid grandiosity." He was interested in Eastern mysticism and along with a friend came to the conclusion that he was a "select, superior being." So he ruled his home "like an Eastern potentate." Only his adoring wife and the children's governess were allowed to enter his room. The children had to stay out, with the result being emotional deprivation, isolation from the family, and, because of the family's bizarre behavior, isolation from the outside world (Lidz et al., 1957b).

The Dolfuss's son became schizophrenic. Significant others gave him little affection, and the father combined this lack of warmth with an "almost insatiable" need for adulation from others. So, the lack of warmth produced a poor "unique" self-image, compounded by the son's learned awareness that any of *his* successes, any possible sources of *his* self-esteem, "threaten the father's need to be the shining life in the home." Now this threat was severe enough in a family where others told the child the father was great, wonderful, superior. But recall the boy's isolation from others; he had no other world and to risk conflict with the father over successes was to risk losing the only "security" life afforded. Better, then, to deny the obvious and lie to self and others. Finally, "the child may recognize that much of the father's greatness exists only in his own self-evaluation and self-deceit," but double-binds come in the form of denials from significant others (for example, the mother and the governess) and once again the child's isolation intervened. If he did not deny his perceptions of reality, he risked increasing the distance between the other people who provided him with his most important definitions of self and world (Lidz et al., 1957b; Fleck, 1960).

Reacting to the attitudes of others, the boy first tried suicide, at least one reasonable reaction to a world where others permit no sense of self-esteem. However, after some time in the hospital, this boy chose to embrace a new image of self and world. He decided he was superior and chose as his model, his father. He neglected his appearance, grew a beard, refused to allow haircuts, and not only looked like the Messiah, but quickly became preoccupied with religious mysticism. On an everyday level, the boy was "autocratic, pompous, and critical"; he stayed in his room and, just like his father, only allowed a few select people to enter. As if to stress his isolation from others, he often talked only in foreign languages; to avoid childhood deprivations, he not only hoarded his food, but during one stage of his hospitalization, "he devised a complicated airline system designed exclusively for transporting and distributing food supplies in such a way that his needs would be gratified from all over the world" (Fleck, 1960).

Without knowledge of his family history, this boy's behavior is inexplicable. His use of religion, his everyday action, is modeled after an all-powerful, unloving father. Probably the boy "decided" to use this readily available model as a way of coming to terms with the things others denied him: love, a sense of esteem and worth, food, coherent and congruent communication, security. In one sense the boy's response is a failure: labeled insane, he is put into a hospital. However, from the boy's perspective, and from the perspective of many children reared in a skewed family with one all-powerful yet disparaging parent, the manufacture of a new identity is a sensible way to gain control over self and world. Now he has the power. Now he is in control. Now he tells others when to come and go. His power assures the success of his food transportation system and, most important, his new definition of self permits him to confront others with some sense of esteem and security. Granted, he is schizophrenic but, safely locked into his new identity, he is "free" from a world that drove him to suicide.

Skewed families are also dominated by the wife and mother. In fact, since this pattern is so common, the literature contains many studies of mothers with schizophrenic children. Tietze said all her mothers were "fundamentally insecure people, who could feel relatively secure only if they could control the situation, . . . only if the situation was set and the rules of the game rigidly adhered to" (Tietze, 1949; Lidz and Lidz, 1949; Reichard and Tillman, 1950). Working in Great Britain, McGhie found the same thing. The "most outstanding features" of his mothers, "which appeared in all aspects of their behavior, was the mothers' capacity to project, deny, rationalize, and distort reality to suit their own needs." This warped their interpretation of events. McGhie was further impressed by the mother's "lack of acceptance of the child's individuality" and the degree to which mothers tightly and irrationally defined the situation for their children. Often these women had problems with sex, generally they rejected their own femininity, and "the most common criticism made by the mothers regarding the patient's father was that he was a weak character, lacking in masculine forcefulness and ambition" (McGhie, 1961a, b; Laing and Esterson, 1970).

Consider the Church family. Claire's label was paranoid schizophrenic. She was usually listless, without feeling; she hallucinated and among her delusions was the idea of an atom bomb inside her plus a feeling that others tormented her by "calling her a prostitute, cutting her up into little pieces, and torturing her without mercy" (Laing and Esterson, 1970).

Claire's mother dominated the family. Claire said "she was more of a managing-director than a mother. She was more interested in business than in being a mother and she brought the business woman's attitude into the home." Affection was absent and, although Claire was unable to explain why, her mother made her feel afraid. Claire said her mother "didn't like me to have my own ideas about things." So she grew up afraid to express her own feelings or ideas, following her mother's way instead of her own.

Although long hours of discussion proved Claire right, Mrs. Church denied everything. Her own problems and experiences dominated the family's life; nothing mattered except her perception of reality. For example, Mrs. Church said she and her daughter were very much alike. This was clearly false, but Mrs. Church simply denied reality and demanded that Claire follow suit. For Claire, everyday life meant a mother who attributed to her "memories, experiences, and actions that were disjunctive with Claire's self-attributions, while also being impervious both to Claire's own feelings and actions plus to her attributions about her self" (Laing and Esterson, 1970).

Combined with a lack of affection, Mrs. Church's actions gave Claire a very poor "unique" image of self, and her denial of Claire's perceptions not only undermined the child's confidence and communicative abilities, they also made certain she had no sure answer to a vital question: Who am I? Laing and Esterson stress that whenever Claire's accurate perceptions threatened Mrs. Church, she defended herself by muddling Claire, by rendering her speechless, by obliterating her memory, by continually inducing a disorganization in her personality (Laing and Esterson, 1970).

Added to all this were Mrs. Church's attitudes toward sex. Sexual feelings were permissible only in marriage, and Mrs. Church condemned "in the strongest terms" sexual behavior and sexual feelings that Claire kept entirely to herself. Spontaneity was forbidden, its manifestation a sure sign of breaking the rules made by Mrs. Church for her daughter.

Finally, the atom bomb. Claire was thirty-six and during World War II her mother allowed her "to work in the top story of a house, at the height of air-raids in one of the heaviest bombed areas, after having narrowly missed being killed when running to a shelter in an early air-raid." Presumably, Claire used these terribly frightening experiences to summarize the persecution she received from others; she had an atom bomb inside her which at any time might explode and destroy her (Laing and Esterson, 1970).

To repeat: today we still lack precise knowledge of how form and content together produce specific aspects of schizophrenia. Undoubtedly, time and effort will move us beyond the general hints we now posses, but to end this discussion, let us focus attention on yet another form of communication that research strongly suggests is an integral part of the family life of children who become schizophrenic.

Wynne and his colleagues call it "pseudo-mutuality," and they use the term to emphasize a "quality of relatedness" found in the families of schizophrenics. The idea is that all interaction is structured in terms of *some* kind of "fitting together"; people meet one another on the basis of shared beliefs, values, expectations, and perceptions of reality that allow them to understand one another, to fit together without major conflict or confusion. In "genuine mutuality," people meet each other owning a positive sense of self "and out of experience or participation together, mutual recognition of identity develops, including a growing recognition of each other's potentialities and capacities." But in "pseudo-mutuality," people are "predominantly absorbed in fitting together, at the expense of the differentiation of the identities of the people in the relation." For whatever reason(s), people need to see the other in a particular way, and in pseudo-mutuality they maintain the idea or feeling of fitting together even if they do not. Indeed, "in pseudo-mutuality the subjective tension aroused by divergence or independence of expectations, including the open affirmation of a sense of personal identity, is experienced as not merely disrupting that particular transaction but as possibly demolishing the entire relation" (Wynne et al., 1968).

Look at it this way. Children inherit others with serious problems in living; those others continually communicate by means of double-binds and, because of pseudo-mutuality, those others refuse to discuss their own problems or their constant contradictions. Come what may, significant others shape, perceive, and demand that children perceive self, others, and world in a manner that says yes to illusion and no to the reality that is actually there.

Our discussion of the mothers of schizophrenics cited a distortion of reality as their principal means of dealing with others. As early as 1950, Reichard and Tillman stressed the illusory quality of relatedness found in schizophrenic families. They said that "much that masquerades as love is really *pseudo-love* in which apparent affection and concern serve to mask the basically selfish demands made upon the love-object . . ." (Reichard and Tillman, 1950). Lidz and his colleagues never used the word *pseudo*, but in a paper discussing the "transmission of irrationality" they defined "masking as the ability of one or both parents to conceal some very disturbing situations within the family and to act as if it did not exist." Commenting on a skewed family dominated by a narcissistic father, they said that "the slightest challenge to his imperious and unrealistic demands provoked a storm of fury. These people must retain the necessary picture of themselves and their family. Some will fight to retain it; but others adhere to their conceptualization, which reality cannot alter or a new situation modify. They perceive and act in terms of their needed preconceptions, which they relinquish only under extreme pressures, and then with all sorts of maneuvers to explain through projection or ignore through isolation" (Lidz et al., 1958a; also Lidz et al., 1958b).

Like blinders on a horse, pseudo-mutuality ensures that children stay on the road that leads to schizophrenia. Indeed, the rule of pseudo-mutuality is the last element in a terrible inheritance from others. Recall that by means of isolation, significant others maintain a homogeneous environment, and then others fill this closed world with double-binds, pseudo-mutuality, and a host of their own very serious problems in living. The wonder is not the development of schizophrenia. The wonder would be sanity.

One final point. Mental illness is a myth. People are forced to undergo the most dehumanizing "treatments" only because they violate the syntax of conduct (Goffman, 1961; Scheff, 1975). O.K. Granted. But do we follow Ronald Laing's bird of paradise and embrace the schizophrenic experience? Do we, should we, seek to "turn on" to the insights of the schizophrenic (Laing, 1967)?

I hope not. Labels are culturally and historically relative, but they are also the best means people have of symbolically representing experience. That of the schizophrenic is one of the most acute anxiety, the most bizarre relations with others, the most terrible psychological pain. That experience has much to tell us about the development of problems in living; hopefully we see that Sullivan was right, schizophrenia is a human process. But I see no benefit in embracing catatonia or paranoia. Laing himself defined schizophrenia as "a special strategy a person invents in order to live in an unlivable situation" (Laing, 1967). I agree. But the schizophrenic's strategy is no solution. Pain, anxiety, and trauma are ever present; the strategy fails because the problems are never confronted. And if we endorse schizophrenia, the strategy will fail for us. Modern life is terrible enough. Must we imitate the schizophrenic and confront life by adopting an unworkable strategy?

Bibliographical References

Bateson, Gregory. "Minimal Requirements for a Theory of Schizophrenia." *Archives of General Psychiatry* 2 (1960): 477-91.

Bateson, Gregory; Jackson, Don D.; Haley, Jay; Weakland, John. "Toward a Theory of Schizophrenia." *Behavioral Science* 1 (1956): 251-64.

Birley, J. L., and Brown, G. W. "Crises and Life Changes Preceding the Onset or Relapse of Acute Schizophrenia: Clinical Aspects." *British Journal of Psychiatry* 116 (1970): 327-33.

Boyers, Robert, and Orrill, Robert, eds. *R. D. Laing and Anti-Psychiatry.* Baltimore: Penguin, 1972.

Brandt, Anthony. *Reality Police: The Experience of Insanity in America.* New York: Morrow, 1975.

Broverman, Inge K.; Broverman, Donald M.; Clarkson, Frank E.; Rosenkrantz, Paul S.; and Vogel, Susan R. "Sex-Role Stereotypes and Clinical Judgments of Mental Health." *Journal of Consulting and Clinical Psychology* 34 (1970): 1-7.

Bugenthal, Daphne; Kaswan, Jaques W.; Love, Leonore R. "Perception of Contradictory Meanings Conveyed by Verbal and Nonverbal Channels." *Journal of Personality and Social Psychology* 16 (1970): 647-55.

Chesler, Phyllis. *Women and Madness.* New York: Avon, 1973.

Coleman, James C. *Abnormal Psychology and Modern Life.* 4th ed. New York: Scott, Foresman, 1972.
Fleck, Stephen. "Family Dynamics and Origin of Schizophrenia." *Journal of the American Psychosomatic Society* 22 (1960): 333–44.
Fleck, Stephen; Lidz, Theodore; and Cornelison, Alice. "Comparison of Parent-Child Relationships of Male and Female Schizophrenic Patients." *Archives of General Psychiatry* 8 (1963): 17–23.
Foucault, Michel. *Madness and Civilization.* New York: Mentor, 1967.
Freud, Sigmund. *The Psychopathology of Everyday Life.* New York: Norton, 1960.
Goffman, Erving. *Asylums: Essays on the Social Situation of Mental Patients and Other Inmates.* Garden City, N.Y.: Doubleday, 1961.
Goffman, Erving. "The Insanity of Place." In *Relations in Public: Micro Studies of the Public Order.* New York: Basic Books, 1971.
Goldfarb, William; Levy, David M.; and Meyers, Donald I. "The Mother Speaks to Her Schizophrenic Child: Language in Childhood Schizophrenia." *Psychiatry* 35 (1972): 217–26.
Haley, Jay. "The Family of the Schizophrenic: A Model System." *Journal of Nervous and Mental Disorders* 729 (1959b): 357–74.
Haley, Jay. "An Interactional Description of Schizophrenia." *Psychiatry* 22 (1959a): 321–32.
Laing, R. D. *The Divided Self.* Baltimore: Penguin, 1965, first published in 1960.
Laing, R. D. *The Politics of Experience.* New York: Ballantine, 1967.
Laing, R. D. *Self and Others.* New York: Pantheon, 1970.
Laing, R. D., and Esterson, A. *Sanity, Madness and the Family.* Baltimore: Penguin, 1970, first published in 1964.
Lidz, Theodore. "Schizophrenia and the Family." *Psychiatry* 21 (1958b): 21–27.
Lidz, Theodore; Cornelison, Alice; Fleck, Stephen; and Terry, Dorothy. "The Intrafamilial Environment of Schizophrenic Patients: Marital Schism and Marital Skew." *American Journal of Psychiatry* 114 (1957a): 241–48.
Lidz, Theodore; Cornelison, Alice; Fleck, Stephen; and Terry, Dorothy. "The Intrafamilial Environment of the Schizophrenic Patient: The Father." *Psychiatry* 20 (1957b): 329–42.
Lidz, Theodore; Cornelison, Alice; Terry, Dorothy; and Fleck, Stephen. "The Intrafamilial Environment of the Schizophrenic Patient: The Transmission of Irrationality." *Archives of Neurological Psychology* 79 (1958a): 305–16.
Lidz, Theodore; Fleck, Stephen; Alanen, Yrjo O.; and Cornelison, Alice. "Schizophrenic Patients and Their Siblings." *Psychiatry* 26 (1963): 1–18.

Lidz, Theodore; Fleck, Stephen; Cornelison, Alice; and Terry, Dorothy. "The Intrafamilial Environment of the Schizophrenic Patient: Parental Personalities and Family Interaction." *American Journal of Orthopsychiatry* 28 (1958c): 764–76.

Lidz, Ruth Williams, and Lidz, Theodore. "The Family Environment of Schizophrenic Patients." *American Journal of Psychiatry* 106 (1949): 332–45.

McCall, George J., and Simmons, J. L. *Identity and Interaction.* New York: Free Press, 1966.

McGhie, Andrew. "A Comparative Study of the Mother-Child Relationship in Schizophrenia: The Interview." *British Journal of Medical Psychology* 34 (1961a): 195–208.

McGhie, Andrew. "A Comparative Study of the Mother-Child Relationship in Schizophrenia: Psychological Testing." *British Journal of Medical Psychology* 34 (1961b): 209–21.

May, Rollo. *The Meaning of Anxiety.* New York: Ronald Press, 1950.

Misler, Elliot G., and Waxler, Nancy E. "Family Interaction Processes and Schizophrenia: A Review of Current Theories." In *Psychosocial Interior of the Family*, edited by Gerald Handel. London: George Allen and Unwin, 1968.

Reichard, Suzanne, and Tillman, Carl. "Patterns of Parent-Child Relationships in Schizophrenia." *Psychiatry* 13 (1950): 247–57.

Rokeach, Milton. *The Three Christs of Ypsilanti* (New York: Knopf, 1964).

Rosen, George. *Madness in Society: Chapters in the Historical Sociology of Mental Illness.* New York: Harper & Row, 1967.

Rosenhan, David L. "On Being Sane in Insane Places." In *Labeling Madness*, edited by Thomas Scheff. Englewood Cliffs, N.J.: Prentice-Hall, 1975.

Roszak, Theodore. *Where the Wasteland Ends.* Garden City, N.Y.: Doubleday, 1973.

Rycroft, Charles. *Anxiety and Neurosis.* London: Penguin, 1968.

Schatzman, Morton. "Paranoia or Persecution: The Case of Schreber." In *Labeling Madness*, edited by Thomas Scheff. Englewood Cliffs, N.J.: Prentice-Hall, 1975.

Scheff, Thomas. *Being Mentally Ill.* Chicago: Aldine, 1966.

Scheff, Thomas, ed. *Labeling Madness.* Englewood Cliffs, N.J.: Prentice-Hall, 1975.

Scheff, Thomas. "The Labeling Theory of Mental Illness." *American Sociological Review* 39 (1974): 444–52.

Searles, Harold F. "The Effort to Drive the Other Person Crazy—An Element in the Etiology and Psychotherapy of Schizophrenia." *British Journal of Medical Psychology* 32, pt. 1 (1959): 1–18.

Sullivan, Harry Stack. *The Interpersonal Theory of Psychiatry*. New York: Norton, 1953.

Sullivan, Harry Stack. *Schizophrenia as a Human Process*. New York: Norton, 1961.

Szasz, Thomas S. *Ideology and Insanity*. Garden City, N.Y.: Doubleday, 1970a.

Szasz, Thomas S. *The Manufacture of Madness*. New York: Harper & Row, 1970b.

Szasz, Thomas S. *The Myth of Mental Illness*. New York: Dell, 1961.

Szasz, Thomas S. *The Second Sin*. Garden City, N.Y.: Doubleday, 1973.

Tietze, Trude. "A Study of Mothers of Schizophrenic Patients." *Psychiatry* 12 (1949): 55–65.

White, Robert W. *Abnormal Behavior*. 2d ed. New York: Ronald, 1964.

Wynne, Lyman C.; Ryckoff, Irving M.; Day, Juliana; and Hirsch, Stanley I. "Pseudo-Mutuality in the Family Relations of Schizophrenics." In *Psychosocial Interior of the Family*, edited by Gerald Handel. London: George Allen and Unwin, 1968.

PART TWO
PERSONALITY IN CULTURE

CHAPTER FIVE

How Is Society Possible?

Note the title of Part Two—"Personality in Culture." Whereas the first four chapters generally kept group influences in the background, now they are up front. For in Chapters Five through Eight, the main goal is to focus attention on the significance of culture and society for determining the actual, imaginary, or implied influence of others on people's thoughts and actions. Overall, we meet a variety of topics, from roles and role-making, to the presentation of self in everyday life, the limits of fabricating reality, and the importance of reference groups for our attitudes toward self and world. However, before we discuss any of these concepts and issues, let us first use Dostoyevsky's Underground Man to pose a very fundamental question: How is society possible?

> *I woke up nights thinking about it. "Why must I always get out of his way?" I panted in a hysterical rage. "Why always me rather than him? There's no law saying that that's the way it should be. Why can't it be fair, as it is when polite people meet—one moves aside a little and so does the other, and they pass respecting each other's dignity?"*
>
> *But that wasn't the case here. I kept stepping aside without his even noticing it. And then I got the most amazing idea.*
>
> *"What would happen," I thought, "if I wouldn't move aside—didn't budge, even if it meant pushing him? What would come of it?"*
>
> *This bold idea took hold of me. I had no peace. I kept thinking of it. . . . But the preparations took a long time. . . . I couldn't just go and*

do this hastily. Everything had to be thoroughly, gradually worked out. . . . I must admit, however, that after several attempts, I began to despair: we seemed desined not to bump into each other. . . .

Everything ended quite unexpectedly and as well as could be hoped. During the night I decided to give it all up and forget my futile plan. So I decided to walk along Nevsky Avenue to see how it felt, having given up my plan. I saw him about three steps away from me. Suddenly I decided. I closed my eyes and we banged hard against each other, shoulder against shoulder. I didn't yield an inch and walked past him as an equal! He never even turned around . . . but I know he was just pretending. I'm sure of it to this day. Of course, I got the worst of the collision, for he was much heavier. But I didn't care. What I cared about was that I had accomplished my goal and behaved with dignity. Without yielding an inch, I had put myself on an equal footing with him in public.

Fyodor Dostoyevsky, *Notes from Underground* (1864)

Odd behavior? Probably. But the situation of the Underground Man still gives rise to a good question: How can people walk crowded streets or packed college corridors without fights occurring at every turn? How can two people march toward one another, excitedly talk to a friend, avoid the oncoming human obstacle, and still continue talking and walking as if nothing happened?

One answer is that, like the Underground Man, we plot our route before beginning a walk. Another answer is that "rules of walking" exist, but we normally take these rules for granted; if pressed, we recall them (for example, step aside for handicapped persons or pregnant women) but normally life proceeds as if the rules were absent. We "know" them; we assume other people "know" them; they assume we "know" them; and together our assumptions serve as an unwritten agreement to "never" talk about our taken-for-granted knowledge. In effect, we normally walk on and by one another without conscious knowledge of the rules that permit peace and prevent conflict.

Now, walking only highlights the "unconscious" conformity that so often occurs among very different people. Taken-for-granted rules also exist for speaking turns in conversations (Duncan, 1972), as well as the physical distance customer and clerk maintain between them (Hall, 1972). And these "petty" examples overlook the numerous assumptions that have traditionally guided relations between, for example, Indians and whites. Only after Indians began to ask basic questions—Who says Indians are savages? Who says Indians must defer to whites? Who says God is white? —did relations between the two groups grow increasingly troublesome. Before then both generally took their inherited social identities for granted, and while conformity always made society unjust, conformity also made society possible. Indians accepted gross injustices in silence while whites loudly proclaimed their superiority. It was a series of assumptions and recipes for living that persisted for literally hundreds of years.

How is this possible? How can millions of different people normally interact so successfully—in areas as "distinct" as color and walking along a street? And if social order is normally possible, what makes it impossible? Can we isolate the factors that foster disorder? Are order and disorder related? Is the potential to remake society inseparably yoked to the ability to make society in the first place?

HOW IS SOCIETY POSSIBLE?

Georg Simmel writes that three things make society possible. First is our symbolic representation—our mental image—of another person. If only because of personal bias or need, these are always subject to error, but Simmel never stresses the mistakes "resulting from incomplete experience, defective vision, or sympathetic or antipathetic prejudices." His concern is the possibility of society and his focus is the distortions that result from seeing other people always generalized to some degree. For example, I see my wife, a unique human being; but I also see a woman, a mother, a journalist, and a wife. The unique person is inextricably embedded in a web of social identities. No escape is possible and that means no alternative. No matter how hard I try, I always generalize—distort—to some degree the uniqueness of another person.

Always is a big word, but that is Simmel's argument. We never see others *only* in terms of their uniqueness. We *also* see them generalized in some measure because uniqueness must be measured against some standard. In society the standard is a humanly made generalization (for example, American, Russian, lower class, upper class), and the unfortunate result of any generalization "is a fundamental change in the quality of the object perceived." After all, each of us is unique, a never to be repeated person. But by their nature generalizations abstract from the heterogeneity of reality and produce homogeneous categories. Although these typifications inevitably blur the unique person—by adding "a relation to other pictures"—Simmel's argument is simple: put up with generalizations or resign yourself to the impossibility of human society.

What are the origins of generalizations? Simmel gives no one answer, but he suggests that a basic cause is a "fact" of human life: "we cannot fully represent to ourselves an individuality which deviates from our own." In re-creating another, we can begin from a basis of similarity or we can try for objectivity by placing distance between ourselves and the other. Either way, "perfect cognition presupposes perfect identity," and Simmel feels that each person possesses "a core of individuality" which, like a locked vault, is not open for inspection. So, since "we cannot know completely the individuality of another," we generalize. It is an imperfect solution, but it is also the only one people can achieve.

Perhaps Simmel is right, but many writers point to another cause of generalizations: life would be very difficult without them. How, for example, would we know what to expect from others if we failed to categorize them? Without terms such as teacher and student, woman and man, customer and clerk, each meeting would be an "isolated and never-recurring experience" (Lidz, 1963). Definitions of the situation are impossible because we lack a basis for definition, and predictions about the future are worthless because each interaction is unique. Finally, without generalizations, how do we learn from experience? With no categories, we lack a basis of comparison; we lack a "set of expectancies" that allow us to look at yesterday and decide if today is different. Could we call ourselves civilized if we had not looked back and decided that some of our historical predecessors were "barbaric," "savage," "primitive" (Lidz, 1963)?

Actually, a search for the cause of generalizations takes us back to a major function of language and thought. Normally we name things or jobs or nationalities because it serves a purpose. Perhaps we want to convey information (He is a Canadian) or warn of dangers (She is a pinko) or transmit values (Black is beautiful) or guide actions (Students eat here). Aims vary, but the underlying cause is the same; interaction is much easier if we are familiar with, and knowledgeable about, the involved element of experience. In fact, if "the whole point of defining terms is to make it possible to go on and say something useful employing those terms" (Brown, 1965), generalizations perform yeoman service by providing answers to innumerable questions. Normally these answers suffice for the purposes at hand; if not, new answers are possible. But either way, generalizations furnish the knowledge necessary for learning from experience, as well as the knowledge necessary to predictably define the situations that characterize our lives (Schutz, 1970).

Although this is a significant achievement, it comes with a price tag: all relations between people "are determined by varying degrees of incompleteness." In the case of love, this incompleteness is small, perhaps even minute. But one beauty of love is its special nature. It is an uncommon relationship; it is rare to know—or want to know—another person as completely as lovers do. So, if we use love as a basis of comparison, we could all place our relationships with others on a scale of incompleteness. Undoubtedly, each scale would differ; a bank clerk's interactions are in sharp contrast to a psychiatrist's. But in society each of us is continually forced to classify others by means of general types. Inevitably, these types enhance (for example, aristocrat) or deflate (for instance, peasant) other people; inevitably, they hide the "pure individuality" of everyone we meet.

Simmel uses the metaphor of a veil. Because of generalizations, "people look at one another as if through a veil. This veil does not simply hide the peculiarity of the person; it gives it a new form." And this new form not only prevents our completely knowing the other; it acts as a barrier against our *wanting* to completely know the other. In the case of value judgments such as black or white, rich or poor, the barriers are removable; they relate to ideas of freedom and equality. But in the case of clerk or doctor or lawyer or barber, I am normally uninterested in completely knowing the others. All I want is a haircut; I will gladly engage in "small talk" but no more. The generalizations (barber and customer) place a welcome barrier between people. Granted, they hide individuality, "but the very alterations and new formations which preclude this ideal knowledge of the other, are, actually, the conditions which make possible the sort of relations we call social" (Simmel, 1970).

Generalizations channel our perceptions as well as guide and direct our actions; but not entirely. For the second factor making society possible is the "extrasocial nature" of women and men. Perhaps this derives from temperament or unique experiences or opportunities to see society from various perspectives. The causes vary, but the result is the same: a person's extrasocial nature "gives a certain nuance to the picture formed by all who meet him (or her)." In effect, no one is a total conformist; even the "perfect" bureaucrat mixes his social picture with all sorts of "nonsocial imponderables." Perhaps, instead of tranquilizers, he feverishly twists rubber bands. Or, instead of eating lunch in the company cafeteria, he goes to the park to share his meal with nature. The possibilities are infinite and the conclusion is that we all add to, or subtract from, even the most confining social identities.

Simmel calls this the "within and the without" of social life. In earlier chapters we saw this in terms of the "I" and the "me." Either way the idea is that people always "stand inside and outside of society at the same time"—the relationship between people and society is dialectical; one acts back upon the other and the result is the ongoing construction of social reality (normally) within the framework set by society. For example, bureaucracies ideally set precise rules for *all* employees. Professionals, however, are independent; they think for themselves. Working within bureaucracies, professionals can resolve the tension in many ways, but one study indicates that professionals turn a deaf ear to the bureaucracy's definition of the situation. They simply do what is professionally right, and while working within the bureaucratic system, their attitudes and actions place them—simultaneously—outside of that system (Haga et al., 1974).

How does this make society possible? The answer is in every way. After all, if people are not simultaneously inside and outside of society, if they cannot say no to the attitudes and actions of others, change is impossible.

Life becomes a series of yesses. I simply agree with what others tell me about self and world—and that is the end of it. I am a perfect social product. Others are perfect social products. And society is static; the dialectic makes way for a continuous mesh between self and world.

In a period overwhelmed by change, the idea of a static world is perhaps appealing. But that would not be society as we know it. Societies always change, with a root cause of change the human ability to stand inside and outside of society at the same time.

One final point. Everyone stands outside of society. But the ability to consciously make self and world the object of our attention—to achieve what was earlier called internal freedom—greatly increases the possibilities of society. For example, pondering the intellectual preeminence of Jewish people in 1900, the American economist Thorstein Veblen argued it was a result of circumstances. Rejecting their own Jewish culture, and rejected (because of anti-Semitism) by European society, Jewish intellectuals were less inside, and more outside, both societies than almost anyone else. This "marginal" position freed them from many biases, thus enabling them to see things closed to typical members of Jewish and European societies. One result of their insights was intellectual preeminence in early modern Europe (Veblen, 1963; Stonequist, 1937).

Few people become intellectually preeminent. But we all possess the ability to consciously step outside of society. Utilized, this ability frees us from many societal biases and opens up the possibility of a new and different society. It would still have generalizations; it need not approve of racism or aggression.

But if we have the ability to consciously rethink self and society, why is this capacity so often dormant? Why (recall the discussion of adolescence in Chapter Three) do few of us radically rethink the values of our parents and society? Why is substantial social change so hard to achieve?

One basic reason is the "preestablished" harmony that normally exists between a society and its infant members. In a sense, society is oblivious; it "takes its course as if each of its elements (people) were predestined for its particular place in it." By means of its cultural beliefs, values, and practices, society sets patterns for all to follow, and it audaciously assumes that "individuality finds its place in the structure of generality . . ." (Simmel, 1970). In short, while leeway is always given, society assumes that individuals internalize a culture in their early years and that, as adults, they are at least generally resigned to inherited patterns of thought and action. Hopefully, of course, people are actually happy to be members of American or Russian or Indian society.

Since most people generally follow societal patterns, Simmel argues that "preestablished harmony" is the third factor making society possible. In fact, it is the most important element of all because generalities typically derive their significance and meaning from preexisting patterns.

How can children stand outside of society until they are first inside it? How can I reject what others tell me to think, do, and have, until they first tell me?

So, we now turn to a discussion of culture and society. Hopefully, this begins to balance the thrust of the first four chapters. Earlier, the stress was on the individual. Here, we emphasize the typical. Our questions are: How, specifically, do preexisting patterns make society possible? And what is the effect of these typical patterns on what you and I—unique individuals—think about self and world?

Let's begin with culture. Culture is ongoingly made only by people, and the "finished" product refers to everything we think, do, and have as members of society (Bierstedt, 1957; Fernandez, 1975). Say, for example, that you and I were born in America in 1950. Before we came out of the womb, other people—our societal predecessors and contemporaries—made us their heirs. Given the chance, we might have said no to our inheritance; but nobody offered choices. Arbitrarily, others gave us the products of human labor; arbitrarily, others taught us what to think, do, and have as members of twentieth-century American society.

No one gets a choice. Everyone arbitrarily inherits a preexisting culture. And that is its power. Culture is external to every infant, and just because its institutionalized patterns of thought and action exist before we do, culture is capable of exerting a very powerful influence over our lives (Durkheim, 1957). Consider, for example, what Berger and Luckmann (1966) call the three moments of sociology: (1) people make culture, (2) culture stands as objective reality (out there), and (3) culture makes people (in here).

While culture always begins with people, no man or woman gets to make culture "from scratch." Instead, we must act back on preexisting patterns. These exist "out there," in the minds and actions of others; at birth and in the process of socialization, we internalize them. As Chapter Two illustrated, this process includes both cognitive and social maturity, but the general content of our thought is always supplied by culture. And even the opportunity to think at the "highest" levels is related to culture. For example, if preexisting patterns successfully define a group of people—say Indians—as inferior, can we expect those people to believe themselves capable of thinking as well as the culture's dominant groups? In effect, why should they try to succeed intellectually if their inherited definition of self says they never can?

While culture's power rests on its preexisting patterns, its influence is clearest when we consider the content of culture. First is what we think; included are ideas about virtually every aspect of our lives. From sex roles to god, from military obligations to the manifest destiny of the political form, from the need for competition to the belief in progress via the machine, from a faith in science to a trust in the virtues of education—all are examples of the pervasive influence of inherited ideas and all underline the extent to which our personal truth is often cultural truth. It is normally like a nearly finished Broadway play. The script is already written, the plot well laid out. Small rewrites are necessary and actors are even allowed to ad-lib, but only if trial runs prove disastrous is any radical revision of the script undertaken. Otherwise the show goes on, with the actors and actresses performing their assigned roles—some happily, some not.

Always, cultural ideas carry a freight of bias. Degree is relative, but all cultures teach their adherents to evaluate other cultures in terms of their own. Sometimes this is only amusing, for example, the American tourist who is shocked to discover that London lacks a McDonald's. But sometimes cultural bias breeds self-righteousness (many missionaries in the Far East), and often it is capable of blinding people to the lessons of history. For example, if culture defines formal education, the more the better, as a blessing, can we learn anything from cultures that train people "on the job"? And if culture defines other groups of people as primitive or uncivilized, do we arbitrarily write them off? Can we learn anything from their patterns of thought and action?

So, culture teaches us what to think and it even provides an interpretation of history. But culture does not stop there. It also plays a vital part in teaching us *how* to think. Alfred Schutz, for example, refers to "interpretational relevances" (Schutz, 1970). Culture teaches us how to interpret experience. Now to some extent this harks back to the question of bias—if we encounter primitives, we know how to interpret the experience—but it also points to something different. Culture places a value on the use of reason and science versus emotion and mystical experience. In interpreting a particular incident, say a faith healer who miraculously cures a paralyzed person, we know beforehand how to define the situation. In the twentieth century it is implausible for most of us to believe in miracles. Our ties are to science, to fact, to empirical investigation; to believe in miracles is to embrace the irrational. Heaven forbid!

Miracles are only one example. For by teaching us how to think, as well as what tools to use, culture constructs a scale of the plausible and the implausible (see Berger, 1967). Certain things are reasonable; others are not. Certain things are possible; others are not. Culture makes the rules, and it becomes our "job" to interpret experience by means of cultural definitions of relevancy. Incidentally, preexisting patterns sometimes conflict, thus threatening to make society impossible but, as in the case of religion versus science, there is no reason to assume that different aspects of the culture always mesh (see, for example, Freud, 1962; Berger, 1969).

Besides what we think, culture also tells us what to do. Sociologists call these *norms*, and the word ably stresses culture's power. Before birth, decisions were already made about society's definitions of normal and abnormal. Consider this story. Along with others, my wife and I were busily sending out invitations to our wedding. My job was to place invitations in envelopes, plus insert a piece of tissuelike paper. This was boring, but I *did* it. Then someone pointed out, after about twenty invitations, that I was putting the paper in the wrong place. It went inside the invitation, not outside of it. Individualist that I am, I unpacked each invitation and then *did* the proper thing. But not without a question: "Who says the paper goes inside the invitation?" Answer: Amy Vanderbilt's book of etiquette. That settled it. I "caved in" and did the normal thing.

The story, I hope, is amusing. But it should also make a point. Others decide for us what it is normal and abnormal to do and, generally, most of us embrace the definitions of others. Perhaps we fear looking silly. Or perhaps doing the proper thing avoids conflict. Or perhaps we wish to appear like the "right" kind of person. Reasons for obedience vary but results are normally the same: we follow collective definitions of the normal and do as we are told.

We all do this. Think of the rigid conformity—in dress or hair style—often imposed by counterculture groups and next time you view a crowded college classroom, look around. Experience indicates that virtually everyone dresses the same. Today, for teachers and students alike, it is the nonconformist who comes to class in a suit and tie or skirt and blouse.

Norms are generally broken down into three categories: folkways, mores, and laws. *Folkways* refers to things we do because custom says this or that is right. Examples are shaking hands rather than kowtowing, eating with a knife and fork rather than chopsticks, or, where Americans sprinkle salt on their food, in England custom says the proper thing to do is to make a little "mountain" of salt on the side of the plate. Then, when salt is wanted, food is dipped into the waiting supply.

Mores are normally more important than folkways. Here culture teaches that improper action threatens the welfare of the society or group. So, it is absolutely necessary to construct rules indicating what is moral or immoral behavior. Examples of mores are conduct toward animals or infidelity between a husband and wife or cheating on examinations, particularly at schools such as West Point or Annapolis.

Laws are norms formally enacted by a government. They can relate to anything, sometimes be changed with ease, and they are always backed by the power of the government. Examples are the income tax laws and the now dormant norm that requires every man in America to register for the draft within ten days of his eighteenth birthday.

Two final points. First, culture is thorough. Every norm is created along with a sanction for those who act abnormally. In the case of folkways, the sanctions are relatively minor; if one eats mashed potatoes with the hands, others will just never eat with him again. But if one breaks a law, the sanctions are often severe. Penalties sometimes include many years in jail, and in some countries lawbreakers still lose their lives.

Second, what we think and what we do are (normally) closely related. Laws supposedly put our ideas into practice, frequent baths apparently indicate civilized standards of cleanliness, and beating dogs or horses makes light of our belief in the value of life—human or animal.

So far, stress is on the power of culture; its preexisting patterns of thought and action furnish ready-made recipes for living and dying. But what about individuals? How do we become committed to the patterns of others? And why do we stay committed?

One obvious answer is that we learn them in childhood and as adults we resist change because it threatens our already established beliefs or vested interests. Another answer—also correct—is that it is hard to change what we never think about. So many of our beliefs and practices "present themselves as not in need of further analysis" that we actually take them for granted. In effect, socialization is so successful that we go through life without seeking to understand our beliefs—and so ourselves—in terms of origin and structure. Instead, we take it for granted that there is only one way to think and act: our way (Schutz, 1967).

Alfred Schutz makes the distinction between the "well-informed citizen" and the "man on the street." The former investigates and analyzes; he or she tries to understand beliefs and practices in terms of origin and structure. For well-informed citizens are dissatisfied unless they "know" how things got to be the way they are. But what about "the man (or woman) on the street"? They are content to accept taken-for-granteds. Beliefs and practices are given; there is no need to analyze or understand (Schutz, 1961).

No one is totally well-informed or totally "on the street." But if a balance sheet were made, most of us would wind up, if not on the street, at least on the sidewalk. Prove this to yourself. Have you ever asked why men wear ties? Have you ever wondered why time is money? Have you ever asked why masculinity is often defined in terms of being able to beat up others? And, before people such as Szasz and Goffman analyzed the idea of mental illness (see Chapter Four), how many of us asked if doctors had a right to send women and men to insane asylums?

Questions such as these are never ending. And for every one we have analyzed, there are countless others pleading for attention. In all likelihood, we simply lack the time to answer every question—but do we want to? Taken-for-granteds save a lot of time. What would life be like if we questioned everything? And, most important, is society possible without the preestablished patterns that so often breed a host of taken-for-granted assumptions?

The answer is no. Undoubtedly, human life would go on without patterns and assumptions, but the dictionary defines *possible* as "that which may be dealt with or put up with, tolerable, reasonable." Well, without patterns and assumptions, society is impossible, life (one suspects) intolerable. No one would know what to expect. No one could take anything for granted. Everything would be formless, life a journey on a road that apparently led to nowhere. In sum, it would be people without society, people without a (more or less) firmly institutionalized set of recipes for living and dying.

Patterns, assumptions, and generalizations are necessary for human society. But preexisting patterns never guarantee a perfect mesh among individual, culture, and society; nor do they guarantee justice. Patterns only make society possible. Perfection and justice are issues that must be tackled separately.

First, let's consider perfection. Simmel wrote that while "social life presupposed an unquestionable harmony between the individual and society, . . ." this harmony never did away with "violent dissonances." For "if social reality were determined by this presupposition of harmony alone, without the interference of other factors, it would result in the perfect society." Everyone would be fully integrated; no one would find any reasons to disagree. However, perfection is impossible because other factors do interfere. Before we spoke of the "within" and "without" of any human society. This is probably the basic cause of disharmony, but it is not—by far—the only one. Consider, for example, the situation of children of immigrants to America. They inherit cultural confusion: their parents are tied to the "homeland," while they live in the "new world." Inevitably they learn two patterns for living, and just as inevitably their life situation guarantees a certain degree of disharmony. Whether at home or at school, at work or at play, their ties to two patterns of living are sure to generate conflict. In the extreme their dual inheritance could make life intolerable.

As a second example, consider contemporary American society. We all inherit a culture whose preestablished patterns of thought often applaud change, as well as individualism. Among other things, this cultural stress produces fast-moving industrial change, daring and ominous biological research, and schools of psychology that direct people toward self-actualization. Can we be surprised, then, that writers speak of "cultural crisis" (Ortega y Gasset, 1957), of a society that exists "between past and future" (Arendt, 1953)? If we stress change, we will probably get it. That could be good or bad; judgments are based on our values. But a cultural stress on change guarantees disharmony between the individual and society. Inevitably it produces an imperfect society and for some, society is increasingly impossible. In a jet-propelled world, too many cherished beliefs and assumptions are cast to the wind. This is very unpleasant for almost anyone.

Now, to repeat, the causes of disharmony vary and the amount of disharmony is relative to the social and historical period under investigation. Sometimes it is small (primitive societies). Sometimes it is large (modern societies). But imperfection is unavoidable. Life is process; social reality is always continuously constructed. Cultural beliefs, values, practices, and taken-for-granted assumptions powerfully influence our lives; and by providing a more or less solid foundation for life, they make society possible. But, they are always grounded in process. Although social scientists can "stop the clock" with concepts such as culture, they cannot change social reality. That is always in the process of being made and remade by its manufacturers: people.

> His first adornment was the sleeveless dimity B.V.D. undershirt. . . . He never put on B.V.D.'s without thanking the God of Progress that he didn't wear tight, long, old-fashioned undergarments, like his father-in-law. . . .
> . . . Babbitt's spectacles had huge, circular, frameless lenses of the very best glass; the earpieces were thin bars of gold. In them, he was the modern businessman; one who gave orders to clerks and drove a car and played occasional golf and was scholarly in regard to salesmanship. . . .
> The gray suit was well cut, well made, and completely undistinguished. It was a standard suit. . . . The only frivolity was in his purple knitted scarf. With considerable comment on the matter to Mrs. Babbitt, he chose between the purple scarf and a tapestry effect with stringless brown harps among brown palms, and into it he thrust a snake-head pin with opal eyes.
> A sensational event was changing from the brown suit to the gray the contents of his pockets. . . . They included a fountain pen and a silver pencil which belonged in the right-hand upper waistcoat pocket. Without them, he would have felt naked. On his watch-chain were a gold penknife, silver cigar-cutter, seven keys, and incidentally a good watch. Depending from the chain was a large yellowish elk's-tooth—Proclamation of his membership in the Brotherly and Protective Order of Elks. . . .
> Last, he stuck in his lapel the Boosters' Club button. With the conciseness of great art the button displayed two words: "Boosters—Pep!" It made Babbitt feel loyal and important. It associated him with Good Fellows, with men who were nice and human, and important in business circles. It was his V.C., his Legion of Honor ribbon, his Phi Beta Kappa key. [Sinclair Lewis, *Babbitt* (1922)]

Babbitt was the perfect conformist. In fact, Lewis's portrait aroused (in 1922) such intense feelings, people despised Babbitt so much, that the word soon became part of America's cultural heritage. Passed on to the young as a generalization, *Babbitt* symbolized a person who said yes—

loudly—to inherited patterns of thought and action. Babbitts never thought for themselves. They allowed others to think for them and they wore the badge of conformity with no obvious signs of bitterness or remorse. Conformity was their way of life.

It is also our way of life. For we are all Babbitts to some degree. No one escapes societal dictates about thought and action—this is true even when we say no to society. Like adults who hate something because their parents liked it (see Chapter Two), our no to society means we are still unwittingly determined by the beliefs and values of others. Especially if our lives are one long no to what others first told us about self and world, we are determined by others, and in our passion to escape their noxious influence, we often join groups that are as conformist as any club that welcomed Babbitt (see Mannheim, 1968, Coser, 1956).

What can we do? Unfortunately, not as much as we would like to. For human life harbors a profound paradox: all people are simultaneously free and socially determined (Fernandez, 1975). We saw this in the chapter on childhood and in the section on adolescence. As children, we must root our images of self and world in the beliefs and actions of others, and it is not until middle adolescence that we normally acquire the ability to consciously stand outside the world and images learned and inherited from others. Only then can we "free" ourselves from what others told us about self and society. Obviously, freedom is always a relative achievement, but the ability to see the causes and consequences of our personal development is a powerful means of facing present and future on the basis of a consciously corrected past.

In the earlier chapters we focused on personality and its core—the self-concept. Here, we stress society. Any separation is arbitrary—"I am black" says something about self and American society. But our aim is to return to the question of social justice. What about the perfect society?

One answer is that it is impossible to achieve (Maslow, 1972). Another is that the question is meaningless unless we first possess an intimate understanding of the origin and structure of our inherited beliefs, values, and practices. Cultural determinism is real; it is a fact of every human life. There is no way to totally escape it but, in the same way that internal freedom furnishes insights into our personal development, it also furnishes insights into the development of any culture and society. Undoubtedly, Maslow is right: "the" perfect society is impossible. But since only people make society and culture, only they can remake it. This can be done through force; people can receive a "better life" at the point of a bayonet. Or change can occur so rapidly that people do not know what is happening to them; they only know they are unable to feel comfortable with the present (Toffler, 1970; Ortega y Gasset, 1957).

Another option exists. People can thoroughly investigate the origin and structure of their beliefs, endure the unavoidable pain of change, and peacefully build a very different tomorrow on the basis of a consciously corrected yesterday. This is possible; nothing human forces us to accept our inherited culture and society. Inevitably, change via internal freedom will threaten to make society impossible; a conscious look back (for example, the women's movement) is certain to undermine institutionalized beliefs and practices. But a very imperfect society is the price we pay for a tomorrow rooted in freedom from inherited beliefs, values, and practices. Peace returns only when we construct patterns of thought and action more to our own liking for example, Fernandez, 1977).

Bibliographical References

Arendt, Hannah. *Between Past and Future*. New York: Viking, 1953.

Berger, Peter. *A Rumor of Angels: Modern Society and the Rediscovery of the Supernatural*. Garden City, N.Y.: Doubleday, 1969.

Berger, Peter. *The Sacred Canopy*. Garden City, N.Y.: Doubleday, 1967.

Berger, Peter, and Luckmann, Thomas. *The Social Construction of Reality*. Garden City, N.Y.: Doubleday, 1966.

Bierstedt, Robert. *The Social Order*. New York: McGraw-Hill, 1957.

Brown, Roger. *Social Psychology*. New York: Free Press, 1965.

Coser, Lewis. *The Functions of Social Conflict*. New York: Free Press, 1956.

Duncan, Starkey. "Some Signals for Taking Speaking Turns in Conversations." *Journal of Personality and Social Psychology* 23 (1972): 283–92.

Durkheim, Emile. *The Rules of Sociological Method*. New York: Free Press, 1957.

Fernandez, Ronald. *The Promise of Sociology*. New York: Praeger, 1975.

Fernandez, Ronald, ed. *The Future as a Social Problem* (Santa Monica, Calif.: Goodyear, 1977).

Freud, Sigmund. *The Future of an Illusion*. New York: Harcourt, Brace & World, 1962.

Haga, William; Graen, George; Dansereau, Jr. "Professionalism and Role-Making in a Service Organization: A Longitudinal Investigation." *American Sociological Review* 39 (1974): 122–33.

Hall, E. T. "Silent Assumptions in Social Communication." In *Communication in Face-to-Face Interaction*, edited by John Laver and Sandy Hutcheson. London: Penguin, 1972.

Lidz, Theodore. *The Family and Human Adaptation*. New York: International University Press, 1963.

Mannheim, Karl. "The Idea of Generations." In *Studies in Social Movements*, edited by Barry McLaughlin. New York: Free Press, 1969.

Maslow, Abraham. *The Farther Reaches of Human Nature*. New York: Viking, 1972.

Ortega y Gasset, José. *Man and Crisis*. New York: Norton, 1962.
Pollner, Melvin. "Sociological and Common Sense Models of the Labeling Process." In *Ethnomethodology*, edited by Roy Turner. London: Penguin, 1974.
Schutz, Alfred. *Collected Papers*. 2 vols. The Hague: Mouton, 1961.
Schutz, Alfred. *The Phenomenology of the Social World*. Chicago: Northwestern University Press, 1967.
Schutz, Alfred. *Reflections on the Problem of Relevance*. New Haven: Yale University Press, 1970.
Simmel, Georg. "How Is Society Possible?" In *The Sociology of Georg Simmel*. Chicago: University of Chicago Press, 1970.
Stonequist, Everett. *Marginal Man: A Study in Personality and Culture Conflict*. New York: Holt, 1937.
Toffler, Alvin. *Future Shock*. New York: Random House, 1970.
Veblen, Thorstein. "The Intellectual Preeminence of the Jew in Early Modern Europe. In *Thorstein Veblen*, edited by Bernard Rosenberg. New York: Crowell, 1963.

CHAPTER SIX

Roles

*How the Monk Put Gargantua to Sleep and of
His Hours and Breviaries*

. . . Gargantua could not sleep, no matter how he lay. Observing this: "I never sleep so well as during a sermon or prayers," Friar John of the Funnels remarked. "I earnestly advise you to try my system. Let us both say the seven penitential psalms: we'll soon find out if you can sleep or not."

Gargantua, delighted with the idea, launched into the first of them; by the time they had reached Beatiquorum . . . or Blessed are the . . . they were both sound asleep. Yet the monk, accustomed to the routine of the cloister, did not fail to awake shortly before midnight. What then should he do but rout out the others by singing at the top of his lungs:

"The morning sun shines down on us
From the bright noonday skies
Wake up and labor, Lazarus
Up, lazybones, arise."

When all were roused, he addressed them as follows:

". . . Let us now begin matins with a stiff drink. . . ."

"To drink so soon after sleep is contrary to all medical science," Gargantua objected. "First we must clear our bellies of superfluity and excrement."

"My arse to your quacks!" growled Friar John. "A hundred devils trample me down if old drunkards do not outnumber old doctors. . . . My drawer, ho!"

> *"Your drawer?"* Gargantua asked. *"What do you mean?"*
> *"My breviary!"*
> *"Your breviary? . . . How do you say these fine prayers?"*
> *"Catch as catch can,"* Friar John replied. *"Three psalms, three lessons, like in Lent. The minimum, what? And sometimes, nothing at all, if the spirit so moves. Why should I tie myself down to hours and sacraments? They were created for man, not he for them. I treat my devotions as I do my stirrup straps, lengthening or shortening them when I think good:*
> *The shortest prayers go quickest to the sky,*
> *The longest draughts drain the decanter dry.*
> *I forget, what major prophet said this?"*
>
> François Rabelais, Gargantua and Pantagruel (1553)

To stress the rapid changes of today, scholars sometimes recall the Middle Ages. Then life was slow and static; powerful institutions such as the Roman Catholic Church set up rigid patterns of thought and action, precise rights and obligations that the occupant of a particular role—say, a monk—was bound to follow. Why? Because there were no alternatives, because the Church was powerful, because socialization supposedly produced a consensus that led everyone to share the same system of "value-orientation" standards (Parsons, 1951; Nisbet, 1973).

Change is a human constant (Moore, 1963). And despite the bias, exaggeration, and hilarity, Rabelais's work represents a trend in medieval thought. Some people wanted change. Like Erasmus in *The Praise of Folly*, they no longer cared about petty disputes on whether to make the sign of the cross with two or three fingers. People came first. Religion was for people, or, as Friar John said, hours and sacraments were created "for man, not he for them."

Friar John's beliefs led him to reject dominant "value-orientation standards." In fact, John not only rejected aspects of the culture, he remade it. "How do you say these fine prayers?" asked Gargantua. "Catch as catch can," "as the spirit moves me," replied the Friar. Or, put differently "I must do as I see fit and, despite the precise rights and obligations codified in Canon Law, I will role-make as I see fit. You tell me what I am supposed to do. I tell you what I will do."

Role-making is a human constant. Always the relationship between institutionalized roles and the person is dialectical. One is always acting back upon the other, and some scholars argue that "the formalized roles are to the full roles as detonators to explosives—merely devices to set them in motion" (Turner, 1962).

Who is right? What is the relationship between formalized roles (say, that of a monk or a teacher or a husband) and the person? And, if formalized roles only set people in motion, how do we define something—a role—that is always different?

ROLES: A DEFINITION[1]

The argument goes back to the earliest definitions of role. Based on work with preliterate peoples, Ralph Linton made a distinction between status and role. Status was a position in a particular group, a collection of rights and duties. Role was the dynamic aspect of status. Occupying a position, people put its rights and obligations into effect when they performed a role. However, not only were status and role "quite inseparable," the distinction between them was "only of academic interest." Apparently, Linton felt that, unlike Friar John, people performed roles as their statuses saw fit (Linton, 1936, 1945; also Neiman and Hughes, 1951).

Linton's definitions make at least two valid points. First, by stressing patterned collections of rights and duties, Linton underlines the fundamental importance of roles. They are "models for organizing the attitudes and behavior of the individual" (Linton, 1936); they are "the basic unit of socialization," the means by which society allocates tasks (for example, father, mother, teacher, firefighter) as well as makes arrangements to enforce their performance (that is, "If you don't teach or fight fires, you don't get paid.") (Goffman, 1961; Gerth and Mills, 1953; Berger and Luckmann, 1966). Second, roles often exist before the person. Part of our cultural inheritance, roles indicate "clusters of behavior norms" (Popitz, 1971); they refer to patterns that structure behavior in a way the society calls normal (Bates, 1956, 1957). For example, despite women's liberation, many wives in 1977 embrace patterns of behavior followed by their grandmothers, their great-grandmothers, their great, great-grandmothers, and so on (see, for example, Morgan, 1975).

The basic problem with these definitions is their indifference to reality. Whether it is Linton's argument that the distinction between status and role is only of "academic interest," or Bates's contention that roles are "part of a social position and not an expression of the position in action" (Bates, 1956; Parsons, 1951), a focus on the normative aspects of role lacks life. Interest is in the ideal, not the real. Interest is in what people are supposed to do, not what they do. Interest is in the enactment of a

---

[1] It is easy to think that *role* and *identity* refer to the same thing: I can think of myself as a father and also act like one. Identity, however, is a transsituational variable; I carry these notions with me "everywhere," and I need not engage in interaction to make them meaningful. For example, I can sit alone in a room and think about my identity as father. In contrast, role refers to the way a *type* of person *acts*. Put another way, the distinction between role and identity underlines "the experiential reality of being a thing (say, a sociologist) in a specific situation, as compared to the nonexperiential contemplation of being the same thing *in general* (Travisano, 1975; emphasis added).

prescribed role, not the process of interaction that may move people to add to, subtract from, or even remake roles (Turner, 1962; Komarovsky, 1973).

Consider some of the many variables that move people to role-make. First is the person. People are not zeros. A unique self-image and personality traits mediate between the prescribed role and its performance (Komarovsky, 1973). For instance, police departments have precise rules and regulations for the "cop on the beat," but some are cheerful, others harsh, some helpful, others condescending, some humane, others brutal. Second is the social situation. Teachers help students to learn, but teachers perform the same role differently when students are in their classroom and when students are in their home. Third is a social fact: interaction is a formative process in its own right (Blumer, 1969). One role means two: mother needs father, teacher needs student. And when a friend of the author's taught in England, his expectations were that students anticipated a formal, impersonal teacher. But in the process of interaction, his expectations were proved wrong. Students did not expect or want a formal role performance, and he reacted to them by remaking the role of teacher.

Below other variables are discussed that allow people to role-make. For now, if we seek to describe reality, we must have a definition of role that is rooted in the notion of behavioral norms but still flexible enough to confront the many variables that move people to perform roles in a way that reshapes the norms.

One good starting point is the idea of "working agreements." In performing roles, a working agreement exists when the "cognitive processes" of one person are not "in gross conflict with the expressive processes of the other person" (McCall and Simmons, 1966). Consider the professors at school. Students enter classes with certain expectations, but (normally) bend to the expressive reality that they find there. Some teachers demand attendance; others could not care less. Some teachers stress exams and quizzes; others do not. The list is long, with one also existing for professors, but the point is that with each professor the student has a working agreement. Probably small conflicts about roles may arise with each professor but, despite disagreements, the student manages to sustain a role relationship that avoids gross conflicts.

Are working agreements the common means used to maintain and sustain role relationships? The answer is yes. Perfect meshes may occur, but when self meets other, the relationship is affected by so many variables that two people are unlikely to achieve perfect satisfaction with each other's role performance.

Consider first the major reason that working agreements are possible: the existence of common normative expectations. Socialized in modern, heterogeneous societies, it is unlikely that my role cognitions will mesh perfectly with your expectations of what I should do.[2] However, socialized in the same culture, at home in the same universe of discourse, we do own a common yet broad framework for interaction. Professors are free to give or not give exams, but even if they only read from the assigned text, they are expected to teach something, as well as show up for class and grade students. And students are allowed to cut classes, but teachers expect them to put in an occasional appearance, as well as take any exams and hand in any assigned papers.

Common normative expectations are the basis for role relationships, but in modern societies the common framework is generally so broad that a precise mesh of self-other expectations is rare. If the role relationship is to continue, working agreements must be entered into and when we add other operative variables—the personalities of self and other, the situation, the process of interaction, the relative amounts of power each has over the other, idiosyncrasy credit—the chance for anything other than working agreements is very small. For example, consider idiosyncrasy credit. Defined as "an accumulation of positively disposed impressions residing in the perceptions of relevant others," the idea is that popular leaders often have the option of deviating "from the common experiences of the group." Well liked, respected, having prestige, self and other may meet owning the same normative expectations, but deviation occurs because the leader has idiosyncrasy credit (see Hollander, 1958; also Shils, 1965).

Because working agreements are the common means used to maintain and sustain role relationships, a definition of role must be based upon what is typical in different performances of the same role. Many scholars have offered similar suggestions, but Ralph Turner's definition seems the best: "role refers to a *pattern* which can be regarded as the *consistent* behavior of a single *type* of actor" (1962, emphasis added).[3]

The beauty of this definition is its firm hold on reality. For roles are patterned and people do act consistently, typically, when they perform roles. But because of working agreements, consistency and typicality are

---

[2] Working in preliterate, relatively homogeneous societies, Linton devised a concept of role that assumed a great deal of cultural consensus about the rights and duties of social roles. Today precise consensus is rare, but remember that degree of consensus is only one variable affecting the existence of working agreements. Preliterates also had personalities and varying social situations that allowed them to role-make every day of their lives. So, while preliterates often entered role relationships on the basis of a solid cultural consensus, the phenomenon of working agreements is a cultural universal. And that means that for preliterates and moderns alike, a definition of role must take account of role-making as well as role norms.

[3] In *Encounters: Two Studies in the Sociology of Interaction*, Erving Goffman comes to a similar conclusion: "role is the *typical* response of individuals in a particular position" (1961, emphasis in original). And William Goode says that role refers "to a set of mutual (but not necessarily harmonious) expectations of behavior between two or more actors with reference to a particular type of situation" (1960).

the closest we can come to describing role performances. This is so because everyday meetings between the ideal and the real only produce more or less consistency in the ongoing process of people enacting more or less institutionalized roles.

ROLES: FREEDOM VERSUS DETERMINISM

The dictionary definition of *determine* is "to limit in extent or scope, to put or set an end to." Well, some roles limit the extent of a person's development; in fact, some roles put or set an end to a person's life before it really begins.

Linton tried to make this point with a distinction between ascribed and achieved roles. Ascribed roles (for example, man or woman) are those assigned to people "without reference to innate differences or abilities." In contrast, achieved roles (say, teacher or garbage collector) are not assigned at birth, but "are left open to be filled through competition and individual effort" (Linton, 1936). Linton said the majority roles in any society were ascribed and "those which take care of the ordinary day-to-day business of living are practically always of this (ascribed) type." Working in preliterate societies, Linton probably exaggerated the number of ascribed roles, but his distinction is still valid. An ascribed role such as *woman* is a pattern for consistent behavior, and it does limit development by saying no to a number of achieved roles. For example, traditionally women were effectively excluded from law and medical schools. Desire was meaningless if society closed the door to a woman's achieving the role of lawyer or doctor.

Perceiving the importance of Linton's distinction, others have tried to make it clearer. Defining role differentiation as "the extent to which the incumbency of one role is independent of other roles," Michael Banton said people possess three types of roles—basic, general, and independent—and he then constructed a scale that measured the extent to which particular roles can be played independently of others (Banton, 1965).

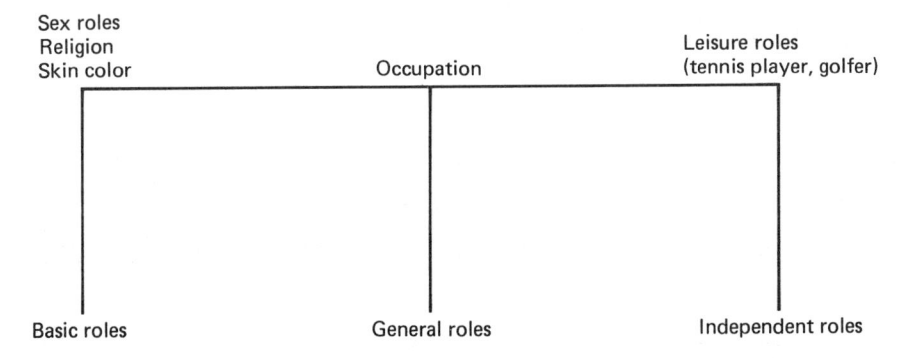

Sex roles Religion Skin color	Occupation	Leisure roles (tennis player, golfer)
Basic roles	General roles	Independent roles

Roughly, basic and ascribed roles refer to the same thing. Whether it is sex, religion, skin color, or caste in India, these roles are assigned without reference to innate differences or abilities. What Banton's scale shows is that because these basic roles are *not* differentiated, because people are *not* permitted to play them independently of others, they have the ability to limit the extent of occupational achievement or the scope and type of leisure roles. As a Catholic in Northern Ireland, I am unable to play this ascribed religious role independently of others. Like an anchor, my religion weighs me down; it closes many schools and jobs to me and it is the reason I will never be a member of certain leisure-time clubs.

Although societies differ in the number of ascribed roles arbitrarily assigned its members, all societies have them, and since roles are the basic means by which tasks are allocated, societies normally put great pressure on those who refuse to have their lives determined by ascribed roles. Remember: since an ascribed role cannot be played independently of others, to challenge it is to threaten the allocation of tasks and privileges in many areas of the society. Indeed, when the threat comes from women, from over one half of the population, the threat could be catastrophic. For to reject this ascribed role is to refuse to cook meals, scrub floors, wash laundry, rear children, or be excluded from certain jobs and clubs—daily and serious threats that cannot be avoided because society is simultaneously being attacked on a variety of role fronts.

Societies try to ensure conformity to role patterns in a number of ways. First is socialization. People are taught to think and act by means of inherited patterns and, if socialization is "successful," people accept their roles, ascribed or otherwise. Second is other people. One role means at least two,[4] and even if a person rejects an inherited role, others may not. In fact, others (for example, a husband, a father, a mother, a mother-in-law) may put considerable pressure on the person to conform to societal patterns. Naturally, people can say no, but a refusal to conform makes the person an alien among the normals: "They're telling me I'm ungrateful, a freak, a weirdo. Perhaps they're right. Perhaps I should retain self-esteem by conforming." Also, if social psychological pressures fail to work, there is always the threat of power: "You, a black person in America, a gypsy in Spain, a Catholic in Northern Ireland, conform or I'll make you wish you had."

Third comes the notion of "role-set." Any role normally includes a number of role relationships (for instance, a wife's role-set includes her husband, her children, her in-laws, her husband's friends at work), and this "interlocking" of roles means that it may be very difficult to fail in one important role obligation without failing in others (Goode, 1960; Merton,

---

[4] For example, doctor needs patient, mother needs child, teacher needs student, clerk needs customer.

1968). A woman might decide that the role of wife spells injustice but continue to perform her role because of the possible effect her departure might have on her children.

Fourth and last is Goode's point that in many roles people have the obligation to serve as models for others (1960). A man might decide that traditional male role patterns are quite conducive to violence and war but be afraid to change behavior because of the effect on his son. In the absence of the old pattern, the man must make a new one and he could conclude this to be too risky for his son. Without a solid pattern to serve as a model, the son could grow up confused, unsure of what a man is or does.

Despite the efforts society makes to enforce conformity to roles, especially to ascribed roles, one characteristic feature of modern societies is the challenge to many ascribed roles (see, for example, Gans, 1972). In America, blacks, women, Chicanos, and Puerto Ricans are all demanding that others allow them to play educational, occupational, and leisure roles, independently of their racial, sexual, and ethnic roles. Undoubtedly, others will respond with pleas for conformity to inherited roles, but if a woman believes she is the equal of a man or a black argues he is beautiful, socialization has failed. If the person is secure about his or her reevaluation or identity and role, efforts to make the person feel alien or peculiar are also likely to fail—leaving others who try to produce conformity with few choices. They can hope that interlocking roles and the obligations of being a model will produce conformity, or they can resort to power. Either way, they are unlikely to undo the social psychological change that the rejection of traditional patterns has produced. That change is "permanent" and conflict can be avoided only if others are willing to allow those who inherited ascribed roles to achieve any they wish.

ROLE-MAKING

Role relationships are rooted in working agreements. People meet each other with different expectations and in interaction they often achieve "creative compromises" that allow them to have a satisfactory role relationship. Perhaps because early theory focused on the normative aspects of role, we still know little about the hows and whys of working agreements, about the factors that facilitate or force people to use normative expectations as no more than a basis for the role-making that produces working agreements. So, since role-making is "an important phase of role theory" (Turner, 1962), some of the factors that move people to role-make are discussed below.

First are cultural beliefs and values. To the extent that a society advocates freedom, individuality, achievement, and social change, people learn in childhood to accept or at least tolerate role differences, as well as receive social support for their own role-making. For example, the belief in a professor's right to academic freedom is widely accepted and it provides teachers with a great deal of latitude in defining their role.

Second, because they lack expertise, are authorities required to permit role-making? A study of dock foremen in Great Britain found that "foremen have freedom to define their own roles and behavior." Apparently, superintendents "arrive with no knowledge of dock custom and practice," no awareness of traditional docking skills, and no systematic managerial training. So, since foremen were in reality responsible for training their bosses, they had great latitude in role-making (Hill, 1973). Incidentally, the importance of expertise has also affected the military, traditionally a very rigid role-definer. Janowitz and Little write "that the impact of technology has forced a shift in the practices of military authorities." Now middle-level officers require a great deal of knowledge and skill to perform their tasks. Generals can try to rigidly define roles but, in the absence of expertise, many now believe "the task of the highest echelons is to maintain a suitable environment within which the middle strata of specialists can coordinate their efforts" (Janowitz and Little, 1965).

Third, do authorities in an organization care if subordinates perform their roles according to laws or precise institutional rules and regulations? For example, Watergate showed that some politicians set fund-raising goals for their subordinates, but did not worry about, nor did they want to know, how subordinates achieved their goals (Magruder, 1975).

Fourth, how much social consensus exists about the way a particular role is to be performed? Studies suggest that the greater the consensus, the more others demand "exact" performances from role occupants. But, the absence of social consensus is one factor that allows people to role-make. A study of social workers in urban and rural settings found that "roles were more broadly conceived" by rural workers. Apparently, the specialized social services found in cities keep those workers within a role pattern defined by the organizational division of labor. However, these specialized services are absent in rural areas, making it necessary for rural workers to "informally" take over more functions than their urban counterparts (Thomas, 1959; also Julian, 1969; Bible and Brown, 1962; Bible and McComas, 1963).

Fifth, does the role require people to "exert influence without legitimate authority"? This is similar to the example from Watergate but here, instead of indifference to legal or organizational rules or regulations, the role is structured in a way that furnishes few "or no provisions for the exercise of legitimate authority" (Snoek, 1966). For example, when he resigned as vice-president, Spiro Agnew spoke of a "post-Watergate morality." Apparently, Baltimore's public officials saw the role problems of people doing business with the city. Success demanded more than a formal submission of bids or a professional presentation of the company's case. In effect, because the society's definition of their roles provided few or insufficient chances for the exercise of legitimate authority, heads of companies "had" to use favors, gifts, and "charitable" contributions. Neither the public officials nor the business executives called these *bribes*. Instead, it was a case of public officials recognizing that executives had to role-make if they were to exert the influence their formal roles denied them (see Cohen and Witcover, 1974).

Sixth, is the role a new one? To the extent that it is, people should be able to role-make. Others are uncertain of what to expect and probably tolerant of deviations from any written rules and regulations: "No one has ever done this before; perhaps we better allow them to behave as they see fit."

Seventh, even if one role partner tries to precisely define the other's role, does he or she have the power to do so? For example, when a child is five or six, a father can "precisely" define the role of his son. But when the son is twenty-five, the father has normally lost this power. The son can role-make as he sees fit and if the father has always tried to rein in his son, the boy may respond by defining the role of a son as a person who never sees his father.

Eighth and last, there is "differing intensity of role-involvement among those in the role-set" (Merton, 1968). Perhaps the key variable is power; perhaps it is love. For whatever reason(s), "the role expectations of those in the role-set are not maintained with the same degree of intensity." So, perhaps you are a husband who loves his wife and children, and another member of the role-set—your wife's father—tries to make you conform to his expectations of the husband role. If your wife asks you to, you might do as her father wishes. But, suppose your wife agrees with you. That leaves you free to disregard the low-intensity expectations of your father-in-law and role-make as you and your wife see fit.

The eight examples focus on why role-making takes place. Generally little has been said about how creative compromises are achieved, about why one partner responds positively to the other's role-making. This is an important theoretical task. For example, if the adolescent son of an open-minded father redefines aspects of their relationship (for example, he now communicates on a first-name basis; he says he respects the man, not the role) and the father generally agrees, what were the key variables that produced compromise? How important is the father's personality, his openness to change? How important are instrumental considerations: If I don't compromise, I may begin to lose my son? How important is the social environment? Were father and son both affected by widespread changes in cultural beliefs and values? And finally, how important was the process of interaction? If the son requested the changes, how important was the manner of his request? Would the father compromise if the son came to him with self-righteous demands?

We lack precise answers to these questions. Exchange theorists (for example, Homans, 1958; Blau, 1964) offer some help, but they themselves stress that all interaction is not governed "by the concern of both (or all) partners with rewards dispensed by the other (or others)." And, more important, if we try to view interaction in terms of the exchange of social rewards, in terms of costs, profits, and losses, won't we often be forced to stretch the meaning of these words until they break? For example, if a traditional Catholic agrees to role-make (for instance, meat can be eaten on Friday; Sunday mass obligations can be fulfilled on Saturday), how helpful is it to say that the rewards dispensed by priests outweigh the losses arising from role-makers? If the person compromised because of a belief that "you can't fight change," is his willingness to role-make a result of rewards dispensed by others? Or if the person compromised because he genuinely believed the Pope was infallible, need we enter into questions of profit and loss? Isn't the belief alone an explanation for the person's willingness to role-make?

ROLE INVOLVEMENT

People assume roles with different amounts and kinds of cognitive, emotional, and physical involvement (Sarbin, 1966). Sometimes a person loves his role; he cannot conceive of being anything other than a teacher. Sometimes a person dislikes a role; my father hated every day of his forty-two years as a machinist. And often, like my father, or yours, a person hates a role but has no choice about playing it.

To describe people's involvement in roles, Erving Goffman uses four concepts (1961). The first is *commitment*. Here reference is "to questions of impersonally enforced structural arrangements." As a result of the "fixed and interdependent character of many institutional arrangements," the person gets "locked into a position and coerced into living up to the promises and sacrifices built into it." Recall our discussion of middle age in Chapter Three: a forty-five-year-old man may want to change jobs but responsibilities to family, as well as twenty years of accumulated pension benefits, commit him to a role he abhors.

Since commitments normally develop only to regularly performed roles, they can easily have serious psychological consequences. The person feels hemmed in, chained to a role with no chance of escape. As one committed receptionist said: "Until recently I'd cry in the morning. I didn't want to get up. I'd dread Fridays because Monday was always looming over me. Another five days ahead of me. . . . One minute to five is the moment of triumph. You physically turn off the machine that has dictated to you all day long. You put it in a drawer and that's it. You're your own man for a few hours. Then it calls to you every morning that you have to come back" (Terkel, 1974).

Attachment is a second kind of role involvement. Here people are eager to perform the role. Emotionally and cognitively in "love" with it, they desire and expect to see themselves enacting it, primarily because of the "self-identifications" the role offers (Goffman, 1961). Generally attachment has positive consequences for the person. Especially if the attachment is to an important role (for example, man, woman, carpenter, lawyer), the person eagerly approaches everyday life. Daily the role offers a variety of emotional and cognitive satisfactions. However, if attachments are positive for the person, they can be negative for the society. Ex-colonel Anthony Herbert loved being in the Army's Ranger program. This made him a "super-soldier," a man who could "kill with his hands as well as use them as a semi-skilled surgeon." At one point Herbert's attachments to the identity soldier and the role soldier led him to search for ex-Nazis, apparently thinking they could teach him something about being a Ranger. So, in an effort to be a "super-soldier," he tracked down war criminals to learn the skills he and his colleagues would later use in Vietnam (Herbert, 1973).

Embracement is a third type of role involvement. Here the person is attached to the role, has shown the ability to do it, *plus* has "an active *engagement* or spontaneous involvement in the role activity at hand." Resembling attachment, embracement goes beyond it. Central to this type of role involvement is a person's "visible investment of attention and muscular effort" his complete disappearance into the "virtual self" offered by the role, his willingness to be "fully seen in terms of the image and to confirm expressively one's acceptance of it" (Goffman, 1961).

Examples of embracement include a police officer feverishly directing traffic, a beaming mother breast-feeding her child, or consider this quote from professional hockey player Eric Nesterenko: "I still like to skate . . . (His eyes are glowing). I haven't kept many photographs of myself but I found one where I'm in full flight. I'm leaning into a turn . . . I'm in full flight and my head is turned. I'm concentrating on something and I'm grinning . . . I'm something else there. I'm on another level of existence, just being in pure motion. Going wherever I want to go, whenever I want to go. That's nice you know. (Laughs softly)" (Terkel, 1974).

Role distance is a fourth kind of role involvement. Here there is an "effectively expressed pointed separateness" between the person and the role; here the person "is actually denying not the role but the virtual self that is implied in the role for all accepting performers" (Goffman, 1961; also Stebbins, 1967). Discussing her life as a prostitute, Roberta Victor says: "I didn't like my work. It was messy. That was the biggest feeling about it. Here's all these guys slobbering over you all night long. I'm lying there, doing math or conjugations or Spanish poetry in my head (Laughs). And they're slobbering" (Terkel, 1974).

Ms. Victor does not deny the role *prostitute;* she is committed to that. What she does reject is the self-image implied in her enactment of role. Society says people who participate in sexual intercourse are supposed to embrace it; they should be actively engaged or spontaneously involved in the role activity at hand. Ms. Victor says, "Are you kidding?" Customers may expect her to embrace them, to enjoy making love to them. She answers no. "I'm committed to the role but the 'real me,' the person I actually am, is not on this bed. You may think I'm embracing the role, but actually I'm maintaining as much distance from it as I possibly can. In short, despite what my behavior implies, I am not who you think I am."

Ms. Victor's comments allow us to discuss an important point about the concept of role distance. Is it a sociological or social psychological concept? The answer is both, but the emphasis is always on the threat to self-image; to desire role distance people must perceive a threat or a shame or a loss of self-esteem because of the virtual self implied in the role performance. For example, Coser (1966) argues that role distance is actually sociological ambivalence; a role or roles contain "incompatible normative expectations of attitudes, beliefs, and behavior," and the person tries to achieve role distance because of institutionalized incompatibilities. Consider Ms. Victor. She is a woman and a prostitute. Should she embrace the role of prostitute, she immediately loses self-esteem as a woman. Taking the role of the generalized other she must say to herself, "They tell me if I enjoy this I'm a slut or a whore. So, I'll maintain distance from the role in order to deny the implied self-image. I refuse to accept the identity slut." Or, consider the single role, Dean of Student Affairs. Normatively the dean is expected to help students with their problems, to be an understanding, compassionate person. But the dean may also be called upon to enforce college rules of discipline that he or she hates. So, while enforcing the rules, the dean maintains distance—through tone of voice, through phrases such as "I didn't make the rules; I only enforce them"—by denying the virtual self, that is, the identity S.O.B., implied in the performance of role.

Now, in both of these examples there are structured incompatibilities; should Ms. Victor or the dean embrace their roles, there are negative consequences for self-image. However, in both examples it is the person's interpretation of the attitudes of *others* that produces role distance. Stebbins makes this point when he underlines the importance of an audience (Stebbins, 1967; Goffman, 1961). In the case of the dean, the audience is actually present, but except for her clients, Ms. Victor is alone. She assumes the role of an implied audience (see Turner, 1956) and, seeing herself in their eyes, she reacts with role distance. Of course, neither Ms. Victor nor the dean had to respond with role distance. Certainly there are deans who see no threat in being labeled "disciplinarians" and that means that, as in roles, the structured incompatibilities act as detonators to explosives: they set people in motion, but role distance occurs only if the person feels it is important to deny the virtual self, the identity in the role performance. Since these incompatibilities are more or less institutionalized, it is likely that people share the same beliefs about role performances. Most prostitutes should react as Ms. Victor does. But whether or not they do is an empirical question. It is eminently a matter of how a person interprets the attitudes of others in the process of interaction.

One final point about role distance is that it often occurs in the absence of structured incompatibilities. Stebbins rightly notes that "these are role expectations which, if one shows attachment to them while performing before significant role others, might bring on some loss of respect and a momentary lack of support for one's self-conception" (Stebbins, 1967). Again it is a person's interpretation of others' attitudes that produces role distance, but when a businessman acts bored while filling out routine forms or when a teacher yawns her way through correcting exams, it is hard to find ambiguity or structured incompatibilities. Instead, we only find role expectations that are generally interpreted as "unenjoyable or distasteful" (Stebbins, 1967).

Commitment, attachment, embracement, and role distance are four types of role involvement. Analyzed separately, they are actually linked. For example, people committed to roles probably often use role distance as a way of responding to impersonally enforced structural arrangements. And attachment to role should lead many to embrace it. Finally, to the extent that roles are ascribed, people have no choice about assuming them. But if master and slave are both willed roles, masters inherit easily embraceable attachments; slaves, commitments that offer self-esteem only if people refuse to see themselves in terms of the self-identifications the role offers.

ROLE CONFLICT

Ludovir's interminable smile now became almost satanic.

". . . You'll tell the Foundation? What if I deny it?"

"Then they can choose which of us they will believe."

"I see. You want me to go to jail. You've always hated me. I've felt that."

"No. I shall simply instruct the Foundation that incontrovertible proof has come to light that Miss Dunham had failed to interest Mr. Hussey in making a grant to the Museum. . . . There will be no reason for them to suspect actual fraud. My information will be perfectly consistent with your forged entry. You need apprehend no prosecution. . . .

"How satisfactory for you, Mr. Chairman. . . . Oh I know your type— . . . Beeky Ehninger, the wise fiduciary, the honest little fellow, the widow's darling. . . . What would you know of passion or sacrifice? When you come into the temple of art to grab another medal you should be exterminated ruthlessly with a moral DDT. . . .

Beeky felt suddenly depleted. He sat down and turned away from the accuser. "As the young people say today, we're not communicating. I must do what I must do."

". . . You ask us, Beeky, if we want to keep money acquired by a crime. We cannot argue about that. We cannot hear ourselves say that we will. We cannot accept your offered resignation from the board. We have to answer: 'Stay with us, Beeky, and do what you must do.' But we can still ask a favor. We can still ask you—without argument, without discussion, without hypocrisy and without pretense—to forget this whole wretched business. Let us, for God's sake, go on as if nothing had happened."

"You ask too much, Mr. Fletcher. I have offered to resign from the board and keep my mouth shut. If I stay, I must go to the Foundation and tell what I know."

What else . . . could he have answered? If he remained chairman of the board—and they had insisted that he do so—he had to act in the only way a decent man could act. What other? what? [Louis Auchincloss, *The Partners* (1974)]

Beeky Ehninger's is a special type of role conflict: that between personality and role. Chairman of a museum's board of directors, Beeky's conflict arises when two members of his role-set want him to forget forgery. He refuses. He offers to resolve his role conflict by resigning, but he makes it clear that if he stays on, he has no choice but to resolve his conflict with the truth.

One theory of role conflict argues that, besides resignation, Beeky had two other options. Taking the road of expediency, he could have kept quiet, as well as kept the money. Or, he could have weighed the consequences between maintaining a moral stance and closing his eyes to forgery. Auchincloss never allows Beeky these options; the man is a type and Auchincloss is saying that an "old-fashioned" Wall Street lawyer always resolved such role conflicts by giving primacy to morality. Beeky acted in the only way a decent man could (see Gross et al., 1966).

Types change and today few of us expect to meet a Beeky Ehninger. But everyone encounters role conflicts. And generally everyone resolves those conflicts by choosing from among the same limited number of options.

What are some sources of role conflict? One is role ambiguity; a second, cultural contradictions; a third, conflicting demands among members of a role-set; and a fourth, conflict between two or more different roles (see Goode, 1960a; Stogdill, 1974; Seeman, 1953). Obviously, different people experience these conflicts with varying degrees of frequency and intensity, but it is hard to imagine a person without role conflicts. For although roles are the means by which society allocates tasks, "mistakes" are inevitable. And in societies that change rapidly, mistakes are bound to join forces with ambiguity and contradiction.

Now, if no one has a choice about experiencing role conflicts, people do have a choice about the means they use to resolve conflicts. Here at least several options are available—deny or suppress the conflict, compartmentalize, extend, delegate, or eliminate a role, combine two conflicting roles, change or alter beliefs, values, and expectations about a role (Goode, 1960; Turner, 1962)—and when we consider the types of conflict, we will also discuss ways to reduce conflict, as well as the pressures and problems people experience when they choose one means rather than another. For example, a combat soldier can try to reduce the conflict between the demands of his religious role and the demands of his military role by desertion. However, this option presents a problem: military law says no to the person's elimination of role.

Role Ambiguity. This occurs when a role is not clearly defined or when people cannot discover the dimensions of their role expectations. Generally, five sources of ambiguity exist: people are confused about role expectations, the boundaries of acceptable and unacceptable behavior, the situations in which the role applies, whether behavior is obligatory or optional, and which of two or more expectations should be given priority (Secord and Backman, 1974; Stogdill, 1974).

A good example of role ambiguity exists in Wilson's study of the Pentecostal minister. Essentially conflicts arise from demands made by organizational leaders and the minister's congregation, from demands made by the statics of rules and regulations and the dynamics of a revivalist ideology. If demands were clear, the minister's conflicts might be easier to resolve. As it is, the minister's problems are heightened by role ambiguity. First, ministers are supposed to encourage speaking in tongues (that is, glossolalia) while simultaneously keeping the order that leaves their authority unchallenged and their spirit election unquestioned. However, since no norms exist for meeting these conflicting demands, ministers are continually unsure about the boundaries of acceptable and unacceptable behavior. Second, superiors stress keeping the excesses and improprieties of early Pentecostalism under control, but that spirit, those excesses, are the ideological essence of a revival movement. Moreover, superiors sometimes counter their order for constraint with literature suggesting free rein to everyone's spirit. So, which of the two role demands is given priority? The minister receives no definite answer; instead, he is forced to wage an inner battle over which demand is most important (Wilson, 1968).

Theoretically, resolving the minister's conflicts can take many forms. But, since most ministers are attached to their roles, elimination is not a serious possibility. Conflict occurs within one role, so there is no chance of combining two; denial is possible but bound to produce failure; and because the minister must check yet simultaneously encourage the spirit, compartmentalization is also no solution. Wilson writes that one approach used by ministers is delegation of role demands. Ministers are leaders, but revival groups prize informality and spirit seeking. So, ministers allocate functions within a meeting and they also ask members to minister to one another. Since this self-ministering conceivably challenges *the* minister's authority, many have responded by altering beliefs about their roles. Today many claim that ministers, qua ministers, are "blessed with the gift of the discernment of spirits"; when someone is speaking in tongues, ministers alone have the ability to distinguish between true and false manifestations of the Holy Spirit (Wilson, 1968).

In reality, the minister can never solve his conflicts. Wilson points out that the movement is in transition from a sect to a denomination, and ambiguity is unlikely to disappear until ministers and members achieve a balance between the demands of the spirit and the demands of organization. However, the minister's problems with role ambiguity do tell us something about the resolution of all role conflicts. First, is elimination a realistic possibility? If, like the minister, a person is attached to a role, eliminating it is unlikely. Or, if, like the soldier with religious conflicts, the person is committed to the role, elimination is again unlikely. Second, is the conflict, the ambiguity, inherent in a social situation or historical process? Like the Pentecostal sect, many organizations change and until they achieve stability any resolution of role ambiguity is bound to be temporary. Third, one easy way of resolving ambiguity is to follow the minister's lead and change beliefs about the role. For example, in a study of insurance agencies, the role of assistant manager was often ambiguous. Assistants and managers both claimed responsibility for some of the same tasks, with assistants uncertain about whether particular functions were optional or obligatory (Stogdill, 1974). Seemingly, the resolution of this conflict is easy: get managers and assistants together and clarify the functions and responsibilities of each. But, will the managers listen? Or, are an assistant's problems a result of the managers' resolving their role conflicts? While questions like these can only be answered by an empirical investigation of the total situation producing ambiguity, they underline the many variables affecting the means used and the possibilities of resolving role ambiguity. Conceivably, if they wish to retain the role, people may be forced to daily resolve unresolvable ambiguities. And, relative to the importance of the ambiguous role, that could be a serious problem.

Cultural Contradictions. These exist when culture, when institutionalized beliefs, values, and practices, say two or more different things about the same role. Especially when the role is basic, and the possibility of eliminating it quite small, role contradictions have the potential to cause serious problems. People may have to search hard for ways of reducing, if not resolving, such basic conflicts.

An example of cultural contradictions can be found in Mirra Komarovsky's work on sex roles. In an early (1946) study she focused on women. Working with college students, she found a basic contradiction between the "feminine" role and the "modern" role. "Throughout their lives" these women met "powerful challenges and strong pressures to excel in certain competitive lines of endeavor and to develop certain techniques of adaptations very similar to those expected of their brothers," but then, if they acted as they were taught, they met strong pressures to act like women, to be submissive, emotional, sympathetic. As one student said: "How to do the job and remain popular was a tough task. If you worked your best, the boys resented the competition; if you acted feminine, they complained you were clumsy" (Komarovsky, 1946).

Some twenty-five years later, Komarovsky studied male sex roles. She found a "tangled web of contradictory values and sentiments associated with men's attitudes." Generally they still believed in sharp sex role differentiation, but time had undermined the ideological support for their belief and that put many of these men in a peculiar position. They supported the right of a woman to the career of her choice, they admired women who "measured up" to the society's dominant values, and they found "modern" women appealing; but, the men also said there was no substitute for the mother's care of young children, they felt the husband should be superior, and they considered the man's career the most important (Komarovsky, 1971, 1973).

How do people resolve these very basic contradictions? Eliminating the role is possible but few choose this option. Delegating the role of man or woman is hard and compartmentalization is also difficult in a role that spills over into so many aspects of everyday life. Changing beliefs about sex roles is obviously one easy solution but neither sex eagerly embraced this option. In 1946 the women generally denied or suppressed their conflicts. No women's movement existed to provide social support for the resolution of conflicts via change of beliefs, and women met a great deal of pressure from family, friends, and lovers to conform to traditional sex roles. Generally, they did so, but Komarovsky suggested that the denial or suppression of conflict was hardest for those women with obvious talents and learned ambition.

In the 1970s the men found it harder to suppress or deny their conflicts. Many did take this route but Komarovsky writes that nearly 50 percent of her sample (college seniors) "expressed mild to acute anxiety over their failure in relationships with women. . . ." Generally these men felt they failed to live up to the *traditional* ideal of masculinity. Generally they felt "*they* violated their own or their partner's normative expectations." As one student said, "One thing that bothers me is the way they always picture men as having to be dominant and strong. That puts a lot of strain on a man. I'd like to share things and you cannot dominate and share at the same time. But girls like a hard exterior in a man" (Komarovsky, 1973).

Maybe they do. But this man is bound to meet girls who do not, and even if he does not, he is still caught in a web spun by his contradictory socialization. Somehow he has learned new beliefs and values for his male role, but he apparently believes that women still want men to behave in terms of traditional sex roles. This student should (and does) have problems suppressing or denying his conflicts. First, unlike 1946 there is at least minority support for his beliefs. If he does not bring his conflicts to the surface, highly visible social movements will. Second, and closely linked to organized movements to produce *and* resist change, these men are subject to cross pressures that make it difficult for them to deny or suppress role conflict. Where the women in 1946 seemingly met the same pressures from friends, relatives, and lovers, the men in 1971 probably met contradictory pressures. Friends may say one thing, a lover another, a relative a third. The man's problem is to resolve these cross pressures. It is not surprising the men failed to do so; it is also not surprising they failed to suppress or deny their role conflicts (Komarovsky, 1973).

Discussing these sex role conflicts tells us something about the resolution of cultural contradictions in general. If the conflicts are about basic roles, and people find it difficult or undesirable or impossible to eliminate those roles, conflict should remain until the roles are defined with a satisfactory degree of harmony. If, as in 1946, there is little social support for one side of the contradictory expectations, people may succumb to pressure and suppress or deny their conflict. In some cases, denial may take the form of passionately advocating the generally supported role behavior. However, if, as in 1971, there is widespread support for both sides of the contradictory expectations, denial or suppression of conflict will be much harder. Probably, those who feel peculiarly threatened by the change, or those who have a strong need to advocate it, will resolve role conflict by reaffirming or changing role expectations, but those without strong needs will have conflicts that others continually bring to the surface. If the contradictions cannot be delegated or compartmentalized, the conflict should continue until the society achieves harmony about role beliefs, values, and expectations. Naturally, the conflict may itself be an important factor in the realization of harmony. For example, a man who believes women should have a career and care for children must do something about his contradiction when it is his wife who refuses to stay home with the baby.

Role-Set Conflict. This occurs when two or more members of a role-set demand different behavior from the occupant of a role, or when two or more members of the role-set demand behavior that conflicts with the normative definition of the role. Either way, the need to resolve the conflict is intimately related to a person's feeling about the role's importance (is she very attached to the role?), as well as the extent to which elimination is impossible because of factors such as cultural ascription or achieved commitments. For example, a twelve-year-old boy caught between the conflicting demands of his mother and father has a compelling need to resolve his role-set conflicts.

One good example of role-set conflict is Priestly's study of the prison welfare officer in England. Normatively, his role is defined as that member "of the prison team with particular responsibility for helping the prisoner in his relationships with individuals and organizations outside the prison. He will be concerned with making plans for the prisoner's after care and will advise and assist in any immediate problems which may arise during his sentence" (Priestly, 1972).

Now, this definition of role focuses on the prisoner's life after release, and Priestly found "high agreement" among welfare officers with a role definition focusing on rehabilitation. However, if welfare officers agreed, members of the role-set did not. Problems with administrators were small; some were oriented toward rehabilitation and they saw welfare officers as a threat to continued employment. But the serious conflicts came from guards and prisoners. Oriented toward control of the men, guards resented the welfare officers' rehabilitative goals; they demanded a role performance "exclusively focused on material and financial problems." Coincidentally, these guard expectations meshed with those of the prisoners. Highly suspicious of anyone working for the prison, inmates felt that all officials were proper targets for exploitation. And, since welfare officers had the authority to grant a number of privileges (for example, visits, letters), prisoners met welfare officers expecting to focus not on rehabilitation but on the prison privileges officers could dispense (Priestly, 1972).

So, the welfare officers expect one thing, key members of their role-set another. How is the conflict resolved? The answer is by the welfare officers changing their beliefs about the responsibilities and goals of their role. Attached to the role, few saw the conflict as a cause for eliminating it. Delegating, extending, or compartmentalizing the role was no solution, and since they planned to continue as welfare officers, it was very hard to deny conflicts with guards and prisoners, the crucial members of the welfare officers' role-set. For example, officers spent a great deal of time at reception and interaction boards, "in processes of assessment, allocation, and review." Although these tasks had little to do with the welfare officers' expectations, they were the daily means of role enactment. Perhaps if the prison system and larger society offered hope of reform, officers might have tried to change the expectations of others. In the absence of such support, and in the presence of consistent demands to adopt a control orientation, most welfare officers responded by accepting "a limited, benefit-conscious, control-minded" definition of their roles (Priestly, 1972).

Resolving role-set conflicts need not lead to conformity with others' contrary expectations. Welfare officers met others who had the same expectations of them; moreover, since guards were often present, or at least knew the results of meetings between officers and prisoners, compartmentalizing role performances was impossible. But consider the case of the stockbroker. To some members of the role-set, they are only brokers; they function as "commission merchants," executing sales or purchases for others. However, sometimes brokers are dealers, buying and selling for their own, rather than a customer's, account. The conflict occurs when a stockbroker, qua dealer, buys stock for his company, and then the next day, qua broker, sells that stock to a customer—without mentioning the personal or company profits the sale produces. Here the conflict among members of the role-set is clear: customers would resent such a profitable sale, members of the brokerage house would be happy about it. The point is that, unlike the welfare officer, the stockbroker is in a "perfect" position to resolve role conflict by compartmentalizing role performances. As long as customers never find out about the broker's profits as a dealer, stockbrokers can ignore the problem of ethics and satisfactorily fulfill the conflicting expectations of role-set members (Evan and Levin, 1966; Goode, 1960a).

A final example of role-set conflict is the Bantu clerk. White supervisors expect the clerk to focus on "respect and obedience to the European authorities," while clerks and other members of the role-set, that is, the Bantu public, expect an emphasis on being "helpful, sympathetic, and kind to the Bantu public." Now to some extent conflict is resolved by compartmentalization: a general lack of communication between supervisors and clerks allows the latter to act one way when supervisors are present, another when they are absent. However, even when supervisors try to produce conformity to their expectations, clerks generally conform to the public's expectations. This ability to resolve conflict by role-making occurs because clerks counter their supervisors' power with a weapon of their own: job security. Confident of remaining on the job, Bantu clerks are able to affirm their strong ties to the black public, normally enacting roles as they and the public see fit (Sherwood, 1958).

Together, these examples point to some of the important variables influencing the resolution of role-set conflicts. If commitments or attachments make role elimination undesirable or impossible, what are the chances for compartmentalization, delegation, or extension of the role? To the extent that one aspect of the role performance takes place in the absence of conflicting role-set members, and to the extent that it is profitable, compartmentalizing roles is the likely means of resolving role-set conflicts. However, if compartmentalization is not possible, and the conflict cannot be suppressed, denied, delegated, or extended (that is, the prison officer), the way in which roles are redefined depends on, first, the support for change that comes from the institution and/or the larger society. If politicians were publicly advocating prison reform, perhaps welfare officers would have refused conformity. And second, does the role possess power that allows the person to role-make? During the Vietnam War, all three American presidents had role-set conflicts between soldiers and civilians who expected them to win a military victory and others who expected them to seek a political victory. Given their power, the presidents were often able to resolve role-set conflicts by defining the role according to their expectations. However, if we bring in another member of a president's role-set, that is, the public, remember that as the war lost popular support, the president lost power and those seeking a political victory gained it. In short, the variables influencing the resolution of role conflict can always be affected by the ongoing processes of social interaction.

Between-Role Conflicts. Here role conflict occurs because two or more different roles demand two or more different types of behavior. One example is the conflict between the role of minister and that of military officer. The first might argue to "turn the other cheek," the second to systematically kill anyone defined as an enemy. Stated in these extreme terms, the conflict is great, but in reality many men easily resolve the conflict by refusing to acknowledge it. In Burchard's study, "over half of the respondents denied any conflict existed between military regulations and religious ideology." Essentially the men resorted to compartmentalization. When conducting religious services, they felt their moral beliefs and values were operative but, when dealing with military matters, they were guided by the military's definitions of right and wrong. In this way they easily resolved their possible role conflicts. However, one of Burchard's findings throws light on this easily achieved solution: most chaplains volunteered for military duty. They wanted to be military officers and this attachment helped solve any possible problems. For these chaplains, their primary allegiance was to the military, not to a religion (Burchard, 1954).

Another example of between-role conflict is that of Soviet physicians. Doctors dedicated to helping others, they are also employees of the political state that says that people must work. Conflict arises when citizens seek a sick certificate that excuses them from work. As state employees, doctors receive orders to suspect everyone, and since patients may actually be state spies, the result is doctors who look "upon the patient as an adversary who wants to deceive him and illegally receive a day off" (Field, 1953). This acceptance of the state's definition of role need not resolve the conflict—doctors often asked themselves, "What good are we doing the people?"—but it does suggest that if power acts to force certain behavior, between-role conflicts can be resolved on a functional level but continue to cause serious moral problems for the occupants of the two conflicting roles. Generally, the extent of these unresolved problems varies with the importance of the conflicting role to the person, as well as the amount of coercion used to force conformity with the other role. For example, if a person were mildly committed to the doctor role and the state used severe threats to enforce its will, the person should not have great difficulty in explaining conformity in terms of the state's use of threats and possible penalties.

A final example of between-role conflict is that of a scientist doing applied research for an industrial corporation. As a scientist, the person may have high role expectations; her job is to cure illnesses or stop pollution. When the corporation assigns a task such as the production of artificial meat or building a better toaster, role conflict comes to the fore: "As a scientist, how can I continue doing such insane work?" One answer is "I cannot"; the person resolves the role conflict by leaving the corporation. However, assuming this to be impossible, that is, the person is either attached or committed to the role, Evan suggests a factor that moves scientists to suppress the conflict. Believing in the norm of reciprocity (Gouldner, 1960), believing that employees owe an obligation to decent employers, scientists perform the applied research because they are being paid to do it. It is their job and, despite conflict, they must fulfill the obligations of their role as corporate employee (Evan, 1962). Especially when the scientific role is important to the person, resolution by reciprocity is probably accompanied by rationalizations about the research's importance. With high personal attachment, and in contrast to the Soviet physician, moderate external justification, the person should be moved to seek some internal justifications for deciding in favor of the corporation (Aronson, 1976; Festinger, 1957).

Assuming an attachment or commitment to the roles, compartmentalization appears to be an especially good way of resolving between-role conflict. However, since the two roles were played simultaneously in all three examples, compartmentalizing roles was difficult, especially for the doctor and the scientist. In no instance could the roles be satisfactorily combined, and neither extending nor delegating roles resolved the conflict. In each case the conflict was suppressed or denied, but in each case people acted for different reasons. And although this underlines the importance of power, personal attachments, and social norms as variables affecting the resolution of between-role conflicts, when operative, power is probably the most significant of the three. For example, while attached to their role as physicians, Soviet doctors resolved their conflicts in favor of the state. And in *The Gulag Archipelago* Solzhenitsyn cites conflicts between the role of trustee and the role of prisoner. Again both roles were played simultaneously, but whenever conflicts arose over obligations to fellow prisoners and obligations to prison authorities, Solzhenitsyn argues the authorities almost always won. For if the trustee decided in favor of the prisoners, he was sure to find himself no longer a trustee. And Solzhenitsyn notes that survival was virtually impossible unless a prisoner received the privileges given only to trustees (Solzhenitsyn, 1975).[5]

Role Accumulation. One generally valid assumption in role theory is that a large number of roles increases the chances for conflict. With more obligations and the need for a more precise allocation of when and where roles are enacted, people have a greater chance of encountering problems (Goode, 1960a, b). Normally researchers highlight only the negative results of accumulating roles, but in a recent article Sieber not only suggests positive results from role accumulation, he also argues that "if multiplicity of roles yielded more gratification than stress, or more stability than disorder, we (researchers) would not be concerned with identifying mechanisms which reduce stress" (Sieber, 1974).

This is wrong. Conflict does not disappear if role accumulation yields more gratification than stress, and it is hard to see why social psychologists would be uninterested in the resolution of the role conflicts of men and women, of a chaplain, of a trustee-prisoner. In all three instances the resolution of the conflict is the *individual's* response to a *social* problem. However, by focusing on the positive results of many roles, Sieber performs a very useful task. For despite conflict, people often seek many roles and Sieber tries to tell us why.

First are role privileges. "Every role carries with it certain rights as well as duties," and Sieber argues that privileges are an inducement to accumulating roles, as well as a cause of role accumulation equaling more gratification than conflict. For example, any American president is simultaneously head of a political party, head of a political state, head of an executive branch, and commander-in-chief of the armed forces. Studies indicate that these many roles often produce conflict, but studies also show that any president's role privileges (for example, personal jet, two

---

[5] This brings to mind a statement made by Gerhard Lenski: "When men are confronted with important decisions where they are obliged to choose between their own, or their group's interests and the interests of others, they nearly always choose the former . . ." (Lenski, 1966).

or more houses, a substantial pension, a retinue of servants) are one powerful source of compensation for role conflicts (see, for example, Hughes, 1973; Goldman, 1969).

Second is what Sieber calls "overall status security." With a number of roles, people have "buffers" that protect them from total failure. For example, a lawyer who enters public life and fails can always return to the lawyer role hopeful of at least preserving some self- and social-esteem. Or a man or woman unhappy at work can try to compensate by gaining a number of roles in voluntary organizations (Sieber, 1974).

A third benefit of role accumulation is a gain in "resources for status enhancement and role performance." People often join voluntary groups such as the Lions, Elks, or American Psychological and Sociological associations to meet the community and professional leaders who will furnish help in furthering their careers. And contacts with a wide variety of people can easily enhance role performance. The businessperson who joins political organizations to meet legislators can later call upon these contacts to help achieve a better role performance. This is especially so if the businessperson adds a contribution to party or organizational membership.

A final benefit of role accumulation could easily prove the most important. Sieber calls attention to the ego gratification, the enhanced self-image, of people who acquire a large number of roles. For example, Franklin Roosevelt loved being president, but he got special pleasure from his role as head of the armed forces. Burns writes that "Roosevelt not only assumed the role of commander-in-chief, he embraced it and lived it." Apparently it gave him a sense of gratification that the term *president* did not. At one state dinner, when Secretary of State Hull was about to propose a toast, Roosevelt "asked Hull to try to address him as commander-in-chief, not as president"; and during the war he preferred to be tested, not as chief executive or chief politician, but as commander-in-chief (Burns, 1970).

Sieber's article emphasizes a neglected aspect of role theory: many roles often produce gratifications, and those positive results may compensate for role conflicts, even acting as important variables in the resolution of role conflict. For example, chaplains decided in favor of the officer rather than the religious role. Burchard's data suggested this was due to role attachments, but the data do not tell us if chaplains liked officer privileges or if they received ego gratifications from the role. Certainly these are possibilities that tell us that the privileges of many roles may be a reason for refusing to see conflicts, or a reason for making privileges more important than conflict. Like the trustees in Russian prison camps, people may perceive their role conflicts but consistently decide in favor of the privileges accompanying those conflicts.

Bibliographical References

Aronson, Elliot. *The Social Animal.* 2d ed. San Francisco: W. H. Freeman, 1976.
Banton, Michael. *Roles: An Introduction to the Study of Social Relations.* New York: Basic Books, 1965.
Bates, Frederick. "A Conceptual Analysis of Group Structure." *Social Forces* 36 (1957): 103–11.
Bates, Frederick. "Institutions, Organizations, and Communities: A General Theory of Complex Structures." *Pacific Sociological Review* (Fall 1960): 59–70.
Bates, Frederick. "Position, Role, and Status—A Reformulation of Concepts." *Social Forces* 34 (1956): 313–21.
Berger, Peter, and Luckmann, Thomas. *Social Construction of Reality: A Treatise in the Sociology of Knowledge.* Garden City, N.Y.: Doubleday, 1966.
Bible, Bond, and Brown, Emory. "Role Consensus and Satisfaction of Extension Advisory Committee Members." *Rural Sociology* (1962): 81–90.
Bible, Bond, and McComas, James D. "Role Consensus and Teacher Effectiveness." *Social Forces* (1963): 225–33.
Blau, Peter. *Exchange and Power in Social Life.* New York: Wiley, 1964.
Blumer, Herbert. *Symbolic Interactionism: Perspective and Method.* Englewood Cliffs, N.J.: Prentice-Hall, 1969.
Burchard, Waldo. "Role Conflicts of Military Chaplains." *American Sociological Review* 19 (1954): 528–35.
Burns, James MacGregor. *Roosevelt: The Soldier of Freedom.* New York: Harcourt Brace Jovanovich, 1970.
Campbell, E., and Pettigrew, T. "Racial and Moral Crisis: Role of Little Rock Ministers." *American Journal of Sociology* 64 (1959): 509–16.
Cohen, Richard M., and Witcover, Jules. *A Heart Beat Away.* New York: Viking, 1974.
Coser, Rose Laub. "Role Distance, Sociological Ambivalence, and Transitional Status System." *American Journal of Sociology* 72 (1966): 173–87.
Evan, William M. "Role Strain and the Norm of Reciprocity in Research Organizations." *American Journal of Sociology* 68 (1962): 346–53.
Evan, William M., and Levin, Ezra. "Status-Set and Role-Set Conflicts of the Stockbroker: A Problem in the Sociology of Law." *Social Forces* 45 (1966): 73–83.
Festinger, Leon. *A Theory of Cognitive Dissonance.* Stanford, Calif.: Stanford University Press, 1957.
Field, Mark. "Structural Strain in the Role of the Soviet Physician." *American Journal of Sociology* 58 (1953): 493–502.

Gans, Herbert. "The New Egalitarianism." *Saturday Review*, October 14, 1972.
Gerth, Hans, and Mills, C. Wright. *Character and Social Structure: The Psychology of Social Institutions*. New York: Harcourt Brace & World, 1953.
Goffman, Erving. *Encounters: Two Studies in the Sociology of Interaction*. Indianapolis: Bobbs-Merrill, 1961.
Goldman, Eric. *The Tragedy of Lyndon Johnson*. New York: Dell, 1969.
Goode, William J. "Norm Commitment and Conformity to Role-Status Obligations." *American Journal of Sociology* 66 (1960b): 246–58.
Goode, William J. "A Theory of Role Strain." *American Sociological Review* 25 (1960a): 483–96.
Gouldner, Alvin. "The Norm of Reciprocity." *American Sociological Review* 25 (1960):161–78.
Gross, Neal; McEachern, Alexander W.; and Mason, Ward S. "Role Conflict and Its Resolution." In *Role Theory: Concepts and Research*, edited by Bruce J. Biddle and Edwin J. Thomas. New York: Wiley, 1966.
Herbert, Anthony, with Wooten, James T. *Soldier*. New York: Holt, Rinehart & Winston, 1973.
Hill, Stephen. "Supervisory Roles and the Man in the Middle: Dock Foreman." *British Journal of Sociology* 24 (1973): 205–21.
Hollander, E. P. "Conformity, Status, and Idiosyncrasy Credit." *Psychological Review* 65, no. 2 (1958): 117–27.
Homans, George. "Social Behavior As Exchange." *American Journal of Sociology* 63 (1958): 397–407.
Hughes, Emmet. *The Living Presidency*. New York: Coward, McCann & Geoghegan, 1973.
Jackson, John A., ed. *Role*. London: Cambridge University Press, 1976.
Janowitz, Morris, and Little, Roger. *Sociology and the Military Establishment*. New York: Russell Sage, 1965.
Julian, Joseph. "Some Determinants of Dissensus on Role Prescriptions Within and Between Four Organizational Positions." *Sociological Quarterly* 10 (1969): 177–89.
Komarovsky, Mirra. "Cultural Contradictions and Sex Roles." *American Journal of Sociology* 52 (1946): 182–89.
Komarovsky, Mirra. "Cultural Contradictions and Sex Roles: The Masculine Case." *American Journal of Sociology* 77 (1971): 873–84.
Komarovsky, Mirra. "Some Problems in Role Analysis." *American Sociological Review* 38 (1973): 649–62.
Lenski, Gerhard. *Power and Privilege: A Theory of Social Stratification*. New York: McGraw-Hill, 1966.
Linton, Ralph. *The Cultural Background of Personality*. New York: Appleton-Century-Crofts, 1945.

Linton, Ralph. *The Study of Man.* New York: Appleton-Century-Crofts, 1936.

McCall, George, and Simmons, J. L. *Identity and Interaction.* New York: Free Press, 1966.

Magruder, Jeb Stuart. *An American Life.* New York: Pocket Books, 1975.

Merton, Robert. *Social Theory and Social Structure.* New York: Free Press, 1968.

Moore, Wilbert. *Social Change.* Englewood Cliffs, N.J.: Prentice-Hall, 1963.

Morgan, Marabell. *The Total Woman.* New York: Pocket Books, 1975.

Neiman, Lionel J., and Hughes, James W. "The Problem of the Concept of Role—A Re-Survey of the Literature." *Social Forces* 30 (1951): 141–49.

Nisbet, Robert. *The Social Philosophers.* New York: Crowell, 1973.

Parsons, Talcott. *The Social System.* New York: Free Press, 1951.

Popitz, Heinrich. "The Concept of Social Role as an Element of Sociological Theory." In *Role*, edited by John A. Jackson. London: Cambridge University Press, 1971.

Priestly, Philip. "The Prison Welfare Officer—A Case of Role Strain." *British Journal of Sociology* 23 (1972): 221–35.

Rose, Arnold, ed. *Human Behavior and Social Processes.* Boston: Houghton Mifflin, 1962.

Sarbin, Theodore. "Role Enactment." In *Role Theory: Concepts and Research*, edited by Bruce J. Biddle and Edwin J. Thomas. New York: Wiley, 1966.

Secord, Paul F., and Backman, Carl W. *Social Psychology.* 2d ed. New York: McGraw-Hill, 1974.

Seeman, M. "Role Conflict and Ambivalence in Leadership." *American Sociological Review* 18 (1953): 373–80.

Sherwood, Rae. "The Bantu Clerk: A Study of Role Expectations." *The Journal of Social Psychology* 47 (1958): 285–316.

Shils, Edward. "Charisma, Order, and Status." *American Sociological Review* 30 (1965): 199–213.

Sieber, Sam D. "Toward a Theory of Role Accumulation." *American Sociological Review* 39 (1974): 567–78.

Snoek, J. Diedrick. "Role Strain in Diversified Role-Sets." *American Journal of Sociology* 71 (1966): 363–72.

Solzhenitsyn, Alexandr I. *The Gulag Archipelago, 1918–1956.* Vol. 2. New York: Harper & Row, 1975.

Stebbins, Robert A. "A Note on the Concept of Role Distance." *American Journal of Sociology* 73 (1967): 247–50.

Stogdill, Ralph. *Handbook of Leadership: A Survey of Theory and Research.* New York: Free Press, 1974.

Terkel, Studs. *Working: People Talk About What They Do All Day and How They Feel About What They Do.* New York: Pantheon, 1974.

Thomas, Edwin J. "Role Conceptions and Organizational Size." *American Sociological Review* 24 (1959): 30–38.

Travisano, Richard V. "Alternation and Conversion as Qualitatively Different Transformations." In *Life As Theater,* edited by Dennis Brissett and Charles Edgley (Chicago: Aldine, 1975), pp. 91–104.

Turner, Ralph. "Role-Taking: Process Versus Conformity." In *Human Behavior and Social Processes,* edited by Arnold Rose. Boston: Houghton Mifflin, 1962.

Turner, Ralph H. "Role-Taking, Role Standpoint, and Reference Group Behavior." *American Journal of Sociology* 61 (1956): 316–28.

Wardwell, Walter. "The Reduction of Strain in a Marginal Social Role." *American Journal of Sociology* 61 (1955): 16–25.

Wilson, B. R. "The Pentecostalist Minister: Role Conflicts and Contradictions of Status." In *Patterns of Sectarianism,* edited by Bryan Wilson. London: Heinemann, 1968.

CHAPTER SEVEN

Frames and the Presentation of Self in Everyday Life

My basic attitude toward the world and society can only be inconsistent. For all my eagerness to be on affectionate terms with them, I was frequently aware of a considered coolness, a tendency to critical reflection, which astonished me. There was, for example, an idea that occasionally preoccupied me when for a few leisure moments I stood in the lobby or dining-hall, clasping a napkin behind my back and watching the hotel guests being waited and fawned upon by blue-liveried minions. It was the idea of interchangeability. *With a change of clothes and make-up, the servitors might often just as well have been the masters, and many of those who lounged in the deep wicker chairs, smoking their cigarettes, might have played the waiter....*

Therefore, my imaginary transpositions sometimes succeeded very well ... I would dine in some elegant restaurant on the Rue de Rivoli or the Avenue des Champs-Elysees or in some hotel of the same quality as my own, or finer if possible, the Ritz, the Bristol, the Meurice, and would afterward take a loge seat in some good theater devoted to the spoken drama or comic opera or even grand opera. This amounted, as one can see, to a kind of dual existence, whose charm lay in the ambiguity as to which figure was the real I and which the masquerade: was I the living commis-de-salle who waited on and flattered the guests in the Saint James and Albany, or was I the unknown man of distinction who looked as though he must keep a riding-horse and who would certainly, once he had finished dinner, call in at various exclusive salons, but was meanwhile graciously permitting himself to be served by waiters among whom I found

none equal to me in my other role? Thus I masqueraded in both capacities, and the undisguised reality behind the two appearances, the real I, could not be identified because it actually did not exist.
Thomas Mann, *Confessions of Felix Krull: Confidence Man* (1954)

Interchangeability. Krull is fascinated by the idea. All one need do is change clothes, speak with the "correct" diction, know what is normal in every situation, and—presto!—a waiter turns into an aristocrat. Or, as in Victorian England, an "epileptic" dresses in neat but threadbare clothes, stands in front of a large church on Sunday, places soap shavings under his tongue, and, when the congregation begins to leave, falls to the ground foaming at the mouth, only to be cared for by sympathetic, very generous Christian souls (Chesney, 1972).

Although changes often work, sometimes they fail. Krull's confidence masks the difficulty of being something he is not. At all times the con artist must try to control the thoughts and actions of others by means of his intimate knowledge of their beliefs, biases, or sympathies. For example, our foaming epileptic can appear only moderately sick. Too convincing a performance might produce enough worry for someone to call a doctor. And that inevitably clean bill of health would lead to another change of identity: from epileptic to convict.

Using the notion of interchangeability, imagine that you are an automobile mechanic. You are repairing someone's car while they are being obnoxious: "Are you doing that properly?" "Are you sure that goes there?" Politely, you excuse yourself to go get a part for the car. While in the storeroom, you fume. *That so-and-so, that ignoramus, if I didn't need his business, I'd tell him where to get off!* But, you do need his business, and when you leave the storeroom, you change your attitude. Anger is masked by a broad smile and you even go so far as to patiently listen to the customer's silly suggestions.

Are you a con artist? Perhaps, but the question is much less important than others: How often are "average" people faced with situations where they must be what they are not? And where did you and I learn the facial expressions, the tones of voice, the "schemes of interpretation" that allow us to successfully turn anger into happiness? And does everyone learn, *as a prerequisite for everyday life,* to split himself into two, to take the role of the other and to sometimes be, not what he is, but whatever they want him to be (Goffman, 1971b)? And, finally, are honest and dishonest presentations of self no more than an indication of the glue that holds social life together? Is it possible to argue that the prime cause of social order is not politics or economics but the learned frameworks (for example, the proper behavior when confronting a sick person who is lying on the ground foaming at the mouth) that allow people to successfully "locate, perceive, identify, label," and, if they wish, manipulate a seemingly infinite number of concrete occurrences (Goffman, 1974)?

It is not only possible to make this argument, but it is also possible to furnish a substantial body of evidence that proves it. But for that we must turn to the work of Erving Goffman.

FRAME ANALYSIS

Over the last twenty years Erving Goffman has written nine books and numerous articles. Much of this work can stand alone, a contribution in its own right, but taken together Goffman's work represents a very important and truly original contribution to social psychology.

What is *originality?* The dictionary says it is "freshness of aspect, design, or style," and the thesaurus lists the following synonyms: *primary, inventive, creative, novel, unique.* Well, Goffman's work is original[1] because it casts a fresh aspect, a different and novel perspective, on people's thought and action. Generally, that perspective is called dramaturgical. Goffman often focuses attention on people as actors. How did our epileptic stage his performance? And what did he do in his act? What facial expressions, phrases, and appeals were used to manipulate others and so ensure the success of his deception? Or, returning to the mechanic—in reacting to the customer, he presented a jovial, polite image of self. That presented self had nothing to do with his real self—how he actually felt toward and about the customer—but under the circumstances it was an image he felt obliged to present.

So, the perspective is dramaturgical because it focuses on how people present themselves to one another, how they act and react to each other. And one reason it is original is that it casts a novel aspect on the self. In Chapter One the self was defined as a person's representation of himself or herself as an object in the world of experience. Well, Goffman asks us to see that a person often has two selves, the one he is presenting to others and the one he really is. In effect, because our role-taking abilities allow us to split ourselves in two, we take the role of the other, present the self we think the other should or wants to see (for example, I am a white person) and, simultaneously, keep our real image of self hidden from public view (I am really a black person). Acutely conscious of ourselves as objects in the world of experience, we refuse to allow others to see how we actually feel about ourselves as objects in the world of experience.

---

[1] No one's work is absolutely original. Phenomenologists (for example, Schutz, 1963, 1967, 1974) have long dealt with issues similar to those raised by Goffman, and over the years Goffman's footnotes have betrayed a heavy if ambiguous debt to structural-functionalists such as Talcott Parsons.

Although presentations of self are a key element of his work, Goffman stresses that his focus is not "aspects of theater" that "creep into everyday life." The "language and mask of the stage" are helpful but only because they throw light on social interaction, because they help us to see that whenever people are in one another's immediate physical presence, the key factor in this structured meeting is "the maintenance of a single definition of the situation, this definition having to be expressed (via a presentation of self), and this expression sustained in the face of a multitude of potential disruptions" (Goffman, 1959). Say you are just entering a subway car. Study shows that, despite being in one another's immediate presence, subway riders try to avoid meeting one another. Eager to go unnoticed, people often take the nearest vacant seat. And by *not* communicating with their eyes, hands, or voices, people present an image of self that offers no information to others, as well as no reason for others to initiate any form of interaction. And, should one rider speak to another, a frequent response is to present an image of self that refuses to recognize the other's existence. Turning a cold shoulder, one person acts as if he did not hear what he did hear (see Levine et al., 1973).

For Goffman subway riding is an instance of "unfocused interaction," an example of those presentations that occur "solely by virtue" of people being in one another's presence. Think of walking through a crowded student union. You are alone but still very conscious of how your clothing, posture, and manner appear to others. However, in contrast to coincidental or unavoidable interactions, people continually agree "to sustain for a time a single focus of cognitive and visual attention." Goffman calls these focused meetings "encounters," and just because they are the substance of everyday life, the study of "situated activity systems" is one of Goffman's main goals. Indeed, for Goffman it is impossible to understand social order without first seeing the central place occupied by encounters such as buying a newspaper, ordering lunch from a waiter, eating it with a business acquaintance rather than a friend or relative, speaking to a faculty member about a grade, asking someone for directions, going for a job interview, purchasing gas at an attended rather than a self-service station (on encounters, see Goffman, 1961a).

Why are so many of our encounters successful? One answer is the presentation of self. Agreeing to sustain a particular focus of attention, we act "properly"; and even if an intense discussion with a faculty member is interrupted, perhaps by a telephone call or someone else coming into the office, we normally present an image of patience or fatalism: to the faculty member's "Excuse me," we respond with, "I'm in no hurry," or, shrugging our shoulders, "What are you gonna do, I'll wait." Second is the script, the frame that furnishes an organizational premise for the encounter. Continually we all present images of self, but Goffman stresses that we normally act by means of already internalized definitions of the situation. When entering the faculty member's office or a McDonald's or a department store, we are sensitive to the situation, aware of the self to be presented, and, while most frames fail to stage an encounter with precision, they always furnish organizational premises that serve as the general guidelines, the broad schemes of interpretation people are supposed to use in encounters (Goffman, 1974).

Frames are part of culture. Generally they are inherited and learned from significant and generalized others, but even if new frames are manufactured (for example, the proper language, gestures, and mood when two "Jesus freaks" meet one another), they are shared by groups of people. And that is why they contribute so significantly to social order. For members of the same culture learn an almost infinite number of frames and especially when socialization is so successful that people are unable to articulate the frames they always use, we enter encounters unaware of the definitions that ensure social order. Think of a college classroom. Yawns are often a good sign of student boredom, but if the teacher's eyes happen to catch a yawning student's, he or she almost always apologizes for "breaking frame." A student acts flustered or immediately presents an interested self or after class explains the reasons for sleepiness. Rarely do students say what is generally true: they were bored. Instead, acting through the frame (that is, students are supposed to be interested and even if they are not, why hurt a faculty member's feelings or, what is probably worse, risk a faculty member's wrath), they present, or apologize for not presenting, an image of self in harmony with the frame shared by members of the culture.

Sometimes people make a study of frames. A con artist's success rests on an ability to act, along with conscious knowledge of the frames other people take for granted. However, since most people are unable to articulate the schemes that guide their actions and presentations of self, Goffman's work tries to fill a void in our knowledge. Intentionally and consciously, he sets out to explain the frames that so often successfully order everyday life.

Goffman begins with primary frameworks, definitions of the situation that do not "hark back to some prior or 'original' interpretation"; instead, a primary framework renders an "otherwise meaningless aspect of the scene into something that is meaningful." For example, if a student quietly sings in class, that otherwise meaningless act acquires meaning: the frame dictates silence or at least no singing; maybe this student wants music, not social psychology? Always frames vary in degree of organization, and it is possible to distinguish between natural and social, primary frameworks. A framework is natural when something is seen as "purely physical." Success or failure is unimaginable because with events such as the weather "full determinism and determinators prevail." No presentation of self alters a typhoon or rain when we seek sun. In contrast to natural frameworks, social frameworks "provide background understanding for events that incorporate the will, aim, and controlling effort" of people. Here full determinism never prevails. Frames guide action but, in sharp contrast to the weather, people can be "coaxed, flattered, affronted, and threatened." In fact, people can even consciously decide to break frame, as well as create new ones. Always social interaction is a gamble (Goffman, 1974, 1971).

Now, keep Goffman's aim in mind: he wants "to develop the study of face-to-face interaction as a naturally bounded, analytically coherent field" (Goffman, 1971). Well, the notions of primary natural and social frameworks are the foundation concepts for that effort. Goffman says "we can hardly glance at anything without applying a primary framework" (Goffman, 1974), and especially with regard to social life, culture provides primary schemes of interpretation for virtually everything we do. Alone, these primary frameworks enable us to act in an orderly manner, but Goffman shows they also act as *the* building blocks for almost all forms of face-to-face interaction.

First are keyings, "the set of conventions by which a given activity, already meaningful in terms of some primary framework, is transformed into something patterned on this activity but seen by the participants to be something quite else" (Goffman, 1974). Consider make-believe. Two children are playing house, they are pretending to be mother and father. Consciously they know they are "making believe," but their game is based on a whole set of primary frameworks: who washes the dishes, who brings the slippers to whom, who pretends to cook, who says "That's delicious, darling."

Based on his notion of primary framework, Goffman tries to show how other forms of interactions are developed. Besides make-believe, he distinguishes four other basic keys: contests (for example, boxing, cross-country meets, horse racing); ceremonials; technical redoings (rehearsals for a job interview, war "games"); and regroundings, openly doing something for reasons or motives "radically different" from those that normally operate (a Las Vegas shill who plays blackjack so the table looks filled with gamblers). In effect, Goffman argues that keys build another frame on a primary frame. Seeing two people fighting and bloody on the street might move us to call the police, but witnessing two people fighting and bloody in a prizefight, we applaud the action and it is sometimes appropriate to boo if no blood is drawn.

Remember: while Goffman tries to coherently analyze face-to-face interaction, he never neglects the presentation of self. For example, whether in a primary framework or a keying, one important motive for people is "the motivational relevance of the event for the other persons present" (Goffman, 1974, 1963b). While attending a prizefight with his father, a son might be sickened by the violence but know the frame dictates applause and admiration. So, he cheers to make his father happy because he knows the scheme of interpretation says a "real man" enjoys a good fight and, of course, he does not want his father to think he is anything other than a "real man."

If keys are one way to transform primary frameworks, fabrications are another. However, where all concerned parties are normally aware of keyings, the essence of a fabrication is deception. For the deceived, "what is going on is *what* is being fabricated"; for the deceivers, "what is going on *is* fabrication" (Goffman, 1974). Consider an example from the 1968 presidential campaign of Richard Nixon. Television appearances often showed the candidate being questioned by unselected and unrehearsed citizens. In reality all questioners were thoroughly screened, and when the gallery of citizens surrounding the candidate spontaneously applauded an answer, they were actually responding to a stimulus, a red light that lit up a sign—APPLAUD—every time spontaneous applause was desired. So, for the candidate, his questioners, and his audience, what was going on *was* fabrication; but for television watchers, what was going on was spontaneous applause for the sound answers of a candidate responding to tough questions (McGinniss, 1969).

Goffman cites two general types of fabrications: the benign and the exploitive. Benign deception is supposedly in the interest, or at least not against the interest, of those deceived. Goffman cites as examples the playful deceit, the experimental hoax (say, of participants in a psychology experiment), training courses that test the loyalty of employees, or the large number of deceits labeled "parental constructions," for example, a father who lies when he tells his son there is no money for candy, or the conspiracy between doctor and family to prevent a patient from learning he is about to die (see Glaser and Strauss, 1965).

Exploitive fabrications are against a person's interests. Sometimes exploiters act within the law (for instance, lies told by police to extract a confession); often they are outside it, but either way, the aim in these fabrications is to "take" the person(s). And while people often assume that exploitive fabrications include two essential parties, the person conned and the person doing the conning, Goffman cites another type of deception: when a fabricator stages an encounter that furnishes a false definition of a second party for a third party. For example, study shows that police sometimes carry weapons they never use. What happens is that extra pistols and knives are taken along so they can be placed at the scene of conflict should police need to prove self-defense. Of course, if someone is dead, police have few worries about exposure, but Goffman notes that this type of con always requires a second party who will not be believed. For the deception to succeed, the fabricators should have a much greater sense of legitimacy than those being misrepresented (Goffman, 1974).

Some structural issues in fabrications will be considered later. For now remember that whether in a primary frame or almost any key, disruptions and even failures rarely destroy the possibility of once again defining things this way with these people. Rehearsals are perhaps the best example here, but think too of rematches between prizefighters or horses. However, whether benign or exploitive, "fabrications introduce the possibility of a different kind of disruption, one in which discovery can sharply alter the capacity for those involved to participate together in that kind of activity again" (Goffman, 1974). Obviously, someone is unlikely to pal around with people who successfully sold him the Brooklyn Bridge, but a less harmful fabrication, the practical joke, can often produce a very sharp reaction. Discovery of the joke can also lead to the discovery that one never wants to see that guy again!

With the concepts of primary framework, keys, and fabrications, Goffman takes a giant step toward achieving his goal; few encounters cannot be placed under one of these three conceptual umbrellas[2] and that means any understanding of how societies define situations is also an understanding of the "scripts" people use for their continual presentations of self. But, if we now possess a general map of encounters, we are still left with at least three important questions: How, when, where did we learn about frames, keys, and fabrications? And, what can we say about the social conditions that demand false presentations of self, as well as the social conditions that facilitate any presentation we decide to give?

Following Goffman's analysis, the acquisition of schemes of interpretation, of definitions of the situation, is first and foremost a study of the learning of primary frameworks. After all, if keys and fabrications build on these primary frames, people can only manipulate others if they have a thorough knowledge of primary frames, of what to expect from people when they are engaged in the many types of face-to-face interaction.

Although we still lack studies that specifically focus on the learning and internalization of primary frames, the social psychological literature offers some important suggestions. Refer again to our discussion of private speech in Chapter Two. From about three to about seven, children talk out loud, and only to themselves, in public. Apparently, whether collective monologue, dialogue, or self-guiding speech, children practice what others tell them about self and world. And what is a central topic of these discussions? It is the frames that Goffman argues are so important for social order.

---

[2] The discussion here of these concepts provides only a broad outline. In *Frame Analysis*, Goffman handles each detail, and with the nuances included, not excluded. See Goffman's work for any thorough analysis of these concepts.

Consider a four-year-old child who is playing cops and robbers. First, he is the "bad buy" who has robbed a bank. Then, sirens screeching, he is a policeman chasing the thief. Finally, he apprehends his opponent who, when caught, sheepishly submits to the orders of legitimate authority.

Reflect on the child's achievements. His dialogue shows that he already understands a primary framework quite well. And not only that, this four-year-old shows a sophisticated ability to key. He consciously knows he is only pretending to be bad guy and policeman; and while he is completely unable to explain how he transformed a primary frame into the key of make-believe, *that* inability does not set him apart from adults. As Goffman notes, people are "likely to be unaware of such organized features as the framework has and unable to describe the framework with any completeness if asked, yet these handicaps are no bar to their easily and fully applying it" (Goffman, 1974; also 1971a).

Based on the attitudes and instruction of others, from the ages of three to seven, children publicly practice primary frames, keys, and fabrications of all sorts.[3] By seven they no longer need to talk out loud in public; now relying primarily on silent inner speech, or thought, children show a capacity to understand a multitude of primary frames. Indeed, since silent speech indicates they no longer need to practice, seven-year-olds are in one sense very much like adults: both are unable to explain frames, both thoroughly take them for granted, and both are able to easily apply frames, keys, and fabrications.

Three qualifications must be made at this point. First, while a child's ability to think *symbolizes* his developed capacity to deal in frames, public practice is based on the attitudes and instruction of others. Take two examples. My wife and I played "peek-a-boo-I-see-you" with our nine-month-old daughter. Usually we simply peeked from behind a doorway and said "peek-a-boo." By eleven months our daughter played peek-a-boo with us. On a very elementary level she was already keying, in this case playing make-believe. Or, take the everyday instruction parents give children about frames. If someone is on the telephone, please do not interrupt, wait. If you do not feel like playing with a friend, why hurt his feelings; perhaps you should just say you do not feel well. And, finally, if you meet someone with a physical handicap, a stigma (Goffman, 1963a), try not to stare or in any way call attention to the stigma. Perhaps it is even better for you to act as if the stigma does not exist.

---

[3] Sometimes the fabrications are benign; consider the child who cries "wolf" only to find parents who hate the joke. And sometimes fabrications are exploitive; for instance, the child who says he ate his vegetables when they are actually in his pocket, soon to be flushed down the toilet.

The second qualification relates to the comparison of children and adults. Able to deal in possibilities, as well as to thoroughly understand and manipulate concepts, adults are generally able to apply their knowledge of frames far more fully than even the brightest seven-year-old. However, the comparison was drawn to underline that by seven, children take a host of frames, keys, and fabrications for granted. And this assurance is essential for everyday social order. For like adults, children are then so sure of the appropriate schemes of interpretation, so confident that encounters are broadly defined in only this way, that they need not enter most forms of face-to-face interaction expecting the unexpected. In fact, once they gain the capacity to think, children need only "automatically" draw from the well that is mind their large store of taken-for-granted knowledge about frames, keys, and fabrications.

The final qualification relates to social change. The faster social change takes place, and the more it concerns important aspects of everyday life (for instance, the frames that define encounters between men and women), the greater the chances of everyday social disorder. For now, Goffman is right; everyday social order is still generally intact. The frames we learn in childhood still serve most of us well as adults. But Goffman consistently argues that cracks in many frames are obvious. For example, in a period of rapid social change, there are bound to be "frame gaps" between the 10 percent of the population over sixty-five and the 45 percent of the population under twenty-five. So, to the extent that social change undermines the validity of frames learned in childhood, or, what is probably worse, to the extent that others furnish weak frames, our presentations of self are likely to be rooted in anxiety and our encounters with others are likely to become increasingly impossible and chaotic.

PRESENTATIONS OF SELF

This section attempts to answer four questions. What are the components of any presentation of self? What are some of the variables that "force" us to present an image of self that is different from our actual image of self? And is everyone, the honest and the dishonest, the sincere and the exploiters, consistently involved in false presentations of self and situation? Is there any way to avoid splitting up the self within and the self without, the self presented to others?

Let us begin with the elements of any presentation. Front is that part of a person's performance "which regularly functions in a general and fixed fashion to define the situation for those who observe the performance" (Goffman, 1959; 1967b; 1971c). In effect, based on the setting of the performance, as well as a person's appearance and manner, we establish for others a definition of self and situation. Setting refers to furniture, decor, physical layout, and other *background* items that stage the performance. Appearance refers to signs of social status, along with a person's "temporary ritual state": Do I appear to be hard at work or am I apparently ready for any form of recreation? Manner indicates "the interaction role I expect to play: am I haughty or submissive or indifferent" (Goffman, 1959)?

Always, front stages a presentation of self, but remember that even the best staged performance can "bomb." For example, consider the experience of one wife who tried to be a "total woman." The house was all set for romance, the woman's manner was both starry-eyed and submissive, and her appearance was different: in order to entice her husband, she was "dressed à la gypsy with beads, bangles, and bare skin." However, despite her efforts with all the aspects of front, this woman's presentation failed. Hearing a knock at the door, she danced over to open it. Turning on an enticing smile while turning the doorknob, she only succeeded in greeting a stunned water-meter reader (Morgan, 1975)!

The most important bases for front are the primary frames we learn from others. For these not only tell us what to expect from others in the way of action, they also point out the proper setting, appearance, and manner for whatever we have in mind. In fact, if you were to break down your daily interactions into frames, think of the many fronts you use, and also consider the many and varied presentations of self that you give every day of your life. How many of those presentations are in harmony with what you actually feel about self in that situation? How much is one's life filled with situations that ask us to present one self while being or feeling like another?

Goffman's answer is quite a few. He writes of "interaction constraints," of factors that play upon people by demanding a false presentation of self. Obviously, some of these constraints are voluntary; when we try to deceive someone, the whole point is to present a convincingly false presentation of self. However, other constraints are involuntary; deeply woven into the fabric of social life, they consistently furnish "good reasons" for presenting a false image of self and situation.

What are some of these constraints? One is a subdivision of benign fabrications: a need for secrecy. Perhaps you have a problem, but do not want your parents or friends to know. Actually worried, perhaps even scared, you present an image of happiness and contentment. Or, say you are tired when your children want to play. Instead of presenting your tired self, you act as if you were eager to play, play, play. A second example is the problem of expression versus action. Perhaps you are a hardworking, excellent employee. But you work in a large corporation and the only way to get ahead is to express yourself, to tell others what a good job you are doing. So, you go to cocktail parties, join clubs, and even eat in the executive dining room. Continually you present a very happy image, while in reality you are unhappy about the self you feel forced to present. Third is a job that not only requires skill but a continually smiling presentation of self. Here service occupations are the best example; you are a clerk in a department store, a receptionist for a large corporation, a waiter or waitress at any of America's many hamburger havens. To keep the job, you must always smile, say thank you, and even add, "Have a good day and please come back again." In reality you hate the job, as well as think it is no reflection on the "real" you but, since any indication of role distance might threaten your job, you smile for a full eight-hour shift! Fourth, and last, think of those many situations when you conclude, "It's not worth it." You are arguing with someone, decide there is no point in talking to this person but, because you see no reason to hurt his feelings, or because the encounter will soon be over, you agree with him or suddenly discover you are sick: "I must leave at once!" Again you present an image of self that bears little relation to the self you really are, at that moment, in that situation.

If we were to include examples of voluntary fabrications,[4] the number of interaction constraints would multiply indefinitely. It is enough that all cultures teach frames that furnish "good reasons" for presenting a false image of self and situation, enough that people who never use exploitive fabrications are still put in situations where they must be what they are not.

Exactly how often do we present a false image of self? The question cannot be answered without considering a number of variables. For example, con artists are continually presenting false images of self, and people with very poor global images of self often present an image of self-confidence. So, rather than try to even grossly quantify the number of false presentations, let us be satisfied with this conclusion. In Chapter One we discussed the self as an image *within* a person; it exists *inside* your mind and mine. Goffman asks us to see another self: the one we present to others, the one they impute to us as a *result* of our performance. Often the self within and the self presented are the same; many people who present an image of self-confidence *are* self-confident. However, because he forces us to see this second self, Goffman forces us to see ourselves as actors, as presenters of a true or (perhaps just as often) presenters of a false image of self (esp. 1955).

---

[4] Goffman discusses the way products are presented to a public. For example, a number of introductory sociology texts are not written by the authors. These "managed texts" are put together by book editors, professional writers, *and* sociologists. However, the sociologists present the image of being authors, while in reality the book is, for the most part, devised and written by others.

PRESENTATION PROBLEMS

CHARLES SURFACE. What! Joseph? you jest.
SIR PETER TEAZLE. Hush!—a little French milliner—and the best of the jest is—she's in the room now.
CHARLES SURFACE. The devil she is!
SIR PETER TEAZLE. Hush! I tell you. *(Points to the screen)*
CHARLES SURFACE. Behind the screen! S' life, let's unveil her!
SIR PETER TEAZLE. No, No, he's coming. You shan't indeed!
CHARLES SURFACE. Oh, egad, we'll have a peep at the little milliner!
SIR PETER TEAZLE. Not for the world!—Joseph will never forgive me.
CHARLES SURFACE. I'll stand by you—
SIR PETER TEAZLE. Odds, here he is.
Joseph Surface enters just as Charles throws down the screen.
CHARLES SURFACE. Lady Teazle, by all that's wonderful!
SIR PETER TEAZLE. Lady Teazle, by all that's damnable!
CHARLES SURFACE. Sir Peter, this is one of the smartest French milliners I ever saw. Egad, you seem all to have been diverting yourselves here at hide and seek, and I don't see who is out of the secret . . . so I'll leave you to yourselves. *(Exits)*
They stand for some time looking at each other.
JOSEPH SURFACE. Sir Peter—notwithstanding—I confess—that appearances are against me—if you will afford me your patience—I make no doubt—but I shall explain everything to your satisfaction.
SIR PETER TEAZLE. If you please, sir.
JOSEPH SURFACE. The fact is, sir, that Lady Teazle, knowing my pretensions to your ward Maria—I say, sir, Lady Teazle, being apprehensive of the jealousy of your temper—and knowing my relationship to the family—she, sir, I say—called here—in order that—I might explain these pretensions—but on your coming—being apprehensive—as I said—of your jealousy—she withdrew—and this, you may depend on it, is the whole truth of the matter.
SIR PETER TEAZLE. A very clear account, upon my word; and I dare swear the lady will vouch for every article of it.
LADY TEAZLE. For not one word of it, Sir Peter!
SIR PETER TEAZLE. How! don't you think it worthwhile to agree in the lie?
LADY TEAZLE. There is not one syllable of truth in what that gentleman has told you.
SIR PETER TEAZLE. I believe you, upon my soul, ma'am!
JOSEPH SURFACE. *(Aside to Lady Teazle)* S' death, madam, will you betray me? [Richard Brinsley Sheridan, *The School for Scandal* (1777)]

Since any presentation of self is "diffusely located in the flow of events" and, at that, relies for success on the correct interpretation of others, any presentation is always open to failure. Like a mortgaged house, presented images are "on loan from society" and unless people conduct themselves in a way that is worthy of the presented self, foreclosure can follow. Like Joseph Surface, anyone can fall on the face he presents to others (Goffman, 1955).

Consider Joseph's problem. He successfully presents an image, a face, to Sir Peter: he is a "rake" with a milliner hidden behind a screen. Then, when the screen drops, he is *"in wrong face"*; the milliner turns out to be Sir Peter's wife. Quickly, Joseph tries to *save face;* despite information that explodes the line he is pursuing, Joseph tries to give the impression that he has not lost face. But no one is willing to *give face* to Joseph, no one is willing to help him with his now problematic presentation of self. Instead, after his face-saving try, Lady Teazle calls him a liar and Sir Peter indicates he never believed Joseph anyway. The result is a failed presentation of self; Sir Peter now sees Joseph's right face, but for Joseph that is the wrong face. In fact, once Sir Peter and Lady Teazle refuse to help, Joseph no longer has any selves to present. He is both shamefaced and *out of* faces (Goffman, 1955, 1974).

Now, consider all the possibilities: we can successfully present a face (that is, an image of self) to others, we can be in the wrong face, we can try to save face, we can give face, and we can also be out of face. All of these exist as possibilities in any encounter and what follows below is an analysis of some of the pitfalls that threaten encounters, along with a discussion of those actions people can take, the "face work" they can use, to make whatever they are doing consistent with the face threatened by their actions.

Four everyday pitfalls in encounters are: external preoccupation, self-consciousness, interaction consciousness, and other-consciousness (Goffman, 1957). Consider other-consciousness. Two friends are happily talking to one another. Then, someone else walks by, and one "friend" leaves the other to talk to the newcomer. Clearly, other-consciousness is offensive; for it breaks an important yet unwritten "ground rule" of many encounters: "Don't treat a person as a thing; don't neglect your obligation to support *my* face along with your own. Do some face work, because if you don't, you not only undermine your presentation of self, you threaten the self *within* me." To use Meadian language: "By leaving he is telling me I am not worth talking to. Why, he is telling *me* I am such a nothing I can be left stranded and alone, forced to do his face work."

Take another example: interaction consciousness. Here, instead of getting involved in the topic of conversation, a person becomes "consciously concerned to an improper degree with the way in which the interaction, qua interaction, is going." Goffman uses the example of host and hostess at a party. It is their responsibility to make sure everyone is having a good time and, if they take their responsibility seriously or the party seems dead, they may try to act to others like the friends they are but actually present an image of self that reflects their true focus of attention: is everyone having a good time? Incidentally, in contrast to other-consciousness, here others are likely to "give face" or at least not take offense. Where there is no apparent explanation for the rudeness discussed above, people at a party are thoroughly familiar with the frame and so likely to understand as well as sympathize with the host and hostess's interaction consciousness.

Self-consciousness occurs when someone who ought to be able to talk about the topic of conversation talks instead about himself or herself. For example, Robert Stebbins lists a number of rules for presenting self in a wide variety of frames. Don't monopolize conversations with self-centered talk. Be candid about weaknesses; don't overemphasize achievements; express approval of others' achievements; and when comparing one's self with others, be charitable. Don't make invidious comparisons (Stebbins, 1972). Whether at a party, a professional gathering, or a casual encounter, violation of these rules breaks a social norm. And when people are trying to present a positive image of self, they must refrain from overstepping the boundaries set by cultural frames. The line between justifiable pride and obnoxious conceit is very thin and it is easily crossed. This is especially so if a very positive face is presented to others who have doubts about the self within (Stebbins, 1972).

Another pitfall often met in social encounters is the presenting of one face and then the quick introduction of another (Gross and Stone, 1964). Pretend that you are a woman student talking to a male professor. For ten minutes the conversation has been academic, but suddenly the professor introduces his sex role. Before, his face was serious, now it is eager, and yours expresses surprise and unhappiness. The professor then counters with his knowledge of face work. Or, referring again to Chapter Three, consider an aged person who, when he is a customer at a gas station, suddenly presents a "dead" self, i.e., the occupational identity he had before he retired. Here society's injunction against continuing work is an assault on the self within, often compelling aged persons to present their dead identities in the most uncalled-for situations. This is embarrassing to others and it is also a symbol of the aged person's pain. Retired, he tries to take role distance by presenting to others a face that was once in harmony, a face that was once the self within and simultaneously the self without, the self he presented to others.

A last example concerns the violation of personal space. For study shows that in learning frames, we also learn the distance that is supposed to remain between members of the encounter. Always the "proper" distance varies with the relationship and the culture, but should people sit too close when the frame dictates distance, or too far away when the frame says close proximity, a problematic presentation of self occurs. The classic example is interaction between an American woman and an Arab man at a cocktail party. Uncomfortable about the closeness of the man, the woman back-pedals until she can no longer escape. Literally cornered, she must do something about what is for the Arab man the normal distance two people use for everyday encounters (Hall, 1966; Hendrick et al., 1974).

Assuming presentation problems, what are the common forms of face work used to sustain the threatened image? One remedy is an account (Goffman, 1971b); like Joseph Surface, the person can try to set things straight with an explanation. And, generally, people are willing to listen; they may not give face but, assuming even a minimal interest in the encounter, others are also committed to the presented self. For example, if presentation problems arise in a public place, a person might listen to an account only because a refusal could easily mean a very embarrassing incident.

Accounts take many forms. A person can say he did not do what he did, and in a public place such as a crowded subway car, someone may be willing to listen. Or, consider the case of Patty Hearst. Presenting a revolutionary image to the world, she now argues differently. Contending that others forced her, or tricked her, into presenting a revolutionary face, she asks us to understand that only circumstances made her present a radical image. In reality, the self within her never changed; she was never what she appeared to be. Or, finally, some accounts plead ignorance. Pretend you are happy and present that face to another. Unfortunately, the other has good cause for grief, and while your plea of ignorance will normally be accepted, you still feel—unjustifiably—like a bungler.

Sometimes accounts are insufficient; the only remedy is an apology, the only way to explain the presented face is to dissociate oneself from it by affirming a belief in the offended rule (Goffman, 1971b). Generally people accept apologies, especially when they are accompanied by "penance or restitution," but if the other responds to the apology with a too critical or "holier than thou" face, apology could easily turn into anger and defense of the offensive face. For people seem to have a "special license to accept mistreatment" at their own hands which they cannot or will not accept from others. In effect, "I won't carry the special license to extremes, but you might." So, in accepting my apology, abide by what Goffman calls the rights and obligations of an interactant, abide by the unwritten rule to treat my presented face as an object of "sacred value" (Goffman, 1955).

A third way to deal with problematic presentations is to prepare people for them. Here, instead of waiting for a problem to develop, a person foresees it and so "asks license of a potentially offended person to engage in what could be considered a violation of his rights." For example, take the case of a middle-level executive who has orders to discipline one of his staff. In order to obey orders, he has to publicly offend the employee, but, before doing so, he tells the staff member that while he knows this is not right, there is no other way for both of them to remain on the job. Then, not only is the employee prepared for the problem, but what could have been seen as an offense is transformed into a gesture of regard for the potentially offended person. I thank you for presenting an offensive image of self (Goffman, 1971c).

Accounts, apologies, and requests: these are the three general types of face work used to remedy problematic presentations of self. Often two are used together—"guilty with an explanation, your honor"—and sometimes none are used at all. For it is entirely possible that a person may care neither about the face he presents to others nor about the self-image of others. Put differently, it *is* an unwritten rule of interaction to take account of another's internal and external images of self. But in many societies people also learn to "get ahead." And to return to the offense of otherconsciousness, one person may, without account or apology, swiftly turn away from one encounter to enter another, one more likely to produce progress in getting ahead.

WATERGATE AND STRUCTURAL PROBLEMS IN FABRICATIONS

So far attention has been focused on the individual. Now let's think of ourselves as members of a team. Defined by Goffman as "any set of individuals who cooperate in staging a single routine" (1959), examples of teams include a public relations department engaged in presenting a favorable image of a corporation, or a company of soldiers working together to present an efficient, capable image to an inspecting officer, or the staff of a fine restaurant who cooperate to present an image of elegance and excellence. Normally teams run a greater risk than individuals of having a failed presentation of self. Numbers alone increase the chance of poor performance, as well as increasing the risk of disloyalty. Like Daniel Ellsberg with *The Pentagon Papers,* one person may reassess his relationship to the team, decide he wants to quit, and in so doing intentionally undermine the team's presentation of self and situation.

Teams, like individuals, operate in different regions. Defined "as any place that is bounded to some degree by barriers to perception," Goffman makes a distinction between front and back regions, between onstage and backstage. For example, a restaurant's front regions are its dining areas; kitchens or staff rooms are its back regions. In a department store showrooms are front regions; stockrooms are back regions. And, finally, when entertaining guests, a family's living and dining rooms are front regions; there the family is onstage. But normally, bedrooms and especially closets are back regions, places closed to almost all visitors (Goffman, 1959).

Regions are of great help in making a successful presentation of self and situation. Onstage the team cooperates in delivering the desired image; meanwhile the closed back regions furnish a place to practice, to show anger forbidden onstage, and to hide secrets that might easily undermine the team's presentation. Generally, the more the team has to hide, the greater the barriers put up to prevent members of the audience from ever getting backstage. For example, the State Department has Room 6510A. Closed to the audience of citizens as well as most members of the State Department team, few officials are ever permitted inside this room. For it does not contain confidential, secret, or "top secret" information; here the department keeps its "super secrets," information so highly confidential that until recently no one even knew there was a government classification of secrets above "top secret" (Wise, 1973).

Although not every team has a Room 6510A, it is hard to imagine a team without back regions that contain secrets. And that means team members must not only cooperate in giving a performance, they must also cooperate in denying the audience access to backstage secrets. Even the best presentation fails if members of the audience somehow lift the curtain and peer into a reality they were never meant to see.

Watergate was a social tragedy. It was also the effort of a sophisticated team to present an innocent image of self to its audience of citizens. Watergate has great historical significance, but here that significance takes a back seat to viewing Watergate as a means of emphasizing a number of structural issues about team and individual fabrications of reality.

News of the break in reached members of the Nixon team in California soon after McCord, security chief of the Committee to Re-Elect the President (CREEP), and his colleagues were arrested. Naturally disturbed, team members chose as one of their first tasks the search for a "secure" phone. Conceivably, someone had already bugged the team's backstage and that would destroy the performance before it began. From Washington Gordon Liddy told Jeb Magruder the military base at El Segundo had a secure phone, but the problem had an easier solution: pay phones are apparently backstage for everyone. So Magruder called Liddy from a pay phone, got the shocking details, and an assurance as well: Liddy's men were members of the team, "they would never talk" (Magruder, 1975).

Magruder immediately got team members together to discuss their problem. Initially they were going to use one of their own hotel rooms but, since their wives were not considered members of the team, they used the room of John Mitchell's bodyguard. In this and other early meetings, Magruder says "no one ever considered there would *not* be a cover-up." That was "immediate and automatic," for "it seemed inconceivable that with our political power we could not erase this mistake we had made" (Magruder, 1975, emphasis in original).

The first try at erasure failed: hoping to get McCord out of jail and then have him disappear, the team was unable to obtain McCord's release. That meant his participation in the break in had to be explained, and in a series of meetings extending over four weeks, Mitchell, LaRue, Magruder, and sometimes Dean and Mardian put their heads together and came up with a story presenting an innocent image of self. However, before we touch on that story, remember that within two days of the break in (it occurred on June 17, 1972), team members had destroyed damaging backstage evidence. Liddy, Strachan, and Magruder all shredded records that might threaten the team's presentation. Moreover, while Magruder and Mitchell were developing a plausible presentation, team leaders at the White House had decided they must lie to team members.

Goffman discusses this in terms of layers. Either a key or a fabrication is a layer on a primary frame; like a coat placed on a nude body, the layer covers up previously uncovered, previously untransformed activity. Well, sometimes, there is a layer on top of a layer; sometimes people engage in an exploitive fabrication and then discover that someone else has built another layer on their layer (Goffman, 1974). In this case the June 23 transcript between Nixon and Haldeman shows both deeply implicated in the exploitive fabrication. But neither man, and especially Nixon, told other team members he knew what they were doing. On the contrary, Nixon's initially convincing presentation of innocence and ignorance was such an effective layering of a layer that some team members worked even harder to protect their innocent boss (White, 1975).

Remember how long this layer on a layer remained uncovered: Nixon presented an image of innocence for over two years, through a series of performances that included fifteen statements or open letters, eight press conferences, and four television appearances (White, 1975). Over time members of the team and members of the audience became increasingly suspicious about the image presented, but it was only when people gained access to the deepest regions of backstage, the White House's "Room 6510A," that the layer was incontestably revealed. And even then reactions varied. Deceived for two years, presidential speechwriter Raymond Price said: "The President had done me a favor by deceiving me. It meant that I'd been able to write for him honestly" (White, 1975).

Through Haldeman and Ehrlichman, the president was trying to use the CIA to stop the investigation in its tracks, but this was a backstage attempt. Onstage CREEP, and especially Magruder, were accounting for their illegal and possibly unscrupulous image of self. Essentially their line was that CREEP had allotted a substantial sum of money for convention security. Certainly this was understandable. With large numbers of radicals running about, CREEP could take no chances. Unfortunately, Liddy did. *He* authorized the break in and while CREEP did admit to a loose distribution of so much money, it was obviously silly to believe that responsible men would sanction such a "third-rate burglary." And, if anyone questioned this account, all they had to do was ask Liddy. But, since members of the CREEP team knew Liddy was not talking, indeed, Liddy had volunteered to be murdered, their account effectively put journalistic investigators into a corner: if they questioned the story, they always had to come back to Liddy and he was not talking.

This presentation of self was based on an accurate perception of the structural issues in fabrications. For Goffman correctly notes that any discrediting of a presented image may "retrospectively undermine a linked series of prior occasions" (Goffman, 1974). Mitchell, Dean, and Magruder knew that a failed presentation would allow its audience to know of many still mysterious campaign events, for example, the tricks played on Senator Muskie. And Nixon, Haldeman, and Ehrlichman, again placing a layer on a layer to many team members, were worried that any failed presentation would expose the plumbers' operations and especially the break in at the offices of Daniel Ellsberg's psychiatrist. So, it was crucial for structural reasons to keep the indictments limited to the seven men who participated in the Watergate break in. Of course, team members were prepared should their attempts fail. Realizing that team members might be tempted to be dramaturgically disloyal (Goffman, 1959), the seven members of the break-in team were well cared for and Dean assured Magruder "the President is very pleased with the way you've handled things. You can be sure that if you're indicted, you'll be taken care of," that is, you will receive executive clemency and your family will have no financial problems (Magruder, 1975).

Now, recall the team's success. Only the seven burglars were indicted. Apparently the structure of fabrications was secure; unlike London Bridge, it did not seem to be falling down. However, despite their most strenuous efforts, teammates knew their presentation was still full of holes. Especially with regard to the laundering of money in Mexico, the team's presentation was quite shaky.

Enter Woodward and Bernstein, two indefatigable *Washington Post* reporters. They had found out about the $89,000 in Mexican checks, the $25,000 check from a former Humphrey supporter, as well as the "slush fund" in the hands of Maurice Stans. Why weren't these mentioned in the indictment of the seven burglars? Bernstein and Woodward meant to find out. And they did. But remember their helpers. Someone called them about the possible role of Donald Segretti, and throughout their tenacious investigations they had the invaluable aid of "Deep Throat," a very high-level example of dramaturgical disloyalty. Woodward met with "Deep Throat" in parking lot garages at two or three in the morning. It was he who suggested they focus on other things besides the break in, who told them about CREEP's attempts to destroy the Democratic opposition, who consistently confirmed or denied facts or suspicions held by the two reporters. And without such high-level confirmation, many of the *Post* stories would not have appeared. And if they had not appeared, team members might have presented, if not a plausible account, at least a successful one (Bernstein and Woodward, 1975; Magruder, 1975; White, 1975).

How did the team react to the *Post*'s continuing revelations? One response was no response: when stories about CREEP's campaign of dirty tricks were published, Press Secretary Ziegler refused twenty-nine times in thirty minutes to discuss the matter. A second response was to take the offensive and present an image of a malicious Eastern newspaper slandering the administration of the silent majority. This was an especially plausible image since teammates knew that its audience "had been softened up" by three years of speeches from Vice-President Agnew. And finally, the team, and particularly the first team at the White House, went right on proclaiming its innocence. Confronted with published stories about White House aide Dwight Chapin's directions to Donald Segretti, Ziegler simply continued to play the part of Snow White: "You know, since the Watergate case broke, people have been trying to link the case to the White House . . . and no link has been established . . . because no link exists . . . I am not going to dignify these types of stories with a comment" (Bernstein and Woodward, 1975).

And generally he did not. But as stories continued to appear, and especially after the establishment of the Ervin Committee on February 7, 1973, the team knew it had to alter its presentation. Claiming innocence and citing executive privilege as a way to keep people out of backstage was effective, but a better line was to give someone else presentation problems. So a new strategy runs through the transcripts of early 1973: flood the newspapers with stories of Democratic dirty tricks. Beat the Ervin Committee to the starting line by having Attorney General Kleindienst come up with a series of backstage information about the other team (White, 1975).

Although this strategy was actually used well in 1974, it failed because no relevations about the Democrats could compete with the charges of James McCord. Despite large sums of money, as well as assurance of executive clemency, McCord broke ranks; yet another example of dramaturgical disloyalty, he charged (on March 23, 1973) that perjury had been committed in the Grand Jury hearings, and he also alleged involvement by Magruder and a relatively unknown member of the team, John Dean.

Now Dean was a White House legal counsel and a real problem for the team's presented image: How could they explain charges that he directed the cover-up? Publicly, the explanation was simple: Ronald Ziegler repeatedly said the president had talked to Dean and we "flatly deny any prior knowledge on the part of Mr. Dean regarding the Watergate matter." However, in private, backstage, the team was quite worried about its image. Since early March Dean had been talking to the president and in the now famous discussion of March 21, Dean told Nixon of a "cancer on the presidency." Keeping layer on layer, the president never revealed to Dean his own early direction of the break in but instead asked Dean to keep the cap on the bottle until they could devise a new strategy for presenting themselves.

Dean agreed to the president's requests, but since Dean had already talked to federal prosecutors by March 21, that discussion was a perfect example of what Goffman calls "containment competition." Backstage, the two men could talk candidly; they need not imitate Ziegler's comments to the press. But Nixon placed a layer over his remarks by never telling Dean of his actual knowledge and involvement in the cover-up, while Dean placed a layer over his remarks by never telling the president he had already been dramaturigcally disloyal. In some of the April conversations, the competition between the two men heightened. Nixon added another layer to his first layer by "bugging the backstage"; when he and Dean talked, Nixon tried to engineer a conversation that showed himself to be innocent. But Dean, no amateur at layering, added another when he suspected the president of taping their conversation. Coolly, Dean continued to talk as if nothing happened, but the president's new layer was nullified by Dean's new layer. In effect, the two men were trying to con each other, each (or at least Dean) knowing the other was trying to con him, but each trying to outcon the other (Goffman, 1974).

Consider the extent of what Goffman calls "transformational depth" (Goffman, 1974). The primary frame is a conversation between two people. Then Nixon added a layer by not telling Dean he knew from the start, Dean added a layer by not telling Nixon he was disloyal, Nixon capped this with a third layer when he bugged the talk, and Dean added a fourth layer when he suspected but did not say anything about the bug. Conceivably, there was even a fifth layer: Nixon might have guessed Dean's suspicions, but acted as if he did not. Ideally, there is no limit to layering, but in reality a point of no return is eventually reached. Seemingly, the complexity of the encounter would overwhelm its participants; after a while there would be no possibility of maintaining a structure with an endless number of layers. How could they talk and simultaneously keep in mind which layer of fabrication they were then using?

But, once again, back to the cover-up. Dean and McCord's revelations forced the team to reconsider its presentation. Now they had to allow the audience backstage: in order to show that the White House and especially the president had nothing to hide, they had to waive executive privilege and allow team members to testify before the Ervin Committee and the Grand Jury. In effect the presented image (on March 30) was one of cooperation: the team was doing its best to uncover the truth and, to show their sincerity, they would let their people testify. Meanwhile, backstage,

Nixon, Haldeman, and Ehrlichman were frantically searching for a scapegoat. Magruder had to go but, once again perceiving that discrediting one image threatened others, team members realized that if Magruder's image collapsed, so would Mitchell's, and then John Dean's. So, the "scenario" was to place total blame on Dean. But Dean refused to take the blame, and when the president failed to convince Assistant Attorney General Petersen not to grant Dean the immunity he sought,[5] Nixon no longer had any choice. In his April 30 television address, he tried to account and even apologize for his failed presentation of self. Now "there has been an effort to conceal the facts," now the president was misled by his subordinates, now Dean, Haldeman, and Ehrlichman were all leaving the administration, now there would be a special prosecutor, and, while the president stoutly maintained his own innocence, now he accepted responsibility for the uncontrolled actions of his overzealous campaign workers (White, 1975; *New York Times*, 1975).

Although overloaded with lies, this was a good presentation of self. Cornered, the president admitted overall responsibility but *no guilt;* playing on the public's presumed sympathies, the essence of the presentation was: "I should have known but I was too busy being your president. You (the audience) and I were both lied to." However, despite this "good" presentation, hindsight shows it was doomed from the start. Two days later details of the Ellsberg break in appeared, the Ervin hearings began on May 17, on May 18 Archibald Cox was named special prosecutor, in late June Dean's testimony implicated the president, and then, a little over two weeks later (on July 16) Alexander Butterfield made a startling remark: the team had bugged itself! Get the tapes and you have an exact record of everything that happened backstage. Get the tapes and no one will be able to present a false image of self; backstage will be onstage.

After Butterfield's revelations, the team presented many images of self: the president who would like to tell all but could not because it would undermine the office of the president; the administration that was being viciously pursued by newspapers and congressional committees; the president who was using the government's total resources to make sure the truth got out; the president who turned over a mountain of transcripts that included "all relevant portions of all the subpoenaed conversations" (Mankiewicz, 1975; White, 1975). Overall, the dominant image was that of innocence, persecution, and, especially as the courts began to agree with the special prosecutor, of a president trying to protect the Constitution by maintaining executive privilege.

How much of this did the team actually believe? That is hard to know. Certain is the fact that all these presentations had the same general goal:

---

[5] Apparently the idea was that, without immunity, Dean would remain silent and silence would protect Haldeman and Ehrlichman.

to keep the audience from reaching the deepest regions of backstage. Eventually the audience got there. And eventuallly the president had to resign. But even then he did it for the audience's good—"to continue to fight through the months ahead for my personal vindication would almost totally absorb the time and attention of the president and the Congress . . ."—and even then the team made certain of a sound presentation of self. For the morning of his departure from the White House on August 9, 1974, the president received the following instructions from teammates (White, 1975):

> 9:30 A.M. You and the First Family pause in the Grand Hallway for Honor and announcement. You enter to "Hail to the Chief" and move directly to the platform along the center of the East Wall and take your positions (stage right to left) as follows: Ed. Tricia. Mrs. Nixon. The President (behind podium). Julie. David.
> Note: There will be tape on the platform indicating where each family member should stand. There will be a slight separation between Mrs. Nixon and Tricia so that Mrs. Nixon will be closer to you as you speak.

Bibliographical References

Archibald, W. Peter, and Cohen, Ronald. "Presentation, Embarrassment, and Facework as a Function of Self; Evaluation, Conditions of Self-Presentation, and Feedback from Others." *Journal of Personality and Social Psychology* 20 (1971): 287–97.

Bernstein, Carl, and Woodward, Bob. *All the President's Men.* New York: Warner, 1975.

Chesney, Kellow. *The Victorian Underworld.* London: Penguin, 1972.

Glaser, Barney, and Strauss, Anselm. *Awareness of Dying.* Chicago: Aldine, 1965.

Goffman, Erving. "Alienation from Interaction." *Human Relations* 10 (1957): 47–60.

Goffman, Erving. *Asylums: Essays on the Social Situation of Mental Patients and Other Inmates.* Garden City, N.Y.: Doubleday, 1961b.

Goffman, Erving. *Behavior in Public Places: Notes on the Social Organization of Gatherings.* New York: Free Press, 1963b.

Goffman, Erving. "Embarrassment and Social Organization." In *Interaction Ritual: Essays on Face-to-Face Behavior,* pp. 97–112. Garden City, N.Y.: Doubleday, 1967c.

Goffman, Erving. *Encounters: Two Studies in the Sociology of Interaction.* Indianapolis: Bobbs-Merrill, 1961a.

Goffman, Erving. *Frame Analysis: An Essay on the Organization of Experience.* New York: Harper & Row, 1974.

Goffman, Erving. *Interaction Ritual: Essays on Face-to-Face Behavior.* Garden City, N.Y.: Doubleday, 1967a.

Goffman, Erving. "The Nature of Deference and Demeanor." In *Interaction Ritual: Essays on Face-to-Face Behavior*, pp. 47–96. Garden City, N.Y.: Doubleday, 1967b.

Goffman, Erving. "On Cooling the Mark Out." In *Human Behavior and Social Processes*, edited by Arnold Rose. Boston: Houghton Mifflin, 1962.

Goffman, Erving. "On Face-Work: An Analysis of Ritual Elements in Social Interaction." *Psychiatry* 18 (1955): 213–31.

Goffman, Erving. *The Presentation of Self in Everyday Life.* Garden City, N.Y.: Doubleday, 1959.

Goffman, Erving. *Relations in Public: Micro Studies of the Public Order.* New York: Basic Books, 1971a.

Goffman, Erving. "Remedial Interchanges." In *Relations in Public: Micro Studies of the Public Order*, pp. 95–187. New York: Basic Books, 1971c.

Goffman, Erving. *Stigma: Notes on the Management of Spoiled Identity.* Englewood Cliffs, N.J.: Prentice-Hall, 1963a.

Goffman, Erving. *Strategic Interaction.* Philadelphia: University of Pennsylvania Press, 1971b.

Goffman, Erving. "Tie-Signs." In *Relations in Public: Micro Studies of the Public Order*, pp. 188–237. New York: Basic Books, 1971d.

Gross, Edward, and Stone, Gregory. "Embarrassment and the Analysis of Role Requirements." *American Journal of Sociology* 70 (1964): 1–15.

Hall, Edward T. *The Hidden Dimension.* Garden City, N.Y.: Doubleday, 1966.

Hendrick, Clyde; Giesen, Martin; and Coy, Sharon. "The Social Ecology of Free Seating Arrangements in a Small Group Interaction Context." *Sociometry* 37 (1974): 262–74.

Ho, David Yau-Fai. "On the Concept of Face." *American Journal of Sociology* 8 (1976): 867–83.

Levine, Janey; Vinson, Ann; and Wood, Deborah. "Subway Behavior." In *People in Places: The Sociology of the Familiar*, edited by Arnold Birenbaum and Edward Segarin. New York: Praeger, 1973.

McGinniss, Joe. *The Selling of the President, 1968.* New York: Trident, 1969.

Magruder, Jeb Stuart. *An American Life.* New York: Pocket Books, 1975.

Mankiewicz, Frank. *U.S. Vs. Richard M. Nixon: The Final Crisis.* New York: Ballantine, 1975.

Morgan, Marabell. *The Total Woman.* New York: Pocket Books, 1975.

New York Times. The End of a Presidency. New York: Bantam, 1975.

Rather, Dan, and Gates, Gary Paul. *The Palace Guard.* New York: Warner, 1975.

Schutz, Alfred. *The Collected Papers* (especially Vols. I and II). The Hague: Martinus Nijoff, 1963.

Schutz, Alfred. *The Phenomenology of the Social World*. Chicago: Northwestern University Press, 1967.

Schutz, Alfred, and Luckmann, Thomas. *The Structures of the Life-World*. London: Heinemann, 1974.

Segarin, Edward. "Etiquette, Embarrassment, and Forms of Address." In *People in Places: The Sociology of the Familiar*, edited by Arnold Birenbaum and Edward Segarin. New York: Praeger, 1973.

Stebbins, Robert A. "Modesty, Pride, and Conceit." *Pacific Sociological Review* 15 (1972): 461–81.

White, Theodore H. *Breach of Faith: The Fall of Richard Nixon*. New York: Atheneum, 1975.

Wise, David. *The Politics of Lying: Government Deception, Secrecy, and Power*. New York: Random House, 1973.

CHAPTER EIGHT
Reference Groups

"You haven't once up to now come into real contact with our authorities. All those contacts of yours have been illusory, but because of your ignorance of the circumstances you take them to be real. And as for the telephone: in my place, as you see, though I've certainly enough to do with the authorities, there's no telephone. In inns and such places it may be of real use—as much use, say, as a penny in the music box slot—but it's nothing more than that. Have you ever telephoned here? Yes? Well, then perhaps you'll understand what I say. In the Castle the telephone works beautifully of course; I've been told it's being used there all the time; that naturally speeds up the work a great deal. We can hear this continual telephoning in our telephones down here as a humming and singing, you must have heard it too. Now, this humming and singing transmitted by our telephones is the only real and reliable thing you'll hear, everything else is deceptive. There's no fixed connection with the Castle, no central exchange that transmits our call farther. When anybody calls up the Castle from here, the instruments in all the subordinate departments ring, or rather they would all ring if practically all the departments—I know it for a certainty—didn't leave their receivers off. Now and then, however, a fatigued official may feel the need of a little distraction, especially in the evenings and at night; and may hang the receiver up. Then we get an answer but an answer of course that's merely a practical joke. And that's very understandable too. For who would take the responsibility of interrupting, in the middle of the night, the extremely important work that goes on furiously the whole time, with a message about his own little private troubles? I *can't understand how even a stranger can imagine that when he calls up Sordini, for example, it's really Sordini that answers. For more probably it's a little copying clerk from an entirely different department. On the other hand, it may certainly happen once in a blue moon that when one calls up the little copying clerk Sordini himself will answer. Then, indeed, the best thing is to fly from the telephone before the first sound comes through."*

"I didn't know it was like that, certainly," said K, "I couldn't know of all these peculiarities, . . . so the only remaining conclusion is that everything is very uncertain and insoluble, including my being thrown out."

Franz Kafka, *The Castle* (1926)

Relevance. Students often demand it. Courses must relate to everyday life. Somehow what is learned in class or read in a text must, like the sun, cast bright light on social and personal life.

Kafka's novels are as relevant as the most current comments on the oil crisis or pollution or the limits of industrial growth. Kafka is looking for God and he is unable to find Him (or Her). Symbolically, the Castle represents heaven, and the passage above is only one small part of K's endless search for the "King" who gives the orders about the beginning and end of natural and human life. K never gets in touch with the King and that leads him to often repeat his gloomy conclusion: "everything is very uncertain and insoluble."

Naturally, many people disagree with Kafka. They know where heaven is and may even have spoken to God. But for those who echo Kafka's conclusion, the result is often personal and social problems: for the absence of God spells the decline of religions, and historically religions were by far the most important normative reference group for men and women.

Reference groups are used for purposes of self-evaluation and attitude-formation. Essentially they indicate groups used by people to compare self and others or groups used by people to set and maintain values, beliefs, and standards (Hyman, 1942; Kelly, 1952; Merton, 1957). When these groups are used to set and maintain standards, they are normative reference groups, and when, as in the case of K, what is arguably the most important reference group is absent or nonexistent, a person is in a peculiar historical situation. For most of our historical predecessors had few problems about ultimate values, beliefs, and standards; members of a religious group, they referred back to group values and standards when confronted with a problematic situation. For example, assume you are attacked by a thief. You defend yourself and, in the process, kill your attacker. Was your action moral? Catholics would answer that question by referring to the law of double-effect. The central value was to love your enemy, so, if you directly willed the death of your attacker, you had sinned, you were guilty. It was permissible to unintentionally kill an attacker, but since the value was to love even enemies, it was a grievous sin to intentionally will the death of any human being (Ramsey, 1961).

Now, perhaps you, like K, are without a reference group on the level of ultimate values. How then do you decide whether it is permissible to burn people alive in war? Or, to take it out of the realm of right and wrong, what is the meaning of life and death?

To the extent that many of us lack answers to these questions, our dilemma highlights the importance of reference groups for everyday life. I respond to what others tell me about self and world and to the extent that I inherit a culture without important normative reference groups or, to the extent that I react to my inheritance with a no, I may be asked to live (or be willing to live) without a set of ultimate values, beliefs, and standards. When someone attacks me, I may be unable to refer to others. Conceivably that is cause for some to applaud: I can make judgment on my own. Perhaps? But since people must live together, it is often helpful if they share a broad consensus about ultimate values, beliefs, and standards. Otherwise the result is societal chaos on the level of ultimate values; the result is people who are attacked, or fight wars, without any shared reference point on the level of ultimate values, beliefs, and standards.

REFERENCE GROUPS AND THE GENERALIZED OTHER

Let's refer again to Chapter One. There we defined *generalized other* as the "social group or organized community that gives people their unity or disunity of self" (Mead, 1934). Essentially, the concept is one of a pair; where the significant other tries to conceptualize the importance and influence of specific individuals on a person's views of self and world, the generalized other tries to conceptualize the importance and influence of many social groups. Born without views of self and world, others influence our development by making us the subject of group attitudes, values, and beliefs. Often people need not belong to a group to be influenced by it. Blacks are not white, but whites certainly have an important influence on black attitudes toward and black beliefs about self and world (Wyne et al., 1974).

Now the attitudes and beliefs of the generalized other often have the impact of a social fact: from birth and external to the individual, attitudes and beliefs are progressively internalized and finally capable of having a constraining effect on a person's thought and action (Durkheim, 1957). When a man and a woman wish to live together but decide instead to marry, it is often because of the constraining effect of beliefs and practices inherited from the organized community that gave them a view of self and society: "to live together without benefit of marriage is to live immorally."

Few students doubt the importance of others for human development, but one admitted problem with the concept of generalized other is its abstractness; the concept tells us little about the effect of specific groups, little about the differential importance of the many groups that together comprise the generalized other. So, here is one reason for the importance of reference groups: "they represent a vast simplification and fairly sharp specification of the other" (Kuhn, 1964; Williams, 1970). Always reference groups are part of the generalized other; they indicate social groups that give people positive or negative attitudes and beliefs about self and world (Turner, 1956). But where the *generalized* other tries to conceptualize the *overall* effect of the social groups that influence views of self and world, *reference* groups indicate the *specific* groups that are used as a basis for self-evaluation and attitude-formation. For example, one consistent finding about firstborn children is a need for dependency that exceeds that of younger brothers and sisters. Many hypotheses exist to account for this difference, but one that makes a great deal of sense is the kind of reference groups available to the firstborn. Consistently they are forced to use adults as a central reference group; and often use of that reference group furnishes a poor image of self. It is simply impossible for a child to compete on an equal footing with an adult; consistently they must meet failure and it is that failure that is one cause of the firstborn's lower self-esteem and dependency on others (Radloff and Helmreich, 1968; Zimbardo and Formica, 1963).

Reference groups are part of the generalized other. And their importance rests on their potential ability to explain the specific ways "in which individual-group relationships" shape a person's thought and action. However, remember that our focus is the effect of groups on the individual. Noting the close relationship between the concepts of reference group and role-taking, Ralph Turner still points out that one is more inclusive than the other. For one can "take account of a reference group without taking the role of a member" (Turner, 1956). As above, one can refer judgment of two people living together to "hometown" beliefs, decide one must marry, and do this without once taking the role of a specific individual. One is constrained, not by the attitudes of Tom, Dick, or Harry, but by the attitudes of the group: "*They* tell me to think and act as I do."

TYPES OF REFERENCE GROUPS

Part of our task here is already completed. Normative reference groups set and maintain standards for the individual. Above religion was used as an example of a normative reference group, but virtually any collectivity can assume this role. For example, in discussing a reference group theory of juvenile delinquency, Haskell notes that delinquents often use the street gang to set and maintain standards. Especially when issues of right and wrong arise, delinquents decide in favor of the gang's norms and beliefs (Haskell, 1960). Or, consider soldiers in Vietnam. Many were troubled by the military's use of certain tactics and weapons, but the conflict was often resolved by using the army as a normative frame of reference. In Vietnam the army set and maintained standards, and the soldier's "only" choice was to follow the norms that dominated (Polner, 1971).

Incidentally, the delinquent example suggests another point: reference groups can be either positive or negative. Often the approval of one group's standards is based on a prior rejection of another's; for delinquents, the family is often the rejected group. But a person need not have a substitute in order to use some group as a negative reference for values and beliefs. Sometimes young people decide to reject their families' standards. And while they lack a positive reference group to substitute for the family, their future is still built on a solid rejection of family values, beliefs, and practices.

If some groups are used to set and maintain standards, others are used as a basis of comparison. Here people evaluate self and others by comparing themselves or their situation to that of others (Kelly, 1952). During World War II married draftees compared themselves to single undrafted men, and the result was anger: "With all my responsibilities, why should I be in the army when those guys are out having a good time" (Stouffer et al., 1949).

Overall, four types of comparative reference groups exist (Kemper, 1968, 1966; Turner, 1956). The first is what Kemper calls the *equity group*. Here others are used "as a frame of reference for judging whether or not one's situation or fate is fair or equitable." Consider feminists—comparing themselves to men results in a sense of injustice. When women college graduates receive an average of $6,000 less than male college graduates for the very same job, there is something radically wrong.

A second type of comparative reference group is the *role model* (Kemper, 1968). Here a group "possesses skills and displays techniques which the person lacks," and so, by observation and then comparison with his or her performance, the group is used as a model for behavior. "I want to be like that"; or "Until I'm like them, I'm a nobody." A famous example is the "Kennedy clan." People who surrounded the late president used his family as a role model and so, apparently, did former President Nixon. Envious of news pictures that often appeared showing the Kennedys sailing on Nantucket Sound or frolicking with their children at Hyannis Port, reporters were asked to photograph the president walking "along the water's edge in solitary splendor." Soon the president came into view, but his presentation of self failed: instead of casual clothes, he was walking in the water wearing a windbreaker, a pair of dress trousers, and street shoes (Rather and Gates, 1975).

A third comparative reference group *legitimates* a person's beliefs, values, or actions. Here people use a group "when a question arises as to the legitimacy of behavior or opinions" (Kemper, 1968).[1] Consider prostitutes. Given the nature of cultural beliefs, their profession is an everyday assault on self-image. So, one way that prostitutes deal with the conflict is to use criminal groups—hobohemians—as the frame of reference. Middle-class people are "dull, frightened, and hypocritical"; in comparison, hobohemians are forthright, exciting, and carefree. Thus, there is no choice to be made; the question of legitimacy is quickly resolved in favor of criminal groups (Jackman et al., 1967).

Always the prime function of all comparative reference groups is self-evaluation and attitude-formation. But since the prostitute example suggests that legitimist groups can also set and maintain standards, remember that the basis for distinguishing between normative and comparative groups is, first, in terms of *primary* effect and, second, "in terms of the *mechanism* of the reference group" (Turner, 1956). While criminals do help set and maintain prostitute values and beliefs, they do so only after a process of social comparison and self-evaluation. Unlike the army for the Vietnam soldier, the prostitute is dealing with two groups and, based on a comparison, deciding that one is better than the other.

A final type of comparative reference group is the *accommodation group*. Here people provide "cues for a complementary response in a cooperative situation" or cues for a parallel response in a competitive situation. Consider American foreign policy. Newspaper reports indicated Secretary of State Kissinger considered Russian support for one side in the Angolan civil war a cue for a parallel response from America. Using the Russians as his frame of reference, Kissinger apparently compared Americans to Russians and decided that, unless America responded in a parallel fashion, the Russians would think America was weak. So, in a show of strength, he accommodated American policy to the Russians. Now both groups were strong (Kaufman, 1976).

A third and last general type of reference group is an audience (Kemper, 1968; Turner, 1956). Ideally these are groups that neither set standards nor serve any of the functions performed by the four types of comparative reference groups. In reality, however, "certain reference groups within each of the preceding types might usefully be regarded as audience groups to the individual" (Turner, 1956). The basic reason for the distinction is to underline presentations of self. Often we act before oth-

---

[1] Kemper's terminology has been used throughout, but for a similar analysis, see Turner, 1956.

ers and often we refer our judgments of correct behavior to what others say they want or what we think others want. Assume that you are going to attend a convention of sociologists. You do not know many people and the group has not set any standards, but you feel they have and so you then use your judgment of their attitudes as a frame of reference for your behavior.

If reference group is itself a fairly sharp specification of the other, the distinctions among types of reference groups hopefully make the importance and influence of others even clearer. But, despite their importance, definitions still only tell us what we are studying. And since the aim of reference group theory is to "systematize the determinants and consequences" of using reference groups to evaluate self or set standards, below we turn to some of the key issues in reference group theory. For example: "Under which conditions are associates within one's own groups taken as a frame of reference for self-evaluation and attitude-formation, and under which conditions do out-groups or nonmembership groups provide the significant frame of reference?" (Merton, 1957).

SOME DETERMINANTS OF NORMATIVE REFERENCE GROUPS

Let's begin with normative reference groups. Why do people choose a particular group to set and maintain societal and personal standards? One reason is a lack of alternatives. And the best example is children. Since children are unable to think about self and world until they are first the subject of other people's thought and action, the child's family inevitably furnishes the standards that are *the* basis for the child's view of self and world. Observe the conversation of four- and five-year-olds. One boy will say "Yeah" and the other, referring back to family standards, will respond, "Don't say yeah, say yes." Or, seated at a table, one boy is talking, the other interrupts, and the talker responds with, "That's rude. If you must interrupt, say excuse me."

To the extent that a child's environment is homogeneous—recall the discussion of schizophrenia in Chapter Four—the ability of the family to set and maintain standards is considerably strengthened. But homogeneity of experience, a lack of alternative normative reference groups, is a factor that adds to the power and use of any group that sets and maintains standards. Consider the Roman Catholic Church in the Middle Ages—or, until recently, the power of whites to set and maintain standards for blacks. Or consider the famous Bennington College studies by Theodore Newcomb. While attending school, previously "conservative" women assumed the "liberal" standards that dominated Bennington. Besides a lack of alternatives, other variables were at work, but especially for dormitory students, the everyday availability of other normative reference groups was significantly decreased (Newcomb, 1948, 1962).

A second factor influencing the choice of normative reference groups is the prestige or reward people attach to the group. Prestige was a factor in the Bennington studies and it was also important in our analysis of adolescent peer groups (see Chapter Three). For an example of prestige and rewards, think of socially mobile Americans who, born Baptist, switch to the Presbyterian or Episcopal religions as they climb the ladder of success (for example, Baltzell, 1964). Naturally, people need not deeply internalize the new standards, but if only maintained publicly, they still use the new religion as an important reference in regard to values and beliefs.

A third reason to accept a normative reference group is vested interest. This can be psychological interest, material interest, or both; the point is that a person feels committed to a group's standards. Consider the issue of rape. Susan Brownmiller shows that in many cases of assault with a weapon, women blame themselves: "For years afterward I felt it was my fault. I tried to figure out what had made him follow me. Was it the clothes I was wearing or was it my walk? It *had* to be my fault, you see?" Now to come to this conclusion, a woman uses men as her normative reference group: "All women want to be raped," "She was asking for it," "No woman can be raped against her will." Conceivably, this woman could see things in a different light, but to do so is to embrace change and pain; it means reevaluating, not only her beliefs about rape, but a host of others also laid down by men. So, for many, the social psychological threat is too great; rather than change, they continue to make judgments by means of the normative standards of men. As one policeman told Brownmiller when she asked why thirty-five rape complaints had led to only two arrests: "You know what these complaints represent? Prostitutes who didn't get their money" (Brownmiller, 1975).

While vested interest is one reason to adopt a normative reference group, this determinant also tells us something about the consequences of use. If a group furnishes the primary standards for a person, has prestige and rewards to offer, and thus establishes a vested interest in group standards, use of that normative reference group may lead a person to take for granted absurd and demeaning conclusions. For example, reliable statistics from four cities show that about 50 percent of rapes are gang rapes; in a careful study of Philadelphia, 71 percent of the rapes were planned; and in a Boston study, 85 percent of the women were either threatened with a weapon or manhandled. Yet, with a reality such as this, women often if not generally conclude they were asking for it; they are to blame for being assaulted. That is a potent influence by a powerful normative reference group: men (Brownmiller, 1975).

A fourth reason to adopt a normative reference group is coercion: if one fails to refer to group norms, he may not get the chance to fail again.

Solzhenitsyn makes this point in the first volume of *The Gulag Archipelago*. To survive, a prisoner had to dispense with everything except the standards set and maintained by the prison administration (Solzhenitsyn, 1974; see also Bettelheim, 1943). And, since concentration camps are an extreme example, remember the everyday position of children. Particularly when parents are harsh disciplinarians, children must refer, at least at home, to the standards set and maintained by their family.

A final reason to accept a normative reference group is disillusionment. In *Report to Greco*, Nikos Kazantzakis describes his disenchantment with Christianity. Unable to accept inherited standards, Kazantzakis felt compelled to seek an alternative. He never found one, but he tried very hard to adopt the values of, first, Buddhism, and then, communism (Kazantzakis, 1965). Naturally, disillusionment was not the only cause of Kazantzakis's search, or that of the many young Americans who now try to embrace Buddhism, but the point is that the rejection of one normative group generally leads people to seek another. For without a set of norms, people encounter self, others, social reality in a more or less chaotic fashion; norms constrain us but they also furnish a stable, and seemingly necessary, basis for people's judgments about self and world (Festinger, 1954; Ortega y Gasset, 1962).

Before turning to a discussion of comparative reference groups, one more point needs to be made. So far we have focused on the acceptance and adoption of reference group norms; in saying yes to the group, one is therefore influenced by it. This is true but it is also correct that a no to a particular group often leads to influence and even determination by it. Recall a telling point made by Karl Mannheim: even if we reject inherited standards, "in negation our orientation is fundamentally centered upon that which is being negated, and we are thus still unwittingly determined by it" (Mannheim, 1969). Now many factors can lead people to reject a normative reference group (for example no prestige, a lack of rewards, cultural beliefs that applaud growth and independent thought, cultural heterogeneity, proof that the group's beliefs are false), but the point is that a no does not necessarily lessen the influence of a normative reference group. For example, particularly if a person has strong personal commitments to a group, rejecting it may cause the person to adopt standards that are exactly the opposite of the rejected reference group. In fact, not only does rejection fail to undercut the group's influence, the rejected group may be the key variable influencing the choice of a new normative reference group. Perhaps the most powerful example here are the hippies and yippies of the 1960s. Rejecting the middle-class standards of their families, many "freely" chose to live on communes primarily because it offered a life that was in dramatic contrast to that of the rejected normative reference group (Reich, 1970).

SOME DETERMINANTS OF COMPARATIVE REFERENCE GROUPS

One of the most interesting findings from early studies of reference groups was the use of nonmembership groups to influence or determine thought and action. It came as no surprise to observe people influenced by membership groups, but to see a sometimes equal or even more important influence from nonmembership groups was both surprising and informative. What was it that moved people to base thought, action, and self-image on comparisons with others they did not know or, in some cases, were not allowed to know (for example, Merton, 1957; Davis, 1959)?

One factor is superiority. People believe nonmembership groups are superior (say, in ability) and since in comparison they are not, one way to become superior is to act like the nonmembership group. Or, even if they are unable to act like "superior" others, they may still use them as an important basis of comparison. Studying the totally blind, Helen May Strauss found that in reference to learning, personal appearance, and character, blind people used the sighted as the basis of comparison. Particularly in regard to personal appearance, fully 77 percent of the blind chose to compare themselves with the sighted: "I'm totally blind and they (sighted people) are telling me I can't compare to them. They are normal; I am odd. They blend into a crowd; I stick out" (Strauss, 1968).

Based on her study, Strauss refuted a hypothesis about the use of comparative reference groups; where theory (see Festinger, 1954) argued that the tendency to compare self with others decreased as the difference between their opinion or ability increased, Strauss found the blind using a group (that is, the sighted) with much greater abilities as a basis of comparison. So, "the concept of similarity in social comparison theory needs considerable qualification and specification in the light of our studies of the blind" (Strauss, 1968).

Strauss is both right and wrong. When the blind use the sighted as a basis for comparing abilities, theory is clearly incorrect; the differences between the abilities of the blind and the sighted are substantial, yet the sighted are still used as an important comparative reference group. However, isn't the ground for this comparison of abilities a fundamental *agreement* in reference to *opinions* about the superiority of sighted people? Strauss writes that the totally blind "may reject the obvious and objective ground of similarity with each other to protect their self-regard, which might be damaged by their accepting membership in a group labeled inferior" (1968). So, in reference to a factor such as personal appearance, theory is confirmed; the blind and the sighted are in substantial agreement about the superiority of the sighted.

How account for a person's willingness to accept the label *inferior*? Strauss makes an important point when she notes that "the perception of the standing of a reference group is certainly a neglected aspect of the theory." If one group is generally considered superior, prestigious, powerful, people may willingly use these nonmembership groups as a basis for comparison. Conceivably, the result of these comparisons may be a very poor image of self, but that is no reason for people to stop making the comparisons. Witness this comment about a white, white-collar, high school graduate: "Rissaro believes people of a higher class have a power to judge him because they seem internally more developed human beings; and he is afraid, because they are better armed, they will not respect him. He feels compelled to justify his own position, and all his life he has felt compelled to put himself up on their level in order to earn respect" (Sennett and Cobb, 1973).

All his life. Rissaro has been making these negative comparisons all his life. And the prime reason is that comparisons of superior-inferior, prestigious-worthless, are often institutionalized aspects of a culture. At birth Rissaro knew little about social classes. But he was taught by the generalized other (and of course by significant others) that his inherited membership in one group made him inferior to another. In effect, Rissaro learned in childhood to specify the generalized other. For him the two key groups were lower and upper class; and for him the basis of his global self-image was a social identity. Taught that the upper classes were superior and that his lower-class membership made him inferior, Rissaro agreed to base his life on an inherited and institutionalized social comparison. "They (the upper classes) tell me I'm not as good as they are. I agree. But just watch me use them as a role model; watch me try to become superior by acting like my betters."

Although other studies (for example, Runciman, 1968) show that inherited comparisons need not produce such a poor image of self, the point made here is that a major reason people use nonmembership groups as a basis of comparison is the institutionalized judgments made by any culture about the superiority-inferiority, normality-abnormality, prestige-worthlessness, of particular social groups. Whether the comparisons involve upper and lower classes, blacks and whites, men and women, blind and sighted, or "straight" and homosexual, the result is often the same: a poor self-image based on an institutionalized and learned comparison with others. Listen, for example, to two black psychiatrists talking about a black woman's feelings of femininity: "Her blackness is the antithesis of a creamy white skin, her lips are thick, her hair is kinky and short. She is, in fact, the antithesis of American beauty. However beautiful she might be in a different setting with different standards, in this country she is ugly. . . . So it may be that after a brief struggle a black woman feels that femininity, as it is defined in these times is something she cannot achieve. Rather than having her heart broken every day, she relinquishes the struggle and diverts her interest elsewhere" (Grier and Cobbs, 1969;

also Griffin, 1961; Goodman, 1964; Stonequist, 1957). In sum, on the basis of a learned comparison with others, on the basis of what they tell her about herself, she agrees she is ugly.[2]

Now, if the generalization is established, if we agree that one major reason to compare self with nonmembership groups is institutionalized comparisons, let us qualify the effect of cultural comparisons. For whether it is Rissaro or a black woman, we have used examples in which the negative comparison was accepted by the person. This need not be the case. First is cultural consensus about the comparisons. Social class is a much more salient fact in British than in American society. Probably, the effect of institutionalized class comparisons is less apparent in America (Lipset and Bendix, 1964). Remember, too, that people can reject positive as well as negative comparisons. One factor in the origin of America was aristocrats who felt they were no better than "common people." Second is homogeneity of experience. If the comparisons refer to what we earlier (in Chapter Six) called basic roles, and no or few alternatives are presented to the person, the effect of the comparisons (whether positive or negative) should be great. However, to the extent that alternatives are present (for example notions about black femininity in 1977), the effect of the comparisons should decrease. Third, and this addresses the issue of basic roles, how important are the comparisons to the person? Black-white, man-woman, upper class-lower class, "straight"-homosexual: these are normally important and very diffuse comparisons; their effect is not limited to one segment or side of a person's life (Turner, 1955). But since others (for example, tall-short, Protestant-Catholic, Democrat-Republican) generally assume less significance, even a negative comparison may have little effect on a person. Fourth and last is unique self-image. Armed with a positive view of self, it should be easier to disregard or at least minimize negative comparisons of self.

Undoubtedly, other factors also qualify the effect of learned cultural comparisons. Suffice it for us that the existence of institutionalized beliefs about superior and inferior groups is a major cause of people's comparing themselves with nonmembership groups. Moreover, the consequences of these learned comparisons persist even after the person has rejected them. As one homosexual noted: "Today I read something that deeply disturbed me . . . a Catholic priest saying that one cannot be a Christian and be a homosexual. That's intellectually sick, but inside me, I say maybe he's

---

[2] Another example comes from Japan. Ashamed of their yellow hue, and convinced that white is beautiful, many Japanese women now have up to fifty inches of their large intestine removed. Apparently Japanese people have larger intestines than whites and this is what gives the skin a yellow hue (see also Johnson and Johnson, 1975).

right. Yet, I know he's not right, and yet I can still believe he could be right" (Kimmel, 1974).

A second reason people compare themselves with nonmembership groups is a societal or personal stress on social mobility. To the extent that a lower-class person believes he or she must rise in the social scale, judgment about self and world will often be referred to the upper classes. Comparisons could include manner of dress, style of speech, type of food, decor of home, leisure-time activities: these and other comparisons are readily available. And if the lower-class person wants to be like the upper class, he or she suffers in comparison. So, one alternative often taken is to use upper-class groups as role models, as legitimists of beliefs about self and world, and even as the basis for deciding that, in reference to equity, the inequalities that exist between social classes are justified: "I (a lower-class person) agree with what you are telling me. They (lower-class people) are generally lazy, shiftless, immoral. They deserve to be where they are" (for example, Josephson, 1934; Hofstadter, 1955).

As in America, some cultures place heavy stress on social mobility; group and (to a relative extent) self-esteem depend on success in climbing the ladder of classes. However, even when societies lack a cultural stress on mobility, people may have no choice about rising, about using nonmembership groups as a basis of comparison. Today many underdeveloped nations are rapidly industrializing their societies, thus reducing the number of manual jobs available. To the extent that modernization is pursued with fervor, if children are to work, they may have no choice but to rise above their parents. Nonmembership groups (for example, the educated) must be used as a basis of comparison if the children are to obtain work in an industrial society (Lipset and Letterberg, 1966).

A third reason to compare self with nonmembership groups is social change. To the extent that cultural beliefs, values, and practices are challenged, undermined, in transition, or all three at once, people are likely to turn to nonmembership groups for solutions to problems or alternative ways to view self and world. For example, consider Orrin Klapp's discussion of fashion. Lacking a set of solid social identities, some people use fashion designers to tell them who they are. One year they adopt the "Cossack look," another year they are Modigliani girls, and then they switch to the Chelsea look. Probably, these changes never touch any basic beliefs but, in sharp contrast to traditional societies, modern societies provide no one proper way to look. Changes are rapid and if people want to be "in," they use nonmembership groups (whether they are fashion designers or Hollywood celebrities) as role models (Klapp, 1969; Riesman, 1950).

Often fashion only symbolizes threats at a deeper level. Today, ties to many basic groups (for example, the family, religion, political parties, male and female) are being challenged. While media often exaggerate the amount and diffuseness of change, it is occurring, and to the extent that change undermines or weakens ties to membership groups, people may be quite willing to compare themselves with nonmembership groups. A good example is what members of the women's liberation movement call a "closet feminist." A woman will contact a feminist organization, immediately try to dissociate herself from women's liberation—"I'm no bra burner"—and then seek aid or advice because of injustices brought to her attention by the women's liberation movement. Because the societal image of a feminist is relatively poor, a woman shuns the social identity—"I'm not one of them and don't tell me I am"—but her conversation shows she has used nonmembership groups (that is, feminists) as a basis for deciding that a particular social situation is unjust.

If social change is often a reason to compare self with nonmembership groups, it can also lead some to a total and angry rejection of inherited comparisons with nonmembership groups. Recall the concept of internal freedom. People have the ability to see how they got to be as they are. So, if blacks or women or Chicanos or members of the lower class decide that, for example, feelings of inferiority are rooted in institutionalized social comparisons, they can reverse course. Normally this reversal is very difficult and painful, but if it occurs, where negative comparisons were once accepted, insight into the origin and development of the comparisons leads to "hostility or derogation" of the nonmembership group (Festinger, 1954). And this is quite understandable. Consider the role of the other. I now see what they did to me. And I'm furious. Moreover, since the society still furnishes little support for my reevaluation of the negative comparison, I'm also a little insecure. Like the homosexual who believed and disbelieved the priest, even though I now reject the comparisons, they are still one original and important basis of my global self-concept. So, my hostility toward the nonmembership group is the result of my insights and it is also the result of a need to convince myself I am who I think I am.

Today social change has led many people to angrily reject inherited negative comparisons. Often this anger produces the same response in others. But if we understand the reference group roots of the anger, perhaps it is more appropriate to respond with empathy and a willingness to together abolish comparisons so harmful to a human being's image of self and world?

PREJUDICE AND COMPARATIVE REFERENCE GROUPS

Likewise, it was Hark who gave expression to that certain inward sense
—an essence of being which is almost impossible to put into words—that

every Negro possesses when, dating from the age of twelve or ten or even earlier, he becomes aware that he is only merchandise, goods, in the eyes of all white people devoid of character or moral sense or soul. This feeling Hark called "black-assed," and it comes as close to summing up the numbness and dread which dwells in every Negro's heart as any word I have ever known. "Don' matter who dey is, Nat, good or bad, even ol' Marse Joe, de white folks dey gwine make you feel black-assed. Never seed a white man smile at me yet 'thout I didn't feel just about twice as black-assed as I was befo! How come dat 'plies, Nat? Figger a white man treat you right you gwine feel *white-assed*. Naw suh! Young massah, old massah, sweet-talk me, I jes' feel *black-assed* th'ough an' th'ough. Figger when I gets to heaven like you says I is, de good Lord hisself even *He* gwine make old Hark feelin like a *black-assed* angel. 'Cause pretty soon I know His line, yas *suh!* Yas *suh*, pretty soon I can hear Him holler out: "Hark! You dere boy! Need some spick and span roun' de throne room. Hop to, you *black-assed* scroundrel. Hop to wid de mop and de broom!" [William Styron, *The Confessions of Nat Turner* (1968)]

Prejudice is "an antipathy based on a faulty and inflexible generalization." A person or group dislikes or hates another on the basis of "unfounded judgments" and even when exposed to the truth, the person or group continues to affirm the generalization: "Those people are inferior; isn't any way you're going to tell me anything else" (Allport, 1954; Rokeach, 1960).

Studies show that one side of prejudice is psychological: "the cognitive processes of prejudiced people are in general different from the cognitive processes of tolerant people" (Allport, 1954). However, another side of prejudice is sociological: positive or negative judgments about racial and ethnic groups are institutionalized aspects of the culture. Hopefully, people develop in a way that permits them to reject unfounded judgments, but no matter how a specific person develops, if prejudice is an institutionalized part of the culture, most people learn the inherited judgments about racial and ethnic groups. Taking the role of the other, they eventually discover that they (for example, a black person) were the subject of other people's positive or negative judgments before they were even born.

Prejudice has many effects. It excludes people from jobs, clubs, schools; it arbitrarily condemns people to work in menial jobs; it often guarantees a life of poverty; it produces, as in South Africa, the most inhuman laws. However, the worst result of prejudice by far is learned self-hate. Based on institutionalized comparisons, people accept the role of the superior group and conclude: "I am as awful as you tell me I am." In its extreme form this kills a human life before it begins. For if one strongly believes himself inferior, even changed social conditions may be meaningless. Perhaps, even if he gets to heaven, he will expect God to treat him like a "black-assed scoundrel" (see, for example, Rollins, 1973).

Above we discussed in a general way the results of institutionalized comparisons. Here we get specific. What do we know about the development of, and consequences for, the child's self-image when an important part of that image is based on institutionalized comparisons between black and white?

The first thing we know is that the meaning of the comparisons develops over time and along with a child's cognitive development. Recall our discussion in Chapter Two. It normally takes six or seven years for concepts to stabilize; before then children may have "verbal fluency," but most are uncertain about what they want to mean or uncertain about the meanings of the words they pronounce and use so well. In short, since self-concepts develop over time and through a process of interaction, it takes children about seven years to begin to grasp the full significance of institutionalized comparisons between ethnic and racial groups (Goodman, 1964; Proshansky and Newton, 1968; Morland, 1968).

Concepts take about seven years to stabilize, but awareness of racial identities exists at three or four years of age. Recall that this is the time when the developing ability to use language shows us that children are trying to make sense of their inherited world; they are beginning to sort people out on the basis of physical differences—hair, skin, clothes—and they are beginning to learn from others that these differences indicate gradations in social power, prestige, and status. In Goodman's Boston study many of the children had at least a low awareness of racial groupings by four years, two months, and none of the five-year-olds lacked at least a low awareness of racial groupings (Goodman, 1964). Along with the Clarks, Stevenson and Stewart found a dim awareness of racial groups as early as three, but since many of the studies were done in nursery schools, the bulk of nearly thirty years' work focuses on children who are at least four years of age (Clark and Clark, 1947; Stevenson and Stewart, 1958; Morland, 1966; Asher and Allen, 1969; Wyne et al., 1974).

Granted, toddlers are aware of racial identities and comparisons. But what do we mean by awareness? Consider this example of a black girl who is four years, five months old. She is putting together a picture puzzle of ten figures that must be fitted into two rows of five each. Five figures are white, five black; and except for color, they are identical. At first Joan put the figures wherever she felt like. Then, surveying the finished product, and without prodding from the researchers, she segregated the puzzle: two white figures were removed from their position next to three black figures and the rows were made homogeneous. In another situation Nadine (black and four and one-half years old) not only thinks the brown doll's hair "doesn't look good," Nadine volunteers that "her sister is lighter" and Nadine's mother says the child asked when *she* will get lighter (Goodman, 1964).

Turning to white children, David is four years, eleven months old.

Shown the picture of a solitary black child, he says "He's black. He's a stinky little boy. He's a stinker—he shits!—Take it away! I want another little boy." Or, consider the case of Debbie, four years, seven months old. She "expresses marked preferences for whites and explicit rejection of blacks." She wants to play with a white boy "because he's lighter," and she states firmly "I don't like the brown ones." But Debbie is also uneasy about her rejection of blacks. Perhaps because she senses surprise on the researcher's face or because she has also been told to be polite to everyone, Debbie clearly understands the society's distinctions between black and white, but she is still unsure about their use. It is as if she asks: "Is it really all right to publicly say such nasty things about a group of people?" (Goodman, 1964; see also Asher and Allen, 1969; Morland, 1966).

The examples used were of children with a high awareness of racial comparisons. Many four- and five-year-olds were unable to deal with the distinctions in such an explicit and knowledgeable manner. However, taken together the studies do permit the following generalization: by four or five, most black and white children "know the relevant words, concepts, and phrases used to describe members of their own and other racial groupings" (Proshansky and Newton, 1968). Often they use the words inconsistently and they seem to be feeling others out: "Is this right? Did I say it correctly? Am I thinking as you told me to?" But, by five, almost all children have learned to break down the generalized other and use black and white as more or less important comparative reference groups.

If children are uncertain at five, by seven or so the continuing process of concept stabilization leads to conclusions about self. As Proshansky and Newton note, "the Negro child's rejection of his own racial group is well founded"; he or she has had three or four years of experience with this inherited knowledge. Now, like water in December, the knowledge hardens into a solid foundation for self-image. For example, a number of the studies (Clark and Clark, 1947; Stevenson and Stewart, 1958; Morland, 1962; Asher and Allen, 1969) cite a decreasing tendency for black children to identify with whites. Apparently, in-group references are strong at three, whites are the dominant reference group at five, and then, at about seven, black children once again identify with other black people. Generally, the explanation for this process is the children's desire to avoid damning judgments about self. Acutely aware of the significance of the group comparisons, the children turn inward to avoid comparing themselves with a group that can only produce a poor self-image. They "must face the fact they are Negroes and that they will be treated as Negroes by members of their own group and, more significantly, they will be treated as Negroes by the very people they wish to be: the members of the white majority" (Proshansky and Newton, 1968).

After seven there seem to be fewer and fewer ways to escape this realization. Recall that along with concept stabilization come other significant intellectual abilities: class inclusion and the capacity to multiply classes. And, since the studies show many black children accepting the inherited and negative comparisons of self, these new abilities are used to weaken even further an already poor self-image. Multiplying classes, the children know they are Negro-Americans; and nesting one class in another, they see a group of people called Americans, and then within this general class, two others: white and black Americans. Given their acquired knowledge about the meaning of white and black, the children's increasing intellectual abilities would seem fated to produce an even poorer self-image. And one way to respond to all this dovetailing knowledge is to turn inward, away from the source of so much pain.

Of course, turning inward by no means lessens the importance of institutionalized comparisons. It prevents assaults on self but to the extent that black children are negative toward their racial identity, that conclusion is only based on an acceptance of the inherited comparisons. Moreover, however understandable, to turn inward is to turn away from the knowledge that could produce a positive image of blackness. Insight into the origins of the poor self-image can only come by facing the development of self by others. Turning inward, the child says yes to cultural inheritance and no to insight into the development of self-image. Consider, for example, Robert Coles's description of the drawings of black children in desegregated schools. Often significant differences appeared in the relative size of blacks and whites. Many drawings showed blacks smaller than whites, or blacks with missing or mutilated body parts. Finally, Coles found an inconsistent use of color. Eight-, nine-, and ten-year-olds did not want to draw themselves as Negroes, while others "compensated" by drawing whites a light shade of brown (Coles, in Proshansky and Newton, 1968).

While the civil rights and black power movements do seem to have helped many black people to gain insight into the development of self (see, for example, Goldman, 1973; Jackson, 1970), there is a very substantial body of evidence which indicates that, at least until recently, the poor image of self acquired in childhood stays with many black people all their lives (for example, Frazier, 1961; Grier and Cobbs, 1969; Griffin, 1961). Obviously, many factors account for the persistence of this poor image, but on an everyday basis perhaps nothing compares with the twentieth-century version of feeling "black-assed." John Howard Griffin says Negroes now call it the "hate stare." And it can come at the most unexpected times. But when a white turns it on a black, "it is far more than the look of disapproval one occasionally gets." This stare, for no apparent reason, is so "exaggeratedly hateful" that for a white (Griffin is white) turned black, "you see a kind of insanity, something so obscene the very obscenity of it (rather than its threat) terrifies you." However, for a person born black, perhaps the gravest result of the "hate stare" is feeling "black-assed," feeling "a discrimination against self," "a contempt for blackness," feeling that whites are superior to blacks (Griffin, 1961).

REFERENCE OTHERS

If the concept of reference group is a fairly sharp specification of the generalized other, what about the concept of significant other? How can we be more precise about the effect of particular people? What variables determine the referring of judgments about self and world, not to a group, but to a specific person?

Since perception is always an interpretative process (see Chapter One), "significance is in the eye of the beholder." Naturally mothers and fathers are significant others (if only negatively) to their children, but this need not be true. Ultimately I decide whether you are significant to *me*, and a number of variables influence my decision (Rosenberg, 1973).

As in reference groups, homogeneity is a factor that makes people significant. Like the schizophrenic girl who was never allowed out unaccompanied by one of her parents, others may suffocate us and become significant to us only because they are our only source of judgments about self and world. We refer our beliefs about self to them because we live in a vacuum they created.

Although complete homogeneity is very rare, the particular people who socialize us are quite likely to be significant to us. After all I become an object to myself based on what they tell me about self and world. Inevitably I must use what they tell me in order to begin thinking, in order to begin talking to myself about myself. So, even if only negatively, it is unlikely that the people who furnished the foundation for my views of self and world are not significant to me.

A second factor affecting the influence of others is the value, belief, practice, or issue in question. Like groups, other people need not have a diffuse influence on our beliefs about self and world (Turner, 1955). For example, if I seek a judgment about the quality of my work in social psychology, I am unlikely to turn to a close friend who is a biologist. Significance in this case is closely related to competence and expertise in social psychology. Moreover, while another person might have a significant effect on my judgment of self as social psychologist, that person is unlikely to have any effect on my view of self as teacher, son, or father.

Remember, too, that someone who has had a significant and diffuse influence need not have the same kind of influence when the issue changes. Conceivably, I may refer my judgments about religion back to my mother, but when it comes to child-rearing I react in this manner: "I had a lot myself when I was young: I know what the belt is, I know what the stick is . . . and I swore I'd never touch my kids" (Newson and Newson, 1965).

A third factor affecting the influence of others is credibility (Rosenberg, 1973). Do I believe what that person is telling me? Obviously, to the extent that I do believe the other, and to the extent that the other is talking about important aspects of self, he or she can be quite significant to me. However, credibility is often closely associated with a person's membership in groups. Today no American president is just Kennedy, Nixon, or Ford. They are also politicians. And since many Americans use politicians as a negative reference group, the credibility of a specific other is inevitably affected by his or her group membership. Or, consider schoolteachers. It is often assumed that teachers have a significant influence on students. Sometimes this is true, but a teacher's effect is mediated, first, by the belief, value, or issue in question and, second, by a student's beliefs about the group of people called teachers. If students enter school hating teachers, the possible effect of any particular one is unlikely to be great.

A fourth factor affecting the influence of particular others is support for a positive image of self. Rosenberg found that "only 38 percent of the students who believed teachers thought poorly of them said they cared very much about their teachers' opinions compared with 81 percent of those who attributed favorable attitudes to their teachers" (1973). Other studies furnish similar evidence. People want others to support their views of self and world, and particularly when the belief or issue is important to the person, the influence of another is likely to be significant only when the other furnishes positive support for self-image. For example, Bailey et al. found that for friendship duration, similar beliefs and attitudes were less important than support for the person's view of self (1975; see also Sherwood, 1965; Kemper, 1966). However, for us to believe the other, we cannot suspect ulterior motives. Support for positive image must come because the other wants to provide it; if we suspect the other is trying to con us or sympathize with us, or if we suspect the other praises everyone, his or her effect is more or less significantly decreased (Kleinke, 1975).

Another factor that moves one to refer to others' judgments is no support for a negative image of self. Assume that I think I am dumb, but a teacher refuses to accept this view: "You're really very intelligent. I don't know how you can think anything else." Here a lack of support for self-image could make someone very significant to me. However, remember that other variables affect my willingness to believe I am not who I think I am. For example, how credible is the other? Do I need to believe I am dumb? Is this image of self a defense I use to avoid facing issues overloaded with threats and anxiety? How much support do I get for a new image of self? All of these variables are capable of mediating and so negating the chance of referring judgments about self to someone who refuses to accept my negative image of self.

A sixth factor affecting the significance of others is prestige. If someone has prestige in groups or activities that are important to me, I am likely to be influenced by him. He is someone I look up to, someone I identify with, and should he say something about me, I may very well refer judgments about self and world to this prestigious other. In China, for example, Mao Tse-tung seemed to be a significant other for many members of the society. Apparently, people consistently refer to the "Little Red Book" for judgments about self and society.

A seventh factor is power, another's ability to force one to act in a particular way. Assume that I am an inmate of an asylum. Continually I may be forced to refer judgments about self to the head nurse or a particular orderly. But my referring to them need not mean any significant influence on my beliefs about self. Perhaps it does. But while their power forces me to refer to them, it need not affect my real beliefs about self and world. I act as they tell me to, all the while believing what I think is correct.

An eighth factor is rigidity, the extent of my closed-mindedness. Obviously, to the extent that my views of self and world are padlocked, I will not refer to others unless they echo my views of self and world.

Although many factors affect our referring judgments about self and world to a particular person, some variables are more important than others. Four together seem to promise greater influence for any particular person: should someone be a major source of our judgments, as well as have prestige, power, and credibility, that person is likely to have a very significant influence on our beliefs about self and world. Probably very few people we meet have all of these characteristics, but two who normally do are our parents—or whoever assumes responsibility for laying the foundation for our images of self and world.

Bibliographical References

Allport, Gordon. *The Nature of Prejudice.* Reading, Mass.: Addison-Wesley, 1954.

Asher, Steven R., and Allen, Vernon L. "Racial Preference and Social Comparison Processes." *Journal of Social Issues* 25 (1969): 157–66.

Bailey, Roger C.; Finney, Phillip; and Helm, Bob. "Self-Concept Support and Friendship Duration." *The Journal of Social Psychology* 96 (1975): 237–43.

Baltzell, Edward Digby. *The Protestant Establishment: Aristocracy and Caste in America.* New York: Vintage, 1964.

Bettelheim, Bruno. "Individual and Mass Behavior in Extreme Situations." *Journal of Abnormal and Social Psychology* 38 (1943): 417–52.

Brownmiller, Susan. *Against Our Will.* New York: Simon and Schuster, 1975.

Brown, Claude. *Manchild in the Promised Land.* New York: Macmillan, 1965.
Clark, K., and Clark M. "Racial Identification and Preference in Negro Children." In *Readings in Social Psychology,* edited by T. M. Newcomb and E. Hartley. New York: Holt, 1947.
Davis, James A. "A Formal Interpretation of the Theory of Relative Deprivation." *Sociometry* 22 (1959): 280–96.
Deutsch, Morton, and Krauss, Robert M. *Theories in Social Psychology.* New York: Basic Books, 1965.
Durkheim, Emile. *The Rules of the Sociological Method.* New York: Free Press, 1957.
Eisenstadt, S. N. "Studies in Reference Group Behavior. In *Readings in Reference Group Theory and Research,* edited by Herbert Hyman and Eleanor Singer. New York: Free Press, 1968.
Festinger, Leon. "A Theory of Social Comparison Processes." *Human Relations* 7 (1954): 117–40.
Frazier, E. Franklin. *Black Bourgeoisie.* New York: Mentor, 1961.
Goldman, Peter. *The Death and Life of Malcolm X.* New York: Harper & Row, 1973.
Goodman, Mary Ellen. *Race Awareness in Young Children.* New York: Macmillan, 1964.
Grier, William H., and Cobbs, Price M. *Black Rage.* New York: Bantam, 1969.
Griffin, John Howard. *Black Like Me.* New York: Signet, 1961.
Haskell, Martin R. "Toward a Reference Group Theory of Juvenile Delinquency." *Social Problems* 8 (1960): 220–30.
Hofstadter, Richard. *The Age of Reform: From Bryon to F.D.R.* New York: Knopf, 1955.
Hyman, Herbert H. "The Psychology of Status." *Archives of Psychology,* no. 269 (1942): 5–38; 80–86.
Hyman, Herbert H. "Reflections on Reference Groups." *Public Opinion Quarterly* 24 (1960): 383–96.
Jackman, Norman R.; O'Toole, Richard; and Geis, Gilbert. "The Self-Image of the Prostitute." In *Sexual Deviance,* edited by John H. Gagnon and William Simon. New York: Harper & Row, 1967.
Jackson, George. *Soledad Brother: The Prison Letters of George Jackson.* New York: Bantam, 1970.
Johnson, Colleen Leahy, and Johnson, Frank Arvid. "Interaction Rules and Ethnicity." *Social Forces* 54 (1975): 452–66.
Josephson, Matthew. *The Robber Barons.* New York: Harcourt, Brace & World, 1934.
Kaufman, Michael T. "Suddenly Angola." *New York Times Magazine,* January 4, 1976.

Kazantzakis, Nikos. *Report to Greco*. New York: Simon and Schuster, 1965.

Kelly, Harold H. "Two Functions of Reference Groups." In *Readings in Social Psychology*, 2d ed., edited by G. E. Swanson, T. M. Newcomb, and E. L. Hartley. New York: Holt, 1952.

Kemper, Theodore D. Reference Groups, Socialization, and Achievement." *American Sociological Review* 33 (1968): 31–44.

Kemper, Theodore D. "Self-Conceptions and the Expectations of Significant Others." *The Sociological Quarterly* 7 (1966): 323–43.

Kimmel, Douglas. *Adulthood and Aging: An Interdisciplinary Developmental View*. New York: Wiley, 1974.

Klapp, Orrin. *Collective Search for Identity*. New York: Holt, Rinehart & Winston, 1969.

Kleinke, Chris L. *First Impressions: The Psychology of Encountering Others*. Englewood Cliffs, N.J.: Prentice-Hall, 1975.

Kuhn, Manford. "The Reference Group Reconsidered." *The Sociological Quarterly* 5 (1964): 6–21.

Lipset, Seymour Martin, and Bendix, Reinhard. *Social Mobility in Industrial Society: A Study of Political Sociology*. Berkeley: University of California Press, 1964.

Lipset, Seymour Martin, and Letterberg, Hans L. "A Theory of Social Mobility." In *Class, Status and Power: A Reader in Social Stratification*, edited by Reinhard Bendix and Seymour Martin Lipset. Rev. ed. New York: Free Press, 1966.

Mack, Raymond. "Riot, Revolt, or Responsible Revolution: Of Reference Groups and Racism." *The Sociological Quarterly* 10 (1969): 147–56.

Mannheim, Karl. "The Sociological Problem of Generations." In *Studies in Social Movements*, edited by Barry McLaughlin. New York: Free Press, 1969.

Mead, George Herbert. *Mind, Self, and Society: From the Standpoint of a Social Behaviorist*, edited by Charles W. Morris. Chicago: University of Chicago Press, 1934.

Merton, Robert. *Social Theory and Social Structure*. New York: Free Press, 1957.

Morland, J. "A Comparison of Race Awareness in Northern and Southern Children." *American Journal of Orthopsychiatry* 36 (1966): 22–31.

Morland, J. "Racial Acceptance and Preference of Nursery School Children in a Southern City." *Merrill Palmer Quarterly* 8 (1962): 271–80.

Morland, J. "Racial Self-Identification: A Study of Nursery School Children." *American Catholic Sociological Review* 24 (1968): 231–42.

Newcomb, Theodore M. "Atttitude Development as a Function of Reference Groups." In *An Outline of Social Psychology*, edited by Muzafer Sherif. New York: Harper & Brothers, 1948.

Newcomb, Theodore M. "Resistance and Regression of Changed Attitudes." *Journal of Social Issues* 19 (1962): 3–13.
Newson, John, and Newson, Elizabeth. *Patterns of Infant Care in an Urban Community.* London: Penguin, 1965.
Ortega y Gasset, José. *Man and Crisis.* New York: Norton, 1962.
Pollis, Nicholas P. "Reference Group Re-examined." *British Journal of Sociology* 3 (1968): 300–307.
Polner, Murray. *No Victory Parades.* New York: Holt, Rinehart & Winston, 1971.
Proshansky, Harold, and Newton, Peggy. "The Nature and Meaning of Negro Self-Identity." In *Social Class, Race and Psychological Development,* edited by M. Deutsch, I. Katz, and A. R. Jensen. New York: Holt, Rinehart & Winston, 1968.
Radloff, Roland, and Helmreich, Robert. *Groups Under Stress: Psychological Research in Sealab II.* New York: Irvington, 1968.
Ramsey, Paul. *War and the Christian Conscience: How Shall Modern War Be Conducted Justly.* Durham, N.C.: Duke University Press, 1961.
Rather, Dan, and Gates, Gary Paul. *The Palace Guard.* New York: Warner, 1975.
Reich, Charles. *The Greening of America.* New York: Random House, 1970.
Riesman, David (in collaboration with Nathan Glazer and Revel Denney). *The Lonely Crowd.* New Haven: Yale University Press, 1950.
Rokeach, Milton. *The Open and Closed Mind.* New York: Basic Books, 1960.
Rollins, Joan Heller. "Reference Identification of Youth of Differing Ethnicity." *Journal of Personality and Social Psychology* 26 (1973): 222–31.
Rosenberg, Morris. "Which Significant Others?" *American Behavioral Scientist* 16 (1973): 829–60.
Runciman, W. G. "Reference Group and Inequalities of Class." In *Readings in Reference Group Theory and Research,* edited by Herbert Hyman and Eleanor Singer. New York: Free Press, 1968.
Sennett, Richard, and Cobb, Jonathan. *The Hidden Injuries of Class.* New York: Random House, 1973.
Sherwood, John J. "Self-Identity and Referent Others." *Sociometry* 28 (1965): 66–81.
Stevenson, Harold W., and Stewart, Edward C. "A Developmental Study of Racial Awareness in Young Children." *Child Development* 29 (1958): 399–409.
Stonequist, Everett V. *The Marginal Man: A Study in Personality and Culture Conflict.* New York: Scribner, 1937.
Steuffer, Samuel; Lumsdaine, Arthur A.; Lumsdaine, Marion Harper; Williams, Robin M., Jr.; Smith, M. Brewster; Janis, Irving L.; Star, Shirley A.; and Cottrell, Leonard S., Jr. *The American Soldier.* 2 vols. Princeton, N.J.: Princeton University Press, 1949.

Strauss, Helen May. "Reference Group and Social Comparison Processes Among the Totally Blind." In *Readings in Reference Group Theory and Research*, edited by Herbert Hyman and Eleanor Singer. New York: Free Press, 1968.

Turner, Ralph H. "Reference Groups of Future-Oriented Men." *Social Forces* 34 (1955): 130–36.

Turner, Ralph H. "Role-Taking, Role Standpoint, and Reference Group Behavior." *American Journal of Sociology* 61 (1956): 316–28.

Turner, Ralph H. "Self and Other in Moral Judgments." *American Sociological Review* 19 (1954): 249–59.

Williams, Margaret Asterud. "Reference Groups: A Review and Commentary." *The Sociological Quarterly* 2 (1970): 545–53.

Wyne, Marvin; White, Kinnard P.; and Copp, Richard H. *The Black Self*. Englewood Cliffs, N.J.: Prentice-Hall, 1974.

Zimbardo, P. G.; and Formica, L. "Emotional Comparison and Self-Esteem as Determinants of Affiliation," *Journal of Personality* 31 (1963): 141–62.

PART THREE

SOCIAL PSYCHOLOGICAL PROCESSES

CHAPTER NINE

Attitudes, Beliefs, Opinions, and Change

The month of Elul. Each morning crowds of women descended to the cemetery to bid the dead farewell; the dead would not reach the holy land as soon as the living; when the Messiah came they would pass to the land of Israel by way of underground caverns. For days the women lay prostrate on the graves, screaming and wailing, begging the forgiveness of the dead for deserting them, explaining that the day of resurrection was near, calling upon them to intercede for their living kin and neighbors in the Hereafter. . . .

Rosh Hashana eve was cool and damp. The sky, which all summer long had been as blue as the curtain of the Torah Ark, and somewhat broader and higher than usual, contracted. Now the town seemed enclosed in a dark canvas tent. The hills, which had been green and evocative of the holy land, disappeared, wiped off the face of the earth. The smoke, reluctant to leave the chimneys, spread over the houses, as though space had shrunken.

Not until sunset did the pious lose hope in the possibility of a miracle. Miracles, they knew, always occur unexpectedly, when people are looking the other way. Perhaps just an instant before sunset the cloud would appear and carry them all off to the holy land. Some had even had a presentiment that it would happen thus. . . . Not until it grew dark and the stars could be seen peeping through the clouds did it become clear to the people of Goray that the Exile was to continue during the High Holy Days. . . .

On both the first and the second day of Rosh Hashana Reb Gedaliya preached before the ram's horn was blown. His face was cinder-red, his eyes flashed, and every word he spoke lightened the heart of the congregation. He argued that this marred holiday was the last of the trials that God was inflicting on his people. Reb Gedaliya compared the present time to the hour before dawn, when the sky must become darkest so that the sun might shine forth in all its splendor. He called on all in the congregation to be steadfast in their faith, and not to despair on this eve of great days. He swore a mighty oath that Sabbatai Zevi was the True Messiah of the God of Jacob; he bade the Jews put away their sadness and gird themselves with trust and joy; he said that the Four Matriarchs had visited Rechele at night to solace her, and they had reported that Satan had leveled a bitter accusation in Heaven against those who wavered in their faith; as a consequence, the end of days had been postponed until such time as the wrath of God should be placated. Before the congregation dispersed, Reb Gedaliya blessed each worshiper with his hands. He lifted the children to kiss them on the head, and called out as the congregation departed:

"Go home and rejoice. We shall all be in the Land of Israel soon, speedily and in our time. Every man shall sit under his vine and under his fig tree."

Isaac Bashevis Singer, *Satan in Goray* (1963)

Assume the role of the other. Sabbatai Zevi said the world was going to end; and, clinging to the prophet's robes, all true believers would follow him to the land of eternal milk and honey. The day arrives; the people are prepared for their journey, eager to meet their Maker. They wait. And wait. And wait. Nothing happens and the assault on self-esteem is tremendous. "I must be a fool. I was totally committed to the prophecies of an impostor. I really believed I would enter the Kingdom of the Lord and all I have to show for my fervent belief is total humiliation. God I am a fool!"

Foolishness is always hard to bear. But when it revolves around a total commitment to ultimate beliefs and values, the burden is often so heavy that people refuse to bear it. Instead of facing reality, they rationalize it away. As with Reb Gedaliya, failed prophecies are turned into divine tests. "Zevi is the Lord's prophet and none of us is a fool. Believe. We will enter the Land of Israel. Believe." Because if you do, the core of your personality is safe. Deny the obvious and your self-esteem will remain both high and intact (for example, Festinger et al., 1956, 1957; Rokeach, 1968; Aronson, 1968; Rosenberg, 1968).

Do people always try to protect themselves? Do they always refuse to change attitudes and beliefs if change means a loss of self-esteem? And what about the use of force? Can one beat you into a change of attitudes, beliefs, and values? Can you be brainwashed into submission?

Questions like these are the focus of this chapter. Above all we seek to uncover some of the more important variables associated with both the persistence and change of people's attitudes, beliefs, opinions, and values.

WHAT IS AN ATTITUDE?

"An attitude is a relatively enduring organization of beliefs around an object or situation predisposing one to respond in some preferential manner" (Rokeach, 1968). Let's begin with the notion of "relatively enduring." Based on learning and past experiences a person has beliefs about a particular object or situation; those beliefs need not be rigid like cement. By "relatively enduring," Rokeach only stresses that the beliefs furnish a basis for interpreting reality and thus a basis for responding to it. Normally the beliefs are organized; not like a rigid bureaucracy but organized in the sense that the beliefs are interrelated. Assume that I hate football under any circumstances. This attitude is rooted in a set of interrelated beliefs: "I believe football makes people violent. I believe football leads to unnecessary injuries. I believe football teaches people to compete when cooperation is what is necessary." And if your attitude toward football leads you to respond to these statements with, "That's ridiculous," what are the beliefs that furnish the basis for your preferential response, your positive attitude toward football?

Since "all attitudes incorporate beliefs," let's make the distinction between attitudes and beliefs clear. It is not based on the idea that attitudes are pro or con while beliefs are always affectively neutral. Both attitudes and beliefs have affective as well as cognitive components. Think of the emotion involved when someone such as Billy Graham says, "I believe in God," and consider the cognitive component of a student's attitude when he says, "I despise lecture classes of seven or eight hundred kids." Clearly, this attitude is based on a number of beliefs (Rokeach, 1968; Osgood, 1974.)

Now, if emotion is not the basis for distinguishing between attitudes and beliefs, the root of the distinction is the summary nature of the attitude concept. Based on a number of interrelated beliefs, attitude indicates "the primary form in which past experience is summed, stored, and organized in the individual" as he approaches any new situation (Newcomb et al., 1965; Rokeach, 1968). Put differently, based on beliefs, attitudes focus our experience or learning by predisposing us to interpret and then respond to an object or situation in a preferential manner. "I love candlelight dinners." "I am wary of all politicians." "I abhor war." "I'm frightened of New York City." In each case the attitude is a "package of beliefs," a summary of "interconnected assertions" that predispose one to say "that certain things about a specific object or situation are true or false, and other things about it are desirable or undesirable" (Rokeach, 1968; also 1960).

If attitudes are based on beliefs, their ultimate sources are values. Defined as "enduring beliefs that specific modes of conduct (say, violence versus nonviolence) or end-states of existence (say, freedom versus equality) are personally and socially preferable" to others, values refer, not to a series of beliefs focused on an object or situation, but "to single beliefs that transcendentally guide actions and judgments across specific objects and situations, and beyond immediate goals to more ultimate end-states of existence" (Rokeach, 1968). For example, say my attitude toward war is abhorrence; say that attitude is based on the beliefs that war is stupid, senseless, unnecessary, and barbaric; but say, above all, that my attitude is rooted in a value, my strong belief in the value of any human life under any circumstances.

Like attitudes, some values are more important than others. And like attitudes, some values are inextricably tied to the core of personality, the self-image. Indeed, the point of these definitions is that attitudes tied to important values and then linked to important beliefs about self should be by far the most resistant to change. There one is threatened at the core. There is generated the dissonance that often requires resistance to even the most demonstrable facts.

DISSONANCE, COMMITMENT, AND SELF-JUSTIFICATION

Dissonance refers "to a relation that exists between pairs of elements." The elements, the "knowledges," could be opinions, attitudes, beliefs, values, images of self; but whatever the nature of the pair, dissonance exists when the elements are in conflict. Assume that I think I'm smart and you tell me I'm dumb. Or say, like the Russian novelist Fyodor Dostoyevsky, I doubt the existence of God but think that a world without God is destined to moral chaos (Fernandez, 1970). In either example the knowledges are in conflict; a person is harboring cognitions that point in opposite directions (Festinger, 1957).

Leon Festinger argues that dissonance is uncomfortable; since people seek consistency in their attitudes, beliefs, values, and images of self, in the presence of conflicting cognitions, they try to eliminate the dissonance. Sometimes it is assumed the need to end conflict is rooted in "human nature": supposedly, people are rational; conflict or contradiction upsets them and they thus seek to restore a rational approach to reality by eliminating dissonance. Perhaps. But the core of Festinger's theory rests on the notion that people are *rationalizing* creatures (Festinger, 1957; Aronson, 1968). Socialized in a culture that highly values rationality, people are often upset by an irrational pair of cognitions. But one of the most striking facts about even the most rational people is that they often resolve dissonance by embracing irrationality. Confronted with evidence that Congress would not support his work at Versailles, Woodrow Wilson turned his back on the facts and sought support from people who had shown they would not give it. Or, consider Lyndon Johnson and his advisers. Confronted with evidence that the bombing of Vietnam was a failure, they refused to believe studies they had commissioned and continued to believe in policies proved unsuccessful by the evidence (Barber, 1972; Janis, 1973; *Pentagon Papers,* 1971).

Hopefully the examples show that, confronted with dissonance, people often choose security before rationality. And the ultimate reason they do so is the anxiety produced by conflicting attitudes or beliefs; at bottom dissonance is psychologically uncomfortable, not because of irrationality, but because of the threats and insecurities that accompany a conflicting pair of cognitions. If I think I'm smart and you tell me I'm dumb, I can eliminate the dissonance in a variety of ways (for example, I can agree with you or I can argue that you are only saying that because you refuse to admit how smart I really am), but Festinger contends that people need to do so because they find it uncomfortable (and often impossible) to live with the anxieties and insecurities caused by a dissonant pair of cognitions (Festinger, 1957, 1964; Aronson, 1968, 1973a, 1973b).

The need to reduce dissonance is relative. And Festinger says it is relative "to the importance of the elements" to the person with conflict. In effect, the greater the importance of the conflicting cognitions, the greater the magnitude of the dissonance, and the greater the person's need to resolve the conflict as quickly as possible. Let's return to our example of Fyodor Dostoyevsky. For him nothing was more important than God; he says in his *Letters* that one idea "has tormented me, consciously and unconsciously, all my life long: it is the question of the existence of God." Dostoyevsky could not decide if God existed and the torment was severe, the need to resolve the dissonance (that is, I believe God exists; I do not believe God exists) was great. So, Dostoyevsky came to a very irrational but very comfortable conclusion. He was prepared to admit that God did not exist; the facts said God was a fiction. But so what! Dostoyevsky refused to accept the truth. In fact, he resolved his dissonance by concluding that the free personality of man is revealed only in Jesus Christ, who is God[1] (Dostoyevsky, 1961; Mochulsky, 1971; Fernandez, 1970).

If the key variable determining the magnitude of dissonance is the importance of the elements to the person, it is possible to be more specific about the meaning of importance. First is the possible involvement of self-image. If the two cognitions torment one, and in addition are linked to focal beliefs about self, the magnitude of the dissonance increases sub-

---

[1] A similar approach is taken by Spanish philosopher José Ortega y Gasset: "The fact is that with respect to the things in my surroundings I need to know on what I can rely. This is the true and original meaning of knowing: my knowing on what I can depend." And, "Man adapts himself to everything, to the best and the worst. To one thing only does he not adapt himself: to being not clear in his own mind what he believes about things" (Ortega y Gasset, 1962).

stantially. Like the followers of Sabbatai Zevi, it is threatening enough to believe in a miracle and then see none, but if the result of no miracle is a serious assault on self-image (that is, I am a fool and a sinner), then all at once the dissonance strikes at key attitudes, values, and images of self. The person would have to work hard at quickly resolving the dissonance (Aronson, 1973b; Worchel and McCormick, 1964; see also Bramel, 1968).

A second aspect of importance is the amount of *new dissonance* that may result if a person chooses one knowledge rather than another. How much does conflict or contradiction about a pair of cognitions (for example, the existence or nonexistence of God) threaten a number of other attitudes and beliefs (one's attitudes toward abortion, premarital sex, killing another person)? To the extent that conflict here means even more conflicts there, the magnitude of dissonance increases and so does the person's need to resolve conflicts (Festinger, 1957; Deutsch and Krauss, 1965).

A third aspect of importance is the notion of commitment (Brehm and Cohen, 1962; Wilhelmy, 1974). If a pair of cognitions trouble a person, involve focal beliefs about self, are capable of producing new dissonance, and then the person decides to do one thing rather than another or chooses one (or more) alternative(s) rather than another or actively engages (*or has engaged*) in one behavior over another, then the person has "resolved" the dissonance by binding himself to the chosen alternative(s). In essence, the person has entrusted his security to one of the knowledges and that bond, that commitment, should increase the importance of the elements to the person and thus the magnitude of dissonance that arises should a commitment be threatened or proved incorrect or stupid or anachronistic.

Now, let's put the variables together. Ideally any dissonance is uncomfortable, but in reality the theory makes its best predictions when the conflicting cognitions are important to the person, implicate focal aspects of self-image, have the capacity to produce new dissonance, and involve a commitment on the person's part to one rather than another cognition. When these four variables are present, the need to resolve dissonance is great, and people often do so by engaging in mental gymnastics. They twist, turn, somersault, do anything except embrace knowledges that threaten to destroy important beliefs about self and world. And while it is true that self-justification often means an effort to protect self, to guard against a loss of self-esteem, the ultimate cause of the need to resolve dissonance is the insecurity that flows from threats to important beliefs. The clinical literature is studded with examples of people who had terrible images of self but found the therapist's efforts at help too threatening. Confronted with positive knowledge about self, people resolved the dissonance by vigorously reaffirming a negative image of self. In Horney's words, these people "tend to deny and eliminate expansive feelings about self such as self-glorification, pride, and arrogance. Pride, no matter what it concerns, is put under a strict and extensive taboo. As a result it is not consciously felt; it is denied or disowned" (Horney, 1950; see also Adams, 1975).

To eliminate dissonance, people must change beliefs about one of the elements. Here many possibilities exist (Brehm and Cohen, 1962; Cohen, 1964), but to show how they operate in reality let us consider a situation where the need to eliminate dissonance was of the utmost importance to the people involved.

Our example comes from Volume 2 of Solzhenitsyn's, *The Gulag Archipelago*. In a chapter titled "The Loyalists," he describes the problems of totally committed Communists. In terms of values, beliefs, attitudes, and self-images, these men had voluntarily committed themselves to Communist ideology, and more specifically, to communism as defined by Joseph Stalin. Then, suddenly, and for no apparent reason, they "fell beneath the ax"; along with enemies of the state, men they spit upon, Loyalists were literally sent to Siberia with sentences ranging from five to twenty years.

Now, consider the role of the other, of the Loyalist. "I am a committed Communist; all my attitudes, even those toward the men I am imprisoned with, are rooted in my allegiance to Joseph Stalin's communism. But I am in prison for no reason and the attitudes and statements of prison authorities give me only one message: I too am an enemy of the state. Indeed, they are telling me I am everything I have committed myself not to be!"

Here the magnitude of the dissonance was great, the need to eliminate the dissonance of the utmost importance. What did Loyalists do? The first thing they did was totally refuse to accept reality. Their need to resist the obvious was essential and, acting in response to that need, Loyalists quickly put on and refused to remove the blinders that hid reality from them. In Solzhenitsyn's words, "impenetrability, that was their chief trait! Armor-piercing shells for iron-heads have not yet been invented. In arguing with them, you wear yourself out, unless you accept in advance that the argument is simply a game, a jolly pastime" (Solzhenitsyn, 1975).

Essentially, arguing was a game because these men eliminated dissonance by responding to reality as if they themselves were boomerangs (Brehm and Cohen, 1962). Confronted with important and unavoidable dissonance, they came back upon themselves and became even more fervent advocates of Joseph Stalin's communism. Instead of facing a very painful reality, they "discovered" their Communist attitudes and values were even more valid than they had imagined: "You're telling me I wasted my life in allegiance to a brutal set of attitudes and values. I tell you you're wrong. Why, in reevaluating the correctness and benefits of communism, this experience has shown me they are even more wonderful than I thought." Translated into everyday life, Loyalists "never" tried to escape because that was "an act of subversion of Soviet power." And generally Loyalists "were devoted to work"; labor was in the service of the state and it was "quite rational that persons refusing to go out to work should be beaten and imprisoned in the punishment block and shot in wartime." Finally, Loyalists felt that "inasmuch as the camp regimen has been established by *us,* the Soviet government, it must be observed not only willingly but conscientiously. The *spirit* of the regimen has to be observed *even before this is demanded or requested by the supervisors*" (Solzhenitsyn, 1975, last emphasis added).

Although passionate reaffirmation of attitudes and values helped Loyalists to reduce their dissonance, to "eliminate" it they still had to come to terms with a very difficult question: What were they doing in prison? Here Loyalists had no choice about an answer for they were unable to change the knowledge producing dissonance: they were in prison and no one was letting them out. So, because they were unable to follow one easy means of reducing dissonance (that is, change one of the knowledges producing it), Loyalists responded by adding a host of new cognitive elements (see Festinger, 1957). This included the following rationalizations: their imprisonment was "the very cunning work of foreign intelligence services"; Stalin knows nothing of the arrests, they are the work of "wreckers" in the secret police; the repressions—they admitted it was repression—"are an historical necessity for the development of our society"; this is all a terrible mistake and "the more people arrested, the quicker those at the top are going to *understand their mistake!* (Solzhenitsyn, 1975, emphasis in original).

Obviously, different prisoners used different excuses, but the need for rationalization had the same basic root: they could not change important attitudes and values, yet they must somehow come to terms with a cognition that would not change. So, their only hope was to add knowledges that satisfactorily explained their contradictory situation. And, should someone produce dissonance about these new cognitions, they would respond with a ferocity born of insecurity. For example, Solzhenitsyn notes that if a prisoner said Stalin was "a dog" and that until he died nothing good would happen, Loyalists "would hurl themselves on such a person with fists, and hurry to denounce him to their interrogator."

A third way that Loyalists tried to eliminate dissonance was by attempting to change the knowledge that would not change: Loyalists sought release from prison. Festinger puts this in the category of reducing dissonance by "changing an environmental cognitive element." Instead of reducing dissonance by a change of beliefs or behavior, the person tries to change the environment. However, such a change implies "a sufficient degree of control over one's environment—a relatively rare occurrence" (Festinger, 1957; Brehm and Cohen, 1962). In the case of Loyalists, they added new elements because they lacked control over the environment, but since a changed environment could completely eliminate dissonance by proving their rationalizations correct, Loyalists never gave up trying. "Six and twelve times a year they sent off complaints, declarations, and petitions." Quickly, their pleas were rejected and just as quickly they responded to this dissonance with another rationalization: "They didn't reach Stalin! He would have understood. He would have forgiven the benefactor!" (Solzhenitsyn, 1975).

Finally, consider the everyday behavior of Loyalists. Theory says they should be active proponents of the Party's line, for another way to reduce or eliminate dissonance is to persuade more and more people that the Communist system of belief is correct and "then, clearly it must, after all, be correct" (Festinger et al., 1956). In effect, could so many people affirm a false or brutal system of beliefs? Obviously they could not, and so Solzhenitsyn notes that Loyalists "made a display of their ideological orthodoxy first to the interrogator, then in the prison cells, and then in camp to all and everyone." And should someone say this pleading was "pigheadedness" or "hypocrisy," Solzhenitsyn says "they argued in the cells in defense of all the government's actions" because "they needed ideological arguments" (and we add the notion of social support) "in order to hold on to a sense of their own rightness—otherwise insanity was not far off" (Solzhenitsyn, 1975).

Remember that the example of the Loyalists stacks the cards in favor of dissonance theory. If the dissonance revolves around unimportant attitudes and values or if it is not linked to focal beliefs about self or if it will not produce new dissonance or if a person made no voluntary commitment to the attitudes and values, the magnitude of the dissonance more or less significantly decreases, the need to resolve dissonance may be weak, or a person may have no vital reasons to defend attitudes and values against a reality that contradicts them. Consider two examples. A friend bought a car that was supposed to get thirty-five miles for every gallon of gasoline; in reality the car gets nineteen miles to the gallon. My friend's response to the dissonance (that is, the dealer said it would get this much mileage; it doesn't get near that) was: "Who cares? Maybe the guy lied to me. Maybe I got a lemon. Maybe the mileage will get better. Who cares? I've got more important things to worry about." Or, consider the case of many Communist Chinese soldiers captured during the Korean War. Told by their leaders that military success was assured, dissonance came when the army suffered defeats. But, where the Loyalists might have reduced dissonance by adding new beliefs (for example, we have faked defeat in order to win everything in the future; the United States used biological warfare), the Chinese soldiers resolved dissonance by accepting reality: they and their leaders were wrong. Apparently, many of the soldiers were impressed into service; their "commitment" to the war was involuntary. And since Communist attitudes and values were not crucial to them, they were relatively incapable of producing new dissonance or striking at focal beliefs about self. So, in the absence of total commitment to a system of attitudes and values, many of the soldiers were able to eliminate dissonance by accepting the reality of military defeat (see George, 1969).

Under certain conditions a person eliminates dissonance by turning away from reality. Under other conditions this same flight from the obvious is true of people working together. Irving Janis calls it "groupthink," and his reference is "to a deterioration of mental efficiency, reality testing, and moral judgment that results from in-group pressures" (1973). In essence, very intelligent men and women sometimes do the dumbest things. Having a set of facts before them, they resist the obvious and instead embrace, not what they see, but what they wish to see. How is this possible?

Janis says the first thing needed is "an illusion of invulnerability." The sources of the illusion can be cultural (for example, it is America's Manifest Destiny "to spread democracy far and wide") or personal (that is, people with tremendous self-confidence) or both, but when present the illusion of invulnerability creates an atmosphere of "excessive optimism"; group members feel they cannot lose. In fact, like the men who surrounded Presidents Kennedy and Johnson, men who sincerely believed that their "sheer intelligence and rationality could answer and solve anything" (Halberstam, 1972; Barnet, 1972), a group's optimism may "encourage" it to take very extreme risks (Janis, 1973). And why not? The group will successfully solve any problem.

Often linked to the notion of invulnerability is "an unquestioned belief in the group's inherent morality." "Our side is right; they are wrong; and that is all there is to it." Naturally, to the extent that group members believe they alone carry the banner of morality, they are unlikely to question even the most brutal policies. And they are also likely to become very defensive if someone says they are immoral. Like a boomerang, assaults on their policies may move them to eliminate dissonance by turning back on themselves, by reassuring themselves they are as moral as they think they are. Lyndon Johnson responded to criticism of the Vietnam War by calling critics immoral, and dissenters often unintentionally fueled the determination of Johnson and his advisers to win in Vietnam. "Appeasement would be disaster" (Barber, 1972; Janis, 1973).

A third source of groupthink are collective efforts to rationalize away the truth and, tied to this, one or two "self-appointed mindguards," people who intentionally "protect" group members from adverse information. At Pearl Harbor, the naval group was convinced "it can't happen here" and, rooted in their shared commitment to this definition of the situation, they helped each other to rationalize away evidence that pointed to a Japanese attack on impregnable Pearl Harbor (Janis, 1973). A "famous" example of a mindguard was W. W. Rostow, President Johnson's national security adviser. Voluntarily, Rostow "shielded the president from criticism and from reality." In group sessions, "he deflected others' pessimism and rewarded those who were optimistic." And, after spending long hours pouring over military information to find one or two positive pieces of news, Rostow would then call Secretary of State Rusk and Secretary of Defense McNamara to announce the great news, to proclaim the victories that would soon produce success in Vietnam (Halberstam, 1972).

A fourth and fifth source of groupthink are social pressures that produce a "shared illusion of unanimity" or, if someone does break the spell, "direct pressure" on a group dissenter to follow the group line. Janis says that at Pearl Harbor the prevailing atmosphere was one of "geniality and security." When the Japanese boats were actually steaming toward Hawaii, group leader Admiral Kimmel joked about such a possibility in a way that showed "he would be inclined to laugh derisively at anyone who thought otherwise." And, tragically, no one who might have thought otherwise said so. Obviously everyone agreed that a Japanese attack was impossible; why such an idea was even laughable (Janis, 1973).

A final source of groupthink is related to the illusion of invulnerability and the unquestioned belief in the group's inherent morality. For these assumptions tend to produce others; they tend to lead to "stereotyped views of enemy leaders as too evil to warrant genuine attempts to negotiate, or as too weak and stupid to counter whatever risky attempts are made to defend their purposes" (Janis, 1973). Throughout the Vietnam War, and despite the evidence of France's defeat, President Johnson and his advisers continually underestimated, or simply refused to credit, the North Vietnamese with intelligence, skill, and determination. It seemed impossible to them that the most technologically advanced civilization in history could not easily defeat a group of people who had barely risen above the level of preliterate tribes (for example, Stavins et al., 1971; Halberstam, 1972).

Like an individual, groups sometimes need to justify themselves. And when, as in Vietnam, that need revolves around a voluntary commitment rooted in important values and beliefs, it is very hard to decide which came first, the need for self-justification or the variables that produce groupthink. Probably the two factors have an interactive relationship. At least in Vietnam the illusion of invulnerability and the belief in the group's inherent morality were rooted in attitudes, values, and self-images important to virtually all of President Johnson's advisers. And while these two sources of groupthink were present at the outset, the need for mindguards, for collective rationalizations, for direct pressure on dissenters, and for shared illusions of unanimity, all increased dramatically as failure and criticism produced serious dissonance about a series of group members' important attitudes, values, self-images, and commitments.

INADEQUATE JUSTIFICATION

One of the most interesting predictions derived from dissonance theory concerns the effects of rewards or incentives on changes in attitudes and values. Paradoxically, dissonance theory argues that if you or I behave contrary to our attitudes and values, but are given no or little incentive to do so, there will be *more* attitude change than if we had received a large reward or incentive. Follow the reasoning of dissonance theory. We behave contrary to our attitudes but have no external justification for doing so; no one gave us a lot of money, no one threatened us, no one beat us into submission. So, in the absence of external justification, we have cognitive dissonance: "I believe this but I did that. Why?" An answer must come from the person; especially if the magnitude of the dissonance is great, he or she can eliminate it only by finding an internal justification for the discrepant behavior. In sum, in order to resolve the dissonance, and in the absence of any external justification, people explain their behavior by changing their attitudes about it (Festinger, 1957; Aronson, 1973a; Festinger and Carlsmith, 1959; Carlsmith et al., 1966; Cohen, 1964; Brehm and Cohen, 1962).

Take as examples the following experiments. For a small reward, students who were strongly against the legalization of marijuana were asked to make a videotaped speech advocating its legalization. Since students were told their speech would be shown to people who were uncommitted on the issue of marijuana's legalization, experimenters hypothesized that students would resolve their dissonance (I'm against the legalization of marijuana; I'm advocating its use for no good reason to people who may very well accept my arguments) by a change of attitudes regarding the legalization of marijuana. In fact, the hypothesis was strongly confirmed. Students who had received a $.50 incentive to make the tape "showed a large amount of attitude change" (Nel et al., 1969). In another experiment, students strongly against a college policy were asked to write essays in support of the policy for a $1.50 reward. Since students were told their essays might result in the unwanted policy's continuance, and since the students were told they would never know the actual effects of their essays, experimenters predicted that students would resolve dissonance (I'm against this policy; I'm writing an essay that may help perpetuate it) by changing their attitudes about the policy. In fact, this did happen; students changed attitudes and they did so even if there was only a possibility their essay might lead to the unwanted policy's perpetuation (Goethals and Cooper, 1975; see also Cooper and Worchel, 1970).

So far we have only presented one side of the theoretical story. The other belongs to incentive theorists[2] (for example, Elms and Janis, 1965; Elms, 1968). Here one of the central arguments is that "when rewards are presented under circumstances where they do not arouse emotional responses which interfere with attitude change processes, highly rewarded role playing produces *more* attitude change than when rewards are low" (Elms, 1968). Consider this experiment as an example. Students were asked to write essays in favor of sending American students to study the Soviet system of government and the history of communism. They were told the essays were sponsored by the U.S. State Department, with rewards ranging from $.50 to $10.00. Experimenters predicted greater change with the high reward students and their predictions were fully confirmed. More attitude change occurred in the high reward rather than the low reward situation (Elms and Janis, 1965).

The results of this study are accurate, but at least here there is no disproof of dissonance theory. This is so because in the situation described there was no dissonance to theorize about. Students were apparently positive about the American government, and they received no information regarding any harmful consequences that might flow from their essays. So, in the absence of dissonance, and in the presence of a high reward and relatively positive attitudes toward the sponsor and the suggested program, why not more attitude change with a high reward? Elms and Janis are correct; under positive conditions, high rewards do produce more attitude change than low rewards. And this is especially clear if the person feels the task is valuable or important; there the high reward should act as an extra incentive, pushing the person to change his attitudes and beliefs even more.

But, what happens under negative conditions? What happens if students are told the Soviet Embassy sponsored the essays? In the Elms and Janis study, "low reward role players showed more (though not significantly more) positive attitude change than high reward role players" (Elms, 1968; Elms and Janis, 1965). Now this result could be interpreted as support for dissonance theory; knowing the Soviet Embassy was the sponsor, students may have experienced dissonance: "I dislike communism; I'm writing an essay sponsored by a group I dislike in order to study the group I dislike." Here, if students experienced dissonance, in the absence of a high reward, they may have resolved dissonance by seeking an internal justification for their behavior. Or, consider an alternative explanation. Knowing the Soviet Embassy was the sponsor acted as a nega-

---

[2] A third that will not be considered here is that of behaviorism (see Bem, 1967).

tive incentive to students. Immediately, their suspicions were aroused, and so, despite the high reward, their suspicions moved them to resist changing their attitudes. Obviously, this interpretation of this experiment fails to explain the changes of the low reward students, but it does offer a plausible explanation for the failure of high rewards to produce attitude change. In effect, it is not dissonance that explains the success or failure of rewards but the extent to which rewards are presented in situations that are totally positive, situations in which people need not suspect the motives of a sponsor or an experimenter.

Although to date no definitive resolution of the problem exists, we are much closer to understanding the limiting conditions of each theory. First, Aronson is correct when he writes that "dissonance and incentive effects can exist side by side"; the two theories are not mutually exclusive (1968). Under positive conditions, high rewards should produce more attitude change than low rewards; and when experiments do not lend themselves to conflicting explanations, when there is little doubt that dissonance exists (for example, one would say it is very hard to interpret the marijuana experiments as other than the existence of cognitive dissonance), the evidence consistently shows that low rewards produce more attitude change than high rewards (Aronson, 1976). However, the effect of negative conditions appears to be relative. Consider the following experiments. Students had to perform a dull task and then lie about it; they had to tell others they enjoyed the task. Where students stated this in an essay, were assured of complete anonymity, and were told only small parts of their essay would be used, high rewards produced more change than low rewards. But, where students had to lie to others face-to-face, low rewards produced greater change. Apparently, the degree of a student's commitment is an important variable determining the effect of rewards. Where students experience dissonance but lack any sense of commitment, the dissonance presents no problems. And why should it? If the magnitude of dissonance is relative to the importance of the elements to the person, in this experiment the lack of commitment makes the dissonance unimportant and that results in the high rewards having a greater effect than the low rewards. But, where students have to make a public commitment, where anonymity is impossible and others will use any part of the argument they wish, a degree of importance is introduced. Dissonance means something to the person and so the low rewards produce more attitude change (see Carlsmith et al., 1966; Aronson, 1968, 1976; Helmreich and Collins, 1968; Wilhelmy, 1974).

In sum, the differences between the predictions of dissonance and incentive theory are often more apparent than real. As long as no dissonance exists, strong incentives should produce more attitude change than weak incentives. However, where dissonance exists, is important to the person (in terms of attitudes, values, self-image, and for commitment), and the incentive is weak, the person should have to find an internal justification for his or her dissonant behavior and this search should produce more attitude change than that experienced by a person whose dissonance can be eliminated by reference to a strong incentive. For example, consider Stanley Milgram's experiments on obedience to authority, discussed in detail in Chapter Ten. Many of the participants felt they were decent, moral men and women, but when they shocked someone enough to kill him, dissonance was often great and the incentive, the external justification, for the shocks was very small—$4.00 for possibly killing someone.

Now in this situation dissonance would predict change—possibly significant change—in attitudes, values, and self-image in order for the person to satisfactorily explain the dissonant behavior. And that is exactly what Milgram often found. Consider the experiment's effect on a thirty-nine-year-old social worker, Mr. Braverman. Although he obeyed all the way to 450 volts, the magnitude of his dissonance was already evident during the experiment: "There was I. I'm a nice person, I think, hurting somebody and caught up in what seemed a mad situation . . . what appalled me was that I could possess this capacity for obedience and compliance to a central idea, that is, the value of a memory experiment, even after it became clear that continued adherence to this value was at the expense or violation of another value, that is, don't hurt someone else who is helpless and not hurting you." Clearly, Mr. Braverman had serious conflicts: How to explain the dissonance between his values and his behavior? And how to explain the possibly terrible consequences for self-image? One explanation was in terms of science: he valued it more than he valued his belief not to hurt someone who is helpless. But, in terms of self-image, Mr. Braverman experienced a significant change. When he told his wife about the experiment, she said: "You can call yourself Eichmann." And in a sense Mr. Braverman did so. Self-confident, and apparently able to face the fact that, like Eichmann, he could be a product of his times, Mr. Braverman came to the conclusion that under certain circumstances he did have the potential to do and be evil. This was a significant change, caused by many interacting factors—the dissonance about important values, the threat to self-image accompanied by a self-confidence and world view that enabled him to confront reality, and, of course, the lack of any external justification for his very contradictory behavior (Milgram, 1974; see also Lifton, 1961; Schein, 1961).

PUBLIC OPINION

A shrill trumpet call has pierced the air. It was the bulletin! Victory! It always meant victory when a trumpet call preceded the news. A sort of electric thrill ran through the cafe. Even the waiters had started and pricked up their ears.

The trumpet call had let loose an enormous volume of noise. Already an excited voice was gobbling from the telescreen, but even as it started it was almost drowned by a roar of cheering from outside. The news had run round the streets like magic. He could hear just enough of what was issuing from the telescreen to realize that it had all happened as he had foreseen: . . . victory—greatest victory in human history—victory, victory, victory.

Under the table Winston's feet made convulsive movements. He had not stirred from his seat, but in his mind he was running, swiftly running, he was with the crowds outside, cheering himself deaf. He looked up again at the portrait of Big Brother. The colossus that bestrode the world! The rock against which the hordes of Asia dashed themselves in vain! He thought how ten minutes ago—yes, only ten minutes—there had still been equivocation in his heart as he wondered whether the news from the front would be of victory or defeat. Ah, it was more than a Eurasian Army that had perished! Much had changed in him since the first day in the Ministry of Love, but the final, indispensable, healing change had never happened until this moment.

. . . He gazed up at the enormous face. Forty years it had taken him to learn what kind of smile was hidden beneath the dark moustache. O cruel, needless misunderstanding! O stubborn, self-willed exile from the loving breast! Two gin-scented tears trickled down the sides of his nose. But it was all right, everything was all right, the struggle was finished. He had won the victory over himself. He loved Big Brother. [George Orwell, *1984* (1949)]

Orwell's Big Brother symbolizes many things. One is mind control. Using the "telescreen" and a variety of sophisticated techniques, political leaders can make us think what they wish. Seemingly, you and I are flexible. Ready for mobilization, eager "to wait until we are told to act," we—the masses of men and women—are willingly at the mercy of those who control society's telescreens. Others give us our public and private opinions, tell us how to behave, and seemingly you and I docilely do as we are told. Paraphrasing Jacques Ellul, today people are "less and less capable of acting by themselves"; always they need the "collective signals" that integrate their actions into the complete mechanism, always they need a political leader's version of truth and happiness (Ellul, 1965, 1967; Kornhauser, 1959).

Although *1984* was first published in 1949, the view that people's public and private beliefs could be easily controlled dates from at least 1915. World War I was unique. Never before had governments assumed such centralized control of the sources of public information; never before had governments made such systematic attempts to propagandize their people. And never before had propaganda had such a dramatic effect. Seemingly the war showed that with the use of centralized control and scientific techniques people's opinions could be molded in any shape their leaders wished (see, for example, Ponsonby, 1928; Lasswell, 1928; Peterson, 1939).

But was this true? And is it true? Are we as docile as some scholars suggest? Are our public and private beliefs so easily changed by those who control the sources of information? In general, the answer is no, but since the reasons are complex, let us begin by defining our terms.

An opinion is "a verbal expression of some belief, attitude, or value" (Rokeach, 1968). Often opinions are private; it is the person's business and no one else's. But sometimes people want to tell others what they believe, and some political systems actively request that citizens speak their minds. When this happens, we are talking about a public, about "a dispersed group of people" interested in, divided about, and engaged in, a discussion of an issue (Turner and Killian, 1972; Blumer, 1969). When these people collectively register their views, it is public opnion. Before we proceed any further, these facts must be kept in mind. First, reference is to *a* public, not *the* public. Rarely (if ever) does the entire public register an opinion about even the most important issue; and when the issues are remote, it is likely that *a* public includes only a small percentage of *the* public (for example, Rosenau, 1961). Second, on any particular issue there are probably at least two or more publics. Turner and Killian rightly underline that a basic assumption of societies that register public opinion is that "people agree to disagree about issues." Third, since public opinion revolves around issues, it is crucial to know how issues are defined. For it is entirely possible that "many and perhaps most changes in public opinion consist of redefinitions of issues" (for example, Are you in favor of American involvement in Vietnam; or, Should America lose its honor and retreat, like a helpless giant, from Vietnam?) that group people differently (Turner and Killian, 1972). Fourth, since public opinion is rooted in attitudes, values, and beliefs, it is at least plausible to assume that if issues touch important attitudes, values, and beliefs, people may be highly unlikely to change. Indeed, they may resist change at all costs.

Now, let's return to the question of mind control. If political or economic or social leaders have the power to mold public opnion, that power is clearly limited, not to *the* public, but to *a* more or less large public. Some people simply refuse to express opinions about public issues, and while indifference may produce obedience, it does not mean control of public and private beliefs. Second, since publics agree to disagree about all issues, even a very successful campaign at molding public opinion rarely (if ever) succeeds with everyone. Normally, even successful "opinion makers" fail to convince some segments of that part of the public that registers an opinion about an issue. Third, and perhaps most important, because public opinion revolves around an issue, the issue "may change without equivalent change in the attitudes and opinions of individuals." Conceivably, part of a public may agree to follow an "opinion maker," not because of a change in attitudes and values, but because a redefinition of the issue moves people to have a different opinion about it (Turner and Killian, 1972). And, to the extent that this is so, perhaps the power of "opinion makers" is not that of easily changing attitudes and values but of defining and redefining issues in a manner that moves substantial parts of a public to say yes to the opinion maker's definition of the issue.

Let's consider a specific example—public opinion about American involvement in World War I. Initially, the issue was how to maintain neutrality, how to be fair to both sides. Then, in February of 1915, came the German declaration of submarine warfare. Wilson and the press could have firmly linked their response to the German declaration, to the British blockade of the North Sea; this would have maintained neutrality. Instead, they saw the German policy as a much more serious and essentially separate problem. Germany would be held to "strict accountability," and while few knew what this meant, the harsher response to Germany was the first fundamental redefinition of the war versus neutrality issue. As of August 1914, that part of the public that had registered an opinion about American involvement was overwhelmingly negative. But with the issue redefined by Wilson and the press, concerned members of the public now realized that war was possible. They also realized that a submarine incident on the high seas could force Wilson to define strict accountability as well as force the public to register an opinion about his definition (see, for example, Osgood, 1953; Millis, 1935; Peterson, 1939).

The incident came on May 7, 1915, with the sinking of the *Lusitania* in only eighteen minutes and the loss of 128 American lives. Both Wilson and the press (throughout the country) were outraged, but only six of one thousand papers called for war (Costrell, 1940) and two powerful Democratic leaders told Wilson he might find it impossible to obtain a congressional declaration of war. So, what to do? Against the views of Secretary of State Bryan, Wilson sent a strong note of protest to Germany: The United States refused to accept any "abbreviation of the rights of American shipmasters or of American citizens bound on lawful errands . . ." and the U.S. "must hold the Imperial German Government to a strict accountability for any infringement of those rights, intentional or accidental." But how was strict accountability defined? Here Wilson set the stage for America's involvement in World War I.[3] Bryan's advice was to define it in terms of claims the U.S. would make *after* the European war was over; rejecting this advice, Wilson defined accountability in terms of an implied threat of war: if Germany attacked our ships, we would fight. Moreover, remember that Wilson had refused to send a protest to Great Britain (about its lawbreaking) when he sent the *Lusitania* notes

---

[3] The intent here is not that Wilson wanted war. He saw the issues in a particular light and he acted on his perceptions.

to Germany. So, he had once again unintentionally redefined the issue and increased the chance of war. For when he was dealing with both countries together, it was plausible to argue that he could never coerce both, leaving the option of doing nothing. When the claims were separated, the option tended to disappear, particularly when opinion makers began to argue that the nation's honor was involved (see May, 1959).

Remember that most Americans were against fighting in Europe's war. But think too of the "new" issue confronting them. Now the threat of war had been made and, at that, to one specific country. Between them, the Wilson administration and the press—the "opinion makers" of the time—had herded its citizens into a corner: new incidents would force America to act on its threats. In March of 1916, the *Sussex* was torpedoed without warning, and Wilson's response was clear: either Germany completely ceased submarine warfare or America severed diplomatic relations, the last step before a declaration of war. Germany gave in, it agreed to America's demands. But now it was up to Germany to decide if Americans went to war; by publicly redefining the issue in terms of a severance of diplomatic relations, if Germany decided to resume submarine warfare (she did on January 31, 1917), America had no choice: she had to sever diplomatic relations and wait for war.

Had people changed their beliefs and attitudes about the war? Did they want to fight in 1917? A few did, but the vast majority of that part of the public expressing its opinions was against American involvement. Wilson had won reelection on the slogan, "He kept us out of war," and a British intelligence report of March 21, 1917, indicated that "the overwhelming majority of the American people still desired most earnestly to avoid war." They would stand behind the president, even in the use of force, but there was no "positive support among the public as a whole" (Peterson, 1939). And when, six days after the eventual declaration of war, Chicago's recruiting officers called for 18,000 volunteers to appear at the Chicago Cubs ballpark, recruiting officers had a bad day. Not one volunteer appeared (Bogart and Matthews, 1920)!

Why then in 1917 did a large public express positive support for a war they did not want to fight in 1914? Consider a point made by Milton Rokeach. People have attitudes and opinions about objects and situations (Rokeach, 1968). Over three years relatively few Americans changed their attitudes or opinions about the war; they did not want to fight, period. But, as the issue was redefined, America's situation changed and with it the opinions of a large public. Most Americans were never enthusiastic about the war. Magazines, newspapers, and diaries record a sense of fatalism, a resignation to the seemingly inevitable coming of war. And that resignation was in response to the new situation created by the redefinition of the issue. In 1917 the issue was far removed from any notions of how to maintain neutrality; the issue was how much longer could

America tolerate Germany's actions without declaring war. Eventually a very large public agreed with Wilson; the answer was no longer, America had to fight. But, if the opinions of a very large public were in agreement with those of Wilson; it was *not* because he or the press or three years of sophisticated British propaganda (see, for example, Squires, 1935) had convinced Americans to change their attitudes, values, and beliefs about war in Europe. Most Americans with an opinion responded only to the ongoing redefinition of the issue, and if a very large public had positive opinions about the need to declare war, their opinions were rooted in an agreement about a redefined issue, America's situation in 1917. For all their efforts, opinion makers never changed most people's negative opinions, attitudes, and beliefs about war in Europe. In fact, when America did enter the war, one of the first things her propagandists noted was that "the great mass of the American people" needed an education. Only a "small group actively favored" the war; for the vast majority it was "vital that all mists should be swept away, all doubts resolved, and all purposes united" (Ford, 1919).[4]

Hopefully the example makes at least two points. First, Turner and Killian are right: since public opinion revolves around issues, it is entirely possible that "public opinion may change without equivalent change in the attitudes and opinions of individuals." Sometimes all that is needed is a redefinition of issues and, even with a subject as important as war, people may hold strong beliefs and then behave contrary to their beliefs (Turner and Killian, 1972; Rokeach, 1968). Second, while the example by no means denies the influence of opinion makers (whether presidents, members of the news media, or business leaders), it does suggest that their power rests, not so much on easily changing attitudes and values, but on defining and redefining issues in a manner of their choosing. Put differently, perhaps the real power of opinion makers is an ability to define issues in a manner that makes them harmonize with both enduring public opinion and the flow of mass communication.

Enduring public opinion refers to institutionalized attitudes, values, and beliefs; relative to factors such as degree of cultural consensus and amount of social change, the assumption is that on any particular issue members of the public already have opinions before the issue is openly discussed. Before any one or any group even tries to change our attitudes or mold our minds, we already have beliefs and values that more or less strongly influence our opinion about an issue (Doob, 1948). Whether it is abortion or nationalization of railroads or the role of the family, shared cultural attitudes, values, and beliefs lay a foundation for our opinions about virtually any public issue; and especially if enduring opinions are

---

[4] For a similar analysis of public opinion in World War II, see Cantril (1942) and Blumer (1943).

taken for granted, are important, and are widely shared, those opinions may be quite resistant to change. Conceivably, if they mean to mold our minds, opinion makers may have to work within the more or less tight boundaries set by enduring beliefs, attitudes, and values.

Consider Joseph Klapper's discussion of the effects of mass communication (1960, 1968). He notes first that "mass communication ordinarily does not serve as a necessary and sufficient cause of audience effects"; always perception is an interpolated act (see Chapter One) and always mass communications "function among and through a nexus of mediating factors and influences." Included here are enduring public opinions, the importance of the issue in relation to enduring opinions, and the contemporary social situation (for example, Is there a social crisis?); but Klapper's overall conclusion is that, taken together, these mediating factors and influences "typically render mass communication a contributing agent, but not the sole cause, in a process of *reinforcing the existing conditions*" (Klapper, 1960, emphasis added; see also Turner and Killian, 1972). In short, the typical effect of mass communication is to echo the attitudes, values, and beliefs already held by members of a public.

Many factors contribute to the often "conservative" effects of mass communication. One is success. Whether it is television programing or advertising or politics, the goal is generally to achieve "the maximum audience size and attention." Normally this cannot be done by threatening established attitudes and values; on the contrary, perhaps the best way to reach the most people is to "tell them what they want to hear" (Turner and Killian, 1972). Second is the flow of mass communication. Often the assumption is that the message reaches us directly; nothing intervenes between a message and those who hear it. However, a number of studies confirm the existence of communication networks. For example, Katz and Lazarsfeld discuss the "two-step flow of communication." Any community or group of people has "opinion leaders," individuals who have a disproportionate influence on the opinions of others. Generally these people are more interested in and informed about public issues; so, "influences stemming from the mass media" often first reach these opinion leaders and they, in turn, "pass on what they read and hear to those of their everyday associates for whom they are influential" (Katz, 1957; Katz and Lazarsfeld, 1955). Naturally, opinion leaders can "filter" communications in ways that stress change, but since the studies agree that opinion leaders "are usually supernormative members of the same groups to which their followers belong," their influence "appears more likely to be exercised in the service of continuity than of change" (Klapper, 1960). And often those who lead opinion consciously recognize this fact. Annually the United States military tries to mold opinion by "picking local leaders, flying them to military facilities, and briefing them on chosen, specific subjects." Generally the trips are quite impressive, and many "alumni" join the Defense Orientation Conference Association, an organization that keeps members informed about "things military." Overall the military chooses and impresses local leaders who will use their expert knowledge to reinforce enduring public opinion: "America needs a strong military and our services are doing their very best to fulfill our needs. Let's give them our support, no matter what the issue" (Fulbright, 1970).

Finally, even if opinion leaders try to change enduring attitudes and beliefs, study shows this is unlikely unless certain conditions prevail. For example, does a social crisis argue that survival demands a change in attitudes and beliefs? Or, is there widespread ambiguity or confusion on the level of enduring opinions? Generalized and significant others need not will us an inheritance of taken-for-granted and widely shaped attitudes, values, and beliefs. And, to the extent they do not, the probability that opinion leaders will produce basic changes is more or less great.

Overall there are three conclusions to be drawn from this discussion. One, the power of politicians or advertisers or the mass media to easily change people's attitudes, beliefs, and values has often been grossly exaggerated. Enduring opinions, local opinion leaders, the opinion maker's desire for success, and immediate social conditions: these and other factors all mediate the communications received by a public and in general these variables move people to hold opinions that generally confirm already institutionalized attitudes, beliefs, and values. Second, perhaps the greatest power of opinion makers is their opportunity to make or not make something a public issue. As Jacques Ellul notes, the foremost example of a "non-fact" was the Nazi concentration camps. For a long time no powerful person or interest group made the camps a political issue and in the absence of an issue there was no significant body of public opinion regarding the camps (Ellul, 1967). Naturally, the public need not respond in any significant way to an issue raised by powerful people or groups (for example, the public's response to Watergate from June of 1972 to, say, March of 1973), but those with access to the means of communication nevertheless have the power to make or not make something a public issue. Third, and last, opinion makers have the power to define an issue. Naturally, other things being equal, their best chance of convincing a public to follow them is to define the issue in a way that harmonizes with enduring public opinions. However, the power to define an issue should not be underestimated. If a person or group has their definition accepted before that of others, it can lay the foundation for public opinions about an object or situation. President Wilson defined the issue in World War I and, to take a conspicuous example from today, there is a great difference between the question, "What is your opinion about a welfare system that allows so many people to live like parasites?"; and the question, "What can we do to improve a welfare system whose recipients overwhelmingly include children, the aged, and the handicapped?"

Bibliographical References

Adams, Paul. *Obsessive Children*. Baltimore: Penguin, 1975.

Aronson, Elliot. "Dissonance Theory: Progress and Problems." In *Theories of Cognitive Consistency*, edited by Robert Abelson, Elliot Aronson, William J. McGuire, Theodore M. Newcomb, Milton J. Rosenberg, and Paul Tannenbaum. Chicago: Rand McNally, 1968.

Aronson, Elliot. "The Process of Dissonance." In *Attitudes*, edited by Neil Warren and Marie Jahoda. London: Penguin, 1973.

Aronson, Elliot. *The Social Animal*. 2d ed. San Francisco: W. H. Freeman, 1976.

Barber, James David. *The Presidential Character: Predicting Performance in the White House*. Englewood Cliffs, N.J.: Prentice-Hall, 1972.

Barnet, Richard. *The Roots of War: The Men and Institutions Behind U.S. Foreign Policy*. New York: Atheneum, 1972.

Bem, Daryl. "Self-Perception: An Alternative Interpretation of Cognitive Dissonance Phenomena." *Psychological Review* 74 (1967): 188–200.

Blumer, Herbert. "Morale." In *American Society in Wartime*, edited by W. F. Ogburn. Chicago: University of Chicago Press, 1943.

Bogart, Ernest, and Matthews, John. *The Modern Commonwealth*. Springfield: Illinois Centennial Commission, 1920.

Bramel, Dana. "Dissonance, Expectation and the Self." In *Theories of Cognitive Consistency*, edited by Robert Abelson et al. Chicago: Rand McNally, 1968.

Brehm, Jack W., and Cohen, Arthur R. *Explorations in Cognitive Dissonance*. New York: Wiley, 1962.

Cantril, Hadley. "Public Opinion in Flux." *The Annals of the American Academy of Political and Social Science* 220 (March 1942): 136–50. Part of this article appears in Turner and Killian, 1972.

Carlsmith, J. Merrill; Collins, Barry E.; and Helmreich, Robert L. "The Effect of Pressure for Compliance on Attitude Change." *Journal of Personality and Social Psychology* 4 (1966): 1–13.

Cohen, Arthur R. *Attitude Change and Social Influence*. New York: Basic Books, 1964.

Cooper, Joel, and Worchel, Stephen. "Role of Undesired Consequences in Arousing Cognitive Dissonance." *Journal of Personality and Social Psychology* 16 (1970): 199–206.

Costrell, Edwin. *How Maine Viewed the War*. Orono: Maine University Press, 1940.

Deutsch, Morton, and Krauss, Robert M. *Theories in Social Psychology.* New York: Basic Books, 1965.

Doob, Leonard W. *Public Opinion and Propaganda.* New York: Holt, 1948.

Dostoyevsky, Fyodor. *Letters of Fyodor Dostoyevsky.* New York: Horizon, 1961.

Ellul, Jacques. *The Political Illusion.* New York: Knopf, 1967.

Ellul, Jacques. *Propaganda: The Formation of Men's Attitudes.* New York: Knopf, 1965.

Elms, Alan C. "Role-Playing, Incentive, and Dissonance." *Psychological Bulletin* 68 (1968): 132–48.

Elms, Alan C., and Janis, Irving L. "Counter-Norm Attitudes Induced by Consonant versus Dissonant Conditions of Role-Playing." *Journal of Experimental Research in Personality* 1 (1965): 50–60.

Fernandez, Ronald. "Dostoyevsky, Traditional Domination and Cognitive Dissonance." *Social Forces* 45 (1970): 385–90.

Festinger, Leon. *Conflict, Decision, and Dissonance.* Stanford, Calif.: Stanford University Press, 1964.

Festinger, Leon. *A Theory of Cognitive Dissonance.* Stanford, Calif.: Stanford University Press, 1957.

Festinger, Leon, and Carlsmith, J. Merrill. "Cognitive Consequences of Force Compliance." *Journal of Abnormal and Social Psychology* 58 (1959): 203–10.

Festinger, Leon; Riecken, Henry W.; and Schachter, Stanley. *When Prophecy Fails: A Social and Psychological Study of a Modern Group That Predicted the Destruction of the World.* New York: Harper & Row, 1956.

Ford, Guy Stanton. "America's Fight for Public Opinion." *Minnesota History Bulletin* 3 (1919–1920): 3–27.

Fulbright, J. William. *The Pentagon Propaganda Machine.* New York: Liveright, 1970.

George, Alexander L. *The Chinese Communist Army in Action: The Korean War and Its Aftermath.* New York: Columbia University Press, 1969.

Goethals, George R., and Cooper, Joel. "When Dissonance Is Reduced: The Timing of Self-Justificatory Attitude Change." *Journal of Personality and Social Psychology* 32 (1975): 361–67.

Halberstam, David. *The Best and the Brightest.* New York: Random House, 1972.

Helmreich, Robert, and Collins, Barry E. "Studies in Forced Compliance: Commitment and Magnitude of Inducement to Comply as Determinants of Opinion Change." *Journal of Personality and Social Psychology* 10 (1968): 75–81.

Horney, Karen. *Neurosis and Human Growth.* New York: Norton, 1950.

Janis, Irving L. *Victims of Groupthink.* Boston: Houghton Mifflin, 1973.

Katz, Elihu. "The Two-Step Flow of Communication: An Up-to-Date Report on an Hypothesis." *Public Opinion Quarterly* 21 (1957): 61–78.

Katz, Elihu, and Lazarsfeld, Paul F. *Personal Influence: The Part Played by People in the Flow of Mass Communications.* New York: Free Press, 1955.

Klapper, Joseph T. *The Effects of Mass Communication.* New York: Free Press, 1960.

Klapper, Joseph T. "Mass Communication: Effects." In *International Encyclopedia of the Social Sciences.* Vol. 3. New York: Macmillan, 1968.

Kornhauser, William. *Politics of Mass Society.* New York: Free Press, 1959.

Lane, Robert E., and Sears, David O. *Public Opinion.* Englewood Cliffs, N.J.: Prentice-Hall, 1964.

Lasswell, Harold. *Propaganda Technique in the World War.* New York: Knopf, 1928.

Lifton, Robert Jay. *Thought Reform and the Psychology of Totalism.* New York: Norton, 1961.

McGuire, William J. "The Nature of Attitudes and Attitude Change." In *Handbook of Social Psychology,* edited by Gardner Lindzey and Elliot Aronson. Vol. 3. Reading, Mass.: Addison-Wesley, 1968.

May, Ernest. *World War and American Isolation, 1914–1917.* Cambridge, Mass.: Harvard University Press, 1959.

Millis, Walter. *The Road to War: America, 1914–1917.* Boston: Houghton Mifflin, 1935.

Milgram, Stanley. *Obedience to Authority.* New York: Harper & Row, 1974.

Mochulsky, Konstantin. *Dostoyevsky: His Life and Work.* Princeton, N.J.: Princeton University Press, 1971.

Nel, Elizabeth; Helmreich, Robert; and Aronson, Elliot. "Opinion Change in the Advocate as a Function of the Persuadability of His Audience: A Clarification of the Meaning of Dissonance." *Journal of Personality and Social Psychology* 12 (1969): 321–27.

Newcomb, Theodore M.; Turner, Ralph H.; and Converse, Philip E. *Social Psychology.* New York: Holt, 1965.

Ortega y Gasset, José. *Man and Crisis.* New York: Norton, 1962.

Osgood, Charles E. "Cross-Cultural Comparability in the Measurement of Meaning." In *Conceptions of Social Life: A Text Reader in Social Psychology,* edited by William Gamson and Andre Modigliani. Boston: Little, Brown, 1974.

Osgood, Charles E. *Ideals and Self-Interest in America's Foreign Relations.* Chicago: University of Chicago Press, 1953.

——— *The Pentagon Papers.* New York: Bantam, 1971.

Peterson, Horace C. *Propaganda for War.* Norman: Oklahoma University Press, 1939.

Ponsonby, Arthur. *Falsehood in Wartime*. New York: Dutton, 1928.
Rokeach, Milton. *Beliefs, Attitudes, and Values: A Theory of Organization and Change*. San Francisco: Jossey-Bass, 1968.
Rokeach, Milton. *The Open and Closed Mind*. New York: Basic Books, 1960.
Rosenau, James N. *Public Opinion and Foreign Policy*. New York: Vintage Books, 1961.
Rosenberg, Milton J. "Discussion: The Concept of Self." In *Theories Of Cognitive Consistency*, edited by Robert Abelson et al. Chicago: Rand McNally, 1968.
Schein, Edgar H. (with Inge Schneier and Curtis H. Baker). *Coercive Persuasion*. Cambridge, Mass.: MIT Press, 1961.
Solzhenitsyn, Alexandr I. *The Gulag Archipelago, 1918–1956*. Vol. 2. New York: Harper & Row, 1975.
Squires, James. *British Propaganda at Home and in the United States*. Cambridge, Mass.: Harvard University Press, 1935.
Stavins, Ralph; Barnet, Richard J.; and Raskin, Marcus G. *Washington Plans an Aggressive War*. New York: Vintage, 1971.
Turner, Ralph H., and Killian, Lewis. *Collective Behavior*. 2d ed. Englewood Cliffs, N.J.: Prentice-Hall, 1972.
Warren, Neil, and Jahoda, Marie, eds. *Attitudes*. London: Penguin, 1973.
Wilhelmy, Roland A. "The Role of Commitment in Cognitive Reversibility." *Journal of Personality and Social Psychology* 30 (1974): 695–98.
Worchel, Philip, and McCormick, Betty L. "Self-Concept and Dissonance Reduction." *Journal of Personality* 31 (1964): 588–99.

CHAPTER TEN

Obedience to Authority

—The Judenrat is responsible for producing the Jews designated daily for resettlement. In order to accomplish that task, the Judenrat is to use the Jewish Order Service. The Judenrat is to see to it that 6,000 Jews are delivered daily . . . beginning July 22, 1942. . . . For the time being, the Judenrat may draw the daily quota of Jews from the general population. Later on, the Judenrat will receive definite instructions as to the parts of streets or housing blocks to be emptied. . . .

Instruction Number Eight . . . gave us all fair notice as to how this resettlement will be carried out:

—Every Jew . . . who undertakes a move which may circumvent or disturb the carrying out of the resettlement, will be shot. Every Jew who assists a move which may circumvent or disturb the carrying out of the resettlement orders will be shot. All Jews not belonging to exempt categories . . . who will be found in Warsaw after the conclusion of resettlement will be shot. The Judenrat is warned that should these instructions and orders not be carried out freely, a proper number of hostages will be taken and shot. . . .

John Hershey, The Wall (1950)

Horror. The twentieth century is filled with it. Perhaps the murder of Jewish people is the worst example, but civilized Australians gassed Aborigines in the 1930s. Is it really possible to say one slaughter is worse than another? From the victim's point of view, one suspects the answer is no.

Explanations of such horror often stress politics. How did Hitler come to power? What made this man hate the Jewish people with such an intense passion? How did he use the legal system to legitimate genocide (see, for example, Bullock, 1961; Stern, 1975; Gilbert, 1950)?

These are important questions. But, for all his hatred, Adolf Hitler's plans for murder had to fail unless thousands of average people willingly obeyed his orders. Remember: Although Hitler gave the initial command, it took years to murder six million people. Hitler needed and got willing obedience from thousands of people, on a daily basis, to the most grotesque orders.

How? How do average, so-called normal people become murderers? And why? Why do people sometimes willingly obey orders that end in a My Lai? (see Hersh, 1970)? Answers to these questions are complex; no simple solution, for example, the idea that people have an innate need to obey (Heilbroner, 1974), is possible. But answers do exist. And one reason they do are the experiments done by Stanley Milgram.

THE MILGRAM EXPERIMENTS

Experiments in social psychology are often frustrating. Researchers endure long hours of tedious laboratory work to discover that their data yield inconclusive results. Perhaps the hypothesis is true; perhaps not. These data prove nothing and they leave us with few choices: we can forget the question, move on to another, or plan a new experiment that may also yield no answers.

In his experiments on obedience to authority, Stanley Milgram undoubtedly met frustration, but in the end his series of experiments led to very significant and very frightening results: many "average" people of both sexes willingly obey authority, even when they are volunteers under no legal constraint and when the order is to administer severe shocks to a man with a heart condition. In one experiment where subjects clearly heard the victim's screams, twenty-six of forty (65 percent) people went "all the way." They administered shocks of 450 volts to a man who had stopped screaming six shocks earlier, at 345 volts. The pay for the experiment was $4.00 an hour, no one was beaten into submission, and experimenters made no strong efforts to sway reluctant subjects. They only requested obedience; the surprise is that so many people said yes.

Let's begin with the laboratory situation. Experiments first took place in Yale University's "elegant interaction laboratory." Subjects were not college undergraduates. Milgram wanted a heterogeneous group of people and he drew from the city of New Haven. An advertisement in a local newspaper told readers that people "with no special training, education, or experience were needed for a study of memory." Pay was $4.00 an hour, plus carfare, and the only stipulations were that recruits be men between the ages of twenty and fifty. High school and college students were told they need not apply.

Nearly 300 people responded to the ad, and once Milgram added to this number via direct mail invitations,[1] he was able to balance each experiment for age and occupational type. In the end each experiment contained 40 percent skilled and unskilled workers; 40 percent white collar, sales, business; and 20 percent professionals. Each occupation interacted with these age categories; people in their twenties, thirties, and forties were assigned to each experiment in the proportion of 20, 40, and 40 percent respectively (Milgram, 1974).

Once people arrived at the laboratory, they met the experimenter. This part was played by a thirty-one-year-old high school teacher. "His manner was impassive and his appearance somewhat stern; he was dressed in a gray technician's coat." The victim's part was played by a forty-seven-year-old accountant, specially trained for the role. He was a likable man; no one would want to hurt him. Subjects, of course, had no idea the victim was working for the experimenter; they met the victim as if he were also a recruit. The experiment was designed to test the theory that people learn things correctly whenever they get punished for making a mistake. Subjects were split into teacher and learner, but the drawing for role was rigged: in each case the accomplice was always the learner.

After parts were set, both teacher and learner were taken to an adjacent room where the teacher saw the learner strapped into an "electric chair." The teacher was told straps were needed "to prevent excessive movement while the learner was being shocked. The effect was to make it appear impossible for him to escape from the situation." After strapping, the teacher watched while an electrode was attached to the learner's wrist and paste rubbed on "to avoid blisters and burns." The subject was told the electrode was connected to the shock generator in the next room and if he expressed concern about the victim's welfare, the experimenter assured him that "although the shocks can be extremely painful, they cause no permanent tissue damage" (Milgram, 1974, 17–19).

The teacher sat in front of a shock generator that contained thirty clearly labeled switches. Labels indicated that shocks ranged from 15 to 450 volts, from left to right, in groups of four switches (for example, 15, 30, 45, 60). A second label placed the shocks in categories; the labels read "slight shock, moderate shock, strong shock, very strong shock, intense shock, extreme intensity shock, Danger: Severe Shock." At the very end of the scale, shocks of 435 and 450 volts carried a separate label: XXX.

Shocks were administered when the subject failed the memory test. Initially the teacher read the learner a series of word pairs. The test was

---

[1] Names were sampled from the New Haven Telephone Directory.

to see if the learner remembered a paired word correctly when the teacher later read the right answer as one of four. For example, if the pair was first given as *blue-box*, the learner was tested by being asked *blue: sky-ink-box-lamp*. If the learner answered incorrectly, a shock was given. This was repeated for each incorrect answer, except that each mistake meant the next shock was 15 volts greater. A teacher continued until he reached 450 volts and if he gave shocks of 450 volts three times, the experiment stopped. Obviously, such a teacher proved he willingly obeyed authority.

Milgram worked a series of "prods" into the experiment. If the teacher questioned his orders, the experimenter responded with one of four answers:

Prod 1: Please continue or Please go on.
Prod 2: The experiment requires that you continue.
Prod 3: It is absolutely essential that you continue.
Prod 4: You have no choice, you must go on.

Prod 4 was never used until the other three were tried first, the experimenter's tone was firm but polite, and "the sequence was begun anew an each occasion that the subject balked or showed reluctance to follow orders." Finally, if the teacher asked about possible permanent injury, the experimenter said there was none. If the teacher said—based on the victim's screams—that the learner wanted to quit, the experimenter also accepted responsibility for injury. If a teacher said, "Will you be responsible if something happens to this guy?" the experimenter said yes. The teacher was only doing his job: responsibility for any injury rested with the experimenter.

Besides the four prods, and the answers to questions, the experimenter made no other efforts to obtain obedience. Neither propaganda nor long explanations of the value of science nor bribes nor coercion were used. The experimenter gave his definition of the situation. The subject was simply asked to agree with it and continue giving shocks until the experimenter said stop.

Surprisingly, the experimenter had to say stop quite often.[2] For example, in the first series of experiments, Milgram varied the distance between teacher and learner. In one experiment the learner was in another room, but there was no voice feedback. In the second experiment the victim's voice was heard. In the third, teacher and victim sat side by side,

---

[2] "Surprisingly" because of predictions made before the experiments began. Virtually everyone Milgram asked—graduate students, faculty, college sophomores, middle-class adults—said only a "pathological fringe" would give shocks of 450 volts. A group of psychiatrists said that one person in a thousand would give the highest shock.

and in the fourth experiment the teacher had to take the learner's hand and personally administer the shock by placing the victim's hand on an "electric" grid. As usual, the victim received no pain at all—the accountant was a good actor—but the subject never knew that. He had to inflict injury on a face-to-face basis.

Milgram's hypothesis was that as the victim got closer to the subject, as the teacher could see firsthand the results of his actions, obedience would lessen. Although Milgram's hypothesis was borne out, the results were still startling. With the victim remote and silent, 26 of 40 teachers went all the way. Voice feedback (for example, screams, protests) produced no real change: 25 of 40 teachers went to the 450-volt level. When teacher and learner sat side by side, 16 of 40 subjects pushed the last button, and even when subjects had to personally administer the shock, 12 of 40 men obeyed authority to the limit.

Results like these proved at least two things. One was a point of theory: Milgram's experiments showed that "any theoretical model of obedience" had to take into account "the concrete, visible, and proximal presence of the victim" (Milgram, 1974, 40). Naturally, the importance of the victim's presence is relative—it mattered in Milgram's experiments; was much less important at the gas ovens in Germany or the search-and-destroy missions in Vietnam (see Gilbert, 1947, 1950; Hersh, 1970)—but Milgram showed that degree of obedience was related to the subject actually seeing firsthand the results of his actions.

A second result of these initial experiments was surprise and sympathy. Everyone was surprised at the number of people obeying to the limit, and many onlookers expressed sympathy with subjects. People were not obeying with pleasure; unlike a child viciously pulling wings off a fly, teachers were tense and their words and actions made it clear "that in punishing the victim, they were often acting against their own values." This is graphically illustrated in a moving picture of the experiments. A man goes all the way but he is quite nervous, seemingly feels that giving the shocks is very wrong, and (in the opinion of my students and myself) wants to hear the experimenter say stop. However, the experimenter responds with the series of prods, and despite his obvious stress, the man refuses to disobey. He gives the 450-volt shock to a man with a heart condition.

Milgram correctly underlines the importance of his subjects' obvious stress. So much obedience could easily be explained if teachers were sadists or had some other psychological need to satisfy. However, since most of Milgram's subjects gained little if any satisfaction from obeying authority, simple explanations were out. Subjects were troubled by their actions; they wanted to disobey; they thought they should and yet they continued to say yes to authority. The question is why.

Milgram tried to provide an answer by changing the experimental situation. Thinking that subjects perhaps responded to the personalities of victim and experimenter, he paired a "hard, technical-looking" authority with a "soft, avuncular, and innocuous" victim; his other team consisted of a "soft and unaggressive" experimenter, paired with a victim "who looked as if he would do well in a scrap." Small changes occurred when personnel were switched, but 20 of 40 subjects still went all the way. Apparently, the personal characteristics of experimenter and victim were not major causes of so much willing obedience to authority.

Milgram then ran an experiment with the authority figure outside the laboratory. Reasoning that the physical presence of authority was an important element in producing obedience, in this experiment the authority figure explained the task to the subject, but he then left the lab and gave orders by telephone. Disobedience increased greatly with an absent experimenter: "only" 9 of 40 subjects flipped the last switch; this was in sharp and dramatic contrast to the 26 subjects who said yes with the experimenter present. So, Milgram's hypothesis was correct. "Obedience to destructive commands was in some degree dependent on the proximal relations between authority and subject, and any theory of obedience must take account of this fact" (Milgram, 1974, 62). However, once again the importance of the variable is relative. A member of the Strategic Air Command could easily receive—via the plane's radio—orders to drop nuclear weapons on heavily populated cities and the evidence indicates that flyers would obey. As SAC commander, Lt. Colonel Wilbur C. Carraway, puts it: "The president has got a lot of smart people advising him. If he gives the order, it means he's decided it's necessary. The only question is, are we going to hit them? I've never lost any sleep over dropping a hydrogen bomb and I never will. The only thing I'm going to lose any sleep over is whether I can get to the target and carry out my mission" (Moss, 1970; also LeMay, 1965).

So far Milgram's experiments showed that both the proximity of the victim and of the authority were important variables in explaining willing obedience to authority. Next came sex: would women obey as readily as men? Yes, they would: fully 26 of 40 women gave the maximum shock. With sex ruled out, Milgram turned to the victim's consent. Previously, subjects had signed a form releasing Yale University from any legal claims arising out of participation in the experiment. Now, Milgram still allowed his accomplice to sign the form but, after doing so, the victim stated—in the presence of the teacher, of course—"I'll agree to be in it, but only on condition that you let me out when I say so; that's the only condition."

Milgram's hypothesis was that subjects obeyed before because victims had voluntarily contracted to participate in the experiment; shocks were the result of their own free choice. But, if the victim's "social contract" ruled out pain, would subjects still obey? Would they say yes even though authority was disregarding its contractual agreement with the victim? Again the answer is yes. Some reduction in obedience occurred—16 of 40 gave the maximum shock—but it was small. Apparently, in this laboratory situation "the social contract doctrine is a feeble determinant of behavior. . . . Subjects were aware of the injustice being done to the victim (who began to complain when the shocks reached the 150-volt level), but they allowed the experimenter to handle the issue as he saw fit" (Milgram, 1974, 66).

Another hypothesis of Milgram's dealt with the possible importance of institutional setting. This was Yale University, a very prestigious school; and the experiments themselves took place in an "elegant" laboratory setting. Would it make any difference if the experiments were taken out of the university? Milgram moved the experiments to Bridgeport, Connecticut, an industrial city. He set up shop in a "somewhat rundown commercial building," furnished his three-room office suite so that it was "marginally respectable in appearance," and told his subjects he represented "a private firm conducting research for industry." Yale was not mentioned.

Results again showed an insignificant reduction in obedience to authority: 19 of 40 subjects went all the way. Although tension in Bridgeport was as high as ever—subjects were very uncomfortable—it never led to a significantly large number of refusals. By pointing out that many of us deposit money in seedy-looking banks, Milgram suggested it is "the category of institution, judged according to its professed function," that wins our obedience, but given his experiment in Bridgeport, he tentatively concluded that (as long as it was a scientific laboratory) institutional setting and sponsorship were relatively unimportant causes of his subjects' willing obedience to authority (Milgram, 1974, 70).

Milgram's next experiment is particularly significant. Here subjects were permitted to choose shock level. Everything else was the same "except that the teacher was told he was free to select any shock level on any of the trials." Results of the experiment were encouraging. With victims showing no sign of discomfort until shock level 5, teachers gave an average shock of 3.6. "Three subjects limited their shocks to the very lowest on the board, 28 went no higher than the first indication of discomfort, and 38 did not go beyond the point where the learner vehemently protested" (Milgram, 1974, 72).

Milgram correctly stresses these findings. All along subjects were tense but obedient; when the experiment permitted them to give shocks without specific orders from authority, the overwhelming majority refused to inflict pain. This obviously undermines explanations rooted in an innate or learned need for aggression; it speaks well for the subjects when they are on their own; and it underlines the importance of trying to understand obedience to authority in terms of underlying and immediate social conditions. For example, does the socialization process in an advanced industrial society produce citizens who are very accustomed to obeying orders? And if experiences in school and factory produce an underlying disposition to obey, what conditions allow this latent willingness to manifest itself (see Fernandez, 1975; Milgram, 1974)?

Since his experiments dealt mainly with immediate social conditions, Milgram next varied the victim's reaction. Instead of protest, when the shock got to 150 volts, the victim now said he wanted to go on; but the experimenter said no. He ordered the subject to stop, and the experiment was a test to see how subjects would obey. They followed authority's orders. In fact, since no one went beyond the 150-volt mark, Milgram concluded "the decision to shock the learner does not depend on the wishes of the learner or the benign or hostile impulses of the subject, but rather on the degree to which the subject is bound into the authority system" (Milgram, 1974, 93).

Another version of the experiment introduced a second accomplice. While the subject still gave shocks, the second accomplice did paper work at the experimenter's desk. Suddenly, a phone call "forced" the experimenter to leave. Although he did so, he asked the subject to continue. Now the second accomplice took over: he knew a good system to use in giving the shocks (that is, one switch higher for each mistake) and suggested they run the experiment based on his idea. All the subjects agreed to this, but Milgram's question was, how far will they go when an ordinary man gives the orders? Not very far. With an N of 20, only 4 subjects went all the way and 12 quit at the "very strong shock" level. Milgram noted the drop in obedience, but added two qualifications. First, since the experimenter's departure was always awkward, this undermined the credibility of the experiment to some degree. Second, even though he left, authority set up the experiment and gave the orders to continue. This was a rationale for those who gave maximum shocks.

It was also a rationale for 11 other men. For Milgram varied the variation. When new subjects refused to continue, the second accomplice took over. This placed the real subject in the position of bystander, and the experiment became a test to see if the subject would stop the second accomplice. Some did so. One man even "lifted the zealous shocker from his chair, threw him to a corner of the laboratory," and kept him there until he cried "No more." However, only 4 of 16 men stopped the second accomplice quickly. One man stopped him at 420 volts, and the other 11 allowed him to go all the way. Apparently, it is much easier to say yes if people only indirectly obey orders. Subjects did protest, but not enough to stop the accomplice from reaching the switches marked XXX.

Next Milgram put authority in the victim's chair. Accomplices gave the orders and subjects had to shock authority. Would they? No. Every one of the subjects refused to continue when the experimenter protested at the 150-volt level. Accomplices vigorously made a case for continuing, but to no avail. Subjects listened to authority.

But, would they obey when two authorities issued contradictory commands? Here Milgram introduced subjects to two experimenters who agreed until the 150-volt level was reached. Then, one said go, the other said stop. Of 20 subjects, 18 stopped when disagreement made its appearance. One man stopped prior to the conflict and another went one switch higher before refusing to continue. Milgram stressed these results: ". . . in other variations nothing the victim did—no pleas, screams, or any other response to the shocks—produced an effect as abrupt and unequivocal. The reason is that action flows from the higher end of a social hierarchy to the lower." Subjects listen to the voice of authority, but that voice must be clear. When it issues contradictory commands, it loses power. For like those subjects who tried to discover which of the two experimenters was boss, people normally want a clear definition of the situation. When authority is hazy, it makes it easy for subjects to disobey.

This is clear from another experiment. Working again with two experimenters, Milgram made it plausible for one of the two to take the victim's chair. Now, instead of authorities being equal, one was clearly defined as the learner, the other as the experimenter. What will subjects do? Generally, they obey. Six did break off at the 150-volt level twice (when the learner-experimenter protested), but 13 of 20 subjects went all the way. Obviously, it makes quite a difference if authorities furnish a precise definition of the experimental situation.

In his final experiments Milgram tried to assess the power of the group. Here three accomplices were used. One was a learner, while the other two sat at the control desk with the real subject. All three were assigned a role in the experiment until the 150-volt level. Then, in response to the victim's protests, one of the accomplices refused to continue. No plea from the experimenter changed his mind; he quit. This still left two people at the controls, but when the shocks reached the 210-volt level, the second accomplice quit. And so did most of the real subjects. Four did give the maximum shock, but 25 of 40 quit at the 210-level and another 9 quit soon after. In sum, the power of the group is amply demonstrated. When subjects have support for disobedience, many disobey. Sometimes this support only confirms the subject's views; one man said, "Well, I was already thinking about quitting when the group broke off." But, for some the group refusal led to disobedience. As one man put it, "The thought of stopping didn't enter my mind until it was put there by the other two" (Milgram, 1974, 120).

In his final experiment Milgram made it "easy" for subjects to obey. Another accomplice gave the shocks while the real subject did peripheral things; he was part of the experiment, but he never gave shocks—he only watched. In this experiment 37 of 40 subjects allowed others to give the maximum shock. Milgram's somber and correct conclusion is that "any competent manager of a destructive bureaucratic system can arrange his personnel so that only the most callous and obtuse are directly involved in violence. The greater part of the personnel can consist of men and women who, by virtue of their distance from the actual acts of brutality, will feel little strain in their performance of supportive functions.[3] They will feel doubly absolved from responsibility. First, legitimate authority has given full warrant for their actions. Second, they have not themselves committed brutal acts" (Milgram, 1974, 122; for examples, see Huntington, 1957; Janowitz, 1960, 1965; Irving, 1963).

What can we say of the experiments as a whole? First, they are obviously a series of brilliant experiments, full of vital insights about an important facet of human life: Why do people willingly obey authority? Second, the experiments underline the willingness of men and women to obey authority. And in a century that has witnessed unprecedented evil toward one another, this willingness—under certain conditions—must be understood. Third, if the experiments have a fault, it is their focus on immediate social conditions. In *Obedience to Authority* (pages 123–34) Milgram tries to place the experiments in a larger social and historical perspective, but his analysis is admittedly tentative. (In the next section of this chapter, we try to present a provisional overview of obedience to authority.)

Fourth, and by no means last, comes the problem of ethics. Given its potential effect on the subject's self-image once the experiment was explained, did Milgram act ethically when he allowed people to be exposed to such potentially harmful effects? Any answer to this question asks us to judge; that is a difficult role for any fair person. So, rather than quickly condone or condemn, each of us must—at least—carefully weigh Milgram's own answer: "The central moral justification for allowing a procedure of the sort used in my experiment is that it is judged acceptable by those who have taken part in it. Moreover, it was the salience of this fact throughout that constituted the chief moral warrant for the continuation of the experiments" (Milgram, 1974, 199).

---

[3] For instance, only 12 percent of the soldiers in Vietnam did any actual fighting.

AN OVERVIEW OF OBEDIENCE TO AUTHORITY

"Decide yourself who was right—you or he who questioned you then? Call to your mind the first question; its meaning, though not in these words, was this: 'You want to go into the world and you are going empty-handed, with some promise of freedom, which men in their simplicity and their innate lawlessness cannot even comprehend, which they fear and dread—for nothing has ever been more unendurable to man and to human society than freedom.'

". . . You wanted man's free love so that he should follow you freely, fascinated and captivated by you. Instead of the strict ancient law, man had in future to devise for himself with a free heart what is good and what is evil, having only your image before him for guidance. But did it never occur to you that he would at last reject and call in question even your image and your truth, if he were weighed down by so fearful a burden as freedom of choice? . . . It was you yourself, therefore, who laid the foundation for the destruction of your kingdom and you ought not to blame anyone else for it. And yet, is that all that was offered to you? There are three forces, the only three forces that are able to conquer and hold captive forever the conscience of these weak rebels for their own happiness—these forces are: miracle, mystery, and authority. You rejected all three and . . . so . . . we have corrected your great work and have based it on *Miracle, Mystery, and Authority*. And men rejoiced that they were once more led like sheep and that the terrible gift which had brought them so much suffering had at last been lifted from their hearts." [Fyodor Dostoyevsky, *The Brothers Karamozov* (1879–80)]

Cynicism is the cornerstone of the Grand Inquisitor's world-view. Lacking any faith in the ability of people to lead themselves, he substitutes order for the chaos that results from the human fear of freedom. Building on a foundation of miracle, mystery, and authority, he releases people from the burden of free choice and receives in return their obedience to his authority.

Is cynicism justified? Milgram's experiments seem to say yes, but recall the instance (for example, when the experimenter left the room) when Milgram easily produced disobedience. Apparently, sheepish behavior—willing obedience to authority—is relative to a number of situational variables. And even these provide only a partial explanation of obedience to authority. For people enter situations *already* possessing certain values, beliefs, and personalities; these variables play a part in any definition of a situation and, at times, underlying values and beliefs are more important than any situational variable. For example, when President Lincoln introduced conscription into the Civil War (in 1863), public opinion generally favored "fighting on." But since conscription went against 200 years of tradition (Boorstin, 1958; Bowman, 1942), most Americans defined the new situation as a grievous infringement of their traditional rights and liberties. In the first four months of the law's existence, "sheepish" Americans killed or wounded ninety-eight of the soldiers who came to register them for the draft. And all over the North—in Wisconsin, Vermont, Pennsylvania, New Hampshire, Ohio, New York—people responded with a loud no to the orders of authority (see, for example, Crowder, 1920; Murdock, 1963; Lonn, 1928).

So, the Grand Inquisitor is guilty of gross oversimplification. At times people do seem eager to give away freedom; J. P. Stern makes this point in his *Hitler: The Fuhrer and the People* (1975). But at other times people passionately resist the orders of authority. The overview that follows argues that the best way to bypass simplification is to root theory in three sets of variables: underlying social conditions, immediate social conditions, and the personalities of those asked to obey.

While underlying social conditions refers to the institutionalized beliefs, values, and practices that dominate a particular society, they exist on two levels of social reality. First is the transinstitutional basis of authority, the axis upon which social institutions revolve. Following Max Weber (1947), it is possible to recognize three overall bases of authority—charismatic, traditional, and legal-rational—and argue that each ideal type has different consequences for the *kinds* of orders people obey, as well as the willingness of people to obey *any* orders they receive. For example, it was noted above that one major reason Americans rejected conscription in the Civil War was their allegiance to tradition. Historically, Americans were permitted to elect their own officers, serve with neighbors, and be led by officers from their own states. When, under the mantle of law, federal authorities bypassed tradition, citizens disobeyed the law and demanded that federal authorities respect 200 years of custom (see Cunliffe, 1968; Lonn, 1928).

Besides the kind of order, the type of transinstitutional authority does or does not place limits on the extent to which people obey *any* orders they receive. Weber stressed this when he wrote that "traditions directly determine the content of the command and the objects and extent of authority" (1947). So, to the extent that traditional authority dominates, citizens normally reject orders that overstep tradition. But, to the extent that "pure" charismatic authority dominates or to the extent that legal-rational authority convinces its citizens that status *is* the person (that is, I am *only* a soldier, I am *only* a corporate employee), people may be willing to obey *whatever* legitimate order they receive. The volumes on My Lai strongly suggest that the learned ability to think of themselves only as GI's was one important variable that moved these men to obey any orders they received (Hersh, 1970; Hammer, 1970).

Now, the type of transinstitutional authority is one aspect of underlying social conditions. But, besides factors common to many societies (for example, degree of bureaucratization, level of industrialization, extent of urbanization), underlying social conditions also refers to "unique" cultural beliefs, values, and practices. Included here are variables such as religious beliefs, ethnic ties, and class situation. Ideally, these mesh with the dominant type of authority, but this relationship is not a given. For example, in World War I American socialists generally accepted legal-rational authority (for example, Weinstein, 1967; Kolko, 1967), but their class ties were a strong barrier against willing obedience to President Wilson's authority. So, while unique cultural beliefs, values, and practices often harmonize with other underlying social conditions, they may call for disobedience, even though people share ties to the same transinstitutional basis of authority.

The primary significance of underlying social conditions is that their claims to obedience exist, not only *prior to* immediate social conditions, but they normally exert a claim that is *superior to,* and so more powerful than, the claims of immediate social conditions. People internalize—in the process of socialization—a number of beliefs and values, as well as experience daily the dominant forms of social organization. If my results are representative (see Fernandez, 1975), that process typically results in taken-for-granted assumptions, conceptions of reality that move individuals to fatalistically accept the world they inherit. However, whether individuals understand and analyze their beliefs or simply take them for granted, underlying social conditions provide the predispositions and preoccupations that are the basis for interpreting immediate social conditions. And, assuming strong ties to underlying social conditions, they should prove superior to, and more powerful than, the claims of immediate social conditions. As in the Civil War, public opinion—say, in the South—may furnish widespread support for the war, but when leaders make claims that contradict their ultimate sources of authority, citizens disobey even though they support the war (see Coulter, 1958).

Central in any consideration of underlying social conditions is the extent to which the transinstitutional basis of authority harmonizes with "unique" cultural conditions. For example, when war began in 1914 Austria-Hungary had seven ethnic groups, and at present many of the underdeveloped nations contain groups whose underlying allegiance to tribe, for example, in Nigeria, will undoubtedly fail to complement any general acceptance of one transinstitutional basis of authority. So, the degree of harmony between the two aspects of underlying social conditions is always a matter for empirical investigation, but if the two sets of variables harmonize, the fundamental basis for willing obedience to authority is extremely strong.

Another consideration on the level of underlying social conditions is the amount of power people believe authorities possess. During World War I the ethnic ties of German- and Irish-Americans were a strong barrier to obeying President Wilson's orders to register for the draft, but political authorities were believed to possess a great deal of power (for example, to levy fines, send citizens to jail, ruin a person's reputation) and the evidence indicates many German- and Irish-Americans obeyed authority only because they feared what could happen to them if they disobeyed (Wittke, 1936; Fernandez, 1975). Finally, the likelihood of power equaling obedience is greater if immediate social conditions (for example, public opinion, a social crisis where authorities are not to blame) mesh with the orders of authority. Potential resisters are much less likely to disobey authority if the large majority of people support it.

A final point on the level of underlying social conditions concerns the nature of the institution giving the orders. The proposition is that the more an institution monopolizes time and mind, the more it resembles a total institution (Goffman, 1961), the greater the likelihood of individuals obeying whatever orders they receive. In effect, with their ability to shut out competition, total institutions furnish the dominant definition of the situation; and they also have great power to enforce their orders. Those in the army or a prison should normally find it quite difficult to disobey the orders of authority; they are, in fact, captive audiences.

However, under certain conditions individuals will disobey orders from the authorities of total institutions. In the Civil War the orders of military authority consistently conflicted with underlying beliefs of the common soldier. In fact, even under threat of stern penalty, soldiers refused to serve under officers they had not elected or who were not from their own states (Lonn, 1928). So, while total institutions normally increase the likelihood of willing obedience, their orders must mesh with, or at least not seriously conflict with, important underlying beliefs of those subject to authority. Finally, it is also possible for disobedience to occur because of conflict on the level of immediate social conditions. Discovering that their families faced starvation, southern soldiers disobeyed orders and returned to their homes (Lonn, 1928).

Where underlying social conditions refers to the ultimate, institutionalized sources of authority, immediate social conditions refers to sources that *have come to exist* because of the movement and continuous interpretation of the historical process. In essence, factors such as dramatic events, public opinion, the social and economic pressures on individuals or groups, the attitude of legitimate authorities, social movements, and emergent social norms, all together produce a definition of contemporary, of present, of immediate social conditions. And this definition has theoretical significance because authorities never issue calls for obedience in a social vacuum. On the contrary, authorities always issue particular social orders under particular social conditions, and that makes it important to understand how those subject to authority define the immediate social situation. Often the ongoing interpretation of history results in one dominant definition of the situation that provides the immediate source for citizen obedience (or disobedience) to authority. However, sometimes no one definition dominates, and no matter what the result of the ongoing and collective interpretation of history, the point is that definitions of immediate social conditions either do or do not provide a source of willing obedience for the particular orders issued under particular social conditions. For example, a president might have the legitimate authority (rooted in law) to call up the National Guard, but the likelihood of willing obedience is greater if immediate social conditions are defined in a manner that "proves" the call is necessary.

On the level of immediate social conditions, the following factors are of particular importance. *First,* how do authorities and citizens define the situation in question? Is there a social crisis? And are authorities responsible for it? Assuming a positive response to underlying social conditions, with little or no perceived responsibility for the crisis (for example, Pearl Harbor), the proposition is that the greater the crisis, the greater the likelihood of obedience and the greater the likelihood the crisis factor will prove more important than any other on the level of immediate social conditions. In fact, assuming a positive response to underlying conditions, a crisis might move people to obey orders that run counter to some underlying beliefs and values. Examples are England and America in both of the World Wars (Marwick, 1968; Pollenberg, 1972).

However, assuming an ambiguous or negative response to underlying social conditions, the likelihood of disobedience is increased. Disobedience would be especially likely if authorities were perceived to be the cause of the crisis.

Finally, disobedience could occur even when the response to underlying conditions is positive. Crises normally demand extreme solutions, and if citizens perceive a need for drastic action, they might disobey orders that seem absurd in the face of the social crisis. Naturally, the response of the public to the response of authority could lead to a reevaluation of underlying beliefs, values, and practices. At all times the relationship between underlying and immediate social conditions is dialectical.

Second, how much time has the citizenry had to prepare for the crisis or simply for the orders of authority in general? Assuming the orders of authority mean social change, the proposition is that the greater the amount of social change, the more citizens are asked to change important beliefs, values, and practices, the more time authorities need to prepare people to willingly obey orders. With conscription in 1917, authorities needed almost three years to convince people to obey, and, at that, they were continually helped by a series of dramatic incidents, for example, the sinking of the *Lusitania* and the *Sussex,* and the Zimmerman telegram (Link, 1954; Tuchman, 1958).

Third, who is the authority figure and how proximate is she or he? In all circumstances, and especially when orders equal social change, obedience is more likely if authorities are well known, well liked, and close by (Milgram, 1974). However, the importance of authority figures who are well known and close by is relative. For example, draftees obey induction notices received in the mail, and those notices are signed by individuals the draftee has never heard of, much less seen. So, while it is helpful to have authority figures who are well known and close by, willing obedience often occurs when authorities are distant and relatively unknown. In fact, assuming a positive response to other social conditions, the need for authority figures who are well known and close by should significantly decrease when the social situation is defined as an unavoidable crisis and the institution is total.

Fourth, and closely related to the factors of social crisis and total institution, what are the consequences of disobedience? For example, disobeying a traffic law means a fine; in the case of a soldier who refuses to fight, the man faces jail, as well as the possibility of bad employment prospects for life.

Fifth, if the orders of authority mean, for example, controlling or coercing or fighting another person or group, who is the person, what is the group? To the extent that the person or group is disliked or hated, obedience is easier to obtain. However, to the extent that the victim is loved (Germans to many German-Americans in World War I), even crisis and a positive response to important aspects of underlying social conditions may be insufficient justification for willing obedience. As in World War I, authorities may have to also stress their power in order to obtain obedience.

Whenever feelings toward another person or group have their deepest roots in underlying social conditions, it is impossible to neatly place the other person's identity into only one of the two overall variables. The other person's identity is here placed under immediate social conditions because there are normally many groups that could be singled out for coercion or control. To understand why this person or group was chosen, it is crucial to know the particular social conditions that produced the orders of authority.

Sixth, if the orders of authority say to coerce or control another person or group, how physically close are they? Normally, "the concrete, visible and proximal presence of the victim" should make it easier for individuals to disobey; it should be harder for men and women to kill one another on a face-to-face basis (Milgram, 1974). However, the importance of the victim's proximity is relative to other social conditions. As noted in the discussion of the Milgram experiments, at My Lai executioners and victims met face-to-face, and except for one soldier who shot himself in the leg, the victim's closeness failed to produce disobedience to authority. Or, take the case of the people who manned the ovens in which that Jewish people were murdered. Guards faced the victims as they undressed and let them into the rooms where they were to "shower." Thus, to the extent that a crisis situation prevails, and the institution is total, the proximity of the victim loses importance as a possible source of disobedience to authority.

Seventh, what is the public's definition of the situation? To the extent that a widespread consensus exists, and that consensus echoes the views of authority, it should be very difficult for individuals to disobey. After all, the dominant available definition of the situation is that of the authorities. Finally, if the orders of authority mean a change of important beliefs, values, or practices, the chances of willing obedience are much greater if there exists a widespread consensus about the issue(s) in question.

Eighth, who is the authority giving the orders? To the extent that he or she has a quality—charisma—that sets them apart from ordinary people, and enables others to treat them as though endowed with highly superior attributes, the chances for willing obedience to authority are greater. For example, in a situation where no public opinion consensus exists, a charismatic leader could sway the balance in favor of willing obedience to authority.

Ninth, to what extent do the orders of authority, as well as the institutional setting, allow individuals to escape responsibility for their actions? To the extent that individuals can place blame on others, their obedience is more likely. In fact, combined with crisis, a total institutional setting, and a positive response to underlying social conditions, the ability to shift responsibility to others could end in individuals obeying *any* orders.

A final variable is impossible to place in either underlying or immediate social conditions. Reference is to the extent that the orders of authority implicate important self-images and significant beliefs and values. In a sense we said this when we asked, "Who is the victim?" but the larger point is that when a particular belief (for example, the rule of law before all else) or issue (that is, war with Germany) is especially meaningful to a person or group, we would expect a greater likelihood of willing obedience if the orders of authority support the belief or issue. Conversely, should the orders of authority go against especially meaningful beliefs, the likelihood of disobedience is increased.

A Typology of Willing Obedience to Authority

	Underlying Social Conditions	*Immediate Social Conditions*
1. Willing Obedience	+	+
2. Probable Willing Obedience	+	−
3. Probable Disobedience	−	+
4. Disobedience	−	−

Using the variables discussed above, the typology lists four alternative responses of societal members to underlying and immediate social conditions. Each of the alternative responses equals a higher or lower probability of willing obedience to authority, and each of the four is examined in detail in the following pages.

Finally, the dictionary defines *probable* as "likely to prove true, having more evidence for than against." In none of the four situations is the probability of willing obedience absolutely positive or absolutely negative. Always, willing obedience to authority is more or less likely. So, in *Situation One* the probability of willing obedience in very high; people find it quite difficult to disobey the orders of authority. In *Situation Two* willing obedience to authority is "likely to prove true," but the probability of willing obedience is good, not excellent. In *Situation Three* disobedience to authority is "likely to prove true," but, once again, the chances are good, not excellent. In *Situation Four* the probability of disobedience to authority is quite high; people find very little cause to willingly obey authority.

Situation One. Here, since the reaction of people is positive to both underlying and immediate social conditions, the probability of willing obedience is quite high. Citizens who wished to disobey would find very little support in the larger society; as in 1941 public opinion on a series of issues might "dictate" obeying the orders of authority, and these immediate claims to obedience would be backed up by the (normally) more powerful claim of the society's ultimate sources of authority. In such a situation, with demands for obedience coming simultaneously from within the person, and from the larger society, the probability of disobedience is very low.

Under any circumstances, a positive response to both underlying and immediate social conditions makes the probability of willing obedience quite high. But the orchestration of the two variables is particularly necessary when the orders of authority demand social change. This was the case in 1917, and the overriding explanation of ten million Americans willingly obeying conscription authorities must be in terms of the "perfect" mesh between underlying and immediate social conditions. In fact, the proposition is that the greater the amount of social change demanded, the more people asked to change important beliefs, values, and practices, the greater the need to eliminate dissonance on both levels of authority and so confront those subjects to authority with the same message everywhere: obey.

Naturally, the motives of those subject to authority vary but, focusing now only on willing obedience, the point is that an orchestration of underlying and immediate social conditions moves citizens to obey for a variety of reasons. Some might believe in the value of the political system and the patterns of behavior; others might accept the authority of existing political institutions, as well as succumb to the constraining effect of emergent norms. However, no matter how many motives, or combinations of motives, one uncovers, the problem for authority—particularly in modern societies—is how to get a heterogeneous group of people to act in the same manner. This is accomplished by an orchestration of underlying and immediate social conditions because, while harmony is interpreted differently by different groups (for example, native and German-Americans), the end result for authority is the same: most citizens willingly obey the orders they receive.

A final point is that the relationship between the four possible situations is always dynamic. In 1914 Americans were positive in terms of underlying social conditions but negative on the level of immediate social conditions. Only after three years did citizens react positively to both sets of conditions and even then the situation was fluid. If, for example, Americans had failed dismally in Europe, and the government had had to call for more men and more sacrifices on the home front, the probability of willing obedience would have decreased. Or, consider the Civil War. Citizens of the North and South were initially positive to both underlying and immediate social conditions. But, as immediate enthusiasm for the war waned (for instance, the changing perception of the war's length), and both administrations were forced to adopt measures that contradicted their ultimate sources of authority (the draft and impressment), citizens quickly became negative, particularly in terms of the legitimacy of orders flowing from either Washington or Richmond (Fernandez, 1975).

So, while each of the four situations is analyzed as if it were static, reality is dynamic. History is process and collectively interpreted process at that. At all times it is possible for a situation of "two pluses" to turn into a situation of "two minuses."

Situation Two. In this instance, response to the underlying sources of authority is positive, but response to immediate social conditions is negative. The proposition is that the end result of this situation is probable willing obedience to authority. This contention is based on the argument that the claim of underlying social conditions is prior to, and normally more powerful than, the claim of immediate conditions. In effect, those subject to the orders of authority might "discount" conflict on the level of immediate social conditions because, for example, they value the traditions that sustain authority, or they fear the power that authorities could employ if disobedience takes place, or fear is combined with a taken-for-granted attitude regarding the authorities in question.

One example of willing obedience under Situation Two is provided by response to the draft during the Vietnam War. At the end of 1968, for instance, only 1 in 278 Americans refused induction into military service (Woodstone, 1970)—.0034 percent—and such a low rate of disobedience was combined with widespread disagreement on the level of immediate social conditions. Now, without a detailed investigation it is impossible to list the "exact" motives that moved American young men to say yes to the draft, but studies indicate that for the vast majority, willing obedience had little to do with a belief in the value of democracy or the draft. On the contrary, young men apparently saw no alternative to obedience. Growing up with a peacetime draft, and seemingly taking its existence for granted, they obeyed authority for two reasons: they feared the consequences of disobedience and their socialization had led them to accept federal authority and the draft as unquestioned facts of life (Moskos, 1970; Polner, 1971; Parks, 1968; Mangiolardo, 1969).

To repeat, only detailed investigation can demonstrate all the factors that moved American young men to willingly obey draft authorities, but it is undeniable that despite widespread disagreement on the level of immediate social conditions, willing obedience to authority did occur, and the evidence indicates that the primary causes of obedience were rooted in underlying social conditions.

However, there is only the probability of willing obedience to authority under Situation Two. For example, in America most women and men accept the authority of national, state, and local governments, but immediate social conditions sometimes move people to disobey the law. Consider illegal abortions. Until recently strict laws prohibited abortions unless the mother's life was in danger, but hospitals throughout the nation often admitted women who had had, what Planned Parenthood calls, "botched" abortions. Since statistics on illegal abortions are obviously unavailable, there is no way to accurately assess the amount of disobedience to authority, but it occurred often enough to allow us to underline that immediate social conditions are sometimes more important than a positive attitude toward the transinstitutional and ultimate sources of societal authority.

Situation Three. Here the probability is for disobedience to authority. People respond positively on the level of immediate social conditions, but authorities give orders that conflict with underlying social conditions. An example is the Civil War. Both Northern and Southern citizens generally responded positively to the war, but when Davis and Lincoln sought to use conscription, people overwhelmingly responded with a no. In effect, the superior claims of underlying social conditions overrode the general support for the war. In the South especially, support for the war was high, and so too was disobedience to the Confederacy's draft law (Fernandez, 1975).

As was the case with Situation Two, however, our argument is qualified. Given the superior pull of underlying social conditions, the probability under Situation Three is for disobedience. But certain interpretations of immediate social conditions might override even a negative attitude on the level of the ultimate sources of authority. For example, the Black Muslim religion is opposed to the authority of the federal government, but it nevertheless counsels obedience to federal authority in all areas except the draft. As Muslims interpret them, immediate social conditions are always generally positive and there is no reason to disobey the law while awaiting the inevitable end of history: the destruction of white people and the coming of a Garden of Eden inhabited only by black people (Essien-Udom, 1963).

Situation Four. Here disobedience is quite likely. Because people are negative in terms of underlying and immediate social conditions, authorities have little basis for obtaining willing obedience. In fact, if obedience comes in Situation Four, authorities must, in all probability, use force. For example, in the eighteenth-century British army, a thousand lashes for certain forms of disobedience to authority were not uncommon. Negative toward underlying and immediate social conditions, most rank-and-file soldiers consistently refused to obey military authorities, and only force kept most men in the army (see Glover, 1963; on France, see Kennett, 1967).

ULTIMATE REASONS FOR OBEDIENCE TO AUTHORITY

Together underlying and immediate social conditions provide a framework for understanding willing obedience to authority. But, beyond all the social and historical causes of obedience, there is another question: What is, what are the individual's *ultimate* reason(s) for willing obedience to authority?

Theory offers at least three answers to this question. Max Weber argues "that the basis of every system of authority, and correspondingly of every kind of willingness to obey, is a belief by virtue of which persons exercising authority are lent prestige" (Weber, 1947). Now there is some ambiguity in this statement. It is unclear whether belief refers to a value; it is also unclear whether willing obedience must always arise from the conscious appreciation of a particular institution or pattern of behavior. But, if we take Weber to mean that people willingly obey commands only because they consciously accept the values that legitimate a particular political system or pattern of behavior, beliefs can be defined differently. As noted in Chapter Five, Alfred Schutz writes that people hold taken-for-granted beliefs. Defined as "that particular level of experience which presents itself as not in need of further analysis," acceptance of taken-for-granted beliefs is not based on "clear and distant insight into, and understandings of," particular beliefs. Instead, taken-for-granteds are normally acquired in the process of socialization and they are internalized as givens, as socially imposed relevances that are unnecessary to understand in terms of origin and structure (Schutz, 1967). Again, Schutz makes the distinction between "the well-informed citizen" and "the man on the street." The former investigates and analyzes; he or she attempts to understand systems or issues in terms of origin and structure. But the man on the street is content to accept taken-for-granteds. Structured by the social order, taken-for-granteds provide habitual "conceptions of reality" that, because they are never questioned, appear to the man on the street as the only way in which the world works. Like the weather, a person lives with taken-for-granteds; there appears to be no other choice (Schutz, 1967).

The argument is that a qualitative difference exists between willing obedience rooted in a conscious belief in the value of something and willing obedience rooted in taken-for-granted beliefs. In one case individuals understand and analyze the basis of their beliefs, values, and practices. In the other case individuals do not consider possible alternatives, nor do they analyze the relevance of their values to social reality. On the contrary, individuals simply accept the world they inherited. It could be American or Russian or French. It is there and it is the only world they know. Except in the most tangential ways, values are irrelevant to an individual whose willing obedience to authority is based on taken-for-granted beliefs.

A third possibly ultimate cause of obedience to authority is power. If we define *power* as "the probability that one actor within a social relationship will be in a position to carry out his will despite resistance" (Weber, 1947), we are not concerned with the use of violence to "win" obedience. Our focus is willing obedience to authority, and our question is to what extent does the *threat* of power, or the citizen's perception that authorities *could* use power, produce willing obedience to authority? In brief, to what extent do people willingly obey authority, not because of a belief in the value of the system, or because they take a system or pattern of behavior for granted, but because they fear the powers authorities could use?

Social reality gives no one answer to the question: What is, what are the ultimate reason(s) for willing obedience to authority? Seemingly, obedience rooted in a conscious belief in the value of a political system or pattern of behavior is rare, but even where obedience is based (at least partially) on a host of taken-for-granted assumptions, different groups of people react to those assumptions in different ways. For example, discussing war in preliterate societies, Lesser writes that "what is found characteristic of primitive, stateless societies are forms of armed aggression in which involvement and motivation [are] deeply personal . . ." (Lesser, 1968). But a major conclusion of the World War II study, *The*

American Soldier, was that "except for a very limited number of men, *little feeling of personal commitment to the war emerged.* The war was accepted passively as a national necessity but this acceptance was not internalized as a sense of personal responsibility" (Stouffer et al., 1949, vol. 1, emphasis in original).

Seemingly, despite obedience rooted in a host of taken-for-granted assumptions (see also Heider, 1970; Matthiessen, 1962; Chagnon, 1968), preliterate societies are still able to produce a sense of deep commitment to arbitrarily inherited beliefs, values, and practices. Undoubtedly, a number of variables account for this sense of personal involvement, for example, the relatively slow pace of social change, the relative homogeneity in the experience of preliterate peoples, the importance of religion in virtually all aspects of preliterate life. However, whatever the causes of the preliterate's sense of deep commitment to cultural beliefs, values, and practices, the contrast with modern societies is both sharp and frightening.

This is so because a number of studies confirm the conclusions of *The American Soldier.* Analysis of obedience to the draft in World War I found the vast majority of men (nearly ten million of them) willingly obeying the orders of authority on the basis of taken-for-granted assumptions and a fear of government power. In the case of German- and Irish-Americans, power was the most important variable in explaining their willing obedience to authority (Fernandez, 1975). And studies from Korea and Vietnam (e.g., Little in Janowitz, 1965; Barrett, 1952; Suchman et al., 1952; Adler, 1967; Moskos, 1970) also indicate willing obedience to authority with little feeling of personal commitment to, or conscious belief in, the value of the political system or any particular pattern of behavior (for example, the draft). As one Vietnam draftee noted, "I know what *I* am fighting for over here in Vietnam—for survival, to stay alive. I don't know what you people back there think we are fighting for. I would like to know" (Mangiolardo, 1969).

Overall, these studies show that, at least for most men in twentieth-century America, willing participation in war is rooted in the power of the state, the power of a very total institution (the military) and, before anything else, allegiance to a host of taken-for-granted assumptions that rarely generate a sense of deep personal commitment.[4] Again, this is in

---

[4] In *The American Enlisted Man,* Charles Moskos writes that to fight, soldiers must have "an underlying commitment to the worth of the larger social system," but this commitment "need not be formally articulated, *nor even perhaps consciously recognized."* Moskos refers to a *"Latent* Ideology" that sustains the soldier; seemingly, even though they do not discuss them, soldiers have "widely shared sentiments" that have concrete consequences for combat motivation. Moskos's "latent ideology" is exactly what is meant here by taken-for-granted assumptions. The "man on the street" possesses habitual conceptions of reality, acquired in the process of socialization, that

sharp contrast to preliterate societies, and it is frightening because obedience that is ultimately rooted in these variables greatly increases the probability of more twentieth-century horror. With his deep personal commitment to a particular set of beliefs, values, and practices, the preliterate "citizen" was unlikely to do *anything;* in all probability, deep commitment to particular beliefs put a tight rein on the kinds of orders he would willingly obey. But, consider modern citizens. Given our underlying commitment to legal-rational authority, as well as taken-for-granted assumptions that produce little sense of personal responsibility or commitment, the "proper mix" of immediate social conditions could easily lead large numbers of Americans (and one could add, for example, Russians or Germans) to obey any legitimate orders they receive. Today people's assumptions and authority's power often produce obedience without commitment. People's ties to culture, particularly to political and religious culture, often lack any sense of deep involvement. And when this absence of personal concern is linked to participation in total institutions that intentionally absolve people of responsibility, the result under conditions of social crisis could easily be mass willing obedience to *any* legitimate order.

Bibliographical References

Adler, Bill. *Letters from Vietnam.* New York: Dutton, 1967.

Arendt, Hannah. *Eichmann in Jerusalem: A Report of the Banality of Evil.* New York: Viking, 1963.

Barrett, George. "That's the Way the Ball Bounces." *New York Times Magazine,* November 23, 1952, p. 17.

Boorstin, Daniel J. *The Americans: The Colonial Experience.* New York: Knopf, 1958.

Bowman, Allen. *The Morale of the American Revolutionary Army.* Washington, D.C.: American Council on Public Affairs, 1943.

Chagnon, Napoleon. *The Yanomamo: The Fierce People.* New York: Holt, Rinehart & Winston, 1968.

Coulter, E. Merton. *The Confederate States of America.* New Orleans: Louisiana State University Press, 1958.

Crowder, Enoch. *The Spirit of Selective Service.* New York: Century, 1920.

---

appear to be the only way in which the world works. When asked to obey a legitimate order, an order that supports taken-for-granted assumptions, modern citizens do not often develop a sense of personal commitment, but their assumptions furnish a key basis for inarticulately defining the situation in a way that helps produce willing obedience to authority (Moskos, 1970, emphasis added).

Cunliffe, Marcus. *Soldiers and Civilians: The Martial Spirit in America, 1775–1865.* Boston: Little, Brown, 1968.
Essien-Udom, E. U. *Black Nationalism.* New York: Dell, 1963.
Fernandez, Ronald. "Conscription in the Civil War and World War I: The Rejection and Acceptance of Authority." Ph.D. diss., University of Connecticut, 1975.
Faulkner, Herbert. *The Decline of Laissez-Faire.* New York: Harper & Row, 1954.
Fried, Morton; Harris, Marvin; and Murphy, Robert. *War.* Garden City, N.Y.: Doubleday, 1968.
Gilbert, Gustave. *Nuremberg Diary.* New York: Mentor, 1947.
Gilbert, Gustave. *Psychology of Dictatorship: Based on an Examination of the Leaders of Nazi Germany.* New York: Ronald, 1950.
Glover, Richard. *Peninsular Preparation.* Cambridge, Eng.: Cambridge University Press, 1963.
Goffman, Erving. *Asylums: Essays on the Social Situations of Mental Patients and Other Inmates.* New York: Doubleday, 1961.
Hammer, Richard. *One Morning in the War: The Tragedy of Son My.* New York: Coward, McCann & Geoghegan, 1970.
Heider, Karl. *The Dugum Dani: A Papuan Culture in the Highlands of West New Guinea.* Chicago: Aldine, 1970.
Heilbroner, Robert. *An Inquiry into the Human Prospect.* New York: Norton, 1974.
Hersh, Seymour. *My Lai Four: A Report on the Massacre and Its Aftermath.* New York: Random House, 1970.
Huntington, Samuel. *The Soldier and the State: The Theory and Politics of Civil-Military Relations.* New York: Random House, 1957.
Irving, David. *The Destruction of Dresden.* New York: Holt, Rinehart & Winston, 1963.
Janowitz, Morris. *The Professional Soldier: A Social and Political Portrait.* New York: Free Press, 1960.
Janowitz, Morris (with Roger Little). *Sociology and the Military Establishment.* 2d ed. New York: Russell Sage, 1965.
Kennett, Lee. *French Armies in the Seven Years' War: A Study in Military Organization and Administration.* Durham, N.C.: Duke University Press, 1967.
Kolko, General Gabriel. *Triumph of Conservatism.* Chicago: Quadrangle, 1967.
LeMay, Curtis. *Mission with LeMay.* New York: Funk and Wagnalls, 1965.
Lesser, Alexander. "War and the State." In *War,* edited by Morton Fried, Marvin Harris, Robert Murphy. Garden City, N.Y.: Doubleday, 1968.
Link, Arthur. *Woodrow Wilson and the Progressive Era: 1910–1917.* New York: Harper & Row, 1954.

Lonn, Ella. *Desertion During the Civil War.* New York: American Historical Association, 1928.
Mangiolardo, Michael. *My Days in Vietnam.* New York: Vintage, 1969.
Marwick, Arthur. *The Deluge.* London: Macmillan, 1968.
Matthiessen, Peter. *Under the Mountain Wall.* New York: Ballantine, 1962.
Milgram, Stanley. *Obedience to Authority: An Experimental View.* New York: Harper & Row, 1974.
Moore, Albert. *Conscription and Conflict in the Confederacy.* New York: Hilary House, 1964.
Moskos, Charles. *The American Enlisted Man: The Rank and File in Today's Military.* New York: Russell Sage, 1970.
Moss, Norman. *Men Who Play God: The Story of the H Bomb and How the World Came to Live with It.* London: Penguin, 1970.
Murdock, Eugene. *Patriotism Limited 1862–1865. The Civil War Draft and the Bounty System.* Kent, Ohio: Kent State University Press, 1967.
Nisbet, Robert. *The Social Bond: An Introduction to the Study of Society.* New York: Random House, 1971.
Owsley, Frank. *States' Rights in the Confederacy.* Chicago: University of Chicago Press, 1925.
Parks, David. *G.I. Diary.* New York: Harper & Row, 1968.
Planned Parenthood Federation. *Facts and Figures on Legal Abortion.* December 1973.
Polner, Murray. *No Victory Parades.* New York: Holt, Rinehart & Winston, 1971.
Schutz, Alfred. *The Phenomenology of the Social World.* Chicago: Northwestern University Press, 1967.
Solzhenitsyn, Alexandr I. *The Gulag Archipelago, 1918–1956.* New York: Harper & Row, 1974.
Stern, J. P. *Hitler: The Fuhrer and the People.* Berkeley: University of California Press, 1975.
Stouffer, Samuel A.; Suchman, Edward A.; De Vinney, Leland C.; Star, Shirley A.; and Williams Jr., Robin M. *The American Soldier.* Princeton, N.J.: Princeton University Press, 1949.
Suchman, Edward A.; Williams, Robin M.; and Goldsen, Rose L. "Student Reaction to Impending Military Service." *American Sociological Review* 17 (1952): 293–303.
Toennies, Ferdinand. *Community and Society.* New York: Harper & Row, 1958.
Tuchman, Barbara. *The Zimmerman Telegram.* New York: Viking, 1958.
Weber, Max. *From Max Weber: Essays in Sociology.* Edited and translated by Hans Gerth and C. Wright Mills. New York: Galaxy, 1956.
Weber, Max. *The Theory of Social and Economic Organization.* New York: Free Press, 1947.

Weinstein, James. *Decline of Socialism in America 1912–1925*. New York: Vintage, 1967.

Wittke, Carl. *German-Americans and the World War*. Columbus: Ohio Historical Society, 1936.

Woodstone, Norma. *Up Against the War*. New York: Tower, 1970.

CHAPTER ELEVEN

Leadership

If the aim of history is the description of the movement of humanity and of nations, the first question which must be answered, or all the rest remains unintelligible, is the following: What force moves nations? To meet this question, modern history carefully relates that Napoleon was a very great genius, and that Louis XIV was very haughty, or that certain writers wrote certain books.

All this may well be so, and humanity is ready to acquiesce in it; but it is not what it asks about. All that might be very interesting if we recognized a divine power, based on itself and always alike, guiding its peoples through Napoleons, Louis', and writers; but we do not acknowledge such a power, and therefore before talking about Napoleons, and Louis', and great writers, we must show the connection existing between those persons and the movement of the nations. If another force is put in the place of the divine power, then it should be explained what that force consists of, since it is precisely in that force that the whole of history lies. . . .

What is the force that moves nations?

. . . This power cannot be that direct power of the physical ascendancy of a strong creature over a weak one, that ascendancy based on the application or the threat of the application of physical force—like the power of Hercules. Nor can it be based on the ascendancy of moral force, as in the simplicity of their hearts several historians suppose, maintaining that the leading historical figures are heroes—that is, men endowed with a special force of soul and mind called genius. This power cannot be based on the ascendancy of moral forces; for, to say nothing of historical heroes, like Na-

poleon, concerning whose moral qualities opinions greatly differ, history proves to us that neither Louis XI nor Metternich, who governed millions of men, had any marked characteristics of moral force, but that they were, on the contrary, in most respects, morally weaker than any one of the millions of men they governed.

If the source of power lies not in the physical and not in the moral characteristics of the person possessing it, it is evident that the source of this power must be found outside the persons—in those relations in which the person possessing the power stands to the masses.

That is precisely how power is interpreted by the science of law, that cash bank of history, that undertakes to change the historical token money of power for sterling gold.

Power is the combined wills of the masses, transferred by their expressed or tacit consent to the rulers chosen by the masses.

Leo Tolstoy, *War and Peace* (1866)

Tolstoy made a complete turn. Rejecting the idea that leaders possessed extraordinary qualities that set them off from others, he left leaders with nothing. To him, leadership[1] was a gift from others—from the masses—to an individual. Seemingly, leaders led because others allowed them to do so. Caesar, Louis XIV, Napoleon: they had no particular gifts, genius, or charisma; instead, like a loan, their ability to lead was borrowed from others. And if others decided to call in their loan, the individuals ability to lead disappeared. Broke, former leaders had to return to the ranks and follow whomever the masses chose.

If Tolstoy's view is the North Pole, the South Pole is the idea that individuals are everything. People follow because they must; like giants, leaders stand above normal people and lead because of their superior qualities. Good looks, intelligence, prestige, popularity, tact, diplomacy, initiative, drive: leaders have these qualities and great leaders have them in abundance. As Napoleon said in speaking to the legislative assembly in 1814, "Whom do you take yourselves for, departmental deputies, to speak as you do? The people do not know you, they know only me" (Lacouture, 1970).

Who is right? The answer is both and neither. For while studies show that leaders often possess a cluster of distinctive characteristics, studies also show that leaders who are effective in one situation, fail in another. Apparently, followers do make a difference; people are but one of the variables that makes leadership easy, difficult, or impossible. But people are only one of the variables; others include the social situation, the task, the power of the leader, his or her legitimacy, and the process of inter-

---

[1] Since a leader plays an active part in developing and maintaining the role structure and goal direction necessary for effective group performance, leadership is defined as a *category of behavior,* as "the initiation and maintenance of structure in expectation and interaction" (Stogdill, 1974).

action between leaders and followers. All together these variables allow some people to lead and they point to the futility of trying to explain leadership solely in terms of the individual or the group. Always leadership is the result of a number of interacting variables and always a change in, say, social situation and group task can make even the most effective leader both ineffective and unwanted (for example, Gibb, 1968, 1969; Hollander and Julian, 1969). For example, as the primary objective of the civil rights movement changed from *obtaining* formal rights to using and implementing rights already *gained,* the need for the "charismatic" leadership of Martin Luther King was greatly reduced. Wanted now were leaders with the administrative skills and the specialized knowledge necessary for the everyday success of the Voting Rights Act of 1965 (see Nelson, 1970).

LEADERSHIP TRAITS

Let's begin with a qualification. Although studies spanning seventy years show certain personality characteristics associated with leadership, those characteristics are at least to some degree culturally relative. Where Americans might applaud the enterprise, initiative, and drive that leads to achievements, in traditional Vietnam a leader had to be "absolutely and fundamentally bent on social order." There, qualities such as tact, diplomacy, and a reverence for the past were more important than the initiative and drive that often lead to change (McAlister and Mus, 1970).

Are leaders old or young, tall or short, fat or thin, handsome or ugly, neat or sloppy? Questions such as these were an early focus of studies on leadership traits. Today few scholars consider physical and constitutional factors important variables in explaining leadership. And the main reason for this view is that the early studies were both inconclusive and contradictory. For example, while a study of business leaders found most over fifty years of age, leaders in intellectual activities were generally much younger. And while appearance mattered in business, one study showed it was unimportant for leadrship in religious and intellectual activities. In short, a 6'4", handsome, 225-pound man of steel is by no means the typical leader (see Stogdill, 1948, 1974; also Gibb, 1969).

If constitutional factors are no help in explaining leadership, the studies are more positive when we turn to variables such as intelligence and personality. Leaders seem to be smarter than followers. In reviewing twenty-eight studies, Richard Mann found that 88 percent of the findings indicated a positive relationship between intelligence and leadership; and in a review of the entire literature from 1948 to 1970, Stogdill concluded there was "uniformly positive" support for the finding that leaders are more intelligent. However, the difference between leaders and followers is *small;* a stream, not an ocean, generally separates them. And, finally, recall our discussion in Chapter One. Since environment plays an important part in determining intelligence, the evidence indicates that leaders are both born and made.

In assessing the significance of personality, a wide variety of traits were studied. One that receives a tremendous amount of support is self-confidence (Gibb, 1969; Stogdill, 1948). Apparently, when leaders think about themselves as objects in the world of experience, they come to positive conclusions. And when interacting with others, that positive self-image plays a part in the role differentiation that "ends" in leadership. A second trait receiving strong support is sociability. Leaders have skill in dealing with others; at times this may mean no more than a false presentation of self, but at its best sociability refers to a leader's faculty for fostering the loyalty, cooperation, and cohesiveness required for a group's successful functioning. A third trait often found in leaders is a drive to excel, a need for achievement. Leaders want to do things and that means they are willing to persist when others have given up or perhaps never even tried. A fourth and final trait is variously labeled "adjustment or personality integration." Obviously, "no single measure of adjustment (for example, to family, to marriage) is likely to be an efficient predictor of leadership, "but there is strong evidence to indicate a positive relationship between an individual's adjustment and the leadership status he is likely to attain" (Mann, 1958; Gibb, 1969; Stogdill, 1974).

One final trait worthy of consideration is extroversion; leaders are supposedly outgoing, gregarious, eager to be with and approved by others. Generally the accumulated studies support this conclusion, but the evidence is by no means overwhelming (Mann, 1958; Stogdill, 1974). In fact, when Gibb suggests it may be possible to predict that elected leaders are extroverts while the powers behind the thrones are "introverts," there is evidence to support his hypothesis. For example, over a twenty-year period, Robert Lovett was a very powerful figure in American politics. A Wall Street lawyer, an undersecretary of state, head of the Defense Department, an adviser to John Kennedy on government appointments, Lovett is described as a man with no need to seek publicity; indeed he is pictured as the "private man par excellence." And, most important, Lovett is seemingly typical. For studies show that many of those who lead "behind the throne" seek anonymity, privacy, and the power that gives them the chance to lead (Halberstam, 1972; also Gibb, 1969; Domhoff, 1967, 1970).

In summing up, it is both possible and correct to argue that leaders are different; substantial support exists to show that, among other traits, leaders generally stand above followers in their degree of self-confidence, need to achieve, overall adjustment, intelligence, and skill in dealing with others. However, remember that "leadership must be conceived in terms of the interaction of variables which are in constant flux and change." Task, degree of power, social situation: factors such as these are often subject to rapid change. And, in comparison, the personal characteristics of the leader are more static. So, while a leader's traits are an essential element in explaining leadership, when we consider how difficult it is to achieve a "good fit" between "stable" personality and "unstable" social situation, it is clear that "any adequate analysis of leadership involves not only a study of leaders, but also of social situations" (Stogdill, 1974; also Cartwright and Zander, 1968).

CHARISMA AND SOCIAL SITUATION

Perhaps the best way to emphasize a leader's dependence on social situations is to discuss the concept of charisma. Defined as a quality of an individual by virtue of which he or she is "set apart from ordinary people and treated as though endowed with supernatural, superhuman, or at least specifically exceptional powers or qualities" (Weber, 1947, 1956), it is sometimes assumed that followers have no choice about embracing the charismatic leader. Overwhelmed by his or her qualities, ordinary people follow because they must. Could anyone refuse to accept a charismatic leader?

Of course they could. Of course they do. When Hitler tried to take over the German government in 1923, his "Beer Hall Putsch" was a dismal failure. Despite his blue eyes and stirring speeches, Hitler lacked support among senior officers in the army. Indeed, since senior officers interpreted his attempted takeover as the insolence of an ex-corporal, they were determined to crush the putsch as quickly as possible. Seemingly, Hitler could argue that he was "born to be a dictator," duty bound to step forward and take over the German government, but at least in 1923 few people agreed. Prospective followers said duty was insolence, destiny the ravings of a mad man (Bullock, 1962).

Always "it is recognition on the part of those subject to authority which is decisive for the validity of charisma" (Weber, 1947, Bendix, 1960; Shils, 1965). Ideally, this recognition is freely given; people believe it is their duty to follow the charismatic leader. However, whether charisma is immediately or slowly recognized, its power to influence others in expectation and interaction, its power to lead, is crucially dependent on others saying yes to a claim of extraordinary abilities. Charisma is *not* a quality that exists in and of itself; charisma is a relationship, an always questionable linkage of one person to others, of one person to the social situation in which the claim of charisma is made (Lacouture, 1970).

Consider the elements of a social situation (Gibb, 1968). First is the character of the culture. Shaped by common forms of thought and action, people are unlikely to accept a claim of charisma unless it makes cultural sense. For example, Hitler not only introduced a conception of "personal authenticity" to public life, he actually said it was "the chief value and sanction of politics." *He* was destined by fate to rule; follow *me* because the forces of history or God are on my side and your side (Stern, 1975). Now in many Western countries such a claim was unlikely to meet with approval. In Great Britain or America, culture taught people to regard claims of personal authenticity as arbitrary and tyrannical; above all the Constitution was the foundation of political life. But in Germany "the Romantics of the early nineteenth century, and after them the right-wing nationalists of the Second Reich" saw in the charismatic personality—the "genuine" or "natural" leader—"the fulfillment of their political hopes." So, when Hitler made his claim of personal authenticity, he was building on a solid foundation of cultural beliefs and values (Stern, 1975; Bullock, 1961).

Culture is one element of a social situation. Another is "the structure of interpersonal relations within the group" (Gibb, 1968). Consider someone trying to lead a country such as the United States versus someone leading the Sealab II expedition, ten men together for a month in a 12′ by 57′ steel cylinder 205′ below the surface of the Pacific Ocean? In each case leadership requires different skills and abilities; what succeeds with two hundred million Americans may fail completely with ten in the depths of the ocean. For example, suppose our charismatic politician is continually able to project an excellent media image; he blends in well with one important element of the structure of interpersonal relations in modern society. However, this same politician detests routine and often does poorly in small primary groups. Well, with such characteristics, all the media charisma in America will not produce leadership in the Pacific. There, a prospective leader would have to expect routine and, more important, possess skill in dealing with people on a crowded face-to-face basis (for example, Radloff and Helmreich, 1968).

A third element of a social situation are "the physical conditions within which the group finds itself constrained to act" (Gibb, 1968). In the airplane crash that left survivors stranded in the Andes, charisma was less important than physical well-being. So many people had been killed or injured in the crash, that one crucial variable constraining choice of leader was good health. Just being in one piece was sufficient justification to be considered for group leadership (Read, 1974).

Fourth are "the characteristics of the group as group" (Gibb, 1968). Is the charismatic leader making his claims for strong, personal leadership in a stable, well-off society or a nation beset by political crisis and economic woes? Both experimental and historical evidence argue that claims are much more likely to be legitimated when people experience crisis or threats. Using people "famous for their need for independence," Mulder and Stemerding found that external threats produced a desire for a "strong leader" (1963), and while Hitler failed in 1923, when he finally "succeeded" he was greatly helped by two years of economic depression, mass unemployment, and a government unable to resolve crisis or eliminate threats (Bullock, 1961; Stern, 1975).

A fifth element of a social situation is the task. Sometimes tasks are well-defined, other times they are quite ambiguous, but always the nature of the task affects a person's chances to have charisma validated. For example, like Dr. King, a man may have his charisma legitimated, but as the movement's tasks change, so does the relationship between leader and followers. Now new tasks demand new leaders, and the relationship sustaining the leader's charisma rapidly deteriorates (Nelson, 1970).

A final element of a social situation is the perception that group members have of the total situation. Based on culture, physical conditions, structure of interpersonal relations, task and group characteristics, people often come to some conclusion about the demands made by all the variables operating together. For example, when Ho Chi Minh asserted his leadership over Vietnam in 1945, he blended quite well into the total social situation. People embraced him because so many factors jointly validated his claims to leadership. Culture taught that major changes came from the top down and, if a revolution succeeded, its leaders had a "mandate from heaven." Physically, the Japanese army might have stopped Ho; instead, it allowed him to lead. Task-wise the goal was to restore a Vietnamese government to the land; few people knew the Vietminh's doctrine in detail, but if it made a good general impression that was sufficient for most Vietnamese. On the level of interpersonal relations, Ho Chi Minh established a centralized government while simultaneously trying to respect the ancient traditions of village life; for instance, to indicate socialism Ho used a phrase specifically designed to emphasize "the traditional village with all its spiritual and social connotations." Finally, the entire society was characterized by social crisis: the war was over, the Japanese were leaving, and before the French tried to reestablish their colonial regime, Ho Chi Minh was able to fill the void, and the hopes of many, with an authentic Vietnamese government. Rarely do charismatic leaders find such an inviting social situation; and rarely is the invitation open-ended. For while the Japanese allowed Ho Chi Minh to solidify himself in the North, before he could turn attention to the South, the British army took control in the name of France (for example, McAlister, 1969; Lacouture, 1968; McAlister and Mus, 1970).

In sum, although charisma is a quality possessed by individuals, charismatics are allowed to act as leaders, to engage in this *category of behavior,* only because of a satisfactory relationship to others and to the many elements of a social situation. Moreover, remember that any claim of charisma validated by others is always subject to reevaluation and rejection. Above all, charisma invokes a relationship.

But what happens when the charismatic leader dies? Does a new charismatic leader appear? Is there a schism in the movement? Or, like Christ placing his faith in Peter—"Upon this rock I will build my church"—is there a peaceful transfer of charisma from the dead to the living?

Since history answers yes to the last three questions, there is no one answer to the query, "What happens when the charismatic leader dies?"[2] However, the question brings us to an important issue in the study of leadership. Consider the late Pope John XXIII. For many this man had charisma in his own right; many felt he possessed extraordinary qualities. But Pope John was also the *institutionalized* head of the Roman Catholic Church and heir to the charisma passed from Christ to Peter and eventually to Pope John. So, if Pope John made many people follow him, was this a result of his leadership abilities or of the authority and power he had as legitimate head of the Roman Catholic Church? And if people followed because of his institutionalized power, was Pope John still engaging in the category of behavior defined as leadership?

In dealing with charisma, we were able to skirt if not totally avoid this problem.[3] In fact, charisma was discussed first because it highlights the intimate relationship between leaders, followers, and the elements of a social situation; perhaps more clearly than any other issue, charisma underlines why any adequate theory of leadership must be based on the interaction of many variables. But, when we turn away from individual qualities to positions within organized groups, we meet variables, for example, power and authority, that have continually aroused controversy among students of leadership. In short, if one initiates structure on the basis of institutionalized power and authority, is that leadership?

LEADERSHIP, POWER, AND AUTHORITY

Let's begin by defining terms. Although authority can be vested in either individuals or positions, the stress here is on the authority of positions. Defined as "the delegated or recognized right to initiate action," *authority*'s hallmark is "unquestioning recognition by those who are asked to obey." Ideally holders of authority need not use force or even persua-

---

[2] The classic account is in Weber, 1947, 1956.

[3] Ho Chi Minh had charisma and he led without any legitimate power or authority in either the prewar or war governments. But Ho Chi Minh was the head of the Vietminh, and to a significant if indeterminate degree, his success was also based on this institutionalized position.

sion; social influence is achieved because of the respect people have for the authority of a particular position or person (Stogdill, 1974; Arendt, 1970). For example, citizens sometimes follow a course of action because of a presidential request; it is not Kennedy, Johnson, or Nixon asking Americans to do this or that; it is the president—as well as all the authority that comes with being president.

Like leadership, power is a relationship; it belongs to a group and is given to individuals. Formally *power* is defined as "the probability that one actor within a social relationship is in a position to carry out his own will despite resistance" (Weber, 1947; Arendt, 1970). "You want to do this, I want to do that, and because I have power, you are likely to do as I wish."

Often power is equated with force; I beat you into submission. Actually coercive power is one of five types, and in many cases people voluntarily accept another's use of power (see French and Raven, 1959).

Consider first expert power. This refers to specialized knowledge. People obey because they accept the apparent or proven expertise of another. In a study by Evan and Zelditch, group members were more likely to accept the orders of supervisors who appeared to be well-informed about the task at hand (1961).

Second is referent power. This is based on a group's identification with a person; because people like or respect a leader, he or she has the probability of more social influence over them (Stogdill, 1974).

Third is legitimate power. This refers to people's agreement that one person has the right to prescribe behavior for them. Generally legitimate power is rooted in a shared belief, value, or standard (Raven and French, 1958a,b). For example, many were unhappy about it, but Gerald Ford had legitimate power over the American people because he achieved his office by the constitutional standards accepted by most Americans.

Fourth is reward power. One person influences another by virtue of the benefits offered. Often a position of authority comes loaded down with reward power. Promotions, money, status: people in authority have the power to dispense these wherever they wish, and others sometimes obey only because they seek the rewards that come with compliance.

Finally there is coercive power. One person has the ability, for example, to fine others, to jail others, and even to kill others. People obey because they have no choice; the consequences of disobedience are too great.

Now, let's return to the argument. Often the powers and authority that come with an institutionalized position (for example, Chair of the Sociology or Psychology Department; executive Vice-President of Marketing) are called headship (Gibb, 1968, 1969). The idea is that a head influences others, not because of spontaneous recognition by group members, but because of a position in an organized group. Deriving authority and power from the position, heads never have followers; instead they dominate others because of their reward, coercive, or legitimate powers. Domination has nothing to do with the spontaneous recognition that is supposedly the essence of leadership (Gibb, 1969; Kochan et al., 1975).

This is the crux of the argument. And it is more than a matter of semantics or definition. Gibb and others contend that "when influence derives from a power given to one or a few individuals by a source external to the group itself," that is not leadership. That exists only when "group structure is internally imposed," only when group members openly discuss an issue and voluntarily confer influence rights on a person without the added variables of external authority and power (Gibb, 1969; Kochan et al., 1975).

The major problem with this notion of leadership is that it results in unnecessary confusion. Apparently, Gibb and others believe that leaders must do it alone; they agree that leadership is a category of behavior, but they then go on to define, not only behavior, but the conditions under which the behavior can take place. That is confusing. Either leadership is a type of behavior or it is not. Obviously, the behavior occurs in different social situations and a person with institutionalized authority and power has a great advantage in deciding who leads, but that still only qualifies the degree to which the individual was helped by factors external to social interaction. Whether achieved alone or with the aid of authority and power, if a person initiates and maintains structure in expectation and interaction, that is the category of behavior called leadership.

In disagreeing with Gibb and his colleagues, let us not neglect the reason for their distinction. Occupants of positions with authority and power need not be leaders. Perhaps a person simply performs—to the letter—his formal functions. Or perhaps the occupant of a position is totally inept. There is no argument with the contention that a leader is defined "not by his position in the formal structure," but "in terms of the frequency and multiplicity of leadership-like functions he performs within a group" (Kochan et al., 1975; Gibb, 1969). However, just because a person has authority and power is no reason he or she cannot exert leadership. Leadership is behavior, and people with authority as well as power can be, and often are, leaders. For example, during World War II sergeants were "notorious for their skill in developing their own structures for supplementing, bypassing, or cutting through bureaucratic procedures. . . ." Without these new structures the system might have failed, but because many sergeants used their authority and power they were able to lead, to improvise structure and so maintain the organization for expectation and interaction (Katz and Kahn, 1966).

EMERGENCE OF LEADERSHIP

Leaders emerge through a process of role differentiation. In many experimental studies this process is relatively "pure"; group members are strangers, and when given a task, leaders emerge as a result of the interaction which leads group members to believe that one person will best promote, for example, task achievement, member satisfaction, group cohesiveness. Of course, outside the laboratory, interaction often assumes less importance in determining a group leader. Factors such as authority, power, status, and previous performance all set the stage before interaction begins; then, to a varying extent, the leader has already emerged before the group begins work (Stogdill, 1974; Burke, 1969; Fisek and Ofshe, 1970).

Let's begin with "personal factors in the emergence of leadership." Seemingly, the self-confidence, need to achieve, and overall adjustment of many leaders make an appearance very quickly. In interaction, emergent leaders talk more often, participate more actively in group discussions, as well as show an ability to sustain and initiate group interaction. In a study done at Stanford, freshman students were asked to participate in small decision-making groups. And despite being strangers, "as early as the first minute of the group members interaction, there existed marked inequalities in participation." In fact, the inequalities in the first minute were nearly as great as those that existed thirty minutes later. Apparently, in these groups "the dominant individual controlled an approximately fixed proportion of the available opportunities to speak at all times" (Fisek and Ofshe, 1970).

Leaders emerge with the cooperation of others. Studies show that people tend to choose leaders whose beliefs and values are similar to their own. In the largest sense this harks back to the cultural or subcultural aspect of a social situation; at least in general leaders' beliefs and values must mesh with those of the people they seek to lead. In a study of prison inmates, jailed persons tended to choose leaders whose offense, sentence, previous criminal record, institutional adjustment, and ethnic status were all similar to their own (Schrag, 1954). And numerous studies of the army and navy show that an education at West Point or Annapolis is often an important factor in emerging as a leader. Karsten argues that "this commonality of profession, this ease and depth of identification among Academy graduates, this 'common cause,' was perhaps the most profound and lasting thing the candidate acquired" (Karsten, 1972; Janowitz, 1960).

If people choose leaders with similar beliefs, that does not mean they neglect the social situation and, especially, group goals and tasks. Hollander and Webb analyzed the relationship between people who were friends and each friend's nominees for leadership. Not only were nominations not a total function of friendship, but friendship "appeared to play only a minor role in the emergence of leadership nominations." Much more important was a friend's "evaluations of an individual's potential for performance" (Hollander and Webb, 1955). And in the prison study cited above, an important factor differentiating emergent leaders was their "achievements"; leaders were "criminally mature," comparatively permanent residents of the prison, as well as more aggressive and violent than their followers (Schrag, 1954).

Other important factors in the emergence of leadership are a person's authority, status, and power. Study shows that status differences are quickly perceived, used as a basis for differentiating a leader, as well as brought back to the group when it meets at other times. In a study of small decision-making groups at a corporate conference, Crockett found emergent leaders usually had a higher position in the corporate hierarchy than followers, and expert power was a factor in role differentiation. Group members tended to take their leads from people known to possess specialized knowledge (Crockett, 1955). And remember the influence of sex. To the extent women learn that men lead while they follow, and to the extent this knowledge produces a lack of self-confidence, as well as no drive to achieve, men are more likely, perhaps much more likely, to emerge as the leaders of almost any group (see Hoffman, 1972; Horner, 1972).

Remember, too, that status, authority, or power also have an effect on emerging leaders. Aware of high status, or posssssing expert or reward power, a person tends to make more attempts at leading. Taking the role of the other (actually of the generalized other), a person who wants to lead knows that others probably think as highly of his authority or status or power as he does: "I can try to lead because they'll tell me my qualities are as important as I think they are." And, should the expectations of a prospective leader and the expectations of group members mesh, leaders may easily succeed themselves; changes in social situation can always undermine an emerged leader, but success lays a sound basis for the expectations that will guide future interactions. For example, in studying the inner workings of a factory, Melville Dalton found that in executive meetings headship did not mean leadership. Mr. Stevens was plant manager but invariably meetings were dominated by his assistant, Mr. Hardy. Apparently, Stevens would or could not lead and over time a routine was established: Stevens opened a meeting with a few remarks and then silently gave way to Hardy. Generally questions were directed to Hardy and eventually everyone took it for granted that his answers "were made without request for confirmation from Stevens." Emerging as the leader, Hardy gained the confidence to step up his attempts, had them reinforced by others, and over time gained the coercive, reward, and referent power that solidified his leadership even more (Dalton, 1959).

Two other factors that influence a leader's emergence are group task and group size. People tend to choose leaders who can do the job, and should the task change, a leader in one group may easily emerge as a follower in another. Also, studies over twenty-five years show that "as the size of the group increases, the potentiality for leadership is reduced to a smaller percentage of members" (Stogdill, 1974). The reasons for this are clear: large groups require some form of organization, and the establishment of even a small hierarchy makes factors such as authority and power quite important for a leader's emergence. For example, Stogdill showed that "large groups make greater demands for leader skill and competence than small groups." Apparently, large groups function poorly without the specialized knowledge required for coordinating complex activity (Stogdill, 1974; Indik, 1963).

So far our discussion has focused on variables that exist prior to interaction. Turning to the process itself, at least four factors contribute to a leader's emergence. First is the prospect of success. In one study even individuals with a strong need for achievement were not eager to assume leadership when conditions were against them (Pepinsky et al., 1958). Second is reinforcement. Positive feedback is more effective than negative, but should group members strike at a prospective leader's self-image, he or she may very well try to lead all the harder (Bowers, 1963). Third is actual success in leadership. Like Mr. Hardy, this not only wins approval from others, but it gives the emergent leader power over others. Fourth and finally is "group motivation and concern" for group tasks and goals. Naturally, to some extent this exists prior to interaction; before anything happens people are happy or unhappy, concerned or indifferent about the group. But if the process of interaction leads to interest in the group, people should be eager to see the emergence of a competent leader (Stogdill, 1974).

Leaders emerge over time and through a process of interaction with and acceptance by others. Seemingly, the most suitable conditions for a leader's emergence are a self-confident person with a strong need for achievement who, possessing status, authority, and power, confronts a group in which the chances of success are good and the group's concern about tasks and goals quite high. However, whether a leader emerges under ideal or awful conditions, remember that all leaders always maintain an interactive relationship with followers. Leaders control others but they are also controlled by others.

Consider Hollander's notion of "idiosyncrasy credit." Like interest on a savings account, the successful leader accumulates positive expectations from others. Over time this positive regard gives a leader leeway; others value the leader so much they will allow deviation "from the common expectancies of the group." Like interest, idiosyncrasy credit has a limit but until that point is reached leaders are able to initiate and maintain structure via means and toward goals that are new to the group (Hollander, 1958).

Now, consider a leader's credit and place it in a real situation. Assume our leader operates in a society dominated by tradition, assume our leader is Henry VIII. The label *leader* was earned, but Henry's leadership was inherited; to a great extent his ability to lead depended on his respecting the traditions that were the basis of his authority, as well as refusing to grossly exaggerate the powers of his office. At first Henry acted with care; apparently aware that even a very popular king led with limits, he asked the Pope for permission to divorce and, using his reward and coercive powers, he had his followers obtain decisions from European universities stating that the Pope could dispense with the law against marrying a deceased brother's wife. But the Pope refused to give in and Henry refused to acknowledge the limits of his idiosyncrasy credit. In the end, unable to secure from many clergy recognition of his supremacy over the church, Henry resorted to coercion. And he did lead. Using his army, he initiated major changes in the structure of British government and society. However, any visitor to England need only inspect the numerous and once magnificent abbeys destroyed by Henry to see that for many he had used up his idiosyncrasy credit. For thousands of people, Henry was no longer a leader. Indeed, in a reversal of the social situation, Henry was now an enemy who had to be resisted (see, for example, Pollard, 1966).

Perhaps Henry VIII is a "loaded" example. Tradition is a heavy burden for any leader to bear. Conceivably, the "pure" charismatic leader has no limits to his or her leadership; believing the leader is God or at least very close to God, followers give the leader unlimited credit. Probably this is so. Some followers can obey any order, no matter how much it deviates from group values, beliefs, and practices. But for the vast majority of people, all leaders, even the most revered of charismatics, have a credit limit. Like Malcolm X, after the discovery that his "savior" (Elijah Muhammad) had violated group beliefs and practices, a dedicated follower may be forced to conclude he can follow no more (Malcolm X, 1966).

LEADERSHIP: STYLE AND EFFECTIVENESS

One topic that has received considerable attention from students of leadership is style. Defined as the manner and tone a person characteristically assumes in interaction, studies have focused on autocratic versus democratic, authoritarian versus egalitarian, production versus human relations, and task- versus group-oriented styles. Throughout, the assumption is that style makes a difference; style affects a person's chances of initiating and maintaining structure in expectation and interaction (for example, Fiedler, 1967; Anderson, 1968).

By far the most detailed and suggestive studies on leadership style are those of Fred E. Fiedler. Presenting a contingency theory of leadership, Fiedler has done literally hundreds of studies focused on two styles of interaction. First is the task-oriented leader. This person is concerned above all with considerations such as group productivity. Often punitive toward poor coworkers, the task-oriented leader "never" worries about being liked. Self-esteem derives from efficient performance of the group task and, even at the risk of poor interpersonal relations, the task-oriented leader concentrates on getting the job done—and well. In contrast, the group-oriented leader keys on establishing rapport and good feelings between and among followers. Here self-esteem derives from being esteemed by others, as well as having good relations with others. To succeed, group-oriented leaders must produce, but they try to do this by orienting themselves and the group toward pleasant, considerate, relaxed interaction (Fiedler, 1962; 1967).

For Fiedler effective use of a style is contingent upon the social situation in which the leader operates. Consider an early study of army and air force crews. Fiedler found that when a task-oriented leader had no choice about his key aide (say, the gunner on a tank-gunnery task), and was incompatible with the aide, group performance suffered. But put a group-oriented leader in the same situation, and the group maintained its effectiveness. Apparently, the effectiveness of leadership style was contingent upon leader-member relations, upon the extent to which the leader was liked by, as well as had the confidence of, group members (Fiedler, 1955, 1967; Gibb, 1969).

Over time results like this led Fiedler to conclude that leadership style is contingent upon three major variables.[4] First is the personal relationship between leader and group members. If the leader is liked and trusted, that should produce compliance with a minimum of effort. Second is the leader's power. Since this is "the degree to which the position itself enables the leader to get group members to comply with and accept his leadership," for Fiedler power includes all the types discussed above (that is, reward, coercive, expert, referent, and legitimate power), as well as the authority that a position offers. Finally, there is the task. Is it structured or unstructured? Particularly if a leader receives a structured task from "on high," he or she can depend on backing from above. "This is what we were told to do. This is what you did. This is your penalty for failure to perform." However, given an unstructured task, leaders must

---

[4] Fiedler's theory relates to interacting groups, groups that "require the close coordination of several team members in the performance of a primary task" (1967).

rely on their own resources to inspire and motivate followers. There can be little appeal to orders from above and that means, with unstructured tasks, leaders lose a valuable aid (Fiedler, 1967).

Now, with his two styles of leadership and three major variables Fiedler constructed the typology below:

	Leader-Member Relations	Task Structure	Position Power
1	good	high	strong
2	good	high	weak
3	good	weak	strong
4	good	weak	weak
5	moderately poor	high	strong
6	moderately poor	high	weak
7	moderately poor	weak	strong
8	moderately poor	weak	weak
8A	very poor	high	strong

Rooted in the idea that different types of groups need different styles of leadership, Fiedler's overall conclusion is that task-related leaders are most effective when conditions are either very favorable or very unfavorable. In groups with moderately favorable conditions, it is the group-oriented style that is most effective.

Consider Fiedler's explanations. In favorable situations (1, 2, 3) group-oriented leaders have few worries. Basing their style on recognition and approval from others, they easily get what they want. In fact, since they can remain "relatively passive, nondirective, and permissive," group-oriented leaders need not exert themselves. But task-oriented leaders do exert themselves. In power, as well as confident about the approval and support of their followers, such leaders can key on what gives them the most pleasure and esteem: getting the job done (Fiedler, 1967, 1968).

Turning to "somewhat unfavorable situations" (4, 5, 6, 7), task-oriented leaders begin to lose their advantages. Worried by the (in situation 4) lack of power and the unstructured task, or (in situations 5, 6, 7) troubled by poor relations with others, task-oriented leaders use what resources they have to get the job done. But if in situation 4, impatience produces a cutoff of group discussion, the leader's failure to make full use of others should impede group productivity. Or, if in situation 5, leaders use their power to achieve the structured task, they risk alienating group members, as well as reducing the motives to work. In contrast, group-oriented leaders should find unfavorable conditions a reason "to interact more intensively with group members." And this consideration of, and responsiveness to, others should be effective. In situation 4, group-oriented leaders are "perfect"; despite an unstructured task and a lack of power, their orientation should allow the group to use and exploit the intelligence and creativity of its members. Or, in situation 7, group-oriented leaders could use the reward powers of their position; where task-oriented leaders might turn to punitive measures, a focus on member satisfactions would move group-oriented leaders to use carrots rather than sticks. The result should be a greater chance of getting the job done (Fiedler, 1967, 1968).

Finally, there are very unfavorable group situations. Here group-oriented leaders lack any resources. But their focus on others tends "to increase the rate and intensity of their interactions with group members." And even if this focus never alienates others, it does take group-oriented leaders away from "the task-relevant aspects of the group situation." Now, like his counterpart, the task-oriented leader is not in an enviable position; by definition, situations 8 and 8A do not lend themselves to successful leadership. However, Fiedler never argues a magical power for task-oriented leaders. His contention is that groups in these situations are often threatened, for example, an unpopular corporal trying to salvage the remains of a battered company. So, if we add threat to the other conditions, a focus on task may be effective. Everyone would desire success and thus be willing to follow directive, perhaps even inconsiderate, leaders (Fiedler, 1967, 1968).

Overall Fiedler's typology represents a substantial contribution to our understanding of the interactions between style and social situation. Certainly there is no evidence that group-oriented or permissive or democratic leadership styles are always or even more effective than task-oriented or authoritarian leadership styles (see Stogdill, 1974). Leadership effectiveness is relative to the social situation, and Fiedler's typology takes many of the important variables into account.

But keep the model's limitations in mind: some elements of a social situation are not included in the typology. For example, we added the threat variable to situations 7 and 8. What happens if we add it to the somewhat unfavorable situations? Does a threat always increase the effectiveness of a task-oriented leader? And does that threat overcome the advantages of group-oriented leaders in somewhat unfavorable conditions? Or, what about culture? A vital element in any social situation, what are the effects of a strong democratic tradition in the very favorable conditions? Task-oriented leaders should do very well in situations 1 to 3, but will their style soon alienate members of the culture? Will a focus on task turn good leader-member relations into poor ones? Does an effective performance of task lead to a desire to get rid of such an effective leader?

At present we lack answers to these questions, but any fully comprehensive theory of the interaction between style and social situation will have to provide them.

Lastly, remember that effectiveness is only one goal of a group. Others include freedom and happiness. Obviously, many groups and societies may be quite willing to sacrifice degrees of effectiveness in order to preserve rights and freedoms. And whether to opt for effectiveness or freedom is not an easy question because answers are very dependent upon socioeconomic conditions. For example, when they came to power, the Chinese Communists had structured tasks, as well as a strong power position. What they often lacked were good relations with their citizens, and they compensated for this lack by using the harshest measures—coercive power pushed to its limits. But today the average Chinese person has clothes that keep him or her warm. This was not true before the use of authoritarian styles of leadership, and the question, a crucial one in so many developing nations, is whether the end justifies the means. Knowing that task-oriented leadership is likely to work is no justification for its use. That is intimately a question of values, beliefs, and socioeconomic condition (see, for example, Terrell, 1972; Heilbroner, 1963, 1974).

Bibliographical References

Anderson, Richard C. "Learning in Discussions—A Résumé of the Authoritarian-Democratic Studies." In *Contemporary Issues in Social Psychology*, edited by Lawrence S. Wrightsman, Jr. Belmont, Calif.: Wadsworth, 1968.

Arendt, Hannah. *On Violence*. New York: Harcourt Brace Jovanovich, 1970.

Bendix, Reinhard. *Max Weber: An Intellectual Portrait*. Garden City, N.Y.: Doubleday, 1960.

Bowers, David G. "Self-Esteem and the Diffusion of Leadership Style." *Journal of Applied Psychology* 47 (1963): 135–40.

Bullock, Allan. *Hitler: A Study in Tyranny*. New York: Harper & Row, 1961.

Burke, Peter J. "Scapegoating: An Alternative to Role Differentiation." *Sociometry* 32 (1969): 159–68.

Cartwright, Dorwin, and Zander, Alvin. *Group Dynamics: Research and Theory*. London: Tavistock, 1968.

Crockett, Walter. "Emergent Leadership in Small, Decision-Making Groups." *Journal of Abnormal and Social Psychology* 51 (1955): 378–83.

Dalton, Melville. *Men Who Manage*. New York: Wiley, 1959.

Domhoff, G. William. *The Higher Circles: The Governing Class in America*. New York: Vintage, 1970.

Domhoff, G. William. *Who Rules America?* Englewood Cliffs, N.J.: Prentice-Hall, 1967.

Etzioni, Amitai. *A Comparative Analysis of Complex Organizations*. Rev. ed. New York: Free Press, 1975.

Evan, W. M., and Zelditch, M. "A Laboratory Experiment on Bureaucratic Authority. *American Sociological Review* 26 (1961): 883–93.

Fiedler, Fred E. "The Influence of Leader-Keyman Relations on Combat-Crew Effectiveness." *Journal of Abnormal and Social Psychology* 51 (1955): 227–35.

Fiedler, Fred E. "Leader Attitudes, Group Climate, and Group Creativity." *Journal of Abnormal and Social Psychology* 65 (1962): 308–18.

Fiedler, Fred E. *A Theory of Leadership Effectiveness.* New York: McGraw-Hill, 1967.

Fisek, M. Hamit, and Ofshe, Richard. "The Process of Status Evolution." *Sociometry* 33 (1970): 327–46.

French, J. R. P., and Raven B. "The Bases of Social Power." In *Studies in Social Power*, edited by D. Cartwright. Ann Arbor: University of Michigan, Institute for Social Research, 1959.

Gibb, Cecil. "Leadership." In *Handbook of Social Psychology*, edited by Gardner Lindzey and Elliot Aronson. Vol. 3. Reading, Mass.: Addison-Wesley, 1969.

Gibb, Cecil. "Leadership: Psychological Aspects." *Encyclopedia of the Social Sciences.* Vol. 5. New York: Macmillan, 1968.

Halberstam, David. *The Best and the Brightest.* New York: Random House, 1972.

Heilbroner, Robert. *The Great Ascent.* New York: Harper & Row, 1963.

Heilbroner, Robert. *An Inquiry into the Human Prospect.* New York: Norton, 1974.

Hoffman, Lois Wlasis. "Early Childhood Experiences and Women's Achievement Motives." *Journal of Social Issues* 28 (1972): 129–55.

Hollander, Edwin P. "Conformity, Status, and Idiosyncrasy Credit." *Psychological Review* 65, no. 2 (1958): 117–27.

Hollander, Edwin P., and Julian, James W. "Contemporary Trends in the Analysis of Leadership Processes." *Psychological Bulletin* 71 (1969): 387–97.

Hollander, Edwin P., and Webb, W. B. "Leadership, Followship, and Friendship: An Analysis of Peer Nominations." *Journal of Abnormal and Social Psychology* 50 (1955): 163–67.

Hook, Sidney. *The Hero in History: A Study in Limitations and Possibility.* Boston: Beacon, 1955.

Horner, Matina. "Toward an Understanding of Achievement-Related Conflicts in Women." *Journal of Social Issues* 28 (1972): 157–75.

Indik, Bernard P. "Some Effects of Organization Size on Member Attitudes and Behavior." *Human Relations* 16 (1963): 369–84.

Janowitz, Morris. *The Professional Soldier: A Social and Political Portrait.* New York: Free Press, 1960.

Karsten, Peter. *The Naval Aristocracy.* New York: Free Press, 1972.

Katz, Daniel, and Kahn, Robert L. *The Social Psychology of Organizations.* New York: Wiley, 1966.

Kochan, Thomas A.; Schmidt, Stuart M.; and De Cotiers, Thomas A. "Superior-Subordinate Relations: Leadership and Headship." *Human Relations* 28, no. 3 (1975): 279–94.

Lacouture, Jean. *The Demigods: Charismatic Leadership in the Third World.* New York: Knopf, 1970.

Lacouture, Jean. *Ho Chi Minh.* New York: Vintage, 1968.

McAlister, John T. *Vietnam: The Origins of Revolution.* New York: Knopf, 1969.

McAlister, John T., and Mus, Paul. *The Vietnamese and Their Revolution.* New York: Harper & Row, 1970.

Malcolm X, *The Autobiography of Malcolm X* (with the assistance of Alex Haley). New York: Grove, 1966.

Mann, Richard. "A Review of the Relationships Between Personality and Performance in Small Groups." *Psychological Bulletin* 56 (1958): 241–70.

Mulder Mauk, and Stemerding, Ad. "Threat, Attraction to Group, and Need for Strong Leadership." *Human Relations* 16 (1963): 317–34.

Nelson, Harold. "Leadership and Change in an Evolutionary Movement: An Analysis of Change in the Leadership Structure of the Southern Civil Rights Movement." *Social Forces* 49 (1970): 353–71.

Pepinsky, Pauline; Hemphill, John K.; and Shevitz, Reuben N. "Attempts to Lead, Group Productivity, and Morale Under Conditions of Acceptance and Rejection." *Journal of Abnormal and Social Psychology* 57 (1958): 47–64.

Pollard A. F. *Henry VIII.* New York: Harper & Row, 1966.

Radloff, Roland, and Helmreich, Robert. *Groups Under Stress: Psychological Research in Sealab II.* New York: Appleton-Century-Crofts, 1968.

Raven, Bertram H., and French, John R. P. "Group Support, Legitimate Power, and Social Influence." *Journal of Personality* 26 (1958a): 400–409.

Raven, Bertram H., and French, John R. P. "Legitimate Power, Coercive Power, and Observability in Social Influence." *Sociometry* 21 (1958b): 83–97.

Read, Piers Paul. *Alive: The Story of the Andes Survivors.* New York: Lippincott, 1974.

Schrag, Clarence. "Leadership Among Prison Inmates." *American Sociological Review* 19 (1954): 37–42.

Seligman, Lester G. "Leadership: Political Aspects." *Encyclopedia of the Social Sciences.* Vol. 5. New York: Macmillan, 1968.

Shils, Edward. "Charisma, Order, and Status." *American Sociological Review* 30 (1965): 199–213.

Slater, Philip. "Role Differentiation in Small Groups." *American Sociological Review* 20 (1955): 300–310.

Stern, J. P. *Hitler: The Fuhrer and the People*. Berkeley: University of California Press, 1975.

Stogdill, Ralph M. *Handbook of Leadership: A Survey of Theory and Research*. New York: Free Press, 1974.

Stogdill, Ralph M. "Personal Factors Associated with Leadership." *Journal of Personality* 25 (1948): 35–71.

Terrill, Ross. *800,000,000: The Real China*. New York: Dell, 1972.

Weber, Max. *From Max Weber: Essays in Sociology*. Edited and translated by Hans Gerth and C. Wright Mills. New York: Galaxy, 1956.

Weber, Max. *The Theory of Social and Economic Organization*. New York: Free Press, 1947.

CHAPTER TWELVE

Aggression and Social Conflict

Though Muller would be delighted to have Kemmerich's boots, he is really quite as sympathetic as another who could not bear to think of such a thing for grief. He merely sees things clearly . . . Kemmerich will die; it is immaterial who gets them. Why, then, should Muller not succeed to them? He has more right than a hospital-orderly. When Kemmerich is dead, it will be too late. Therefore Muller is already on the watch.

We have lost all sense of other considerations, because they are artificial. Only the facts are real and important for us. And good boots are scarce.

Once it was different. When we went to the District Commandant to enlist, we were a class of twenty young men, many of whom proudly shaved for the first time before going to the barracks. We had no definite plans for the future. Our thoughts of a career and occupation were as yet of too unpractical a character to furnish any scheme of life. We were still crammed full of vague ideas which gave to life, and to the war also, an ideal and almost romantic character. We were trained in the army for ten weeks and in this time more profoundly influenced than by ten years at school. We learned that a bright button is weightier than four volumes of Schopenhauer. At first astonished, then embittered, and finally indifferent, we recognized that what matters is not the mind but the boot brush, not intelligence but the system, not freedom but drill. We became soldiers with eagerness and enthusiasm, but they have done everything to knock that out of us. After three weeks it was no longer incomprehensible to us that a braided postman should have more authority over us than had formerly our parents, our teachers, and the whole gamut of culture from Plato

> to Goethe. With our young, awakened eyes we saw that the classical conception of the Fatherland held by our teachers resolved itself here into a renunciation of personality such as one would not ask of the meanest servant—salutes, springing to attention, parade-marches, presenting arms, right wheel, left wheel, clicking the heels, insults, and a thousand petifogging details. We had fancied our task would be different, only to find we were to be trained for heroism as though we were circus ponies. . . .
>
> Erica Maria Remarque, *All Quiet on the Western Front* (1929)

Circus ponies, automatons, slaves, robots. The words differ but all are commonly used as stereotypes for the modern soldier. In fact, some people go further: "It's always been that way. History is a broken record. No matter what the civilization, soldiers have always been forced to act, not think, to kill, not worry why."

Like most stereotypes, this one contains only a kernel of truth. In the Mexican-American War most of General Zachary Taylor's troops wore no uniforms and, just as he was about to attack Mexico City, many of his men deserted. One-year volunteers, their time was up and not even imminent victory enticed them to fight any longer (Singletary, 1960). Or, consider a famous story from the Middle Ages, about Duke Louis of Bourbon and one Regnaud De Monteferrard, a noble squire. The Duke was besieging a castle commanded by Regnaud. After a month's labor, the Duke's men completed a tunnel into the interior of the castle. Would any of the castle's knights like to meet another warrior in the tunnel—a passage about eighteen inches wide? The castle lacked any knights but would a noble squire do? He would. And the two immediately met in cramped-quarters combat. However, when the squire learned his opponent was Duke Louis of Bourbon, he was all thanks: "I praise God that he has today done me the grace and honor to fight so valiant a prince." Indeed, Regnaud so appreciated the glory won from fighting the Duke, he offered to surrender the castle if the Duke would dub Regnaud a knight. The Duke did so, the castle was surrendered, and all who heard of the affair "were filled with admiration for the courtesy of the two participants" (Painter, 1957).

The examples make two points. First, the motives and manner of conducting war are socially and historically relative. Is it possible to imagine a modern officer surrendering his ship because his opponent is famous? On the contrary, today the rules are reversed. As was the case with Commander Lloyd Bucher on the spy ship *Pueblo,* we demand that military men refuse to surrender, even when faced with impossible odds and certain destruction. Second, if war is socially and historically relative, perhaps there is hope for humanity. Arguing that fighting was instinctual, Freud said "there was no likelihood of our being able to suppress humanity's aggressive tendencies" (Freud, 1933), but if the motives and manner of war vary, perhaps the causes of violent conflict are social rather than biological? Of course, it is possible to argue that instinct underlies all manifestations of war, but what of those societies that lack the institution of war? Among others, the Eskimos, the Lepchas of Sikkim, and the Aurohvacos of Colombia all do (or did) without war (Mead, 1964; Davie, 1929). Are these people biological freaks? Did they somehow lose what the rest of us possess? Or is it possible that all forms of violent conflict have social roots? To answer these questions, let us turn first to a discussion of aggression in the individual.

AGRESSION: A SOCIAL PSYCHOLOGICAL ANALYSIS

In defining *aggression* as an "offensive assault on another person, group, or thing," there is no doubt that human life is filled with aggressive acts. Today, we seem to believe that aggression is more common than ever before, but based on available statistics it appears that murder occurred less often (per capita) in America of the 1960s than during the 1920s (Clark, 1971). And if we turn, say, to fourteenth-century England, the situation was even worse. Without a police force—one was established only in 1830—"murder, rape, beating, and robbery by violence were everyday incidents" (Trevelyan, 1967).

Granted, aggression is commonplace and pervasive. But is it instinctual? There are at least three reasons to answer no.

The first is recent research on the brain. Instinct[1] theorists talk about the intensity of innate impulses to aggression (Storr, 1968), but studies show that "any animal, regardless of its species, reacts to a life-threatening attack with one of two patterns of behavior: either with flight or with aggression and violence—that is, fight" (Mark and Ervin, 1970). Both responses are "closely linked to one another," and Fromm asks important questions: Why stress Homo aggressivus? Why not a theory built on people's "uncontrollable flight instinct"? Threatened, people can respond either way and that means a theory centered on the "instinct to flee" is "neurophysiologically as sound as one centered on the instinct to fight" (Fromm, 1973).

A second reason to reject instinct theories of aggression is the consistent use of unjustified analogies. Writers switch from other animals to humans without any apparent awareness they are discussing phenomena that may be different. Citing work by Lorenz, one writer notes that well-fed dogs

---

[1] *Webster's Seventh New Collegiate Dictionary* gives the following definition of *instinct:* "complex and specific response by an organism to environmental stimuli that is largely hereditary and unalterable, does not involve reason, and has as its goal the removal of a somatic tension."

still love hunting and then goes on to say that "sports, science, and so many other activities certainly have connections with internal factors of this kind." How? Why? Where is the proof for such an assertion? The answer is there is none. As Lehrman notes, "it is obvious that this argument is based on the most casual and unanalytical kind of comparison, and a lack of concern with the specific origins of the behavior patterns at issue" (Lehrman, 1953; Montagu, 1968; Lorenz, 1967).

A third reason to reject the notion of instinct is that it includes so many meanings, its explanatory value is nil. Normally, the concept is used to refer to the *cause* of an activity, the *goal* of an activity, as well as the *rigid* activity itself (Gerth and Mills, 1953). Consider the predicaments this produces. Motives for aggression include religion, family, love, honor, power, adventure, money, social status. These are only some of the things that move people to aggression and, at that, these causes of conflict are abstract. All motives are always embedded in a cultural framework and while it is correct to argue that religion is a cause of aggression, the particular god(s) must be specified. For example, the Yanomamo fight because of links to the god Periboriwa (Chagnon, 1968). They will not fight for Jesus or Muhammad or Buddha. They fight for Periboriwa and it is unnecessary to use instincts to explain their aggression. The causes, goals, and manner of Yanomamo warfare are relatively specific to Yanomamo culture and to argue the Yanomamo fight because of an instinct to aggression is to tell me nothing about why they act as they do (Chagnon, 1968).

Nothing? Yes, nothing. Because the weakness of the concept in explaining specific instances of aggression shows its illusory character. To accept instincts is to make a leap of faith. Given all the causes of aggression, all its goals, along with its anything but rigid manifestations (for example, the spear as opposed to the crossbow as opposed to cannon as opposed to intercontinental ballistic missiles), we are asked to accept that underlining all the specificities attached to culture and personal history are instincts. We are asked to believe this in the face of societies without war, people who are pacifists, as well as a historical record that shows soldiers often fight only because they are beaten into submission.[2]

The leap is hard to make. For, given the large number of aggressive motives, goals, and means, the evidence indicates "that the impulse which controls aggression is not primary but derived" (Malinowski, 1941). For instance, although the Jibaro engage in wars of extermination, they always leave enemy territory as soon as possible. Inevitably, enemy sorcerers fill roads, forests, and houses with witching arrows; any can strike

---

[2] In fourth-century Rome, desertion was so widespread that officials resorted to tattoos. At least that way deserters were easily identifiable (see Phillips, 1960). In George Washington's army the instinct to aggression was so aroused that only 30 to 50 percent of the soldiers deserted (Bowman, 1943).

without warning and any are capable of forcing the Jibaro to flee (Karsten, 1967). Now, the Jibaro had to derive this knowledge in the process of social experience; it was not present at birth. Equally important, the factors that ignite the "instinct to aggression" and the "instinct to flee" are both determined by cultural beliefs, values, and practices. It is unnecessary to resort to instinctual explanations since the evidence shows that the human "impulse to aggression" is so *nonspecific* that it easily attaches itself to a multitude of objects; and what those objects are is not determined by biology. It is determined (or at least guided) by culture and personal history.

If biology fails to explain human aggression, what does? Historically, a most influential answer is frustration. As Dollard et al. said in 1939, "aggression is always a consequence of frustration." In fact, ". . . the occurrence of aggressive behavior always presupposes the existence of frustration, and, contrariwise, the existence of frustration always leads to some form of aggression" (Dollard et al., 1939).

Let's begin with the first half of the proposition: "aggressive behavior always presupposes the existence of frustration." Two general exceptions to this rule are "instrumental" and "learned" aggression. Sometimes people fight and kill one another to achieve a goal. In Vietnam air crews systematically and impersonally engaged in "surgical strikes"; one man compared himself to a television technician: he was just doing an efficient job of bombing (Littauer and Uphoff, 1972). However, because of his efficiency, many people were killed and the Vietnamese rightly saw the bombing offensive as an aggressive act. The problem is to find the frustration (Berkowitz, 1962).

For examples of learned aggression, consider the experiments that show how easy it is to create situations where children readily imitate aggressive models (for example, Bandura et al., 1973), or, in real life, reflect on those children and adults who model their aggressive behavior on television programs that applaud violence, or, what about the memoirs of the nineteenth-century writer Alfred de Vigny? He wrote: ". . . as I sat on my [father's] knee, I found war seated at my side. He showed me war in his wounds, in the parchments of his ancestors, in their coats of arms, and in their huge armoured portraits that hung in an old chateau in the Beauce. As I saw things, the nobility consisted of one big family of hereditary soldiers, and my sole thought was to grow tall enough to join their ranks" (De Vigny, 1964).

Despite these exceptions to the rule, there is widespread agreement that aggression quite often rests on a foundation of frustration (for example, Aronson, 1976; Berkowitz, 1962). But what is frustration? For example, if I attack when you step on my toes, is my reaction a response to frustration? Or, if you cut me off while driving on a highway and I react by trying to force you into an accident, is my aggression caused by frustration?

The answer is it all depends on your definition of frustration. Dictionaries say *frustration* means to "induce feelings of discouragement"; synonyms for *frustration* include *hinder, thwart, baffle, balk,* and *circumvent.* So, to stretch or not to stretch, that is the question. Berkowitz answers by broadening the concept to include stepping on toes (you hindered my movements), attacks (the mugger is frustrated by the absence of money), and children's fights over toys (you thwarted my playing with that truck). There is nothing wrong with this if we remember the abstractness of the word *frustration.* While it sensitizes us to factors (for example, thwarting, hindering, balking) that provide a solid base for aggression, to move away from the level of grand generalizations, we must introduce other variables.

Consider, for example, culture, personality, and social situation. What frustrates a Mexican might not hinder, thwart, or discourage an American. And what frustrates Tom might not make Dick or Harry balk. So, while it is correct to argue that aggression quite often presupposes frustration, to begin to comprehend the aggression of a society or an individual we must know what *they* consider frustrating, the degree to which those frustrations are institutionalized or are likely to occur, as well as the "unique social and historical situations which increase or decrease the number and intensity of important frustrations." For example, many Americans find it very frustrating to vigorously seek a job and find none. Sometimes this frustration leads to violent crime, and James Q. Wilson notes that the dramatic rise in the number of violent crimes during the sixties is closely associated with a set of social conditions that gave fewer jobs to a rapidly burgeoning portion of the population, youngsters between the ages of sixteen and twenty (Wilson, 1975). So, while high unemployment was certainly not the only cause of a dramatic increase in violent crimes,[3] the point is that, since specific social situations can easily increase or decrease frustration, we must take these into account when trying to explain either mass or individual aggression. Otherwise we remain at the level of an accurate but abstract generalization: aggression quite often presupposes the existence of frustration.

The second half of Dollard et al.'s proposition reads: "the existence of frustration always leads to some form of aggression." Often this is true, but frequently the aggression is indirect (for example, a man hits his wife rather than his boss) and, as above, there are exceptions to the general rule. First is understanding. You might push me, but if we were in a crowded subway car and you said, "Excuse me," I suspect I would not react with aggression. In fact, the frustration might be the start of a pleasant friendship. Second is anger. Frustration often produces anger without any

---

[3] In 1962 the murder rate was 4.5 per 100,000 population; in 1964 the figure was 4.8, in 1966, 5.6, and in 1972, it was 9.4 (Wilson, 1975).

resort to aggression. Assume that you cheated me on a real estate deal, thwarting my attempts to gain a much desired property. Undoubtedly, I would be very angry, but what about a resort to violence? Perhaps. But it is just as likely that I would consider the legal penalties for assault and decide to take you to court instead of a hospital. Third is the person's definition of frustration. Always that definition intervenes between frustration and response and always it is possible to define frustration as beneficial. In America many attend "the school of hard knocks" and teachers say "hard knocks, hard work, long hours, and constant plugging produce results." Here people have no time for frustrations to equal aggression. Setbacks and disappointments are only stumbling blocks on a path leading to success. As the McGuffey readers used to declare: "Try, try again. Why, what other folks can do, why, with patience, should not you? Only keep this rule in view: try, try again" (Wyllie, 1966; Wills, 1971).

Now, while the exceptions show that frustration fails to always produce aggression, a substantial body of evidence argues that frustration is a major cause of aggression (for example, Aronson, 1976). Consider first direct aggression. When the successes of Malcolm X frustrated plans of the Black Muslim leadership, they decided something had to be done; murder was the option chosen (Goldman, 1973). And when the union activities of Cesar Chavez hindered farm owners in California, they resorted to a wide variety of attacks, on persons, on property, on anything that would eliminate this major source of frustration (Matthiessen, 1969).

While direct aggression is one common response to frustration, sometimes a person is unable to attack the source of frustration. Perhaps the frustrater is absent; your father left instructions that you were to stay home—period! Or, perhaps you learned it was wrong to attack the frustrating source; would you hit your grandmother? Or, perhaps the penalties for direct aggression are too great? A number of possibilities come to mind, but no matter how or why direct aggression fails to occur, theory contends the aggression will make an indirect appearance. For example, "the greater the degree of inhibition specific to a more direct act of aggression (for example, hitting one's grandmother), the more probable will be occurrence of less direct acts of aggression" (Dollard et al., 1939). Or, "the stronger the aggressive tendency relative to the restraints against aggression, the more similar this object (the substitute) will be to the frustrater, while the substitute target will be less similar to the instigator the stronger the inhibitions relative to the aggressive tendencies" (Berkowitz, 1962).

Let's consider three examples. Psychologists frustrated young children by placing a wire fence between the youngsters and an attractive pile of toys. Conceivably, the children could have kicked the direct source of frustration—the psychologists—but they managed to control themselves and only gave vent to their frustrations when allowed to play with the toys. Then the children kicked, smashed, and destroyed the toys they were given (Aronson, 1976). Or, in Vietnam soldiers were often frustrated by an enemy that attacked and ran; frequently the direct source of soldier frustration refused to make an appearance. So soldiers consistently took out their aggressions on people they had no inhibitions about hurting, people who were very similar to the direct source of frustration—innocent Vietnamese villagers (Parks, 1968). And third, consider an overseer of slaves in nineteenth-century America. Should he be thwarted by his boss, or in some other way frustrated by him, strong inhibitions existed against striking a plantation owner or other similar whites. But there were few inhibitions against striking members of a group of people very different from the overseer's employer. Consistently, slaves served as a substitute target for overseer aggressions (Stampp, 1956).

In sum, frustration is a major cause of aggression. And if a person is unable or unwilling to attack the direct source of frustration, he or she will often seek to displace aggressions on a substitute target. Always, the need to be aggressive and the intensity of response is dependent on a number of variables—for example, the importance of the frustration to the person or group, culture beliefs that foster or inhibit violence, the immediate positive or negative influence of others—and always it is possible that even the most serious and important frustrations need not lead to aggression, to a desire to injure others. The British missionary-explorer David Livingstone worked two years and managed to possibly convert one native to Christianity. Believing he had a mission to spread the Gospels, Livingstone was obviously frustrated by continual failure. However, instead of trying to injure others, Livingstone's overall response was optimism. He concluded that Christianity must wait until the African continent was wide open for European colonists. And so, despite frustration after frustration, Livingstone died trying to find a way for "legitimate commerce" to begin the Christianizing of Africa (Jeal, 1973).

So far the discussion has neglected the individual. Now we briefly turn to the development of personality, and more specifically, the "unique" self-image. For some people possess aggression as a personality trait; they are much more likely than others to respond to frustration with quick and intense aggression. And while a number of variables can help to explain aggressive personalities, a very important one is the influence of significant others on the development of attitudes toward self and world.

Refer again to our discussion of parental discipline (in Chapter Two). While warmth is associated with self-esteem, hostility is associated with self-hatred and aggression (Becker, 1964; May, 1972; Frank, 1967). This is so for many reasons. Harsh discipline is frustrating; children's anger often turns into aggression against others. The classic example is the bully. Second, aggressive parents provide a model for the child's behavior. Children need not identify with parents in order to imitate them; and especially if the model exists without any mitigating forces (for example, love from one of the parents), children are likely to embrace it (McCord and McCord, 1957). Third, and perhaps most important, is the "I's" response to the hostility of others. For example, the evidence indicates that growing up in a hostile environment, Adolf Hitler developed intense feelings of inferiority. But his response to these feelings was to deny them by emphasizing his own greatness and displacing his aggression on others. Tragically, history allowed him to link this assertion of greatness to cultural themes (identification with the Aryan "race," desire to overcome German's humiliation at Versailles, hundreds of years of anti-Semitism) with the eventual result being Nazi Germany (Gilbert, 1950; Bullock, 1962; Fromm, 1973; Stern, 1975; Speer, 1970).[4]

Now it was not stated that Hitler's self-image produced Nazi Germany. The Nazis' rise to power was a very complex process. But Hitler's ability to link "unique" self-image to cultural themes allows us to make an important point about many aggressive people; in everyday life their "unique" self-image is linked to social identities and often they use these identities to gain esteem as well as get rid of aggressions.

Consider two examples, the first Sirhan Sirhan, the assassin of Robert Kennedy. Apparently, Sirhan had a very difficult childhood, one that produced a poor enough image of self to convince Sirhan that people were constantly trying to hurt him. Now in everyday life Sirhan might have tried to mask his fears and aggressions, but when Robert Kennedy made statements supporting Israel, Sirhan decided to embrace the identity of patriot. For the war was important to Sirhan and since Kennedy was obviously trying to hurt Arab interests, Sirhan decided to kill him. In effect, the need to be a patriot had its deepest roots in a terrible unique image of self and, by embracing a prestigious social identity, Sirhan achieved a sense of esteem normally absent. As one court psychiatrist noted, "He apparently preferred to think of himself as a sane patriot and be convicted of the assassination—rather than face his psychotic behavior . . ." (Coleman, 1972).

Another example comes from the literature on prejudice and ethnocentrism. Prejudice is learned by "everyone" as part of the cultural inheritance, but studies show that some people need to hate others. Often a hostile childhood wills the person a very poor self-image, and the individual responds by combining underlying self-contempt with self-glorification. Instead of facing their own intense doubts, like Hitler, many people pro-

---

[4] In *Spandau*, Albert Speer wrote that Hitler loved the destructive force of fire. It "stirred a profound excitement in him." Speer recalled Hitler's "ordering showings in the Chancellery of the films of burning London, of the sea of flames over Warsaw, of exploding convoys, and the rapture with which he watched those films" (Speer, 1976).

ject their feelings of hostility on to groups whose inferior status is confirmed by the culture. And while any culture furnishes a variety of targets, "the nearest to the all-duty scapegoat is a religious, ethnic, or race group. Having permanence and stability, they can be given a definite status and stereotyped as a group." In sum, for psychological problems, the society furnishes ready-made social-psychological solutions (Allport, 1958; also Adorno et al., 1969; Rokeach, 1960).

The outline of factors associated with aggression shows that, like prejudice, aggression is both sociological and psychological. Some people need to take out aggression on others, and many of us learn identities (for instance, soldier) that demand aggressive behavior—even if we lack personality problems—in a wide variety of social situations. In real life these underlying variables (for example, self-concept, learned aggression) combine with factors on the level of immediate social conditions, and any comprehensive theory of aggression must show how underlying predispositions are linked to everyday situations. However, in the absence of a grand theory, and as a preface to our discussion of war, let us try to sort out some of the relationships among a learned identity (man), personality, and the aggressions that occur in many modern societies.

MANHOOD AND AGGRESSION

Only people make culture. And only people have the ability to institutionalize a set of beliefs, values, and practices that, acting like a doubled-up branch, snaps back upon the holder and does violence to self or others. Naturally, the branch need not snap back; but the potential is always there. Tension and the power to hurt are inherent in any doubled-up branch; and they are also inherent in contemporary beliefs about the meaning of manhood.

David and Brannon (1976) argue that others teach manhood by stressing four themes. First is "no sissy stuff." For as the dictionary notes, a sissy is "a timid or cowardly person." And since men need to be bold, brave, and courageous, others teach boys to be men by using women as a negative reference group (see Chapter Eight). Ideally, "a 'real man' must never, never resemble women" for they possess timid and cowardly characteristics. Very early boys involuntarily assume the attitudes of others: "They're telling me that if I think or act like a woman I embrace a negative identity. So, I better shun any of the 'soft' characteristics in order to be what others want me to be: a man."

A stress on "no sissy stuff" is negative; the boy learns what he is not, he learns what he must avoid if he wishes to have self-esteem. But attached to negative attitudes about self and world are a host of beliefs and practices that root a man's self-respect in a learned approval of violence and aggression. Take the stress on "the sturdy oak." David and Brannon define this as the demand that boys display an "air of toughness, confidence, and self-reliance." For example, during the fifties in Brooklyn a boy respected by his peers was "hard," and those most esteemed were "rocks." Apparently, a man has to be unbreakable; to open up (for example, about personal problems) is to show the vulnerability of a woman, and to be less than tough and strong suggests an unwillingness to fight, a reluctance to engage in the battles that are a proving ground for manhood.

A third theme of man-makers is "the Big Wheel." Men are expected to succeed, to reach a rung on the ladder of success that grants status by forcing others to look up to those who had the wherewithal to make the climb. Generally others applaud large amounts of success in anything (David and Brannon, 1976), even musical conducting or intellectual work, but if an individual manages to succeed in the military or in sports, his achievements are especially noteworthy. At once the person is a "sturdy oak," successful, and a perfect model for the fourth stress of man-makers, "the aura of aggression, violence, and daring."

David and Brannon call this the "Give 'Em Hell!" theme. Seekers of power, men must be prepared to fight for what they want. In adolescence, lower-class boys often "give 'em hell" by engaging in gang fights, for stomping an opponent to a bloody pulp is proof the boy is a "tough customer," a person no one can push around. And while upper-class boys normally avoid gang fights, they still know how to "give 'em hell." In fact, should an upper-class man become president, he could mirror the beliefs of the late President Kennedy. Afraid that Premier Khrushchev might think he was young and inexperienced, that he "had no guts," Kennedy felt he had to act. And since Vietnam was the only place there was a real challenge, America would make its power credible, and Kennedy would give Khrushchev hell, by daring to use violence in Indochina (see, for example, Fasteau, 1974; Halberstam, 1972; Barnet, 1972).

All together these four themes (no sissy stuff, the sturdy oak, the Big Wheel, Give 'Em Hell) ask boys to become men who will at least see the need for, and respect the use of, power and aggression in everyday life. Ideally, all men should always applaud the use of violence, but in reality other beliefs and values (for example, love thy enemy, make peace not war, cooperate rather than fight) compete with the themes of manhood, and the result is a society in which most men are able to walk through life without daily engaging in a series of conflicts and fights. However, the stress on strength, toughness, and guts is still *the* foundation for our society's definition of the social identity *man* and, if most men normally avoid violence, when they meet frustration or harbor a poor unique image of self, they often solve their problems by becoming "real men."

Consider first an example from Hans Toch's *Violent Men* (1969). The subject "was flooded all his life with strong feelings of not being able to be what he should be." Especially in any sort of verbal exchange, he was easily scared. Continually, he felt he would fail; at bottom he had a very poor "unique" image of self. So, since the self is a transsituational variable (see Chapter One), this man carried the image of failure with him at all times. In fact, as a youngster, he was afraid "that if he got into physical combat he would not be able to take punishment" (that is, they're telling me I must be a sturdy oak). But, over time he found he could take a beating and he also discovered that if he carefully chose his opponents, he could beat others. This was very helpful. Others began to praise him (that is, he earned esteem by giving 'em hell) with the result that this man resorted to violence whenever he was plagued by "a feeling of guilt, of being scared and of a lack of worthwhileness." As Toch noted, this man "goes out of his way to provoke fights to show he isn't afraid. He tackles the first 'bully' he meets in a juvenile institution; he calls another one 'punk' shortly thereafter; he arrives at a party mad at one of his friends and proceeds to show him how well he could have licked him by assaulting the first man he comes across. . . . And in every instance in which his little demonstration succeeds, he feels great. . . . There are a few moments of regret . . . but by and large he feels good both after picking a fight and after stomping his opponent" (Toch, 1969).

If the social identity "real man" furnishes one violent means of compensating for a poor "unique" image of self, a similar process is at work in many crimes of rape. However, here the motivating focus is often typical rather than unique. For what statistics we have indicate that the vast majority of rapes are committed by lower-class men on lower-class women (Brownmiller, 1975; Griffin, 1975). Apparently, the stress on toughness and aggression is emphasized with peculiar force in the lower classes, and one result of this decided stress (for example, Brown, 1970) is rape. Often it is a group of boys out for a "good time"; the society and particularly the lower-class subculture has few inhibitions about attacking a woman, and the boys prove their manhood by sexual aggression. Or, in some cases, rape is committed by one individual. Naturally, motivations vary, but a prime cause appears to be the frustrations that lower-class men consistently meet. Unable to get jobs, much less get ahead, the men are unable or unwilling to vent their aggressions against the larger society. But there are few inhibitions about attacking a very convenient substitute, women, and there are few better ways for real men to assert their power, strength, and virility than by engaging in sexual intercourse. All at once the man gains esteem, power, and, apparently, pleasure (Brownmiller, 1975; see also Lang, 1969).

So far the examples have been "pathological." Perhaps it is true that the social identity *man* teaches people to be aggressive and perhaps it is also true that when men meet frustrations (for example, about jobs or about unique self-images), any aggression that follows is often both rooted in, and strengthened by, the social identity *man*. But what about normal men, those who never even think of rape, those who rarely if ever engage in violent behavior? Can we show a close association between the social identity *man* and the violence that normal men sometimes commit?

We can. And the example is war. Rhetoric has it that men fight in wars because they are patriotic or because they love their system of government or because they wish to eradicate the world's wrongs. Sometimes rhetoric is right. But generally it is quite wrong. Most men (or at least those Americans who fought in World Wars I and II, Korea, and Vietnam) take part in war because they saw few viable alternatives, and while a number of factors explain behavior once men enter the military (see, for example, Marshall, 1947; Gray, 1970; Janowitz, 1964; Moskos, 1970), an important source of combat motivation is the social identity *man*. Consider World War II. Seeking to find a sense of personal commitment to the war, investigators discovered none. But they did find "that behavior in combat was recognized as a test of being a man." In fact, the ideal of masculinity filled a good part of the void left by the absence of patriotic or altruistic motives. Not only were "courage and aggressiveness (guts)" a "prime ingredient of the combat man's notion of a good soldier," for privates and noncommissioned officers, they were the characteristics "mentioned more often than any others." In the words of one soldier:

> One time me and another guy were in a hole. The guy says, "Let's get out of here." I talked to him (tried to calm him down) but he never was a soldier—did typewriting, ran errands for officers. He was a suck-ass for a colonel, not a real soldier. A real soldier is a guy—he'll drink and swear—but he relies on himself; a guy that can take care of himself.[5]

To summarize: First, I have tried to suggest some of the relationships that exist between aggression and the unique and typical frustrations of men. Frustration produces aggression, but it does so in league with and (to a relative degree) because of the social identity of man. Second, I have tried to show that the social identity *man* is an important and learned cause of aggression in many modern societies. Finally, I have tried to show that one important reason men fight in wars is their desire to show self and others they are "real men." Of course, that desire tells us little about the manner or frequency of wars, but it does hopefully provide a fitting preface to the next question in this chapter: What is war?

---

[5] For World War I, see Fernandez, 1975; for Korea, Janowitz, 1964; for Vietnam, Moskos, 1970.

WHAT IS WAR?

The first consideration to note about war is the prime importance of group, of sociological factors. Aggression may be a human constant but aggression is not war. Thousands of men never enter a battlefield because Jack or Sam or Harry is boiling over with aggression. Thousands of men enter a battlefield and fight in a similar way because of common beliefs and practices. To take one example, consider Harold Lasswell's early study of propaganda in World War I. Lasswell showed that propaganda cannot work unless it makes sense to "all" the people. The atrocity stories, stresses on war guilt, analyses of war aims: these are common themes of all nations at war. What is different is the way in which each nation tells the truth. The American assumed he was fighting to save democracy, the German to preserve "kultur," the Englishman to purge the world of German militarism. In brief, a propagandist's success "depends upon traditional prejudices, objective conditions between nations, plus the changing level of popular irritability. And no matter how skillful the propagandist may be in organizing his staff, selecting suggestions, and exploiting instruments of transmission, his manipulative skills will go for nought if there is no favorable juxtaposition of social forces to aid them" (Lasswell, 1928).

Agreed. War is at bottom a sociological phenomenon. But what is war? War is a social invention, a tragic product of people's ability to make and remake social reality. Among preliterate groups there were many origins and causes of war: they settled disputes, appeased the gods, attained prestige for the warriors, and sometimes occurred because of economic factors. But the one constant is that war was and is socially constructed; everywhere it is the end product of only human manufacturers (Turney-High, 1948; Mead, 1940).

Unfortunately, because war has served some important purposes, no matter where we find it, we also discover that war is *institutionalized*. War is humanly made, but when the initial inventor dies, the creation becomes a part of the cultural heritage. Of course, as time passes others add to, and subtract from, the original product. Yet the net result is the same: with alterations, war becomes an established part of the cultural heritage. For in the same way that people embrace beliefs and practices associated with religion or economics or politics, they embrace war beliefs and practices that direct them down the approved cultural paths.

By far institutionalization is the most important underlying principle of human behavior found in all wars, no matter what the historical period. For while hatred and warmongering militarists are sometimes central to explaining war, institutionalization is the key to any adequate understanding of the power and persistence of war throughout human history. For example, the Dugum Dani of New Guinea often fight wars. But the Dani fight because their gods say they must. The Dani do not, and would not, fight for Jesus or Muhammad or democracy or communism. They fight in a particular manner (for example, they use spears and engage in raids more often than formal battles) and for causes that are relatively unique to Dani culture. Their warfare can only be understood in terms of the development of that culture and of the effects of making war a dominant institution in it (Heider, 1970; Matthiessen, 1970).

Better than anyone else, Emile Durkheim understood the significance of institutionalizing certain beliefs and practices. He stressed that by making something an established part of the culture, people also "guaranteed" that those beliefs and practices would exert a constraining—even determining—effect on the exposed individuals. Durkheim called such phenomena "social facts." And that is exactly what war is: a social fact. For wherever war is found, it is a complex of beliefs and practices that, by means of socialization, constrains groups of humans to think and act in a particular manner (Durkheim, 1958).

Consider three more examples. In the seventeenth-century Spanish army the rank and file often went on strike. When dissatisfied with their treatment, the entire force might refuse to obey orders. Only after "collective bargaining" settled the issues would soldiers submit to the wishes of their officers (Cruickshank, 1966). Or, take the Roman soldier's concern with livers. Before a declaration of war, a sacrifice was performed, and since the Stoics maintained that the liver was a microcosm of the working universe, the condition of the sacrificed animal's liver was an important omen of success or failure. In Rome a group of sixty citizens—haruspices—existed to interpret the meaning of a sacrificed animal's liver (Ogilvie, 1970). Or, finally, consider a custom common in eighteenth-century Europe and America: the honors of war. When a fortress surrendered, and especially if the besieged had been brave, the victors accorded the vanquished the honors of war. Defeated soldiers were allowed to leave a fortress with their arms, to play music of their own choosing, and to carry provisions to feed themselves on the way to their destination. At the French fortress of Hille in 1708, the besieged conducted themselves with so much valor that the defeated Marshall Boufflers was allowed to write the terms of his own capitulation (Wright, 1963).

The examples should make a point: while war is socially and historically relative, wherever it exists, it is also a social institution, a complex of preexisting beliefs, values, and practices that constrains people—in and through socialization—to accept the particular institution of war they arbitrarily inherited. Always people decide to remake or reject their inheritance, but since they can do so only after *first* receiving the inheritance from others, if others accept the institution, the probability is high that children will say yes to their significant and generalized others.

Now, while war is a social institution, it never stands alone. Always it is a more or less integrated aspect of the cultural whole; and always explanations of war's influence are possible only if we also know how war does or does not harmonize with the rest of the culture. The historian Alfred Vagts once defined militarism as "every system of thinking and valuing and every complex of feelings which rank military institutions and ways above the way of civilian life, carrying military mentality and modes of acting and decision into the civilian sphere" (Vagts, 1959). Well, social psychologically, a culture is militaristic if religious, political, economic, and kinship institutions teach and affirm beliefs, values, and practices conducive to war.

Consider an example from religion. Since medieval times, Christian churches have preached the doctrine of "just war." People must love their enemy and that means war is justified only when a king or a country's intentions are pure, that is, war is always defensive. But, despite this serious attempt to limit war, a problem with "just war" theory is the nature of perception. It is always interpolated and the historical result has almost always been the ability to "doctor and manipulate" intention (Merton, 1971) so that every king or every nation always fights a just war. Conceivably, church leaders could force a potentially significant role conflict—between the person as citizen and the person as Christian—but when they agree that a war is just, religious institutions harmonize with the war and political institutions. God's imprimatur is placed on the banner of war (Wells, 1967).

In sum, war is a complex of institutionalized beliefs, values, and practices. Wherever it exists, it is a more or less established and more or less harmonious part of the cultural whole. And this means that war's relationship to military institutions and to the larger culture is dialectical. By establishing the norms of belief and conduct, war sets the norms of behavior for soldiers; but by sometimes rejecting and changing those norms, soldiers reconstruct war. Equally important, while war can change culture (for example, by establishing precedents for presidential power), culture can change war. In fact, two of the propositions discussed in the next section focus on the degree to which political, economic, and scientific changes have—since about 1800—revolutionized the war institution.

PROPOSITIONS ABOUT WAR

1. To the extent that a society is highly industrialized, it has the potential to mobilize much larger portions of the population, for much longer periods of time, than societies with little or low levels of industrialization.

Right up to 1914 it was unusual for any society to mobilize more than 1 or 2 percent of a population. At times Napoleon managed to mobilize 5 percent of the French people, but the real change came in 1914. When Germany had four million men under arms and the British eventually reached five million, fully 10 percent of the total population of the two nations was mobilized. And in World War II the figures were even higher; the percentage of the people mobilized was Germany, 14 percent; Japan, 13 percent; the United States, 12 percent; France, 13 percent; the Soviet Union, 13 percent; Great Britain, 12 percent (see Wright, 1964; Preston et al., 1965).

Machines offer one explanation for the sudden and dramatic increase in the number of people mobilized. For in preliterate warrior bands, the armies of Hannibal and Caesar, or the British and Russian forces in the Crimean War (1854), the ability to transport men and supplies was limited by a lack of technology. Poor roads were an obvious example, but right up to the twentieth century the animal-drawn vehicle was the chief means of supplying soldiers. Railroads began to change this, but men in trains were relatively unable to defend themselves; they could not be brought to the battlefield in trains, and it was certainly unwise to carry trainloads of supplies to the front. Instead, men and supplies were deposited at a depot and then slowly and ponderously taken by animals to the scene of battle. But even then the columns of supply had to be limited. Otherwise the roads would become clogged and the possibility of maneuvering limited to a "straight forward advance" (Maurice, 1928; Wright, 1964; Ropp, 1962).

With the appearance of the internal combustion engine, the "problems" that had faced Hannibal, Caesar, and Moltke[6] began to disappear. By 1914 Europe had a complete network of trains; the truck traveled six times faster than a horse and carried three to four times the load of even the strongest animals (Maurice, 1928). Suddenly trains could deliver the goods and trucks could then get much larger amounts of ammunition and food to the soldiers, much more quickly than the horse, and without the problem of clogged roads. Obviously, as trucks were improved, and along with them, trains, roads, boats, and airplanes, the chances of supplying soldiers increased proportionately.

Machines are one part of the story. Another is science, especially medicine. Before 1914 disease often killed more soldiers than even the fiercest enemy. Cholera was the problem in the Crimea, malaria when Americans fought the Spanish in Cuba. But with the advance of science came the possibility of keeping huge armies healthy for long periods of time. All at once millions of men could be supplied and sent out to kill one another without fear of disease.

---

[6] Head of the German forces in the Franco-Prussian War of 1871.

Now, despite their importance, better machines and medicines only give people the potential to mobilize and maintain good health for large portions of the population for long periods of time. No one had to use trucks to supply soldiers and no one had to take over factories, ration civilian consumption, use the society's productive capacities to keep the soldiers in the field, or channel unprecedented power into the hands of political and military leaders. Always machines provide a potential, but people decide to use or not use that potential. For example, except for some use by Americans in Vietnam, since its introduction during World War I, people have generally refrained from chemical and biological warfare. Probably, the motive is fear, that is, if one side uses it, the other will too, but the point is that people always have the ability to say no to even the greatest technological "advances." Machines are not to blame; the responsibility lies with people, the only makers of culture.

2. To the extent that a society is rooted in allegiance to traditions, there is an institutionalized limit on the kind and amount of violence that will normally occur. However, to the extent that a society is rooted in an allegiance to law, reason, and science, the limit tends to collapse; indeed, societies rooted in reason institutionalize the need for ever more terrible strategies, tactics, and weaponry (for example, Weber, 1947).

By definition a tradition looks back in time. It is a behest from the past that inheritors are not supposed to change. So, if a society is rooted in tradition, the tendency is toward repetition; and in the extreme, yesterday, today, and tomorrow all bear close resemblance to one another. Militarily the result is a commitment to fight, generation after generation, in the same way.

Consider these examples. In Plains Indian warfare the aim of combatants was to touch an opponent with a coup stick and then quickly depart from the battlefield. If this was impossible, armed conflict took place, but tradition still had it that the main aim of battle was the number of coups amassed. Or, take the Roman soldiers use of the sword and pilum. Because of their allegiance to tradition and the (linked) relative absence of technological advances, Roman soldiers used these same weapons for nearly seven hundred years. Or, finally, consider the pleas (in the 1740s) of the French Marshal de Saxe. Tradition had it that when a battle ended, the victors never pursued the defeated. De Saxe said this was ridiculous; wipe out the enemy at once. But, despite his pleas, de Saxe noted that his colleagues always had one response: " 'Tis contrary to custom" (Phillips, 1960; Hoebel, 1960).

By means of its allegiance to the past, any society rooted in tradition put an inherent check on social change; after all, if the old ways were revered, why seek new methods of killing one another? And of course people disobey traditions; the norms of any society were violated. But to the extent that traditions were followed, there was normally a limit on the kind and amount of violence that occurred. For example, despite an avowed aim of exterminating the enemy, the Jibaro would often fail to achieve their goal. For enemy territory was filled with a host of "secret supernatural dangers," and the Jibaro always tried to leave enemy territory as quickly as possible (see Karsten, 1967).

In modern societies, societies dominated by law, reason, and science, traditions lose their sense of legitimacy. Naturally, the process is never complete (for instance, the family), but once reason is in the saddle, unchanging and unquestioned patterns of thought and action no longer make sense (they are unreasonable) to large portions of the population. Slowly but persistently, efficiency, effectiveness, competency, and technical skills become important goals of many people; and to the extent that they do so, a taken-for-granted acceptance of traditions becomes anachronistic.

Consider this example. When the French under Napoleon defeated the Prussians at Jena and Auersted in 1806, the defeat led to revolutionary changes in Prussia's military organization. Leaders saw the irrelevance of many traditions and decided to prepare for future wars by relying heavily on reason. For example, where nobility had been the eighteenth-century requirement for leadership, now it became knowledge and education. Ideally, anyone who had the skill and ability could lead Prussian troops. And, to institutionalize this emphasis on reason, Prussian leaders established (in 1810) the Kriegsakademie, the first war college where people made a concerted effort to make war a science, and officers, rather than inept aristocrats, were to become skilled professionals (Craig, 1956; Shanahan, 1945; Huntington, 1957; Liddell-Hart, 1946).

Overall, the Kriegsakademie became significant for at least two reasons. First, when other Western nations made major changes in their military institutions, the Prussian army was almost always the ideal. For instance, Prussia was in Elihu Root's thought when he reorganized America's military at the turn of the twentieth century. Second, when war becomes a science, the desire for change, for possible rejection of tradition, is institutionalized. Now war is studied objectively and if inherited strategies and tactics no longer suffice, they must be scrapped and replaced by the products of reason (Hittle, 1961; Irvine, 1935).

To "prove" this point, consider the effects of World War I on military strategy. Officers were surprised by the war's length; was there no way to break the deadlock of trench warfare? Yes, there was. Instead of killing soldiers, attack civilians. Destroy the factories that supply soldiers and undermine the morale of the labor force by a campaign of terror bombing that will frighten civilians into demanding their government's surrender (Liddell-Hart, 1925; Mead, 1966; Vernier, 1966; Spaight, 1930).

Now this tactic—strategic bombing—made great sense. It did not have to succeed, but it was at least a logical and reasonable means of avoiding the deadlock of 1914–18. Unfortunately, this strategy went against nearly three hundred years of tradition. Since the end of the Thirty Years' War civilians were a forbidden military target. Naturally, war did kill innocent people, but up until the twentieth century soldiers felt it was immoral to systematically and deliberately attack civilians. As the American naval captain, W. S. Pye, said in 1925, theories of strategic bombing struck "at the root of civilization. . . . Is this nation which fought for the preservation of international law and the sacredness of treaties to adopt this theory of ruthlessness? . . . Are we to become the baby killers and the 'boches' of the future? The civilized world would stand aghast at any such decision made by the United States of America" (Spaight, 1930).

Perhaps Captain Pye was right in 1925. But by 1940 many military men (and especially those in Great Britain) were committed to a policy of strategic bombing. And as the years went by, tradition rapidly gave way to reason and military necessity. The British were the first to begin systematic terror bombing (in March of 1942) and when General Curtis LeMay arrived in the Pacific theater in 1945, his tactics were eminently sensible. Japanese buildings were made of wood and, in contrast to Germany, industry was not concentrated in factories, but widely dispersed. So, use magnesium and napalm. ". . . Magnesium makes the hottest fire, and it'll get things going where probably the napalm might not. But the napalm will splatter further, cover a greater area. We've got to mix it up" (LeMay, 1965; see also Spaight, 1944).

And they did. The first attacks on Tokyo burned up "sixteen square miles of the world's largest city." And with fires that were seen from a distance of 150 miles, the bombing killed over 98,000 people. That is 20,000 more than died at Hiroshima. Or, in General LeMay's words, *"No other air attack of the war, either in Japan or Europe, was so destructive of life and property"* (LeMay, 1965, emphasis in original).

Strategic bombing is only one instance of war utilizing reason. And the examples from Great Britain and America could easily be supplemented by others from Germany, Japan, or, today, Russia and China. However, the overall point is that if war becomes a science, new strategies, tactics, and weaponry are not only to be expected, they are *required* by the institutionalized demands of war colleges, air universities, and research and development firms (think tanks). Always traditions (whether of strategy or morality) can resist change, but if a society's citizens sink their deepest roots into values such as efficiency, effectiveness, and expertise, the resistance is usually weak and short-lived. For example, the Nuremberg trials supposedly affirmed immutable principles of morality, but seven years later, in Korea, United Nations troops systematically bombed dams in North Korea. And they did it in May because destruction then would destroy the rice crop and hopefully produce the famine that was the strategy's ultimate goal (Rees, 1970).

3. To limit war, it is crucial to have powerful social institutions that never blindly accept its onset and continuance. To the extent that these institutions are nonexistent, wars are easier to begin, difficult to question, and harder to end.

This proposition follows from the definition of war as a social institution. Always war does or does not harmonize with the society's other institutions and, where it fails to harmonize, the possibilities of limiting and questioning war are more or less great, relative to the social power of the dissenting institution(s). For example, the Roman Catholic Church was powerful during the Middle Ages and it often succeeded in limiting war. Conflict was forbidden on certain days of the week and the Church acted to prevent introduction of the crossbow because the weapon was deemed uncivilized. Or, to jump to today, Barnet and Müller argue that multinational corporations are increasingly using their great power to check and limit war. For companies such as GM or ITT, nationalism is anachronistic. Their market is the world,[7] their chief goal profit-maximization, and that means "it is in their (the multinationals') interest that the game of nations be transformed from a military duel which no one can win and which threatens all their dreams." As one General Electric executive noted, "I think getting GE into China and the Soviet Union is the biggest thing we can do for world peace" (Barnet and Müller, 1974).

Only time will tell who is right, but in assessing the executive's remarks one should recall a book written by Nobel Peace Prize winner Norman Angell in 1909. The book was *The Great Illusion,* and its theme was the argument that war was no longer profitable. World leaders believed war produced benefits but Angell argued that European economies were so intertwined that even if Great Britain defeated Germany, the loss of British investments in Germany would later attack Britain's economy. So, given the realities of the world economy (in 1909), it was senseless to fight a war that would destroy a nation's capital and its future profits.

Angell's book was an instant success. It was read by many, agreed with, and then discarded in 1914. Economic institutions proved less powerful than traditional political rivalries and far less powerful than the notions of national honor and patriotism. Perhaps things are different today. This is possible. But Angell's book is stressed here to suggest that despite the great power of economic institutions, perhaps other institutions and beliefs are more powerful than the lure of profit. Perhaps if we seek to limit war, we should focus on the kinship institutions that are "the" sources for notions of masculinity or on the political institutions that applaud ideas such as nationalism, power, patriotism, and national honor.

4. At birth people are neither good nor evil; they are potential. But to

---

[7] Barnet and Müller note that the top 298 United States-based multinationals earn 40 percent of their entire net profits outside the United States.

the extent that political, economic, and religious leaders are pessimistic about human nature, they will use their pessimism as a justification for recourse to violence. And since war sets up a set of social situations designed to bring out the worst in people, war confirms the leaders' beliefs about human nature and so continually proves an assumption dangerous to themselves and their people: wars are necessary and inevitable (Merton, 1971).

At bottom this proposition deals with role-taking. Can anyone accurately assess another's role if he enters interaction assuming the other is wicked or bad? Isn't it incumbent on the assumer to look for hidden motives in a perhaps innocent proposal? And isn't empathy difficult, if not impossible, when one person is sure the other is out to "get him" as soon as the opportunity arises? If a conflict develops, doesn't the presumption of malevolence call for force? Isn't it the only thing these people understand? And, finally, if the assumer leads a world power, doesn't the presumption of malevolence produce a superior image of self? With all those people harboring a "universal taste for violence," isn't it his duty to maintain order? And using the violence lovers as a comparative reference group, aren't we, the civilized few, the only ones capable of squaring the circle, of using force to produce peace (Barnet, 1972)?

Since different cultures (and subcultures) teach different assumptions about human nature, the presumption of malevolence is socially and historically relative. But wherever Christianity has established itself, many people often accept the idea of innate evil, a return to the concept of original sin. People are born evil and only by submitting themselves to God can they be cleansed. And even then people must be on guard; the world is full of sinners and a host of temptations. Watch out for the Eves offering apples or, as the Calvinists taught when they took the notion of evil to its logical conclusion, "Trust no one. Only God should be your confidant," (for example, Weber, 1958).

Now, in analyzing particular wars, it is often difficult to accurately assess the significance of a presumption of malevolence. In Vietnam, for example, many government leaders expressed profound pessimism about human nature, but since their remarks were generally intertwined with a hatred of communism, it is impossible to say whether pessimism about people was more important than a hatred of communism in moving these men to say yes to war. However, since pessimism is more basic and diffuse than a hatred of communism (for example, a leader can be on guard against fascists, monarchies, and other democracies) and since it can easily serve as the cornerstone of a person's world-view, it is reasonable to assume that a presumption of malevolence distorts role-taking abilities in many more situations than the hatred of any particular ideology. Indeed, perhaps a presumption of malevolence provides the firmest and deepest source of our willingness to accept—as a societal taken-for-granted—the existence of war as a powerful and permanent social institution.

Reflect, for example, on the following statement by the Protestant theologian Reinhold Niebuhr, a man whose thinking has influenced many of America's recent leaders. Niebuhr argues: "All social cooperation on a larger scale than the most intimate social group requires a measure of coercion." And those who deny this fail to see "that the limitations of the human imagination, the easy subservience of reason to prejudice and passion, particularly in group behavior, make social conflict an inevitability in human history, probably to its very end" (Niebuhr, 1960).

To sum up: Since war is an institutionalized complex of beliefs and practices, it exerts a constraining effect on the people who inherit it. And that means if we seek to limit, much less eliminate war, we must analyze the institution and its relationship to other aspects of the culture. Only then can we accurately assess the enemy (for example, taken-for-granted assumptions about masculinity or the relationship between strategic "progress" and our commitment to values such as efficiency or objectivity) and only then can we begin to destroy an institution that may soon destroy us.

Bibliographical References

Adorno, T. W.; Frenkel-Brunswik, Else; Levinson, Daniel J.; and Sanford, R. Nevitt. *The Authoritarian Personality*. New York: Norton, 1969.

Allport, Gordon. *The Nature of Prejudice*. Garden City, N.Y.: Doubleday Anchor, 1958.

Angell, Norman. *The Great Illusion*. New York: Putnam, 1909.

The Armed Forces Officer. Washington, D.C.: Government Printing Office, 1965.

Armine, Michael. *The Great Decision*. New York: Putnam, 1959.

Aronson, Elliot, ed. *Readings About the Social Animal*. San Francisco: Freeman, 1973.

Aronson, Elliot. *The Social Animal*. 2d ed. San Francisco: Freeman, 1976.

Bandura, Albert; Ross, Dorothea; and Ross, Sheila. "Transmission of Aggression Through Imitation of Aggressive Models." In *Readings About the Social Animal*, edited by Elliot Aronson. San Francisco: Freeman, 1973.

Barnet, Richard. *The Roots of War: The Men and Institutions Behind U.S. Foreign Policy*. New York: Atheneum, 1972.

Barnet, Richard, and Müller, Ronald. *Global Reach: The Power of the Multinational Corporations*. New York: Simon and Schuster, 1975.

Batchelder, Robert. *The Irreversible Decision*. New York: Macmillan, 1961.

Becker, Wesley. "Consequences of Different Kinds of Parental Discipline." In *Review of Child Development Research,* edited by Martin L. Hoffman and Lois W. Hoffman. New York: Russell Sage, 1964.
Berkowitz, Leonard. *Aggression: A Social Psychological Analysis.* New York: McGraw-Hill, 1962.
Bohannan, Paul, ed. *Law and Warfare.* Garden City, N.Y.: Natural History Press, 1967.
Bowman, Allen. *The Morale of the Revolutionary Army.* Washington, D.C.: Public Affairs, 1943.
Brown, H. Rap. *Die Nigger Die!* New York: Dial, 1970.
Brownmiller, Susan. *Against Our Will.* New York: Simon and Schuster, 1975.
Bullock, Alan. *Hitler: A Study in Tyranny.* Rev. ed. New York: Harper & Row, 1962.
Buss, Arnold. *The Psychology of Aggression.* New York: Wiley, 1961.
Chagnon, Napoleon. *The Yanomamo: The Fierce People.* New York: Holt, Rinehart & Winston, 1968.
Clark, Ramsey. *Crime in America.* New York: Pocket Books, 1971.
Clausewitz, Carl Von. *On War.* Baltimore: Penguin, 1968.
Coleman, James. *Abnormal Psychology and Modern Life.* 4th ed. Glenview: Scott, Foresman, 1972.
Craig, Gordon. *Politics of the Prussian Army, 1640–1945.* New York: Oxford University Press, 1956.
Cruickshank, C. G. *Elizabeth's Army.* New York: Oxford University Press, 1966.
David, Deborah S., and Brannon, Robert, eds. *The Forty-Nine Percent Majority: Readings on the Male Sex Role.* Reading, Mass.: Addison-Wesley, 1976.
Davie, Maurice. *The Evolution of War.* New Haven: Yale University Press, 1929.
De Vigny, Alfred. *The Military Condition.* New York: Oxford University Press, 1964.
Dollard, John; Doob, Leonard; Miller, Neal E.; Mowrer, O. H.: and Sears, Robert R. *Frustration and Aggression.* New Haven: Yale University Press, 1939.
Durkheim, Emile. *The Rules of the Sociological Method.* New York: Free Press, 1958.
Fasteau, Marc Feigen. *The Male Machine.* New York: McGraw-Hill, 1974.
Fernandez, Ronald. "Obliteration Bombing." *The Humanist* (March–April 1973): 14–18.
Frank, Jerome D. *Sanity and Survival.* New York: Vintage, 1967.
Frederick the Great. "The Instruction of Frederick the Great for His Generals, 1747." In *Roots of Strategy,* edited by Major Thomas R. Phillips. Harrisburg: Military Service Publishing Company, 1940.

Freud, Sigmund. *Why War?* Open Letter Series, vol. 2. Paris: League of Nations International Institute of Intellectual Cooperation, 1933.

Fromm, Erich. *The Anatomy of Human Destructiveness.* New York: Holt, Rinehart & Winston, 1973.

Gerth, Hans, and Mills, C. Wright. *Character and Social Structure: The Psychology of Social Institutions.* New York: Harcourt, Brace & World, 1953.

Gilbert, Gustave. *Nuremberg Diary.* New York: Signet, 1947.

Gilbert, Gustave. *The Psychology of Dictatorship: Based on an Examination of the Leaders of Nazi Germany.* New York: Ronald, 1950.

Goffman, Erving. *Asylums: Essays on the Social Situations of Mental Patients and Other Inmates.* Garden City, N.Y.: Doubleday, 1961.

Goldman, Peter. *The Death and Life of Malcolm X.* New York: Harper & Row, 1973.

Gray, Glenn. *The Warriors.* New York: Harper & Row, 1970.

Griffin, Susan. "Rape: The All-American Crime." In *Sexual Deviance and Sexual Deviants,* edited by Erich Goode and Richard Troiden. New York: Morrow, 1975.

Halberstam, David. *The Best and the Brightest.* New York: Random House, 1972.

Heider, Karl. *The Dugum Dani: A Papuan Culture in the Highlands of West New Guinea.* Chicago: Aldine, 1970.

Hittle, James. *The Military Staff.* 3d ed. Harrisburg: Stackpole, 1961.

Hoebel, E. Adamson. *The Cheyennes: Indians of the Great Plains.* New York: Holt, Rinehart, & Winston, 1960.

Huntington, Samuel. *The Soldier and the State: The Theory and Politics of Civil Military Relations.* New York: Random House, 1957.

Irvine, Dallas. "Origin of Capital Staffs." *Journal of Modern History* 10 (June 1935): 165-79.

Irving, David. *The Destruction of Dresden.* New York: Holt, Rinehart & Winston, 1965.

Janowitz, Morris, ed. *The New Military.* New York: Norton, 1964.

Janowitz, Morris. *The Professional Soldier: A Social and Political Portrait.* New York: Free Press, 1960.

Jeal, Tim. *Livingstone.* New York: Putnam, 1973.

Karsten, Rafael. "Blood Revenge and War Among the Jibaro Indians of Eastern Ecuador." In *Law and Warfare,* edited by Paul Bohannan. Garden City, N.Y.: Natural History Press, 1967.

Lang, Daniel. *Casualties of War.* New York: McGraw-Hill, 1969.

Lasswell, Harold. *Propaganda Technique in the World War.* New York: Knopf, 1928.

Lehrman, Daniel. "A Critique of Konrad Lorenz's *Theory of Instinctive Behavior.*" *The Quarterly Review of Biology* 28, no. 4 (1953): 337-63.

LeMay, General Curtis. *Mission with LeMay*. New York: Funk and Wagnalls, 1965.
Liddel-Hart, Sir Basil. *Paris; or, the Future of War*. New York: Garland Publishing, 1969, first published in 1925.
Liddell-Hart, Sir Basil. *The Revolution in Warfare*. London: Faber & Faber, 1946.
Littauer, Raphael, and Uphoff, Norman, eds. *The Air War in Indochina*. Boston: Beacon, 1972.
Lonn, Ella. *Desertion During the Civil War*. New York: American Historical Society, 1928.
Lorenz, Konrad. *On Aggression*. New York: Bantam, 1967.
McCord, Joan, and McCord, William. "The Effects of Parental Role Model on Criminality." *Journal of Social Issues* 13 (1957): 66–75.
Malinowski, Bronislaw. "An Anthropological Analysis of War." *American Journal of Sociology* 5 (1941): 521–50.
Mark, Vernon H., and Ervin, Frank R. *Violence and the Brain*. New York: Harper & Row, 1970. Cited in Fromm, 1973.
Marshall, Samuel L. A. *Men Against Fire: The Problem of Battle Command in Future War*. New York: Apollo, 1947.
Matthiessen, Peter. *Sal Si Puedes—Escape If You Can: Cesar Chavez and the New American Revolution*. New York: Dover, 1969.
Matthiessen, Peter. *Under the Mountain Wall*. New York: Ballantine, 1970.
May, Rollo. *Power and Innocence: A Search for the Sources of Violence*. New York: Norton, 1972.
Mead, Edward Earle, ed. *Makers of Modern Strategy*. New York: Atheneum, 1966.
Mead, Margaret. "Warfare Is Only an Invention—Not a Biological Necessity." In *War*, edited by Leon Bramson and George W. Goethals. New York: Basic Books, 1964.
Merton, Thomas. *Thomas Merton on Peace*. New York: McCall, 1971.
Montagu, M. R. Ashley. *Man and Aggression*. New York: Oxford University Press, 1968.
Moskos, Charles. *The American Enlisted Man: The Rank and File in Today's Military*. New York: Russell Sage, 1970.
Niebuhr, Reinhold. *Moral Man and Immoral Society*. New York: Scribner, 1960.
Ogilvie, R. M. *The Romans and Their Gods in the Age of Augustus*. New York: Norton, 1970.
Painter, Sidney. *French Chivalry: Chivalric Ideas and Practices in Medieval France*. Ithaca, N.Y.: Cornell University Press, 1957.
Parks, David. *G.I. Diary*. New York: Harper & Row, 1968.
Phillips, Brig. General Thomas R., ed. *Roots of Strategy*. Harrisburg: Stackpole, 1940.

Preston, Richard A.; Wise, Sydney F.; and Werner, Herman O. *Men in Arms: A History of Warfare and Its Interrelationships with Western Society.* Rev. ed. New York: Praeger, 1965.

Rees, David. *Korea.* Baltimore: Penguin, 1970.

Rokeach, Milton. *The Open and Closed Mind.* New York: Basic Books, 1960.

Ropp, Theodore. *War in the Modern World.* Rev. ed. New York: Macmillan, 1962.

Rostovtzeff, Mikhail. *Social and Economic History of the Roman Empire.* 2 vols. New York: Oxford University Press, 1957.

Scott, J. P. *Aggression.* Chicago: University of Chicago Press, 1958.

Shanahan, William. *Prussian Military Reforms, 1786–1813.* New York: Columbia University Press, 1945.

Sherrill, Robert. *Military Justice Is to Justice As Military Music Is to Music.* New York: Harper & Row, 1970.

Singletary, Otis. *The Mexican War.* Chicago: University of Chicago Press, 1960.

Spaight, J. M. *Air Power and the Cities.* London: Longmans, Green, 1930.

Spaight, J. M. *Bombing Vindicated.* London: Geoffrey Bles, 1944.

Spatz, General Carl. "Strategic Bombing." *Foreign Affairs* 26 (April 1947): 385–96.

Speer, Albert. *Inside the Third Reich.* New York: Macmillan, 1970.

Speer, Albert. *Spandau.* New York: Macmillan, 1976.

Speier, Hans. *Social Order and the Risks of War: Papers in Political Sociology.* Cambridge, Mass.: MIT Press, 1969.

Stack, Rodney. "Collective Police Violence." In *The Sociology of Dissent,* edited by R. Serge Denisoff. New York: Harcourt Brace Jovanovich, 1974.

Stampp, Kenneth. *The Peculiar Institution.* New York: Knopf, 1956.

Stern, J. P. *Hitler: The Fuhrer and the People.* Berkeley: University of California Press, 1975.

Storr, Anthony. *Human Aggression.* New York: Atheneum, 1968.

Stouffer, Samuel; Lumsdaine, Arthur A.; Lumsdaine, Marion; Harper, William, Jr.: Robin, M.; Smith, M. Brewster; Janis, Irving; Star, Shirley A.; Cottrell, Leonard S., Jr. *The American Soldier: Combat and Its Afterward.* Princeton: Princeton University Press, 1949.

Toch, Hans. *Violent Men: An Inquiry into the Psychology of Violence.* Chicago: Aldine, 1969.

Trevelyan, G. M. *English Social History.* London: Penguin, 1967.

Turney-High, Harry H. *Primitive War: Its Practice and Concepts.* Columbia, N.C.: University of South Carolina Press, 1948.

Vagts, Alfred. *A History of Militarism.* New York: Free Press, 1959.

Vernier, Anthony. *Bomber Offensive.* New York: Holt, Rinehart & Winston, 1965.

Weber, Max. *Protestant Ethic and the Spirit of Capitalism.* New York: Scribner, 1958.
Weber, Max. *The Theory of Social and Economic Organization.* New York: Free Press, 1947.
Wells, Donald A. *The War Myth.* New York: Pegasus, 1967.
Wills, Gary. *Nixon Agonistes.* New York: Signet, 1971.
Wilson, James Q. *Thinking About Crime.* New York: Basic Books, 1975.
Wright, John Womack. *Some Notes on the Continental Army.* Cornwallville, N.Y.: Hope Farm Press, 1963.
Wright, Quincy. *A Study of War.* Edited by Louise L. Wright. 2d ed. Chicago: University of Chicago Press, 1964.
Wyllie, Irvin G. *The Self-Made Man in America.* New York: Free Press, 1966.

CHAPTER THIRTEEN
Collective Behavior

The next thing Tod knew, he was torn loose from Homer and sent to his knees by a blow in the back of the head that spun him sideways. The crowd in front of the theatre had charged. He was surrounded by churning legs and feet. He pulled himself erect by grabbing a man's coat, then let himself be carried backwards in a long curving swoop. He saw Homer rise above the mars for a moment, shoved against the sky, his jaw hanging as though he wanted to scream but couldn't. A hand reached up and caught him by his open mouth and pulled him forward and down.

There was another dizzy rush. Tod closed his eyes and fought to keep upright. He was jostled about in a backing cross surf of shoulders and backs, carried rapidly in one direction and then in the opposite. He kept pushing and hitting out at the people around him, trying to face in the direction he was going. Being carried backwards terrified him.

. . . He struggled desperately for a moment, then gave up and let himself be swept along. He was the spearhead of a flying wedge when it collided with a mass going in the opposite direction. The impact turned him around. As the two forces ground against each other, he was turned again, like a grain between millstones. . . . He was slowly pushed into the air.

. . . Not being able to touch was an even more dreadful sensation than being carried backwards. . . .

Another spasm passed through the mob and he was carried toward the curb. He fought toward a lamp post but he was swept by before he could grasp it. . . . This rush ended in a dead spot. Here his neighbors were all shorter than he was. . . .

> *In this part of the mob no one was hysterical. In fact, most of the people seemed to be enjoying themselves. Near him was a stout woman. . . . She paid no attention to him and went on talking to the woman at her side.*
>
> *"The first thing I knew," Tod heard her say, "there was a rush and I was in the middle."*
>
> *"Yeah, somebody hollered, Here comes Gary Cooper, and then wham!"*
>
> *"That ain't it," said a little man wearing a cloth cap and pullover sweater. "This is a riot you're in."*
>
> Nathanael West, *The Day of the Locust* (1939)

Although this very accurate description of crowd behavior was first published in 1933, conventional wisdom still lags far behind. Heir to the theories of Gustave Le Bon's *The Crowd,* most people seem to believe that crowds act on the basis of unanimity; like germs, people are exposed to the moods of others, and as the infection quickly moves through the crowd, everyone soon acts in unison because they have no choice: contagion has struck (see Le Bon, 1960).

This is wrong. Consider first the notion of permeability (Milgram and Toch, 1968). Any crowd has boundaries that work in two ways. It may be easy to enter a crowd but, as in Tod's case, it may be impossible to leave—no matter how strong the desire. For example, in 1932 General Douglas MacArthur had the task of clearing Washington's streets of Bonus Marchers. Unfortunately, MacArthur began the cleanup at 4:30 P.M. Twenty thousand government employees had just finished work and, massed on the sidewalks, they were unable to escape as soldiers sought to disperse the crowd of Bonus Marchers. Major George S. Patton, Jr., gave the order and his men charged "without the slightest warning into thousands of unoffending people." Many were trampled, among them Connecticut's Senator Hiram Bingham (Manchester, 1974).

Now consider the notion of unanimity. Tod's locating of a "happy" part of the mob points to a common fact about crowds: unanimity is never found. Members of the crowd, government employees in 1932 wanted no part of it. Similarly an analysis of political demonstrations in Indonesia found crowd members with many motives for participation; some were leaders, some followers, some hired participants, some out for the fun of it, some literally forced into being enthusiastic political supporters (Willner, 1972).

So, instead of contagion, people may be forced or paid to participate in crowds. And instead of unanimity, crowd members often act in the same way for different reasons. Inevitably, these facts undermine traditional explanations of crowds, and they also point to another insight: the accumulating evidence about all forms of collective behavior suggests very complex processes that always defy simple explanations—traditional or otherwise.

WHAT IS COLLECTIVE BEHAVIOR?

The answer is that collective behavior is different. First, whether in crowds or social movements, interest centers on the group, not on the individual. And this is so because all forms of collective behavior characteristically exhibit a set of "interindividual, relational, and interactional properties which cannot be reduced to purely intraindividual terms" (Zygmunt, 1972; also Turner and Killian, 1972). For example, during World War I a rumor swept through England that angels had saved British troops. Apparently, just as they were about to attack, the German troops stopped pursuit, allowing the English soldiers to escape unharmed. The real explanation for the German action was an absence of supplies, but this knowledge was lacking in Great Britain, and the construction of the angel rumor cannot be understood in intraindividual terms. Necessary for any explanation of this rumor is an analysis of the level of collective excitement, the general mood of defeat in Britain, and the way in which the process of interaction led to responsibility being placed on the wings of angels rather than the tall staff of Ireland's Saint Patrick (Shibutani, 1966).

A second reason that collective behavior is different is that "it is concerned with large group activity which comes into being and develops along lines that are not laid out by preestablished social definitions" (Blumer, 1957). Where an institution such as the family operates by established beliefs, values, and practices that are rooted in tradition, crowds, social movements, or rumors develop along paths not mapped out by an already built culture. At the outset, collective behavior lacks defined procedures for selecting and identifying either leaders or followers; those procedures, perhaps very loose, are "forged" in the process of coming to grips with undefined or unstructured situations. Thus, the task in studying collective behavior is to identify the emerging sources of coordination, as well as to explore the relationship between, say, riots and five thousand orderly people leaving together from a factory (Blumer, 1957; Turner and Killian, 1972).

Remember, too, that since cultural taken-for-granteds are in the background, crowds or social movements show a degree of fluidity uncommon in everyday life. Inevitably, the absence of established definitions allows much room for the world-making abilities of people; inevitably, the lack of solid guidelines means that in collective behavior it is especially important to focus attention on the process of interaction. For example, when an angry mob approached a convent (in 1834), mob members only demanded to see a nun being held by the Mother Superior. Probably, the nun's appearance would have quieted the crowd. However, in response to their demand the Mother Superior acted defiantly and condescendingly.

She scolded the mob, said she would receive a "decently conducted delegation" the next day, and then, as the crowd began to leave, added: "Disperse immediately, for if you don't, the Bishop has twenty thousand Irishmen at his command in Boston, and they will whip you all into the sea." Not surprisingly, in response to this remark, in the ongoing process of defining the situation, mob members "saw red." Quickly, a few hundred people grew to four thousand and before the night was over, the convent was sacked and burned to the ground (Chaplin, 1959).

Collective behavior is different. It cannot be explained in intraindividual terms, it tries to define undefined or unstructured situations, and it manifests a degree of fluidity uncommon in everyday life. Generally, six forms of collective behavior are cited: rumors, crowds, social movements, fads, crazes, and public opinion (Blumer, 1969, 1957). Here we focus only on crowds and social movements, beginning with the theoretical approaches that supposedly furnish models for understanding collective behavior.

CROWDS

One theoretical model was already mentioned: contagion theory. Here collective behavior is explained "on the basis of some process whereby moods, attitudes, and behavior are communicated rapidly and accepted uncritically" (Turner, 1964). Sometimes contagion is called "circular interaction," but whatever the label, the argument is similar: people interact, their interaction creates a common mood, and the result is "simple ideas or images shared by all by virtue of the experience in this crowd" (Klapp, 1972).

Contagion theory has many problems; its greatest is the empirical evidence about crowds. Here the data is from different centuries, as well as being cross-cultural. Crowds contain people in different moods and by no means do all crowd members share the same simple ideas or images. For example, Rude notes that members of political crowds during the French Revolution were sometimes recruited by "intimidation or persuasion"; myth sees a mob roaring approval for democratic ideals, reality sees a heterogeneous group of people acting for different reasons and sometimes on the basis of the simple idea that absence from the crowd equals the use of violence by others. Or, take an example from Great Britain in the 1960s. Crowds of young "mods" and "rockers" met on the beaches, with conflict the probable result. But "in every instance," the young people constituted "a series of interlocking crowds" and "even at the peaks of crowd activity there were very diverse patterns of participation" (Cohen, 1973; Rude, 1964).

Besides its false assumption about shared moods that are uncritically accepted, another weakness of contagion theory is that it has "nothing" to tell us about the organization of collective behavior. After all, if crowds contain different groups of people who often act in the same or a similar way, how is coordination achieved? And how are functions differentiated? Relying on an explanation of shared mood, and finding instead a number of different moods, contagion theory collapses when it deals with the organization of crowds (Turner, 1964).

One response to the weaknesses of contagion theory is convergence theory. Here crowd behavior is explained on the basis of the same or similar predispositions and preoccupations. Assume that our aim is to explain the many food riots that took place during the French Revolution. Convergence theory would focus attention on people's predisposition to blame societal elites and, noting that the amount of a laborer's income devoted to buying bread rose from 50 percent in 1788 to 83 percent in 1789, convergence theory would cite the rise in prices as the cause of the people's preoccupation with the price of bread, as well as their need to do something about lowering it (for the figures, see Rude, 1973).

A stress on predisposing conditions is valuable and informative. Certainly the rise in bread prices was a cause of the food riots. The question, however, is does it explain all or even many facets of crowd behavior? And the answer is no. First, keying on predispositions fails to explain shifts in crowd behavior. Can the burned nunnery be explained without recourse to the Mother Superior's attitude and remarks? Second, Turner points out that people have many predispositions and preoccupations. *Which* of these becomes an element for crowd action is an empirical question that must include the process of interaction that selects some, and disregards other, latent beliefs and values. Finally, relying only on predispositions leads to assumptions about the direction and intensity of crowd behavior (Turner, 1964). Given the amount of income devoted to bread, the assumption might be riots of great intensity. And that assumption often proved true. But it was always also based on a process of interaction[1] and sometimes, despite a predisposition to violence, interaction produced none. For example, with rioting expected, the Paris police forbid a rise in bread prices and this response from authority temporarily satisfied potential rioters (Rude, 1973).

If neither contagion nor convergence theory furnishes a satisfactory model for analysis, emergent norm theory does. Here unanimity is regarded as an illusion and the key problem is "to explain the development and imposition of a pattern of differential expression that is perceived as unanimity." Here "equal weight" is placed on predispositions and preoc-

---

[1] Rude notes that the Revellion Riots occurred because of the predisposing factors *and* because two prominent manufacturers made a public statement about lowering workers' wages (1973).

cupations; less weight is placed on suggestibility, contagion, or circular interaction; and "greater stress" is given "to locating the conditions and sequences under which a new or special rule—the emergent norm—comes to be recognized and accepted as the basis for a coordinated response" (Turner and Killian, 1972; Turner, 1964; Milgram and Toch, 1968; Weller and Quarantelli, 1973; Gurr, 1972).

Consider a Berkeley "police riot" in 1968. Hostility between police and youth had been brewing for a long time; words such as "creep" and "freak" were "almost routinely used" by officers to refer to young people. In Berkeley the police were predisposed to expect trouble from crowds of students. However, in this instance everyday biases were increased by a warning: The FBI had told Berkeley police that outside agitators were flying in from New York, Chicago, and New Orleans. At a Young Socialists rally planned for Friday night, these radicals would rise up and "overturn law and order" (Stark, 1974).

So, predisposed to expect trouble, and preoccupied with the FBI warning, police were ready on Friday night. Only two hundred people appeared at the rally and when police overreacted to a remark made by one student, conflict quickly erupted. However, the streets were cleared by midnight and it was only the next day, when accurate reports of police brutality circulated, that a mass meeting was called for that evening (Stark, 1974).

Now, while the predispositions are obviously crucial, one must keep in mind the emerging norm. Police are ready for trouble; they find it, and in response to their discovery, interaction among young people produces enough anger for a large crowd to show up at Saturday's rally. Now the police are really worried. Their worst fears and the FBI reports have been fully confirmed. For example, where Friday night's crowd included many middle-class "straight" people, Saturday night's crowd was mostly juveniles, many having come over from Oakland and Richmond "to see what was happening."

By 9:30 P.M. about two hundred people were at the rally. Rumors spread that the police were about to attack but nothing happened. Actually, police were deciding what to do. Reinforced by outside officers who felt strongly negative about long hair and "peculiar" dress, the police had used Saturday to prepare for anything. The large crowd increased their concern and finally led to the emergence of a norm that defined the situation for police: "If a battle was to be fought, it had best be fought at a time and place of the police's choosing." Otherwise "losing the city was a real possibility" (Stark, 1974).

By 11 P.M. the police decided to clear a thinning crowd, and at 11:30 "the police struck suddenly, violently, and in great numbers." Gas was everywhere, and when someone threw a Molotov cocktail at a highway patrolman, the rumor spread among police "that the patrolman had lost his genitals as a result of the firebomb and was near death." This produced the night's "most furious outburst of violence." All told investigators found twenty-seven people who had been beaten unconscious and left by roving bands of police. This represented only a small portion of those injured by the police rioting (Stark, 1974).

Recall that the focus in emergent norm theory is to explain the development and imposition of a pattern of differential expression that is perceived as unanimity. Above we followed the development of a norm—"strike first or risk the loss of law and order"—that acted as a constraint on those subject to it. In effect, emergent norm theory argues that, like rules of dress for a formal party or recipes governing proper behavior at a job interview, norms are external to the individual, and just because they exist "out there," supposedly sanctioned by everyone, they are capable of imposing their definition of the situation on a crowd of people, many of whom disagree with the norm. For example, while it seemed that all policemen were indiscriminately beating long hairs, in reality a pattern of differential expression existed. Some police did eagerly seek out victims, but others "merely" stood by shouting encouragement. Others participated only because they did not want colleagues to think they were less zealous than anyone else, while still others "appeared to find the whole affair disgusting": they stood to the side as the beatings occurred (Stark, 1974).

Consider the power of the emergent norm. Some police join in only because they perceive it to be the behavior demanded; like people who dress formally for a party even though they dislike wearing tuxedos and long dresses, the norm is powerful enough to force behavior that is objectionable to the individual. And remember the police bystanders. Although disgusted by the beatings, the norm is powerful enough for them to tolerate its demands. And finally, recall the process of interaction. Based on predispositions and the emergent norm, the rumor about the castrated patrolman meets a very suggestible audience. Many police find this story quite plausible and, within the context of the riot, it acts to increase the norm's power. For example, would disgusted police try to stop, or more important, believe it possible to stop, colleagues who accepted both the norm and the rumor?

A focus on norm theory enables us to answer questions that are not answered by contagion and convergence theory. One, instead of circular interaction or shared moods, crowd coordination is explained by means of the imposition of a collectively constructed definition of the situation. Two, by studying predispositions and the conditions and sequences that lead to crowd behavior, emergent norm theory explains why one of many latent beliefs becomes most important. Above we emphasized the end product, the emergent norm, but any overall analysis of crowd norm construction must also come to terms with rumor, with keynotes, and with symbols.

Turner and Killian correctly argue that rumor is "the characteristic mode of communication in collective behavior." Like the two thousand young people at Berkeley, or the ten thousand at Chicago's Democratic Convention in 1968 (Walker, 1968), people in crowds use rumor as "a form of collective problem solving." Caught in an ambiguous situation—Will the police attack or leave us alone? Will the National Guard be called out?—crowd members try "to construct a meaningful interpretation of it by pooling their intellectual resources." In this sense rumor is "improvised news"; it represents a collective attempt to define an inadequately defined situation (Shibutani, 1966; Turner and Killian, 1972).

Rumor is crucial for understanding crowds because it is an important element in comprehending the sequence of conditions that lead to the emergence of a norm, to the emergence of an adequate definition of the situation that is also the basis for crowd action. For example, when a "mad gasser" struck Mattoon, Illinois, in 1944, many people felt they "were locked in deadly combat with a phantom who struck in the night spraying poisonous gas into his victims' bedrooms and then vanished into the darkness leaving them paralyzed, nauseated, and suffering from swollen, bleeding lips." Trying to identify a phantom was difficult, but people did it because they "had to." For many, danger lurked behind every bush and rumors served an important function: they imposed a measure of order on a very ambiguous and frightening situation. For example, one rumor said the gasser was a mad scientist who made gas in a basement laboratory and then sprayed it through people's windows with a high-pressure gun. Another said the gasser was a "sex fiend" who "overcame women in a novel manner for his own dark purposes." Either way, rumor gave groups of shotgun-packing citizens a clue as to what to shoot at (Chaplin, 1959).

Generally, conventional wisdom contains a number of false assumptions about rumors. First, people rarely, if ever, accept anything. The extent of suggestibility varies with the degree of collective excitement, with the public's need to eliminate ambiguity (Shibutani, 1966), but most rumors are consistent with people's predispositions and presuppositions. After Friday night's attack, it made sense for Berkeley's Saturday crowd to construct rumors about an impending police assault, and in Mattoon the mad gasser first struck women in their bedrooms: Wasn't it reasonable to assume sexual interests for the gasser? Second, if collective excitement is moderate, rumor construction occurs through a process of "deliberation." People demand that rumors make sense, generally dropping what they feel are absurd conclusions. Waiting for an official announcement about the execution of Nazi war criminals in 1946, a crowd of reporters rejected the true rumor that Göring had committed suicide. As one reporter said, "A man could ruin himself in five minutes by broadcasting a silly report like that" (Shibutani, 1966). Finally, rumors end in many ways. When Valentino died, sixty thousand people waited outside the funeral home, and one rumor had it that "The Shiek" was interred in a ton-and-a-half solid bronze coffin. This rumor was dispelled when people were allowed to file by the actual coffin. Or, rumors may die out from lack of interest. Although Americans wonder about Warren Beatty's love life or Jacqueline Kennedy Onassis's marital status, interest is generally mild and many people refuse to keep building rumors. Or, lastly, rumors could end as a basis for crowd action. In the Tampa, Florida, riot of 1967, rumor falsely had it that a white policeman had shot a black youth in the back while the boy had his hands above his head trying to surrender. This rumor was accepted as true, and it furnished a firm basis for the crowd's emerging definition of the situation: white cops are racist and brutal; let's act on them before they again act on us (Report of the National Advisory Commission on Civil Disorders, 1968).

Rumors are part of a process. In Tampa they built on a solid foundation of predisposition to believe police were brutal, and it was also "helpful" to have such a potent symbol as the "white cop." Turner and Killian note "that an essential part of the preparation of crowds for action is the development of a shared image of the object" (1972). Both "the material and the product of rumor," these symbols often perform a yeoman's labor in coordinating crowd behavior. Ambiguity gives way to clarity as the symbol furnishes a simple yet powerful focus for attention or action: now people know what to worship or what to flee or what to attack. In Great Britain the initially ambiguous battles between crowds of young people produced many explanations: the teenagers were "ill-conditioned odious louts"; they were "retarded vain young hot-blooded paycocks"; they were "grubby hordes of louts and sluts" who acted like apes. Eventually, these "explanations" led to two shared symbols: mods and rockers. Each group had a distinctive pattern of dress and these obvious characteristics were the symbols that separated normals from the "grubby hordes of louts" (see Cohen, 1973).

If rumors build on predispositions and often help produce a collective symbol, action sometimes requires a keynote. This is "a gesture or symbolic utterance" that puts a cap on the bottle; it tells people what to do—now (Turner and Killian, 1972). For example, in the Tampa riot the rumor about the boy's murder led hundreds of people to assemble on the street. And even though a definition and symbol (that is, the white cop) existed, a black officer's attempt to quiet the crowd seemed to be working when, suddenly, "a young woman came running down the street screaming that police had killed her brother." That scream and the woman's words were a keynote. They "galvanized" the crowd, as well as "told" people what to do. Immediately, some crowd members began throwing rocks, and police cars that were driving into the area were stoned. A riot had begun (Report of the National Advisory Commission on Civil Disorders, 1968).

Many classifications of crowds exist (for example, Brown, 1954; Smelser, 1963), with the best perhaps Turner and Killian's argument for four general types of crowds. *Acting* crowds have as their goal action on some person(s) or object external to them. Examples are riots, lynchings, mobs, panics. In contrast, *expressive* crowds lack an object, a desire to change the relationship of crowd members to some aspect of the outside world. Expressive crowds seek instead "to change the mood, the imagery, and the behavior" of crowd members. Examples are religious groups, especially those listening to preachers such as Billy Graham, or political gatherings where candidates try to turn an indifferent group into a cheering band of loyal supporters.

A third type of crowd is known as *conventional*. People gather "in the hope their assemblage will be transformed into a crowd." Examples are sports events, theater going, parties, and concerts, whether classical, country-western, or rock. The label *conventional* is attached because here crowds are repetitive. People have done this before, they know what to expect, as well as how to act. Naturally, a conventional crowd can easily turn active (for example, in Great Britain the fear of riots at soccer matches forced authorities to build fences between the opposing teams' fans), but the repetition of the event normally leads to some standardization of behavior (Turner and Killian, 1972).

Diffuse is the word used to describe the last type of crowd. Here, in contrast to the compactness that characterizes members of an audience or mob, crowd members are dispersed over a wide area, and yet they develop similar sentiments, moods, and behavior. Examples are the fad, the craze, and the national reaction of panic to Orson Wells's radio broadcast of 1938. Quickly, people separated by thousands of miles developed the mood of fear and the behavior of flight. Accepting a play as reality, they took Wells at his word and tried to combat the invading Martians in a similar way (see Cantril, 1940).[2] Or, if we define a *craze* as "a new idea that suddenly becomes important in the life of a community" but does not disturb the existing social order (Penrose, 1952), consider the Royal Porcelain Craze of the 1750s. In China every aristocrat had to have examples and all over Europe widely dispersed members of the upper classes sought to outdo one another in their search for splendor. Soon "no aristo-

---

[2] For sound discussions of behavior in disasters, see Quarantelli, 1960, and Killian, 1952. These articles successfully undermine many stereotypes about collective behavior in disaster situations.

cratic drawing room was complete without a vase, a figure, or a dish"; indeed the craze reached such proportions that "the fabulously rich began to eat off it, drink from it, wash in it, even spit in it" (Plumb, 1972).

Placing crowds into categories is a way of dealing with variety; it should not lead to the conclusion that crowds are prisoners of their categories. Fluidity is one of collective behavior's defining characteristics and in dealing with any form of crowd it is always important to focus on the process and results of interaction. Recently (in 1975) expressive political crowds in Portugal have often turned into riots and the possibility of panic exists in any conventional crowd; it is perhaps only necessary for a practical "joker" to scream "Fire!"

Given the wide variety of crowds, space alone prevents any extended discussion of each. So, rather than give a cursory treatment to all, the analysis below tries to summarize the knowledge we now have about one important type of acting crowd: the riot.

RIOTS

Let's begin with a loose distinction between riots in preindustrial and riots in industrial societies. Before, say, 1789, riots were small-scale, local in scope, spontaneous (that is, lacking in formal organization), and often rooted in people's "attachment to the *traditional* ways (or believed traditional ways) of the old village community or urban craft . . ." (Rude, 1973; also Tilly, 1972). Rude says food riots were by far the most common form of preindustrial disturbance, but examples of resisting change include antidraft riots (for the United States, see Murdock, 1967), collective violence toward tax collectors, and the numerous attacks on machines that took place in early nineteenth-century England (for example, Hobsbawm and Rude, 1968).

Riots change character as society changes. Centralization of political power in the hands of a national state transforms the nature of political loyalties and political problems. Now, in industrial society, thinking of themselves as Frenchmen before Parisians, Americans before Ohioans, citizens look to the central government because it is the source of power and because only the central government can solve the crucial problems, for example, control of the economy, racism, labor relations, conservation, peace or war. When these political changes are linked to urbanization, as well as "the proliferation and rise to political prominence" of complex special purpose groups such as parties, unions, corporations, and associations, it is no wonder that crowds in *industrial* societies are generally large-scale, frequently led by leaders of formal organizations, oriented toward national issues, and, when the crowd turns into a riot, often rooted in people's demands for a rejection of traditional beliefs and practices. Examples include the civil rights disturbances of the sixties, efforts (say, in Chicago in 1968 or Chile in 1972) to bring down a national government, and the many violent labor disturbances that characterized America in the late nineteenth and early twentieth centuries (Tilly, 1972; Rude, 1973).

If industrialization changes the size, scope, and "purpose" of riots, there are many common characteristics between the riots of today and yesterday.

First, as a general rule, the upper classes still do not participate, while the lower and lower-middle classes do.

Second, riots in both types of societies include many unwilling participants. "Pressing" people into action was common in the British agricultural disturbances of the early 1800s (Hobsbawm and Rude, 1968) as well as the American labor disturbances of the 1900s.

Third, all riots seem to include a number of "zealous" participants who bear a disproportionate share of the responsibility for starting or continuing a riot. In the British agricultural riots "contagion" was often spread by a few men who used the following tactics: "In their progress they take the men of the parish they have left with them; and, having finished their business in the second parish, they send back the men of the first parish and take the men of the second with the third parish and so on" (Hobsbawm and Rude, 1968). And in Detroit in 1968 looters seemed to be well organized, for observers noted a number of cars returning again and again, their occupants methodically looting stores (Report of the National Advisory Commission on Civil Disorders, 1968; also Janowitz, 1969).

Fourth, instead of "mad dogs" fueled by unstoppable passion, rioters are often discriminating and controlled. In the Luddite riots of 1812, people often chose selected targets; there were certain employers whose machines would and would not be destroyed (Rude, 1964). And in at least nine of the riot cities studied by the President's Commission on Civil Disorders, the damage was at least partly "the result of deliberate attacks on white-owned businesses characterized in the Negro community as unfair or disrespectful toward Negroes" (Report of the National Advisory Commission on Civil Disorders, 1968).

Fifth, the riot process is always affected—often dramatically—by the response of authorities.[3] When the antidraft riots broke out in New York in 1863, the governor was in New Jersey. Since he was a powerful and prominent figure, Governor Seymour's appearance might have helped

---

[3] For an extended discussion, see Gurr, 1972; also Wedge, 1972.

quiet rioters; at the least it would have coordinated police efforts. However, Seymour (apparently by intention) took a day to return, and when he finally arrived his calls to stop rioting were totally ineffective (Murdock, 1967). Or, consider a Harlem riot in 1964. Facing an "angry but otherwise peaceful crowd," police decided to clear an intersection by swinging their clubs and, apparently in imitation of Theodore Roosevelt, yelling "charge." Unfortunately, crowd members responded by beginning to riot (Marx, 1970; also Shellow and Roemer, 1966).

Sixth, no matter when or where they occur, a basic cause of riots is a series of underlying social conditions that predispose people to violence. Gurr makes this point when he argues that "the necessary precondition for violent civil conflict is relative deprivation"; people must perceive a discrepancy between their "value expectations" and the society's ability or willingness to deliver (Gurr, 1972). For example, Luddites valued hand craftsmanship, but elites were pushing the machine and the factory. Or, laborers seek decent wages and employers respond by refusing to discuss their claims. In either instance, using employers as a reference group equals a preoccupation with the sources of injustice as well as a predisposition to use violence if necessary or appropriate (see also Milgram and Toch, 1968).

Seventh, since injustice has always been a fact of social life, what factors are associated with its appearance at a particular time and place? One is a persistent inability to solve problems through more peaceful means. In the French Corn Riot of 1775, prices had been rising for two years, appeals to Finance Minister Turgot failed, and when people's pleas to their local magistrate also produced no change, peasants took the law into their own hands (Rude, 1964). Or, when rioting occurred in Springfield, Massachusetts, in 1975, the spark was a police shooting of a Puerto Rican, but underlying the riot were over two years of attempts by the Puerto Rican community to hire Puerto Rican police officers as well as eliminate some apparent biases in law enforcement.

Eighth, riots are more likely if social norms support this type of action (Gurr, 1972). Tradition "approved" of food riots in eighteenth-century France, and while numerous speakers said no, many "leaders" of the war protest at Chicago's Democratic National Convention in 1968 thought violence the only way to "bring down" the establishment (see Walker, 1968).

Ninth, and last, riots are more likely if people feel they are protected from retribution (Gurr, 1972). At one food riot in 1792, the French National Guard, instead of stopping the rioters, joined them (Rude, 1964). And in Chicago in 1968 police wore uniforms but no identifying symbols. Just before attacking the crowd, they removed all badges and some even tore off arm insignias. Free from any possible retribution, they could act as they wished (Walker, 1968).

Together, these nine variables underline many of the constants in riot behavior. But to show how they operate in a particular instance, let us examine some of the factors associated with one type of riot, the race riot.

Here again we meet types. First is the "communal" riot. These center on a struggle between whites and blacks over contested residential areas. Generally, the predisposing factor are groups of whites and blacks who live in segregated areas where the traditional forms of racism are slowly breaking down. So, tension is always high, minor skirmishes frequent. Then, blacks drink at a "white" bar or swim at a "white" beach. Whatever the precipitating incident, it builds on the constant tension and "symbolically, the riot [is] an expression of elements of the white community to kick the Negro back into his place." Examples of communal riots are East St. Louis (1917), Chicago (1919), and Harlem (1935 and 1943) (Janowitz, 1969).

Another type of race riot is the "commodity" riot. Here, rather than violence erupting at the periphery of the black community, it begins within the ghetto. And instead of whites against blacks, the riot is begun by blacks as a response to perceived injustices. Generally, the riot vents its aggression against public property and retail establishments; always there is looting by segments of the acting crowd. Examples of commodity riots include Harlem in 1964 and Detroit in 1967 (Janowitz, 1969).

In the case of the commodity riot, predisposing factors are many. First, people must perceive the injustice of their situation *plus* be willing to do something about it. They must be alive to the issues in question *plus* have expectations that the society is failing to meet. For example, one reason whites were able to riot in Chicago in 1919 was the willing compliance and help of the white police. However, where police brutality was "accepted" in 1919, by the 1960s it was a prime underlying cause of the commodity riots (for example, Milgram and Toch, 1968). Second, if people feel relatively deprived, it is normally caused by three or four different issues. Police brutality is one of these, exploitation by white and black store owners is another, a third is the level of unemployment coupled with the people's desire to work, and a fourth is the people's perception of political leaders. If citizens try to achieve change by peaceful means, but gain nothing, the chances of authorities exerting social control are greatly weakened. And legitimacy is especially important when an incident occurs. If people feel justice will not be done, they are unlikely to vent their anger by working "within the system" (see Lieberson and Silverman, 1965; also Dahlke, 1952).

Although any number of incidents can start a riot, "they tend to be transgressions of strongly held mores by a representative of the other group." Always the incident builds on the predisposing causes and generally rumor plays a significant part in the emergence of a norm. For example, in the Harlem riot of 1943, a black soldier tried to help a black woman who was being arrested for disorderly conduct. In the ensuing fight the soldier and the police were both injured, but the rumor that spread through the community was that a black soldier had been shot in the back by a white policeman in the presence of the soldier's mother (Lieberson and Silverman, 1965). Here the rumors provided a definition of the situation and it also furnished a perfect symbol to begin this riot: white police brutality.

Now, assume the norm has emerged, rioting has begun. Of particular interest are a series of findings about the Watts riot of 1965 (Stark et al., 1974). Researchers worked from a list of 1,878 crowd incidents that broke down in this way: 926 fires, 138 false alarms, 555 lootings, 174 incidents of rock throwing, and, stressing that this category was probably underrecorded, 85 crowd assemblies, in which nothing else occurred. Now, knowing what happened, researchers then plotted the location of the incidents on a map of Los Angeles. They found a riot of "tremendous scope" (it spread across the 46.5 mile curfew area) with "few tracts in which no crowd activity of any kind occurred," and they also found most tracts "had a wide range of crowd actions in varying frequencies." However, a surprising discovery was that "tracts experiencing high rates of one crowd action type (say, looting) were not necessarily high incidence tracts in another event-type category (say, fire)" Stark et al., 1974). In short, while the riot spread to almost every tract, it spread with different intensity and in a different way.

Going beyond this initial finding, researchers also noted the overlap between looting and fires. They found that where fires occurred in a tract for the first time, they were *not* generally accompanied by looting. For example, on August 12 the overlap was only 43 percent, on August 13, 50 percent, and on August 14, 22 percent. Moreover, analysis showed that even where overlap occurred, the figures "greatly exaggerated" the amount of similarity existing in the temporal-spatial spread "of these two riot activities." This was so because fires and looting generally occurred at different times of the day. So, even if a tract showed fires and looting for the first time on the same day, that was no assurance of "contagion." Quite possibly, the two events occurred at different times, begun and carried out by different people (Stack et al., 1974).

A last finding is perhaps the most important of all: "In only 21 percent of the instances of riot spread to a new geographical area did contagion involve a geographically contiguous area" (Stark et al., 1974). In fact, as the riot progressed, the phenomenon of spread to adjacent areas decreased. New tracts continued to enter the riot for the first time, but they were increasingly distant from tracts already rioting.

How can these findings be explained? Probably least difficult is the generally separate occurrence of fires and looting. Rooted in an attempt to explain differential expression that is perceived as unanimity, the emergent norm approach expects to find riot participants acting for different motives. People committed to the cause of racial equality, or bitter about the results of racism, might easily start fires aimed at destroying the immediate sources of their hatred and frustration. But people who only seek to exploit the riot, or who feel that the injustices of racism entitle them to food or a television set, would not start fires that destroy the goods they seek to rob; these people would take what they can and leave the burning to others. Remember, too, that the large number of crowd assemblies is very characteristic of riots. Spectators assemble to watch, and while they often applaud actual rioters, nonparticipating onlookers are a common part of any riot (Turner and Killian, 1972; Report of the National Advisory Commission on Civil Disorders, 1968).

Harder to explain is the spread of the riot. Contagion is of no help when rioting takes place in one tract, fails to occur in contiguous tracts, but begins in other geographically separated tracts. Seemingly, the only way to begin to explain the riot's spread is to "address rioting as a complex, diverse, dynamic, and interactive process" (Stark et al., 1974). Put differently, once a norm has emerged, it is still always subject to being remade by people in the process of interaction, and, even assuming a stable norm, a number of variables mediate between the norm and the people who act by it or against it. For example, studies of rioting in Detroit show that neighborhoods experiencing high riot activity had different characteristics from those showing low rates of activity. In some areas, where people were oriented to the white community, and hopeful of leaving the ghetto, residents not only refused to riot, they engaged in counterriot activity. Eager to protect their property, they sought to prevent its destruction by rioters (see Warren, 1969).

So, one way of explaining the spread of the Watts riot is in terms of the characteristics of particular neighborhoods. If one tract contained many people with no hope, and another many people filled with hope, there would be no reason to expect the riot to spread to the contiguous tract. On the contrary, assuming community links like those found in Detroit, we might even expect counterrioting to occur. Moreover, any city contains residential and business districts. It is at least plausible to assume that rioting would be concentrated in business areas. If so, certain tracts would experience little rioting.

Type of neighborhood is one plausible hypothesis for explaining a riot's complex spread. Another is the process of interaction. With so many crowd assemblies, as well as the presence of police and (on the third day) National Guard, the chances for new precipitating incidents were high. Conceivably, incidents occurred in geographically separated tracts, with each incident a partial explanation for the new rioting in noncontiguous areas.

Undoubtedly, further research will shed more light on the spread of rioting, as well as provide a much more comprehensive explanation for the separate appearance of activities such as looting and fires. However, even though we still have as many questions about rioting as we do answers, the evidence is clear on one point: there is no hope of finding answers unless we treat riots—and for that matter, crowds—as complex, diverse, dynamic, interactive processes (Stark et al., 1974).

SOCIAL MOVEMENTS

Everybody's god. In that case he must have more than little power. What does he base it on?

On love.

Love? Well, why not. . . . But tell me, why do you bear his name on your slave's disk?

Because I belong to him, Sahak said, again with a slight tremor.

Indeed? Belong to him? How can you do that? Do you not belong to the State, just as this stamp signifies? Are you not a State slave?

Sahak made no reply. He merely stood looking down at the floor.

At last the Roman said, but not at all unkindly:

You must answer this. We must be quite clear on this point, don't you see? Do you belong to the State? Tell me now.

I belong to the Lord my God, said Sahak without looking up. . . .—And you? Do you also believe in this loving god? Barabbas made no reply.

Tell me. Do you?

Barabbas shook his head.

You don't? Why do you bear his name on your disk then?

Barabbas was silent as before.

Is he not your God? Isn't that what the inscription means?

I have no God, Barabbas answered at last, so softly that it could hardly be heard. . . .

But I don't understand, he (the Roman) said. Why then do you bear "Christos Jesus" carved on your disk?

Because I want to believe, Barabbas said, without looking up at either of them. [Pär Lagerkvist, *Barabbas* (1951)]

Two thousand years ago there were "Jesus freaks." Today there are "Jesus freaks." However, in those two thousand years a social movement, a "change-seeking enterprise," went through the most profound transformations. For example, success "forced" the movement to quickly develop elements of bureaucratic organization and, although "there is no evidence whatever of Christians in the Army" before the decade A.D. 170–180, around that time things begin to change. Apparently a successful social movement could not expect to win state approval unless it at least permitted its members to fight for the state. In his *Apology* (written in A.D. 197), Tertullian "refuted the charge of misanthropy leveled against the Christians by pointing to their presence in the palace, the senate, the forum, and the army" (Bainton, 1960).

Christianity is typical. All social movements "originate within concrete historical contexts," and all "are conditioned in their development by the socio-cultural systems within which they seek to operate" (Zygmunt, 1972). It is wrong to argue that success inevitably spells compromise and conservatism for a social movement (for example, Michels, 1959), but, whatever its response, any social movement always maintains a dialectical relationship with the larger society. Always the two act back on one another and sometimes that relationship "forces" a social movement to turn its original ideology upside down.

If Christianity is typical, so is Barabbas. Often it is assumed that only a match between personal motives and ideological appeal prompts affiiliation with a movement, but Barabbas cares little about Christian ideology. He wants to believe, he wants security, and his attraction to Christianity is based on the perception that he is not like Christians. He joins because he is different, because he wants to be what he is not, and when he does join, Barabbas shows the links that bind him to many of today's "Jesus freaks." As one young man said, "I was into Buddhism, Hinduism, astrology, scientology, and even witchcraft. But I just went around in circles. Each one made more questions than answers. . . . After awhile I got really hungry for something I could hang on to. Like I got tired of questions; it was time to find some answers" (Mauss and Petersen, 1973; on theory, see Zygmunt, 1972).

Seemingly, this young man joins Jesus because the movement may give him what he lacks: answers. And like Barabbas, this young man allows us to stress a major theme of this section: people join movements for many reasons and because movements are conditioned by the societies in which they operate, their motives may change as the movement does. For example, in the Preparedness Movement of World War I, early joiners generally believed in the movement's ideology. But later, as the movement gained great strength, some people joined because it was the thing to do and others joined because of the social pressure applied by early movement members (Fernandez, 1975).

ORIGINS OF SOCIAL MOVEMENTS

If we define a *social movement* as "a collectivity acting with some continuity to promote or resist a change in the society or group of which it is a part" (Turner and Killian, 1972), we already have an idea about the origins of social movements. Some people are unhappy. Some people are "chafing" because of the authoritative status of a particular social arrangement. Bothered by segregated restaurants or frightened by rampant secularism or convinced that the government is controlled by Communists, people band together and perhaps, like today's Minutemen, "begin immediately to prepare for the day when Americans will once again fight in the streets for their lives and their liberty" (Thayer, 1968).

Movements grow out of social unrest. Generally, growth is a slow process but no matter what the pace, "the primary significance of social unrest is that it is a process by which people redefine or recast their world and so prepare themselves to act toward the world" (Blumer, n.d.). Normally social unrest builds on many factors.[4] First are predispositions. If people are to join together to resist or advocate a social change, many should be predisposed to perceive the problem and predisposed to chafe when someone discusses a particular social arrangement. Naturally, the greater the number of people predisposed to chafe, the greater the chances for a large and successful social movement. Second are dramatic events. Often people take even unjust social arrangements for granted, and dramatic events—a sheriff letting loose dogs on Martin Luther King in Alabama or Senator Joseph McCarthy finding hundreds of Communists in the federal government—have the ability to "incite, focalize, and bring predispositions to bear on a concrete situation" (Blumer, n.d.). Suddenly dramatic events make it likely that latent predispositions will become manifest.

Third is interaction among the participants, among the people who are beginning to chafe. Movements must define what they are for and against; interaction is an important element in understanding the definition that eventually emerges. For example, the impetus for the Minutemen was a duck-hunting trip. One man jokingly remarked that if the Russians ever invaded, hunters could at least take to the hills and fight as a guerrilla band. No one laughed at the joke. Instead, the men took it seriously, deciding to closely study the problem. The result of their study, of their interaction, was the conclusion that "in the last seventeen years [it was 1960] the Communists had succeeded in taking over seventeen sovereign nations." But the men were "surprised to learn that only one had been taken over by military conquest. The other sixteen were lost to communism by internal subversion or negotiations." So the men decided the key problem in America was internal subversion. Indeed, the American government was already in Communist hands and that meant only a dedicated band of guerrillas offered any hope of a free America (Thayer, 1968).

Fourth are the effects of overt expressions of social unrest. Collective dissatisfaction need not lead to a social movement. As in Spain, authorities might kill or jail anyone bold enough to express public dissatisfaction.

---

[4] These five factors are discussed in Blumer's brilliant unpublished paper.

Or, it is also possible that authorities might undercut a blossoming movement by agreeing to make requested changes. Or, as with the American civil rights movement, public expressions of discontent can produce sympathy from the majority group, as well as generate many potential recruits for a social movement. Always the effects of overt expressions of unrest are uncertain, and always those effects have the potential to increase or decrease the likelihood of a full-blown social movement.

Fifth, and closely related to overt expressions of unrest, are the labels that the larger public, and especially the authorities, give to protesters. Conceivably people could say yes to the protesters demands, but resistance is much more likely and the nature of the resistance plays an important part in shaping the social movement's development. For example, if authorities say protest is illegal, the discontented may go underground, seeing no choice but revolution. Or, if protesters are scorned and ridiculed, they may see no hope of changing society and decide instead that only by leaving society is there any chance of achieving social change (Blumer, n.d.).

So, the career or fate of social unrest is dependent on many interrelated factors. Alone predispositions do not make a social movement. Always they act in concert with variables such as dramatic events and the response of authorities, and always the relative importance of predispositions is an empirical question. For example, before war began in August of 1914, many "patriotic" Americans had tried to arouse people to the dangers of America's unprepared military situation. Right up to the war's beginning, their pleas fell on deaf ears. But the war, this very dramatic event, made some Americans listen. And when war was combined with a negative response from authority, as well as interaction among interested participants, the result was the Preparedness Movement. Incidentally, as a result of the war, interaction among participants, and authority's negative response, the movement that was formed in December of 1914 was very different from the movement that was envisioned by those who first began efforts to arouse Americans to their unprepared condition (Fernandez, 1975).

TYPES AND CONCERNS OF SOCIAL MOVEMENTS

One type of social movement is not, by definition, a social movement. Reference is to general movements, to those gradual and pervasive changes in people's values that Blumer calls "cultural drifts." Here the general movement (for example, women's liberation, the labor movement, the peace movement) has no particular membership or organizational apparatus. Instead, the concept tries to underline similarities often found in a number of different movement organizations (the Teamsters, the AFL-

CIO, the grape workers). In effect, because of broad changes in the larger culture, many people come to a similar conclusion: change will not occur unless social movements are formed. Always it is a specific movement organization that crystallizes collective unrest, hope, and desire, but often it is the gradual yet pervasive cultural changes that provide the broad framework within which specific movement organizations are formed (Blumer, 1969; Turner and Killian, 1972).

Even though specific movements operate within the same broad framework of beliefs, values, and goals, they often define the situation differently, as a recent (late 1975) split in the women's movement shows. One way to capture these differences is to use a movement classification developed by Turner and Killian. Noting that any movement organization needs an ideology, power relations favorable to the movement, as well as the promotion of membership gratifications, they argue that one way to understand specific movements (and the battles among them) is to see how movements handle the "ubiquitous tension" among value, power, and participant orientations (Turner and Killian, 1972).

Movements need a set of values and beliefs. These tell members, potential recruits, authorities, and the general public what kinds of change the movement seeks. Is the movement religious, political, social? Does it seek small changes, large ones, or will it only be content with a revolution? The movement's ideology normally answers these questions. It need not be clear or coherent, and it will often change with the passage of time, but an ideology performs the essential task of proclaiming a movement's values and goals.

Let's be more specific. A detailed ideology is a map, a guide that tells members what the goal is, how to reach it, how to interpret events that take place on the journey, and, with very detailed maps, the way stations members may stop at when following the prescribed paths. For example, in traditional Marxism the goal was communism. This was achieved by forging class consciousness among the proletariat, setbacks were easily explained as bourgeois attempts to maintain capitalism, and members learned that on the way to communism there was first the fall of capitalism and then the short transitional period of socialism. The map supposedly answered all questions, and any deviation from it was called heresy (for example, Koestler, 1950).

Besides acting like maps that place the movement in a "moving time perspective," ideologies also have the ability to create the movement's villains, as well as "translate self-interest into an ideal by identifying group interest with the general welfare" (Turner and Killian, 1972). For example, Jewish people were *the* villains in the Nazi ideology and their murder was justified as necessary for achieving the "racial purity" that was—as convinced Nazi's saw it—in the general public's interest.

Given the many variables associated with a movement's ideology, contrasting definitions of the situation are understandable. Feminists may agree that men are the enemy, but some lesbians believe any contact is anti-women's liberation. And disagreements can also occur about the amount of change desired, as well as the time when those changes can and should be expected. Within the general movement for civil rights, specific organizations such as the NAACP and the Black Panthers had very different ideas about the kinds of change needed, as well as the amount of time required to achieve them (for example, Carmichael and Hamilton, 1967). In sum, disagreements are "natural," but ideological disputes, especially bitter ones, weaken the thrust of the movement in at least two ways: they furnish ammunition to movement critics (How can we make changes when movement members don't know what they want?) and they lessen the movement's chances of performing an essential task (the establishment of power relations favorable to the movement).

Recall the "ubiquitous tension" among value, power, and participant orientations. Although any movement needs an ideology, if goals are to become reality, a movement must cultivate power as well as use it on those people or institutions capable of enacting changes desired by the movement. Generally, movements exercise power by persuasion, bargaining, or coercion (Turner and Killian, 1972), but it is obvious that bargaining power is reduced if ideological splits prohibit movements with similar goals from forming the coalitions that might enable them to confront the larger society with significant amounts of, say, political or economic power.

Besides ideological disputes, values and power are linked in other ways. First, ideology may dictate the way in which power is sought. Committed to nonviolence, Martin Luther King could never use terror or guerrilla warfare tactics as a means of achieving social change. Second, ideology may exclude the need for certain forms of power. For Black Nationalists, political power is useless: movement ideology says the world will end in the year 2000 and in the meantime Muslims need not concern themselves with a short-lived commodity such as political power (Essien-Udom, 1963). And third, a necessary focus on power demands that movements at least consider other people's values. For example, both the Irish Republican Army in Ireland and the Basques in Spain have at times changed their tactics because their emphasis on violence conflicted with the values of very powerful social groups.

A final point is that the relationship between value and power orientations is dialectical. Ideally a movement tries to maintain a satisfactory balance between values and power, but it is entirely possible that, for example, a failure to achieve one may lead to a concerted focus on the other. For example, some early members of Dr. King's Southern Christian Leadership Conference were committed to nonviolence and convinced that persuasion would soon produce the desired changes. However, wherever they went, attempts at persuasion were met with violent attacks on movement members. Over time some members dropped their commitment to nonviolence and focused on power because experience taught them that without it black people had little hope of change (Lester, 1968). Or, to reverse the example, the dominant orientation of the National Security League in World War I was to acquire the political power needed to make universal military training a federal law. Over time, however, the movement gained so much power that it changed its ideological goals. Suddenly (in late 1918) a preparedness movement organization focused on civilian concerns. Suddenly it was the league's duty "to create a greater respect for representative government as distinguished from mass administration," and it was also the league's duty to "protect our national legislators from dangerous proletarians" (Ward, 1960).

Movements need an ideology, seek power, and must also promote member gratifications. Sometimes this is done through gigantic rallies (think of Nazi crowds cheering Hitler), other times small gatherings of the faithful worship together (in Meriden, Connecticut, a Brother Julius, who is also Jesus, sees troubled members face-to-face), but always a social movement must make efforts to satisfy the personal needs of movement members. And this is especially important if the movement contains large numbers of people who are not "attracted and held" primarily by the movement's values and goals (Turner and Killian, 1972; Zygmunt, 1972). Seeking status or trying to escape loneliness or eager to experience a sense of community, some movement members join only because of the gratifications they hope to receive, and movements must satisfy these needs if they hope to increase or at least maintain the number of movement members.

Perhaps the most interesting examples of movements oriented to their members are millennial movements. Here people seek help from the supernatural. Rejecting (although often incorporating parts of) orthodox religion, and in search of salvation, they construct an ideology that generally prophesies the destruction of contemporary society and its supernatural transformation into a world blissfully fit for only movement members (Wilson, 1973; Allan, 1974). For example, the Ras-Tafarians of Jamaica believe that whites are inferior to blacks, that Jamaica is a hopeless hell, and that Ethiopia is heaven. In the past, whites forcibly brought blacks to Jamaica from Ethiopia, but soon Haile Selassie, the living God, will repatriate Ras-Tafarians and they will then get their revenge on whites, as well as transform a hopeless hell into the heaven that is rightfully theirs (Watson, 1973).

At least two things explain a millennial movement's need to focus attention on member gratifications. First, members of the larger culture think the movement is peculiar; taking the role of the other, movement members may agree unless they are constantly reassured by people who also believe in movement prophecies. Second, movement members often expect divine help while waiting for the millennium to arrive. In the Tigarr cult of West Africa, one important source of success was the movement's claim to protect members from witchcraft. Every six weeks the movement had a three-day ceremony; animal sacrifices were also part of the movement's activities, and, if the magic failed, the cult would help members to locate the witches responsible for evil-doings (Wilson, 1973; see also Cohn, 1961; Worsley, 1970).

Millennial movements are an extreme example. Most movements must maintain that impossible balance among value, power, and participant orientations. Generally, the need to focus on member gratifications is highest when a movement enjoys special failure or success, but no movement can long neglect its members and, as always, the relationship among the three orientations is dialectical. For example, during the thirties the million member Townsend movement centered on ideology; the main idea was to simultaneously provide guaranteed income for the aged plus stimulate the economy. However, Social Security undermined one aspect of the movement's ideology and prosperity via war the other. So, by 1950 the much-depleted movement sold seeds for income and used its "meetings" as a source of recreation. No longer oriented to ideology, members now came to meetings to socialize and, most important of all, to play cards (Messinger, 1969).

SOCIAL MOVEMENTS: GROWTH, DECAY, CHANGE

One framework used for studying social movements is the life cycle. Growing out of social unrest, a movement gains popularity in the larger society, that increasing approval "demands" a formal movement organization, and over time the movement becomes an institutionalized (and generally more conservative) part of the established society (for example, Blumer, 1969).

Although reality often furnishes little support for the life cycle approach, it has value. Using it allows us "to discover the additional conditions that have to be present if a movement is to proceed from any given stage to the next" (Turner and Killian, 1972). In short, granting the dialectical relationship between movement orientations and the larger society, what are some of the specific variables that push a movement in one direction or another?

First, what are the movement's goals and values? To the extent that a movement requires members to grant maximum degrees of commitment, and to the extent that a movement aims to change members' lives (for example, a millennial movement), it is "less susceptible" to pressures for toning down ideology or maintaining the organization to the detriment of movement values and goals (Zald and Ash, 1966). Consider the "Jesus people." While they have obviously received approval from many people, they are unlikely to make the changes required for acceptance by "average" Americans. Because they aim to change people's lives, and because that desire for change is generally rooted in a total rejection of the "establishment," they are "protected" against pressure to tone down movement ideology. Remember, too, that maximum commitment alerts movement members to any changes that threaten to corrupt movement purity. Obviously, no protection is total (for example, Christianity), but movements like those that embrace Jesus need never enter certain phases of every movement's life cycle (Mauss and Petersen, 1973).

Second, "movement organizations with relatively specific goals are more likely to vanish following success than organizations with broad general goals" (Zald and Ash, 1966). Here the idea is that one or two goal movements have nothing to do once they achieve movement aims; they succeed themselves out of business. For example, the Preparedness Movement of World War I produced the following specific organizations: the Military Training Camps Association, the American Legion, the American Defense Society, the Maryland Defense League, the American Foreign Legion, the Special Aid Society for American Preparedness, the Universal Military Training League, and the National School Camp Association. Each of these movement organizations had specific preparedness aims and, with the tremendously increased military spending that followed America's entrance into World War I, they no longer had any reason to exist. Some tried to continue with new goals, but all failed.[5] And success was the primary factor that stopped them from reaching the last stage in their life cycle: institutionalization (see Tinsley, 1939).

Third, a movement may fail, or at least suffer serious setbacks, "because its legitimacy as an instrument is discredited" (Zald and Ash, 1966). For example, in Great Britain the Committee of 100 was organized in 1960 to plan protests against nuclear weapons. Headed by many famous people, among them, philosopher Bertrand Russell, playwright John Osborne, and novelist Doris Lessing, the committee quickly achieved successes. Thousands marched for peace, and at their largest rally (12,000 people) more than 1,300 persons were arrested, among them actors, scientists, writers, even a Member of Parliament. This was exactly the kind of publicity sought by the movement, but when part of the committee lost interest, new, more radical members took over. Confident of success, the replacements planned sit-downs at several NATO air bases for December 9, 1961. Using every means at their disposal, organizers gave the protests

---

[5] The American Legion that exists today is not the preparedness organization established in early 1915.

widespread publicity, even proclaiming that 50,000 people would attend the new protests. Only 5,000 to 6,000 did so, and the sit-downs proved to be a disaster for the movement's legitimacy with the vast majority of British citizens. First, a substantial decrease in protesters (from 12,000 to 6,000 people) made it look as if the movement had lost steam; humiliation does not attract supporters. Second, and most important, as it became clear that control of the committee had shifted to radicals, moderates turned away from the movement, and sympathetic Members of Parliament were unwilling or afraid to publicly approve of the committee, while many "average" citizens were totally alienated by it. In short, a movement with some chance of success consistently undermined its own legitimacy with the very people it needed to achieve its goals (Meyers, 1971).

Fourth, a becalmed movement is the one most likely to embrace institutionalization, plus a toning down of movement values, goals, and energies (Zald and Ash, 1966). Now a becalmed movement is one that achieves neither success nor failure. Many people join and remain in the movement, it gains some of its goals, it is accepted and integrated into the society, but "growth has slowed down or ceased." So, while movement goals are still relevant to society, the chances of success are dim and the result is often apathy among members and complacency among movement leaders. In fact, leaders can decide that pursuit of radical goals, perhaps the initial basis of the movement, threatens their secure organizational positions. So, lacking any serious pressures or competition from movement members, oligarchical leaders pursue a policy that does not endanger their power or their access to material rewards. The best contemporary example of a becalmed yet powerful movement organization is the AFL-CIO (Zald and Ash, 1966; also Weber, 1946).

Fifth, and last, movement organizations "which aim to change individuals and employ solidary incentives are less likely to vanish than are movement organizations aimed at changing society and employing mainly purposive incentives" (Zald and Ash, 1966). Here the central idea is that if a movement focuses on changing people and so orients itself to movement members, the person's commitment is probably greater, the solidary incentives much more important than, say, money or a change in the laws. Put differently, even if a movement successfully changes its members, the movement still has solidary incentives to keep it in existence. But a movement aimed at social change and oriented to purposive incentives has less of a pull on its members while waiting for success and no purposive pull at all once success is achieved. So, an organization such as the National Mobilization Committee to End the War in Vietnam is much more likely to never complete its life cycle than an organization such as the Emmanuel Holiness Church, a movement specifically organized in 1916 (and still in existence) to change its members' lives (Warburton, 1968).

Although these five examples by no means exhaust the variables associated with the life or death of social movements, they do stress the degree of contingency, the relative lack of determinism inherent in the growth, decay, and change of social movements. Always the life cycle is an ideal, a means of finding the variables that must be present for movements to proceed from one stage to another.

MOTIVES OF MOVEMENT MEMBERS

Why do people join social movements? Answers vary but generally analysts try to find the links that bind personal motives to movement traits. Perceiving a problem, people are predisposed to do something about it, and if they also feel that change is both conceivable and attainable, they are "susceptible," open to movement membership. However, since "social movements—like other advertisers—must show they can respond to the needs of their clients," movement "appeals acquire meaning because they address themselves to susceptibilities." In fact, "the crux of the social psychology of social movements . . . is to isolate the psychological bond that ties appeals and susceptibilities to each other" (Toch, 1965; also Cantril, 1963).

Crux is a big word and the problem with focusing on the bonds that link appeals and susceptibilities is that it "stops the action." People are predisposed to do something about a problem, along comes an appealing social movement, and the two marry, perhaps happily ever after.

Neither alienation from a particular social arrangement, nor attraction to a social movement, can be understood only or even primarily in terms of appeals and susceptibilities (Zygmunt, 1972). First, while virtually no scholar denies the importance of understanding individuals, to focus attention on personal susceptibilities neglects an important point: "the major 'units' of alienation are 'broad collectivities' like social classes, generations, or ethnic groups." For example, one response to groups such as the Black Panthers has been a "white ethnic movement." Italian- and Polish- and Jewish-Americans have come together to form organizations that assert *their* interests. And while particular individuals may have personal motives for perceiving a problem, the basis of that perception is a collective identity, that is, "I am Italian, . . . Jewish, . . . Polish" (Weed, 1973).

Second, movements "are not merely vehicles through which already existing alienation may be expressed and remedied; they are themselves agents of alienation" (Zygmunt, 1972). For example, analysis of recruitment to the sit-in movement shows that people with "relatively stable, permanent deprivations," people who should have been quite predisposed to join the movement, were "relatively late joiners." Apparently, these people had to be convinced that their deprivations were not permanent; they had to be shown that change was possible. When the movement did this, the poorest people began to join sit-in groups, but to comprehend their alienation and subsequent recruitment to the movement, we must focus on the role of movement agitation as a cause of their deciding that racism and poverty were things to resist, not accept (Pinard et al., 1970; also Pinard, 1967).

Third, and this harks back to our discussion of social unrest, a stress on the links between susceptibilities and appeals neglects the role of "interaction among disaffected individuals" as another cause of developing "alienative predispositions" (Zygmunt, 1972). In the women's movement, many young women worked in radical elements of the New Left. Generally women's liberation was not a crucial issue, but discrimination by "radical" men made many of the women angry, and over time and through interaction that anger produced the alienation that helped start a number of women's movement organizations (Freeman, 1974).

Even when seen in "emergent and interactional terms," alienation from a social arrangement is only a necessary cause of movement membership. People need not act on their alienation and even when they do so, a variety of choices is often available. So, why are people attracted to one movement rather than another?

One answer is culture. Rooted in religion, people in the Middle Ages and today many people in the underdeveloped nations accept the legitimacy and importance of "ultimate" explanations of social problems. When alienated by, say, the coming of white colonialists, their culture teaches them to perceive reality in religious forms (Worsley, 1970; Wilson, 1973). Or, to turn to a subculture, alienated women, rooted in radical politics, could not align themselves with middle-class, bourgeois, professional women. Years of movement work taught them to reject "traditional political institutions and abjure all traditional political skills" (Freeman, 1974). So, even though the nature of their alienation was quite similar, radical women could not be attracted to a "bourgeois" group such as the National Organization for Women.

Another source of attraction to a movement is its ideology: people find, as a result of reading movement literature, attending meetings, and having someone explain things to them, that a movement furnishes a particularly appealing definition of the problematic situation. As one member of the Jesus movement said: "She could see I was bummed out, and she put her arms around me and said, 'I love you.' All night long the other kids talked to me and told me of Christ's love and of their love for me. It was really far out. I felt so good. I knew right then that this was a really groovy thing they were getting on" (Mauss and Petersen, 1973).

A third cause of attraction is a charismatic leader. With many movement organizations to choose from, some chose the Southern Christian Leadership Conference only because of their attraction to the words and leadership style of Dr. Martin Luther King (for example, Meier, 1971).

Fourth is the public's evaluation and response to a social movement (Turner, 1964; Zygmunt, 1972). If, like the preparedness and Americanization movements of World War I, the public responds with approval and applause, people are attracted to the movement because of its popularity or because of its ability to help people "get ahead" or because of fears that nonmembership may be interpreted as a lack of approval.

Fifth, and last, besides being "an ideological conveyance and champion of change," a movement is also "a circle of interaction, a network of social relationships." And that means that some people join movements because membership relieves "pangs of loneliness" or because it offers an "exciting set of social experiences" (Zygmunt, 1972; Turner and Killian, 1972). As another member of the Jesus movement said, ". . . I was so lonely. To fight off this loneliness, I went downtown and looked for someone to talk to. About five minutes after I got downtown, some guy came up to me and said, 'Jesus loves you, and he wants to set you free.' I thought about what he said when I got home and found that I couldn't sleep. Then I did something I could never do. I gave up to Jesus and he really set me free. This was three months ago, and I found what I was looking for, love" (Mauss and Petersen, 1973).

Alienated by a particular social arrangement, and attracted to a movement organization, people also undergo a process of conversion, a resocializing that shapes them to meet movement values, beliefs, and goals. Naturally, the extent of resocialization depends on the nature of the movement; a millennial movement tries, and is probably allowed, to engage in a resocialization of members that recruits to a pollution movement would judge both unnecessary and wrong. However, the point is that any movement must convert its members; it must move people to redefine self and world in terms of movement values, beliefs, and goals. This need not produce "motivational homogeneity," but it must produce—for movement success—the harmony that allows individual motives to link up with organizational aims (Zygmunt, 1972; also Toch, 1965; Cantril, 1963).

Suppose the processes of alienation, attraction, and conversion are complete. The person is a committed member of a social movement. Even then, efforts to comprehend members' motives must continue. Movements change over time. How do they continue to hold members who joined for different reasons? And, even if beliefs and goals do not change, members do. A worker who joined the labor movement because of a serious commitment to its goals may change his beliefs but continue his membership because he has friends in the movement or because the process of conversion succeeded in teaching him to value his identity as a member of the labor movement. Always the possibilities are many. And always that is because people and "social movements live and operate in the dimension of time and are, themselves, subject to transformations in their ideological and structural design, as well as in their relations to the broader society" (Zygmunt, 1972).

Bibliographical References

Allan, Graham. "A Theory of Millennialism." *British Journal of Sociology* 25, no. 3 (1974): 296–311.

Bainton, Roland H. *Christian Attitudes Toward War and Peace.* Nashville: Abingdon, 1960.

Balswick, Jack. "The Jesus People Movement: A Generational Interpretation." *Journal of Social Issues* 30 (1974): 23–42.

Blumer, Herbert. "Collective Behavior." In *Principles of Sociology,* edited by Alfred McClung Lee et al. 3d ed. New York: Barnes & Noble, 1969.

Blumer, Herbert. "Collective Behavior." In *Review of Sociology,* edited by Joseph B. Gittler. New York: Wiley, 1957.

Blumer, Herbert. "The Development of Social Unrest." Unpublished paper, n.d.

Brown, Richard Maxwell. "Historical Patterns of Violence in America." In *The History of Violence in America,* edited by Hugh Davis Graham and Ted Robert Gurr. New York: Bantam, 1969.

Brown, Roger. "Collective Behavior." In *Handbook of Social Psychology,* edited by Gardner Lindzey and Elliot Aronson. Reading, Mass.: Addison-Wesley, 1954.

Cantril, Hadley. *The Invasion from Mars.* Princeton, N.J.: Princeton University Press, 1940.

Cantril, Hadley. *The Psychology of Social Movements.* New York: Wiley, 1963, first published in 1941.

Carmichael, Stokely, and Hamilton, Charles. *Black Power: The Politics of Liberation in America.* New York: Random House, 1967.

Chaplin, J. P. *Rumor, Fear, and the Madness of Crowds.* New York: Ballantine, 1959.

Cohen, Stanley. *Folk Devils and Moral Panics.* London: Paladin, 1973.

Cohn, Norman. *The Pursuit of the Millennium.* New York: Harper & Row, 1961.

Dahlke, H. Otto. "Race and Minority Riots—A Study in the Typology of Violence." *Social Forces* 30 (1952): 419–25.

Denisoff, R. Serge, ed. *The Sociology of Dissent.* New York: Harcourt Brace Jovanovich, 1974.

Essien-Udom, E. U. *Black Nationalism.* New York: Dell, 1963.

Evans, Robert, ed. *Social Movements: A Reader and Sourcebook.* Chicago: Rand McNally, 1973.

Fernandez, Ronald. "Conscription in the Civil War and World War I: The Rejection and Acceptance of Authority." Ph.D. diss., University of Connecticut, 1975.

Freeman, Jo. "The Origin of the Women's Liberation Movement." In *The Sociology of Dissent,* edited by R. Serge Denisoff. New York: Harcourt Brace Jovanovich, 1974.

Gurr, Ted Robert. "Psychological Factors in Civil Violence." In *Anger, Violence, and Politics,* edited by Ivo K. Feierabend, Rosalind L. Feierabend, and Ted Robert Gurr. Englewood Cliffs, N.J.: Prentice-Hall, 1972.

Gusfield, Joseph. *Protest, Reform, and Revolt: A Reader in Social Movements.* New York: Wiley, 1970.

Hartmann, Edward. *The Movement to Americanize the Immigrant.* New York: Columbia University Press, 1948.

Hobsbawm, Eric, and Rude, George. *Captain Swing.* New York: Pantheon, 1968.

Janowitz, Morris. "Patterns of Collective Racial Violence." In *The History of Violence in America,* edited by Hugh Davis Graham and Ted Robert Gurr. New York: Bantam, 1969.

Killian, Lewis M. "The Significance of Multiple-Group Membership in Disaster." *American Journal of Sociology* 57 (1952): 309–14.

Klapp, Orrin E. *Currents of Unrest: An Introduction to Collective Behavior.* New York: Holt, Rinehart & Winston, 1972.

Koestler, Arthur, et al. *The God That Failed,* edited by Richard Crossman. New York: Harper & Row, 1950.

Le Bon, Gustave. *The Crowd.* New York: Viking, 1960.

Lester, Julius. *Look Out Whitey, Black Power's Gonna Get Your Mama.* New York: Grove, 1968.

Lieberson, Stanley, and Silverman, Arnold R. "The Precipitants and Underlying Conditions of Race Riots." *American Sociological Review* 30 (1965): 887–98.

McLaughlin, Barry, ed. *Studies in Social Movements.* New York: Free Press, 1969.

Manchester, William. *The Glory and the Dream: A Narrative History of America, 1932–1972.* Boston: Little, Brown, 1974.

Marx, Gary T. "Civil Disorder and the Agents of Social Control." *Journal of Social Issues* 21 (1970): 19–57.

Mauss, Armand L., and Petersen, Donald W. "The Cross and the Commune: An Interpretation of the Jesus People." In *Social Movements: A Reader and Sourcebook,* edited by Robert Evans. Chicago: Rand McNally, 1973.

Messinger, Sheldon L. "Organizational Transformation: A Case Study of

a Declining Social Movement." In *Studies in Social Movements*, edited by Barry McLaughlin. New York: Free Press, 1969.
Meyers, Frank E. "Civil Disobedience and Organizational Change: The British Committee of 100." *Political Science Quarterly* 86 (1971): 92–112.
Michels, Robert. *Political Parties*. New York: Dover Books, 1959, first published in 1915.
Milgram, Stanley, and Toch, Hans. "Collective Behavior: Crowds and Social Movements." In *Handbook of Social Psychology*, edited by Gardner Lindzey and Elliot Aronson. Reading, Mass.: Addison-Wesley, 1968.
Meier, August. "On the Role of Martin Luther King." In *Conflict and Competition: Studies in the Recent Black Protest Movement*, edited by John H. Bracey, August Meier, and Elliot Rudwick. Belmont, Calif.: Wadsworth, 1971.
Murdock, Eugene. *Patriotism Limited*. Kent, Ohio: Kent State University Press, 1963.
Oberschall, Anthony. *Social Conflict and Social Movements*. Englewood Cliffs, N.J.: Prentice-Hall, 1973.
Penrose, L. S. *On the Objective Study of Crowd Behavior*. London: Lewis, 1952. Cited in Turner and Killian, 1972.
Pinard, Maurice. "Poverty and Political Movements." *Social Problems* 15 (1967): 250–63.
Pinard, Maurice; Kirk, Jerome; and von Eschen, Donald. "Processes of Recruitment in the Sit-In Movement." *Public Opinion Quarterly* 30 (1970): 355–69.
Plumb, J. H. *In the Light of History*. New York: Delta, 1972.
Quarantelli, Enrico I. "Images of Withdrawal Behavior in Disasters: Some Basic Misconceptions." *Social Problems* 8 (1960): 69–79.
Report of the National Advisory Commission on Civil Disorders. New York: Bantam, 1968.
Rude, George. *The Crowd in History, 1730–1884*. New York: Wiley, 1964.
Rude, George. *Paris and London in the Eighteenth Century: Studies in Popular Protest*. New York: Viking, 1973.
Shellow, Robert, and Roemer, Derek V. "The Riot That Didn't Happen." *Social Problems* 14 (1966): 221–33.
Shibutani, Tamotsu. *Improvised News*. Indianapolis: Bobbs-Merrill, 1966.
Stark, Margaret J. Abudu; Raine, Walter J.; Burbeck, Stephen L.; and Davison, Keith K. "Some Empirical Patterns in a Riot Process." *American Sociological Review* 39 (1974): 865–76.
Stark, Rodney. "Collective Police Violence." In *The Sociology of Dissent*, edited by R. Serge Demisoff. New York: Harcourt Brace Jovanovich, 1974.
Thayer, George. *The Farther Shore of Politics*. New York: Simon and Schuster, 1968.

Tilly, Charles. "Collective Violence in European Perspective." In *Anger, Violence, and Politics*, edited by Ivo K. Feierabend, Rosalind L. Feierabend, and Ted Robert Gurr. Englewood Cliffs, N.J.: Prentice-Hall, 1972.

Tinsley, William. "The American Preparedness Movement." Ph.D. diss., Stanford University, 1939.

Toch, Hans. *The Social Psychology of Social Movements*. Indianapolis: Bobbs-Merrill, 1965.

Turner, Ralph H. "Collective Behavior." In *Handbook of Modern Sociology*, edited by Robert E. L. Farris. Chicago: Rand McNally, 1964.

Turner, Ralph H., and Killian, Lewis M. *Rights in Conflict*. New York: Bantam, 1968.

Warburton, T. Rennie. "Organization and Change in a British Holiness Movement. In *Patterns of Sectarianism*, edited by Bryan Wilson. London: Heinemann, 1968.

Ward, Robert D. "The Origin and Activities of the National Security League." *Mississippi Valley Historical Review* 47 (1960): 51–65.

Warren, Donald I. "Neighborhood Structure and Riot Behavior in Detroit: Some Exploratory Findings." *Social Problems* 16 (1969): 464–84.

Watson, G. Llewellyn. "Social Structure and Social Movements: The Black Muslims in the U.S.A. and the Ras-Tafarians in Jamaica. *British Journal of Sociology* 24 (1973): 188–204.

Weber, Max. *From Max Weber: Essays in Sociology*, edited by Hans Gerth and C. Wright Mills. New York: Oxford University Press, 1946.

Wedge, Bryant. "Students and Political Violence: Brazil 1964 and the Dominican Republic, 1965." In *Anger, Violence, and Politics*, edited by Ivo K. Feierabend, Rosalind L. Feierabend, and Ted Robert Gurr. Englewood Cliffs, N.J.: Prentice-Hall, 1972.

Weed, Perry. *The White Ethnic Movement and Ethnic Politics*. New York: Praeger, 1973.

Weller, Jack M., and Quarantelli, E. L. "Neglected Characteristics of Collective Behavior." *American Journal of Sociology* 79 (1973): 665–85.

Willner, Ann Ruth. "Public Protest in Indonesia." In *Anger, Violence, and Politics*, edited by Ivo K. Feierabend, Rosalind L. Feierabend, and Ted Robert Gurr. Englewood Cliffs, N.J.: Prentice-Hall, 1972.

Wilson, Bryan. *Magic and the Millennium*. London: Heinemann, 1973.

Worsley, Peter. *The Trumpet Shall Sound*. London: Paladin, 1970.

Zald, Mayer N., and Ash, Roberta. "Social Movement Organizations: Growth, Decay, and Change." *Social Forces* 44 (1966): 327–41.

Zygmunt, Joseph. "Movements and Motives." *Human Relations* 25, no. 5 (1972): 1–22.

GLOSSARY

The numbers in parentheses after each definition indicate the chapter in which that definition is discussed in detail.

Accommodation: People provide cues for a complimentary response in a cooperative situation or cues for a parallel response in a competitive situation. (8)

Acting crowds: Goal action is focused on some person or persons or an object external to them. (3)

Aggression: An offensive assault on another person, group, or object. (12)

Attitude: A relatively enduring organization of beliefs around an object or situation predisposing one to respond in some preferential manner. (9)

Authority: Its hallmark is unquestioning recognition by those who are asked to obey. (11)

Basic trust: Given to infants by others, it refers to the awareness of infants that others will consistently and continually satisfy their physical needs, as well as calm them when unmanageable anxieties produce feelings of insecurity. (2)

Between role conflicts: Two or more roles demanding two or more different types of behavior. (6)

Coercive power: People obey because they have no choice; the consequences of disobedience are too great. (11)

Cognitive dissonance: A relation that exists between pairs of elements in which the elements are in conflict. The result is varying degrees of psychological discomfort; people need and want to resolve the conflict. (9)

Collective behavior: A set of interindividual, relational, and interactional properties that cannot be reduced to purely intra-individual terms. (13)

Comparative reference group: Used by one to evaluate self and others by comparing oneself or his or her situation to that of others. (8)

Competence motivation: The need of infants to interact effectively with their environment. (2)

Complete continuity: The basic psychological process and the manifest form of behavior remain the same over time. (1)

Contagion theory: Collective behavior that is explained on the basis of some process whereby moods, attitudes, and behavior are communicated rapidly and accepted uncritically. (13)

Conventional crowds: People gathered in the hope their assemblage will be transformed into a crowd. (13)

Convergence theory: The explanation of crowd behavior on the basis of the same or similar predispositions and preoccupations. (13)

Cultural contradictions: These exist when culture, when institutionalized beliefs, values, and practices, say two or more different things about the same role. (6)

Diffuse crowds: Although crowd members are dispersed over a wide area, they still develop similar sentiments, moods, and behavior. (13)

Double bind: The form of communication found in families of schizophrenics; the child's position; simultaneously receiving, often from the same person, two contradictory messages; occurs about specific things. (4)

Egocentrism: Essentially a young child's inability to make a clear distinction between self and others. (2)

Egocentrism in adolescence: Because of their ability to think hypothetically, adolescents tend to become preoccupied with themselves and their behavior. (3)

Emergent norm theory: Unanimity is regarded as an illusion, and the key problem is to explain the development and imposition of a pattern of differential expression that is perceived as unanimity. (13)

Equity group: The use of others as a frame of reference for judging whether or not one's situation or fate is fair or equitable. (8)

Expert power: People obey because they accept the apparent or proven expertise of another. (11)

Expressive crowds: They seek to change the mood, the imagery, and the behavior of crowd members. (13)

Frame: Definitions of the situation that furnish organizational premises for social encounters. (7)

Front: Anything used to stage a presentation of self. (1)

Generalized other: The social groups or organized community which give people their unity or disunity of self. (8)

Genotypic continuity: The psychological process remains stable but the form of behavior changes. (1)

Genuine mutuality: People meet each other owning a positive sense of self; mutual recognition of identity develops. (4)

Global self-image: An overall view of self; the organization of qualities the person thinks he or she possesses. (1)

Groupthink: Refers to a deterioration of mental efficiency, reality testing, and moral judgment that results from in-group pressures. (9)

Guilt: Relatively independent of others, it occurs when the self disapproves of a contemplated or already completed act. (2)

I: The response of the individual to the attitudes of others; the response can be a yes, a no, or a maybe. (1)

Identification: A form of imitation, meaning wanting to be like another person. (2)

Ideology: Performs the essential task of proclaiming a movement's values and goals. (13)

Immediate social conditions: The sources of authority that have come to exist because of the movement and continuous interpretation of the historical process. Examples include dramatic events, public opinion, and the response of societal authorities. (10)

Keys: The set of conventions by which a given activity, already meaningful in terms of some primary framework, is transformed into something patterned on the activity, but seen by the participants to be something quite else. (7)

Leadership: A category of behavior, the initiation and maintenance of structure in expectation and interaction.

Legitimate power: People's agreement that one person has the right to prescribe behavior for them. (11)

Legitimator: The group people use when a question arises as to the legitimacy of behavior or opinions; legitimates a person's beliefs, values, or actions. (8)

Marital schism: A situation in which two people with serious problems in living irriate themselves to the point of desperation by marrying each other. (4)

Marital skew: One partner who is extremely dependent or masochistic marries another who seems a strong and protecting parental figure. (4)

Me: The attitudes of others that one assumes. (1)

Mind: Inner control based on information acquired by the individual. (1)

Normative reference group: The group used to set and maintain standards. (8)

Opinion: A verbal expression of some belief, attitude, or value. (9)

Participant orientation: The promotion of members' gratifications. (13)

Permeability: Any crowd has boundaries which work two ways; it may be easy to enter but it may be impossible to leave. (13)

Personality: What makes people distinctively themselves; equivalent to individuality. (1)

Phenotypic continuity: The behavior remains stable but the underlying psychological process changes. (1)

Power: The probability that one actor within a social relationship is in a position to carry out his will despite resistance. (11)

Power orientation: Movements exercise power by persuasion, bargaining, or coercion. (13)

Prejudice: An antipathy based on a faulty and inflexible generalization. (8)

Primary frame: Definitions of the situation that do not hark back to some prior or original interpretation. (7)

Primary socialization: The process by which infrahuman animals gain social attachments. (1)

Private speech: When, oblivious to the social implications of their talk, children talk out loud and to themselves in a public place. (2)

Pseudomutuality: Used to emphasize a quality of relatedness found in the families of schizophrenics. All interaction is structured in terms of some kind of fitting together; people meet one another on the basis of shared beliefs, values, expectations, and perceptions. (4)

Reference group: The group people use to compare self and others, or the group they use to set and maintain values, beliefs, and standards. (8)

Referent power: Based on a group's identification with a person; people obey because they like or respect the leader. (11)

Residual rule-breaking: Thought or action generally labeled sick; refers to norms where the culture provides no firm definition of the situation; formal means of social control do not apply. (4)

Reward power: One person's influence over another by virtue of the benefits offered. (11)

Role: A pattern that can be regarded as the consistent behavior of a single type of actor. (6)

Role-ambiguity: Occurs when a role is not clearly defined or when people cannot discover what their role expectations are. (6)

Role-attachment: People are eager to perform the role; emotionally and cognitively in love with it, they desire and expect to see themselves enacting it, primarily because of the self-identification it offers. (6)

Role-commitment: Reference is to questions of impersonally enforced structural arrangements; the person gets locked into a position and coerced into living up to the promises and sacrifices built into it as a result of the fixed and interdependent character of many institutional arrangements. (6)

Role-distance: An effectively expressed pointed separateness between the person and the role; the person is actually denying not the role but the virtual self that is implied in the role for all accepting performers. (6)

Role-embracement: The person is attached to the role, has shown the ability to do it, and has an active engagement or spontaneous involvement in the role activity at hand. (6)

Role model: A group possesses skills and displays techniques the person lacks; consequently, by observation and then comparison with his or her performance, he or she uses the group as a model for behavior. (8)

Role-set conflict: Occurs when two or more members of a role set demand different behavior from the occupant of a role, or when two or more members of the role-set demand behavior that conflicts with the normative definition of the role. (6)

Role-making: An important phase of role theory; people meet each other with different expectations and in interaction they often achieve creative compromises which allow them to have a satisfactory role relationship. (6)

Schizophrenia: A general term used to group people whose behavior is characterized by gross distortions of reality (in many cases total withdrawal from reality), disorganized and fragmented perception, thought, and emotion. (4)

Self: A person's representation of himself or herself as an object in the world of experience. (1)

Self-percepts: Transitory representations of self. (1)

Shame: Needing others to make it appear, it is a person's unpleasant reaction to an actual or imagined negative judgment of self by others. (2)

Significant other: Anyone who has had or still has an important influence on a person's thoughts about self and world. (1)

Social identities: Representations of self that establish what and where one is in social terms. (1)

Social movement: A collectivity acting with some continuity to promote or resist a change in the society or group of which it is a part. (13)

Underlying social conditions: The institutionalized beliefs, values, and practices that dominate a particular society. (10)

Unique self-image: A person's images of self that are the result of his or her singular experiences with others. (1)

War: A human invention which over time becomes a social institution, a powerful complex of inherited beliefs, values, and practices. (12)

INDEX

accommodation group, 258
achievement
   in infancy, 57–58
   and leadership, 337
adolescence, 85
   aggression and, 365
   egocentrism in, 110–12
   and generation gap, 115–17
   occupational choice in, 112–15
   peer groups and, 120–24
   sex and, 117, 120
adulthood, young, 124–32
aggression, 16, 355–77
   frustration and, 359–62
   manhood and, 364–67
   self image and, 362–64
   war and, 368–77
Ainsworth, Mary, 55
anger, reference groups and, 266
anxiety, 100, 130
   in children, 69, 72–73
   dissonance and, 285
   in infancy, 59, 64–65
   menopause and, 135–36
   middle age and, 132–34
   sex and, 117–18
association, brain, 21
asylums, 156–57
attachment, and role involvement, 209
attitude, 283–84
audience, as reference group, 258–59
authority, 307–30, 394–95
   chart, 323
   leadership and, 341–47
   Milgram experiments and, 308–16
   social movements and, 402

balance theory, 8
belief, 283–84
   dissonance and, 287–88
   leadership and, 344
   social movements and, 403
behavior
   animal, 16–20
   collective, 383–412
   crowds, 386–93
   riots, 393–99
   social movements, 399–412
   commitments and, 125
   leadership and, 343
   mental illness and, 159–63
   moral, 97
   sex roles and, 87–93
behaviorism, 8
bias, cultural, 190
biochemistry, and schizophrenia, 164–66
biology
   aggression and, 356–69
   human development and, 34
   influence of, 16
   language and, 25–56
   see also determinism
Bowlby, John, 54–55
brain, the, 20–23
breast feeding, 56–57

categories, perception and, 185–87
change, social
   movements and, 409–11
   reference groups and, 265–66
charisma
   leadership and, 338–41
   obedience, 323

423

charisma (*cont.*)
   social movements and, 410–11
childrearing, effect on parents, 131–32
children, 63–65
   aggression and, 361–63
   institutionalized, 52–54
   old age and, 147
   prejudice and, 268–69
Chomsky, Noam, 25–26
class, socioeconomic
   self-image and, 82
   occupational choice and, 114–15
   reference groups and, 264–65
   riots and, 394
   school achievement and, 97–98
   status and, 100
Cleaver, Eldridge, 27
concrete operations, 85
coercion, and reference groups, 260–61
cognition
   class inclusion and, 85–87
   development of, 8, 60–65
cognitive development theory, 8
commitment, 125–27
   dissonance and, 286
   roles and, 208–9
communication
   animal, 18–19
   public opinion and, 301–2
   schizophrenia and, 168–69
   see also language; symbols
Comte, Auguste, 6–7
competence motivation, 57–59, 68
concept, 83, 91–92
   stabilization of, 83–87, 92
conflict
   in childhood, 68–69
   and manhood, 364–67
   social, 355–77
   war and, 368–77
conformity, 195
   in adolescence, 121–22
   social roles and, 204–5
conscience, 93–97
consciousness, frame analysis and, 240–41
continuity, personality, 35–56, 44

convergence theory, 387
creativity, language and, 27–28
credibility, reference groups and, 272
crises, obedience and, 321–22
crowds, 386–93
   types, 392
culture, 189–96
   aggression and, 359–60
   authority and, 318–19
   collective behavior, 385
   comparisons of, 264
   conflict and, 212–13, 215–16, 376–77
   conscience and, 96
   identification and, 76
   frames and, 231
   leadership and, 336, 338–39, 347
   personality and, 34
   public opinion and, 300–1
   self-esteem and, 73
   sex roles and, 89–92
   social movements and, 410
crying
   in children, 68
   in infants, 52, 58

Darwin, Charles, 7
death, 148–50
   of spouse, 135, 137–38
delinquency, juvenile, 257
depression
   menopause and, 135–36
deprivation
   in children, 55
   in infants, 54
determinism
   biological, 7, 16–20, 29, 88–90, 92–3
   cultural, 195–96
   social, 42
development
   cognitive, 60, 87, 94
   moral, 94–95
   of prejudice, 268–71
   psychosexual, 56–57, 87–93
discipline
   for children, 71–72
   moral values and, 95

diseases, genetic, 29–30
disillusionment, reference groups and, 261
dissonance, 284–95
divorce, 132
  for young adults, 127–28

egocentrism, 65–67
  adolescent, 110–12
  private speech and, 179
embracement, role involvement and, 209
emergent norm theory, 387–92
Enlightenment, the, 4–5
environment
  competence development and, 58
  for infants, 52
  intelligence and, 31–32
equity group, 257
esteem, self, 100–1
  aggression and, 362
  of children, 70–74
  culture and, 73
  leadership and, 348
  in middle age, 132–34, 139
  occupation and, 113
  schizophrenia and, 165, 171–73
  sex roles and, 91, 112–13, 118–19
  of young adults, 130–31
evolution, human, 20–21
extroversion, leadership and, 337

fabrications
  frame analysis, 233–34
  secrecy and, 237–38
  Watergate and, 243–50
family, the
  schismatic, 170–71
  schizophrenia and, 165–72
  skewed, 171–73
Fiedler, Fred E., 348–50
folkways, 191–92
frame analysis, 229–50
freedom, 8–9
  cultural, 195
  internal, 87, 188
  in middle age, 136–37
  sexual, 118–20

freedom (*cont.*)
  in young adults, 130
Freud, Sigmund, 63, 159
frustration
  aggression and, 359–62
  riots and, 397–98
  social movements and, 400–2

gender; *see* sex
genetics, 29–33
  intelligence and, 31
  temperament and, 32–33
  schizophrenia, 163–64
generalization, prejudice and, 267–68
generalized other(s), 42–43, 80–81
  as reference group, 255–56, 263
  sex roles and, 88, 91
  teachers as, 98
generation gap, 115–17
goals, social, 406–7
Goffman, Erving, 229–48
gratification
  oral, 56–60
  and role accumulation, 222
groups
  authority and, 315–16
  leadership and, 339–40, 346, 349–51
guilt, 93–95

hand-eye coordination, learning in infants of, 58
health, 144
Herbart, Johann, 6
heredity; *see* genetics
hormones, sex
  behavior and, 88–90
hostility; *see* aggression

I, the, 43–45
  aggression and, 363–64
  cognitive development, 63
  controls and, 71–74
  egocentrism and, 65
identity, 38–40, 75–77
  in adults, 126, 129–30
  aggression and, 364–67

identity (*cont.*)
  conscience and, 96
  with mother, 54–56
  occupational, 112–15
  in old age, 148
  peer groups and, 121
  prejudice and, 268–71
  in retirement, 145
  schizophrenia and, 170
  sex roles and, 41, 87–93, 99
  social, 82, 99, 185, 187
  social movements and, 403–5
ideology, and social movements, 403–5, 410
image, self, 38, 41, 45
  adolescent, 116–17
  adult, 126–29
  aggression and, 362–64
  concept stabilization and, 84
  conflict and, 69
  dissonance and, 285–86, 295
  fabrication and, 237–38
  in infancy, 60
  in middle age, 133–34
  negativism and, 167
  in old age, 141
  prejudice and, 268–71
  reference groups and, 263, 272
  schizophrenia and, 170, 174
  school achievement and, 97–98
  sex roles and, 91–92
  trust and, 51–56
imprinting, 17
income, and retirement, 143–44
individuality, and parents, 70
induction, 95–96
infancy
  competence development and, 57
  deprivation in, 54
  language and, 26–32
  mother and, 54–56
  oral phase of, 56–57
  self concept and, 41–42
  socialization of, 50–51
  temperaments of, 32
  trust and, 51–54
  and young adults, 131–32
inhibitions, and aggression, 361–62

instincts, 20
  and aggression, 357
institutions
  authority and, 313, 318, 320
  leadership and, 342–43
  war and, 368–77
intelligence, 30–32, 63
  in adolescence, 111, 122
  and conscience, 96
  leadership and, 336–37
intention
  in infancy, 62
interaction, 36
  frame analysis and, 230–50
  leadership and, 346
  roles and, 201
  social movements and, 401, 410
  trust and, 60
invulnerability, and dissonance, 290
I.Q. tests, 30–32
  of institutionalized, 53
issues, public opinion and, 297–98, 302

justice, and riots, 395
justification, dissonance and, 292–95

keyings, 232–33
Kohlberg, Lawrence, 94–95

language, 19, 23–28
  brain centers for, 23
  changes in, 27–28
  children and, 53, 67–68
  generalizations and, 186–87
  private speech and, 77–81
  sex roles and, 92
laws, 191–92
leadership, 334–51
  authority and, 341–43
  charisma and, 338–41
  culture and, 338–39
  emergence of, 344–47
  power and, 342–43
  style of, 347–51
  traits of, 336–51
learning
  in animals, 17–18

learning (*cont.*)
  aggression and, 359
  in children, 66, 84
  primary frames and, 234
  schizophrenia and, 167
legitimacy, and reference groups, 258
life review, 148–49
literacy, impact of, 28
loneliness
  divorce and, 132
  social movements and, 405
  widowhood and, 146
love
  perception and, 186
  see also trust

McDougall, William, 7–8
manhood, aggression and, 364–67
marriage, and young adults, 127–28
me, the, 43–45
  cognitive development and, 63
  controls and, 71–74
  egocentrism and, 65
  negativism and, 64, 67
Mead, George Herbert, 42–47, 78–80
memory
  in animals, 17–18
  see also learning
menopause, 135–36
mental illness, 156–63
middle age, 133–39
Milgram, Stanley, 308–16
models, 5, 257–58
  of Johann Herbart, 6
  of William McDougall, 7–8
monkeys, and communication, 19
monologue, collective, and private speech, 78–79
Montesquieu, Charles de Secondat, 5
morale
  and old age, 147
morality
  of group, 290
  occupational choice and, 113
  sexual, 118–20
mores, 191–92
motherhood
  during infancy, 54–56

motherhood (*cont.*)
  and child's self esteem, 70–71
mourning, 149-50
movements, social, 399–412
  change in, 406–9
  members of, 409–12
  origins of, 400–2
  religion and, 405–6
  types of, 402–6

negativism, 64–67, 70
  in middle age, 139
  in old age, 148
Newton, Issac, 3
norms, cultural, 191

obedience, 307–30
  Milgram experiments, 308–16
  chart, 323
  see also authority; peer groups
occupation
  adolescent choice of, 112–15
  and middle age, 136–37
  and young adults, 128
old age, 141–50
opinion, public, 295–302
  obedience and, 323
  see also belief; attitude; value
oral phase, 56–58

paranoids, 40
parenthood, 70–74
  effect on young adults, 131–32
peer groups, 98–100
  adolescent, 120–24
  old age and, 147
  widowhood and, 146
perception, 44–45
  concepts and, 83
  in infancy, 52, 59
  generalization and, 185–87
  leadership and, 340
  reference groups and, 262–63
  significant others and, 271
  war and, 370
permeability, and collective behavior, 384

personality, 34
  aggression and, 362–64
  cognitive development and, 60–63
  competence and, 58–60
  conflict and, 68–69
  identification and, 75–77
  leadership and, 337
  paranoid, 168
  roles and, 212
  schizophrenia and, 163
  self image and, 40–42
  sex and, 87–93
  trust and, 44, 51–56
Piaget, Jean, 60–63, 85, 94
politics
  mental illness and, 158–59
  riots and, 393–94
power
  leadership and, 342–43, 348
  obedience and, 319–20, 328–30
  public opinion and, 301–2
  reference groups and, 273
  social movements and, 404–5
predispositions
  crowds and, 387–88, 391
  riots and, 395
  social movements and, 401
prejudice
  aggression and, 363–64
  reference groups and, 266–71
preoccupation, external, 240
prestige
  and reference groups, 260, 273
  see also status; class
private speech
  frame analysis and, 234–35
  sex roles and, 92
  see also language; symbols
propaganda, 296–301
pseudo-mutuality, 174–75
psychoanalysis, 8
psychology, social
  definition, 2
  background, 3–9

race, 268–71
rape, 260, 366
rationalization, 287–91

reference frames, 253–73
  comparative, 262–71
  normative, 254–61
regions, self-presentation, 244
reinforcement, leadership and, 346
rejection, of reference groups, 261
response
  personal, 44
  trust and, 54
retirement, 141–45
reversibility, 86
rigidity, and reference groups, 273
riots, 393–99
  characteristics of, 394–96
  rumor and, 396–97
  types, 396
role(s), 199–222
  accumulation of, 221
  ambiguity and, 213–24
  children and, 33, 66–67, 131–32
  conflict of, 211–12
  cultural, 205–6, 215–16
  involvement, 208–11
  leadership and, 344–47
  models, 257–58
  occupational choice and, 112–13
  old age and, 142–43
  prejudice and, 267
  private speech and, 79–80
  sexual, 87–93, 215–16
  social conflict and, 376
  socialization and, 75–76
Ross, E. A., 7
Rousseau, Jean Jacques, 4
rumor
  and crowds, 390–92
  and riots, 396

schizophrenia, 160, 163–76
  summary of types, 166
school, 97–98
scientific revolution, 3–4
security; see trust
self, the, 38–45
  in adolescence, 111–12
  cognitive development and, 60–63
  competence, 58
  conflict and, 68–69

self, the (*cont.*)
　conscience and, 93–97
　discipline and, 74
　in divorce, 132
　in frame analysis, 230–50
　identification and, 77
　in infancy, 53–54
　justification and, 286–88
　mental illness and, 160–63
　middle age and, 139
　mother and, 54–56
　negativism and, 64, 67
　peer groups and, 122
　personality and, 74
　presentation of, 236–50
　retirement and, 142
　school achievement and, 97–98
　sex roles and, 87–93
　trust and, 51–56
self-esteem; *see* esteem, self
self-image; *see* image, self
sensory-motor period, 61–63
separation, family, 55
sex, 87–93
　adolescence, 117–20
　aggression and, 366
　identity and, 9
　leadership and, 345
　obedience and, 312
　occupational choice and, 112–14
　old age and, 145
　peer groups and, 99, 122
　schizophrenia and, 164
sexism
　and mental illness, 161
　and occupations, 128, 137
shame, 93
sign, 24
significant other(s), 42–44, 56, 65
　and reference groups, 271–73
　and schizophrenia, 165–68, 170
　and sex roles, 88
　teachers as, 98
socialization
　childhood, 50–101
　culture, 192
　homogeneity and, 271
　identification and, 75–76

socialization (*cont.*)
　obedience and, 319
　occupational choice and, 113–14
　peer groups and, 121
　primary, 16
　roles and, 90–92, 200
　temperament and, 33
　war and, 368–69
society, 4, 193–96
space, personal, 241–42
speech, private, 77–81
stability, and reference groups, 261
status
　adolescents and, 121–22
　aggression and, 365
　leadership and, 345
　peer groups and, 99–100
　prejudice and, 268
　retirement and, 142–3
　role-accumulation, 222
　in social movements, 405
stimulation, infant, 54, 57
stress
　in children, 55–56
　cultural, 193–94
　see also anxiety
style, in leadership, 347
sucking, 57–58, 60
suicide, and self-esteem, 172
superiority, and reference groups, 261–62
symbolic interactionism, 8
symbols, 24
　for adolescents, 122
　in childhood, 67–68, 85
　in infancy, 62–63
　language and, 20
　learning and, 18–19
syntax, 25

teams, and frame analysis, 243–50
temperament, 32–33
tradition
　and riots, 395
　and war, 372–74
　see also culture
trait, 36
　inconsistency in, 36–37

trust
  in infancy, 53–56
  interaction and, 60
  leadership and, 348
twin studies, 30, 34

unconscious, the, 6
utopias, 28

values, 283–84
  dissonance and, 295
  leadership and, 344
  mental illness, 158
  moral, 94–95
  obedience and, 311, 327–28

values (*cont.*)
  reference groups and, 254–56, 265–66, 271–72
  social movements and, 403–7
variables, trans-situational, 41

war, 368–77
  technology and, 371–73
  institutions and, 375
White, Robert W., 58–60, 128–29
widowhood, 137–38
  and old age, 145–46
  and retirement, 143
work; *see* occupations; retirement
Wundt, Wilhelm, 7